PLANT HERE *THE STANDARD*

Also by Dennis Griffiths

THE ENCYCLOPEDIA OF THE BRITISH PRESS (*Editor*)
200 NOT OUT

'The choice of a name then claimed our attention. The object was to make a stand against the inroad of principle; contrary to our Constitution in Church and State; a very appropriate motto was chosen by Dr Giffard (the Editor)

Signifer, statue signum,
Hic optime manebimus

Plant here *The Standard.*
Here we shall best remain.

and on the 21st May, 1827, *The Standard* was reared, hauled as a rallying point and was speedily followed by the raising of *Standards* in the Provincial and Colonial Conservative Press. Even Foreign newspapers have adopted the name.' — Charles Baldwin, Publisher

Plant Here *The Standard*

Dennis Griffiths

MACMILLAN

First published 1996 by
MACMILLAN PRESS LTD
Houndmills, Basingstoke, Hampshire RG21 6XS
and London
Companies and representatives
throughout the world

ISBN 0–333–55565–1

A catalogue record for this book is available
from the British Library.

10 9 8 7 6 5 4 3 2 1
05 04 03 02 01 00 99 98 97 96

Printed and bound in Great Britain by
Antony Rowe Ltd
Chippenham, Wiltshire

Contents

List of Plates

Acknowledgements

Many people have kindly assisted me in my research, but special mention is due to Mr Charles Wintour, former Chairman and editor of the *Evening Standard*, and to Dr Joseph O. Baylen, Regents' Professor of History Emeritus, Georgia State University. I must thank also most warmly Viscount Rothermere, Chairman, Daily Mail & General Trust, for his co-operation and for graciously writing the foreword. I owe a great debt also to Dr Aled Jones, of the History Department, University of Wales, Aberystwyth; to the late Professor John Dodge, first Director of the Graduate Centre for Journalism, City University; to the present Director, Professor Hugh Stephenson; and to his colleagues Henry Clother, Robert Jones and Stuart Patrick.

Special mention must also be accorded to the late Stephen Koss, Professor of History, Columbia University, who died in October 1986 at the age of 44. He not only read the opening chapters but was also instrumental in directing me to the Disraeli, Peel and Salisbury Papers, and I have also drawn upon his magnificent two-volume study, *The Rise and Fall of the Political Press in Britain*, which covers the periods 1850–1900 and 1900–85. The Earl of Halsbury, Chancellor of Brunel University, was most gracious in providing access to his family's history, with particular reference to Dr Stanley Lees Giffard, first editor of *The Standard*; and Hardinge Giffard, a future Lord Chancellor of England. The present Earl provides a direct link with the first days of *The Standard*, and in conversation was able to recall boyhood talks with his grandfather, Hardinge Giffard, who had worked with his father, Stanley Lees Giffard, as assistant editor before achieving fame at the Bar.

For any student of the early days of newspapers, *Politics and the Press c.1750–1850* by the late Arthur Aspinall, Professor of Modern History, University of Reading, is indispensable. Much help and advice was also rendered by Dr Lucy Brown, formerly Senior Lecturer in History, London School of Economics, who read the early script; her seminal work, *Victorian News and Newspapers*, is a major source of reference. I would also thank Dr David Jeremy and his colleagues of the Business History Unit, London School of Economics, for their advice.

Among the many other academics, archivists and librarians who have rendered assistance, special thanks are accorded to Professor Ray Boston and David Linton, editors of *The Newspaper Press in Britain: an annotated bibliography*, for sharing their wide knowledge of the British press; Dr B. S. Benedikz, sub-librarian (special collections) at the University of Birmingham; Judith Dunn, Information and Services Librarian, News International Newspapers Ltd.; the late Alec Harrison, honorary librarian, London Press Club; Robert Heron, owner of one of the largest collections of newspapers in the United Kingdom; Gordon Phillips, formerly archivist of *The Times* and *Today*; Anne Piggott, formerly archivist of *The Times*; Stephen Stacey, of the Bodleian Library; Justine Taylor, archivist, Reuters; and C. Woolgar, archivist, University of Southampton.

For early research, I am indebted to R. Rosenberg for his work on the Baldwins; to Ian Maxwell, librarian, University of Exeter, for his advice on London publishers; to Richard and Marjorie Bond, the University of North Carolina, for their investigations into the Minute Book of the *St. James's Chronicle*; and to Robert Wilkinson-Latham for incisive information on Victorian war correspondents and the campaigns they reported. On other matters, the archivists of Lloyds Bank; the Royal Literary Fund; Oriel College, Oxford, and Staffordshire County Council were of great assistance, but I am especially grateful to Miss Robin Myers, honorary archivist of the Worshipful Company of Stationers and Newspaper Makers.

Much of the research was done at the Public Record Office, the House of Lords Library, the British Library, the Guildhall Library and the Barbican, Uxbridge and Buckinghamshire libraries. Two libraries which were especially important were St. Bride Printing Library (where James Mosley, Nigel Roche, Dr Louise Craven and Gwyneth Haslam merit warm thanks); and the British Newspaper Library, Colindale, where the Head, Geoffrey Smith, and the former Heads, Geoffrey Hamilton and Eve Johansson, and their colleagues, Graham Cranfield and John Westmancoat, facilitated my extensive use of *The Standard* files. I am greatly indebted also to Andrew Phillips, Director, Humanities and Social Sciences, The British Library, for his help and for permission to quote from letters held by the Library.

In the newspaper world, I must thank Ivor Cole, legal director, Associated Newspapers; Rt. Hon. Michael Foot, former editor *Evening Standard*; and Angus McGill, columnist, *Evening Standard*; for reading various chapters and offering wise advice. I am indebted also to Lord Hugh Cudlipp, former editorial director of the *Daily Mirror* and *Sunday Mirror*; Paul Dacre, editor the *Daily Mail* and former editor of the *Evening Standard*; Robert Edwards, former editor of the *Daily Express* (twice), *The People*, the *Sunday Mirror* and leader writer of the *Evening Standard*; Max Hastings, editor of *The Daily Telegraph*, former special correspondent for the *Evening Standard*; Simon Jenkins, former editor of *The Times* and *Evening Standard*; Sir John Junor, former editor of the *Sunday Express* and deputy editor of the *Evening Standard*; Louis Kirby, former editor of the *Evening News* and *Evening Standard*; George Newkey-Burden, honorary archivist of *The Daily Telegraph*; Craig Orr, managing editor *Evening Standard*; Tom Pocock, former war correspondent of the *Evening Standard*; Stewart Steven, former editor of the *Mail on Sunday* and editor of the *Evening Standard*; and Jocelyn Stevens, the chairman of English Heritage, formerly managing director of the *Evening Standard*.

Other newspaper personalities to whom I owe thanks include John Beadell, Chief Executive, Audit Bureau of Circulations; Anne Chisholm and Michael Davie, authors of *Beaverbrook: a life*; David Elliot; Vyvyan Harmsworth, Director, Corporate Affairs, Associated Newspapers; Admiral Sir Ian and Lady Hogg; Ed Ram, Circulation director, *Evening Standard*; Leo Simmonds, former Personnel Director, Express Newspapers; Anne Sebba, author of *Battling for News: The Rise of the Woman Reporter*; and George Malcolm Thomson, distinguished leader writer and, at 94, the oldest former member of the *Evening Standard* editorial staff.

For the supply of illustrations, I am indebted to the Associated Newspapers' picture library; the former *Evening Standard* picture library, with special thanks to Ron Brierley and the late John King: the *Daily Express* picture library (Keith Beard); the Hulton-Deutsch picture library, the Beaverbrook Foundation, the Board of Trustees of the Victoria and Albert Museum, *Punch* and John Frost. At Macmillan, I would like to thank Tim Farmiloe, editorial director, who commissioned the book, Belinda Holdsworth, Keith Povey and Stephen Rutt, business publishing director, for their encouragement and advice. Finally, and above all, I must thank my wife, Elizabeth, and my family for their understanding during the writing of this book.

DENNIS GRIFFITHS

The author and publishers wish to thank the following for permission to use copyright material: Guardian Newspapers Ltd for extracts by Michael Burn in the 26 August 1985 issue of *The Guardian* – Copyright © 1985 The Guardian; David Higham Associates on behalf of the author for material from A. J. P. Taylor, *Beaverbrook*, Hamish Hamilton, 1972; Ewan MacNaughton Associates for 'Fleet Street's Standards', 29 April 1975, *Daily Telegraph* – Copyright © 1977 The Telegraph plc; Times Newspapers Ltd for an extract from Simon Winchester, 'Invaders' flag flies in Port Stanley', 3 April 1982, *The Times* – Copyright © 1982 Times Newspapers Ltd; HarperCollins *Publishers* Limited for material from N. Nicolson (ed.) *Harold Nicolson Diaries 1930–39*. Every effort has been made to trace all the copyright-holders, but if any have been inadvertently overlooked the publishers will be pleased to make the necessary arrangement at the first opportunity.

Standard Names and Spellings

Throughout its history, the *Evening Standard* has had a variety of name changes: *The Standard, Evening Standard, New Standard, The London Standard, The London Evening Standard* and, now, *Evening Standard.* Please note, though, that after 1917, where the word *Standard* has been used it refers to the *Evening Standard* or any of its derivatives.

Please note that where text has been quoted the original spellings and punctuation have been retained.

Foreword

A few years ago the *Evening Standard* ran an advertising campaign with the slogan 'A great newspaper for a great city'. It was a proud, not to say, a bold claim but, unlike some statements in the advertising world, it was and is rooted in a fundamental truth.

London is a great city; one of the world's greatest. The *Evening Standard* is part of that greatness echoing London themes, charting the foibles and follies of its residents, complaining with its commuters, sampling its restaurants, enjoying its theatre. Its ability to reflect the hopes and aspirations of Londoners, to help and to amuse them in their daily lives, to find them work and to help them choose their entertainment, and to add significantly to that overall mix which makes London special, is what makes the *Evening Standard* a great newspaper.

No other city in the world can boast of an evening newspaper with a circulation close to the 500,000 per night regularly sold by the *Evening Standard.* Nor for that matter can several national newspapers. That circulation is more than most quality papers achieve with the whole country to aim at, and even those downmarket tabloids with huge circulations nationally cannot outsell the *Evening Standard* on its home ground, within the metropolitan area. Its readers care for it just as it cares for them.

It is unique, too, because, at a time when many local evening papers have allowed their editorial stock to be undermined by the complacency which comes with monopoly, or have lapsed into parochialism, and have had their advertising base attacked by free sheets and give-aways, the *Evening Standard* has fought against any decline in its standards. As a result of its editorial flair it is the paper which sets the agenda for the next day's newspapers, radio and television. Courted by politicians, feared by the bureaucrats, it is once again at the heart of London life, and through London has its finger on the pulse of the nation.

Dennis Griffiths has seen in this paper a story to tell, and a history worth repeating. In fact, as he skilfully shows, there are almost as many stories about the *Standard* as there are stories in it. And that is as it should be. As one of the oldest papers in Fleet Street, it is part of publishing folklore and this history will ensure that the principles of journalistic and commercial excellence, on which the *Evening Standard* is built, will be available for future generations. They could do worse than copy them.

VISCOUNT ROTHERMERE

1

An Outspoken Publisher

The Standard, London's sole surviving evening newspaper, first appeared at two o'clock on the afternoon of Monday, 21 May 1827, in the reign of George IV, during a heatwave. It was launched by Charles Baldwin, already owner of the successful thrice-weekly *St. James's Chronicle*, with the backing of the Tory Party, in opposition to Catholic emancipation.

However, the story of *The Standard*'s origins really goes back to the time of Oliver Cromwell and the Protectorate, for it was then, on 12 June 1653, that Richard Baldwin, great-grandfather of Charles, was born in High Wycombe, Buckinghamshire. The son of Thomas, a hemp-dresser, Richard[1] was bound at the age of fourteen for seven years from August 1668 to George Eversden, a printer, who had a business at the Adam and Eve, St. John's Lane, in the City of London, where he specialised in the publication and sale of theological books.

Richard's father, Thomas Baldwin, was a well-known figure in High Wycombe, and is mentioned in the First Wycombe Ledger Book.[2] At the Guildhall on 17 June 1663, alongside seventeen aldermen and others, he took the Oath of Allegiance to the King. The following year, on 23 March, 'accordinge to Charter Mr Thomas Bauldwin was elected Bayleiff and then sworne and at the same tyme took the oathe mentioned in a late Act for the Regulacion of Corporacions and Alleagiance and Supremacy'.

It was a difficult time in English history to be a printer and publisher, for during the Protectorate of Oliver Cromwell there had been effectively a state monopoly of news under the supervision of a government censor, with the licensed press being suppressed from October 1649 to June 1650 and again from 1655. At the Restoration, five years later, the system was transferred to the Royalists, and under the comprehensive Printing Act of 1662 the press was formally placed under tight parliamentary control.

Because of these strictures, publishing was a precarious business, and any titles that offended parliament were immediately suppressed, a great number of the authors and printers being fined and imprisoned. As for the hawkers or mercuries (many of whom were women) who sold the publications in the street, they were often treated as common rogues and whipped or sent to gaol. Despite these risks, a great number of newsbooks appeared during this period, some often short-lived, but the desire was there for a free press. Samuel Sheppard, a clergyman/publisher, who had himself been imprisoned, wrote at the time: 'What a pannique possesses the souls of the Universe when the hawkers come roaring along the streets like the religious singers of Bartholomew Fayre.'[3]

With the press still under parliamentary control, there sprang up a series of licensers, of whom Sir Roger L'Estrange was foremost. He has been described as the most distinguished writer of the reigns of Charles II and James II, and the journalist of the Restoration. He was the first English journalist to sit in the House of Commons, the first English journalist distinguished by the favour of the Crown, and the first English writer to make journalism a profession. In contrast, for his work as Surveyor of the Press, L'Estrange was paid £3,200 a year and he carried out his duties with a conscientiousness bordering on the obsessive. In 1663, he published *Considerations and Proposals in Order to the Regulation of the Press* in which he recognised the connection between the poverty of the printers and the incentive to seditious printing: 'One great evil is the multiplicity of printers, who for want of public and warrantable employment, are forced to play the knaves in corners, or want for bread.'

L'Estrange let it be known that informers would be rewarded at his office in Ivy Lane. He did not have long to wait, for within months of publishing his *Regulations of the Press* the premises of John Twyn, of Cloth Fair, were raided in October 1663. Twyn was to be the most unfortunate of all the victims, for he was found guilty of printing sheets which expounded that 'If the magistrates prevent judgement, the people are bound by the law of God to execute judgement without them and upon them.'[4] For this, the unhappy Twyn was hanged, disembowelled and quartered.[5]

But, despite all the fears of parliament, the printing industry in London remained small. A survey of 1668 reported that there were 26 masters, 24 apprentices and 148 journeymen, making a total of 198 men employed on sixty-five presses. Of these, the King's Printer had six presses; there were two printers with five; three with four; five with three; nine with two; and six with only one press. The King's Printer employed eighteen workmen and the larger offices from seven to thirteen, but most had less than half a dozen and several only one or two.[6]

The Stationers' Company still retained its role as arbiter of the printing trade, but its power had been slowly declining for more than twenty years. When Charles II restored the monarchy in 1660, the master printers were in dispute with the merchants of the Company, and had suggested that they should be given the authority to regulate the industry. L'Estrange, in his role as Surveyor of the Press, was quick to dismiss their claim: 'It were a hard matter to pick out twenty master printers who are both free of the trade, of ability to manage it, and of integrity to be trusted with it: most of the honester sort being impoverished by the late times, and the great business of the Press being engrossed by Oliver's creatures.'

FIRST APPRENTICE

It was against this background that young Richard Baldwin, having served his apprenticeship, was admitted to the freedom of the Stationers' Company on 25 August 1675. Within twelve months, Baldwin had taken on his first apprentice, Joseph Rydale, of Great Hampden, Buckinghamshire, and had set up shop at Ball Court in the Old Bailey.

In 1679, Parliament allowed the Printing Act to lapse, and as a direct consequence there was an immediate increase in the number of new publications. However, many of these were suppressed through the use of royal proclamations and the law of seditious libel. Among the new publishers the name of Richard Baldwin was to stand out as a champion of English political freedom, and this continued to be so until his early death in 1698. His support of the Protestant cause was then carried on by his widow, Anne, until 1713.

The Baldwins rank among the foremost of the Fourth Estate, being forthright in their denunciation of the Stuarts and bitterly opposed to the imperialist machinations of King Louis XIV and the intrigues of the Vatican. For more than thirty years a succession of books, tracts and news-sheets poured from their premises. From the beginning, Baldwin deemed himself a political person, and in 1681 there appeared the first publication bearing his imprint: '*The Certain Way To Save England...By a Prudent Choice of Members to serve in the Next Ensuing Parliament.*'[7]

Having recently avoided imprisonment through 'Printing and publishing a Book Intituled *The Protestant Plot*', on Monday, 10 October 1681, he launched *Mercurius Anglicus*, a single folio sheet printed every Monday and Thursday. Baldwin immediately made a plea begging the indulgence of his readers for any errors and misreports which 'are the common fate of Discourses relating to Publick Affairs. Care shall be taken in collecting the contents of the said papers ...nothing shall be inserted which be false'. The *Mercurius Anglicus* carried few advertisements, the majority of its space being devoted to current local and foreign news, and there were strong attacks upon the Bourbons and the Papists. He criticised the Papists in his first issue, charging them with hiring 'certain Hawkers and other indulgent persons to disperse about this city and suburbs several scandalous Libels and Pamphlets, tending to create in People a disbelief of the Plot, and to shift it from their Party to the Presbyterians. They hire Ballad-Singers to sing about the Streets, and to disperse certain Songs and Ballads of the same tendency. The said Papists do send these villainous Papers into several parts of the kingdom by Posts, Carriers and Private Conveyances'.

Unfortunately, the paper was not a success and was discontinued after only three issues. Six months later, in April 1682, Baldwin launched the *London Mercury*, which was printed for him by Thomas Vile, an equally enthusiastic anti-Bourbon colleague. The *London*

Mercury followed the same style and format as the official state organ, *The London Gazette,* but differed essentially in its political stance. It was, however, to be another short-lived bi-weekly and lasted only until the following October.[8]

GLORIOUS REVOLUTION

For Baldwin, still a young man at 27, the year had marked the beginning of his publishing awareness; and during the next seven years, until the Glorious Revolution of 1688 and the downfall of James II, he was to issue more than forty books, of which twenty-seven had a distinct political bias: anti-Stuart, anti-French and anti-Tory. Still as violently anti-Papist as ever, Baldwin, on 24 April 1682, launched yet another newspaper, *The Protestant Courant, Imparting News Foreign and Domestick.* A two-sided sheet with just four columns, it did, however, carry about 25 per cent of advertising matter, including those for purging and purifying the blood. Also included was a poem 'upon the death of the late usurper, Oliver Cromwell, written by Mr John Dryden'. Born in 1631, John Dryden was at the time still Poet Laureate, with a stipend of £300 a year.

From the first issue, Baldwin was determined that the *Protestant Courant* should live up to its name and prove a worthy competitor to the loyalist papers, the *Observator* and the *Heraclitus Ridens.* However, publication of the *Courant* was not without its difficulties as he so sublimely declared in the issue of May 1–6:

> Whereas this paper (according to our Promise) have come out on Thursday last. These are to give Notice that some of the Popish Crew...despairing of totally suppressing it, were resolved to try an experiment on the Printer, which they did and detained him so long in Merry Company, that he wanted time to finish the Paper by the day appointed, so that now we have changed our Printer and our Days, and hereafter these Papers will be published every Wednesday and Saturday.

With the paper less than a month old, the *Protestant Courant* sprang to the defence of the Earl of Shaftesbury, who had found himself in serious legal difficulties. Sensing an injustice, Baldwin immediately published a scathing attack on the legal system, reviling the judges and several peers of the realm. Not surprisingly, he was promptly brought to court and arraigned before Justice George Jeffries, 'who severely checked him ... made a sharp complaint and moved that all the news and pamphlet publishers be severely punished'. In mitigation, Baldwin 'pleaded that he had good bail ready and prayed they might be accepted'. There is no evidence that he was imprisoned and it is likely that his 'good bail' was accepted, effecting his eventual release.

Unfortunately, the *Protestant Courant* was to be another short-lived venture, and within weeks it had closed, but not before Baldwin, in its fifth issue, had had an opportunity of attacking Sir Roger L'Estrange. On the front page, he was described as a 'Papist, proved by several Depositions upon Oath, etc., or for Declaring him as an Enemy of Parliament and the Protestant Religion'. Surprisingly, L'Estrange, still Surveyor of the Press, took no action.

However, Baldwin's repeated libels of the Stuart regime did not find favour with the officers of the Stationers' Company, and in the spring of 1682 his house was searched and he was 'perfidiously taken in Execution in a Publick Coffee House'. He was subsequently fined £10.6s for his derogatory remarks, and was informed that the writ for his seizure had been issued at the request of the Master of the Company, Thomas Vere.[9] The reply was swift and scathing: In the next issue of the *Protestant Courant*, Baldwin described Vere as 'one of so High Birth that he is ignorant of the Original of his Family; but to be sure he claims Adam for his first Ancestor'. With just a few issues of the paper to run, Baldwin once more found himself in trouble with the authorities; and on this occasion it was with the Grand Jury of Bristol who declared that its political and religious convictions had been grossly misrepresented in the *Protestant Courant*. As a rebuttal to these allegations, it was ordered that 'the several libels be, at the rising Court, publicly burnt by the Beadle or Common Executioner'. It is interesting to note that, although the country's road system was in its infancy, and the circulation of the *Courant* was barely a thousand copies, the paper had, indeed, found its way to Bristol.

Despite his short-lived ventures into newspapers, Baldwin was now a successful publisher, and from his new premises near the Black Bull in Old Bailey there continued to pour forth a succession of anti-Stuart pamphlets and books, which were to involve him in further trouble. His next adversary was the dreaded L'Estrange, who, in January 1683, wrote to Sir Leoline Jenkins: 'Had my importunities to have had the sifting of Baldwin prevailed, he should have either delivered up some persons more considerable than himself or not have been in a condition this day to do more mischief. Today is published by him a libel entitled a *Defence of the Charter and Municipal Rights of the City* written by Hunt of venomous malice against the King and the Duke, so far as I can judge by dipping into it.' It was to be six months, however, before the case was settled, when the Attorney General declared that 'the books in Baldwin's hands may be seized by warrant from any judge of the king's bench and detained till the matter be determined'. Bearing in mind the unfortunate experience of fellow-printer John Twyn in his brush with L'Estrange and the law, Baldwin must be considered a lucky individual.

In November 1688 came the moment that Baldwin and his colleagues had long been waiting for: the Glorious Revolution and the landing of William of Orange at Torbay, followed by the fleeing, within days, of James II, his wife and baby son to the court of Louis XIV. With William and Mary now ruling, Baldwin issued another of his famous pamphlets; and after their accession until his death ten years later Baldwin was to publish almost 250 books, of which 150 have a political slant, and of these, seventy-five were anti-French in their content.

In March 1688, Baldwin launched yet another newspaper, with the quaint title of *An Account of the Proceedings of the Meetings of the Estates of Scotland*; and within the next three years he sponsored *The Dublin Intelligence*, a newspaper for Irish Protestants living in London, and followed it with *The Scotch Mercury*, which was designed to give 'a true account of the daily proceedings and most remarkable Publick Occurrences in Scotland'.

With the increase in his publishing business, Baldwin and his wife, Anne, had to move into larger premises, and by 1691 they were producing from 'near the Oxford Arms, in Warwick Lane'; and there they were to remain, in the shadows of Wren's masterpiece, the rebuilt St. Paul's Cathedral. Three years later, on 11 August 1694, Baldwin's most successful and enduring newspaper, *The Post-Man* was launched; a publication that was to outlast him by more than thirty years. It began as the oddly-titled *Account of the Publick Transactions in Christendom*, and was called, briefly, *The Holland Paquet Book*.

For the first time, the press was about to be set free, for in 1695 censorship was allowed to lapse, and Milton's dream of 'liberty of unlicensed printing' was finally realised. As a result there appeared a small flurry of new titles. Among them was *The Post-Man* on October 22 – after an abortive amalgamation with the rival *Post Boy* of Abel Roper. Other newspapers to be launched at this time were *The Flying Post*, *The English Courant* and *The Weekly Messenger*. In London there was to emerge a new breed of scribes, among them Jean de Fonvive, a Huguenot exile, who was later to edit *The Post-Man*. As one of the capital's leading newspapers, *The Post-Man* appeared every Tuesday, Thursday and Saturday, and retained correspondents in Italy, Spain, Portugal, Flanders and Holland. Its renown was such that the Duke of Marlborough insisted that it alone carry his front-line despatches.

Fonvive, reputed to be earning £600 per year, laid out his paper's policy in one of the early issues: 'I shall write to you as often as I shall have any subject matters, but you must not always expect from me extraordinary things; so neither must you expect that I should take notice of all little trifles. This is the Province of the most Common News-Writers, with whom I do not deign in the least to interfere.'

One of the chief sources of information for these news-writers was the coffee-house – and it also provided the basis for their newspapers' circulations. At the time of the freeing of the press, there were almost 500 such premises in London, each with its own distinctive clientele. Describing the role of the news-writer, Thomas Macaulay wrote that he

> rambled from coffee-house to coffee-house collecting reports, squeezed himself into the Sessions Houses at the Old Bailey if there was an interesting trial, nay, perhaps obtained permission to the gallery in Whitehall and noticed how King and Duke looked. In this way he gathered materials for weekly epistles destined to enlighten some country town or some bench of rustic magistrates. Such were the sources from which the inhabitants of the largest provincial cities, and the great body of the gentry and clergy learned almost all they knew of the history of their own time.[10]

Meanwhile, in the autumn of 1695, Baldwin and his editor, Fonvive, were to commence a war of words with former associate Abel Roper, and in the October 16 issue of *The Post-Man* there appeared the following statement:

> Whereas I have for several months published a News Paper called the *Post Boy*, and the Historical Account I have now for some reasons thought fit to continue my Historical Account by the same Author, with the additional title of *The Post-Man* and to give notice that what advertisements shall be sent to me, shall be incerted in my News Paper as formerly.

Roper's retort was rapid:

> Whereas R. Baldwin did on Thursday last publish a Paper called the *Post-Man* where he could insinuate that the same was writ by the author of the *Post Boy*. This is to give notice that the Same is altogether False, for the author of the said *Post-Man* and Historical Account is Monsieur de Fonvive and that the *Post Boy* is, always was, writ by me and no other. If any has occasion to insert Advertisements therein, they are desired to send them to A. Roper, J. Moxon and R. Beardwell.

A feature of the period was the Postscript, and in the issue of *The Post-Man*, dated 4–6 February 1696, Baldwin announced: 'This paper having found a General acceptance the Publisher has thought fit to add a Postscript on the 3d [third] side of the whole sheet which shall be done upon good Paper, and shall contain all the most Remarkable occurences of any Gentleman or News Writer shall think fit to make use of them, etc.' The paper would be printed off a full rather than a half sheet, leaving pages 3 and 4 blank, and any late news could then be written on these blank sides. Baldwin asserted, with some pride, that 'They may have them at a very reasonable rate at the Publisher at Oxford Arms in Warwick Lane, and there will be space left, for business or what other means they shall think proper to incert, they are designed to be publisht at 4 in the afternoon every Post day and will begin next week.' The success of this brought a horde of imitations and forgeries; and so concerned were the publishers of *The Post-Man* that they were forced to list the booksellers and news hawkers from whom the newspaper was available.

Problems with forgers were still apparent a decade later, for in the issue of 23–25 April 1706, it was reported: 'There being a Sham Post-script published last night, with an Advertisement, intending to impose the same upon People a Postscript to the *Post-Man*. We think fit to desire our Readers to buy no Postscripts to the *Post-Man* from Hawkers they do not know, as the only means to stop the Villainous practice; and when there is any material News, we shall take care to publish a Postscript, provided it be a Post-day and not too late.'[11]

But still the forgers were busy copying the postscripts; and, in a final bid to defeat them, the publishers issued the following notice in the newspaper:

> Since the counterfeiting of Papers under the Title of Postscripts, etc., is so much in fashion, that People are not ashamed of that Villainy, the Author of the *Post-Man* has thought fit to have a particular sort of Paper made for his use having these words *THE POST-MAN* in the Margin, wrought in the making of the Paper, whereby his Postscripts may easily be distinguished from all others, for such where there is no such Mark are none of his. N. B. That the *Post-Man* and True Postscript shall for the future be printed on this new Paper; and 'tis hoped that the Paper-makers have not amongst them such scandalous People as to counterfeit this Mark, but if they do, they shall be prosecuted according to Law.

SIX ISSUES

Baldwin, meanwhile, apart from two short-lived newspaper ventures – *The Pacquet of Advice from France* which appeared for six issues in April 1691 and *Mercurius Reformatus or The New Observator* which ran from April to November 1691 – had maintained a sure touch. A string of publications had issued from his press, and among these were *The Gentleman's Journal; or The Monthly Miscellany,* which numbered contributions from Dryden and songs from Purcell. Another was *Mis-*

cellaneous Letters, a literary journal, which included selections on 'English Books printed in London' and a digest of foreign books.

Now a prosperous businessman, Baldwin had in December 1692 been admitted to the livery of the Stationers' Company;[12] and from his premises he continued to be a guardian of the press, remaining ever scornful of the Bourbons and Papists. He had, however, been unwell for a considerable time, and the stresses and pressures of the previous twenty years were now finally about to take their toll. After much suffering from consumption, he died at his premises and was buried in his native High Wycombe on 24 March 1698.

His long-standing friend and customer, John Dunton, summed up the man in a fulsome and worthy tribute:

> Mr Richard Baldwin. He printed a great deal, but got as little by it as John Dunton. He bound for me and others when he lived in the Old Bailey; but, after removing to Warwick Lane, his fame for publishing spread so fast, he grew too big to handle his small tools.
>
> Mr Baldwin having got acquaintance with Persons of Quality, he was now for taking a shop in Fleet Street; but Dick, soaring out of his element, had the honour of being a Bookseller but few months. However, to do Mr Baldwin justice, his inclinations were to oblige all men, and neglect himself. He was a man of generous temper, and would take a cherishing glass to oblige a Customer. His purse and his heart were open to all men that he thought honest; and his conversation was very diverting. He was a true lover of King William; and, after he came on the Livery, always voted on the right side.
>
> His wife, Mrs A. Baldwin, in a literal sense was an helpmate, and eased him of all his publishing work; and since she has been a Widow, might vie with all the women in Europe for accuracy and justice in keeping accompts: and the same I heard of her beautiful daughter, Mrs Mary Baldwin, of whom her Father was very fond. He was, as it were, flattered into his grave by a long consumption; and now lies buried in Wickam parish, his native place.[13]

The death of Richard did not, however, mark the end of the House of Baldwin, for in his widow, Anne, he left a person determined to maintain his standards in an outspoken Protestant press. Under her guidance, and the editorship of Fonvive, *The Post-Man* had grown to become one of the most successful newspapers of the period, with a circulation of between 3,800 and 4,000. However, the largest-selling title remained *The Gazette,* which, printed on Mondays and Thursdays, sold 6,000 copies. Four newspapers – *London Post, English Post, Flying Post* and *Review* – had circulations of less than 400, while the *Daily Courant* sold 800; *Observator* 1,000 and Abel Roper's *Post Boy* 3,000.

Production of the newspapers was still basic; using the hand press the printers could ink and pull only 250 single sheets in an hour. By working in relays, 2,000 copies could be produced in eight hours from two presses; and with a popular newspaper such as *The Post-Man* four presses would be required and the paper would be set twice so as to speed up the production. Make-up remained simple, generally consisting of a single folio half-sheet, with two columns front and back, and a decorative masthead and initial drop letter.[14]

Apart from the coffee-houses, the news vendors, or mercuries, were the chief means for the distribution of the newspapers. They controlled a circulation of some thousands in and around London, and, as a consequence, bore the brunt of the prosecutions against the papers they distributed. John Dunton wrote of them: 'I might also characterise the honest (mercurial women), Mrs Baldwin, Mrs Nutt, Mrs Curtis, Mrs Mallett, Mrs Croome, Mrs Taylor, and I must not forget Old Bennett, that loud-mouthed promoter of the *Athenian Mercury*.'

More than forty years later they were still proving a problem for the authorities – only by then they were better organised. The Attorney General himself could complain of the proprietors of unstamped newspapers: 'By their Mercuries and Hawkers [they] not only dispose of them in great numbers in the streets of London and Westminster but in all contiguous counties and have lately taken up a practice and have found means to disperse them 50 to 60 miles from London by their agents and hawkers some travelling on horse and others on foot going from town to town and house to house'.

CLASSIC AGE

On 8 March 1702, King William died, ushering in the reign of Queen Anne. In many ways Queen Anne's reign has been regarded as the classic age of English literature. It was the time of Jonathan Swift, Joseph Addison, Richard Steele, Alexander Pope and Daniel Defoe, and the period of *The Tatler* and *The Spectator* – and Mrs Baldwin was involved with them all. Her period of activity as a publisher and bookseller was to span the next dozen years. Against the background of an almost free press, between 1700 and 1710 she published nine of Defoe's pamphlets, including *The Present State of Jacobitism Considered*, and *A Speech without Doors*. Regarded as 'the father of English journalism', Defoe was undoubtedly the first journalist of major standing, being a frequent contributor to the principal journals and a regular pamphleteer. It was his writing of a savagely ironic pamphlet, *The Shortest Way with Dissenters*, in 1703 that led to his arrest and imprisonment in Newgate. Pleading guilty at the trial, he was sentenced to stand three times in the pillory, to pay a fine of 100 marks, to remain in prison during the Queen's pleasure and to find sureties for his good conduct during the next seven years. Dreading the ordeal, Defoe was locked into the pillory on 31 July 1703, alongside Temple Bar, but he was received not with eggs and abuse but with flowers, and men toasted his health.[15]

Meanwhile, *The Post-Man* had been sold by Mrs Baldwin to Francis Leach, of Elliot Court. However, it remained a profitable venture, for its production costs could be covered on sales of only 600 copies, and, although heavier distribution charges would bite into the 3,000-plus newspapers sold three times a week, there was a growing revenue from advertising. The style of these advertisements remained simple in presentation, but the following passage from issue dated 1–3 February 1704 must stand out as a classic in any age:

> A large collection of curious Original Paintings, Italian, Dutch and English, Ancient and Modern, viz Guido, Michel Angelo, Rubens, Vandyke, Dobson and other Masters, will continue to be expos'd to view this present Thursday being the 3d day of Feb. and continue to be daily expos'd until the Auction begins, of which timely notice shall be given, in Crown Court in the Old Change near St. Paul's.

The one-time owner herself used the newspaper as a medium to advertise her wares:

> There is published and sold by Mrs Baldwin in Warwick-lane, The Necessity and Usefulness of the Dispensaries lately set up by the College of Physicians in London, for the use of the Sick poor: together with Answers to all the Objections rais'd against them by the Apothecaries, or others. Wherin 'tis proved, that Physicians have a right and a necessity to prepare and give Medicines, but that Apothecaries have neither a right nor capacity to practice Physick.[16]

It was during this period that the popularity of *The Post-Man* encouraged Mrs Baldwin to publish a French translation for distribution among the London Huguenots and for sale on the Continent. Apart from newspapers and pamphlets, she continued to sell her own books and those of colleagues, and she was responsible for several political journals, including *The New State of Europe* and *The Politick Spy*. For the Whig Party, from October 1710 to August 1711, she issued on Mondays and Fridays *The Medley*. It was edited by Arthur Maywaring, a member of the Kit-Kat Club, and he was assisted by Steele, John Henley and John Oldmixon. Their outspokenness brought criticism from Swift, who referred to 'those devils of Grub Street, rogues that write the *Flying Post* and *Medley* in one paper, will not be quiet. They are always insulting Lord Bolingbroke and me'.

Two of her more esoteric publications at this time dealt with trade prospects and the weather. *The British Merchant of Commerce Preserved,* apart from attacking pro-French groups, discussed tariffs, exports and imports of wines, silks, linens, paper and kidskins. The other publication was *The Monthly Weather Paper* which was designed as a guide to the fogbound Londoner, the timid traveller and the cautious visitor. The paper contained 'Boroscopical discoveries from what Part or Parts of the Compass the Wind may likely flow, with what other sorts and alterations of the weather may be expected every Day and Night in March'.

However, it is for *The Tatler* and *The Spectator* that Anne Baldwin is perhaps best remembered. Three months after Steele had launched *The Tatler*, there was presented to the fashionable of London, on 8 July 1709, *The Female Tatler.*[17] It was edited by Mrs Crackenthorpe, 'A Lady that knows everything'. She was, in fact, Mrs Mary de la Rivere Manley,[18] the first woman editor, and author of an infamous book, *Secret Memoirs and Manners of Several Persons of Quality of both Sexes. From the New Atlantis.* Its publication was both a sensation and an embarrassment, and in October 1709 she was arrested for libelling public men in the work; fortunately, she was discharged the following February. In Swift she had an admirer who was to urge that she should be rewarded for her services to the Tory cause, describing her as a woman of 'very generous principles for one of her sort, and a great deal of sense and invention; she is about forty, very homely and very fat'.

After a row with one Benjamin Bragge, from issue Number 19 *The Female Tatler* was transferred by its editor to Mrs Anne Baldwin, since she [Mrs Crackenthorpe] had been 'disingenuously treated' by Bragge. Here, indeed, was to be a fearsome female combination. The periodical was now in competition with *The Tatler* but was published on 'contrary days'. Although *The Female Tatler* was first and foremost a gossip sheet, Mrs Crackenthorpe masked the text with high ideals. She was one of the first 'agony aunts', as her advice in the issue of October 1709 showed: 'The young lady in the Parish of St. Laurence near Guild Hall, that lately went to the Coffee House in Man's Cloathes with two 'Prentices, called for a Dish of Bohee, smoak'd her Pipe, and gave herself an abundance of Stroddling Masculine Airs, is desir'd to do so no more.'

Despite being a success, *The Female Tatler* was not without its critics, especially among those who had been libelled, and late in 1709 Mesdames Baldwin and Crackenthorpe found themselves indicted by the Grand Jury of Middlesex[19] which declared that 'A Great Number of printed papers are continually dispersed under the name of the *Female Tatler* sold by A. Baldwin and other papers under other Titles ... which ... reflect on and scandously abuse several persons of honour and quality, many of the magistrates and abundance of citizens and all sorts of people'.

Mrs Crackenthorpe was by then proving to be a liability even to the redoubtable Mrs Baldwin, and a month later the ladies parted company. As for Mrs Crackenthorpe, she regretfully announced her retirement because of 'an affront offer'd to her by some rude citizens, altogether unacquainted with her person'. For the remainder of its short life, until March 1710, *The Female Tatler* was to be conducted by 'A Society of Ladies'.

Since its launch in April 1709, *The Tatler* had been in the hands of Richard Steele, and of the 271 issues until it ceased publication Addison wrote only forty-two. From its first appearance, as a two-page, thrice-weekly journal, it became the favourite of the coffee-houses and of all who enjoyed civilised discussion.[20] But, even while Steele and Addison were achieving success, their thoughts were on launching a daily periodical, *The Spectator*, and as a result *The Tatler* was closed. Its loss was greeted with sadness by its readers. John Gay wrote: 'The coffee-houses realised that it had brought them more Customers, than all their other News Papers put together.'[21]

Within days of *The Tatler*'s demise, the indefatigable Mrs Baldwin had sponsored a *New Tatler*, edited by William Harrison, a young poet and protégé of Swift. It made its first appearance on January 13, 1711, and Swift writing to his pupil and friend, Stella, reported:

> Today little Harrison's *New Tatler* came out. There is not much in it, but I hope he will mend. You must understand that upon Steele's leaving off, there were two or three Scrub *Tatlers* come out, and one of them holds on still and today it is advertised against Harrison's. I am afraid the little toad has not the true vein for it.

Swift's fears were well founded, for within weeks the periodical was in serious financial trouble and in May 1711 it ceased publication.

Two months earlier, on 11 March *The Spectator*[22] had made its appearance and was an instant success. Virtually a daily paper, it ran until December 1712, and in this period 555 issues were produced, of which Steele was responsible for 236 and Addison for 274. Besides Mrs Baldwin, who was in charge of circulation and the soliciting of advertisements, the paper had the backing of Samuel Buckley, who, since 1702, had been producing the *Daily Courant*, the first daily newspaper.

In an age of small circulations, *The Spectator* reached a wide audience and every copy had many readers; within weeks, its sales had risen to more than 4,000. Because not all who wanted to read the paper could afford to buy it daily, it was collected and bound periodically, affording further opportunities for Mrs Baldwin and her helpers. A first printing of 10, 000 copies of the bound volume was not unusual.

The number of coffee-houses in London now numbered more than 2,000, and *The Spectator* was read and discussed everywhere. Other papers were also prosperous; and, as Addison wrote, 'About half-a-dozen ingenious men live very plentifully about this curiosity of their fellow-subjects.' *The Spectator* reigned supreme: the antics of Sir Roger de Coverley and his friends were greeted everywhere with delight; and, as conceived by Addison, Mr Spectator was the very epitome of the new journalist: a man who knew everything and everybody. From his lofty position, Addison could comment on the rest of the press and its treatment of the news: 'They all of them receive the same advices from abroad, and very often in the same words; but their way of cooking it is so different that there is no citizen, who has an eye to the public good, that can leave the coffee-house with peace of mind, before he has given every one of them a reading.'[23]

But the good times of an unfettered press could not last; on 1 August 1712, after seventeen years of freedom, and in response to a plea from Queen Anne for a remedy to the 'scandalous libels', parliament levied a stamp tax of a halfpenny on papers up to a half-sheet, of a penny up to a sheet, and of two shillings on more than a whole sheet (this last was apparently not enforced). Advertisements were to be taxed at a shilling irrespective of length.

Writing to Stella on 19 July, Swift commented: 'This Grub-street has but ten days to live.' Three weeks later he was to observe:

> Grub-street is dead and gone last week; no more Ghosts or Murders now for Love or Money .... *The Observator* is fallen, *The Medleys* are jumbled together with the *Flying Post*, the *Examiner* is deadly sick, the *Spectator* keeps up, and doubles its price. I know not how long it will hold.[24]

Addison's thoughts were equally pessimistic: 'this is the day on which many eminent authors will probably publish their last words'. Alas, as far as *The Spectator* was concerned, they were to be prophetic: the paper did, in fact, double its selling price, but by the year's end had ceased publication.

Now past middle-age, Mrs Baldwin was beginning to find the demands of more than thirty years in the publishing business excessive. Although there remains some doubt as to the date of her death, by November 1713 her imprint had ceased, and her premises in Warwick-lane had been taken over by James Roberts,[25] described as 'a printer of great eminence'. So came to a close the first generation of the Baldwin family, a family that was to remain a dominant factor in the newspaper world for the next 150 years; but there is little doubt that Richard and Anne Baldwin must rank high among the early champions of the press, establishing standards that were to be aspired to by their successors.

2

The Chronicle is Launched

The introduction of the stamp tax by Parliament did not have the desired effect of permanently reducing the sales of the newspapers, as trade was increasing and with it the size and power of the commercial classes. Despite this punitive measure, by 1750 the combined circulations had trebled.[1] One immediate effect, however, was a decline in the sales of daily newspapers and those of an essay-type nature. The death of *The Spectator* had marked the end of an era, as few people were now prepared to purchase this style of publication: the future belonged to the thrice-weeklies, such as *The Post-Man* (which were intended mainly for country distribution) and, above all, the weekly newspapers.

The Stamp Act of 1712, which was to be the basis of newspaper legislation throughout the eighteenth century, required that the sheets of paper should be stamped at the Head Office while they were still blank. Immediately before the Act's introduction, Addison wrote in *The Spectator* on 31 July: 'A sheet of Blank Paper ... must have this Imprimatur clapt upon it, before it is qualified to communicate anything to the Publick.' Its appearance was greeted by Swift in writing to Stella on 7 August: 'Have you seen the red stamp the press are marked with? Methinks, it is worth a halfpenny, the stamping of it.'

In an effort to bypass the Act, astute publishers took to issuing papers consisting of one-and-a-half sheets (six pages)[2] and so common was this between 1714 and 1724 that new legislation was introduced for George I on 5 April 1725. One result was that the proprietors of both the six-page journals and the thrice-weeklies were forced to raise their prices to 2d and 1d respectively and curtail the size of their papers to four pages.[3] It did not take the printers long, however, to realise that there was an omission in the Act: the restriction on the size of the page. This led, increasingly, to a large number of four-page newspapers as half-sheets, from which was to evolve a change in the make-up of the page from two to three columns.

Despite these strictures an unregistered press continued to flourish, and it has been estimated that there were at least thirty such titles circulating in London during this period. This underground press has been cited by Samuel Negus, a government agent, who was himself a printer, as the principal cause of the late [1715] rebellion and disturbances. All printers, whether registered or not, were held responsible for the legal contents of their papers: They considered it their duty not to pass on the name of any offending writer to the courts, even if they themselves would have escaped liability. The printing craft, generally, was very strict on this code, although in 1719 John Matthews was found guilty, on the evidence of two of his apprentices, of high treason in a publication.

During the dramas of the Stamp Act and among the growing unregistered press, the next generation of the Baldwin family was engaged in the more prosaic pursuits of the book trade. Richard, Baldwin's son (also called Richard) was born in 1691, and was apprenticed on 2 August 1708 to Robert Whitledge as a bookbinder. He was freed from the Stationers' Company on 2 May 1716.[4] From there he became a bookbinder and bookseller at Creed Lane, between 1726 and 1731, and at St. Paul's Churchyard. He lived to the great age of 86, dying on 4 June 1777 in Birmingham, leaving a widow Elizabeth. Their son, (also Richard, and also in the trade) predeceased them both in January 1770.

Robert, the brother of the elder Richard, did not go into publishing, but was in business in Farringdon in Berkshire, as an apothecary, although there is no record of his having been admitted to The Society of Apothecaries. His eldest son, Benjamin, was to qualify as a surgeon, but it was to be with his two other sons, Henry and Robert, that the publishing fortunes of the House of Baldwin were to be revived – a revival that was to involve such famous literary figures as Dr Samuel Johnson, James Boswell and Oliver Goldsmith.

ADMITTED TO THE LIVERY

Henry Baldwin, destined to be the better known of the two brothers, was born on 26 December 1734, and was apprenticed to Mary Say on 5 September 1749, being freed and admitted to the livery of the Stationers' Company on 7 December 1756.[5] Mary Say and her husband, Charles, were newspaper publishers, and among their titles was *The Gazeteer*, which was to involve them and Henry Baldwin in contempt proceedings instituted by parliament.

The Gazeteer holds a unique place in the development of the English newspaper, as it was the first-known publication to be run as a joint stock company.[6] It was founded in 1735 as *The Daily Gazeteer or London Advertiser*, and thirteen years later Articles of Agreement were drawn up declaring that 'the Property of the said Paper shall be divided into Twenty shares of which each subscribing Party shall be entitled to one'.

Apart from his apprenticeship under the Says, Henry Baldwin also received guidance from Mr Justice Ackers of Clerkenwell, the original printer of *The London Magazine*.[7] Founded in 1732, it had in its early days won fame for its unofficial reporting of parliamentary debates.

Although not current, these reports had caused great concern, so much so that in 1738 the House resolved that:

> It is a high Indignity to, and a notorious Breach of the Privilege of this House, for any News-Writer, in Letters or other Papers ... or for any Printer or Publisher of any News-papers, or of any Denomination, to presume to insert in the said Letters or Papers, or to give therein any Account of the Debates, or other Proceedings of this House ... as well during the Recess as the Sitting of Parliament.

To counteract this, *The London Magazine* reported the proceedings of a Roman Assembly, with speeches by Scipio Africanus and Tullius Cicero, among others. A key was provided in a supplement, but the readers were titillated by trying to guess the identities of the orators. *The Gentleman's Magazine*, in opposition, engaged Dr Johnson to cover the speeches, and as a subterfuge reported the debates of the Parliament of Lilliput. Both magazines, though, went too far and were brought to account in 1747 for their reporting of the trial of Lord Lovat, following his part in the 1745 Rebellion.

It is apparent that, even as a young man, barely out of his apprenticeship, Henry Baldwin was already a radical and moving in similar political circles: his grandfather would have been proud to have known that the family tradition was being maintained. However, it was to be with *The St. James's Chronicle* that he was destined to make his mark.

At the time of the launch of *The St. James's Chronicle*, in March 1761, London was served by three morning papers:[8] *The Public Advertiser*, famous for publishing the 'Letters of Junius'; *The Daily Advertiser*; and *The Gazeteer and London Daily Advertiser*, owned by Charles Say. Apart from the morning papers there were several evenings, including the *London Evening Post*, the *General Evening Post* and the *Whitehall Evening Post*.

The literary giant of the day was Dr Samuel Johnson who, aside from compiling his great *Dictionary of the English Language*, had also contributed to *The Gentleman's Magazine*, the *London Chronicle* and the *Universal Chronicle* – it was in the last-named that he ruminated on the state of the press and the merits of his fellow scribes. On 27 May 1758 he wrote:

> The compilation of newspapers is often committed to narrow and mercenary minds, not qualified for the task of delighting or instructing, who are content to fill their paper with whatever matter is at hand, without industry to gather or discernment to select. The tale of the morning paper is told in the evening, and the narratives of the evening are brought out again in the morning.

Six months later he was to comment:

> A news-writer is a man without virtue who lies at home for his own profit. To these compositions is required neither genius nor knowledge, neither industry nor sprightliness, but contempt of shame and indifference to truth are absolutely necessary.

It was Dr Johnson himself who set the tone of *The London Chronicle*, when, in its first issue on 1 January 1757, he wrote in the opening article:

> We pretend to no peculiar Power of disentangling Contradiction or denuding Forgery. We have no settled Correspondence with the Antipodes, Nor maintain any Spies in the Cabinets of princes. But as we shall always be conscious that our Mistakes are involuntary, we shall watch the gradual Discovery of Time, and retract whatever we have hastily and erroneously advanced.

Dr Johnson's great confidant, Boswell, was to write that the *The London Chronicle* had a more extensive circulation on the Continent than any other English paper and 'it has all along been distinguished for good sense, accuracy, moderation and delicacy'.

There seems little doubt that Baldwin was deeply influenced both by its contents and its presentation when he launched his *St. James's Chronicle.* At that time, the press was once again under attack from the government, for in 1757 the Stamp Act had been amended. This now imposed a duty of one penny on all newspapers, whether printed on a half-sheet or a full sheet, and there was a further imposition on the advertisement tax, which was raised to two shillings. Despite a vigorous protest from the press – far more vocal than in 1712 – the new Act was introduced. One effect was a fall-off in the number of newspapers, as owners were compelled to cease publication, and a consequent drop in duty paid to the government. However, for the remaining publishers, the new duty on the size of the sheet meant that it was now more economical to produce four-page newspapers, even though the price had to be raised to $2^1/_2$d.

THOROUGH TRAINING

Having undergone a thorough training, Henry Baldwin's first-known venture into the world of newspapers was as printer of *The London Packet.* This was almost certainly from his premises at Swan Alley, Aldersgate, but in 1761 he was in business in Whitefriars, and it was from there on 14 March that *The St. James's Chronicle: or, the British*

Evening Post was launched as a thrice-weekly evening paper. Shortly before its launch, Baldwin purchased from fellow-printer William Rayner *The London Spy, Read's Weekly Journal* and *St. James's Evening Post or British Gazette. The Spy* and *The Journal* were amalgamated to form a Saturday paper, and the *St. James's Evening Post* became *The St. James's Chronicle.* Baldwin, no doubt influenced by his experiences on *The Gazeteer,* formed a joint stock company to secure financial support on the paper's launch.[9]

The shareholders' meetings of *The St. James's Chronicle* cover fifty-four years and its Minute books are the most detailed of any eighteenth-century newspaper. As such, they provide a fascinating glimpse into the management of the press at that time. The notebooks containing the Minutes were only discovered during the past thirty-five years. Contained in three volumes, they detail more than 550 meetings held between 15 May 1761 and 9 August 1815.

There were 20 shares in the new company, and the shareholders included Baldwin, who held 3 shares; Bonnell Thornton, 4; Ralph Griffiths, 3; Thomas Beckett, $1\frac{1}{2}$; and Thomas Davies, 2. Most meetings were held in the Globe Tavern or the Bedford Head, not far from the Britannia Printing office where *The St. James's Chronicle* was published. Some meetings were even held in Henry Baldwin's home at New Bridge Street. To a large extent, the proprietors left the management of the business to Baldwin, who brought his records to the monthly meetings for inspection; and at one of these meetings held on 10 June 1761, it was noted that the 'Price for printing the first Thousand of *The St. James's Chronicle* should be Three Pounds Seven Shillings'.

From the outset, Baldwin and his co-proprietors were determined that their paper would lead the way, both in presentation and in the organisation of the news, and, apart from the domestic intelligence, the paper carried economic, foreign, military and political matters. Political matters were especially important as, with the accession of George III in 1760, the press had entered one of its most exciting periods, and interest in politics and public affairs had never been greater. George III had two main aims: to end the bloody war that came to be called the Seven Years' War and to remove William Pitt the Elder from office. To achieve these objectives he enlisted the aid of the press and its support ensured his success.

Against this background, *The St. James's Chronicle* appeared on Tuesdays, Thursdays and Saturdays, in order to catch the provincial mails. Distribution of newspapers from London to the country was a long-standing problem in the first half of the eighteenth century, despite the fact that 400 Road Acts had been passed; and in the next fifty years this figure was to exceed 1,000. The stage coach did not appear until mid-century and it was not until 1784 that the mail coach came into being. A daily coach service to most parts of the country was developed, and this was complemented by a steady increase in the number of cross-posts between provincial towns.[10]

From the seventeenth century the Clerks in the offices of the Secretaries of State had acted as the main retailers of London papers, sending copies to the provinces at reduced rates. The role was held by six Post Office Clerks of the Road, whose responsibility was for services to different parts of the country, making them ideal agents for the traffic of the London papers.[11] Although not without their faults – including vulnerability to political bribery – the Clerks performed a useful function, and their services were extensively used. As an example, a parliamentary investigation revealed that in seven days during March 1764 the Clerks had distributed more than 20,000 London papers, mainly on Tuesdays, Thursdays and Saturdays, however, by the end of the decade, it was possible for individuals whose names were registered at the Post Office to have their copies franked individually. There was a heavy demand for this service with Members of Parliament using the system, and by June 1789 the weekly number of newspapers posted had reached 63,177, compared with 12,909 for the Post Office Clerks and only 756 by the Secretaries' office.

As for the newly-launched *St. James's Chronicle*, which took full advantage of the Clerks' services from its first issues, its make-up consisted of four folio pages measuring 18 inches by 12 inches, with each page containing four columns. As a circulation ploy, the initial issue carried the words 'Given Gratis' in its masthead 'then 2d till Thursday March 26 when it will be advanced to the usual price of a *Chronicle* which is two-pence half-penny'.[12] Unlike its competitors, though, it was neatly produced and set a standard that others tried to emulate.

Within a few months of the paper's launch, Baldwin was joined by Nathaniel Thomas, fresh from Oxford University, who became editor. Thomas started at a guinea a week 'for translating the Mails, and making Extracts and giving accounts of such Books and Pamphlets as may be recommended, or he may think of worthy Notice, and doing other Matters for the Service of the Paper'. A few months later, his salary was increased 'in Consideration of the Care he has taken', and in 1765 it was set at 120 guineas per annum. After sixteen years he became a proprietor. He died in 1795, and was described as 'a gentleman of great learning and sound judgment and singular modesty'. He was succeeded by a Mr Tromlins, who received the same amount of salary.

From the outset, booksellers and authors were well represented among the proprietors: they regarded the paper as a double asset. On the one hand their connections in the publishing trade would help to establish the financial stability of the *Chronicle*, and on the other they could use its pages to advertise their books on favourable terms. At only the second meeting, it was resolved that 'the Printer would be at Liberty to insert Partner's Advertisements, not exceeding two per Week of each Partner's, charging such Partner's Advertisements with the Duty only'.[13]

Apart from the booksellers, three of the partners were figures of literary and theatrical eminence: Bonnell Thornton, George Colman and David Garrick. A great wit,[14] Thornton was a prominent person on the literary scene and he founded the Nonsuch Club, which dined every Thursday at his home in Covent Garden. It was he who was responsible for the publication of the *Chronicle Year Book* in 1762, which reprinted from *The St. James's Chronicle* the writings of Colman and himself. Thornton died comparatively young – at the age of 44 in 1768 – and is interred in Westminster Abbey.

His great friend, George Colman,[15] also educated at Oxford, practised at the Bar for a short period, but his heart was really in drama. A close colleague of David Garrick, he became involved in the Drury Lane Theatre and it was there that he staged his play *The Jealous Wife*, derived in part from *Tom Jones.* An immediate success, it starred Garrick, Mrs Pritchard and Mrs Clive. Two further plays, *Philater* and *The Deuce Is In Him*, followed in quick succession. With Garrick he wrote *The Clandestine Marriage*, which opened on 26 February 1766, and led to correspondence from Voltaire.

With *The St. James's Chronicle*, Colman is best remembered for his Genius series, which ran for fifteen months in 1761–2, with a deft style and a quick wit. Following a legacy from his mother, Colman then became a proprietor of the Covent Garden Theatre, and it was there that he introduced Oliver Goldsmith as a playwright, first with *The Good-Natur'd Man* and then, in 1773, with his lasting success, *She Stoops to Conquer.* For the following twenty years, Colman led a busy life in the literary and theatrical fields, but in 1793, he became 'feeble in mind', and had to be put under restraint in Paddington, where he died on 14 August 1794, at the age of 64. As a writer, he was much admired by his peers, as Byron testified in his memoirs: 'Let me begin the evening with Sheridan and finish it with Colman. Sheridan for dinner, Colman for supper.'

The early days of the *Chronicle* were indeed heady, as Nicholls was to recall more than thirty years later in his *Literary Anecdotes*:

> Baldwin, with the assistance of a phalanx of first-rate wits, brought it to a height of literary eminence till then unobtainable in any journal. From an early association with these men of eminence, both in the literary and fashionable world, he acquired elegant habits, and without any profound stock of literature he sufficiently cultivated a mind naturally strong to render his company and his conversation in the highest degree acceptable.

For the first few months, as one would expect, the *Chronicle* was published at a loss, but within a year the proprietors could declare a dividend, and by the end of the decade the annual profits were more than £1,900. From that moment, profits became regular, with the 1770s contributing £18,000 per annum, £16,000 in the 1780s, and £12,000 in the 1790s.[16] At the outset, the proprietors were explicit about the type of newspaper that they wished to produce. The price of grain, and the births and deaths from the weekly bills of mortality would be inserted, plus the 'List of Letters left at the General Post Office'. Some years later they resolved that the '*Hague*, the *Amsterdam* and the *Brussels Gazette* be retained, and the other three foreign Prints rejected'. It was also decided that all the county newspapers should be discontinued.

THE GOLDEN AGE

Of the original proprietors not already discussed, David Garrick was undoubtedly the most famous. Born in Lichfield in 1717, he was a pupil of Dr Johnson and moved with him to London in 1740. The following year he took the capital by storm with his portrayal of Richard III. From that moment, his fame as an actor was assured, and within six years he had become joint manager of the Drury Lane Theatre, where he remained for twenty-eight years, producing plays and acting in most of them.

Another of the partners was Thomas Davies, also an actor, who kept a bookshop in Russell Street, Covent Garden – a building still standing – and it was there, on 21 May 1763, that he experienced his finest moment: the introduction of James Boswell to Dr Samuel Johnson. Writing in his *Life of Johnson*, Boswell described the occasion in choice detail:[17]

> Mr Johnson, said I, 'I do indeed come from Scotland, but I can't help it'.
>
> Johnson retorted: 'That sir, I find, is what a very great many of your countrymen cannot help'.

Boswell was long associated with the proprietors of *The St. James's Chronicle* and was a regular at their literary gatherings. In later years he was to provide scholarly advice in discussions with Henry Baldwin's young son, Charles, the future founder of *The Standard.*

In 1762, after it had made numerous complaints, the House of Commons resolved that it was a 'high indignity, and a notorious breach of privilege of this House' to print any account of its proceedings. It was to be another three years, though, before the *Chronicle* became embroiled with the authorities. In its issue of 18 May 1765 it described a mass demonstration of impoverished London weavers, who were protesting against a proposed Silk Bill. The paper reported that 'About Two O'clock a Message was delivered them from the Lords, signifying that they could not proceed to the Re-consideration of their grievances 'till next Session, when every possible Step should be taken for their Advantage.'

Three days later, Baldwin, his past-master, Charles Say, of the *Gazeteer*, and Henry Woodfall, of the *Public Advertiser*, were summoned to the House of Lords. Woodfall said he had used the story from the *Chronicle*; Baldwin explained that he had copied it from the *Gazeteer*; and Say pleaded the cause of 'a Family of Six Children'. Each printer was fined £100, or detained in Newgate until paid. That same issue of the *Chronicle* was to bring another fine of £100 on Baldwin, for the Lords took exception to a paragraph reflecting on one of its Members. The total costs of these fines plus expenses was £225 10s 8d, which was duly recorded in the Minutes.

During the next five years, *The St. James's Chronicle* was to be involved in two incidents which were to have a profound effect on the British press. The first concerned John Wilkes, a parliamentarian, libertine and publisher of the *North Briton*. As a journalist, he was responsible for securing the tacit removal of the ban on reporting parliamentary debates, and he believed passionately in the right to criticise the government. His public victories were, perhaps, even more widespread: the vindication of the freedom of the electorate and the abolition of the general warrant.

On 5 June 1762, some twelve months after the launch of the *Chronicle*, Wilkes started the *North Briton* as a weekly journal of six pages. Week after week he published scurrilous attacks on the Earl of Bute and the Scottish influence on the court of the newly-crowned George III. In the first issue Wilkes wrote: 'The liberty of the Press is the birthright of a Briton, and is justly esteemed the finest bulwark of the liberties of this country.'[18] The attacks reached their peak on 23 April 1763, with the famous issue 'Number 45', a number that was to haunt the ministerial mind for many years. Wilkes wrote a long and highly damaging article on the King's Speech: 'Every friend of his country must lament that a prince of so many great and amiable qualities whom England truly reveres, can be brought to give sanction of his sacred name to the most odious measures, and to the most unjustifiable declarations, from a throne ever renowned for truth, honour, and unsullied virtue ... I wish as much as any man in the kingdom to see the honour of the crown maintained in a manner truly becoming Royalty. I lament to see it sunk even to prostitution'.

George III and his government were appalled at the remarks, and within days the Attorney-General and the Solicitor-General held that the article was 'an infamous and seditious libel, tending to inflame the minds and alienate the affections of the people from his Majesty, and to excite them to traitorous insurrections against his Government, and therefore punishable as a misdemeanour of the highest nature'. A general warrant authorising the arrest of the printers, writers and publishers – in all, forty-eight people – was issued, and the arrests began. Wilkes, a Member of Parliament, promptly issued a writ of *habeas corpus*, and appealed to the court in masterly fashion: 'My Lords, the liberty of all peers and gentlemen, and, what touches me more sensibly, that of all the middling and inferior set of people, who stand most in need of protection, is in my case this day to be finally decided upon a question of such importance as to determine at once whether English liberty shall be a reality or a shadow.'

Lord Chief Justice Pratt upheld the plea of privilege, and Wilkes was released from custody to be borne back in triumph to Westminster. The crowds now took up the cry 'Wilkes and Liberty!' He quickly followed up this success by taking action against the government for illegal arrest, a point seized upon by the others. All were ultimately awarded heavy damages and the Lord Chief Justice ruled that the issue of a general warrant was illegal. The case cost the government more than £100,000 in damages and expenses.

However, the matter was not to rest there, for in the ransacking of Wilkes' house a copy of *Essay of Woman*, a pornographic parody of Pope's *Essay on Man*, had been found. The House of Lords now ruled that it was 'a most scandalous, obscene and impious libel'. The peer chosen to move the resolution was Lord Sandwich, a one-time member of the Hellfire Club with Wilkes and one of the greatest rakes of his day. Following this resolution, Sandwich was henceforth named 'Jemmy Twitcher', after the character in *The Beggar's Opera*, for having thus turned on his fellow libertine. In a verbal clash on another occasion, Sandwich had received from Wilkes one of the most devastation retorts on record. 'Wilkes you will die of pox or on the gallows,' he had said. 'That depends, my Lord,' came the immediate response, 'whether I embrace your principles or your mistress.'

A motion was now passed in the House of Commons that the privileges of parliament did not extend to the writing or the publishing of seditious libels; and, as a consequence, Wilkes was formally expelled. Legal proceedings started afresh and he was found guilty of republishing the *North Briton* and of publishing the *Essay of Woman*. Wounded in a duel, Wilkes prudently departed for France, and in his absence was declared an outlaw. An attempt to burn copies of the *North Briton* outside the Royal Exchange led to a riot, and the law officers were roughly handled.

In 1768, Wilkes returned from exile, and, although technically still an outlaw, he stood for the City of London in the parliamentary election, but was rejected. Standing next for Middlesex, where the electorate included tradesmen and artisans, his reputation as a champion of liberty secured him victory by more than 400 votes. Twice he was refused his seat, and a third time the Ministry put up its own candidate, Colonel Luttrell, who was elected even though he polled fewer votes. London was in an uproar and everywhere the sign '45' was to be seen. Benjamin Franklin noted that 'there was not a door or window to be found in the City that was not marked with the figures 45, and this continued here and there quite to Winchester which is sixty-four miles.'[19]

During this period of the Middlesex elections and his constant rejections, Wilkes was in jail, having been fined £1,000 and sentenced to 22 months' imprisonment for the reprinting of 'No. 45' and the publishing of *Essay of Woman*. Even though incarcerated, his popularity with the people never waned, and as Edmund Burke so aptly observed: 'Since the fall of Ld. Chatham there has been no man of the Mob but Wilkes.'

If parliamentary parties could overrule the wishes of the people and install their own men, who were open to corruption and who would vote accordingly, then elections meant nothing. The mobs readily seized upon this and London was rife with excitement: it reached its peak with the Massacre of St. George's Field on 19 May 1768, when a dozen rioters were killed by the military.

During the next six months, passions gradually cooled until Wilkes published in *The St. James's Chronicle*[20] on 10 December a copy of a most indiscreet letter sent by Lord Weymouth to the local magistrates before the massacre. This urged the use of troops 'when the Civil power is trifled with and insulted, nor can a military Force ever be employed on a more constitutional Purpose, than in Support of the Authority and Dignity of the Magistracy.' Making the most of the situation, Wilkes noted in his introduction to the letter 'how long the horrid Massacre in St. George's Field had been planned and determined upon, and how long a hellish Project can be brooded over by some infernal Spirits without one Moment's Remorse.'

Wilkes was not alone in his fight. In April 1769, William Beckford, the Lord Mayor, and other supporters launched *The Middlesex Chronicle or Chronicle of Liberty*, a thrice-weekly newspaper 'to vindicate the cause of depressed liberty by exhibiting in full view of the people every measure that has already been taken and every attempt that may further be made.' Among the contributors was the precocious Thomas Chatterton, soon to commit suicide at the age of seventeen, who wrote letters for the paper in the style of 'Junius'.

Apart from Wilkes, 'Junius' was to have a greater impact in the battle for a free press than any other man. Although there still remains a doubt as to his identity, he was almost certainly Sir Philip Francis, who was fortunate in having the total backing of a completely fearless publisher in Henry Woodfall. Not only by their brilliance and force, but also by their regularity, the 'Letters of Junius' made public opinion a genuine voice in politics. The first letter appeared in the *Public Advertiser* on 21 January 1769,[21] and from the start were much admired for their style and incisive writing.

It was apparent that 'Junius' was privy to inside information – nothing and no one was sacred – and all were open to attack. But it was in the Letter of 19 December 1769 that he was to achieve lasting fame. It was addressed to the King, and the following extracts provide just a flavour of its biting invective:

> Sire – it is the misfortune of your life ... that you should never have been acquainted with the language of truth, until you heard it in the complaints of your people. It is not, however, too late to correct the error. You could 'shelter under the forms of parliament, and set your people at defiance' or you could 'Discard those little, personal resentments which have too long directed your public conduct ...Come forward to your people...Tell them you are determined to remove every cause of complaint against your government; that you will give your confidence to no man who does not possess the confidence of your subject'.

The Letter concluded in the most telling of phrases, one that has been repeated on countless occasions:

> The prince who imitates their conduct should be warned by their example; and while he plumes himself upon the security of his title to the crown, should remember that as it was acquired by one revolution, it may be lost by another.

Two days after its appearance in the *Public Advertiser*, Baldwin reprinted it in the *Chronicle*. So important was this letter that it was also reproduced in Say's *Gazeteer*, John Miller's *London Evening Post*, George Robinson's *Independent Chronicle* and John Alum's *London Museum*. Reacting with alacrity, the Government prosecuted all the newspapers, and the first to be tried was not Woodfall, who had printed the original letter, but Alum, who had merely copied it. Under the direction of Lord Chief Justice Mansfield, the jury found him guilty. Against Baldwin and the others, he said that the court alone had the power to say whether or not an offending publication was libellous, and the jury had only to decide whether the defendant was the publisher.

Woodfall was found guilty only of printing and publishing; Baldwin and Miller were acquitted; and Say and Robinson were apparently never tried. A fortnight after Baldwin's trial, the proprietors of *The St. James's Chronicle* resolved to take the opinion of Mr Serjeant John

Glynn, the distinguished defence counsel, as to 'whether a fair Action will lie against the Attorney general for the Expense of the late prosecution.'[22] 'Months later, the paper paid Mr Glynn £88 5s 10d for this advice.

Wilkes, like 'Junius', was now very much in favour with the proprietors, for there is a note in the Minutes regarding bad debts for advertisements. It was agreed that a bill and receipt should be sent to the great man for his non-payments, but the editor himself 'was desired to deliver them in such Way as his Discretion shall dictate.'

One result of the 'Junius' trial was an increase in the reporting of parliamentary debates and in their accuracy. In a bid to stop this, the House, on a motion from Colonel Onslow, moved on February 1771 that a resolution of 1738 prohibiting the publication of its proceedings be reaffirmed. This was, of course, quickly seized upon by the press, especially by John Wheble's *Middlesex Journal*. The item was immediately reproduced in the *Gazeteer*, and both printers were summoned to appear before the House. As neither printer put in an appearance, an irate Onslow now extended the writ to cover *The St. James's Chronicle, Morning Chronicle, London Packet, Whitehall Evening Post, General Evening Post* and *London Evening Post.*

As a result, Baldwin was made to kneel in penance before the Speaker – the last ever to do so. After being reprimanded he was discharged on paying his fees.[23] Baldwin rose in silence, ostentatiously brushed his knees, and in an audible aside remarked: 'What a damned dirty House'. Worried at putting Baldwin at risk once again, the proprietors of the *Chronicle* resolved on 4 March: 'That it is advisable to take the Proceedings of the House of Commons under the title of Details of the Representatives of the People of Utopia; and the Printer to be desired to take his measures accordingly.'

A month later, Wilkes took the case a stage further, allowing Wheble to be arrested by a fellow printer in the City. He was then brought before Wilkes, the Sitting Alderman at the Guildhall, and discharged. A similar occurrence took place with Miller, who had been apprehended on the authority of a warrant signed by the Speaker. At the Guildhall, Oliver, Wilkes and Lord Mayor Brass demanded on 'what authority could a citizen of London be arrested within the jurisdiction of its magistrates?' The Speaker's warrant, they declared, was illegal.

It was now a direct conflict between Parliament and the City: the Lord Mayor and Oliver were arrested, found guilty of breach of privilege and sent to the Tower. At the end of the parliamentary session they were released, to the roar of a 21-gun salute, and escorted in triumph by more than fifty carriages to the Mansion House. To the crowds, a great victory had been won: the press was finally free; the right to report Parliament decided.

3

A Phalanx of First-Class Wits

During these years of great change in the reporting of Parliament in the press, newspapers still endeavoured to provide a service describing the latest social affairs and nowhere was this more apparent than in the coffee-houses – especially those in the Covent Garden area. The centre for the proprietors of *The St. James's Chronicle* was the Bedford. As George Colman and Bonnell Thornton remarked: 'This coffee-house is every night crowded with men of parts. Almost every one you meet is a polite scholar and a wit; jokes and *bon mots* are echoed from box to box; every branch of literature is critically examined, and the merit of every production of the theatres weighed and determined.' It was here that the phalanx of first-class wits provided many of the exclusive stories for the *Chronicle.*

As for its chief proprietor, Henry Baldwin was now a successful printer and publisher, and a leading member of the Stationers' Company of which he was appointed Master in 1792.[1] Married to the former Eleanor Graham, he had three sons, Robert, George and Charles; and it was Charles who was destined to take the business to yet higher levels with his founding of *The Standard.* In 1772, Henry Baldwin moved to new premises at 108 Fleet Street, opposite Bride Lane, 'where advertisements etc. are taken and no-where else', and he remained there until 1778.

Although the press was now politically free, it was still prey to the laws of libel and, until Fox's Libel Act of 1792 restored to juries the right to decide upon every indictment whether the defendant was guilty or not guilty, newspapers were at the mercy of the judges. One of the first to be affected was, not unnaturally, Henry Baldwin, for printing a letter in the *Chronicle* on 29 January 1774. Addressed to the First Lord of the Admiralty – the profligate Earl of Sandwich, it asked what were his reasons 'for appointing a Man to Command one of his Majesty's Ships, who has behaved notoriously ill in a neighbouring Service, and dismissed from it with ignominy?'

The man in question was Captain John Elphinston, who had been present at the capture of Quebec, had served as a rear admiral in the Russian navy and been the subject of both English and Russian criticism. He sued in the King's Bench for the printing of a libel which impugned his 'Character and Reputation among diverse of his Majesty's Officers and other good and worthy subjects of this Realm'. A verdict of guilty was reached in scarcely fifteen minutes, and damages were set at £500, with £38 costs.[2] This was the largest such loss that the paper had suffered.[3]

The year 1774 also saw the death of one of the *Chronicle's* most distinguished contributors, Oliver Goldsmith. A close friend of the proprietors, he had been educated at Trinity College, Dublin, was rejected as a cleric, studied medicine in Edinburgh, and by 1757 was employed in Salisbury Court, off Fleet Street, as a reader. Four years later he met Samuel Johnson, and a lasting friendship developed. In 1766, Goldsmith published *The Vicar of Wakefield,* followed by his most famous poem, *The Deserted Village.* At the same time he was making his name in the theatre, his first success being with *The Good-Natur'd Man,* produced by George Colman in 1768. His final work – his masterpiece *She Stoops to Conquer* – was written in 1773, the year before he died.

A fellow student of Goldsmith at Trinity College, Dublin, was Edmund Burke, who also wrote for the *Chronicle.* Entering Parliament in 1765, he rose rapidly to lead the new Whigs with Charles James Fox, but broke with him later. A keen defender of American independence, Burke was also an avowed opponent of the East India Company, and led the case for the impeachment of Warren Hastings. Unlike Henry Baldwin, however, Burke fought hard for Catholic emancipation and he supported Wilberforce in his opposition to the slave trade. And it was Burke who first called the press 'the fourth estate', in the House of Commons in 1774: 'There are three Estates of Parliament; but, in the Reporters' Gallery yonder, sits a Fourth Estate more important far than they all.'

Other well-known figures writing for the paper at this time included William Cowper[4] and Richard Brinsley Sheridan. Born in 1731, Cowper had been a friend of Bonnell Thornton at Westminster School, a friendship that was to lead him to the intimacy of the Nonsuch Club and the companionship of the proprietors. It was during this period that Cowper contributed to *The St. James's Chronicle*:

> How shall I speak thee, or thy power address,
> Thou god of idolatry, the Press?
> By thee religion, liberty and lows
> Exert their influence and advance their cause.
>
> (*Progress of Error*)

Sheridan's connections with the paper were through his friendship with David Garrick, and in 1778 he purchased his share in the Dury Lane Theatre. The following year,[5] Sheridan wrote his masterpiece, *The School for Scandal,* and in 1779 *The Critic, or a Tragedy Rehearsed,* a burlesque on the dramatic fads of the time. 'The newspapers ... Sir, they are the most villainous – licentious – abominable – infernal – Not that I ever read them – no, I make it a rule never to look into a newspaper.' There is little doubt that, like many others, he was attracted to the literary circle of *The St. James's Chronicle.* Few papers since have been able to list writers of the calibre of Goldsmith, Burke, Cowper, Sheridan, Thornton and Colman, with assistance from Boswell, George Stevens and Garrick – it is a roll call of the famous.

Sheridan, long a supporter of Charles James Fox, gave up writing for the theatre and entered Parliament in 1780, where he became a celebrated speaker. With Edmund Burke, he was responsible for the impeachment of Warren Hastings in 1787–8. As a one-time practising newspaperman, he was able to wax eloquently on the Freedom of the Press in a speech which he delivered in the House of Commons in 1810:

> Give me but the liberty of the Press, and I will give the minister a venal House of Peers, I will give him a corrupt and servile House of Commons, I will give him the full swing of the patronage of office, I will give him the whole host of ministerial influence, I will give him all the power that place can confer upon him to purchase submission and overawe resistance, and yet, armed with the liberty of the Press, I will go forth to meet him undismayed, I will attack the mighty fabric he has reared with the mightier engine, I will shake down from its height corruption, and lay it beneath the ruins of abuses it was meant to shelter.[6]

GORDON RIOTS

Despite the occasional trouble with the authorities, the *Chronicle* continued to flourish. One such lapse, though, had occurred on 9 June 1774, when the paper published an advertisement in support of the American colonists, which led to a prosecution from the government. Although the man behind the advertisement, John Horne, was fined £200 and imprisoned for a year, Baldwin was far more fortunate, with just a fine of £100.

Six years later, in June 1780, Baldwin, with John Wilkes and others, was involved in fighting off the mobs during the Gordon Riots. For five days the City of London was subjected to mob rule by followers of Lord George Gordon, leader of the recently-formed Protestant Association. They were objecting to the Catholic Relief Bill of 1778, which for those prepared to take an oath of allegiance offered the ordinary civil rights of a citizen, although there was no move to give full political equality to the Catholics.[7]

Having sacked and set fire to Newgate Prison, freeing all the prisoners, the mob – urged on by the cry of 'No Popery' – turned its attention to Fleet Prison and within hours this was just burnt-out rubble, with all its inmates released. From his father's house, six-year-old Charles Baldwin saw Lord George at the head of the rioters passing through Fleet Street on their way to Parliament: they filled the whole street as far as he could see and numbered many thousands. In later years he would recall how his parents had packed up their 'valuables and necessaries' in case their house was burned. He saw the smoking ruins of Newgate, and remembered one of the Horse Guards shooting a rioter who had attacked him.[8] Private houses in Fleet Street, Fetter Lane and Shoe Lane were set on fire, and one honest citizen climbed to the top of St. Bride's spire to escape the rioters. The troops were called out on the express authority of the King and as a first priority they were ordered to guard the Bank and the Mansion House.

Having burned Fleet Prison, the mobs were met at the foot of Fleet Street by the Guards who, after firing a volley into the crowd, set to with bayonets. Twenty mutilated corpses were left on the street and thirty-five other rioters were seriously wounded. In all, 210 were killed, 248 wounded and 135 taken prisoner, of whom twenty-one were hanged. As for Lord George, he was later tried and acquitted but, after insulting the French government, he spent the last five years of his life imprisoned in the Tower of London, where he died in 1793.[9]

Saved from the mobs and the flames, the business of Henry Baldwin continued to prosper, and in addition to the successful *St. James's Chronicle* he also published the *London Journal*, which was a compilation of the best items from the *Chronicle*. This paper was, in fact, an amalgam over the years of the *London Spy* and *Weekly Journal*, which then formed the *Spy-Journal*. In 1762, Baldwin had purchased Mechell's *Weekly Chronicle* and *The Old British Spy*, and he joined them with the *Spy-Journal* to form the new Baldwin's *London Journal*. From its early days the paper was never a real profit-maker, with an average return of only £28 per year; and, no doubt in a bout of generosity, the other proprietors had in 1766 handed over the paper to Baldwin, giving him the option of returning it if 'he should not think it worth his while to continue the same'. But Baldwin and his son, Charles, were to keep the paper until 1803, when it closed.

In 1781, the proprietors faced their last great clash with the authorities: on 20 January the *Chronicle* reported that meetings had been held between Viscount Stormont, one of the Secretaries of State, and His Excellency John Simolin, Her Russian Majesty's Envoy Extraordinary and Minister Plenipotentiary. The item which first appeared in the *London Courant* said that 'the Ministry have had Reason to suspect his Excellency to be little better than a Spy, and last week had the good Fortune to get a Packet of his' and as a consequence 'he was charged with living here and in the Habit of furnishing the Enemies of Great Britain with Intelligence'.[10]

As a result, the printer of the *London Courant* was gaoled for a year and forced to stand in the pillory before the Royal Exchange for an hour; the printer of the *Noon Gazette* went to prison for eighteen months and was fined £200; the publisher of the *Morning Herald* and two printers of the *Middlesex Journal* each received twelve months' imprisonment and a fine of £100 each; and Mary Say, the printer of the *Gazeteer*, had her punishment cut by half because of her sex – to six months' imprisonment and a fine of £50. As for Henry Baldwin, 'making it appear, he had used every Endeavour in his Power to atone for having indiscretely copied the offensive Article in Question [he] was fined £100 without any imprisonment'.

On 13 December 1784, Dr Samuel Johnson died; but Boswell, who was in Scotland at the time, did not return to London until the following March, and by May 'puffs' of him and his forthcoming pamphlet, *A Letter to the People of Scotland on the Alarming Attempt to Infringe the Articles of the Union*, began to appear in *The St. James's Chronicle*. Boswell had, in fact, been a contributor to the *Chronicle* for more than twenty years, and Henry Baldwin was Boswell's printer.

THE LONDON PRESS

This was now a period of considerable significance for the London newspaper proprietors and their commercial colleagues, and in 1785 there was the first confrontation between management and men.[11] The number of master printers was now 124, between them employing 500 compositors and 180 apprentices. In the pressroom there were a further 200 journeymen and some 80 apprentices, while 180 journeymen worked as bookbinders. Dissatisfied with their wages, the compositors presented a petition, and in response the masters held a general meeting and appointed an *ad hoc* committee, of which Henry Baldwin was a key figure. There was, however, no direct negotiation at this time, since the masters did not believe that the men had a right to address them collectively; but from these discussions was to emerge the Compositors' Scale of Prices, which, with many modifications, was to last for more than 200 years.

London at this time had eight morning papers and nine evenings, but there seemed little integrity among the majority of the men who wrote for them. Dr Johnson's observations of some years earlier still held good: 'They habitually sold their abilities, whether small or great, to one or other of the Parties that divide us; and without a Wish for Truth or Thought of Decency.' Politically, Johnson was correct, for the press was now facing significant changes. The loss of the North American colonies, and Lord Cornwallis's ignominious surrender to Washington's forces at York Town, had ensured that the government of Lord North must fall. The Whigs, now in power, were determined to stop the war and to restrict the interference of George III in the workings of Parliament. William Pitt the Younger was the new Prime Minister, and he led a party which for the first time since the Commonwealth was the result of a genuine uprising of public feeling.

With the press free, parliamentary reports were of even greater importance for the newspapers and were considered to be sure circulation boosters. However, the triumph of Pitt was to herald a critical change in the political control of the press, for despite his efforts to secure newspaper support he was subjected to unprecedented abuse. Determined to overcome this, he began to use the funds of the Secret Service to buy off the opposition; and persuaded the government to deny recalcitrant proprietors inside information and official advertisements. The government could also make trouble at the Stamp Office, thereby effectively restricting newspaper distribution.

In his first year of office, Pitt bought the support of five newspapers: three dailies – *Public Ledger, London Evening Post* and the *Morning Herald*; and two tri-weeklies – *The St. James's Chronicle* and the *Whitehall Evening Post.* The money was paid to the newspapers through third parties, thus 'Mr Harris for Mr Longman to be divided between the editors of the *Ledger, Saint James's* and *London Evening Post* £300'. Thomas Harris was the proprietor of Covent Garden Theatre; and Longman was the bookseller and printer. Secret Service records show that *The St. James's Chronicle* was receiving a subsidy of £200 a year until at least 1793.[12]

Apart from his buying off the editors, Pitt was no friend of the press, for during the 1780s he several times raised the stamp duty and increased the advertisement tax, and even made it illegal for people to hire out newspapers, 'whereby the sale of newspapers is greatly obstructed' and made them liable to a penalty of £5 for each offence. In addition to bribing the editors and proprietors, a large number of journalists were in the pay of the Treasury, receiving sums which ranged from a few guineas for an article to as much as £500 per annum for special cases.

Apart from the emergence of the Compositors' Scale of Prices, the year 1785 had seen one other significant date in newspaper history: the first issue, on 13 January of the *Daily Universal Register,* a paper of four pages, principally designed to show the public a new invention of printing with types representing words and syllables instead of only letters. The printer and proprietor was John Walter, of Printing House Square, who suffered great annoyance and losses in his attempts to introduce this logographical system into common practice.[13] Undaunted, three years later, on 1 January 1788, after realising that the name of his paper was unsatisfactory, Walter relaunched it under the title of *The Times*, and the rest is history. For much of the nineteenth century *The Standard* was to be its closest rival.

Meanwhile, Henry Baldwin, finding his premises in Fleet Street too small, had moved a few hundred yards away to New Bridge Street, and there, at No. 38, on the corner of Union Street, he built his new works, and opened for business in 1789. In the summer of that year, on 7 July, while Paris was in uproar, and the mobs were storming the Bastille, Charles was bound to his father as an apprentice compositor. In Charles Baldwin, *The St. James's Chronicle* was to find a young man with even greater gifts and talents than his father.

'So quickly did he attain the knowledge of the business that at 18 Mr Baldwin senior confided in him the entire superintendence of the working part of his establishment; and at 21 he was called upon by the Committee of the Master Printers appointed to revise the state of the trade from time to time, and to regulate and adjust any differences or demands that might arise between workmen and the employers.'[14] For more than fifty years of his life Charles Baldwin was actively employed and exerted considerable influence in the newspaper trade.

Towards the end of the eighteenth century, however, the General Post Office was once again going through a financial crisis. In 1787 it set up the Newspaper Office to receive and sort all newspapers, made up in bundles according to districts. These bundles were distributed to the postmasters by the Clerks of the Roads for the postal divisions of the country. Prior to this date, the newspapers had arrived at the Post Office late and 'in so wet a state as to deface the directions of many of the letters which went in the same bags'.

In 1796, a Bill was presented to the Commons 'for regulating the conveyance of newspapers'. The result was a curtailment of the role of the hawkers and the handing over of the monopoly to the already entrenched Clerks of the Road, who now, in effect, became wholesalers to the country postmasters; and the Post Office – with the exception of booksellers and hawkers in London – became the national distributing agency. From that year, newspapers were to be carried post-free. However, the Post Office was determined to keep a tight reign on the stamping of the newsprint sheets, as an article of 19 March 1798 pointed out:

> The new postmaster General, Lord Auckland, has begun very extensive reforms in that department. On Saturday night all the Newspapers were examined, to see that no writing was put upon the stamped sheets, so as to defraud the Revenue of postage. This is assuredly proper. No person has a right to abuse the privilege of free carriage which the Newspapers enjoy for the encouragement of the stamp duties by smuggling under the cover of private correspondence.

PRODUCTION COSTS

During the last decade of the eighteenth century, the cost of producing newspapers did not vary greatly between offices. After the new duties of 1789, paper cost Henry Baldwin £2 2s for 500 sheets, yielding 1,000 copies. The old tax on double demy, the size used for newspapers, had been 8s 4d a bundle weighing 106 lbs: less than 1d a pound. But the new duty was 2½d a lb, which for a bundle of 106 lbs, was 22s 1d, an increase of 13s 9d. On the publishing side, the hawkers were normally allowed a penny margin on each paper and given two papers in every quire.

An increase in compositors' wages in 1793 had brought the rates of full hands up to £1 16s, an extra 4s 6d since the introduction of the London Scale of Prices in 1785. Supernumeraries had received an increase of two shillings and were now paid 17s a week. With the costs of the pressmen, flyboys and readers to be added, it is doubtful if the total weekly wages bill of *The St. James's Chronicle* was in excess of £40, and of this sum the Printer would have received £3 3s, which was the going rate.

Apart from paper and wages, other costs were relatively low, although the price of dipped tallow candles for lighting was 8s 4d a dozen; and founders' type increased in price after August 1793, with pica at 1s 1½d and small pica at 1s 3½d a 1b. Two-line letters cost 1s 1d, leads (six to pica) 1s 6d.

In 1793 the compositors in London organised themselves into a society with a permanent committee which collected regular contributions, arranged meetings of delegates from the distant offices, and, most importantly, tried to limit the number of apprentices. Its headquarters were at the Hole-in-the-wall, Fleet Street.[15] By the end of the century the compositors had decided the time was ripe for amalgamation of the various factions, and in 1801 the Union Society was founded. Its purpose was to correct irregularities, and 'to endeavour to promote harmony between employers and the employed. By bringing the modes of change from custom and precedent into one point of view, in order to their being better understood by all concerned'.

Not all the negotiations, however, between employers and employees were of a friendly nature: in 1786 the compositors had failed to obtain an injunction against John Walter, proprietor of *The Times*, forbidding him to set up as a master printer, on the grounds that he had not served an apprenticeship in the trade. The government, alarmed at the spread of revolutionary ideas from France, passed in 1799 and 1800 the Combination Acts, which made all journeymen's trade societies illegal, and provided for summary convictions of offenders. These convictions could now be dealt with by magistrates and not trial by jury. Within weeks of the first Act being passed, pressmen, who had attempted to negotiate with the masters on the limitation of apprentices, were prosecuted for conspiracy. Although it was shown that the accused were, indeed, members of the Pressmen's Friendly Society, whose headquarters was the Crown, near St. Dunstan's, Fleet Street, the prosecutor charged that this was only a subterfuge:

> It was called a Friendly Society; but, Gentlemen, by means of some wicked men among the society degenerated into a most abominable meeting for the purpose of conspiracy: those of the trade who did not join their society were summoned, and even the apprentices, and were told unless they conformed to the practices of these journeymen, when they came out of their time they would not be employed.

Another case which won widespread attention was that of the nineteen *Times* compositors, who in 1810 were found guilty of 'conspiracy' and imprisoned, with one of them, Malcolm Craig, dying in jail. In reality, these two cases were the exceptions in the printing industry, for in most instances the masters were prepared to meet representatives of the men's societies in order to agree wages and conditions of employment. But it was not until 1825, largely through the efforts of Francis Place, that the Combination Acts were repealed.

On the technical side, very little had changed in the methods of composing newspapers by the end of the eighteenth century. Type was still set by hand but, in 1798, there was an improvement in the press-room. The Earl of Stanhope introduced his iron press, but it did little to increase the pressman's speed, which remained at about 250 impressions per hour.

As the new century opened, so young Charles Baldwin became more and more involved in the family business, and in 1801, at the age of 27, his endeavours were recognised when his father changed the firm's name to Henry Baldwin and Son. Charles himself had three years previously married Elizabeth Ann, daughter of the Revd Hugh Laurents, a native of Jersey. The union between Charles and Elizabeth was to produce fifteen children, five of whom died in infancy, and lasted for fifty-four years.

As for Henry Baldwin, having been a liveryman of the Stationers' Company for many years, he had won further honours when he had been elected Master in 1792. He was now aged 67 and could look back as 'the man who had started it all', a craftsman of 'the Old School, bred under the original Printer of the *London Magazine*'. Over that distance of time he had been the responsible publisher in legal matters, and it was due to his direct efforts that this 'great phalanx of wits' had been brought together. Over the years, the Minutes of *The*

St. James's Chronicle bear elegant testimony to his diplomacy and initiative: he had, indeed, been the figurehead of the business. Now, after forty-seven years as the principal, he decided to retire and relinquish his two shares to his son, Charles.

John Nicholls, in his *Literary Anecdotes*, published in 1812, wrote:

> Henry Baldwin brought it [*The St. James's Chronicle*] to a height of literary eminence till then unknown by any preceding Journal, and retired in the full enjoyment of his faculties to the comfort of domestic life; resigning his business to a son, Charles, who, uniting to habits of business an unusual pleasantry of manners, cannot fail of securing the esteem of all who know him.

A year later, on 21 February 1813, Henry Baldwin died, leaving a widow, two sons and three daughters. He was, except for one, the oldest member of the Stationers' Company, and was a liveryman for almost sixty years. In the issue of *The St. James Chronicle*, dated Saturday, 20 February to Tuesday, 22 February, one has to look long to find any record of his passing. No fulsome eulogies, no funereal borders, just a simple obituary of some half-a-dozen lines:

> On Sunday 21 inst, at his house at Richmond, Surrey, in the 79th year of his age, Henry Baldwin Esq., upwards of 40 years a Proprietor and Printer of this paper; but who was long retired from business and enjoyed in the bosom of his family, the merited rewards of his honourable industry. The rectitude of his mind, the real tenderness of his heart, and sincerity of attachments, were best known in his circle and to his close friends.

By 1805, the *Chronicle* bore just the imprint of Charles Baldwin, and all correspondence was now addressed to 'The Printer Charles Baldwin'. The previous decade had opened with the paper paying the highest quarterly dividend of £36, but then the profits had gone into a steady decline. However, in 1808,[16] through gift, exchange and purchase, Charles Baldwin became the owner of seven of the eight shares now remaining. For the next seven years, he and Christopher Moody, who held the other share, met only infrequently, and in 1815, following Moody's death, the Minutes stopped – Charles Baldwin was now in total control. He had certainly been an active proprietor during the preceding years, for the dividends had generally exceeded £60 for a half year, and the annual figures had rivalled those of most of the early period. His major investment had been the purchase of the *London Evening Post*. Founded in 1727, the thrice-weekly *Post* had been the scourge of the Establishment for almost eighty years; in its infancy, it had taken particular delight in exposing Sir Robert Walpole. And in

1771 John Miller, of the *Post,* was apprehended under a warrant from the Speaker for 'misrepresenting speeches and reflecting on several members'. Ultimately, Miller appeared before John Wilkes and other magistrates and the charge was dismissed.

HANGING OF LUDDITES

At the time that Charles Baldwin assumed full control of *The St. James's Chronicle,* England was a country suffering from its own internal problems. Between 1811 and 1813, the troubles with the Luddites and the smashing of new machinery had won great prominence in the press; in the very issue containing the obituary notice of Henry Baldwin the *Chronicle* reported the hanging of Luddites in York. The established press was now complaining about the anarchists who dominated the weeklies and who infiltrated the dailies 'inflaming the turbulent temper of the manufacturers, and disturbing the quiet attachment of the peasant to those institutions under which he and his father have dwelt in peace'.

But the beginnings of the Industrial Revolution were not confined to the weaving machines of the North; in November 1814 *The Times* used a steam press to print newspapers for the first time in Britain – just five months after Stephenson had built the first steam railway engine. The inventor of the press was a young Saxon, Friedrich Koening, working in association with another German, Andreas Bauer, and its introduction meant that the output of 250 copies per hour from the Stanhope iron hand press could be increased to more than 1,000 impressions per hour.[18] The paper could now go to press much later, with up-to-the-minute news, and there was no longer the need to duplicate the setting of the formes, providing a saving in setting charges of between £2,000 and £3,000 a year. By using the steam press, *The Times* was able to print more than 7,000 copies of an eight-page paper every night, and this not only provided the opportunity for increased revenue from sales and advertisements, but it also gave John Walter II, its proprietor, independence from political parties.

Peace in 1815 brought with it a slump, which, after the boom times of the Napoleonic War, was difficult for the working classes to appreciate; always in the background there were the fears of the unknown, of the social and economic changes following in the wake of the Industrial Revolution. It was a time, too, of resurgence in radical journalism, but a journalism directed at the artisan and the labourer. It was also a crusading journalism with a purpose: to mould public opinion. Leading the fight was William Cobbett, whose *Political Register,* with its demand for parliamentary reform, was winning ready support from the working classes. Even though its price of more than a shilling for 16 quarto pages was beyond the pocket of the average reader, working-men clubbed together to buy it and read it aloud. His idea was quickly followed by lesser imitations: *The Black Dwarf, The Gorgon, The Reformists' Register, the Republican, Weekly Commentary*, and the *Medusa*.

However, the Home Secretary, Viscount Sidmouth, considered that there was no difference between the established and the more radical newspapers and said that the 'Newspaper Press was a most malignant and formidable enemy of the Constitution to which it owed its freedom'. It was Sidmouth who, in July 1819, instructed the Lord Lieutenant of Lancashire to take all measures necessary to preserve order, including the calling out of the Yeomanry, in an attempt to control the Reformists. Within a month, his instructions had been carried out to the letter, for in August 1819 a meeting was held in St. Peter's Field, Manchester, and addressed by the Radical, Henry 'Orator' Hunt, who called for parliamentary reform.

A crowd of 50,000, claimed by the organisers to be the largest meeting ever held in England, was met by 400 constables, while, out of sight, the Manchester Yeomanry and the 15th Hussars were kept at the ready. After the reading of the Riot Act by the magistrates – mostly unheard – the Yeomanry arrested Hunt, and then completely lost control, charging the crowd with drawn sabres. The result was the Peterloo Massacre: more than a dozen killed and some 420 wounded.

During that long, hot summer of 1819, two stories had dominated the newspapers: Halley's Comet, visible from many parts of England; and the ever-increasing passions aroused by the Reformists. For many months, the growth of the Reformist Movement, with its meetings, marches and occasional riots, had been covered in depth by the *Chronicle* and it is interesting to follow the events in its columns leading up to the tragedy at Peterloo.

On Saturday, 17 July, the paper noted the disturbances at Stockport; and in its leader commented that Viscount Sidmouth[19] had on 7 July written to the Lord Lieutenant of Cheshire:

> True bills of indictment had been found against Sir Charles Wolsely and Harrison, the Dissenting Minister, for speeches delivered by them at Stockport on the 26th Ult, 'with intent to excite tumult and insurrection within the realm'. This is the right conduct to be pursued by the Government. The laws will be found abundantly strong: they only require to be called into action.

Four days later, the Reformists – more than 20,000 strong – gathered at Smithfield, London, where they were addressed by Henry Hunt. In a delicious phrase the paper reported that the meeting which 'included the idlers who came from curiosity and the pickpockets who attended professionally', had passed without incident.

On 16 August came the meeting and massacre at Peterloo, which was covered in great depth by the *Chronicle*,[20] with accounts from local Manchester reporters John Edward Taylor and Archibald Prentice, and almost certainly a rejig of John William Tyas's copy for *The Times*. However, the newly appointed editor of the *Chronicle*, Dr Stanley Lees Giffard, commented: 'Here *The Times* Reporter, who not being known, has evidently lost his temper, and has obviously written under angry feelings which we feel should have been corrected and repressed by the editor of that paper.'

Giffard and Charles Baldwin obviously had strong feelings against the Reformists, as is shown by the opening paragraph of the leader:

> What has long been desired by every friend of order has at length taken place. The strong arm of the law has been put forth to put, we trust, a final stop to the assemblage of the ignorant and the seditious, which can produce nothing but evil, and which cannot be permitted under any form of Government, nor, indeed, in any state of social existence.

These sentiments were long to remain with Baldwin and Giffard, as they were to show in the launch of *The Standard*, and its opposition to Reform.

It was at this time that Baldwin purchased the *London Chronicle*, once edited by Dr Johnson, for £300 from Lt. Colonel Robert Torrens, and absorbed it into *The St. James's Chronicle*.

TRUST OF PROPRIETOR

As for Giffard, he had only recently been appointed editor of *The St. James's Chronicle* and was to retain the trust of Baldwin from 1819 until his death in 1858. He was also the man selected in 1827 as the first editor of *The Standard*. He was born in Dublin on 4 August 1788, the youngest son of John Giffard, of Dromartin, Co. Dublin, and received his early education under Thomas White, the schoolmaster of Sheridan and of Moore, the poet.[21] Giffard then studied at Trinity College, Dublin, where he proceeded to take his BA in 1807 and his MA four years later. He afterwards took the degree of LL.D, entered at the Middle Temple and was called to the Bar in 1811. Making no progress as a barrister, he turned his attention to literature and was quickly recognised as the most distinguished and powerful political writer of the day. After six years of continuing success as a journalist on *The St. James's Chronicle*, he was rewarded with the editorship.

Giffard as an editor was in the true Baldwin tradition: violently anti-Catholic and bitterly opposed to emancipation. It was said that 'he looked upon the Roman Church as simply a political conspiracy carried on under the name of religion'.[22] He was also a leading supporter of the Irish Church labouring under the distress of a tithe war. Coming from a Protestant family – during the 1798 Rebellion his father had been Sheriff of Dublin and afterwards Accountant-General of the Irish Customs – he had never forgotten how his brother William, a serving officer, had been hacked to death while on leave in Dublin.

Now gradually, under the conduct of its highly-skilled editor, *The St. James's Chronicle* was having a greater influence on the Tories; and suggestions were often made that it should be changed from being a thrice-weekly to a daily newspaper.

On 17 February 1827, Lord Liverpool, the Prime Minister, suffered a stroke and was forced to resign. Three people qualified to be his successor: the Duke of Wellington, Sir Robert Peel and George Canning. In April 1827, Canning was summoned by George IV to form a government, and the majority of the Old Tories who had been his colleagues for almost five years went into opposition. However, Canning's coalition quickly won approval from the public, which led Peel to remark that the press was almost all on one side. Charles Arbuthnott, another leading Old Tory, was also annoyed with the pro-Canning press and hoped that steps would be taken to secure at least one paper for the party.

Arbuthnott was particularly concerned that the reputation of the Duke of Wellington (who had recently given up command of the Army, for which he had been heavily criticised) should be restored. To this end he sought the aid of William Huskisson, President of the Board of Trade. Huskisson, however, was not to be an ally: he replied that 'he had never had any connexion with the newspapers and was convinced that they had not been under any special influence since the formation of the new Government and they had not been encouraged to speak disparagingly of the Duke'.[23]

Attempts to turn *The Watchman* into a daily paper, and to save *The Courier* failed. The thoughts of Arbuthnott and his fellow Tories turned more and more to Charles Baldwin.

4

Plant Here *The Standard*

At 2 p.m. on Monday, 21 May 1827, the hopes of Arbuthnott, Wellington and Peel were realised, when the first edition of the new daily, *The Standard*, appeared. Charles Baldwin, however, had no intention of exposing his successful thrice-weekly, *The St. James's Chronicle*, as he revealed in his own words:

> I was not willing to risk the continuance of my old and valued journal; I preferred the heavier risk of establishing at my own expense and hazard, a Daily Evening Paper to be conducted on the same principles and by the same editor. I also engaged the assistance of Dr Maggin and other celebrated writers.
>
> The choice of a name then claimed our attention. The object was to make a stand against the inroad of principle; contrary to our Constitution in Church and State; a very appropriate motto was chosen by Dr Giffard, 'Signifer, statue signum. Hic optime manebimus' (Plant here the *Standard*. Here we shall best remain) and on the 21st May, 1827, *The Standard* was hauled as a rallying point, and was speedily followed by the raising of *Standards* in the Provincial and Colonial Conservative Press. Even Foreign newspapers have adopted the name.[1]

It was not, however, the first newspaper to adopt that title; on 28 February 1804, Lord St. Vincent, the First Lord of the Admiralty, wrote to Hiley Addington that the son of Major-General ('Rocket') Congreve had 'in the most disinterested manner' started a paper, the *Standard*, 'for the sole purpose of vindicating the Government against the vile charges of Cobbett and other miscreants of his description'.[2]

Twenty-three years later, Charles Baldwin and his editor, Dr Stanley Lees Giffard, in announcing their aims to the new readers of *The Standard* could proclaim: 'Aware that in our character as Journalists, we were not unknown to the people of England, and with voluminous testimonies before us, that we were not uninvited to the task... why possessing and directing *The St. James's Chronicle*, the most popular evening journal in the empire, we encumber ourselves with the additional labour and responsibility of another Journal. ... To the services of a country we have devoted a Daily Journal ... With this offering we devote also what more we have – English and Protestant principles and inflexible integrity and resolution in maintaining them

– qualifications that would seem humble were they not unfortunately so rare.'[3]

The leader did, however, contain a number of typographical errors which seem to have been reflected in the final paragraph of the opening issue: 'Our readers will, we hope, forgive the omission for the present, of some routine articles of information in consequence of the hurry in which we have been compelled to make our arrangements.'

In the following day's paper, Giffard noted, with a touch of pride, in his leader column: 'We cannot but hail an auspicious commencement of our New Journal, that its first number was published simultaneously with the first public meeting ever held in the metropolis of the empire, to promote the complete reformation of the Irish people.'

Published from 5 New Bridge Street, *The Standard* cost 7d and for that the reader received a four-page broadsheet, five columns per page, each page measuring 21 inches by 14.75 inches. The main story on the front page of the first issue had been the flooding of the Thames tunnel under construction between Wapping and Rotherhithe. The tunnel had filled with water in 12 minutes, forcing the miners to swim for their lives. *The Standard* had this on the authority of Marc Isambard Brunel, who had himself delivered a letter to the paper dated 18 May ('I feel it is a duty incumbent on me to make known to the public an accident which occurred this evening') before he had even told his directors. Brunel (father of the great Isambard Kingdom Brunel) clearly knew where his priorities lay in providing such a scoop. Fortunately, because of a safety shield in use in the tunnel, no lives were lost.

From the first issue, *The Standard* included a gossip column, under the heading 'Chit Chat'. Typical of its contents was 'Sir Robert Peel has purchased two Mulready paintings at the Royal Academy for the splendid price of 500 guineas each.' In the advertisement columns, a life assurance company claimed that, instead of limiting cover to healthy lives as usual, it was prepared to quote for persons afflicted with gout, asthma and other diseases. Shipping news was considered to be of some importance, as *The Standard* noted: 'by this day's post the *Dolphin* of Guernsey was run down in the Cattegut on the 24th ult. The *Express Hall* had arrived at Plymouth with loss of sails and want of provisions.' There could, however, be a distinct bluntness in the reporting, as the issue of two days later noted: '23 May 1827. City 1 pm: The transactions this morning have been scarcely worth noting. Court of Chancery: The Proceedings this morning in the Court of Chancery were entirely devoid of interest. Court of King's Bench: This being the last day of Term the Court was occupied until 11 o'clock in hearing motions from Junior Counsel at the Bar of no public interest.'[4]

But, despite this somewhat laconic style, and a circulation of barely more than 700, by the year's end *The Standard* was becoming accepted as the leading daily devoted to the anti-Catholic cause. And so pleased were the Tories with its stance that Lord Ashley wrote to Mrs Arbuthnott, the great confidante of the Duke of Wellington, on 26 December 1827: 'How good the *Standard* has been of late!'

One story circulating at the time – later confirmed as being true by the present Earl of Halsbury – concerned Giffard and the Duke of Newcastle. According to James Grant and other press historians, '*The Standard* was but a few weeks old, when early one morning a splendid carriage with magnificently liveried coachman and servants stopped at the door of Dr Giffard's house in Pentonville, where a small parcel was delivered. On opening it, Giffard found it contained notes to the amount of £1,200 from the Duke of Newcastle.' In the accompanying note, the Duke stated that he begged Dr Giffard's personal acceptance of the amount as a practical expression of his admiration of the masterly article which had appeared in *The Standard* of the previous evening in opposition to the Roman Catholic claims. It is said that 'while accepting the princely gift of the Duke of Newcastle he did not apply the sum to his own individual use, but shared it among his staff'.[5]

Apart from Sundays, the paper was published every day, including Christmas Day, although it was noted that as the main public buildings were closed for the holiday 'there was not much news'. From the first issue, stock market prices were featured, which bore a 2 p.m. time stamp. It took only a matter of weeks for the paper to be accepted by the Government's Messenger of the Press – and when there came a demand to reduce the number of journals taken, *The Standard* was one of those that was retained.

INJUDICIOUS ARTICLE

However, the paper was now proving much too enterprising even for its patrons, and matters came to a head with an injudicious article published a fortnight before the Duke of Wellington became Prime Minister. While out of office, Wellington had felt himself free to express his genuine thoughts on Catholic emancipation and other thorny issues. But on the eve of his premiership, his attitude changed, and he was not at all pleased with the persistence of *The Standard*. His close friend, John Wilson Croker, wrote:

> I saw Herries (a former Chancellor of the Exchequer) and we talked about a paragraph of about ten days ago in *The Standard* which proclaimed that the Tories could not come in without stipulating for

the dismissal of the Lord George Steward Coynghan [husband of George IV's mistress].[6]

We agreed as to the mischievous effect of that paragraph as it was known that the Duke of Wellington and Peel countenanced that paper, and he told me that a certain person took care that it should go down to Windsor that very night it was published. The King is so displeased with Peel and so indignant at that paragraph in *The Standard* that he is, they say, resolved to continue what he calls a mixed government but from which all Tories will recede. The Duke of Wellington lost his temper over the business. 'What can we do with these sort of fellows?' he exclaimed. 'We have no power over them, and for my part I will have no communication with any of them.'[7]

Notwithstanding the harm that he thought *The Standard* had inflicted on him, Wellington was appointed Prime Minister on 8 January 1828. Some fifteen months later, on 16 March 1829,[8] there appeared in the paper a remarkable letter from Lord Winchilsea announcing that he had cancelled his subscription of £50 to King's College, London, because the Duke of Wellington was associated with its foundation. The Duke, as Prime Minister, had taken the chair at the opening of King's College during the previous summer, on 21 June, when, surrounded by three archbishops and seven bishops, he had reaffirmed the place in education of religious teaching. At the time, Winchilsea had also voiced the need for a new college based on the King's faith, but the prospect of Catholic emancipation filled him with horror. So incensed was he, that he wrote to Giffard for publication:

I considered that the noble Duke at the head of his Majesty's government had been induced on this occasion to assume a new character, and to step forward himself as the public advocate of religion and morality.

Late political events have convinced me that the whole transaction was intended as a blind to the Protestant and High Church party, that the noble Duke, who had for some time previous to that period determined upon 'breaking in upon the constitution of 1688', might the more effectually, under the cloak of some outward show of zeal for the Protestant religion, carry on in this insidious design, for the infringement of our liberties, and the introduction of Popery into every department of the State.[9]

Twice the Duke wrote to Winchilsea asking him to retract and apologise, but Winchilsea refused unless Wellington stated publicly that he had not contemplated Catholic emancipation when he had inaugurated King's College. The Duke was now forced into the one dramatic step that he had never before taken in his long and illustrious career as a soldier – a duel: 'I now call upon your Lordship to give me the satisfaction for your conduct which a gentleman has a right to require, and which a gentleman never refuses to give.'

The duel took place at eight o'clock the following morning,[10] on 21 March 1829, 'about half a mile on the other side of the river' over Battersea Bridge. The seconds were Lord Falmouth and Sir Henry Hardinge: the weapons, pistols. John Hume, the Duke's doctor, had been awoken at 6.45 am by Sir Henry for 'an affair of honour between gentlemen', and was 'overwhelmed with amazement and greatly agitated' when the Duke suddenly rode up to him saying: 'Well I dare say you little expected it was I who wanted you to be here.'

With some spectators already gathering, the Duke shouted: 'Now then Hardinge, look sharp and step out the ground. Damn it! Don't stick him up so near the ditch. If I hit him, he will tumble in'. As Sir Henry had lost an arm at Waterloo, Dr Hume loaded the pistols. The Duke fired and missed: Lord Winchilsea, in turn, solemnly and chivalrously fired into the air. His second then announced that he was ready to sign and to publish 'an apology in every sense of the word'. With the apology accepted, the Duke said: 'Good morning, my Lord Winchilsea; good morning my Lord Falmouth', touched the brim of his hat with two fingers, mounted his horse and, with his second, rode quickly off the field. By lunchtime the news of the duel was all over the capital, creating a public sensation. The king was delighted and remarked that 'gentlemen must not stand upon the privileges', adding that he would have done the same thing in the Duke's place.

Having carried the original letter, *The Standard* now reported the duel as its main item in the leader column, with the apology from Winchilsea:

SATURDAY EVENING, March 21

MEETING BETWEEN HIS GRACE THE DUKE OF WELLINGTON AND THE EARL OF WINCHILSEA

A meeting took place this morning between his Grace the Duke of Wellington and the Earl of Winchilsea. After receiving the noble duke's fire, Lord Winchilsea discharged his pistol in the air. The Earl of Falmouth then, on the part of Lord Winchilsea, interposed, and put into the hands of Sir Henry Hardinge the following acknowledgement, which was accepted on the part of his Grace by Sir Henry Hardinge.

March 21, 1829

Having given the Duke of Wellington the usual satisfaction for the affront he conceived himself to have received from me through my public letter on Monday last, and having placed myself in a different situation from that in which I stood when his grace communicated with me through Sir Henry Hardinge and Lord Falmouth on the subject of that letter, before the meeting took place, I do not now hesitate to declare, of my own accord, that in apologising I regret having unadvisedly published an opinion which the noble duke states in his memorandum of yesterday to have charged him with 'disgraceful and criminal motives in certain transactions which took place nearly a year ago'. I also declare that I shall cause the expression of regret to be inserted in the *Standard* newspaper, as the same channel through which the letter in question was given to the public.

(signed) WINCHILSEA AND NOTTINGHAM

In Monday's issue of the paper there appeared the complete correspondence of the controversy – some eighteen letters in all – and there rested a remarkable incident in the history of *The Standard.* The final word on the matter, however, came some months later, from the Duke himself: 'The truth is that the duel with Lord Winchilsea was as much a part of the Roman Catholic question, and it was necessary to undertake it ... as was to do everything else that I could do to attain the object which I had in view.'

HIGHLY RESPECTABLE CHARACTER

After more than forty years in the newspaper world, Charles Baldwin was an extremely successful businessman. A person of highly respectable character and a magistrate for Surrey, he was 'said to be worth upwards of £100,000'. The circulation of *The Standard* had risen to more than 1,500 daily by the early 1830s, and it was believed by one competent critic that 'it owed its success to the fluctuating policies of *The Courier* at the period when the seeming liberalism of the Government led to a sort of coquetry with a better and higher policy'. However, Eugenius Roche, editor of *The Courier,* having been accused by *The Standard* of shady stock market speculations, now sued for libel (with the help of the Foreign Office) Baldwin and Giffard. Baldwin, now aged 55 and contemplating retirement, was said to be a timid person and he was terrified of receiving a visit from government officials. He said that if they did come he would put an end to *The Standard* immediately, provided that by so doing he would avoid a prosecution.[11]

Writing to Joseph Planta at the Foreign Office on 24 August 1829, Roche noted that 'if Baldwin was so excessively eager to sacrifice the existence of his paper to his personal safety the Government might easily get rid of a troublesome and hostile journal by merely issuing an *ex officio* information for libel, which, in the absence of legal proofs of guilt, need not be followed by an actual prosecution.[12]

Within a matter of days, an article appeared in *The Standard* which James Scarlett, the Attorney-General, deemed to be libellous. Giffard admitted that he was the author and asked that he alone might suffer for it. Writing to the Duke of Wellington, the Attorney-General said 'the proprietor who habitually derives emoluments from the trade of slander was more worthy of punishment than the agents he employed. ... At present all that is wanting to make the fortune of a newspaper is a scapegoat who has no objection to earn moderate wages in prison, where he insures, moreover, a moderate compensation for other men's crimes. The fines and damages are often never paid.'[13] Fortunately, for Baldwin and *The Standard*, the Duke did nothing.

In the management of both *The Standard* and *The St. James's Chronicle*, Charles Baldwin had for a number of years been assisted by his eldest son, Edward. Unlike his father and grandfather, Edward had not gone straight into the family business; he had first taken his MA at Oxford University. With his father, Edward had arranged a plan for obtaining the earliest information from all parts of Europe; in some instances by the use of carrier pigeons but more frequently by relays of couriers who mounted at a moment's notice ready-saddled horses, and conveyed the despatch to the next post on the route. The speed and efficiency of the courier service had been proved in the autumn of 1828: 'News of the fate of Varna [Bulgaria] on the 11th of October, 1828, reached *The Standard* office and was published about a fortnight before the arrival of the Government courier. On its confirmation the excitement was very great, and had a decided influence on the circulation of *The Standard*.'[14]

The Times was not at all amused at being beaten on this story; and there developed a circulation fight between the two newspapers, with *The Globe* also entering the fray. *The Times* referred to *The Standard* as that 'stupid and priggish print which never by any chance deviated into candour'. Later, *The Standard* replied to the 'base and filthy insinuations put forward by *The Times*', and called *The Globe* 'our blubber-headed contemporary'. During its formative years, *The Standard* had also come under attack from *The Morning Chronicle*, at that time a newspaper of some importance. It believed that *The Standard* 'is a journal which has lately crawled into existence, and is fast hastening towards dissolution'. In the event, it was *The Morning Chronicle* that met an early demise.

PARLIAMENTARY REFORM

With the Catholic Emancipation Act having received a reluctant royal assent on 13 April 1829, the way was now clear for parliamentary reform. The system at this time was full of anomalies: migration of the population to new industrial regions had created urban areas that were unrepresented, while leaving old constituencies with a handful of electors. Besides these rotten boroughs there remained the pocket boroughs, where aristocratic patrons could secure the return of their nominees.

It was against this background of malpractice and misrepresentation that on 22 March 1831 Lord John Russell, for the recently-elected Whigs, introduced the first Reform Bill into the House of Commons, and, after a heated struggle, the second reading was carried by a majority of one. *The Standard*'s long and detailed account covered three-quarters of the paper, and in its leader commented: 'We neither like the policy, nor much rely upon the fidelity of gentlemen who blurb a measure upon a first or second reading, with the design of strangling it in committee. The Attorney General made exactly such a speech as, if it had been made elsewhere, ought to have been prosecuted by the Attorney General.'

King William IV now dissolved Parliament and a General Election took place. 'The Bill, the whole Bill, and nothing but the Bill' was the cry heard everywhere; and leading the cry was *The Times*, which 'thundered for Reform'. It proclaimed: 'Once again we warn them (the Boroughmongers) to desist – not if they value the lives and happiness of theirs, for they are too selfish to be moved by considerations, but if they value their own.'[15] According to *The Standard* and *The St. James's Chronicle* these words were an incitement, but, when the results were counted, seats which had been Tory-held for generations had changed hands – and the Whigs were returned with a majority of more than a hundred.

On 25 June 1831 Lord John Russell again introduced a Reform Bill, and it was successful, by a large majority, but in early October, the Reform Bill went to the Lords, where it was thrown out by forty-one votes. It was a night of high passions, as *The Standard* reported in its leader on 5 October:

> Not the least striking incident of the night, and that which we would earnestly recommend to general invitation by all the Protestants of the Empire, was the cordial reunion of two noblemen who lately stood in absolute and uncompromising opposition – the Earl of Winchilsea and the Duke of Wellington. We would most unjustly insult these noblemen, if we for a moment left it to be supposed that such a reconciliation cost them effort, no, when opposed, they were

opposed not as personal enemies but as the champions of adverse principles.

SECURE A NEWSPAPER

On 13 May 1830, *The Morning Journal*, a supporter of the Tory Party ceased publication. For a number of months its finances had been unstable, and in the autumn of the previous year there had been a proposal to amalgamate it with *The Standard* under the title of *The Morning Standard*. Charles Baldwin was to become proprietor, which would have included his assuming liability for *The Morning Journal*'s debts, but the deal fell through.

The Tories, out of office for the first time in nearly a quarter of a century, had been anxious to secure a newspaper to present their viewpoint in the great debate on Reform. Baldwin, never slow to miss a business opportunity – especially when it coincided with his own beliefs – approached the Tories with a proposal to launch a paper in their support based on the same lines as *The Times*.

As *The Standard* already had the best writers and foreign correspondents, it was considered that the start-up costs would be the only obstacle, and for this Baldwin required an immediate advance of £10,000.[16] However, after deep consultations, his offer was declined. Twelve months later, the Tories still did not own a newspaper, despite the efforts of some wealthier members who had succeeded in raising more than £30,000 for the purchase of the *Morning Herald*. Unfortunately, in that case, the proprietors backed out of the negotiations. Once more the Tories turned to *The Standard* and talks were resumed with Baldwin and Giffard.

Lord Lowther, one of the proposed backers, said:

> It is no easy matter to establish a morning paper on the same scale as *The Times* and *The Herald*. The first cost would be £30,000 to £60,000. There are all kinds of people volunteering, taking management and being employees and to spend Tory money. But it is not a sum very easily raised, and, if it was, unless there was someone at the head, who, really, truly and honestly felt an interest in its prosperity, it must be a matter of trade, and unless Murray, Baldwin or some such man, that have prospered by Tory literature, undertook it, as a matter of trade, there was no hope of success.

Five days later, on 29 November 1831, Baldwin met Lord Lowther and other backers and told them that he drew most of his profits from his printing business and *The St. James's Chronicle* and very little from *The Standard*. He stressed the financial risk of setting up a morning paper on the same scale as *The Times*, and repeated that he would undertake it only under a guarantee of at least £10, 000. The debate as to whether Baldwin's offer should be accepted continued into the following year and on 12 February 1832 Lord Lowther reported: 'The capital and the extent of the management required is very extensive. Reporters for Parliament, Courts of Justice, public meetings – correspondents in all parts of Europe – separate editors for foreign affairs, home affairs – another for Finance. ... It is the variety and early intelligence that sells a paper, its politics and doctrines are only accessory.'[17]

Apart from *The Standard*, the Tories had very little other support. One small crumb had been *The Albion*, but, at the time of the decision not to proceed with the new daily, its sales had slumped to 1,100 copies a day. Efforts were made by Lord Lowther and his friends to raise sufficient financial backing, including by regular subscriptions. Alas, it was to be of no avail, for *The Albion*, which had absorbed *Lane's Star* in 1831 and *The British Traveller* in May 1833, was itself soon to be absorbed by *The Standard*. It was now the only important evening paper that the High Tories possessed. Since its earliest days, *The Standard*'s editorial staff had been situated in three Queen Anne houses in Shoe Lane, which were owned by the Tory Party; and, arising from this arrangement, in return Giffard was fed a daily ration of paragraphs favouring the party line. It was also believed that Lord Londonerry was providing the editor with confidential Court news for publication.[18]

'AN HONEST ORANGEMAN'

Giffard himself was now something of a celebrity, and was described by Sir Dennis Le Marchant as 'an honest Orangeman, and as violent and fanatical as most of his faith'. However, he was also the intimate of Charles Phillips, a Catholic barrister, who was in Lord Brougham's confidence, and was willing to publish many articles on law reform in which the Lord Chancellor was warmly praised. The power that Giffard now possessed was too much for some, and Croker regretted that 'the whole Conservative cause was then in the hands of Giffard. He is too honest – too honest because of over-zealous patriotism, but he is obstinate, wrong-headed and impracticable'.[19]

Despite the fact that the Tories and *The Standard* management had not been successful in launching their new daily, throughout the remainder of the decade the paper remained true to the party's principles, and in the autumn of 1834, as editor, Dr Stanley Lees Giffard wrote to the Duke of Wellington:

Myddleton Square. 17th November, 1834 – At the risk of being thought obtrusive, I take this abrupt mode of placing at your Grace's service *The Standard* newspaper – and the other newspaper under my control – circulating more than all the other London evening papers, of all parties, put together.

Eight years ago *The Standard* was indeed established at the sole cost and risk of its proprietor, for the same service – but deviating from the other direct course of communication which I now adopt at all hazards. We were deceived by the official persons who made use of your Grace's authority – and this led to consequences which I must continue to regret.

The offer which I now make is wholly without reserve – the newspapers shall be absolutely at your command – and if it be necessary to your Grace's interest that they take a line which I cannot approve of – I shall be at any time ready to retire in favor of a successor of your appointment – and I have no doubt of being able to prevail upon the proprietor to agree to such an arrangement.

Your Grace will, I hope, pardon one word more – which however I am ashamed to write, through the common practice of political writers renders it necessary. I want nothing – I look for no favor, present or remote. I think I may say the same for my friend the proprietor of *The Standard*, etc. Hitherto we have done our best for Conservative principles freely – and will continue to do so. I send this letter by post, because some years ago a letter which I tendered in person at Apsley House was refused.[20]

The Duke replied immediately, on 18 November 1834.

I received your letter last night upon my return home. I have never had any communication with a newspaper or with any gentleman connected with the Press; but nothing can be more open and fair than your proposition.

It was perfectly well known that the arrangement of the Government at present made is only temporary. I think, therefore, that it is but fair towards you to urge you to pause before you decide upon taking so determined a course as you have proposed to take. You will see hereafter the advantage of that which I recommend to you. In the meantime I recommend to your candour & fairness the temporary arrangement of which I have the conduct.[21]

Charles Greville, the diarist, noted the following:

[Lord John] Lyndhurst has just been here – he has seen the Duke, who had already opened a negotiation with [Thomas] Barnes [Editor of the *Times*] through Scarlett.

I offered to get any statement inserted of the causes of the late break up and he will again see the Duke and consider of inserting one. He said: 'Why Barnes is the most powerful man in the country.' *The Standard* has sent to offer its support – The Duke said he should be very happy, but they must understand that the Government has not yet formed, etc.

While Giffard and Wellington were having their exchange of correspondence, Lord Melbourne, the Whig Prime Minister, was seeing the King (William IV) at Brighton. There he was informed that his Government had been dismissed. Sir Robert Peel formed an administration, and, at the general election which followed, issued the Tamworth Manifesto, which is accepted as marking the foundation of the Conservative Party. In an address to his constituents he accepted the fundamental reforms that had been carried out by the Whigs under Earl Grey and Lord Melbourne as 'a final and irrevocable settlement of a great constitutional question'.

The Standard was quick to offer its services to the new Government, as this letter from Giffard to Sir Robert Peel shows:

8th December, 1834. – Sir, I take the liberty of offering for your service *The Standard* newspaper. *The Standard* circulates more than any other evening paper, except *The Globe* which it nearly or altogether equals in circulation – and with *The St. James's Chronicle* and other journals belonging to the same owner conducted by the same editor – and for the most part printed from the same types – circulates more than all the other evening papers put together – the *Globe* included.

In offering *The Standard* to your service, no return of any kind, present or future, is expected, but much of the confidence of the Government as must be necessary to render any service to it effectual: it is right, however, to explain what experience has demonstrated and what you, sir, yourself may observe in the case of the late Government – that it is much better for an administration to do without newspapers altogether than to have rival and jarring papers.

If, therefore, you think it worth while to take *The Standard* into your service, you will feel that it ought to be the only evening paper so taken. There are, I believe, but two evening papers likely to come into competition with *The Standard* – the *Albion* and the *Courier* – but *The Standard* alone (without *The St. James Chronicle*, etc.) circulates a great deal more than both put together. And though it may be and doubtless is inferior in talent (the public has, however, made a different award) it can bring to the aid of any Government which it supports a weight of character such as no other journal can – and a corresponding claim upon the confidence of Conservatives.

If necessary to facilitate an arrangement, the proprietor of *The Standard* is prepared to buy – at a rate higher than persons acquainted with the value of that kind of property will appraise it at – the property of the *Albion* and *Courier* or both.

I cannot be ignorant, sir, that you have good cause for objections personal to myself. I am, however, prepared to break all connecion with *The Standard* and its kindred journals, and I have no interest whatever in any of them. I offer these assertions upon the pledge of a word which no man has a right to doubt. My sole motive in addressing you is to obviate the possibility that this power which I have the means of erecting should operate to embarrass the formation or progress of a Conservative Government to any degree, however slight, and also to learn as early as possible what is to be my own position.[22]

Two days later, Sir Robert Peel replied:

10th December, 1834. – Harassed as I am by public business, I will not defer the acknowledgement of your letter, and by the expression of my sincere thanks for the very liberal and handsome offer which it conveys.

I am the more unwilling to postpone its acknowledgement from a desire to assure you that no comments made by *The Standard* upon any part of my public conduct have left the slightest hostility or ill will towards you. Such has been my admiration of the ability with which that newspaper has been conducted, that I have uniformly read it, being pleased to bear with its occasional severities upon myself than to forego the satisfaction of reading the able and powerful and eloquent comments upon public affairs which it so frequently contained.

I neither have nor ever had the slightest connexion in any shape with either the *Albion* or the *Courier*. Personally, I am entirely free to give a full and fair consideration to the proposal you make, and I will give it that consideration at the earliest moment that I am disengaged from the very pressing matters which at present absorb my whole attention.[23]

The offer was not taken up by the Prime Minister, but for the remainder of the decade Giffard and *The Standard* were to be of immeasurable assistance to the Tories.

BLISTERING ATTACK

At the time of the Reform Bill debate there had been a great increase in the number of newspaper readers, but many of these were purchasers of the unstamped titles; and in a blistering attack on 10 September 1833, Giffard commented.

> Everybody is aware of the miscellaneous multitude of cheap publications which the last two or three years have called into existence. Some of these have had a very considerable sale; but we have in evidence that all, without any exception, of an innocent and respectable kind, have been sold, not as cheap publications, but in collected numbers, at prices such as the upper and middle classes are accustomed to purchase. We do not hesitate to say, therefore that those classes which have been the object of eleemosynary education, have not availed themselves of the cheapness of innocent and respectable reading ... perhaps they have been reading – doubtless they have, and we are enabled, from an authentic source, to give some account of their reading ... It is a list of the unstamped political publications in defiance of the law, with the late average sale of each: *Poor Man's Guardian* – 16, 000 circulation; *Destructive* – 8,000 circulation; *Gauntlet* – 22, 000 circulation; *Cosmopolite* – 5,000 circulation; *Working Men's Friend* – 7,000 circulation; *Crisis* – 5,000 circulation; *The Man* – 7,000 circulation; and *Reformer* – 5,000 circulation.
>
> These are the principal unstamped publications of London – the reading with *The Times* and *The Weekly Despatch*, of the educated democracy of the metropolis. Are men to be turned loose upon such garbage as this? In the country there are also unstamped newspapers – particularly at Leeds, Bradford and Manchester, etc., all taking their tone from the *Poor Man's Guardian* and others, which we described as the penny press of London. These are the primitiae, the first fruits of the late active exertions in behalf of indiscriminate education.[24]

Within three years, the protestations of *The Standard* were heeded, and in 1836 the reduction of the stamp duty was hailed by the middle classes as a great stride towards the freedom of the press. By reducing the differences in price between the stamped and unstamped newspapers, it led to the latter's decline. As *The Northern Star* ruefully noted: 'The reduction upon stamps has made the rich man's paper cheaper, and the poor man's paper dearer.'

The year 1836 was notable also for another event on the press scene. In its annual report the London Union of Compositors observed that an inquiry had been undertaken by the compositors of *The Times* into working conditions.[25] Apart from *The Times*, which had been closed to union labour since 1816, five other newspapers were investigated: *Morning Herald, Ledger, Courier, Sun* and *Standard.* The report showed:

THE STANDARD

Full hands. The full hands on *The Standard* commence at five o'clock am, and are required to get the galley out by nine o'clock. The finish begins at nine, ends at three o'clock, making six hours, during which time they are expected to produce a quarter per hour. There are no extras on the first work. After three o'clock, 10½d per hour is charged. The nick, half an hour is paid. It appears doubtful whether any extras can be charged before half-past three o'clock. Supernumeraries – None.

Assistants. The assistants, who are all elderly men, come in at six o'clock, but have no specified time for commencing, and sometimes do not get any copy before half-past nine or ten o'clock. They do not declare out of the galley at any particular time, nor do they make any charge for standing still. They are not called on to assist in correcting, nor are they expected to wait for second editions, which are done by bookmen in the house, and who are likewise employed on the paper whenever there is a press of copy. If the full hands are not there by six o'clock, the assistants are expected to occupy their frames, but this is only an arrangement amongst the companionship.

Second Editions commence at half-past five o'clock, and are charged by the line if exceeding a quarter of a galley, but an hour is charged for any quantity under that.

The number of lines in a Bourgeois galley is 112; Brevier 106; Minion 94; Nonpareil 64.

The number of letters in a Bourgeois galley is 5040; Brevier 5194; Minion 5170; Nonpareil 4544.

The number of men employed is: Full Hands 13; Assistants 4. Total 17. Average earnings amount to: Full Hands £2 4s 4½d; Assistants £1 10s.

5

Bright, Broken Maginn

During the formative years of *The Standard*, two writers more than any others stood out: Dr William Maginn and Alaric Alexander Watts. 'Bright, broken Maginn' is immortalised by Thackeray as the Captain Shandon of *Pendennis*; and, at the end of the nineteenth century, there was a messenger named Jensen who could remember as a small boy daily bringing Maginn's articles from Fleet Prison to the paper's offices in Shoe Lane.

William Maginn was born on 10 July 1794 in Cork, where his father maintained a private school for boys. There his brilliance in classical studies was so remarkable that he entered Trinity College, Dublin, at the age of eleven and after graduation taught classics at his father's school. He achieved the LL.B degree in 1819, became an LL.D of Trinity, and before the age of twenty-five was fluent in seven languages.[1] Little wonder that Maginn's biographer, Edward Kenealy, could assert that 'His memory was prodigious, the strongest in the world. It was a rich storehouse of all learnings so that it might with propriety be called, like the sublime Longinus, the living library.'

Maginn began in journalism by contributing to the *Literary Gazette* and *Blackwood's Magazine*. In 1824 he joined the *Representative* as its Paris correspondent, being taken on by a young Benjamin Disraeli.[2] Within six months, the paper had folded and John Murray, one of its founders, recalled Maginn from Paris and, strangely, increased his salary to £700 per annum. With this extra income, he was more than able to indulge his weakness for drink – a weakness that was ultimately to wreck his career and lead him into fecklessness and debt for the rest of his life.

Apart from contributing to *Blackwood*'s and *The Literary Gazette*, he was writing for *The Quarterly Review*, edited by John Gibson Lockhart; and he was also involved with Theodore Hook's *John Bull*, a not very reputable weekly. By then a well-known figure in Fleet Street, Maginn had many friends of influence, one of whom was Thomas Barnes, editor of *The Times*. But it was to Charles Baldwin and *The Standard* that he turned in 1827, and there he became assistant to fellow Irishman and Protestant, Dr Giffard. From the very first days, Maginn's brilliant writings and acerbic wit were features of *The Standard*, and although he wrote anonymously his style was easily recognisable and won him many admirers. One contemporary described him thus:

> A bright genius undoubtedly he was, with lovable qualities that bound friends to him amid all his dissipation, his want of principle, his discreditable dodges to escape for a time the consequences of his mode of life; and in the thick of it all, harassed by creditors and hiding from Bailiffs, he sent out to the Press papers that display acute insight, scholarship, and critical skill, and trifles of rollicking entertainment and rare humour. He would write a leader in *The Standard* one evening, answer it in *The True Sun* the following day and abuse both in *John Bull* on the ensuing Sunday.[3]

Maginn is also credited as being one of the first people to call *The Times* 'The Thunderer'. In an article that appeared on 15 February 1830 in the *Morning Herald* he described *The Times* as 'The Great Earwigger of the Nation, otherwise the Leading Journal of Europe, otherwise The Awful Monosyllable, otherwise The Thunderer – but more commonly called the Blunderer.'[4]

One of his faithful friends was William Makepeace Thackeray, and he has described how his love of newspapers was fired by Maginn:

> My interest in journals and magazines of all kinds had always been there – I knew and bought them all and had toyed for a long time with the idea of becoming somehow involved in them, either as a contributor – vain hope – or in the production, which interested me almost as much. Does this surprise you? Then you don't know what an exciting business the putting together of a newspaper is. It does not just put itself through the letter box on its own – the print does not jump onto the page by itself and the pages do not cut and bind themselves alone and the illustrations aren't done on each copy by the artist – the whole process is extremely complicated and skilful and I am always astonished to this day that it can happen at all and at such speed. I remember being taken by my friend William Maginn to *The Standard* in London one Wednesday night where he showed me the mysteries I have outlined above and quite fired my imagination to have a hand in it all.[5]

Thackeray described his visit to *The Standard* offices in this passage from his novel, *Pendennis*:

> They were passing through the Strand as they talked, and by a newspaper office, which was all lighted up and bright. Reporters were coming out of the place or rushing up to it in cabs; there were lamps burning in the editor's room, and above, the compositors were at work: the windows of the building were a blaze of gas.

'Look at that, Pen,' Warrington said. 'There she is – the great engine – she never sleeps. She has her ambassadors in every quarter of the world – her couriers upon every road. Her officers march with armies and her envoys walk into statesmen's cabinets. They are ubiquitous. Yonder journal has an agent, at this minute, giving bribes at Madrid; and another inspecting the price of potatoes in Covent Garden. Look! here comes the Foreign Express galloping in. They will be able to give news to Downing Street tomorrow: funds will rise or fall, fortunes will be made or lost – and Mr Doolan will be called away from his supper for he is foreign sub-editor.'

Thackeray so impressed Giffard that he offered him the post of *Standard* correspondent in Madrid for £300 per annum – an offer which Thackeray turned down.

Despite his undoubted genius as a writer, though, Maginn was intent on destroying himself with drink. In 1836, following an article in *Fraser's Magazine*, he was challenged to a duel by Grantley Berkeley, considered to be a crack shot. Fortunately for Maginn, Berkeley missed with his three shots, and Maginn's second, Hugh Fraser, then insisted that the duel be broken off.[6] The years of heavy drinking were now taking their toll, and Kenealy, another loyal friend, wrote of him: 'He is a ruin, but a glorious ruin, nevertheless. He takes no great care of himself. Could he be induced to do so he would be the first man of the day in literature.' By 1836, however, Maginn's financial situation was desperate, and, despite help from the King of Hanover, Sir Robert Peel and Thackeray, he was thrown into Fleet Prison for debt. This did not, however, prevent his contributing to *The Standard* and to *Punch*. Compelled to obtain his discharge as an insolvent, he emerged broken-hearted and in an advanced stage of consumption. On his release from prison, broken in health and spirit, he moved to Walton-on-Thames, where he died on 21 August 1842.

DESERVING OF ADMIRATION

Alaric Alexander Watts, however, was a very different character, who during his years on *The Standard* was a most loyal and valuable servant to Giffard. 'I know of no man' averred Giffard, 'whose integrity is more pure; no man whose genius is of a higher order; whose conduct, in all relations of life, is more deserving of admiration; no man in whose friendship I feel more highly honoured.'[7] Watts more than repaid that trust when, as a result of Giffard's serious illness, he acted as editor of *The Standard* for three months in the late summer of 1839. In a warm acknowledgement of Watts' service, Giffard told him: 'You and I have known each other for fifteen or sixteen years, a very great part of the allotted life of man, and we have never had a difference of political or private opinion.'[8]

Apart from the *Courier*, he was also editing *The Literary Souvenir*, which had been founded in 1824. Soon his work on the *Souvenir* was bringing him back more and more into London life and as a consequence he resigned as editor of the *Manchester Courier* in 1826 to become editor and proprietor of *The Literary Souvenir*.

Born in London on 16 March 1797, Watts led a varied life as a tutor to the family of the Prince Regent's dentist[9] and as a temporary clerk in the office of the controller of army accounts before working as a sub-editor on the *New Monthly Magazine* in 1818. He soon became well known in London literary circles and began to write for the *Literary Gazette*. As a result he was offered and accepted the editorship of the *Leeds Intelligencer* at a salary of £300 per annum. Always outspoken, he published attacks on Yorkshire mill owners and advocated the fencing in of machinery in the factories. One effect was the large number of cancellations for the *Intelligencer*. Nevertheless, he remained in Leeds until 1825, when he left for Manchester to edit *The Courier*.

At the same time he started part-time newspaper publishing: he arranged that provincial newspapers, with their titles and leading articles set up, should be printed at 1 Crane Court, Fleet Street, and 'that the local intelligence and local politics should be added in the country by the local bookseller and printer by whom the paper was published and who was, titularly, its proprietor'. As his son, Alaric Alfred Watts, was to write in his father's biography, *Alaric Watts, A Narrative of his Life*, in 1884:

> This was the origin of what, in the printing trade, is, I believe, designated 'Partly-printed newspapers'. For the credit of having originated this method of newspaper issue there have been many claimants. For whatever it may be worth, it belongs to my father, and certainly not to a newspaper company established in 1850, as claimed some years ago by a writer in a leading journal.

In 1827, though, Watts' wide experience led to his being asked by Charles Baldwin to assist Giffard in the launch of *The Standard*, and he became a valued and esteemed colleague from the first issue. James Grant, the newspaper historian, who worked on the paper, later remarked: 'I may observe that he [Watts] never occupied on *The Standard* newspaper the position usually understood in newspaper parlance by the term sub-editor.' Watts spent much of his time writing the leaders for *The Standard* and he was to describe these experiences, in humorous vein, in his book of essays entitled *Scenes of Life and Shades of Character*, published in 1831: 'Here figures the editor and uttering his oracular opinions on the affairs of the world, abroad and at home, leaves the more plebeian task of procuring facts, to his minors; who, under various names, more or less complementary, fill the subordinate departments. And these, his articles, are called the leading articles.'

Although Maginn and Watts were colleagues on *The Standard*, there was never any real bond between them – despite Watts assisting him financially.

Maginn, meanwhile, was using *Fraser's Magazine* to attack all and sundry, and prominent among those selected were Watts and his friends.[10] After suffering these attacks in silence, Watts at last replied – but in verse. Unfortunately, this was not the end of the affair, for in 1832 Watts had his portrait painted by a Mr Howard and it was hung at the Royal Academy. This was too good an opportunity for Maginn to miss, and in *Fraser's Magazine* there appeared a libellous but irresistibly comical caricature portrait by Maclise representing 'Watts carrying off pictures with a decidedly furtive expression'. Maginn wrote the facing caption: 'We are not particularly sure what our friend the etcher means by exhibiting Watts in this position in which he is shown on the opposite page.'

Watts, after writing to Lockart, the editor, decided to sue the magazine and Maginn, bringing forth warm support from Giffard: 'This affair gives me great pain. I cannot advise you to forego a legal vindication; but the effect of giving more publicity to the attack, while it cannot raise your high character, will not fail to do mischief to our common cause. I cannot forgive the unthinking fool who has created the difficulty for mere wantonness of malice.'[11] The libel action was never in doubt: Watts was awarded £150 damages and the magazine faced costs of more than £1,000. But despite this vindication, Maginn's barbs had hurt, and *The Literary Souvenir*, which had been successful for so long, now began to decline and expired in 1833. Watts then became co-founder of *The United Services Gazette*.

The demise of *The Literary Souvenir* also led Watts to become what Maginn contemptuously called 'head nurse of a hospital of rickety newspaperlings', the truth of which description was admitted by Watts' son.[12] These speculations, chiefly minor provincial papers established in the Conservative interest, were to involve him in litigation with his partner in *The United Services Gazette*. As previously mentioned, when Giffard became seriously ill in 1839 Watts stood in as editor of *The Standard*, leading Giffard to write on 10 October: 'I resigned my place as principal editor of *The Standard* to you, with an expectation that my friends in Bridge Street would feel the advantage of securing your services as my permanent successor, and had it not been for your very kind offer, I should have died in harness. I firmly believe this.'[13]

With his earnings from *The Standard* and *The United Services Gazette*, Watts was receiving more than £1,000 per annum. But despite the efforts of Charles Baldwin, he now became involved in litigation with his partner over the *Gazette*, and with debts of more than £3,000 Watts lost the court action and co-ownership of the *Gazette*. But his troubles were not yet over, as 'he was arrested outside his beautiful home at the suit of a paper-maker'. Unable to pay, Watts was declared bankrupt in 1850. However, his fate was not to be the tragic ending of Maginn. In 1853, Watts accepted an appointment in the Inland Revenue Office, where his son held a high position, and after pleas on his behalf he was awarded a Civil List pension of £100 a year by the Prime Minister, Lord Aberdeen, in 1854. His later days were thus spent in some comfort, including editing the first issue of *Men of the Time*. He died on 5 April 1864, in Notting Hill, and was buried in Highgate Cemetery.

VICTORIA'S ACCESSION

Two events more than any other dominated the pages of *The Standard* in its early years: Catholic emancipation and parliamentary reform. Now a decade later, in 1837, the death of William IV and the accession of his niece Victoria at the age of eighteen was to bring about a profound change in the character and relationships of the national leaders. Her standards were those of the growing middle classes. In his first leader after Victoria's accession, Giffard wrote: 'Let then the people do their duty to the young and most interesting Sovereign whom heaven has called to the throne. The most devoted loyalty, the most anxious patriotism, here concur, with ever a selfish love of order and peace, in calling every man to aid the Queen in staying the progress of revolution.'

Twelve months later, on Friday, 29 June, the paper published its largest-ever issue – eight pages – to celebrate the Coronation of Victoria;[14] and there were more than five pages of graphic descriptions of the ceremony and activities. Among the list of business firms displaying decorations and bunting, it was reported that *The Standard* offices bore a brilliant star with the letters VR. It was also noted that at Fleet Prison 'the warden with his wonted liberality bestowed half-a-gallon of porter upon each prisoner'.

The talking points in the first decade of Victoria's reign were corn and Chartism, and the reportage of these was extensively covered in the newspapers of the day. Leading the fight for the abolition of duties on imported corn was the Manchester-based Anti-Corn Law League, which advocated free trade. Led by Richard Cobden and John Bright, it was the first great national radical movement, employing all the methods of well-organised agitation – mass meetings throughout Britain, lobbying of MPs and the use of the growing railway system plus the new penny postage to send pamphlets to every elector in the land.

The Standard, ever consistent, supported the Corn Laws; and on 24 January 1839, Charles Greville, long-time Clerk of the Privy Council, noted in his diary:

> The question of absorbing interest is how the repeal or alteration of the corn laws, and the declaration of war against them on the part of *The Times* has produced a great effect, and is taken as conclusive evidence that they cannot be maintained.[15] The rest of the Conservative press, *The Morning Herald, Post* and *Standard,* support the corn laws, and the latter has engaged in single combat with *The Times,* conducted with a kind of chivalrous courtesy, owing to the concurrence of their general politics, very unusual in newspaper warfare, and with great ability on both sides.

In the summer of 1841, Giffard's old adversary, Thomas Barnes, the editor of *The Times,* died, and John Walter II replaced him with the 23-year-old John Thadeus Delane. Despite his youth and lack of experience, Delane was the proprietor's first and only choice, but Walter fully intended to keep a watchful eye and if necessary assume control. Walter wrote to a Conservative Party Manager:

> In consequence of my conversation with you this morning I made an immediate visit to my young friend [Delane] at Blackfriars. I there imparted to him, in a great degree what has passed between us – and I thought it ought to be satisfactory to him, as I am sure it would have been to me in early days, that the Government communications should be made impartially – to all the Government Journals, without any reference to their several sales, or their presumed influence upon the ground. ... *The Times, The Standard, The Post* and *The Herald* should be upon the same footing.[16]

On the political front, Peel was again Prime Minister and was immediately confronted with the problem of the poor harvests throughout the realm. He was convinced that if free trade in manufactured goods had benefited the people, then the time had come to apply the same principles to agriculture and to repeal the Corn Laws. For Giffard and *The Standard,* amid the political turmoil, it was yet another occasion to pledge their allegiance to the Tory Party. On 31 August 1841, he wrote to Peel: 'I hope that in placing unreservedly at your command *The Standard* and the several other papers under my control, I shall be thought to have no personal object nor other object other than the power of being useful to the country and of testifying my gratitude to you.'[17] Within two days, Peel had replied: 'I will again communicate with you upon the subject of it when I am less harassed by business which presses for instant despatch.'

Meanwhile, under Delane's editorship, the policies of *The Times* were increasingly diverging from those of *The Standard*, with their differences over the repeal of the Corn Laws and Roman Catholicism being debated in their columns in the most passionate terms. The row over Catholicism was particularly apparent in the spring of 1845 concerning the Maynooth grant – Peel's proposal to subsidise the Roman Catholic College at Maynooth out of public funds. On 5 May 1845 *The Standard*, in a violent attack on the Papacy and its teaching methods, declared:

> To whatever motive our conduct may be ascribed we must warn all parents and teachers to keep *The Times* of this day from the eyes of young persons under their control. The journal to which we refer has thought it not indecent or criminal to publish a cento of the worst extracts from the filthiest part of the most filthy book by which Roman Catholic priests are made to prepare themselves for the duties of the Confessional, and these extracts are either in plain English or in such Latin that a school-boy or girl – for Latin is now properly a part of female education – can understand them.[18]

Three days later, *The Standard* charged that: 'Three years ago *The Times* was approaching the end of the only access of honourable and consistent conduct in its history; but we imagine that had been an access of some years' duration; we therefore thought well of *The Times* three years ago, and we wrote as we thought; but we imagine that no one will see anything more than civility due to an ally.'

Events reached a climax in the autumn of 1845 when the force of the Anti-Corn Law League, assisted by a devastating blight on the Irish potato crop, evoked a powerful clamour against the Corn Laws and none was more vociferous in this protest than *The Times*. On October 29, it informed its readers: 'Once we might not have declared a free trade in corn, now we must.' This statement was followed by a fierce attack on Peel, and, on 6 November, by a demand for his resignation.

Meanwhile, Richard Cobden and John Bright, in leading the fight against the Corn Laws, were barn-storming throughout the nation, and on 28 November more than 8,000 of their supporters crowded into the Manchester Free Trade Hall to hear them demand the immediate repeal of the corn duties. Bright was in devastating form, and *The Standard*[19] was a major target of his invective when he told the mass meeting:

> *The Standard* newspaper – which alternates between an affection of superior piety (laughter) and the most unblushing effrontery and audacity in its statements – *The Standard* has at last found out that ... no human being, not one of her Majesty's subjects must perish of

hunger, *The Standard* has for seven years heaped all its slanders and poured all its venom, especially upon the men accustomed to address you from this platform ... *The Standard* has supported, without intermission, a law whose especial object was to bring about such a state of things that, though the rich might have enough, and the moderately rich might not starve still the poorest must be driven into the earth.

On 4 December *The Times* announced that Parliament would be summoned in the first week of January and that the Speech from the Throne would recommend the Repeal of the Corn Laws. For *The Standard*, the report could not be true and in an immediate riposte delivered in Giffard's best manner asserted that it was an 'Atrocious Fabrication by *The Times*'. Indeed, Giffard declared that every one of the propositions put forward by Delane was false. As the row raged on between the papers, Giffard wrote on 10 December:

> Let the protecting duties be abolished, and they must follow the corn-laws and the whole mass of British labour. We ask the artisan is he prepared for a reduction of half his earnings in order to have bread, perhaps two-pence in the four-pound loaf cheaper? We will not go out of our own department to put the question. We ask the working printer will he be contented to exchange his present working conditions for twelve shillings a week wages, and bread at three halfpence a pound?[20]

That same evening, at the Manchester Free Trade Hall, Bright once again assailed *The Standard* and its position, charging that '*The Standard*, true to its old principles, true to its anti-national character, is doing its very utmost to rouse the passions of the disappointed class to resist the calls which the almost universal people of England is making upon the Government, that these accursed Corn Laws should be abolished.'

Meanwhile, following Peel's resignation on 4 December as a result of his Cabinet's split on the repeal of the Corn Laws, Lord John Russell endeavoured to form a government and failed in his attempt. The Queen again summoned Peel, and he at once agreed to accept the challenge. On 22 January 1846, the new parliament assembled and Peel made a long speech in which he announced his determination to repeal the Corn Laws, as the only remedy for the Irish famine.[21]

In the Queen's Speech, Peel had spoken of the relaxation of protective duties. To *The Standard* leader writer it was 'next to impossible to believe ... that as the adviser of such an injunction Sir Robert Peel can contemplate so sudden a change'. The debate raged throughout the spring of 1846, and despite the bitter invective of

Benjamin Disraeli and his cohorts, the joint forces of the Peelites and Whigs ensured a majority of 98 over the Tory Protectionists on May 15. A month later, the Duke of Wellington carried out his last service to Peel by steering the repeal of the Corn Laws through the House of Lords.

NEW BITTERNESS

For Giffard, who was not in good health, this was the ultimate blow. His struggles against Catholic emancipation and parliamentary reform had been unsuccessful and now he felt that he had lost the final battle. *The Standard*'s support for Peel could never be the same again, and its new bitterness was reflected in the following extracts from the paper's advertisement in *The Newspaper Guide* of 1851, the first to be published after the repeal:

> Nor was its fidelity to the cause diminished by the difficulties the leader encountered in the administration of national affairs; but it continued to lend him the efficient aid, combatting with equal energy his old opponents and his disaffected allies, till he abandoned the principles of protection, when *The Standard* abandoned him; and, with *The Herald* ranged itself with the adherents of the Country Party.

Looking back with the advantage of hindsight, the author of Giffard's obituary in 1858 quite correctly remarked:

> In the controversy with the Anti-Corn League, Dr Giffard by name was sufficient proof how the weapons of *The Standard* had reached the political enemy. During the period Dr Giffard undertook for a short time the management of the political department of *The Morning Herald*. After the sudden, and at all events, unexpected repeal of the Corn Laws by Sir Robert Peel, he adopted the section, which looked on Sir Robert's conduct as wanting in honesty towards his previous followers, and dealt with the event as members of a deserted party will.[22]

But for Giffard, the 1840s were a time for reflection; and in the General Election which followed the fall of Peel's ministry in the summer of 1846 he decided to stand as a Tory candidate for his old college, the University of Dublin – more to challenge Peel and the Peelites than with any serious intention of sitting in Parliament. In a violent campaign, he was challenged by Mr Shaw, Recorder of Dublin, 'to come out from behind the lair of anonymous types'. Giffard, though, was received by a great mass of electors with much enthusiasm; but he contended himself with 'stating his opinions to the College, justifying his conduct to the Dublin Corporation Bill, offering Mr Shaw what explanation he pleased, and then retiring from the contest'.[23]

The 1840s had been a decade when Giffard's fortunes had been at a low ebb. In fact, for most of his life he was beset with money worries, and, with ten children from his two marriages to bring up and educate, life was hard – especially as his independence of spirit would not allow him to be beholden to any man. Throughout the period he had also suffered bouts of illness and depression; and this is reflected in his long correspondence with his friend, Dr Bliss, editor of *The Herald*, Oxford:

> 1838: I have more than one warning that I shall not be alive at the end of 1840: I have therefore no time to lose.
>
> June 27, 1839: I find that overwork has completely exhausted me and that without a change in my health which I can scarcely dare to hope for I must forgo the gratification and advantage of my connection with the *Herald*. It will make a few months difference, for as I have been declining for the past month or two; a few months more and it will be all over as far as I am concerned.
>
> October 23, 1840: What I foresaw when I last wrote to you has occurred. My utmost exertions have failed to meet the debts for which I am able. I have deprived myself for six months of the society of my family. I have left them to live upon two or three pounds a week in France. I have lived in London for a few shillings a week. I have mortgaged my life assurance for the last penny they are worth. I have trespassed upon my friend Mr Baldwin to the utmost that my duty to his family and my feelings will permit. I have been for months a prisoner in my house, never, I may say with perfect truth, feeling the fresh air but on Sundays. I have tried to borrow, but though my friends profess willingness to relieve my wants as a beggar they shew no disposition to treat me as an honest and industrious man, competent and, if life be spared, be able to repay them.[24]

Within a few months, his creditors were at the door once more, and he wrote to one as follows:

> Sir – I request the honour of your company at this house on a date to be arranged. The occasion of my proposing this trouble to you is as follows. I have lately discovered to my surprise that I am considerably in your debt and indebted to other gentlemen. I have

> no reason however to suppose that my debts much exceed £200 which, with an income of about £720 a year, I can, I hope, settle to your satisfaction in a few months by exertion on my part and such forbearance on your side as I am grateful to acknowledge.

As the decade came to a close, Giffard was still faced with demands:

> Kings College, 29th July, 1850. Sir – I beg to enclose you an account for £22 10s due by you to this College. You are doubtless aware of my having been under the necessity of making many applications to you for payment of this account. It is my duty to inform you now that if not paid within the present week ....

At the foot of the demand, Giffard has written 'I leave this as a warning to my children and to their descendants never to expect gratitude or even decent behaviour from Parsons of the Church of England. I was one of the first promoters of Kings College and subscribed £25 to its creation'.

Although his political ambitious had been dashed and he had been in debt, the 1840s were to provide some consolation for Giffard, as it was then that his son, Hardinge Stanley, joined him on *The Standard*, before being called to the Bar in 1850.[25] Hardinge never went to school but was educated at home by his father, learning Latin, Greek and Hebrew before entering Merton College, Oxford, in 1842. Father and son were close friends and were both the most uncompromising of Tories. For five years, Hardinge acted as assistant editor to his father, and on many occasions wrote the leaders. 'There were very few horse-drawn buses running in London at that time, and each morning two strong, thickset figures – the editor in his full-skirted frock coat, double folded stock, fob and high hat, and his son, probably less conventionally attired – would set out from their home in Myddelton Square, Pentonville, bound for *The Standard* offices in Shoe Lane.'[26]

Hardinge, though, was to seek a legal and political career, achieving Silk in 1865, and, following attempts to obtain a seat in Parliament in the general elections of 1868 and 1874, he was in November 1875 appointed Solicitor General by Disraeli, and knighted. Ten years later, Lord Salisbury, in his first administration, appointed Hardinge Lord Chancellor. He was elevated to an earldom during his third tenure of the chancellorship, which he retained until 1905. He is best-known for his work, *Halsbury's Laws of England.*

PUBLIC DUTY

Charles Baldwin had also tried his hand at politics. In 1837 he had 'received a requisition, signed in 25 hours by above 600 electors of

Lambeth, to contest the representation of that borough. He had no hope of success and one of his opponents, Sir Benjamin Hawes, was a personal friend; nevertheless he considered it an act of public duty to accede to their request. He failed as expected'. It was just as well that he did not abandon journalism for politics. As a contemporary journalist observed: 'Mr Baldwin set up *The Standard* at a time little promising of profit for the speculation, but he set it up to support the Protestant cause, and the political principles which he had seriously entertained. It would be unjust to consider it a mere party journal – it is eminently the journal of liberty. Let an invasion of liberty, a cause of oppression arise, and *The Standard* has always been the first to hurry to the defence.'

Despite criticism from *The Sun* – '*The Standard* is in a singular state of political optimism, we may add, alarming to its friends and its party ... Its extreme unction portends that rite to its party' – it was generally accepted that the paper 'was particularly distinguished by its gentlemanly tone, which was maintained without any sacrifice of the force of argument or the vigour of style'. One anonymous MP of opposition opinions was heard to remark: 'Mr Charles Baldwin was remarkable as the most consistent politician he had ever known; he had never made a political or a professional blunder.'

Having reached the age of 70, Charles Baldwin decided to retire, and from 1844 left the active management of his business to his son, Edward. He continued, however, to attend the Stationers' Hall, of which company he had twice been Master, in 1842 and 1843, and the meetings of the Literary Fund Society.[27] His name was the last inscribed in the list of members of the Society by David Williams, who founded it in 1799. He was elected to the council in 1850, and appointed one of the three treasurers in 1852. He held these offices until 1857, when he resigned in his 84th year.

Apart from his charitable activities, Baldwin was also a Justice of Peace, and held the unique record of being 'the oldest volunteer in the Kingdom'. He had joined the corps under Colonel Kensington (called the Silk-stocking Corps, from all its members being gentlemen) at the turn of the century, and served in it for a number of years. His most vivid memory was of being called out and kept under arms for three days to defend Fleet Prison from a threatened attack of the mob.

He was fortunate not only in living to the great age of 95, but he also retained to the very end his faculties. It was said of him 'that his genial disposition, amiable manners and lively conversation endeared him to a large circle of younger friends with whom he was held in affectionate regard'.[28]

Unlike Henry, his father, Charles Baldwin had been fortunate in his dealings with the Establishment; on looking back he could reflect with pleasure at the great strides that had been achieved with his *Standard* – both as a political force and as a commercial proposition. From its early beginnings the circulation of some 700 or 800 copies each evening had risen within a matter of years to more than 3,500, and there had been a corresponding increase in the number of advertisements. For the first year, the number of advertisements had been considerably less than a column, but within three years it had increased, on average, to more than four columns an issue. With expenses being kept down, the increased circulation and advertising meant that 'before it was five years old profits could not have been less than from £7,000 to £8,000 a year'.

The Standard's position had been strengthened by the lowering in 1833 of the tax on advertisements, from 3s 6d to 1s 6d; and three years later, on 15 September 1836, the stamp duty on newspapers was reduced from fourpence to one penny a copy,[29] and a reduction in the duty on paper was also made. The newspaper owners immediately introduced one of the earliest restrictive practices – they collectively agreed not to pass on the full tax relief to their readers, and to lower the price of the newspapers by only 2d instead of 3d – from 7d to 5d.

Apart from *The Standard* and *The St. James's Chronicle*, Charles Baldwin was also the sole owner of the *London Packet*, published twice a week, and the *London Journal*, once a week – 'all got up with scarcely any expense out of *The Standard*'. And it was estimated that by 1835 his income from the newspapers was more than £15,000 per year.

Throughout this period, *The Standard* continued to be produced as a four-page broadsheet. There were, however, the occasional eight-page issues, the Coronation of Queen Victoria being one such example, selling at 5d. But in 1838, Baldwin even produced a one-page Special Supplement. Late on February 28 he came out with:

SUPPLEMENT TO
The Standard
EXTRAORDINARY EXPRESS FROM CANADA
SEIZURE OF BOIS BLANC
BY REBELS

Baldwin's success in building up his small chain had led to criticism from some of his contemporaries, who considered that the London press was in the hands of too few people. William Clement and Henry Colbourn were other newspaper proprietors who came under attack. It was believed by their critics that the punitive effects of taxation on sales and advertising – despite the recent reductions – and the large concentration of capital required to establish a paper had now made it impossible for anyone except 'trading speculators' to own the press. As an example, before 1820 it was estimated that the costs of setting-up an evening newspaper such as *The Standard* could vary between £2,000 and £5,000, but by the early years of Victoria's reign these had escalated to between £30,000 and £50,000, and it was considered that it would lose at least £100 a week until it became established. The salaries of reporters had also risen during this period – from two guineas a week at the turn of the century to five or seven guineas by the 1840s, while the pay of full-time compositors had increased from £1 16s to almost £3.

Now, with *The Standard* accepted by the parties as a political force, and with the paper on a sound financial footing, Charles Baldwin decided that the time had come to retire and hand over succession to his son. He was confident that in Edward there was a well-educated, highly-trained person who could take the group to even greater heights.

6

Enter Edward Baldwin

For the new proprietor of *The Standard*, Edward Baldwin, it was a time to further expand the business, and his first task upon his father's retirement was to develop *The Morning Herald*, which he had recently purchased from the Thwaites family. Ever since the eighteenth century, when the Revd Henry Bate (he later changed his surname to Dudley) had been editor, the paper had led a lively existence: in 1786 William Pitt, the Prime Minister, had sued *The Herald* for libel, the paper having charged him with gambling with public funds. Pitt demanded £10,000 damages, but the jury awarded only £150.[1] Despite the notoriety from the libel suit, the circulation did not exceed 1,200 copies – to a large extent it was the revenue from its advertisements which enabled the paper to exist precariously until 1820.

Then all changed. Under the editorship of Alexander Chalmers, *The Herald* hit upon the novel idea of reporting the courts in a humorous manner. The results were almost immediate, and in a little over a year the circulation had trebled, to more than 3,600 copies per day. The author of this new style of reporting the cases at Bow Street Court was a Mr Wight, and the feature was a gross exaggeration, yet cleverly done, of whatever grotesque or ludicrous cases came before the magistrates.

A selection was made from these reports and published as a volume with illustrations by George Cruikshank, entitled *Mornings at Bow Street*, and this had a large sale running to twenty editions. But it was not to last, for, seeing that the reporting was reducing the stature of the court through ridicule, the magistrates prohibited further publication of proceedings. Wight, however, received his just rewards, being given a handsome increase in salary, appointed a partner and finally awarded the editorship.

A Mr Thwaites, as chief holder of the sixteen shares, had a great deal of influence in the politics and management of the paper, but a Mr Glassington, the next largest shareholder, having quarelled with Thwaites, threw the paper into the Chancery Court. Thwaites, however, was determined that Glassington should not receive a penny, and spent any profits on improving the paper.[2] He increased the number of parliamentary and law reporters, established correspondents in the main provincial towns and appointed 'stringers' in the leading capitals of Europe. The result of sparing no expense was a marked improvement in the paper, and as a consequence *The Morning Herald* overtook

The Times in circulation. The official stamp returns of 1828 put it 1,000 copies per day ahead, with a sale of 10,000.

Until his death in 1834, Thwaites continued as manager of the paper and also wrote many of the leading articles, but its heady days were already in the past: *The Times* had swiftly recovered its lost ground and was ahead once more. With the paper now in the hands of Thwaite's descendants, people with little or no newspaper experience, the decline continued, until, at Edward Baldwin's purchase, it had fallen to under 5,000 copies per day. At that time, his other titles, *The Standard* and *The St. James's Chronicle*, were selling 2,950 and 4,000 copies respectively.

In writing of the purchase, James Grant described Edward Baldwin as a thoroughly enterprising and enlightened trader in journalism,

> who two decades after Dudley's (Bate's) death, bought *The Morning Herald* from the little group of fifth-rate capitalists to which it had gone. He at once entered on a course of spirited rivalry to *The Times*, which set all its resources in motion to crush the new competitor. So excellently did his Continental intelligence service work that, very early in his proprietorship, *The Herald* won European reputation for the promptitude, the accuracy and the fulness of its despatches from beyond the seas.

Giffard, apart from his editorship of *The Standard*, was also given control of *The Morning Herald*, and one of his first acts was to reject a message from the Duke of Wellington. Almost an order, it had directed him to take a particular course in *The Standard* – and to ensure that the editor of *The Herald* followed suit. For long afterwards, Giffard never spoke of this incident without the greatest indignation of Wellington's conduct in trying to unduly influence the press. However, Baldwin's main preoccupation now was to recover the lost ground from *The Times*, and as a first step he decided to engage the best editorial talent available, almost regardless of cost, and one of his first acts was to raise the honorarium paid for leading articles from three to five guineas.

For the first few months, the *Herald*, with its highly-paid staff, was running at a loss, but then its circumstances changed dramatically. In 1845, Great Britain was swept with railway mania, which led to wild speculation alternating with periods of panic. There was a perfect mania of railway companies and so great was the influx of long advertisements of new companies that *The Morning Herald* had sometimes a sufficient number to require not only a second sheet, but a supplement of four pages. This made the paper on each day on which it occurred consist of twenty pages, or 120 columns.[3]

The advertisements were charged at one shilling a line – double that of the ordinary advertisements – and for a time Edward Baldwin was making profits of more than £3,000 a week. This lasted for almost four months and then came the railway panic, when the mania of forming new public companies suddenly and completely collapsed. Not only had *The Morning Herald* gained large sums from its advertisement columns but its sales had also increased, and during 1845 it achieved a daily average of 6,400 copies – the highest since 1837, when its figure had been 6,000. But in the panic year of 1848 it dropped to 4,800, and by 1854 had fallen to 3,700. On 17 November 1845, *The Times* exposed the competing schemes, showing that there were more than 1,200 projected railways seeking to raise more than £500 million. While the boom lasted the papers waxed rich – but not the government, because the duty on the long advertisements was exactly the same as that on the dozens of smaller ones which had been left out for lack of space: one shilling and sixpence.

Baldwin, however, believed that the good times would return and he continued to conduct his business in a most extravagant manner, even increasing the pay of his parliamentary reporters from five guineas to seven guineas as a week – and all the while his circulation continued to fall. But for *The Times* it was now a different tale. In 1837 its daily average had been only 10,700, while in 1845 the sales had reached 25,000. Two years later the circulation was 29,000 and in 1852 it exceeded 52,000 – ten times that of *The Morning Herald.*

An idea of the weekly costs of producing a daily newspaper at that time is given by H. R. Fox Bourne in his *Fourth Estate.* Payments to senior journalists on *The Standard* and *The Morning Herald* were, in fact, higher than those listed:

Editorial: Chief editor, £18 18s; sub-editor, £12 12s; second sub-editor, £10 10s; foreign sub-editor, £8 8s; writers (about four guineas a day) £25 4s; sixteen parliamentary reporters, £86 7s.

Foreign: Paris correspondent, £10 10s; reporter for Chamber, £3 3s; Paris Postage, £18 13s. Agents in Boulogne, Madrid, Rome, Naples, Vienna, Berlin and Lisbon, £26.

In addition it would also be necessary to have paid correspondents in Malta, Athens, Constantinople, Hamburg, Bombay, China, Singapore, New York, Boston, Massachusetts, Halifax, Nova Scotia, Montreal and Jamaica.

There would also be the need to employ reporters in Britain – either staff or linage – at, say, Dover, Southampton, Liverpool, Manchester, Leeds, Birmingham, Bristol, Dublin, Plymouth, Pembroke, Falmouth, Portsmouth, York, Wakefield, Chatham, Sheerness, Woolwich, Gravesend, Glasgow, Cambridge and Oxford. Costs of covering the various courts in London – Lord Chancellor's, Rolls, Bankruptcy, etc. – amounted to £25 a week, with a further £6 allotted for the provincial circuits. For reporting the London police courts a sum of £20 a week would be allowed.

The City salaries were given at £9 9s, and there would also be a need to subscribe to the *Stock Exchange Lists*, to Lloyd's, and the Jerusalem Coffee House. In addition, 'penny-liners' would cover the principal markets in London. Provision would also be made to cover the Royal Court, fine arts, sport and turf. A large number of foreign and provincial papers was taken daily and these could total more than 150, plus copies of *Hansard's Debates, Acts of Parliament, Votes of the House* and other parliamentary papers, *The London Gazette*, the *Coal Market List* and the *Packet List.*

To service the editorial staff, between fifty and seventy production personnel would be needed:

Printing: Number of men employed – printer, an assistant printer, a maker-up of advertisements, three readers, three assistant readers or 'reading boys', and about forty-five to fifty compositors regularly employed, also about eight or ten 'grass' men not regularly employed but who wait for engagement of work in place of regular hands who may be absent through illness or otherwise.

Time of working: Copy is given out by the printer from about half-past seven to eight in session of parliament time, and from eight to nine during the recess. The compositors are obliged to attend about three hours before the copy is given out, for the purpose of distributing the type used in the previous day's paper, which will be required for the night's work. Composition is usually closed about three o'clock; the men are usually occupied about ten hours in the office.

Wage rates: The printer earned between £5 and £6 per week; the assistant printer and advertisement man, £3 10s to £4; the reader from £2 10s to £3; assistant readers, £1 1s to £1 10s; the compositors, from £2 10s to £3, averaged over the whole year. About four to six men were generally employed by the printer after the composition was closed, to assist in putting the paper to press. These men averaged between £3 10s and £4 a week. There were some 460 compositors working on the daily press in London, three-quarters of whom were men of superior intelligence, habits and respectability, a great improvement having taken place in the previous eight or ten years.

Machine room: Machinist and assistant machinist, chief engineer and assistant engineer, sixteen men and boys to feed the machines and take out the paper, one wetter down to prepare the paper.

Publishing room: Publisher at five guineas a week, assistant and four or five errand boys.

Business management: Secretary, cashier and accountant, three advertisement clerks, night porter, day porter and errand boy.

Total costs: Including rent, gas, wear and tear of plant, interest on outlay, plus other charges, were: editing, writing and reporting a double paper, during the Session of Parliament, £220; foreign and local correspondence, £100; printing, machining, publishing and general expenses, double paper, with occasional second or third edition; and an evening edition three days a week, £200. *Weekly cost*: £520.

It was also at this time, 1846, that C. Mitchell published the first ever *Newspaper Press Directory*; both *The Standard* and *The St. James's Chronicle* featured prominently:

STANDARD

Daily 5d. Established 1827

Advocacy. Conservative – Ministerial – Moderality Protectionist – Church of England. This old established and highly esteemed journal has ever been known for the force and ability exhibited in its writing – on evidence of the high literary qualification of its conduct. Eloquently, warmly conservative, it bore its part well – during the period of Sir Robert Peel's opposition – in keeping alive the spirit of his party, by appeals of the most argumentative and impassioned description; nor has its fidelity to the cause been diminished by the difficulties the leader encountered in the administration of national affairs; but it has continued and continues to lend him the most efficient aid; combating with equal energy his old opponents and disaffected allies. So has it remained steadfast to the full Church of England principles – supporting them with surprising power against all attacks, whether external or internal, and for the ability and the zeal with which it has ever adhered to the church it has acquired in a very great degree the confidence and attachment of the Clergy.

Published by Charles Baldwin, 38, New Bridge Street, Blackfriars

ST. JAMES EVENING CHRONICLE

Tuesday, Thursday and Saturday. Price 5d. Established 1761

A reprint of the *Herald* and *Standard*, allowing for the difference of politics, and for the various tussles likely to be qualified by the style and the tone of the papers above named. These reports circulate among the same sort of class. *The St. James's Chronicle* has long been an especial favourite with the clergy.

It is interesting to note that, even though the papers were under the proprietorship of Edward Baldwin, the advertisements carried the imprint of his father, Charles.

UNDERLYING DISPUTE

While *The Standard* and *The Times* continued to air their differences with one another in the columns of their newspapers there was an underlying dispute: the fight to be first with the news from the Continent. This was to be outlined by Edward Baldwin in *The Standard* on 1 January 1846:

> Up to 1843, *The Times, Morning Herald, Morning Chronicle* and *Morning Post* addressed their Indian letters to the agents of their respective papers at Marseilles, and upon arrival of the steam-boat the despatches for the four journals were given to one courier who proceeded on horseback to Paris and thence to Boulogne, where a special steam-boat was always lying waiting where one could be procured, and upon the arrival of this boat at Folkestone a special engine brought the despatches to London.
>
> In 1844, the new proprietor was not allowed to join. On the very first occasion upon which the *Herald* commenced its single-handed exercise our courier performed the distance from Marseilles to Paris in 48 hours – that is two hours less than was ever before accomplished. Such was the system that continued throughout the whole of the year 1844 – the average time occupied by the *Herald* express between Marseilles and London being 67 hours.
>
> From 1845, the *Morning Chronicle* and the *Morning Post* withdrew. *The Times* and the *Herald* were therefore left alone to fight out the battle. The distance between Marseilles and Paris being too great to allow one courier to carry the despatches, twice a month we determined upon dividing the distance, and by appointing two couriers instead of one, thus lessening the fatigue, we calculated upon bringing the despatches from Marseilles to Paris in 42 to 44 hours instead of 48 or 50 as before.
>
> This should always have been accomplished had it not been for the unfair practices adopted by *The Times* agents, who, unable to beat us manfully upon the road, have had to recourse to all sorts of devices to retard our couriers, by hiding their bridles and saddles and in some instances actually by stopping them *vi et armis* until *The Times* courier was enabled to overcome the express.[4]

The Times account of the rivalry was, not unexpectedly, somewhat different: the French administration suddenly withdrew the facilities for *The Times* courier, who covered the Marseilles–Paris–Boulogne route and required that the despatches should be forwarded by the ordinary channels of the French Post Office. Despite protests from *The Times* to François Guizot, the Prime Minister, and to the Minister of Posts, the French government would not budge. To bypass this, *The Times* in October 1845 had arranged through Thomas Waghorn that the Indian mail arriving at Suez would be sent by a man on a swift camel, who, riding non-stop across the desert, would deliver it the next day to Waghorn himself, waiting on an Austrian ship, with steam already up. He would cross the Mediterranean to Dwino, 12 miles from Trieste, and then travel through Bavaria, Baden and Belgium to the channel ports.

The French government retaliated immediately, and Guizot entered into a partnership with Edward Baldwin and *The Morning Herald* to prove that the Marseilles route was quicker than that from Trieste. *The Times* at once sought to join in the venture, but Guizot replied, 'this is a joint affair of ours and *The Morning Herald*, and consequently we cannot – and we regret it – allow *The Times* to participate in an advantage for which *The Morning Herald* is at the greater expense'. A French naval vessel was loaned for the service, and by the end of December 1845 *The Morning Herald* was able to publish the Indian news 48 hours in advance of *The Times.* After appearing in *The Herald*, the news was immediately reprinted in *The Standard.*

For *The Times* it was a bitter blow, and they could do no more than express concern that 'a public man and the Prime Minister of France, prosecuting a public undertaking, enters into a private partnership with the proprietor of a newspaper, and, on the grounds of private interest, excludes all the world, save its partner alone, from a share of the advantage. We are more proud, however, of our defeat than of our remarkable success. We have spared no expense and no exertion, but we would not purchase M. Guizot's favour by slavish adulation; and if success can only be achieved at such a price, we are well contented to copy, as we do now, our intelligence from the *Morning Herald*'. This admission of defeat in *The Times*[5] on 31 December 1845, was just the fillip that Baldwin needed, hence his article on the success of his venture in *The Standard* the following day.

On 21 January 1846, the first issue of *The Daily News* appeared, edited by Charles Dickens at a salary of £2,000 a year, a huge sum in those days. From the outset, costs were deemed to be secondary, and a large staff, with generous salaries was engaged, including Dickens' father, who was responsible for the parliamentary reporting.[6] The only attempt at economising was in Dickens entering into partnership with Edward Baldwin on the collection of foreign news. It was estimated that the expenses of such a service were in excess of £10,000 a year, and Baldwin was as glad as were *The Daily News* that this heavy outlay should be shared between them.[7]

Despite the success of the early issue, Dickens' tenure was to be brief, and he only edited seventeen numbers of *The Daily News*. On 9 February he wrote to John Forster, one of the chief leader writers, saying that he was 'tired and quite worn out'. He then left the paper, and his only contact thereafter was the publication over the next few months of his letters on Italian travel and English social questions.

Charles Wentworth Dilke, who was at the time editing his own paper, *The Athenaeum*, took over the management of *The Daily News* from Dickens, and immediately reaffirmed the arrangements with Baldwin. However, they were not really satisfactory for *The Daily News*, and their termination was announced in the paper on 28 October 1846. Many years later, in his *Paper of a Critic*, published in 1875, Dilke gave a full account of the troubles with *The Morning Herald*, and wrote: 'There must have been treachery or concert somewhere'.

Meanwhile, in the continuing dispute between *The Times* and *The Morning Herald* as to who would be first with the overseas news, the Austrian government now came to the aid of *The Times*: it developed into a race between two warships, Austrian and French, bringing the news from Alexandria. On one occasion, with a severe storm raging over the Western Mediterranean, the French ports were sealed off, but the Austrians were able to land their news near Trieste – and for *The Times* it meant a fortnight's lead over *The Morning Herald* and *The Standard*. Thus it raged until 1850, when the rivalry ceased, and henceforth it was to be a purely political difference. Even the cost of hiring special trains from Paris, steamers from Boulogne and Calais and locomotives from Dover was shared. Baldwin and John Walter of *The Times* were now in concert ... but while it lasted it had been a rare battle.

REVOLUTION IN EUROPE

Throughout Europe in 1848, revolution was rife – France, Italy, the Austrian lands, Hungary, the German lands, all were affected; and, with few exceptions, the agitation was the work of middle-class intellectuals in alliance with working-class radicals. Although not backed by any one organisation, there was undoubtedly a strong underlying theme: economic unrest brought about by bad harvests and famine in the countryside, linked with urban unemployment and a recession of trade in the towns.[8]

In England the theme was one of Chartism: universal male suffrage, annual Parliaments, vote by ballot, payment of MPs, equal electoral districts and the abolition of the property qualification for MPs. A decade earlier, the London Working Men's Association had published the *People's Charter* which had advocated the above six points. The Industrial Revolution had succeeded in producing a vast working class, of whom five out of six were left without the vote, in spite of the introduction of the Reform Bill in 1832. As Disraeli so aptly wrote in his novel, *Sybil*: 'Two nations between whom there is no intercourse and no sympathy; who are as ignorant of each other's habits, thoughts and feelings, as if they were dwellers in different zones or inhabitants of different planets. ... The rich and the poor.'

To *The Standard*, the reasons were clear-cut:

> This is the fruit of the incendiary speeches and writings of 1831 and 1832, the natural and necessary result of letting loose the fierce passions of an uninstructed and indigent population, and of teaching them that their will ought to stand above the law. And who have been the prompters in this course of crime? The men who first taught that laws are to be trampled on – the men who countenance political unions – who corresponded with them, who called for 'threats of physical force' from them, encouraged the menace of a rebel army to march upon London to frighten the House of Lords into a desertion of its duties.

Here the leader writer was commenting on the full-scale rising in Newport, Monmouthshire, on 13 November 1839 when twenty-four Chartists were killed. The reports in *The Standard* of the riots make gripping reading:

> TUESDAY EVENING, NOVEMBER 5
>
> ALARMING CHARTIST RIOTS AT NEWPORT
>
> With deep regret we record today another of the frightful consequence of Whig–Radical teaching – another dismal offering of British blood to the Reform idol. The deplorable tragedy is thus described in the second edition of *The Times* and *Morning Herald*.
>
> (From *The Times*)
>
> We have received the following from our correspondent at Newport:
>
> Newport, Monday, Eleven o'clock a.m.
>
> The Chartists have almost entire possession of the Town. There are 7,000 or 8,000 marched in from the hills and attacking the Westgate Inn, where the magistrates are sitting. I have heard 30 or 40 shots fired, and learn that several of the Chartists as well as soldiers are killed.
>
> What the end will be God only knows; they are firing now. I write by post, but fearing the mail may be stopped I send this in addition ....

The Morning Herald correspondent, from Bristol, reported:

Newport, Two o'clock

The Chartists are in possession of the town. This morning alone about 8,000 of the most desperate, headed by Frost, the ex-magistrate and Chartist demagogue, marched into Newport from the hills armed with muskets, guns, pistols, pikes, swords and other offensive weapons (and, as I have been told, two small pieces of cannon) and commenced a violent attack on the Westgate Inn, where the magistrates were sitting. The military was promptly called out, and the attack was of the most ferocious and bloody character. They were obliged to fire upon them, and several have been killed, accounts vary between 10 and 20.

I myself have seen several in our yard ... Besides the nine Chartists I have seen dead, I have since seen several whose wounds are such as would almost certainly prove mortal. The 45th soldiers acted bravely – they acted like men, and but for their noble exertions the town would probably by this time have been a mass of smoking ruins – they charged the Chartists and put them to flight in all directions, leaving several hundreds of their weapons in the street.[9]

Between 1840 and 1842, the Chartist movement was widely split, but a second massive petition was presented to Parliament in May 1842 and, as with its predecessor three years earlier, was rejected. Following this rejection, the movement had fallen under the influence of Feargus O'Connor, and now in1848, the 'Year of Revolution', the time was ripe to make one final demand.

On 10 April, following a huge meeting on Kennington Common, a monster petition containing the Six Points was to be presented to Parliament. *The Standard* commented on the day's events as follows:

MONDAY EVENING, APRIL 10

THE CHARTIST MEETING ON KENNINGTON COMMON (THIS DAY)

Let us tell in a few words the history of the Kennington meeting. The Chartists began to assemble in anything like numbers at about eleven o'clock; the whole assemblage certainly did not exceed 9,000 or 10,000 at the very most (of those about 4,000 passed our office at half-past 10, chiefly the lower class of Irish labourers, bearing banners with all the mottoes of Irish sedition). Shortly after the arrival of the delegates, and the completion of the arrangements, an inspector of police carried a communication to Mr Feargus O'Connor, when a murmur arose that a person had been arrested.

Mr O'Connor, however, hastened to explain that such was not the case, but that he had received a message, declaring that the Government would disperse the meeting, and suggesting that it would be convenient if the persons assembled would anticipate any forcible interference by separating voluntarily. Mr O'Connor added his own advice – to obey the Government as the Chartists were unarmed; the advice, thus supported, was promptly obeyed, and at two o'clock there were not more than 200 on the ground.

We write in the commencement of a day of such anxiety as the people of London of the present generation have never witnessed. The anxiety of which we speak is not the anxiety of alarm, or of any feeling akin to alarm. It is the anxious expectation with which men await the trial of a desperate experiment on a grand scale ....

Two hundred special constables already enrolled (at 10 a.m.) to be augmented, we have no doubt by noon, to more than half the adult population, give ample warrant for the ultimate preservation of order. The movers of the sedition will be disappointed . . . . And we ask is it reasonable or is it just that under the threatened penalties of rapine, conflagration and murder, the people of London shall be exercised in £100,000 sterling, if not twice the sum, at the pleasure, forsooth, of Mr Feargus O'Connor, Mr McGrath, Mr Cuffy, Mr O'Brien and the rest of the offshoots of the Repeal Association; and with this no other possible effect than the making of a diversion in favour of an Irish rebellion, or inviting America or France to invade this country.[10]

Advocating that the ringleaders should be prosecuted for treasonable conspiracy, the leader writer concluded: 'We expect courage from Lord John Russell, if we cannot hope for wisdom; and with courage we expect honesty. Twenty-four hours will tell us of what stuff the noble lord is made.'

Following the leader there was one final paragraph on the day's happenings:

Before taking leave of the Chartists and their description let us offer one other remark upon the audacious petition presented to the House of Commons. The petition is said to bear the names of five million and a half signatures. The number would never be counted for it would take fifteen weeks of twelve hours a day to count so many, but however closely written five million and a half of signatures would cover some tons of parchment, whereas the petition actually presented did not apparently weigh more than a few hundredweight.

An eye-witness of the Chartist demonstration was young Hardinge Giffard, and in 1907, as Lord Halsbury, he was to recall:

> Sixty-one years yesterday, I was a Special Constable on Blackfriars Bridge. I remember very well that John Frank and I went to the offices in the New River Building and were duly sworn in. Then they wanted us to take charge of the Parish in place of the ordinary policeman, but I did not fancy that. I walked down to Kennington Common, where the giant Chartist meeting was held.
>
> I came across a big policeman, twice as big as myself, who was being sent with a message to Feargus O'Connor, the head of the movement, and I went with him. He said, I suppose with some irony, 'I suppose, Sir, you are protecting me.'
>
> We came back to Blackfriars Bridge, and received our orders not to stop absolutely all persons from crossing the Bridge, but only to allow them to go in small groups. There were occasionally little rushes, but we were too strong for anything like a fight, and one of the assailants dropped a somewhat formidable-looking dagger, but they soon found it was hopeless to attempt to cross in any organized body, and by three o'clock in the afternoon the whole thing was over; but notwithstanding that nothing happened, the Paris papers the next day announced that London was *en feu et flame.*[11]

During the two days after the demonstration, the clerks at the House of Commons had a chance to examine the petition, and on 13 April *The Standard* reported:

> The whole number of signatures amounts to one million nine hundred thousand; enough of all conscience, but no less than three million, seven hundred short of Mr O'Connor's deliberations. The misstatements of the actual number of signatures, such as they are, is not, however, the most disgraceful part of this affair.
>
> The signatures are for the most part forgeries. The Duke of Wellington's name appears seventeen times repeated, the Queen's name and Prince Albert's name are again and again repeated; the like liberties are taken with the names of all distinguished public men of all parties; and in addition to those there is a huge miscellaneous muster role of ludicrous, filthy and even impious and obscene designations under the form of names. Of the numbers of persons represented by the *bona fide* names, an idea may be formed from the fact stated by a correspondent of *The Times* that one errand boy had signed the petitition more than 1,250 times.

In the laughter and ridicule that followed, the days of Chartism were numbered and the movement died a natural death. Unlike the Anti-Corn Law League, it had failed because of weak leadership, lack of co-ordination or contact with the trade unions, and because its objectives were not clear-cut. Nevertheless, the four main Chartist demands were to be enacted within the next seventy years.

FORTUNES ON WANE

By the end of the 1840s, the fortunes of Edward Baldwin were on the wane: *The Standard* had begun the decade with an annual circulation of 1,040,000, or 3,320 copies per day; by 1850, its sales had slumped to 492,000, or 1,220 per day. *The Morning Herald* was similarly affected: from a peak of 2, 018,025 a year in 1845 – the time of the railway mania – it was now down to 1,139,000 or 3,635 per day.[12] For Baldwin and Giffard – and their *Standard* – inexorable events were about to occur which would have a profound effect upon the paper's fortunes. It was also a time of change in the political world, for within two years both of England's leading statesmen were to depart the scene. On 1 July 1850, *The Standard* reported that Sir Robert Peel had 'sustained a most serious accident by the fall of his horse'; within forty-eight hours he was dead. Two years later, on 15 September 1852 the paper announced:

DEATH OF THE DUKE OF WELLINGTON

> The greatest man of our age – the greatest military commander of any age or nation – the man whose fame has for half a century filled the civilized world, restored by his matchless achievements from thraldom and anarchy – the Duke of Wellington has been taken from us.
>
> A consumate military commander – the greatest of military commanders – he certainly was; a great statesman he certainly was not; tried by the vulgar test, success, his political capacity had been plainly found wanting, for all his principal measures have failed of the effect expected by himself.
>
> His Grace was, however, though, peremptory enough for a time, in the end a conceding politician, certainly not the statesman by which a free state can be best served . . . . Willingly, however, we return to the claims which he has established by his military service upon the gratitude of his country. These claims are boundless and they do not die with them who has established them; for he has not only left us honour, peace and security; but also a body of leaders trained under his instruction and by his example qualified to defend the empire against a world in arms.

For more than two months, preparations were in hand for the Duke's state funeral. During this period, while *The Standard* and *The*

Times continued to air their differences, there was the occasional leader from Giffard in somewhat lighter vein. On 30 October 1852, he declared:

> The writers for newspapers as they choose to call themselves, 'public instructors', are subject to a difficulty with which, we fear 'the public' our pupils have little sympathy – the difficulty, we mean, of finding daily something to say that may be thought worthy of being read. To the supply of this *desideratum* two conditions are necessary; first a subject deserving attention; next an opportunity of treating the subject with some little approach to novelty. They who have not exercised themselves in the labour day after day, month after month, year after year, can scarcely appreciate how hard it is always to compass these conditions.
>
> It is true that opposition journals have an inexhaustible subject in the abuse of the ministry, and it may be hastily presumed that journals not in opposition have their *pièce de resistance* of equal value in the defence of the ministers abused; but such is not the case. Accusation and abuse are generally sure of a better acceptance than defence or praise; and as regards defence, especially, its interest must depend to a great extent upon the quality of the attack that it is to meet. If the attack be vague and general the defence must be even more vague and general.
>
> Still the leader columns, 'Like a nest of new-waked rooklings caw for provender', and their want must be supplied. To those who endeavour to meet the right, there is no doubt consolation, that in the dearth of subjects, the most perverse must sometimes, however reluctantly, deviate into truth, though, after all, we are as journalists, by getting back to our own arguments and opinions, dressed up by former adversaries. *Toujours perdrix* palls, let the cook be changed never so often. Let us, however, enjoy the moral triumph, though it lends little to professional convenience.[13]

Politically, the death of Wellington left a great void, for no longer could there be an opportunity to seek his counsel. The recent general election, held in July 1852, had ended in stalemate, with the Peelites reduced to forty in number, but still holding the balance. Disraeli was now trying hard to persuade the Conservatives formally to abandon protectionism, and for that he needed more support in the press. Lord Stanley wrote to him on November 3, saying how concerned he was at the lack of allies for the Conservative side: '*The Times* with 40,000 circulation was in general on the Liberal side; *The Morning Advertiser* supported liquor and Russophobia; *The Morning Chronicle* was Peelite; *The Globe* was Palmerston and *The Daily News* was Liberal.' On their side, he felt he could rely on *The Morning Post* with 2,000 circulation and *The Standard* with 2,400. *The Morning Herald* was so ultra Tory and bigoted that it was regarded as being 'more harmful than beneficial'.[14]

The following day, *The Standard* returned to the attack against *The Times,* and described Lord Aberdeen's involvement with Printing House Square as

> illustrating some or other of the categories in Swift's (or Arbuthnott's treatise of 'political lying' as being a falsehood self-convicted by its gross extravagance ...). No, *The Times* and its fellows must be left to work out their own defeat, or if the public chooses to be gulled by such clumsy fabrications, eating up one week by the falsehoods of the week before, we cannot help it.

FRENCH INFLUENCE

Rumours were now also rife that, due to Edward Baldwin's friendship with the deposed King of the French, Louis Philippe, *The Standard* and *The Morning Herald* were in the pay of his successor, the Prince President, Louis Napoleon. In 1851, *The Times* had attacked the Prince President in its columns, leading his ambassador to write:

> Someone has told you, Prince, that the hostility of *The Times* and *The Morning Chronicle* was provoked by pecuniary subsidies. Nothing could be more false than such an assertion and believe me, on such an important subject I would not make a statement without being absolutely certain. It is possible that third-rate papers like the *Sun, Standard,* etc., etc., might be purchased. But the enterprises of *The Times* and *Morning Chronicle* are backed by too big capital, their political management is in too many hands, for it to be possible to buy them for any price .... .
>
> The prosperity of *The Times* is founded on a very large number of readers, who give it more advertisements than to any other newspaper. Moreover, it is an axiom among the founders of this paper that to retain a great number of readers it must anticipate public opinion, keep it alive, animate it, but never break a lance against it and give way every time it desire itself in any direction and even when it changes its attitude to change with it.

Not at all pleased with his ambassador's reply, Louis Napoleon turned to threats and attempted to persuade the British government to restrain *The Times.* The whole affair was brought up in Parliament, where it gave Lord Derby an opportunity to discuss the independence of the press and its responsibilities:

> If, as in these days, the press aspires to exercise the influence of statesmen, the press should remember that they are not free from the corresponding responsibility of statesmen, and that it is incumbent on them, as a sacred duty, to maintain that tone of moderation and respect even in expressing frankly their opinions on foreign affairs which would be required of every man who pretends to guide public opinion.

The whole affair was later to become the subject of a *Punch*[15] cartoon on 15 February 1856, with the caption 'The French Emperor, with *Le Moniteur* in his back pocket, dispenses bribes to the *Morning Post. The Standard* and *The Morning Herald* wait their turns.'

It was during this period, too, that *The Standard* and *The Morning Herald* began attacking Queen Victoria's husband, Prince Albert, the Prince Consort.[16] Writing in his diary, Charles Greville noted that there had been an extraordinary attack against the Court, most particularly against Prince Albert. On 15 January 1854, he wrote: 'It began a few weeks ago in the press, particularly in *The Daily News* and *The Morning Advertiser*, but chiefly in the latter, and was immediately taken up by the Tory papers, *The Morning Herald* and *The Standard*, and for some time they have poured forth article after article and letter after letter full of the bitterest abuse and all sorts of lies.'

Anxious to redress the balance, John Thadeus Delane, editor of *The Times*, approached Lord Aberdeen, the Prime Minister, and offered, if it was thought desirable, 'to take up the cudgels in defence of the court'. Aberdeen, after consulting the prince, said they were of the opinion that it was better not to rebut the charges in the press but wait until Parliament met and take the opportunity to repel the charges there. Disraeli was very angry about the whole affair, and wrote to Lord Henry Lennox: 'I am disgusted with the silly *Herald* and the stupid *Standard* mixing themselves up in the mud. There were plenty of scavengers among the *canaglia*.'

A week later, on 21 January 1854, Greville wrote:

> For some days past the Tory papers have relaxed their violence against the court. There can be little doubt that the Tory leaders got alarmed and annoyed at the lengths to which their papers were proceeding, and have taken measures to stop them. One of the grounds of attack in *The Morning Herald* and *The Standard*, particularly, has been the illegality of the prince being a privy councillor. In reply to this I wrote a letter in my own name showing what the law and practices are.

The following day the Queen was pleased at 'an admirable article in the *Morning Chronicle* defending the prince. "Has Lord Aberdeen any idea who could have written it?" she asked. The Prime Minister gave the credit to Gladstone, "although he would not wish it to be known", and he welcomed "a very sensible letter in the same day's *Standard*".'[17] On 31 January the Royal Address provided a proper setting for Aberdeen in the Commons and Russell in the Lords to vindicate Prince Albert; but by then the controversy was already running its course and newspaper readers were more concerned with the possibility of hostilities in the Crimea. A month later, on 28 February, *The Times*[18] was able to print the ultimatum from Great Britain and France to Russia in its leading article. In reply to criticisms from Lord Derby on the leader, the paper said: 'We hold ourselves responsible not to Lord Derby or the House of Lords, but to the people of England, for the accuracy and fitness of that which we think proper to publish.' Indeed, the printing of the secret Anglo-French ultimatum set the pace for *The Times'* success during the Crimea War, both in the securing of military news and in the exposing of administrative abuses. And for this they owed an immense debt to their correspondent, William Howard Russell, who was undoubtedly the star reporter of the war. Russell was determined that there would be no repeat of what happened to his first big story for *The Times* – the trial of Daniel O'Connell in Dublin in 1842. Through the use of a fast ship, train and cab, he arrived at Printing House Square with his 'scoop', only to be accosted at the door by a bystander who said that he was pleased to learn that O'Connell had been found guilty. A gullible Russell replied: 'Oh, yes! All guilty but on different counts.' Within minutes the 'bystander' was at *The Standard* offices relating the account to his editor ... and once more Giffard had stolen a march over his rival.[19]

A decade later, a much wiser Russell knew when to hold his counsel, but once more his only rival was to be a *Standard* man, Nicholas Woods, who was also covering the war for his sister paper, *The Morning Herald*. Arriving at Scutari, Woods was appalled by the stench and the chaos of the British military encampments but within days he was off to Varna where the organisation was even more confused. His reporting of these horrors incurred the wrath of the commander-in-chief, Lord Raglan, who announced that he would not recognise the press in any way or give them rations or assistance, and 'worse of all, it is probable that he will forbid our accompanying the troops'. Matters were not helped when Woods exposed the poor quality of the shells issued to the Black Sea fleet. Some, he reported, were more than twenty-five years old and some even manufactured before the Battle of Waterloo, and 'not ten per cent of which exploded'. Of all the correspondents reporting the war, Woods and Russell stood out, and their vivid coverage did much to inflame public opinion against the government of Aberdeen.

Woods himself, was fast making a name for the accuracy of his reporting, and one such description – Sir Colin Campbell's precautions against a Russian attack – caused great annoyance among the Army staff. In his history of the war, E. Nolan wrote: 'The correspondents of our London morning papers not only communicated intelligence which but for them had never reached the British public but gave opinions in reference to military facts and possibilities'. Everywhere, Woods was in the thick of the battle, with his vivid reportage conveying the full horrors of war to the readers of *The Standard.* On 15 October, he covered the defence of the 92nd Highlanders at Balaclava – the 'Thin Red Line', as Russell was to dub them. But there was a difference in their reporting. Woods' account states that the Russian cavalry did not even close up on the Highlanders for their volley to be effective.

Within hours, Woods was reporting the Charge of the Light Brigade, news of which first appeared in *The Standard* on 1 November. Although Varna, on the Bulgarian Black Sea coast, was linked to France by cable, and then to Britain by submarine cable, its use was confined mainly to army commanders needing access to their governments. For the correspondents, it was a case of ensuring that their messages reached a European cable line, enabling news items to be received by their papers within days rather than weeks. But it was not from Woods but on the basis of intelligence from St. Petersburgh that *The Standard* reported the early news of the Battle of Balaclava and the Charge of the Light Brigade:

> ST. PETERSBURGH
>
> A report from General Manschikoff dated October 25 states that General Leprondi attacked on that day a detached camp of the English. It also states that he captured four redoubts which defended the camp. The report further states that at the same time the Russian cavalry attacked the light cavalry of the English and inflicted on them much loss.

Three days later *The Standard* was able to give the news from the English side:

> **SIEGE OF SEBASTOPOL**
> **Official Intelligence**
> **from**
> **THE SEAT OF WAR**
>
> At length we are in possession of authentic, if not minute, intelligence of the events in the Crimea on the 25th and 26th ult, so variously represented in previous accounts. This intelligence is

> contained in a despatch of Lord Stratford de Redcliffe, dated Constantinople, October 28, at midnight. Our readers will be pleased to have the despatch before them in the first instance.
>
> The captain of an English steam-transport, which left Balaclava on the evening of the 26th confirms in great part the information brought this morning by a French ship, and transmitted immediately to London by way of Manala. It appears that the Russians attacked the forts in the vicinity of Balaclava on the 25th. Their numbers are supposed to have been about 30,000 men. The attack was unexpected. The Cossacks preceded the infantry. To resist them at first were Ottoman and Scotch troops. The Turks gave way and even spiked the guns which, seized by the Russians, were turned against them.
>
> The Scotch on the contrary remained firm in their position. Other forces arrived and the Russians were obliged to yield the ground remaining nevertheless masters of two forts, from which they fired upon our troops. Three regiments of English light cavalry, exposed to the cross fire of the Russian batteries, suffered immensely.

The defeat, glorious as it was, is best summed up in the words of the French commander, General Bosquet, who was an astonished onlooker: *'C'est magnifique, mais ce n'est pas la guerre.'*

7

A Change of Ownership

The war in the Crimea dragged on for nearly another eighteen months, bringing with it the horrors of Scutari and news of the appalling lack of medical attention – until the arrival of Florence Nightingale – all dutifully reported in the London papers. Day after day *The Standard* printed long lists of the troops who had died, many from cholera, dysentery and associated diseases. Thanks to Delane, and Russell's hard-hitting despatches describing the misery and the chaos, the circulation of *The Times* continued to soar, and by the preliminary peace in February 1856, it was selling more than 40,000 copies daily.

It was a very different tale, though, for Edward Baldwin; the sales of his paper were steadily declining and by the mid-1850s the circulation of *The Standard* was down to barely 700 copies a day. Even with those low sales, however, it was still considered to be the most authoritative of the afternoon papers. 'There is no subject, celestial, or terrestrial,' commented *The Saturday Review*, 'on which it has not a fixed, familiar opinion.' This was a state of affairs, though, that could not last, and in the spring of 1857 there appeared a short notice in *The Times*[1] announcing the bankruptcy proceedings of Edward Baldwin – and with it the end of almost 200 years of his family's involvement in the London newspaper world:

> Edward Baldwin, Shoe-lane, printer, to surrender March 5 at half-past 11 o'clock, April 2, at the Bankrupt Court. Solicitors: Messrs. Barker, Bowler and Peach, Grays-inn square; official assignee Mr Johnson, Basinghall-street.

The new owner was James Johnstone and he bought *The Standard, The Morning Herald* and *The St. James's Chronicle* during the summer. As for Edward Baldwin, he moved to 1 Streatham Hill, where he lived to the great age of 87 and died on 31 January 1890. In his obituary it was noted that 'his connexion with the Press belongs to a past generation, but in his time he played a prominent part in the newspaper world and was an ardent supporter of the early policy of Lord Derby and Mr Disraeli'.[2]

Discussing the sale of *The Standard,* James Grant wrote:

> But afterwards the latter journal fell into the hands of the son, and the latter having become bankrupt, both papers were ordered to be

> sold by the Court of Bankruptcy. Mr James Johnstone, who had for many years held an official appointment of considerable pecuniary profit in that court, bought the newspaper property thus put up for sale. I believe I am making no disclosure to which Mr Johnstone would object when I mention that the price which he paid for *The Morning Herald* and *The Standard* together, including what is called the 'plant' – that is presses, types, everything, indeed, necessary for working the paper was £16,500.[3]

James Johnstone himself was now aged 42, and a senior partner in the firm of Johnstone, Wintle, Cope and Evans; accountants. For many years he had held an official appointment in the Bankruptcy Court which he immediately resigned on purchasing his newspapers. He was described as 'a shrewd man of business, cheery, and fond of his job who developed into an able, though not perhaps strikingly brilliant newspaper director. He was on more familiar terms with his staff than most modern proprietors, which the severe division of labour isolates in a measure from those in their employ'.

Having no knowledge of the newspaper world, he took as his counsellor John Maxwell, a publisher, who was for a time a partner in the business. It was he who advised Johnstone in regard to the purchase of the papers and their management. Maxwell, however, was to retire early from newspapers in order to expand his own publishing concern. In truth, James Johnstone was clear-headed and strong-minded enough to need no other counsellor, but he did engage a manager from one of his partners in the accountancy firm, D. Morier Evans, and it was Evans whom Johnstone made responsible for the business side.

Writing of Johnstone almost half a century later, a one-time colleague noted: 'The first offices were three old Queen Anne houses in Shoe Lane, and there was no attempt at style, either inside or out. I remember going to see Johnstone there; his room was approached by a flight of old-fashioned stairs, while the room itself was devoid of carpets, and the writing-table and few chairs were old and worn.'[4]

For the first few weeks, the new proprietor continued to conduct *The Standard* and *The Morning Herald* in the same manner as had Edward Baldwin; but finding that he was operating at a loss, decided that drastic measures were called for. He therefore reduced the price of *The Standard* from fourpence to twopence, doubled the pagination to eight and converted it into a morning paper. In the issue of Thursday 18 June 1857, two display advertisements above the main leader announced the changes:

ALTERATION OF PUBLICATION
ON AND FROM MONDAY, 29th JUNE
THE STANDARD will become a
FIRST-CLASS MORNING NEWSPAPER
Consisting of EIGHT FULL-SIZED PAGES
The same as "The Times"
Containing all the NEWS of the DAY
Advertisements inserted at 6d per line
Office: 129, Fleet-street, London

On and from Monday, 29th JUNE
THE STANDARD will become a FIRST-CLASS MORNING NEWSPAPER. Double in size; and REDUCED to half its present PRICE, or TWOPENCE DAILY
consisting of EIGHT FULL-SIZED PAGES
And containing all the NEWS OF THE DAY

THE STANDARD will enter upon a new career; and will endeavour to supply the want of the age – a really cheap newspaper large enough to report all passing events with ample fulness and sufficiently independent and fearless to expose wrong-doing.

As nothing will be allowed to appear in THE STANDARD that can shock the purity of social life, it is confidently hoped that the Heads of Families will appreciate the attempt to give all the News of the Day, Home and Foreign, uncontaminated by details which can neither usefully enlighten the public mind nor advance morality.

THE STANDARD may be regarded as alike adopted for the Counting House and the Domestic Circle; its intelligence will be full and faithful.

THE STANDARD will be published Daily, at the same hour as all other Morning Newspapers. Price 2d.

Advertisements will be inserted at 6d per line. Office: 129, Fleet-street, London.

The main item in the leader column of its last issue as an evening, on Saturday, 27 June 1857, had been devoted to the presentation by Queen Victoria at Hyde Park of the Victoria Cross to sixty-one recipients. The editor noted: 'The Victoria Cross is a poor, dull looking thing, but its establishment as an order is the commencement of a new era.' On Monday, 29 June 1857, *The Standard* converted successfully to a morning paper – issue no. 10,257 – and in the leader the editor set out his reasons and his hopes:

> The announcement we are about to make will appear startling, and, perhaps, to some incredible; but it is nevertheless strictly true, and will be fulfilled to the letter. We commence this day an undertaking without parallel for boldness and liberality in the history of the newspaper press, and realising for the first time the *desideratum* of a first-class journal purchasable for the price hitherto paid for only reading one. Henceforth, the *STANDARD*, enlarged to the size of *The Times*, and conducted on a scale or liberality in all its departments equal to that of the best morning paper, will be published daily and sold for TWOPENCE.
>
> It quits the ranks of the Evening Journals and today takes its place besides *The Times* and its contemporaries, to compete with them in every excellence, to be less only in price ... the buyers of *The Standard* will have first-class reports of the debates in Parliament, the proceedings before the law and police courts, home and foreign news, the operations in various markets, and all the usual articles of political, social and commercial intelligence.
>
> The political and City articles, reviews of literature, music and the drama, the criticisms of the fine arts, will be written by men thoroughly acquainted with the subject alloted to them. It will also devote a considerable portion of its space to sporting and turf intelligence – a department placed under highly competent superintendence, and will give full accounts of acquatics, cricket, pedestrianism, and all the manly sports of the people.
>
> Of the manner in which all this will be put before the public – of the paper, the type, the printing, we need say nothing. Our readers can ask no better proof of the mechanical resources of *The Standard* than the impression before them. As for its political principles, they will be thoroughly independent, devoted to the great interests of the common good, and wholly untrammelled by party ... Such is the tender we make for public support: Quantity, quality, cheapness and independence.[5]

The main story in the paper was an account, by 'Extraordinary Express', of the outbreak of the Indian Mutiny; and one interesting feature was a serial – an innovation for Fleet Street. Written by William Russell, the famous war correspondent, and latterly of *The Times*, it was entitled 'Leonard Harlowe, or The Game of Life'.

The removal of stamp duty,[6] which had encouraged Johnstone's new venture, now meant that *The Standard* was preparing to challenge *The Times* and the recently-launched *Daily Telegraph* head-on. *The Daily*

Telegraph and Courier had been launched one day before the removal of stamp duty, on 29 June 1855, and in its first leader announced:

> Our mission is to extend in this country the benefit of a cheap and good Daily Press, and now that Parliament has wisely knocked off the last shackle which fettered the progress of the Press, in this great metropolis, we take our stand, availing ourselves, the first possible moment the law permitted, of the Repeal of the Stamp Duty, to issue our Journal at the price of TWOPENCE, as a candidate for the popular favour.[7]

It was against this background that Johnstone embarked upon his plan to convert *The Standard* to a morning paper. The first result of doubling the pagination and halving the price to twopence was a large increase in circulation, but it was still not enough to make the paper profitable. In running the *Herald* and *The Standard* he exercised great economies, and followed the example of his predecessor: the news columns were similar, although the leaders were different, and the papers, while voicing the same opinions, were supposed to be entirely independent of one another. This closeness between the two sister papers lead to *The Standard* becoming popularly known by the nickname of 'Mrs Harris', while *The Morning Herald* was dubbed 'Mrs Gamp'. The first mention of 'Mrs Gamp' and 'Mrs Harris' had been, not unnaturally, in *Punch* as early as 1845, and for almost thirty years the magazine kept up the fun. Its most famous cartoon ridiculing the papers appeared in May 1862 and featured Disraeli with Lord Derby.[8]

FIRST CONSIDERATION

With Johnstone, the papers were always his first consideration and he quickly acquired a knowledge of the mechanical and financial aspects of management. He was quick, also, to obtain financial assistance from the Tory Party. In one respect he was true to the traditions of the paper: he would not knowingly employ a Roman Catholic on the staff.

The introduction of this new-style *Standard* now posed a direct threat to *The Times*. As *The Times* wrote in its official history:

> The ability with which the twopenny *Standard* was conducted – Robert Cecil, later Lord Salisbury, was one of its leader-writers – contributed an undeniable threat to the supremacy of *The Times*. Even *The Daily Telegraph* considered the 2d. eight-page *Standard* to be a very desirable money's worth in comparison with its own four pages for 1d.

However, on 4 February 1858,

> the entire town and country trade was staggered by an announcement that *The Standard* was about to reduce its price to 1d without any reduction in size.[9]

On the first day of the one-penny paper, the editor headed his leader column with the following:

> THE PRICE OF *THE STANDARD* IN
> FUTURE WILL BE
> **ONE PENNY**
> THURSDAY, FEBRUARY 4
>
> On this day we publish *The Standard* at the price of ONE PENNY, which, we venture to predict, will yet become the current charge for newspapers throughout the kingdom. This is no hasty or temporary reduction to catch an ephemeral success of popularity, but the fixed price of the journal by which we are determined to stand. …
>
> *The Standard* shall know no dimunation in size, in intelligence, in independence, in ability. This paper is not an experiment of yesteryear, or of the last few years. Founded in 1827 as the evening edition or exponent of an old-fashioned daily contemporary – by the great force of its special talents – by the evidence of independent master mind displayed in its columns – it soon achieved a marked and exclusive existence. …
>
> The politics of *The Standard* are those of the age – enlightened amelioration and progress; our religious principles are staunch Protestantism, without narrow sectarian bigotry of polemical zeal. Bound to no party, our only object and aim are to make this journal the earnest and honest representative and exponent of true English spirit, interests, prosperity and freedom; striving manfully for the permanent advance and greatness of the entire British Empire.

At the same time of introducing the eight-page *Standard* as a morning paper, Johnstone had also launched a new Tory evening entitled *The Evening Herald*, in connection with the long-established *Morning Herald*. Priced 2d, it was not a success – even though much of the material was lifted from its sister paper – and it died on 26 May 1865. While the sales of *The Standard* had continued to soar, those of *The Morning Herald* fell sharply. Even though the stamp duty had now been abolished, *The Herald* was still priced at threepence – no competition whatsoever for the cheaper, larger *Standard*; and people wondered at Johnstone's tactics: 'But Mr Johnstone understood what he was about; and the result showed that he was a far-seeing man. Had he reduced

The Morning Herald to the same price as *The Standard*, the probability is that both would have suffered in price and matter between them'.

As for *The St. James's Chronicle*, which had for so long been the bedrock of the Baldwin family fortunes, there had been no future for it in the Johnstone plan. Johnstone sold the paper to Charles Newdegate, a Tory MP for North Warwickshire, who, within a matter of months, had converted it into a weekly.

Both *The Times* and *The Daily Telegraph* were now rightly concerned at the eight-page, one-penny *Standard*. *The Telegraph* realised that it must produce larger papers, and on 29 May 1858 announced that with its new press room strengthened by one of the latest Hoe machines, printing eight pages at the rate of 15,000 copies per hour, an average circulation of 30,000 was being produced.

For *The Times*:

> It was clear enough that *The Daily Telegraph*, catering as it did for the 'million', affected *The Times*' sales very little, if at all. It was unfortunately only too sure, however, that *The Standard* was successfully competing with *The Times* almost on its own level – and at a quarter of the price. The Indian Mutiny assisted *The Times*, but days and weeks and months of a well-edited and well-produced penny *Standard* gradually brought down the sales of *The Times*.

While sales of *The Standard* continued to rise, there were ever-increasing pressures placed on its production area and it was not always possible to meet the demands for extra copies. The growth of the railway system meant that it was now possible for many readers to receive the paper at breakfast time, but there were still those (in Wales and the West Country, for example) who were unable to obtain copies at all. To meet these increased demands, Johnstone ordered an eight-feed press from Augustus Applegath. Erected by Thomas Middleton of Southwark, it was capable of 12,000 impressions an hour.

It had been a long project, but on Monday, 9 May 1859, in its first leader, the paper was able to announce success:

> More than fifteen months have elapsed since we gave to the public the first broadsheet of the Penny *Standard*. The venture was a bold and, except with our readers, an unpopular one ... From that first day of the publication of *The Standard* at its present price, the demand for it throughout the country has steadily risen ... It is, then, with no ordinary gratification and pride that we find ourselves enabled this day to respond fully to the growing demand for our paper. And we should be doing an injustice to Messrs. APPLEGARTH, the inventors, and Messrs. MIDDLETON, the engineers and erectors of our new printing machine, if we did not

give them the fullest credit for the success which has attended their labours.

We have by the erection of this machine, which it is calculated will enable us to print from 16,000 to 20,000 sheets in the hour, placed ourselves on a par with the largest newspaper establishments in the country. We look to the public for the continuance of the support which it has hitherto ungrudgingly offered, and we do so the more hopefully because we feel that we are advocating a cause with which the most vital interests of every citizen in this free country are connected.

This news of the installation of the new press resulted in the receipt of two letters, one from Applegath's brother, and the other on 14 May 1859 from a disgruntled, though sanguine, reader in Devon:

TO THE EDITOR OF THE STANDARD

Sir, – In the name of the Conservatives of my native town, I congratulate you and our common cause on the importance of the fact alluded to in your leader of last Monday. I assure you that down in the West of England there are hundreds of us who would gladly read your paper could we only get it supplied by our agents. But we are always met by the same story, that London and the large towns take all the issue. We hope now you have got your machine to work, to obtain your paper regularly down here. Wishing you success,

I am, your well-wisher,

A CONSERVATIVE

EVENING EDITION

Encouraged by the success of the new-style *Standard* and the increased press capacity available, Johnstone decided that the time had come to revive the evening edition, which had ceased publication three years earlier. The title was easily agreed: *The Evening Standard*, and it was felt that, with the advent of the electric telegraph – although still in its infancy – there was a growing demand for up-to-the-hour news. The increasing importance of the stock market, and, in summer, the great interest shown in sport, especially cricket, were also contributory factors. But, whereas *The Standard*, through the growth of the railway system, was essentially a national paper, its evening counterpart was designed for London – and the City businessman. Throughout the first week of June 1860, readers of *The Standard* were able to read:

TO OUR LONDON AND COUNTRY READERS

On and after MONDAY, JUNE 11th, will be PUBLISHED at 3.15 p.m. DAILY, *THE EVENING STANDARD*, Price One Penny, a full-sized paper containing all the LATEST INTELLIGENCE up to one hour of going to press, including the LETTERS from our PARIS, VIENNA, HAMBURG, MILAN, INDIA and other Correspondents, with the PRICES OF THE FUNDS, and SHARES, LAW and POLICE, and the NEWS of the DAY.

The first issue comprised eight pages, with the front and back pages solid with classified advertising, each advertisement distinguished by a dropped capital letter and cut-off rules. In a long leader, the paper declared its policy :

> The evening newspaper is an indispensable requirement of these times of rapid intelligence. We cannot keep up with the news of the day without it. The telegram of one hour would almost grow stale waiting for the morning, so speedy is intercommunication everywhere, so urgent the demand for the latest information. ... The electric wires are running the whole of the twenty-four hours; it is not asking too much of their usual medium of publication – the Press – that it do effective duty half this time. The evening newspaper is the necessary complement of daily journalism.
>
> *The Standard* was reserved for a better fate. From an evening journal of great weight and influence, of established character and high reputation, it merged into a morning paper destined to diffuse its principles through the masses of the British population ... It is a proud feature in the history of the old evening *Standard* that the morning *Standard* is so decided a success ... Perhaps all that was wanted to consummate the thorough success of its career was this *Evening Standard*, which is now for the first time issued to the public.
>
> We must own we have a cause to advance in this extension of *The Standard* to the evening. We desire to leven the country thoroughly with Conservative principles and opinions. We wish to counteract the baneful efforts of Radicalism and infidelity wherever met. *The Standard* has done its part in the arduous struggle. *The Evening Standard* will be no less zealous in advancing our one paramount object. ...

Under Johnstone's direction, *The Standard* and its sister paper, *The Morning Herald*, now had a new editorial chief, Thomas Hamber, and one of his first tasks was to appoint Charles Williams to take responsibility for *The Evening Standard.* However, Hamber himself remained in supreme control.

Born in Coleraine and educated at Belfast Academy, Charles Williams [10] had a most varied career in the newspaper world. After emigrating to America he returned to England in 1859, whereupon he assumed editorial control of *The Evening Standard.* But his forte was really as a special correspondent, and he covered the Franco-Prussian War in 1870–1, the Armenian Crisis in 1877 and the Afghanistan Campaign in 1878–9. He was then appointed editor of the pre-Harmsworth *Evening News*, before joining the *Daily Chronicle* – and he represented that newspaper at the Battle of Omdurman in Egypt in 1898.[11]

Succeeding Williams on *The Evening Standard* was John Moore Philp, who was to remain in charge until 1864. He had begun his career in 1838, when he was indentured to J. A.Valpy, a printer of Red Lion Court. After his apprenticeship, Moore Philp worked as a proof reader, firstly at Messrs, Spottiswood, the Queen's Printer, and later at Messrs Bradby and Evans. He joined the sub-editors' table of *The Standard* in 1857, before replacing Williams on the evening paper in 1860. He then left for *The Daily Telegraph* but rejoined *The Standard* as a sub-editor in 1880, and remained there until his death in 1903.

As for Thomas Hamber,[12] the new editor-in-chief and the man mainly responsible for the circulation problems at *The Times*, he was the son of a former colleague of Johnstone in the insolvency Court. Educated at Oriel College, Oxford, Hamber – described as 'a thin, spare but manly figure' – was a contemporary of Lord Robert Cecil, a future Prime Minister; of Lord George Goschen; and of Ward Hunt, a future Chancellor of the Exchequer. Upon leaving Oxford, Hamber joined, during the Crimean War, the Swiss Legion, not as was sometimes alleged, the brutal Turkish mercenary Bashi Bazouks. Many years later, Thomas Escott, a leader writer on *The Standard* and long-time friend of Hamber, commented: 'Whatever his services in the field may or may not have been, they had given him the titular rank of captain, and had invested him with a bluff genial manner, which he has, I think, never lost.'

On entering journalism, he was immediately known as Captain Hamber, and throughout the 1860s and 1870s he remained as familiar a figure in Pall Mall as in Fleet Street. 'Hamber in his best days united great intellectual quickness with many political opportunities, with wide social popularity, and with a certain magnetism which made him a leader of men'. He succeeded the great Stanley Lees Giffard as editor. Giffard had been unwell for a number of years, and by the spring of 1855 he had been bedridden for three months. On May 22 of that year he wrote a letter of reconciliation to his sister:

The first use I make of my increased strength, after thirteen weeks of confinement to my bed, from an almost hopeless sickness and a frightful operation of two hours under the knife, is to reply to your short note communicated through my unhappy Sarah. As for forgiveness, if I have anything to forgive you have my forgiveness many, very many years ago.[13]

Giffard now realised that after more than a quarter of a century of editing *The Standard*, and almost forty years' devoted service to the Baldwin family, that his heart was not with the new ownership and the time had come for him to leave. The onerous years on the paper had, without doubt, taken their toll. In 1857, profoundly shocked by the death of his youngest daughter, Catherine, an 18-year-old upon whom his devotion was centred, he retired from the world, and died a year later at Folkestone, in his seventieth year. His final illness had involved an agonisingly painful cancer which he endured with great courage to the end.

He was not to be forgotten by the paper which he had so lovingly served: on 9 November 1858, *The Standard* carried as its main news story on page 5:

DEATH OF
DOCTOR GIFFARD

It is with sorrow that is not often expressed so sincerely in the columns of a newspaper that we have to announce today the death at Folkestone, in Kent, of Stanley Lees Giffard, Esq., LLD, of Trinity College, Dublin, and the Middle Temple, Barrister-at-law who was much better known to statesmen, men of letters and the public as having exercised for considerable more than a quarter of a century the office of editor of *The Standard* ... His first engagement as a journalist he made with *The St. James's Chronicle*, where, as to learning and readiness, he was not an unworthy successor of two of his illustrious countrymen who had contributed to the same columns, Edmund Burke and Oliver Goldsmith. ...

From that period (repeal of the Corn Laws), public questions were not of that importance that demanded any very brilliant effort from a journalist, and Dr. Giffard's failing health and wont of interest in questions that were not of the spirit of his time, induced him to retire from the press, especially as the journal to which his name had been so long indentified was about to assume a form and system more suited to the commercial spirit of the present time. In the obduracy of his sympathies and antipathies in politics he was a man after Dr Johnson's own heart; and with him departed perhaps the last of the school of Georgian political writers, who brought so great a fund of learning to the pursuit of the press.[14]

Hamber's style of editorship, though, was far different from that of Giffard. A much-travelled man, Hamber, after Oxford, had been a student at German universities, and as a result of living in both Berlin and Paris was fluent in German and French. It was this background that made it possible for him to conduct idiomatic correspondence with Continental publicists or politicians upon critical questions. It was said that the waiting rooms in Shoe Lane were in his day filled with foreign refugees of all nationalities, seeking employment as translators or with early and exclusive news from Continental embassies and chanceries to sell. Such people abounded in the 1860s, but they received short shrift from Hamber.

'Of Napoleon III and his personal surroundings,' wrote Thomas Escott, 'Hamber's first-hand knowledge equalled Borthwick's, and so of course gave rise to the rumour that *The Standard* as well as the *Post*, was in the pay of the Tuileries. In the case of *The Standard* this was as ancient a legend as it was in the case of the *Post*; for, when in Baldwin's day it had been an evening paper, it was spoken of as existing mainly on a Napoleonic subsidy.' Giffard, of course, had always strenuously denied this.

Socially, Hamber was known as an agreeable and sometimes brilliant person, with a large fund of fresh anecdotes which he told with mordant humour. He was also known for his singing of French comic songs – 'and his animal spirits and physical courage missed few opportunities of asserting themselves.'[15] One example of Hamber's physical courage was witnessed by Escott himself outside *The Standard* building in Shoe Lane :

> Tom Hamber had driven down with Mrs Hamber to the office, leaving her in the cab for a few minutes to complete his business inside. While he was away, the driver addressed her in tones she did not like. 'Tom,' she said, when her husband appeared, 'This man has spoken impertinently.' 'Get down from your perch at once,' said the journalist. The man, with a coarse oath, descended. Hamber boxed first one ear, then the other. When the driver squared up to him, the Tory organ's militant chief scientifically slipped a right and left to his opponent, polishing him off very neatly, so, I have heard from others who saw it, he annihilated an abusive bargee at Henley some three decades antecedently.[16]

Under Hamber's editorship, *The Standard* now began to attract a better calibre of writer, and one of these was Lord Robert Cecil, who later, as Lord Salisbury, was to become Prime Minister. Educated at

Christ Church, he had been a friend of Hamber at Oxford, and was one of his first appointments. He soon proved his worth as a leader writer, specialising in free trade and foreign policy, but in 1860 he gave up journalism and entered Parliament as the member for Stamford – and quickly won a certain notoriety in opposing the Bill to abolish the paper duty. As he grew prominent in the party, so the need to have a firm supporter in *The Standard* increased in importance, and it was then that his early training and his easy relationships with the editorships of Hamber, and, later, Mudford were to prove invaluable. For much of that time he enlisted the services of Alfred Austin – and he was certainly not above reworking the leaders. When he was Prime Minister, Lord Salisbury confessed that in his youth he had eked out his means by writing for newspapers. At the height of his powers, in 1895, he agreed with T. H. S. Escott that they had worked together more than thirty years earlier; and that 'he had lingered in the office' of *The Standard* in Shoe Lane.

Throughout much of the second half of the century, Escott was a key figure on *The Standard* staff. He served two periods at Shoe Lane, and such was his fame as a writer that he was featured in an Ape cartoon in *Vanity Fair* in May 1885. After leaving Oxford, Escott first joined the *Glow-worm*, a short-lived satirical weekly which supported the Tory cause. From its office in The Strand he moved to *The Standard* in 1865 as a leader writer and was to continue to write for the paper for almost three decades.

Apart from Escott, other leader writers included H. E. Watts formerly editor of the *Melbourne Argus*, and Percy Gregg. All these young men 'in their political slashers' consistently and emphatically advocated Colonial Preference and an Imperial Tariff – long before Disraeli had spoken on the subject and before these ideas had been officially recognised by the Conservative establishment.

CLOSE RELATIONSHIP

Between Hamber and Disraeli there was to develop a close relationship which lasted some fifteen years, and during that time they exchanged a long series of letters, but there is little doubt that the editor did not 'call the tune'. In 1860, less than three years after Hamber had assumed control of *The Standard*, Harry W. Carr, a senior Tory, wrote in confidence to Disraeli:

> The other great disadvantage under which he has been labouring, viz.: the dearth of cabinet and information from the leader of the Conservative party is, I trust, now removed, and you may rely upon it that he will do his best to strengthen your hands. I wish to bear

testimony to the ability and knowledgeable character of Mr Hamber, because I have been informed that a very unfair prejudice has been raised against him in some quarters.

Carr, in his letter, also took the opportunity of suggesting to Disraeli:

> With reference to the newspapers I am told that the proprietor would be satisfied if the Conservative Party would purchase 1,000 copies of *The Morning Herald* a day. It might be true that this would put money into Mr Johnstone's pocket, but it is certain that some of the money would go to increase the salaries of the gentlemen who form the editorial staff ... The proprietor would strongly object to any plan which robbed him of the political direction of the paper ... this may be arrived at, if the proper kind of influence is brought to bear upon him in the proper way.[17]

In his bid to overtake *The Times*, Johnstone had unfortunately overstretched himself: largely because he had re-equipped the pressroom. Now, three years later, on 20 March, 1862, Hamber was given the melancholy task of seeking assistance from Disraeli:

> Dear Sir – I acquainted myself of a very unpleasant task in presenting you with Mr Johnstone's balance sheet. Consistently with the service I owe to him, I could not without discourtesy decline to be its bearer, but I hope never to be entrusted with a similar announcement. I have only entered into this explanation because I am most anxious that no misapprehension should arise in your mind as to the motives with which I have sought and involved myself of your every kind of flattering confidence. Nothing would grieve me more than to do anything to impair it. I beg therefore you will not trouble yourself to answer this letter.[18]

The brief 'Statement showing the Profit and Loss during Mr Johnstone's Proprietorship' was almost certainly drawn up by Morier Evans, the deputy financial manager, and is signed by Johnstone himself. Hamber added a footnote, vigorously underlined: 'During the whole period Mr Johnstone has been the Proprietor of the above newspapers from May 1857 to the present date, he has not in anyway drawn one farthing from the concern.'

The accounts showed a loss of £16,641 7s 5d over the four-and-a-half year period, and against this were to be set profits of only £2,596 6s 2d. The largest loss was for the year ending December 1858 – £8,510 17s 2d – and this was almost certainly brought about by the charges for the new Applegath press. To these losses a further figure of £17,500 was added being 'the interest of capital brought in by Mr Johnstone and for his services as Financial and General Manager at £3,500 per annum'. With a total loss of £31,500, *The Standard* and *The Morning Herald* were in deep financial trouble.

There is no record of any response from Disraeli, although four months later, on 17 July, Hamber wrote : 'I acknowledge the receipt of your cheque with many thanks. The slight trouble I have had has been very much more than repaid.' From the tenor of his reply, it seems more probable that this was 'payment in kind' for Hamber to ensure his loyalty rather than any attempt at easing his paper's financial straits. Hamber's letter to Disraeli only seems to confirm what many people had long suspected: that *The Standard* was in the pay of the Conservative Party. Just a few weeks earlier, on 3 May, *Punch* had published a telling cartoon captioned:

> Mrs Harris (a struggling Newsvendor): '*Stanerd! Stanerd!* Only a Penny! Please support an old 'ooman, dear gents!'
> (Derby to Dizzy): 'For goodness sake give her a penny, and tell the old goose we don't want her cackle – people will think she belongs to us – just opposite the club too!'[19]

AMERICAN CIVIL WAR

The fortunes of *The Standard,* however, were now about to change. In 1861, the American Civil War broke out, and this was to provide an opportunity for the paper to score over its old rival, *The Times,* and simultaneously to increase its sales. At the outbreak of hostilities, *The Standard* had at once taken the side of the South, and, in addition to its leading articles, published a series of letters from 'Manhattan' which were even more fiercely anti-Unionist. These letters were talked about by everyone and 'sent up the circulation of the paper by leaps and bounds'. The author of these letters was Joseph A. Scoville, based in New York, and his despatches from the North were later to be so critical of President Lincoln's administration that he was incarcerated in Fort Lafayette Prison and released only in 1864, just before he died. The activities of the Southern Confederacy were covered by Philip Day, who wrote his column from Atlanta.[20]

In the vivid reporting of the war in America, including the defeat of the Federal (Northern) Army at Bull Run on 5 August, there was little doubt that the sympathies of the majority of the British upper classes continued to be with the South. There was a great outburst of anti-Northern feeling, which culminated in the *Trent* affair, an incident that almost led to war between the two countries. In the November, a Northern warship intercepted the British steamer *Trent* and removed two leading Confederate agents, Mason and Slidell, who were travelling to England and the Continent on a diplomatic mission.

The Standard was outraged, and in his leader on 4 December 1861, Hamber fulminated:

> The summary of President Lincoln's Message to the Federal Congress which we publish in another column will be read with interest by the country. It makes no mention of the *Trent* outrage but breathes war and defiance to the country. The terms of the recent circular of Mr Seward, calling on the governors of the States to put their coasts in a state of defence are exceeded ... In the present instance the Senate and the House of Representatives would appear to be unanimous in their approval of what is virtually war with this country while the President is manifestly as hot-headed as the rest.

Strangely, in view of his later imprisonment, 'Manhattan's' letters at this time also presented the Northern viewpoint, which led to this disclaimer:

> We continue to publish 'Manhattan's' Letters notwithstanding much that is offensive in them to English ears at the present crisis, believing that it is desirable our readers should have reliable information as to the spirit in which the recent outrage is regarded by the powerful section of the American community of which he is the representative.

Indeed, 'Manhattan' had declared:

> There is not a single shrewd person in any Atlantic city that does not see that the British Ministers are driving England to overwhelming destruction. The trap is set and baited, and the British Ministry will be caught ... If England goes to war with us, the President knows that while she may with her fleets destroy the blockades at some ports south, he will have control by land with one division of the army, while 400,000 men, as soon as Spring opens, will take and hold Canada.

Fortunately, sanity prevailed, and, assisted by the tact of the Prince Consort and the diplomacy of Charles Francis Adams, the American Minister, Lincoln directed Seward, his Secretary of State, to release the captured Southern emissaries and this was done in late December. Mason and Slidell proceeded to London, but with tempers now cooling little interest was shown in the Confederate cause.

For the people of England, the year 1861 was to end on a note of deep sorrow. The Prince Consort was stricken with typhoid fever – allegedly contracted from the drains at Windsor Castle. On 16 December, *The Standard* appeared in full mourning with reversed column rules on all its eight broadsheet pages. On Christmas Eve, the paper published a long account of the funeral, including 'cuts' of a funeral urn and the coffin:

> The grave has now closed over the mortal remains of the Prince Consort ... He had no love for the pageantry of power in life, and there was as little as possible of it to interfere with the nation's tears at his tomb. His tastes led him to the quiet and retirement of private life, and quietly and privately he was borne to the grave. But his memory will long live in the hearts of the people.

During the war in America, Hamber was intent that Disraeli, with proper regard to the Confederacy, should be made fully aware of the situation, and on 13 July 1862 he wrote: 'I enclose Saunders and Ottley's account, so far as it is completed. The sale, I think, is very good. ... The feeling in this country seems to be almost entirely one of exhultation over the defeat of the north.'[21] Four days later he returned to the theme: 'I am inclined to think [General] McClellan's defeat almost inevitable if the Southerners are not too much exhausted to take advantage of the opportunity. At any rate, it seems probable that the Federals will have plenty on their hands in the defence of Washington.'

The reportage of the war was now having a distinct effect upon the paper's finances, with the circulation on some days exceeding 100,000 copies, a huge sale in those times. A jubilant Hamber wrote on 27 October 1862: 'You will be pleased to hear that our circulation is increasing almost daily. We published last week a greater number than we have ever issued – and this at a dull season of the year.' And so the correspondence on the war continued, up to his last documented message to Disraeli, on 2 June 1864: 'I have an important letter on American affairs from M. Gozi, who is now in Paris, which I should be pleased to read to you, if you have a few minutes disengaged tomorrow at noon.'

Apart from Hamber's personal sympathies with the South, there were also rumours that payment determined *The Standard*'s stance. The reason for these allegations were the activities of Henry Hotze, the Confederate agent in London.[22] On 25 April, 1862, Hotze informed the Confederate Secretary of State, Judah Benjamin, that 'Two more newspapers, *The Herald*, Lord Derby's organ, and *The Standard*, have voluntarily placed themselves at my disposal. The Editor in chief of both called on me, and offered the use of the columns of both, including editorial columns, of which offer I have, though guardedly, availed myself.'

Although Hotze denied the charge of paying *The Standard*, he may well have given a retainer, because in 1862 he founded *The Index*, a propaganda weekly, and employed journalists to write for the paper on a part-time basis. Twelve months later Hotze declared that seven journalists employed by London dailies were working for him, with four of them 'colleagues of one editorial corps'. This was almost certainly *The Standard*, and the following statement strongly indicates that Thomas Hamber was one of them: 'I have been fortunate enough to receive as permanent contributor to *The Index* the Chief Editor of one of the leading daily journals – for obvious reasons I omit the name.'

Similarly, Hotze reported to the Secretary of State that 'disbursements such as boxes of cigars imported from Havana through the aid of Mr Helm, American whiskey, and other articles which not being generally procurable, form acceptable presents, it is of course out of the question to give vouchers (to the Confederate government accounting for expenditures)'. In addition to the probable gifts 'in kind', Hamber was also being supplied with a regular service of news items and leaders and he was not slow to object if he found that *The Times* had inadvertently been supplied with information in advance of *The Standard*. Thus, Hotze noted: 'It appears that Hamber who is intimately connected with *The Index* office was told of the report on Wednesday morning before Hopkins knew that it was to be exclusively for *The Times*. When he, Hamber, learned of this fact in the evening he was indignant of what appeared to him an intentional slight.'[23]

Aside from its own correspondents – and the information fed by Hotze – *The Standard* was to rely heavily upon the new telegraphic services provided by Paul Julius Reuter. On 22 July, 1864, James Johnstone, the paper's proprietor, had signed a three-year agreement with Julius Reuter. For the sum of £83 6s 8d per month, Reuter would provided 'a copy of every Telegram which I supply to the other daily papers' to the *Morning Standard* and *Evening Standard*. And for a monthly sum of £41 13s 4d a similar arrangement was reached with the *Morning Herald* and the *Evening Herald*. The only other condition was that the telegrams should be headed 'Reuters Telegrams' or 'The following telegrams have been received at Mr Reuter's Office'.[24] Its efficiency was more than proved when it was first with the news of the surrender of the main Confederate Army in the spring of 1865.

Isolated Southern resistance, though, continued for another seven weeks, but for all real purposes the war was over, a war that was responsible for more than 620,000 deaths on the two sides. *The Standard* carried the news of the Confederate surrender in its issue of

24 April, 1865. Two days later there was a sensation when the steamer *Nova Scotian* arrived at the telegraph station, near Londonderry, bringing a Reuter's despatch of the assassination of President Lincoln. Hamber duly accorded it extensive treatment as the lead story on page 5, an account which covered more than half the page; and in his main leader the following day commented:

> More astounding news from that brought from New York by the *Nova Scotian* was never borne across the Atlantic. President Lincoln has been shot dead in the theatre, Mr Seward stabbed and is feared mortally, while lying in the sick bed, and his son, Frederick, killed in defending his father. The utmost horror pervaded the city of New York.

STAR CORRESPONDENT

The extensive and acclaimed reportage of the American Civil war had drawn an increased readership to *The Standard* and to meet their needs for overseas news Hamber was determined that his correspondents should be second to none. He was fortunate, therefore, to have on his staff a young man, George Alfred Henty,[25] who was to win fame as a war correspondent and as a writer of books for boys. For almost fifty years, Henty was associated with the paper and was its star correspondent. Born at Trumpington, Cambridgeshire, in 1832, he was educated at Westminster School and Caius College, Cambridge, before leaving, without taking his degree, for service in the Crimean War in the Purveyor's department of the Army.

Upon his return he began to write for *The Standard*, and in 1859 acted as correspondent during the war between Piedmont-Sardinia, France and Austria, and throughout Garibaldi's campaign in Sicily and Southern Italy. He later covered the Abyssinian Expedition of 1868, when he accompanied Sir Robert Napier's Brigade, which defeated the followers of King Theodore II at the Battle of Arogee, on Good Friday, 10 April, 1868. After reporting the gala opening of the Suez Canal in November 1869, he was in action once more, with the German Army during the Franco-Prussian War; and, following the French collapse, was in Paris during the Commune.

His next service abroad was to West Africa in 1873–74, when he covered the Ashanti Expedition. The campaign ended with the destruction of the Ashanti capital, Kumasi, and Henty's three-column despatch, of 5 February, 1874, gave a most graphic account. He was fortunate, though, in not losing his life. During a lull in the fighting, he had been invited by Henry Morton Stanley (renowned as the man who had found in East Africa, the missing explorer, Dr David

Livingstone), who was now covering the West African conflict for the *New York Herald,* to accompany him on his paper's small power-driven boat.

They travelled to the mouth of the Volta river to see the supporting forces of Captain Glover, who were about to mount an attack to the east of Kumasi. Henty was almost drowned in an accident, and later wrote: 'No doubt it does seem a stupid sort of thing to do. If it had been an Englishman I would draw back; but if Stanley can do it, I can; and I am not going to let any Yankee say he was ready to do anything, but an Englishman funked going with him.'[26]

Fresh from his triumphs in Ashanti, Henty was next sent to Spain to cover the outbreak of the Carlist insurrection, and later accompanied the Prince of Wales to India. His last service for *The Standard* was to report on the Turco-Serbian War of 1876, when he was attached to the Turkish forces. After this, he went to California, to see life in the mining camps at close quarters, and from that time onwards devoted himself chiefly to writing stories for boys, although almost to the end of the century he remained a valued contributor to *The Standard.*

As the decade grew to a close, so the profits of *The Standard* continued to improve; but for the man who had started it all there was to be no recognition. On 17 February, 1869, Charles Baldwin, founder of the paper, passed away at the great age of 95. In *The Standard* there was not a line to mark his death: no obituary appeared; it was if he had passed anonymously through its pages. It was left to *The Newspaper Press* to announce on 1 March:

> The death on the 18th ult at his residence Sussex-gardens of Mr Charles Baldwin, at the advanced age of 95 years. Mr Baldwin, in the earlier period of his career, was a partner in one of the largest publishing firms in the city of London. Subsequently, about the time of the agitation for Catholic emancipation, and in conjunction with the late Dr Giffard, Dr M'Ginn, and others of the most brilliant political writers of that day, he established *The Standard* newspaper, of which he continued the sole proprietor for many years.
>
> He was also of many years proprietor of *The Morning Herald.* He was a magistrate for the County of Surrey, had long been the father of the Stationers' Company, and was one of the founders of the Royal Literary Fund.[27]

A N

A C C O U N T

O F T H E

PUBLICK TRANSACTIONS in Christendom.

In a Letter to a Friend in the Country.

Saturday, August 11. 1694. L I C E N S'D.

S I R,

THE Gazette *and* News-Letters *being so common in your Country, I was not a little surprized to find that you should desire me to write to you once a Week what I hear concerning the* Publick Transactions *of the World, and what Reflections our Friends make on them. This, I am sure, is a harder Task than you imagined for me at first, and I think the Reasons I gave you in my last, in order to obtain your excuse, were very pertinent and sufficient; but seeing nothing can satisfy you, and that you are resolved to have a Letter of mine, I shall write to you as often as I shall have any Subject Matters; but as you must not always expect from me extraordinary things, so neither must you expect that I should take notice of all little Trifles; This is the Province of the most Common* News-Letters, *with whom I do not design in the least to interfere.*

We have been this Week in great impatience for want of News, and the *Holland* Mail we had on *Thursday*, has not yet quenched our thirst; for what we heard was not very material. The Letters from *Vienna* of the 31st of *July*, say, That the Imperial Forces were arrived at their *Gazette* says were arrived at *Belgrade*, it proves to be one of its ordinary wilful mistakes. Tho the Summer is so far spent, yet by these Preparations of the Imperialists, it seems that they design to do something; and if we may believe these Letters, the *Turks* are hardly in a Condition to oppose them. This backwardness of both Parties shews how much a Peace is necessary for them, and that they lie under a kind of impossibility to continue the War. I know that the *Turks* are sullen, as generally all Loosers are, and loth to quit the Play; but amongst other Reasons, if the *Arabian*'s Insurrection continues, I am sure they will be glad to accept of Terms. Of these Commotions you have already an Account in one of our *Gazette*'s, which is confirmed by the last Letters from *Transilvania* and *Venice*, with some other particulars. They write in short, That the Czeriff of *Arabia* having got a considerable Army together, had march'd towards *Mecca*, and defeated the Bassa of *Asia*, who intended to oppose him; that he possessed himself afterwards of that place, as well as of *Medina*, causing himself to be proclaimed Emperor; and that having seized on the Treasures of those Towns, he was marching into the *Up-*

1 *An Account of the Publick Transactions in Christendom* published by Richard Baldwin.

A
Poſtſcript
TO THE
POST-MAN.

London, *Auguſt* 11. 1710.

This Day came in an Expreſs, with the welcome News of a Victory obtain'd by the King of Spain, *over the Forces of the Duke of* Anjou. *Which is in Subſtance as follows.*

THE Duke of Anjou being inform'd, That 5000 Palatines were on their March from Gironne, to join the King of Spain near Balaguer, reſolved to decamp the 26th of July from Ivars, and repaſs the Segra. Whereupon King Charles ordered General Stanhope with 14 Squadrons of Horſe and Dragoons, and a Detachment of Grenadiers, to march, and endeavour to fall on their Rear.

Accordingly General Stanhope advanc'd, though he had an Ague upon him, and attack'd the 27th their Rear, conſiſting of Twenty Six Squadrons, which were put into Diſorder; Whereupon the Duke of Anjou ſent all the Cavalry of his Army to ſupport them; and King Charles doing the like, the Engagement became general between the Horſe of both Armies. The Action laſted ſome Hours, but at laſt the Troops of the Duke of Anjou gave way. The General who commanded them, with ſeveral other Perſons of Note were taken Priſoners. The Slaughter was very great, both on the Field of Battel, and in the Purſuit. The Duke of Anjou retired with his Foot to Lerida. The Allies loſt ſome conſiderable Officers, and General Stanhope received a Contuſion in his Right Shoulder.

The Expreſs who brought this News to Prince Eugene and the Duke of Marlborough, went through Ghent in his way to the Army; and they have Printed there the following Account: Which perhaps in ſome Particulars is ſomewhat exaggerated.

Ghent, Aug. 18. Laſt Night an Expreſs arrived here from Milan, (from whence he ſet out the 8th Inſtant) in his way to the Army, with Diſpatches from the King of Spain for the Princes of Savoy and Marlborough. He reports, That the Army of his Catholick Majeſty has entirely defeated in Catalonia the Forces of King Philip. That on the Side of the Enemy, Two Lieutenants-General were killed, with Six Majors-General, Six Brigadiers, 20 Colonels, 24 Lieutenant-Colonels, and 7000 Private Men, beſides a great Number of Priſoners, amongſt whom are 700 Officers. They took from them 30 Pieces of Cannon, and ſeveral Standards and Colours. The Queen of Spain writ this News with her own Hand to her Father, the Duke of Wolfembuttel. The King of Spain was ſtill purſuing his Enemies, when the Expreſs came away.

Printed by *D. Leach* in *Elliot's Court*, in the *Little-Old Baily*, for the Author.

2 *A Postscript to the Post-Man* published by Anne Baldwin.

The *St. James's* CHRONICLE, OR, *BRITISH* EVENING-POST

Price Two-pence Half-penny.] From TUESDAY, September 17, to THURSDAY September 19, 1771. No. 1649.

WEDNESDAY, Sept. 18.

FOREIGN AFFAIRS.

Warsaw, August 31.

FROM Wilkourk in Lithuania we have received an Account, that the Confederates had taken Lieut. Gen. Grabowski from his Country Seat there; but fearing they should not be able to overcome the Russian Detachment which was sent after them, they gave Gen. Grabowski two dangerous Cuts in the Head, and left him in that State. We are not yet certain whether the said General can recover, his advanced Age makes us rather in fear of his Life.

SHIP NEWS.

Deal, Sept. 16. Wind S. by W. Came down and remain with the Ships as per last, the Prosper, Hall, for Bristol. Arrived and sailed for the River, the George, Trenham, from Jamaica, and Crook, Duffield, from St. Vincent's.

Arrived.

At Ant, Hero, Johnson, from Antigua.
At Jamaica, Meredith, Peacock, from London.
At Maryland, Hope, Hooper, from London.
At Leith, Minerva, Alexander, from South Carolina.
At Dover, Nancy Graham, Lynch, from Maryland and Kitty, Wood, from St. Kitt's.
At Dover, Alexander, Reed, from the Grenades.
At Virginia, Hansford, Willon, from the West Indies.
At Jersey, Triton, Collas, from Honduras.
At Philadelphia, Globe, Cartiques, from Cork.

LONDON.

St. James's, Sept. 17. His Majesty has been pleased to grant unto Lewis Bagot, M. A. the Canonry or Prebend in the Cathedral of Christ Church, in the University of Oxford, void by the Resignation of Dr. John Moore.

Lord Chatham speaking of the Struggle likely to be in the City for the Office of Lord Mayor, declared, that Mr. Wilkes acted very imprudently to make his Designs so public: "He is so eager (said this great Man) to engross all the Employments to his own Circle, that his true Motives cannot remain long concealed; and the Moment the Livery discover that he is only labouring to make himself their Master, they will see their Independency as much in Danger from him, as it is from an abandoned Administration."

The new Excise Office in Broad-Street, is to be opened on Tuesday the 24th inst. for the Transacting of Business there.

Cathcart Taylor, Esq. is appointed Captain-Lieutenant in the 2d Regiment of Dragoon Guards.

Francis Hugonin, Gent. is appointed Lieutenant in the 4th Regiment of Dragoons.

Lieut. Geo. Petrie, Gent. is appointed Adjutant to the 31st Regiment of Foot.

The General Howard, Huntrin, from North-Carolina to Bristol, sprang a Leak lately, was obliged to put back, and is condemned.

A Letter from India mentions the Death of Capt. Cooke, of the Earl of Elgin East-Indiaman.

We hear that Mademoiselle Clairon, the celebrated French Actress, is just put into Prison, on Account of some disrespectful Words she let drop against the Government. This Lady has been addicted to a Slightness for some Time, very near bordering on Insanity.

The Rev. Mr. Johnson was a few Days since presented to the Vicarage of Playstone, in the County of Wilts and Diocese of Salisbury, void by the Cession of the late Incumbent.

On Monday Night as Robert Bentham, Esq. of St. James's Street, was returning to Town from Kensington, he was attacked in Hyde Park by two Footpads, who robbed him of his Watch, a Diamond Ring, and about 4l.

Yesterday Edward Burch and Matthew Martin were tried at the Old Bailey, on an Indictment for feloniously publishing, as true, a certain Hand-Writing purporting to be the last Will and Testament of Sir Andrew Chadwick, knowing the same to be forged with Intent to defraud the Heirs at Law of the said Sir Andrew, when they were both found guilty.—The Trial lasted from about half an Hour past Nine in the Morning, till near Twelve at Night, after which the Jury were out about half an Hour.

The Business of the Court was stopt some Time on Account of the Will, produced in Evidence against them, being mislaid; it was handed about to different Persons in Court, and by some Accident dropped on the Ground.

The forged Will bore Date in 1764, and a wholesale Paper-Maker, who was very instrumental in convicting the above Men, swore by the Stamp, or Mark, that was upon the Paper, that he made the said Paper in 1768, four Years after the Will was dated, which Circumstance had great Weight with the Court.

Sir Andrew Chadwick's Estate was about 7000l. per Ann. and 14,000l. in the Stocks, which is now possessed (except the Cash) by James Taylor, Esq. of Center-Place, in Lancashire, who married Miss Lowes, second Cousin to Sir Andrew.

The Cross Roads in Scotland, it is said, are to be farmed out in the Manner those of England were some Years ago by the late Ralph Allen, Esq.

At Monmouth Races on Tuesday the 50l. Weight for Age, was won by Sir Richard Phillipps's Horse, Le Brun, beating the Duke of Beaufort's Old Lad. Mr. Ward's Careless broke down on Sunday in his Exercise.

Wednesday the Give-and-Take Plate was won by Dr. Kinneir's Twinger, at three Heats, beating Mr. Dutton's Windrush, which won the first Heat, and Sir Richard Phillipps's Macaroni. There was good Sport this Day. The first Heat was hard run between Windrush and Macaroni, and Twinger just saved his Distance. The Odds were now greatly on the Side of Windrush: but the next heat Twinger went off at Score and maintained it throughout, beating Windrush by two Lengths. The third Heat Macaroni was drawn, and Twinger won it hollow.

On Thursday there was no Race for want of Horses.

DERBY RACES.

Tuesday the 3d inst. the Purse of 50l. was run for by five Horses, &c. and won by Mr. Malkin's bay Colt, Rowland.

Wednesday the 4th three started for the Purse of 50l. which was won by Mr. Morgan's grey Mare, Damsel.

Married.] Yesterday Mr. Lisle, Apothecary, in Newgate-Street, to Mrs. Beauchamp, of South Ockingdon, in Essex.—Yesterday James Maxwell, Esq. of David-Street, Grosvenor-Square, to Miss Elizabeth Playdell of Marlborough-Street.

Died.] A few Days ago John Harvey, Esq. at his Seat at Ickwelburg, in Bedfordshire.—Monday at his House at Bow, Capt. James Harvey, formerly in the Virginia Trade.—A few Days ago at Dunkirk, Mr. Wilson, Grocer, in Carey-Street.—Saturday at Reading, in Berkshire, Mrs. Harrison, Mother of Mr. Thomas Harrison, Printer of the London Gazette.—Thursday last Mr. Gilbert Hearne, a great Antiquarian, of the City of Hereford.—Monday at his House at Kensington Gore, aged 92, the Rev. Mr. Fleming, a nonjuring Clergyman.—Monday at his Country House at Hillingdon, near Uxbridge, ——— Bell, Esq.

For The St. James's Chronicle.

Extracts from celebrated Authors, concerning imposed Subscriptions to human Explications of the Scripture.

[*Continued from No. 1633.*]

THERE is nothing more ridiculous than for a Man, or Company of Men, to assume the Title of Orthodoxy to their own Set of Opinions, as if Infallibility were annexed to their Systems, and those were to be the standing Measures of Truth to all the World; from whence they erect to themselves a Power to censure and condemn others for differing at all from the Tenets they have pitched upon. The Consideration of human Frailty ought to check this Vanity; but since it does not, but that with a Sort of Allowance it shows itself almost in all religious Societies, the playing the Trick round sufficiently turns it into Ridicule: For each Society having an equal Right to a good Opinion of themselves, a Man, by passing but a River or a Hill, loses that Orthodoxy in one Company, which passed him up with such Assurance and Insolence in another, and is there, with equal Justice, himself exposed to the like Censure of Error and Heresy, which he was so forward to lay on others at home. When it shall appear, that Infallibility is intailed upon any one Set of Men of any Denomination, or that Truth is confined to any Spot of Ground, the Name and Use of Orthodoxy, as it now is in Fashion every where, will in that one Place be reasonable. Till then, this ridiculous Cant will be a Foundation too weak to sustain that Usurpation raised upon it.—*Locke's second Vind. of the Reas. of Christianity.*

Christianity is a Religion suited to vulgar Capacities, and the State of Mankind in this World, destined to Labour and Travail. The Writers and Wranglers in Religion fill it with Niceties, and dress it up with Notions, which they make necessary and fundamental Parts of it; as if there were no Way into the Church but through the Academy, or Lyceum.—*Locke, on the Reas. of Christianity.*

If you consider their (the Papists) ecclesiastical State and System in general, as a Body Politic, and as a spiritual Power, it is certainly calculated to keep the Commonalty in Ignorance, and in an implicit Faith, and a blind Submission to human Authority; and, under the plausible Pretence of Unity and external Peace, to discourage Liberty of Conscience, and free and rational Examination. But, to say the Truth, there has been too much of the determining and domineering Spirit in most Christian Societies of every Denomination. I wish I could except one!—*Jortin's Serm. V. 1. P. 13.*

Men will compel others, not to think with them, for that is impossible, but to say they do, upon which they obtain full Leave not to think or reason at all; and this is called Unity, which is somewhat like the Behaviour of the Romans, as it is described by a brave Countryman of our's in Tacitus—*ubi solitudinem faciunt, pacem appellant.*—*Jortin's Remarks on Eccl. Hist. Pref.*

Scripture, say the Protestants, is the only Rule of Faith; and they say well. There is no other Christianity than this; no other Test of Doctrines than this; no other Centre of Union than this. Whatsoever is not clearly delivered there, may be true, but cannot be important. *Haec mea est sententia, neque me ex ea ullius unquam aut docti aut indocti movebit oratio.*—*Jortin's Remarks on Eccl. Hist.*

To the Printer of the S. J. CHRONICLE.

SIR,

HAVING read, in your last Saturday's Paper, an Extract from a Pamphlet entitled, "Advice from a Bishop," in a Series of Letters to a young Clergyman," it brings fresh to my Remembrance a remarkable Circumstance of a real and well known Matter of Fact, which is as follows. In the Month of September, many Years ago, upon Occasion of a publick Ordination in a certain Diocese, there came many Candidates for Holy Orders from both our Universities, who acquitted themselves exceedingly well in the several Parts of their Examination, to the Approbation of the Bishop and other neighbouring Divines then present; indeed one young Student from Cambridge, much celebrated for his shining Talents, which, however, it seems he exercised more for the Theatre than the Pulpit, was found altogether deficient, to the great Astonishment of all, as will appear to your Readers. The first Question asked him was; how do you prove the Existence of God? He was instantly struck as with a Convulsion, continuing in profound Silence, rolling his Eyes upward and downward by turns for some Time, then toward the Window on his Right Hand, and lastly to the Door on his Left, as if he wanted to make his Escape, still without uttering a Syllable. The Arch-Deacon then hinted to him, that surely the Objects he had seen, and the Sense of his own Existence, might have furnished him with a full and proper Answer. Soon after a second Question was proposed, viz. How many Natures has our Lord and Saviour? but he remained stupid and dumb as before. After some considerable Pause the third Question was; What meanest thou by the Word Sacrament? To which no Answer being made, the Arch-Deacon remitted him to his College with peremptory Orders to learn his Catechism before he pursued any other Studies, especially Theological. Here the Bishop interposed, and desired the young Gentleman to follow him into another Room; but the Arch-Deacon prevented, assuring his Lordship, that he neither would, nor conscientiously could recommend him as fit for Ordination. Upon this the Candidate retired, hastened to the Inn, mounted his Horse, and rode Post to his Alma-Mater, for a restorative Draught to raise his Spirits, &c. &c. &c.

Now, Sir, if you choose, and think it will be agreeable or edifying to any of your Readers, intended for the sacred Function, I will willingly, through the Channel of your Paper, communicate the Advice, Directions, and Injunctions, both of a late Arch-Bishop and Metropolitan also to their Candidates for Holy Orders, how to prepare themselves duely for Examination.

Your's, &c.

VERAX.

ON Monday, October the 7th, G. FORDYCE, M. D. Physician to St. Thomas's Hospital, will begin his Lectures, viz.

On the Practice of Physick and Materia Medica, at Eight in the Morning.

On Chemistry, at Nine, at his House in Henrietta Street, Covent Garden, where Proposals may be had.

IN Soho Square, the Corner of Charles Street, is to be Sold by public Auction, or private Contract, on or before the 5th Day of October next,

All the fashionable, genuine, rich, and elegant FURNITURE of a House situate as above, the Property of a Gentleman gone abroad; consisting of blue and crimson Silk Damasks, Chintz, Moreens, &c. &c. together with all the Pictures, &c. The Whole remaining as when occupied, quite complete for the immediate Use of a Family, for whose Reception the House, with a Coach House, and Stabling for six Horses, with Room to make an Enlargement thereto adjoining, may be taken on Lease. And as the late Possessor spared no Pains to render the Premises thoroughly commodious, and finished in the present Taste, makes it beyond a Doubt that the same, with the Furniture, will be singularly advantageous to any Family of Fashion, desirous of being directly settled without any Trouble.

For further Particulars, enquire for S. S. at the Bar of the Antigallican Coffee House, behind the Royal Exchange; or of Mr. Noble, Appraiser, in Long Acre.

TO be Sold by Auction, by Mr. Pond, at Newmarket, on Thursday October the 3d, which is in the next Newmarket Meeting,

The entire Stud of Brood Mares, Colts, and Fillies, which did belong to Richard Cowles, Esq. deceased.

To be viewed till Thursday, September the 26th, at West Harling, in the County of Norfolk, and on Monday, the 30th, at Newmarket, till the Sale, which will be about two Hours before the Races begin.

☞ West Harling is twenty five Miles from Newmarket, and six from Thetford.

Catalogues to be had of Mr. Pond, in Bridges Street, near Russel Court, Covent Garden.

TO be Sold by Auction by Mr. POND, on Friday the 4th, and Saturday the 5th of October,

Several valuable Brood Mares, Colts, and Fillies; Goldfinder (who to all Appearance is now perfectly sound) Petruchio, Khalen, Mr. Arabian, and the Grey [illegible] Horse Forrester, which did belong to JENNISON SHAFTO, Esq. deceased. To be viewed at Wratting Park, eight measured Miles from Bourne Bridge, and nine from Newmarket, and at Newmarket on the Day of Sale, which will begin about two Hours before the Races.

Catalogues to be had at Mr. Pond's, in Bridges Street, near Russel Court, Covent Garden.

Navy Office, Sept. 16, 1771.

THE principal Officers and Commissioners of his Majesty's Navy give Notice, that on Tuesday the 24th Inst. at Noon, they will be ready to treat with such Persons as are willing to supply his Majesty's several Yards with dryed Bullocks Hydes with the Hair on on a standing Contract.

TO be Lett, from Michaelmas next, for one, two, or three Years, furnished with all useful and elegant Furniture,

A very commodious DWELLING HOUSE with every Convenience, fit to receive a large Family. Good Stabling for twenty Horses, and a large Coach House; walled and other Gardens, on an excellent Soil, and a very pleasant Shrubbery and Terrace Walk, with about thirty Acres of fine Pasture [illegible] Land, and Orchard. It is situate in the Western Part of the County of Somerset; about one Mile from a good Market and Post Town, and the same Distance from the great Turnpike Road, leading from Exeter to Bath and Bristol.

For further Particulars, enquire of Mr. Prockter Thomas, Attorney at Law, in Wellington, Somerset; Messrs. Popham and Sanxter, at New Inn, London; or Mr. Blake, Apothecary, on the South Parade, Bath.

TO be Lett for a short Term, to enter upon immediately,

A Capital MANSION HOUSE, ready furnished, situate in the West Riding of Yorkshire, within six Miles of the Town of Leeds: There are six Rooms on a Floor with Closets; the Offices are large and commodious, consisting of a Brew-house, Laundry, and 3 Coach-houses, Dove Cote, Barn, Stabling for upwards of twenty Horses, and many other Conveniencies. The Garden, in which there are Stoves and Hot Walls, is well planted and very fruitful, and Part of it is laid out in Pleasure Ground. There is a large Paddock before the House with Deer in it, which will be either let with the House or not, as agreeable to the Tenant, and any other Quantity of Land not exceeding thirty Acres. The Manor is well stocked with Game, which the Tenant will have Leave to kill.

Further Particulars may be had by applying to Mr. Dyneley, at his Chambers in Gray's Inn, or of Mr. [illegible], Attorney in Leeds.

TO be Sold, on Friday the 11th of October next, at Twelve o'Clock at Noon, at Lloyd's Coffee House, in Lombard-street,

Several Freehold and Leasehold Messuages or Dwelling Houses, well situated near and adjoining to the General Post Office in Lombard Street, and now in the Occupation of Messrs. Blossom, Ostrich, Hanbury, and Co. Messrs. Lawrence, and Knight, at several yearly Rents, amounting in the whole to 459l. 10s. per Annum. A very small Part of the Premisses is Leasehold, and the Remainder is Freehold, and the same will be sold in five distinct Lots.

For further Particulars apply to Mr. Reade, No. 6 in Copthall Court, London; or to Mr. Kirby or in [illegible].

TO be Sold by Auction, on Tuesday the 8th Day of October, between the Hours of Four and Seven in the Afternoon, at the White Hart Inn at Thrapston in the County of Northampton, subject to such Conditions of Sale as shall be then and there produced,

A FREEHOLD ESTATE, situate in the Parish of Brighton, within five Miles of Kimbolton, six of Thrapston, and about seven of Oundle, consisting of a good Farm House, Barns, Stables, [illegible] with 43 A. 3 R. 33 P. of inclosed Pasture and Meadow Land; 19 A. 2 R. 7 P. of common Field Pasture, [illegible] 1 R. 33 P. of inclosed Arable Land and 144 A. [illegible] of common Field Arable Land. The above Farm is now in the Occupation of the Widow Maynard. The Estate is well wooded and watered, the common Fields lie very contiguous to the Town, and the Premisses are in good Repair.

For further Particulars enquire of Mr. Thomas Batcher, at Copie, near Bedford, or the Widow Maynard, who will shew the Premisses.

Land to be Sold by Auction.

TO be Sold by Auction, on Tuesday the 1st of October, 1771, at Three o'Clock in the Afternoon, at the Swan, in Atherstone, Warwickshire, if not sold before by private Sale,

A FREEHOLD ESTATE, lying in the Parish of Witherly, in Leicestershire, within about three Quarters of a Mile of Atherstone, in Warwickshire, now in the Tenure of Thomas Slack, at the annual Rent of 80l. The Premisses consist of about 63 Acres and an Half of good Pasture and Meadow Land, well watered, have a good Fold Yard, a large Barn, and three Brick Stables, and a Brick Kiln thereon erected.

Also a Quantity of Clay Dug for making Brick and Tyles. At the same Time and Place will be Sold two Houses, and [illegible] Land, in Atherstone, with their Rights of Commons, now in Tenure of Joseph Smith and Charles Beal.

For further Particulars, enquire of Mr. William Ebertel, Attorney at Law; or of Mr. John Williday, both of Atherstone.

To the Nobility and Gentry travelling the Kent Road from London to Dover.

THOMAS TEMPLEMAN, at the Red Lion and Post Office, at Sittingbourn, takes this Method to acquaint the Publick, that he has provided the best four-wheeled Post Chaises, with able Horses, which he intends to run at Nine-pence per Mile. And as he will be ever studious to merit the Encouragement of those who please to favour him with their Company, he keeps a professed Cook, has the genteelest Attendance, and best Accommodations. And as he has been well assured, that the Inn Keepers of Rochester and Canterbury have endeavoured to injure him, by preventing Company coming to his House, he hopes their Malevolence and Ill Nature will prove ineffectual, as he has no other Wish, but by a strict Attention to his Business, to prove himself the Publick's most grateful,

And obliged humble Servant,

T. TEMPLEMAN.

Canal Navigation from Chesterfield to the River Trent, Sept. 5, 1771.

IN pursuance of an Order made at the General Assembly of the Company of Proprietors of the said Navigation, held at Retford [illegible], the said Proprietors are requested to pay into the Hands of Mr. George [illegible], in Retford; Mr. Allwood Wilkinson, in Chesterfield, the Treasurers to the said Company; or to Messrs. Smith, Wright, and Gray, Bankers, Lombard Street, London, on the [illegible] Day of December next, such Sum of Money as together with what already paid by each Proprietor, will make the Sum of Ten Pounds for each, and every Share, which the said Proprietors are respectively possessed of, or entitled to in the said Navigation.

☞ A Penalty of Five Pounds per Share is, by the Act, inflicted upon every Person who shall neglect to pay his Call on or before the Day appointed for Payment of the same.

ANTH. LAX,

Clerk to the said Company.

3 *St. James's Chronicle* published by Henry Baldwin.

4 (*above*) No. 38, New Bridge Street: Offices of *St. James's Chronicle* and *The Standard* (building behind obelisk).

5 (*below*) First edition of *The Standard*.

The Standard.

Signifer statue Signum: Hic optime manebimus.

Plant here The Standard: Here we shall best remain.

MONDAY, MAY 21, 1827.

Valuable Reversionary Freehold Estates, at Kingston, in Surrey, Stratford, Ilford, and Chingford, in Essex, Kent-road, Southwark, Smithfield, Aldgate, Bethnal-green, &c., on the death of a Gentleman, in his 70th year.—By WINSTANLEY and SONS, at the Mart, on Friday, June 29, in 12 lots.

VERY valuable Reversionary Freehold Estates, on the death of a Gentleman, now in his 70th year; consisting of the well known and old established inn and posting house, called the Castle, situate in the market-place at Kingston, in Surrey. The old established inn and posting house, the Angel, at Ilford, Essex. The Crown Public house, in West Smithfield. A genteel and compact Residence, at Chingford, with 10 acres of land. Six houses, Nos. 1, 2, and 3, Newton's-place, near the Turnpike, at Stratford, and Nos. 26, 27, and 28, in Two Brewer-row. A piece of Ground, with building thereon, forming part of the Roebuck Brewery, in the Kent-road, Southwark. An extensive range of sheep and cattle sheds and pens, with arched vaults, in Harrow-alley, Aldgate. Range of stabling, coach houses, sheds, and small tenement, in Black Horse-yard, Aldgate. A large piece of vacant ground, and 18 brick built tenements, in Seven Step-alley, Hounsditch. Two Houses, Nos. 48 and 49, Petticoat-lane, and four tenements behind, and a brick built house, No. 24, Patriot-square, Bethnal-green. Principally let on leases; the present rents and annual value amounting to near 800l. per annum. The land tax is redeemed on a large portion of the property. To be viewed by permission of the respective tenants; printed particulars will be ready for delivery 21 days prior to the sale, and may then be had of Mr. Arthur Clarke, solicitor, Bishopsgate church-yard; at the Castle, Kingston; the Yorkshire Gray, Stratford; the Angel, Ilford; the Castle Woodford; the Crown, West Smithfield; at the Mart; and of Winstanley and Sons, Paternoster-row.

CLERICAL, MEDICAL, and GENERAL LIFE ASSURANCE SOCIETY.
GEORGE PINCKARD, M.D. Chairman.
DIRECTORS.

Rev. Christopher Benson, M.A.	Hon. Jas. Cholmondeley, M.D.
Rev. James Macdonald, M.A.	James Kibblewhite, Esq.
G. G. Babington, Esq.	Samuel Merriman, M.D.
George Birkbeck, M.D.	Samuel Mills, Esq.
Robert Bree, M.D. F.R.S.	F. J. Perceval, Esq.
B. C. Brodie, Esq.	Sir George Pocock
James Carden, Esq.	Ashby Smith, M.D.
Arthur Chichester, Esq. M.P.	George Vance, Esq.

The following are among the distinguished features of this Society.

1. In addition to the general Business of granting Assurance on healthy lives, extending the benefit of Life Assurance to all classes of persons, instead of excluding those afflicted with "Gout, Asthma, Ruptures," and the other diseases usually specified.

2. A diminished Rate of Assurance, especially on the younger lives, calculated on the improved state of public health, and the increased duration of human life.

3. Giving to the assured the advantage of sharing the profits, without being exposed to any risk of loss.

4. Granting the privilege of assuring any fixed sum to become due at the time of decease, by making a single payment—by making annual payments during a limited number of years—or by annual payments of a smaller amount during the whole term of life.

5. Calculating the profits every five years, and giving to the assured the option of having them added to their policies for the benefit of their survivors, or to taking them in diminution of their annual payments of premiums for their own benefit during life.

Persons desirous of becoming Agents to this Company, in Places and Districts where Appointments have not been previously made, are requested to address their application and references to the Secretary.

J. PINCKARD, Resident Secretary.
Office, 38, Great Russell-street, Bloomsbury.

ON THE CATHOLIC QUESTION.
Published by JOHN MURRAY, of Albemarle-street.

Just published, price 6d. the Sixth Edition of
THE OBJECTS, ADVANTAGES, and PLEASURES of SCIENCE.
Being a Discourse introductory to a Series of Treatises, to be published under the superintendance and management of the Society for the Diffusion of Useful Knowledge, and intended to form
A LIBRARY OF USEFUL KNOWLEDGE.

. In these Treatises it will be endeavoured to convey, in the easiest, plainest, and most familiar manner, and at the same time in the cheapest possible form, a full and practical knowledge of the various Sciences and Useful Arts; including the Histories of Nations and of Eminent Individuals.

A full Prospectus of the plan of this work, comprising also the Rules of the Society, and the names of the present Committee, may be had, on application, through any bookseller, to Messrs. Baldwin, Cradock, and Joy, London.

‡‡ The Treatises already published are HYDROSTATICS,—HYDRAULICS,—and PNEUMATICS.

Just published, price 5s. No. I. of
THE JURIST; or, Quarterly Journal of Jurisprudence and Legislation.
Contents:—I. The Criminal Code.—II. Progress of Jurisprudence in the United States.—III. Office of Coroner.—IV. Consolidation of the Bankrupt Laws.—V. Legislative Measures in India for Restraining the Freedom of the Press.—VI. Law of Evidence.—VII. Proposed Alterations in the Courts of Common Pleas and Exchequer.—VIII. Wager of Law.—IX. French Law of Literary Property.—X. Introduction of Trial by Jury among the Natives of Ceylon.—Parliamentary Proceedings; Parliamentary Papers; Proceedings before Magistrates.
London: printed for Baldwin, Cradock, and Joy.

LIFE OF BURKE, SECOND EDITION, ENLARGED.
In 2 large vols. 8vo. price 28s.
MEMOIR of the Right Hon. EDMUND BURKE; with Specimens of his Poetry and Letters, and an Estimate of his Genius and Talents, compared with those of his great Contemporaries. By JAMES PRIOR, Esq. With Autographs, and a Portrait. The Second Edition, enlarged to 2 vols. by a variety of original Letters, Anecdotes, Papers, and other additional matter.
London: printed for Baldwin, Cradock, and Joy.

"In treating of the earlier part of Mr. Burke's career, in times which have been thrown into comparative obscurity by the interest, at once nearer and higher, of more modern events, Mr. Prior has added to the ordinary stock of public information, and has for ever established the claim of Burke to many services affecting the freedom, the laws, and the constitution of England, which had studiously been cast into the shade by his numerous revilers, or slighted and overlooked by his injudicious advocates. . . . . . On this point (Burke's private life) we are bound to commend the work of Mr. Prior, by whom the details are judiciously selected, and related with excellent feeling; many of them had been hitherto unknown to the public; and they are neither too numerous, nor too trivial to encumber the narrative of the political life, to which they give relief and interest."—Quarterly Review, No. 68.

In 2 large vols. 8vo. illustrated with original Maps, numerous Views, &c. price £2 boards.
TRAVELS in CHILE and LA PLATA, including accounts respecting the Geography, Geology, Statistics, Government, Finances, Agriculture, Commerce, Manners and Customs, and the Mining operations in Chile, collected during a residence of several years in these countries.
By JOHN MIERS.

. The long residence of the author in the countries he describes; his constant intercourse with the most influential persons, as well natives as foreigners; the business in which he was engaged, making a correct knowledge of the mining and agricultural capabilities of Chile necessary; the number of natives he employed; and his frequent journeys to different parts of the country, enabled him to collect a mass of curious and useful information, which he will be found to have used with equal impartiality and judgment. From the variety of subjects the book contains, and the way in which they are treated, it may be inferred that it will be acceptable to every

but all their efforts proving unavailing against the increasing rush of the water, they were forced to retreat towards the shaft. The instant the accident occurred, a general consternation prevailed amongst the workmen, and they simultaneously rushed towards the shaft—*sauve qui peut* was the universal sentiment, and in their hurry several ludicrous accidents took place. It is with pleasure we announce, that no life was lost on the occasion, though the engineers, and particularly Tallatt, narrowly escaped drowning. It appears that at a quarter before seven o'clock, the 12 shields, or frame-works, were in the act of being propelled forward at the end of the tunnel, to enable the workmen to excavate more securely; and at that time the tunnel extended 580 feet under the Thames. The workmen employed in propelling No. 11 and 12 shields, observed the soil to give way between these shields, and in a few seconds afterwards the water poured in through an aperture about six inches in diameter. Tallatt, the engineer, screwed up three door-ways as he retreated towards the shaft, and he was obliged to swim a considerable distance. A workman named Gutis was also in the water for some time. Tallatt being a good swimmer, remained at the top of the water, about ten feet below the top of the shaft, till Messrs. Brunel, junior, and Gravatt, came to his assistance. Mr. Brunel, junior, plunged into the water, and affixed a rope round Tallatt, and he was drawn up in a state of exhaustion to the top of the shaft. From the time the water first broke in, till the tunnel and shaft were filled to the level of the river, twelve minutes elapsed. The engineers are quite confident that they shall be able to repair the injury, and that the only consequence which will arise from it, will be the retarding of the work for about a fortnight. This day Mr. Brunel will descend in a diving bell, to ascertain the extent of the injury, and to adopt means of stopping the aperture caused by the influx of the water. Should the means proposed to be used be successful, the water in the tunnel will be drawn up, by means of steam engines in a few days.

The following is a letter, from the principal engineer, on the above subject:—

"Mr. Editor—I feel it a duty incumbent on me to make known to the public an accident which occurred this evening to the tunnel, by the water from the Thames overpowering the exertions which, at the time, could be

6 Dr. Stanley Lees Giffard, first editor of *The Standard*.

7 Duel between the Duke of Wellington and Lord Winchilsea.

8 Dr. William Maginn.

9 Alaric Watts.

10 Edward Baldwin, proprietor of *The Standard* and the *Morning Herald*.

26 PUNCH, OR THE LONDON CHARIVARI.

MRS. HARRIS'S EXPRESS.

THE fuss MRS. HARRIS is making about her one express reminds us a good deal of the cackling of the old hen over her one egg. She has been at considerable pains to show the public how she managed to accomplish this feat, probably fearing that unless it can be shown in detail how it was done, no one will believe that she ever contrived to do it.

For our own parts we are inclined to think, that, to accomplish this great achievement, there must have been some witchcraft at work, and we suspect that our engraving throws some light on the m by which the affair was carried into execution. We believe MRS. HARRIS rode over the Channel, on her umbrella, in the style in w the witches of old were accustomed to travel about across the bac their broomsticks. We shall perhaps be able, in our next, to give amusing details of the difficulties the old lady had to encounter i. course of her one exploit.

42 PUNCH, OR THE LONDON CHARIVARI.

MRS. HARRIS'S EXPRESS STOPPED BY THE "TIMES'" COURIER.

11 'Mrs. Harris's Express' (*Punch* cartoons).

12 James Johnstone, proprietor of *The Standard* (*Vanity Fair* cartoon).

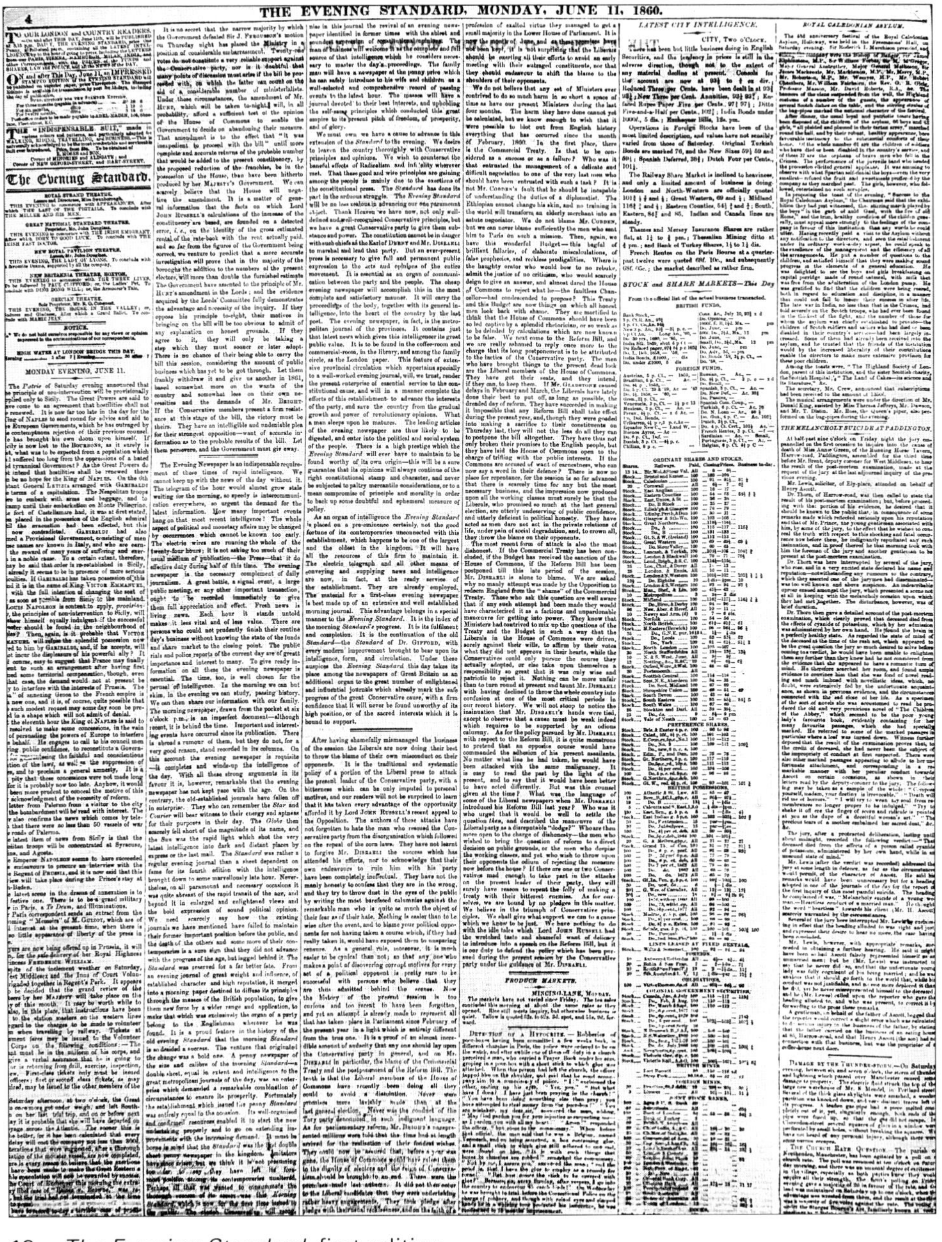

THE EVENING STANDARD, MONDAY, JUNE 11, 1860.

The Evening Standard.

MONDAY EVENING, JUNE 11.

13 *The Evening Standard*, first edition.

14 Charles Williams, first editor of *The Evening Standard*, and one of the great war correspondents.

15 'The Fight for *The Standard*' (cartoon published in *Judy, or the London Serio-Comic*, August 1870).

16 John Eldon Gorst, briefly editor of *The Standard*, architect of Conservative victory and later Solicitor-General.

17 Thomas Escott, *Standard* leader writer and confidant of Lord Randolph Churchill and Joseph Chamberlain.

18 William Mudford, editor/manager *The Standard*.

19 Advertisement hall of the new *Standard* building, St. Bride Street.

Evening Standard
Standard
DAILY SALE—242,062 COPIES
MONDAY, OCTOBER 29.
THE TROOPS IN EGYPT
FEARS RESPECTING WITHDRAWAL
CHINA AND THE TONQUIN DISPUTE
FURTHER IMPORTANT DESPATCHES
THE BRIGHTON & CHATHAM LINES
IMPORTANT WORKING AGREEMENT
M. WILSON & THE FRENCH MINISTRY
WINTER EXHIBITIONS—SPECIAL
MARRIAGE OF LADY MAUD CECIL
DEATH OF CARDINAL BONNECHOSE
FISHERIES AND RAILWAY RATES
RACING NOTES—ASMODEUS

20 *Standard* bill.

21 C. Arthur Pearson, proprietor of *The Standard*.

8

Captain Hamber Departs

The great change in the fortunes of *The Standard*'s finance through the extra circulation from its coverage of the American Civil War, and increased advertising meant that, at long last in 1863, the debts outstanding to the Conservative Party (in lieu of which it had held the mortgage on the paper's premises – three Queen Anne houses in Shoe Lane) could now be paid off. Apart from the strong involvement with Disraeli, the party whips had been in the habit of sending an almost daily quota of leader paragraphs to follow the main article; but on the day the mortgage was redeemed it was reported:

> Mr A – sent his usual communique, with the customary hint to place it after the leaders. The editor, however, was then a free man, and he was determined to assert his freedom, so he packed the pars in an envelope and returned them with the accompanying note:
> 'Dear A – I will see you hanged first!'[1]

Although the paper's debts had been paid off, and Hamber could cock a snook at the Tory whips, he was still beholden to Disraeli. His whole manner is apparent from correspondence dating back to the summer of 1862: 'I have with some difficulty written a leader in the *Herald* on the proceedings of last night ... but I should be sorry to act in any manner contrary to your views and if you would kindly drop me a line to say 'yes' or 'no' I should be gratefully obliged. I ask this favour because tomorrow is my one holiday'.[2] Four further examples of Hamber's homage to the Tory leader are evident from the following correspondence:

> October 30, 1862
> Many thanks for your correction. I have been disappointed about the leaders. I placed them in the hands of two writers: both have failed. The truth is, it is a difficulty to find men who have taken the trouble to think over a good article ...

> October 31, 1862
> I cannot restrict the impudence to offer you my sincere congratulations on your admirable speech. The expression of my individual opinion is of course not worth a great deal, but I have been about in various quarters today, and the feeling is unanimous that it is a

masterpiece of oratory, one of the most successful if not the most successful of your later efforts, and that it must so largely influence public opinion. I cannot hope to do adequate justice to it in my columns, but it may serve me as a text book for days to come, and I trust I may succeed in placing its importance before the nation.

November 4, 1862
I will answer *The Times* immediately. I should have done so before but I lack a great influx of subjects and few available hands. I thought *The Times* leaders singularly weak ... a mere erasure of the points of your speech.

April 18, 1864
I hope you will not think that I have gone too far in *The Standard.* There is horse play somewhere, and those who play with edged tools must expect to be cut. I propose to see Garibaldi tomorrow ... and if you have five minutes to spare I will come in and let you know any particulars.[3]

THE FUTURE POET LAUREATE

Two years later, in the autumn of 1866, Hamber engaged a young leader writer in the person of Alfred Austin, who in later years was to be appointed Poet Laureate. Austin wrote to the editor, with whom he had no personal acquaintanceship, asking if he could be of any use as a writer of leading articles. But, unknown to Austin, the editor was already aware of his talents, and as far back as April 1862 had instituted inquiries on Disraeli's behalf: 'From two sources, on which I can place implicit reliance, I learn that Mr Austin is a gentleman by birth and character, a law student, of independent means, addicted to literary pursuits. This is all I can glean, and I trust it will be satisfactory.'[4] The editor now replied to Austin that the author of 'The Season', a satire which had been well received in *The Athenaeum,* ought to be able to write anything, but that the leading article was a special craft in itself.

Austin has described this correspondence in his autobiography:

Would I therefore, he added, select my own subject, write a leader and send it to him? It so happened that Victor Emmanuel and Garibaldi were on the point of meeting in recently liberated Venice, and I selected that as my subject. On opening *The Standard* on the Monday following I saw my leader occupied the first place, and was 'leaded'; and this was followed by a request from the editor that I would write five leaders a fortnight, the subjects of which would be sent to me.

This was in the days when the press, like the world generally, took things more quietly than they do now; and I was able to write in the daytime and despatch by train what I wrote in time to appear in the paper of the following day. Never, I suppose, did one have so easy an entrance into journalism, and from that hour in 1866, to 1896, when I was appointed to the Laureateship, I was uniformly treated by three successive editors of *The Standard* with a consideration and generosity not a little, in my opinion, in excess of my services or my deserts.

But I think I may say I never sought to take advantage of the privileges thus extended to me, but did all that was possible for the paper within the limits of my capacity; always, however, giving the editor to understand that, while such was and would be my practice, I must be allowed to consider, in all I wrote, the interests of my country and the State.[5]

FRANCO-PRUSSIAN WAR

In the summer of 1870, tensions were high on the Continent because of the rivalry between the French Second Empire and the Prussian-dominated North German Confederation. Relations worsened when the French discovered that the Prussians were supporting the candidature of a Hohenzollern prince for the Spanish throne. On 13 July the French Ambassador met the King of Prussia at the German spa of Ems to discuss the matter. A telegram reporting the meeting was sent by the King to Otto von Bismarck in Berlin, who doctored the text, making it seem as if insults had been exchanged.[6] Upon publication in the press, national feelings were even more aroused in Paris and Berlin; and on 19 July the French declared war on Prussia.

For Hamber, after his paper's success in reporting the American Civil War, this was to present a further opportunity for *The Standard* to gain prestige and circulation. His choice as correspondent to cover the conflict was, in a sense, unexpected but perspicacious: he chose his chief leader writer, Alfred Austin.

At the outbreak of hostilities, Austin[7] had no doubt that the French would lose. His brother-in-law asserted: 'Of course, the French will go to Berlin.' 'On the contrary,' Austin replied, 'the Prussians will march to Paris.' For *The Standard* and for Austin it was to be a momentous occasion, and his despatches swiftly added to his fame. He immediately set out for Berlin and noted 'Prussian troops were being conveyed to the Seat of War along every railway line. They were in the highest spirits shouting '*Nach Paris! Nach Paris!*''

Word was passed to Bismarck at his headquarters that *The Standard* correspondent sought permission to go to the front. At once came his reply, 'Tell Mr Austin to go to the War Office, where official permission to join us will be given.' Buying a horse and hiring two attendants, Austin set off on his journey westwards. The battles around Sedan and Metz were now raging, and Austin arrived at the scene in the aftermath of a bitter French defeat. His experiences at Sedan, where he walked, notebook in hand, through the fields of the dead and the dying, left an indelible mark on his mind. For the sensitive poet that Austin was, this was a nightmare: 'I passed from Scylla to Charybdis .... '

Two days later he reached the Prussian headquarters at Rheims, and there on successive evenings talked with Bismarck.[8] On September 5, *The Standard* reported the interviews, including one where Bismarck said: 'She [France] must therefore be made harmless. *We must have Strasburg, and we must have Metz.* ... We will fight ten years sooner than not to obtain this necessary security.' The interviews created a sensation in England, and were widely reproduced in other newspapers.

With the investment of Paris about to begin, Austin made for Versailles, where he once more met up with Bismarck. 'I said to him I hoped I had given a faithful account in *The Standard,* that had been so widely copied, of the conversation he had been so good as to hold with me at Rheims. He replied that he had not read it, but that Abeken [his aide] had, and he had said it was excellent.'

For *The Times* and its famous correspondent, William Howard Russell, the much-quoted interviews had been a bitter blow. Russell had succeeded in meeting the Crown Prince who gave him an exclusive account of the private talk between the King of Prussia and Napoleon III following the latter's surrender at Sedan. Bismarck would have none of it, and through Austin authorised *The Standard* to say that the story was completely without foundation.[9] A chastened Russell confronted Bismarck with *The Standard*'s story. The Iron Chancellor dismissed him with: 'When you hear things from that dunderhead the Crown Prince you should know better.'

Apart from the hospitality shown by the Prussian Army – 'whenever I addressed myself to German officers I have been treated as one of themselves' – Austin was able to mix with the relatives of his proprietor. By one of those strange quirks of fate, Mr Johnstone had relations of his name living in Versailles, and Austin frequently dined with them on Sundays. Austin was later to say: 'How I found material for an almost daily letter to *The Standard* remains a wonder to me; for I was utterly ignorant then of military tactics and strategy'.[10] Nevertheless, he did succeed – and succeed brilliantly – with his despatches; but it was to be Austin's one and only essay into the realms of the war correspondent.

Covering the war from the French side was Richard Hely Hutchinson Bowes, who had been Paris correspondent of *The Standard* and its sister paper, *The Morning Herald*, since 1857 – a post he was to retain for more than forty years,[11] becoming the doyen of English correspondents in Paris. He had been born into the profession, and when a mere youth had begun his newspaper career by helping his father, who was at that time the editor of *Galignani's Messenger.* Though nearly all his life was spent in the French capital, he remained English to the core, and it was said of him that he was 'The most English of Parisians'.[12] He remained constantly at his post in Paris and France with only two exceptions. In 1873, he came to London to take temporary charge of the managerial department of *The Standard*, and was afterwards sent as a special correspondent to Serbia during the Turco-Serbian War. Bowes died in Paris in November 1898, aged 67, 'and his latest contribution to *The Standard*, telegraphed on the Monday night, had not been published when he breathed his last.'

Another correspondent at the front for *The Standard* was John Augustus O'Shea, who was in Metz during the Franco-Prussian War. It was there that he was sentenced to death as a spy by Marshal Bazaine. The other correspondents made a personal appeal to the Emperor, and O'Shea was released. Subsequently, he was at the siege of Paris. Born in Dublin, O'Shea had been educated at the Catholic University of Ireland, and was a medical student before becoming correspondent for the *New York Herald* in the seven-week war between Austria and Prussia during 1866. In 1868, he joined *The Standard*, and, apart from reporting the Franco-Prussian War, covered the civil war in Spain in 1873 and 1875, and later accompanied General Grant when he made his world tour. Two years later, he was in India during the famine of 1877–8. When not travelling, he was renowned in Fleet Street as a practical joker, and on one occasion, for a wager, dressed up as an Indian and rode an elephant in the Lord Mayor's Show.[13] In later years, however, he suffered from ill-health, and a subscription was raised by his friends to assist him.[14] He died at Clapham on 14 March, 1905.

Although Austin was rightly ranked as the 'star' of *The Standard*, Hamber employed other first-rate men in the field. Burton Blyth covered the Continental papers, especially in the German states. On all military matters Charles and Henry Brackenbury were acknowledged to be experts and they were aided by Colonel H. W. Knollys and Henry Hozier.

RELATIONSHIP WITH DISRAELI

While Hamber was intent on providing the best possible coverage of the Franco-Prussian War, he was still anxious to preserve his relationship with Disraeli, and in the summer of 1870 he was delighted to receive an invitation to Hughenden, Disraeli's country estate near

High Wycombe in Buckinghamshire. Three months later, on 30 October, he once more accepted a summons to Hughenden: 'I shall avail myself with real pleasure of ... your hospitable invitation. Up to the present moment I have not been able to leave here during the present crisis. But although I am far from believing that the end of the war is near I fancy that for the next three or four weeks we shall have few political events.'[15]

Although the editor was by then heavily involved in Disraeli's political machinations, it had, in many ways, been an easier year at Shoe Lane, because the decision had been taken to close down *The Morning Herald* after a life of ninety years. Both Johnstone and Hamber realised that the paper had outlived its usefulness: *The Standard* was now profitable, while *The Herald*'s sales had declined disastrously. On 31 December 1869, the paper appeared for the last time; and, in the main leader, Hamber wrote:

> And now the day has come to write the last article, and add – *Finis.* But we have the consolation of knowing that the place *The Herald* leaves vacant will be thoroughly well filled. Its *raison d'être* ceased when *The Standard* became a real power in journalism. *The Standard,* flourishing and popular, with a circulation not second to that of any paper in the kingdom, will continue to advocate those Constitutional principles which have hitherto been supplied by *The Herald* and *The Standard* in concert, and it is in a great degree with a view to devoting the individual strength of the establishment to *The Standard* that the old paper is sacrificed.[16]

Although Hamber retained this close relationship with the Tory leader – a relationship which had been further strengthened by the editor's attacks on Gladstone over the Disestablishment of the Church of Ireland Bill – there was now an undercurrent of dissatisfaction among the party's managers. It was felt that 'if the paper were to render the party services as undoubtedly were in its power, its conductor must take counsel with the party managers as well as ask for information from them.'[17] Even some of Hamber's staff were expressing uneasiness to the proprietor about the secret doubts they had long held on the paper's policy 'which chiefly consisted of charging a granite wall'. It was being instilled into James Johnstone's thoughts that while Hamber 'won cheers by the constant raising of impracticable war cries, he also had his own axes to grind'.

Hamber, however, continued to ignore any thoughts of direction or co-operation with any Conservative official from Parliament Street. Even the members of his own club, The Carlton, were astounded at his audacity, and prophesied that he would soon find he had reached the end of his tether. The time had come for editor and proprietor to part company, but it was not a task that Johnstone himself was willing to undertake. On an October morning in 1872, Johnstone's solicitor called at Hamber's home in Chiswick to indicate that his services would no longer be required. It was said that 'the dismissed editor carried off the crushing sentence with a resigned and even cheery composure'.[18] Hamber was not down for long, though, for he quickly assumed the editorship of *The Conservative Weekly Paper*, described by Thomas Escott as 'a wealthy man's organ ... fairly progressive in its features'.[19]

But the pace of editing a weekly was too slow for Hamber: he desperately missed the bustle of the daily battle, and on 7 February 1873, he wrote once more to Disraeli: 'I am as you are aware no longer connected with *The Standard*, but I have a newspaper enterprise of some magnitude on hand, with reference to which I would like very much to ask your advice on one or two points.'[20] The enterprise was *The Hour*, a morning paper, which made its first appearance on 24 March 1873. Assisting Hamber to raise the necessary capital was Morier Evans, who, as general manager of *The Standard*, had also left the newspaper: 'No more genial manager than Mr Evans ever handed a contributor a cheque. But he was a man of over-sanguine temperament'.

One of the first to join the new paper from *The Standard* was the effervescent Escott, who described it thus: 'My own services seemed superfluous in Shoe Lane. When, therefore, preparations for *The Hour*, under the Hamber–Evans duumvirate were complete, I gladly accepted the opening, and with my own pen wrote the first leader which ever appeared in the new print, as well as probably the last, with several hundreds in between.' Within a week of joining, Escott was writing to his old friend Thomas Blackwood: 'The paper has made a good start, is being generally taken up, and will, I doubt not, prove in the long run a success.' Even a month later, on 6 May, he was still hopeful: 'The success of *The Hour*, I am glad to say, is no longer problematical.'[21]

SHARP DIFFERENCES

For James Johnstone this new paper was a threat which could not be ignored. Upon Hamber's dismissal he had turned to his eldest son, James Johnstone Jnr, and John Eldon Gorst to supervise editorial affairs. Although James Johnstone Jnr was the titular editor, it was with Gorst that the real power lay. They were assisted by Burton Blyth and A. P. Sinnett, a former editor of the *Allahabad Pioneer*, and, 'esoteric Buddhism notwithstanding, a first-rate newspaper hand'. However, as a result of sharp differences between Johnstone and his son, Johnstone Jnr's tenure as editor was to be brief, lasting less than twelve months.[22]

The man who had been advising Johnstone Jnr, making up for his lack of political experience, was John Eldon Gorst, the Tory party agent, and a person destined to play a key role in Conservative politics for the remainder of the century. He now took over the editorial chair.

Born in Preston in 1835, he was educated at the local grammar school, where he edited a periodical called *The Scholar,* which was suppressed by the authorities because of its mocking spirit. From there he entered St. John's College, Cambridge, and within a few months of coming down went to Germany to learn the language. He then spent a period looking after his dying father, before setting off for New Zealand in 1859. The voyage out, like much of Gorst's early life, was adventurous. Not only was he involved in quelling a ship's mutiny but he also met his wife to-be, Mary Elizabeth Moore of Christchurch, New Zealand, and they were married in Sydney.[23]

After his marriage, he immediately became involved in New Zealand politics and was appointed by the Governor, Sir George Grey, as civil commissioner for the Waikato District. He held this post for a year, and towards the end edited a newspaper *Te Pihoihoi Mokemoke* ("The Sparrow that sits alone upon the House Top"). Gorst set up his printing office on the instructions of the Governor, who was determined to counter the arguments and complaints of the local Maori paper, *The Hokioi.* In its first issue, Gorst bitterly attacked the Maori king, declaring he deserved punishment, and exposed the lawlessness of the Waikato district. The locals were inflamed, asking: 'Why is not the press broken up and the Government officer driven away?' When the fifth issue was being printed, a party of eighty armed Maoris surrounded the newspaper office, broke in, removed the cases of type and dragged out the press; it was alleged that much of the type was melted down to make bullets. Gorst, fortunately, was out of the district that day, and Edward John von Dadelszen, a young Englishman, and later Registrar-General of New Zealand, who was printing the paper, was unharmed.[24]

With the press having been taken away by bullock drays, the rioters, under their chief, Rewi Maniapoto, now occupied the newspaper office, but, after discussions with a Revd A. Reid, agreed to withdraw. On the day after the sacking of the newspaper office, Rewi Maniapoto wrote to the Governor:

Te Awamutu, 25 March, 1863

FRIEND GOVERNOR GREY,
Greeting. This is my word to you. ... The press has been taken by me. They are my men who took it – eighty armed with guns. The reason is, to drive away Mr Gorst, that he may return to the town: it is on account of the great darkness caused by his being sent to live

> here, and tempt us; and also on account of your saying that you would dig round our King till he fell. Friend, take Mr Gorst back to town; do not leave him to live with me at Te Awamutu. If you say he is to stay, he will die. Let your letter be speedy to fetch him away within three weeks.

In Gorst's own words: 'The Governor resolved to take no notice whatever of Rewi's letter, and general instructions were sent to me that in the event of there being any danger whatever to life I was to return to Auckland with the other Europeans in the employment of the Government on the station.'

For almost a month there existed an uneasy peace, but then Gorst was approached by friendly Maori chiefs, who urged him to leave:

> They had come out of kindness, to urge us to go to Auckland at once. We had seen how Rewi treated us in time of peace; and we might judge what he would do in time of war. They begged us to go at once, and not to put off from day to day, waiting till the bad news came from Tarranaki; it would be too late to go then. Being without arms, and at the mercy of the first assailant, I had no choice but to abandon Te Awamutu. At the same time, most of the European settlers left the district.

This was written on 18 April 1863. More than forty years later, Gorst, now a distinguished politician, paid an official return visit, to find that time had long healed the differences of the past.

His appetite for adventure satisfied, Gorst returned to England and was called to the Bar at the Inner Temple in 1865. After standing unsuccessfully for Parliament in Hastings in 1866, he was returned for Cambridge and during the next two years attracted the attention of Disraeli. He lost his seat, however, in 1868, and was then asked to reorganise the Conservative Party on a popular basis. He devoted the following five years to this task, and the Conservative victory of 1874 owed much to his efforts. Gorst expected office in the administration of that year, but was disappointed, and his relations with the party leaders, with the exception of Disraeli, were from that time somewhat strained. It was during this period that he became heavily involved with *The Standard.*

But Gorst's reign as editor of the newspaper was also brief, Johnstone soon realised that Gorst was yet another editor who was to a large degree intent on ignoring his proprietor's wishes. Certainly, Gorst's criticisms of Conservative colonial policy seriously undermined the proprietor's position. He was also involved with differences over his leader writers, of whom Alfred Austin was the most vociferous. Much later, Austin was to comment upon those years:

I could not help feeling that *The Standard*, when I first wrote for it in the autumn of 1866, and for some little time onward, was under the reign of King Log. It is not surprising, therefore, that the proprietor of the paper, as journalistic competition became keener and more strenuous, grew dissatisfied with such easy-going management. This dissatisfaction ended by the editor receiving notice that his services were to be dispensed with, and by the proprietor's eldest son being appointed as his successor. Not from any neglect or incapacity on the part of the new editor, though probably his not having been familiar previously with journalistic experience was a grave disadvantage to him, but for strictly family reasons, the arrangement was of brief duration, the office being conferred for a time on a man [Gorst], dead for many years, who, though, not without practical capacity, was a 'pig-headed Tory' – for there are always such persons – of an extreme kind. It was only necessary for a Party or a policy whether at home or abroad to be called Conservative for him to defend it through thick and thin – a course that has never recommended itself to me.

A glaring instance arose when he lent the strongest support to the Duc de Brogile and Marshal MacMahon [during the first decade of the Third French Republic]: this seemed to be fatuous, since not only was it based on a misnomer, but was certain to end, as it did, in utter failure. Accordingly I refused to write in that sense. Thereupon, though I had been only passive, the proprietor interfered, and quite irrespectively of any opinion of his own, told the editor that my view must be acted on. He bowed to his decision and nothing further occurred.[25]

The change in the gathering of overseas news, now meant that the more leisurely days of the leader writer were about to come to an end: As Austin noted:

Meanwhile, the substitution of telegraphic for postal correspondence from abroad, and the necessity of despatching copies of the paper into the provinces by earlier morning trains, had rendered the conditions less easy and agreeable to its contributors; and, though I was still treated with kindly and privileged consideration, it became necessary for me, every now and again, to go to London late in the evening, and spend the night there, in order to write a leader on the Continental news arriving from hour to hour. This condition was perfectly reasonable and I accepted without demur. For a considerable time I had remained sceptical concerning the influence of the press, but, by degrees, I felt forced to modify that view. This gave me much more interest in journalistic work, while subordinating it to my interest in literature, and most of all in poetry.

STRENGTH TO STRENGTH

As for *The Standard,* the paper was now going from strength to strength; and on 14 February 1874, its success was noted by *Vanity Fair,* when James Johnstone was accorded the honour of being featured in its gallery of 'Men Of The Day'. The coloured lithograph caricature by 'Ape' (Carlo Pellegrini) is simply entitled *The Standard,* and shows the proprietor, paper in hand, pointing to the average daily sale of 185,276 copies. On the reverse of the cartoon is a detailed account of Johnstone's prosperity, written by Thomas Gibson Bowles, the editor/ owner of *Vanity Fair.*

> Many years ago a young man succeeded to his father in a lucrative appointment in the Court of Bankruptcy. He was active and energetic beyond anything that had ever been known in sleepy judicial records; and having at first simply been 'young James' he soon earned for himself the title of 'perpetual motion'. Nothing seemed to suffice to fill his time. Warned by the example of his father who was an advanced Liberal, he became a thorough-paced Tory and 'no-Popery' man, and he was so keen on politics that having made a few small savings he invested them in the purchase of land for the sole object of acquiring thereby a vote.
>
> Soon he became a member of a firm of City accountants, and occupied himself in the preparation and manipulation of figures. In 1857 there came upon the market the decayed and apparently hopeless property of *The Morning Herald* and *The Standard,* and Mr Johnstone bought them for the comparatively small sum of £16,500 in the determination to create what then did not exist, a Tory power in journalism. For such an attempt the times were anything but propitious, nor did it seem possible that any amount of energy could make either of the two journals a commercial success. Mr Johnstone, however, soon effected the double revolution in *The Standard* of increasing its size and reducing its price to one penny.
>
> The circulation of it was then little over 700 and the move was a bold one, nor did it seem at all likely to succeed for many years or so until a vast capital had been sunk. The fate of the journal hung long in the balance. Mr Johnstone poured into it the whole of his fortune, the Party it supported lent a sum of money on mortgage, and the whole of the available resources seemed exhausted to scarcely any effect when the question arose of the abolition of the Paper Duty. This was a vital change for a Penny Paper, yet Mr Johnstone true to his Party opposed it with all the force of *The Standard,* got up a petition of 6,000 citizens against it in forty-eight hours, and when it was effected reaped the advantage of the measure without having compromised himself by advocating it.

The American War of Secession brought him in 'Manhattan' a correspondent whose writing first called serious attention to *The Standard*, and in 1863 matters began so much to mend with it that the daily circulation reached fifty thousand. By the end of 1864 it had further increased to sixty thousand, in 1866 it was eighty thousand, and in 1869 Mr Johnstone, who hitherto had not drawn a farthing from the property, began to experience the sweets of profit.

Last year was a critical one for the *The Standard*. Some of those who held themselves to be the best of its staff seceded to found a rival journal, but this instead of injuring has in its result greatly benefited the paper, while the Conservative reaction has also so far aided it that the number of copies printed weekly now exceeds a million. Mr Johnstone has long ago paid off all the loans he had contracted, he is the sole proprietor of the journal and his profits from it are very large.

END OF *THE HOUR*

While *The Standard* had been undergoing its changes of editorship, it was realised that *The Hour* was now no longer a serious rival. Its first flush of success had long disappeared, and in January 1874 Escott was complaining to the ever-patient Thomas Blackwood of the insolvency of Morier Evans, a main subscriber: 'He deceived both Hamber and myself as to the amt. of capital he had to support it.'[26]

For Hamber, it was to be a spring of hardship, and he now realised that his remaining 'capital was insufficient to the enormous outlay incidental to the conduct of a London daily paper'. Once more he turned to his old friend, Disraeli, and on 18 May sought

> support of the proposal I have to submit to you ... a well-known banker had offered a sufficient sum ... provided the hint be given to him from good quarters that the work ... will be regarded by the heads of the party. You know the circumstances of *The Hour*. I think it is doing good work. ... Unfortunately our capital is insufficient. A word from you, however, indirectly given, would suffice. Am I asking too much in soliciting that word?

As Prime Minister, it was not Disraeli's intention to be associated with failure: Hamber was a spent force; Disraeli therefore did nothing. The finances of Hamber were desperate, and he was fighting a daily battle to pay the printer's bill. He possessed 'many of the qualities which make a born leader of men, or half-a-dozen times his printers in the composing room at Clerkenwell where the paper was set up would have stopped short their work, rent him to pieces and abruptly discontinued the journal'. His friends began to rally round, and, as Escott noted: 'I remember to this day a gallant officer of the Indian Horse, who had heard of our difficulties, after a good night's whist in the Junior, driving down in the small hours to the Clerkenwell office and producing a bag of notes and gold for Hamber to pay his men.'[27]

However, with all the help from his friends spent, and rejection from Disraeli, there was only one person left to whom Hamber could turn. On 17 September 1875, he wrote to his long-time companion of Oxford days and on *The Standard,* Lord Salisbury:

> *The Hour* has failed. It has not sufficient capital, it is in the wrong hands. Even if it survives occasional crises, it can never be of service to the party or a credit to London journalism under its present regime. I find myself, having given up the best part of my life to Conservative journalism, powerless as to the future, yet full of power and the will to work.

Nevertheless, the paper struggled on for almost another twelve months until, in August 1876, Disraeli 'heard with a pang that *The Hour* was no more'.

It was not, however, the end of Hamber's adventures in Fleet Street; in January 1877 he replaced N. de la Fleuriere as editor of the *Morning Advertiser,* 'at a salary of £800 a year soon raised to £1000'. But within five years Hamber's financial position was causing concern and he was given a short leave of absence to sort out his affairs. Declared bankrupt on 25 July 1882, he wrote to Salisbury in great distress: 'today I have been arrested and am in custody'. As a token of their long acquaintanceship, Salisbury forwarded £100. Hamber returned to edit the *Morning Advertiser,* but 'the proprietors claimed that his private affairs were bringing the paper into disrepute, and in November 1886 he was dismissed with three months' salary'.[28]

On 21 February 1890, William Mudford, the editor of *The Standard,* was asked by Salisbury for information about the 'late' Captain Hamber. 'He was alive six weeks ago and I have not heard of his death,' Mudford replied, 'I do not know anything of the son. I knew a good deal of the father twenty years ago, but your enquiry does not refer to him. I will just add, I am glad it does not.'[29] Hamber, though, was not dead, for having purchased the weekly *Licensed Victuallers' Guardian* for £125 in 1887, the following September he changed its name to the *Weekly Advertiser.* In May 1889 the paper ceased publication, and after this Hamber became a freelance writer for a number of newspapers until his death on 8 April 1902 at Mortlake, Surrey.

9

Mudford Takes Over

Following the differences with his son, and Gorst's dismissal, James Johnstone now decided that *The Standard* needed an experienced newspaperman as editor. He first looked to W. D. Williams, the chief reporter, but, upon discovering that Williams was a Catholic, dismissed him. After trying several others without success, he wrote to Mr Mould, who headed the paper's parliamentary staff of twelve journalists, and offered him the post. Mould, an unambitious person of middle age, felt unwilling to take on the responsibility, and eventually suggested W. H. Mudford, whom Johnstone duly appointed as editor in 1874.[1]

William Heseltine Mudford was, undoubtedly, one of the great editors of the nineteenth century, being full of courage, energy and firmness of purpose. He exercised absolute control over each department, and among his first moves were the improvement of the foreign news service, and the introduction of headed articles as well as occasional leaders from writers not on the staff. In some ways, the appointment of Mudford had been a strange choice, because during the time he was on the parliamentary reporting staff, he was singularly reserved and spoke to very few people. It was said that he always reached the House of Commons gallery just before his appointed time, took his turn – generally half an hour in those days – invariably wrote his copy alone, inquired about his next turn, and left the gallery.

An expert and accurate writer of Gurney's shorthand system, his copy was turned out more quickly than that of any other member of *The Standard*'s parliamentary corps. His facility with shorthand seemed to make him impatient with longhand, however, so that his ordinary writing was almost undecipherable. One day, a compositor went to him from the printer to say that no one in the composing room could read his copy and would he please write more plainly. His answer was: 'Please tell Mr Bentley it is my business to write the copy and his to read it.'[2]

Mudford started his newspaper career on his father's paper in Kent, and it was while acting as local correspondent for *The Standard* that he made 'the hit' which brought him to Shoe Lane. A celebrated politician of the period was making a speech at Maidstone. The special staff from *The Standard* missed the train, so the editor was compelled to telegraph to the local correspondent with instructions 'to do his best'. Mudford obliged with a tightly-written piece of three-quarters of a column, which was deemed more readable than the verbatim account in *The Times*.[3] He came to London when *The Standard* 'was in the hollow of the wave', and as a contributor took the keenest interest in all phases and aspects of town life. It was said that no one at the time had a keener enjoyment of society or a larger circle of friends.

But with his appointment as editor there came a distinct change in his manner. It was the high-time of dining out but, while the editors of the rival papers were seen everywhere, Mudford remained aloof. 'He was not to be seen at a dinner party, a reception or any social entertainment; he refused all the invitations which at one time were freely offered. He sent his envoys to Secretaries of State and Under-Secretaries to learn their views. Sometimes he wrote to Lord Salisbury, the Duke of Devonshire and other statesmen, but he avoided making their acquaintance.'

The Times said of him: 'He carried out the same system in his office. Amid the turmoil of conducting the business of a great newspaper, he lived like a recluse. He was a kind of Chinese Emperor, Japanese Mikado in Shoe Lane.'[4] Leader writers, in later times, could recall that they had worked for years at *The Standard* office without ever seeing his face. His instructions would be conveyed either by one of his close associates or by letter. Those memos in his own awful writing, based on Gurney's shorthand, were characteristic; and to decipher them was 'like reading a corrupt Greek text'. It was even said that one old-established and much-trusted correspondent used to cut the manuscript into pieces and set the members of his family to work out the fragments.

Mudford was an excellent judge of men, and he surrounded himself with a highly efficient staff. George Byron Curtis and A. Venables became very capable and dependable assistant editors, and S. H. Jeyes was not only an accomplished scholar but also a good critic and a man of the world. However, within a few weeks of being appointed, Mudford's tenure almost ended. A leader had appeared in the paper discussing a law suit affecting Baron Albert Grant, one-time newspaper proprietor and one of the greatest financial 'entrepeneurs' of the nineteenth century. Grant considered the editorial comment to be libellous and demanded a public apology. Mudford contended that the leader was not libellous, and, even if it were, the paper ought to contest Grant's claim. Johnstone, laid up at the time with a serious illness, consulted his solicitor, and as a result ordered the editor to apologise. The solicitor wrote out the apology, which the proprietor submitted to Mudford for editorial revision. Mudford, acknowledging the fact that the proprietor had supreme control, gave way and published the apology – but immediately resigned, as he completely disagreed with the course taken. Johnstone appealed to Mudford to reconsider his resignation, and after a long correspondence he finally returned to the editorial chair.

SINGULARLY OUTSPOKEN

The Standard was now about to become the favourite of the City, although its singularly outspoken and instructive criticism of financial affairs was not always to the taste of the Stock Exchange. Its London circulation among the merchant, professional and cultured classes was soon to be larger than any of its penny contemporaries – and under its new editor the paper was to represent the more severe and more businesslike element, but always allied with political opportunism. There was also a growing relationship between proprietor and editor, but unfortunately, with Johnstone still desperately ill, this was not to last, and on 22 October 1878, the paper announced the death of its proprietor:

> **Mr James Johnstone**
>
> With deep regret we have to announce the death yesterday at Hooley House, Coulsdon, of Mr James Johnstone, who had been for more than twenty years sole proprietor of this journal. ... Owing to various reasons which need not here be specified *The Morning Herald* and *Evening Standard* had, before passing into his hands, sunk almost to the very lowest ebb. Mr Johnstone purchased them, having in mind a very definite view which he steadfastly pursued to the end. His desire was to found a Conservative newspaper, in the largest sense of the term. ... Mr Johnstone's private character can hardly be spoken of impartially by his friends in a journal which remains in the possession of his family. ... It was a manly, strenuous energetic and influential life that came to its close yesterday.

Within a matter of weeks, the future of the paper was revealed in Johnstone's will; apart from substantial legacies to his wife and children, there was one important clause: 'By a codicil of the will the testator directs that Mr Mudford is to remain as editor of *The Standard* for his lifetime or until such time as he shall voluntarily resign the editorship; and further directs that the paper is to be carried on in every respect as it was at the time of his death.'

To be awarded complete editorial and managerial freedom of *The Standard* for life at a salary of £5,000 per year was one of the most extraordinary acts of faith in nineteenth-century journalism – and indeed there can be few other examples in the British press of one man being granted such absolute power over a national newspaper. Even so, one of Mudford's first acts upon assuming overall control was to approach Austin, his chief leader writer, and offer him the editorship of *The Standard*.[5] Austin has left a detailed account of the interview:

> But in 1878 an entire revolution took place in the conduct of the paper, the offices of both editor and manager being conferred for life on Mr W. H. Mudford. ... No sooner was he appointed than he sought a personal interview with me, and ... hinted that, if I would accept, I could be appointed editor of the paper under his general management at a salary more than double, I believe, of that enjoyed at the time by the editor of any other daily paper. In order to preclude the possibility of the suggestion being entertained by him, I said, in the friendliest manner, that an offer ten times the sum suggested would never induce me to give up my country life.
>
> He then asked me if I should object to having a telegraphic wire to Swinford, to place me in connection with Ashford and so with London, in order that he might communicate to me about five o'clock in the evening the latest news to serve for the subject of a leader for the following day. The rent of the telegraphic wire would be defrayed by the paper; and, knowing that I wrote with exceptional rapidity, he assumed I should have no difficulty in dispatching it from Ashford by train at a little after eight o'clock. The number of leaders he engaged to accept per week was named; and he added that a yearly holiday of five consecutive weeks would be at my disposal, without any deduction from the regular honorarium.

Mudford's suggestion of installing a telegraphic wire to Austin's home in Kent was an interesting innovation, for the use of the telegraph was very much in its infancy. Mudford was a keen supporter of the new medium, however, and used it for regular communication between his home and *The Standard* office. It was said that he 'evinced no liking for life in Shoe Lane'. Half an hour at most generally covered his attendance at the office in later days.[6] The remainder of his work was done by messengers from his house or by telephone messages to his deputies, Byron Curtis and Samuel Jeyes.

It was at this time, too – April 1879 – that Mudford made contact with John MacDonald, manager of *The Times*, to share the costs of the newly-introduced weather forecasts from the Meteorological Office. MacDonald, in rejecting the request, wrote:

> But it is only fair to the Meteorological Council to state that the observations on which the 6 p.m. report is founded are at present far from being complete as they should be; and that they think that the application of another newspaper to publish which *The Times* now had exclusively a good opportunity for selling weather telegrams on a wider area by increased outlay to which of course you would be expected to contribute.[7]

There was also during this period a steady exchange of letters regarding the employment of staff on the two papers, and the giving of references. Mudford, however, on occasion, was not averse to using *Times* personnel without MacDonald knowing; and during the 1880s a distinguished leader writer from that paper occasionally furnished *The Standard*, 'to oblige his friend, W. H. Mudford', with an article on a subject he had made his speciality – Balkan politics. On one occasion, both papers published on the same day articles from the same writer on an identical subject, but they were so skilfully treated and from different points of view that it was impossible for the identity of the author to be suspected. An outsider, in comparing the two leaders, said to Mudford that whatever appeared in *The Times* must be superior to anything in a paper 'price one penny'. Mudford remarked: 'Strange such difference there should be 'twixt tweedledum and tweedledee, and all the stranger because this particular tweedledum and tweedledee were both written by the same man.'

WONDER AND IRRITATION

One of the key members of Mudford's staff at this time was Francis Bowater,[8] who had joined the paper in 1859, and who was to complete fifty years' service as the editor of the estate market reports for *The Standard*. Known as 'Bo' to everyone, he was a well-known figure in the City and was responsible for obtaining thousands of pounds' worth of advertising for the paper. The top hat that he invariably wore was a source of wonder and irritation to all who worked on the paper, and, in later years, in answer to his young critics, he would take it off and reply: 'That hat, my sons, is historic. It knits the Victorian and Edwardian regimes, has been present at the rise and fall of ministries, saluted beautiful women and reflected the art of many Royal Academy shows. Its predecessor adorned my head from AD 1851 to 1881. When Disraeli fell, it succumbed also. A good, nay, sirs, a great, faithful and a loyal topper.'

By the end of the decade, Mudford was sure enough of *The Standard*'s success – sales were nearing 200,000 copies – to show a certain independence with his own party. Added to this, of course, was a fierce pride in his paper; and an example of this was provided when, on 16 April 1879, he wrote to Rowland Winn, Lord of The Treasury in Disraeli's government, and ensured that the Prime Minister received a copy:[9]

Dear Sir,

My attention has just been drawn to the report of you at Wakefield on Tuesday night in which you are made to say that the articles recently in *The Standard* have been a 'perfect disgrace' to it. Will you kindly inform me whether this report which appeared in *The Sheffield Telegraph* of yesterday is correct?

Your opinion about the articles in *The Standard* is of course a matter of complete indifference to me, if I am to understand that it was expressed merely in your private conversation. But if you were speaking as a member of the Government it would be a different matter, and I should feel bound to offer certain observations on your speech in an early issue of my paper. I must add that in that case I should also have to consider whether I should not ask the committee of the Carlton Club to consider my recent election to it, especially as you did me the honour of seconding my nomination to the Club.

In the event, Mudford's honour must have been satisfied, for he did not resign from the Carlton; and, although not a great club man, it did provide for him, on the odd occasion, a useful meeting place for discussion with Conservative politicians. Another, and perhaps more cutting example of Mudford's pride and his insistence on privacy, occurred almost twelve months later, on 19 February 1880, in his reply to Lord Salisbury at the Foreign Office:

The Editor of *The Standard* asks permission to return the enclosed telegram (just received from his assistant manager) which has been addressed to *The Standard* by Lord Salisbury's House Steward. The Editor of *The Standard* may, perhaps, be allowed to add that he is not much in the habit of receiving telegraphic instructions from House Stewards; not even when they are in the Household of the Secretary of State for Foreign Affairs.[10]

Mudford was now a well-known figure in press circles on both sides of the Atlantic. On 26 August 1880, *The Nation*, published in New York, announced:

That *The Standard* under Mudford qualified as the only distinctly and professedly Conservative journal among the morning news of London. But this did not deter it from showing a certain independence with regard to its own party ... much fairness of mind in relation to its opponents, the source of a standing quarrel between it and the leaders of successive Conservative governments.

Even Gladstone, as leader of the Liberals, would have endorsed those remarks, for following *The Standard*'s coverage of the election that year he remarked that it was a paper he always liked to read because he always found it to be fair and honest: 'When I read a bad leader in *The Standard*, I say to myself Mr Mudford must be taking a holiday.' Mudford, of course, would have been pleased with Gladstone's remarks, but in no way would he have allowed them to sway his judgement.

CAUSTIC COMMENTS

Apart from Austin, who continued for much of the time to lead his country existence, and was seemingly above criticism, the other leader writers often suffered the editor's caustic comments. To Escott, who had recently rejoined the paper following the demise of *The Hour*, Mudford wrote: 'I think you had better rest a day or two. Your Friday's leader was hardly up to yr. mark & the one last night must fall under the same criticism.' On another occasion, he remonstrated: 'You're too much of a Radical to write my political leaders. I love the H. of Lords – you loathe it.'[11] T. E. Kebbel, a long-serving writer, was another who had been reproached by the editor, although he described him as 'a kind-hearted man – nay a warm-hearted man – in reality, though his manner was often cold and a trifle constrained, arising, I often thought, from nervousness rather than from any want of real sympathy.'[12]

As well as the leader writers, there was, of course, a highly-skilled editorial team. Mudford found little difficulty in attracting people of the right calibre to such a prosperous newspaper. Many of the journalists were new to *The Standard*, as one of Mudford's first acts upon assuming the editorship had been to dismiss most of the existing staff.

Under his old mentor, Mould, the parliamentary team of a dozen people was well admired and reckoned second only to *The Times*. Most of the morning dailies furnished their readers with 'no more than a snippety and very unsatisfactory account of parliamentary work, but *The Standard* report, without effecting a descriptive style, is always thorough and accurate. The same may be said of its accounts of political speeches on both sides'.

The paper was now accepted for the depth of its City reporting, and leading the team was A. J. Wilson, a strong free trader, who had previously been associated with *The Times*. On the scientific side there was Dr Robert Brown, a well-known traveller and explorer. Hely Bowes, in Paris, led the foreign staff; and other correspondents included Dr Abel (in Berlin); Dr Waldeck; J. Baddely; F. J. Scudamore and E. A Bradford, of the *New York Times*, who was the cable correspondent in the United States. In building up his team, Mudford declared that there was no European capital where *The Standard* was not represented by its own correspondents, and no expense was to be spared in the transmission of news or opinions. As examples, he paid more than £1,000 to have details of the bombardment of Alexandria telegraphed from Egypt, a further £800 for one cable despatched during the Afghan War, and his news during the war in Transvaal was sent regardless of the cost of eight shillings a word.

But it was to the United States that he determined to have a regular cable line. Previously, *The Times* had been the only paper with its own cable correspondent, in Philadelphia, but its despatches were often meagre. In the summer of 1881, therefore, Joseph Hatton,[13] London correspondent of the *New York Times*, was invited by Mudford to 'add a new wire to the telegraphic bureau, so that *The Standard* was in direct communication with New York and through New York with all the cities of the Republic'. Hatton's mission was a success from the start, and almost immediately he had a magnificent scoop: the assassination of President Garfield. The despatch was more than five columns long and was the longest message ever sent through the cable.

Even before the event, on 25 June, *Harper's Weekly* in New York had commented on the new service: 'American travellers in Europe know what it is to take up a London daily paper and find the news of the United States compressed into a few lines, and packed away in an obscure corner. This Transatlantic irritation is to be terminated by the enterprise of Mr Mudford, the broad-minded editor of *The Standard*.'

An English point of view was given by *The Liverpool Mail* on 16 July:

> It must be admitted, however, that *The Standard* beat all its contemporaries in its accounts of the attack on President Garfield. The journal was exceptionally fortunate. It so happened that Mr Joseph Hatton, a gentleman whose energy and ability as a journalist is quite American in its character, had gone out to the States on various literary missions, and among the rest to 'work the wires' for *The Standard*. He could not have gone at a more opportune moment, and hence the mass of interesting anecdotal and incidental matter which our contemporary was able to secure on the day after the attempt.

By the early 1880s, *The Standard* was once more a power in the land, with a circulation in excess of 240,000 copies daily, and the newly-built offices in St. Bride Street fully reflected this importance. The new premises consisted of a four-storey building with a magnificent advertisement hall demonstrating all the grandeur of Victorian enterprise. It could say of itself in the *Newspaper Press Directory*:

> While maintaining Conservative principles, *The Standard* reserves to itself the right to apply the principles to the questions of the day, without regard to party politics, or special devotion to the view of party leaders. The paper has of late paid great attention to foreign correspondents from all parts of the world; more particularly as is

> forwarded by telegraph. ... In literary and dramatic criticism it exercises a careful selection of productions worthy of notice for praise or blame; but the complete display of home and foreign news is its chief distinguishing feature. Reports regarding markets, racing, cricket and boating are very fully given.

To provide for this greatly-increased service, the production facilities had been enhanced, and the paper was now printed on eight presses, seven of which ran at the rate of 14,000 copies per hour. There were also six machines in reserve in another building [the old *Daily Telegraph* site] and a separate font of type was stored there, so that if an accident happened at the offices in St. Bride Street the whole paper could be composed and printed in Shoe Lane at the rate of 12,000 copies per hour. L. W. Massingham reported at the time:

> The number of hands employed on the morning edition is sixty-three; on the evening edition twenty-six – a total of eighty-nine. The formes for the morning edition go down to the foundry at intervals commencing from 12 o'clock midnight, the last forme, with the Parliamentary or other important intelligence, being received in the foundry at 2.30 to 3 o'clock. The eight plates are all produced and handed to the machine room in thirty-three minutes.
>
> The *Evening Standard* is published in four separate editions, the number of plates that are required varying according to the news received. The *Morning Standard* is printed in one hour and fifty minutes, and the *Evening Standard* second edition in fifteen minutes, the third edition in thirty minutes, the fourth edition in twenty minutes and the special edition in forty-five minutes.
>
> The duplicate plant of machinery for use in case of accident, by fire or otherwise, is being replaced at the present time by machinery made and patented by Mr Joseph Foster, of Preston, Lancashire. The new machine is called the Standard Web Printing Machine and is only twelve feet six inches long, occupying half as much space as the other web machines. Its height is five feet six inches and the width being the same as the other machines, plates cast for the Hoe machines will fit on the new machines as well.
>
> The collecting motion of these new machines is arranged by a 'tape race', without guides or switches, and flies six sheets at one time and seven at another, which repeated is a London quire, viz, twenty-six, and the fly-board moves in such a manner as to separate each quire. The machines are constructed so as to print 14,500 per hour, netting 12,500 copies, and do not require so much steam-power for working as other web machines, the friction of the machinery being less.

The paper used on either plant of machinery is prepared on wetting machines, invented and patented by the firm, two machines being placed in each building. The amount of paper used during the year 1880 for *The Standard* was 3,412 tons, equal to a length of 36,609 miles, and for the *Evening Standard* 855 tons, equal to a length of 13,377 miles, the two quantities making a total of 4,277 tons or 49,986 miles of paper, an average of over thirteen tons, or 160 miles per day.[14]

Thomas Escott had his own views on *The Standard*'s costs:

Let us take the case of one of the leading penny papers of the metropolis. Here is a journal whose annual total expenditure is from £260,000 to £270,000 a year and whose average annual profit is from £55,000 to £60,000. If these figures are respectively divided by 313 – the number of working days in a year – we shall have the daily expenditure and profit of a London paper sold for the twelfth part of a shilling. It will then be found that the expenses per diem of such a paper amount, roughly speaking, to £860, and that the daily profit is close to £200.

James Grant, a one-time *Standard* man, also gave a vivid account of production at Shoe Lane in his book, *The Newspaper Press*:

I doubt if there be a human being in the world who has to perform such hard work as the Publisher of a daily paper during the time the publication of the journal lasts. He is, during that time, in a perfect agony of excitement and labour: in the coldest days of winter you may see him all over with perspiration, his face flushed and everything about him showing how great his mental and physical efforts are to get through his work with all the expedition which the clamours of his customers call for.

Scores of newsboys are in the publishing department, each struggling and calling with deafening noise for the number of the day's impressions which he requires. This would be confusing enough for any publisher to hear, but the confusion is 'worse confounded' by the uproar which is caused by the larking which goes on among the newsboys who are waiting. No description could give an adequate idea of what the scenes are which are seen, morning and evening, on the publication of a daily paper.

And any person who is anxious to see the publication of one, without getting up at half-past five in the morning to witness it, will be furnished with a very good idea of the thing, if he places himself any evening about seven o'clock at the door of the *Evening Standard* office, in Shoe Lane, when the Special Edition of that journal is in the course of publication.

SPECIAL CORRESPONDENTS

During Mudford's editorship, he was fortunate that he could rely on first-class special correspondents in the field – G. A. Henty is a classic case. In 1871, the Earl of Stanhope, at a meeting of the Royal Literary Fund, when discussing the Franco-Prussian War, had declared:

> I cannot help thinking that in the past year there is something in addition which calls for particular observation. I allude to the services of the special correspondent at the seat of the recent war. ... From the correspondents of the London Daily Press in an especial manner I think it impossible to withold the highest need of our admiration for the eminent literary talent, the courage and indefatigable energy which they displayed during the late war.

Not all correspondents, however, lived up to those words; and one in particular, Hector Macpherson, when covering the Second Afghanistan War in 1879 was to incur the wrath of General Sir Frederick Roberts and bring shame to *The Standard.* Unlike Sir Garnet Wolseley in the Ashanti campaign, Roberts was a firm believer in consultation and considered that correspondents should have every opportunity to render full and faithful accounts of the army. Indeed, as he later wrote: 'I took special pains from the first to hear the correspondents with confidence, and gave them such information as it was in my power to afford. All I required from them in return was that the operations should be truthfully reported.'[15]

Unfortunately, *The Standard* was in trouble for publishing a report of an incident that occurred on 7 January 1879. Afghans were discovered attempting to creep into General Roberts's camp and 'at the sound of the first shot, the prisoners all jumped to their feet, and calling to each other to escape attempted to seize the rifles belonging to the Guard'.[16] Following a warning, which was ignored, the duty officer ordered his men to open fire. Six prisoners were killed and thirteen wounded. Macpherson, however, reported that ninety prisoners tied together with ropes had been slaughtered, and the report caused a storm in Parliament.

This was not the first time that Macpherson had abused Roberts's good nature. Thus Roberts noted that: 'Judging from his [Macpherson's] telegrams, which he brought me to sign, the nerves of the Correspondent in question must have been somewhat shaken by the few and very distant shots fired at us on November 28. These

Telegrams being in many instances absolutely incorrect and of the most alarming nature were not of course allowed to be despatched until they were revised in accordance with the truth'.

It seems that Macpherson, having been discovered altering a telegram after Roberts had countersigned the despatch, had been brought before the commander and had promised not to do it again. But the prisoner episode had seemed too good an opportunity to miss, and Macpherson despatched a telegram to *The Standard* without Roberts's approval. It was not until copies of the newspaper arrived back in Kurram that Roberts became aware of what Macpherson had done. Incensed by what he deemed to be a betrayal of trust, Roberts commented: 'I felt it to be my duty to send the too imaginative author to the rear. What to my mind was so reprehensible in the correspondent's conduct was the publication in time of war, and consequent excitement and anxiety at home, of incorrect and sensational statements, founded on information derived from irresponsible and uninformed sources'. But, despite these strictures, *The Standard* man was still able to get his messages through, much to the satisfaction of the Prime Minister, Benjamin Disraeli (now Lord Beaconsfield). Thus, on 11 May 1879, Beaconsfield confided to Lady Chesterfield: 'The Afghan news is very good and I credit it; but, strange to say, the Government has not yet received any telegram confirming it. But we cannot compete with *The Standard* newspaper which does not hesitate to expend £500 on a telegram.'[17]

While Roberts was engaged in his campaign in Afghanistan, the harassed Tory government became involved in another war in South Africa. Since the beginning of the century, the Zulu nation had become a formidable military power, led by its warrior kings. Now, under Cetewayo, the Zulus menaced the Boer republic of Transvaal, which turned to Britain for help. On 12 January 1879, a British force, led by Lord Chelmsford, invaded Zululand, and with the main column rode *The Standard*'s man, Charles L. Norris-Newman, a former army captain known affectionately as 'Noggs'. He was the only English correspondent in Natal and claimed to be the first white man to cross the river into Zululand. Norris-Newman's account of the aftermath of the massacre at Isandhlwana, in which more than 1,300 British troops perished, was particularly poignant:

> We began to stumble over dead bodies in every direction, and in some places the men were found lying thick and close as though they had fought till their ammunition was exhausted and then been surrounded and slaughtered. How that terrible night passed with us I fancy few would care to tell even if they could recall it. During the night we noticed fires constantly burning on all the surrounding hills and in particular one bright blaze riveted our attention

> throughout as it seemed to be near Rorke's Drift, and we feared for the safety of those left in that small place, knowing how utterly powerless we were to aid them in any way before morning.[18]

Without waiting to bury the dead, Chelmsford's force, finding the British force at Rorke's Drift still intact, retreated into Natal, and from there the commander immediately despatched a telegram informing London of the disaster. Accompanied by Norris-Newman's chilling account, Chelmsford's report was put aboard the *Dunrobin Castle* sailing for England, and from the Cape Verde Islands, the ship's first port of call, it was sent by cable to London, arriving on 11 February. For *The Standard* and its correspondent it was a great triumph.

Less than two months later, Chelmsford returned to Zululand, and one of his first tasks was to relieve the besieged town of Eshowe. A member of the garrison later wrote in *Blackwood's Magazine* the following account of the arrival of Chelmsford's force, in which Norris-Newman was prominently mentioned:

> On the afternoon of April 3rd, the column ... left the fort under General Pearson to meet the relief column. ... A solitary horseman was seen towards 5 p.m. galloping up the new road to the fort. He had an officer's coat on, and we could see a sword dangling from his side. Who is he? He proved to be the correspondent of *The Standard* ... a second horseman appeared, approaches the fort, his horse apparently much blown. Who is he? ... The Correspondent of *The Argus* (Cape Town). They had a race who would be first at Eshow, *The Standard* winning by five minutes![19]

Three weeks later, on 20 May, Norris-Newman, now accompanied by other correspondents, returned to Isandhlwana with the burial parties and found the whole site of the conflict overgrown with grass thickly intermingled with great and growing stalks of oats and mealies. Concealed among these lay the corpses of the soldiers in all postures of decay: 'I had the melancholy satisfaction of discovering my own tent ... and immediately behind it the skeletons of my horses with the bodies of my servants just as I had left them'. On 4 July, the dead of Isandhlwana were avenged, when Cetewayo's forces were vanquished at Ulundi – and the king was captured.

JOHN CAMERON

With a new Liberal (second Gladstone) government in power, and free from the Zulu threat, the Transvaal Boers now sought to free their country from British suzerainty. But in June 1880, the Boers were informed by the Gladstone ministry that 'the Queen cannot be advised to relinquish her sovereignty over the Transvaal'. The dispute dragged on through the autumn until, at a mass open-air meeting in Paardekrael on 8 December, the Boers insisted on the complete restoration of the sovereignty of the Transvaal republic. A week later hostilities commenced in what became the first Boer War, a conflict which lasted only nine weeks, during which the British suffered three humiliating defeats.

Among the London correspondents hurriedly sent to the Transvaal was John Cameron, of *The Standard*, who was to achieve renown for his reportage of the rout of a British force at Majuba Hill on 26 February 1881. Cameron's 2,500 word account of the battle for *The Standard* was outstanding, and was later used, in note form, by the *London Illustrated News*, with sketches by Melton Prior. During the conflict, Cameron had been captured by the Boers, but was allowed to return to the British base to obtain medical treatment for the wounded.

Less than a month later, on 21 March, he was present with other correspondents at the peace conference, where there ensued a long, anxious wait outside O'Neill's Farm for news of the parleys. Many of the correspondents had their horses saddled ready for the dash to the nearest telegraph at Mount Prospect Camp, some two miles away. Melton Prior, who was on friendly terms with General Woods' aide-de-camp (ADC), had requested the officer to let him know when the Boers had signed the agreement. Strolling over to Cameron, Prior told him quietly to have his horse ready but out of sight behind the hill, and he would repay his debt for the information used in the Majuba sketches by raising his helmet to show that peace had been signed. The ADC emerged shortly afterwards to smoke a cigarette and mentioned casually to Prior, 'They have signed'. Prior immediately raised his helmet and Cameron galloped off to Mount Prospect. Twenty minutes later, General Woods emerged and announced to the correspondents what Prior had already known, but added that 'the wire to England is closed and all communications until my despatch has gone'. However, Cameron's message had already anticipated the embargo and *The Standard* was able to publish an extra late edition that same day announcing the peace even before embarrassed officials in Whitehall had received the news.[20]

Within two years, Cameron was again in action, covering the bombardment of Alexandria on 11 July 1882, following a massacre of Christians in the port. As a reprisal, an Anglo-French fleet was sent to Egypt, and, after the withdrawal of the French squadron, Admiral Sir Frederick Seymour bombarded Alexandria. Leading the assault was Lord Charles Beresford who, in his gunboat *Condor*, moved in close to the batteries with great coolness and daring. It was Cameron's report of Seymour's signal, 'Well done *Condor*!', which made Beresford a national hero. For *The Standard* it was to be a first-class story, and, cabled regardless of expense, it caused a sensation. Cameron's despatch covered more than eight columns, carried on successive days and was virtually an hour-by-hour account: 'The dead calm which has succeeded the tremendous row of artillery which has gone on for so many hours seems strange and unnatural, and we can scarcely realise that the first great sea fight with artillery of the modern type has been fought and won.'

While Alexandria was being bombarded, General Sir Garnet Wolseley was on his way to Egypt, with orders to crush the forces of Arabi Pasha, the Egyptian nationalist. Using the war correspondents to his advantage, Wolseley fed them false information, but more seriously, Major Bruce Tulloch, his intelligence officer, sent a fake telegram in Cameron's name to Mudford at *The Standard*. Later, Tulloch explained:

> I knew well the correspondent of *The Standard*, Cameron, a splendid fellow ... would be too patriotic to object to my taking his name in vain when it was for the good of our work; so I wired the editor ... as if from Cameron, to the effect that rumours of a possible occupation of the canal by the English are now disposed of. M. de Lesseps, who has the French Government behind him, has settled that the neutrality of the canal shall be rigidly observed. It is now an open secret that whilst the British portion of the force will move from Alexandria and attack Kafr Dewar, the troops coming from India will move from Suez direct to Cairo.[21]

Somewhat over a month later, on the morning of 13 September 1882, Cameron was an eyewitness at the battle of Tel-el-Kebir, when Wolseley's army engaged Arabi's forces. As dawn rose, they stormed the Egyptian entrenchments, and the result was a resounding victory, the prolongation of Britain's occupation of Egypt and the direction of the Suez Canal by the British. While a British-dominated government was being established in Cairo, further south in the Sudan the Mahdi and his followers had risen in revolt, determined to rid his country of Egyptian forces. The Gladstone government now faced the dilemma of either enforcing Anglo-Egyptian control of the Sudan or abandoning it to the Mahdi, especially after an ill-equipped army of 10,000 under the command of a British officer, General Hicks Pasha, had been destroyed by the Mahdi earlier in 1883 at Shekan.

By 3 December 1883, with the Mahdi poised on the frontiers of Egypt, Gladstone decided to abandon the Sudan, rescuing only the Egyptian garrisons, especially those troops in Khartoum. A week later, while Gladstone was ill with a chill, and the Queen complaining that 'The govt. does nothing!', the Cabinet decided to act: Following an agitation led by W. T. Stead in *The Pall Mall Gazette*, the decision was taken to send General Gordon to report on the situation with a view to the evacuation of the Egyptian forces. 'Chinese' Gordon, aged 51, was a man of whom the Queen approved, and on 18 January 1884 he left London to undertake his mission. While Gordon was en route, another military disaster occurred in the Sudan with the defeat of an Egyptian force under General Baker Pasha near Trinkiat on the Red Sea coast, which had aimed to relieve the besieged Egyptian garrison of Tokar. For *The Standard*, Cameron, who was in the thick of the fray, telegraphed an exciting account of the disaster:

> As the cavalry rode wildly in, the order was given for the infantry to form a square – a manoeuvre in which they had been drilled daily for weeks. At this crisis, however, the dull, half-disciplined mass failed to accomplish it. Three sides were formed after a fashion, but on the fourth side two companies of the Alexandria Regiment, seeing the enemy coming on leaping and brandishing their spears, stood like a panic-stricken flock of sheep, and nothing could get them to move into their place. Into this gap thus left in the square the enemy poured, and at once all became panic and confusion. The miserable Egyptian soldiers refused even to defend themselves, but throwing their rifles away, flung themselves on the ground and grovelled there, screaming for mercy. No mercy was given, the Arab spearmen pouncing upon them and driving their spears through their necks or bodies. Nothing could surpass the wild confusion, camels and guns mixed together, soldiers firing into the air, with wild Arabs, their long hair streaming behind them, darting among them, hacking and thrusting with their spears.[22]

Three weeks later, on 28 February, General Sir Gerald Graham landed with reinforcements at Trinkiat, determined to relieve Tokar. Moving towards El-Teb, they found the remains of Baker's defeated army and as Graham advanced he was assailed by the Mahdist Dervishes. Describing the fierce onslaughts, Cameron wrote: 'So hotly do the Arabs press forward that the troops pause in their steady advance. It becomes a hand-to-hand fight, the soldiers meeting the Arab spear with cold steel, their favourite weapon and beating them at it. ... At this critical moment for the enemy, the Gardener guns open fire and the leaden hail decides matters.'[23]

Meanwhile, with the Sudan ablaze, General Gordon had arrived at Khartoum on 18 February 1884, and exactly a month later the Mahdi laid siege to the city. With Gordon trapped in Khartoum, the Queen warned Gladstone: 'If anything happens to him the result will be awful.' Harassed by the Queen, public opinion and the press, in the summer of 1884 the Gladstone government belatedly ordered Sir

Garnet Wolseley to leave for the Sudan with a force to rescue Gordon. By the end of the year, Wolseley's expedition had only reached Korti after a most difficult journey in whalers up the Nile. Gordon, completely cut off from the outside world, seemed resigned to the fact that he would not be rescued and in the final entry in his journal on 14 December 1884, wrote: 'Now mark THIS, if the expedition ... does not come in ten days, the Town Hall May Fall, and I have done my best for the honour of our country. Good Bye. C. G. Gordon.'

Meeting stiff resistance, Wolseley engaged the enemy at Abu Klea on 17 January 1885, and Cameron reported that 'The hand-to-hand fighting was terrific, but not one of the Arabs that got inside left the square alive.' It was to be his last despatch, for two days later in the engagement at Abu Kru *The Standard*'s distinguished correspondent was mortally wounded. As bullets ricocheted everywhere, it was inevitable that there would be casualties, and Cameron was the first to fall. On learning of Cameron's demise, his colleague and friend in many campaigns, Melton Prior said: '[He] was a well tried man from north of the Tweed, who never tired of letting us know it with pride ... sharp eyed, imperious, but keen as a razor at his work.' With the skirmish over, Cameron's colleagues, Bennett Burleigh of *The Daily Telegraph*; Frederick Villiers of *The Graphic*; Alex MacDonald of *The Western Morning News*; H. H. S. Pearse of *The Daily News*; and Melton Prior of *The London Illustrated News* carried his body on a stretcher to a freshly-dug grave, where Lord Charles Beresford read the burial service. For Mudford, in Shoe Lane, it was a bitter personal blow. Not only had he lost a good friend, but also a distinctive and distinguished special correspondent.

Later that year, G. A. Henty, another colleague from *The Standard*, speaking at a dinner at the Savage Club, remarked on the death of his friend and of six other correspondents in the Sudan: '... why gentlemen, from the days of the Crimea when William Howard Russell, Nat Wood, and in a humble way, myself, began the work of the correspondents with the British army, all the wars, all the campaigns together, have not caused such a mortality as this'.

But Cameron and his colleagues were not to be forgotten, for in the crypt of St. Paul's Cathedral is a tablet commemorating 'The Gallant Men who in the discharge of their duty as Special Correspondents fell in the Campaigns of the Soudan 1883–1884–1885', and among the names listed is:

JOHN ALEXANDER CAMERON, 'Standard', Abu Kru,
January 19, 1885

10

The New Journalism

The Standard was now a power in the land; everywhere it was regarded as being the oracle of the propertied and the mercantile classes. It was the exponent of solid Conservative respectability, and was said to represent the thoughts of the 'villa resident' order of Englishmen. Mudford's touch was sure, and he was constantly being supplied with Cabinet information, much to the chagrin of the *Daily News*, the official Liberal paper .

The thirteen months from June 1885 have been considered by some to have been among the most complicated in British political history.[1] The state of the parties was by then almost equal, with two powerful leaders in William Ewart Gladstone and, (less securely) Lord Salisbury, backed by a solid group of veterans. And in the wings waiting to take their places were Joseph Chamberlain and Lord Randolph Churchill. When Gladstone's second government fell in June 1885, it was not possible to hold a general election until the autumn, as the new electoral register arising from the Third Reform Bill was not complete. Therefore, Salisbury, despite some misgivings, and with the tacit approval of Gladstone, assumed his first premiership in 'The Ministry of Caretakers' on 23 June 1885, and for Churchill, with ever-increasing power in the party, it meant his becoming Leader of the House, while also being responsible for the India Office. Within a week, Chamberlain, speaking at West Islington, had warned that Lord Randolph had planted 'his foot on Lord Salisbury's neck'.

Meanwhile, Salisbury had been having his initial meeting with a representative from the press, G. E. Buckle, editor of *The Times*, and told him; 'You are the first person who has not come to see me in the last few days who is not wanting something at my hands – place, or decoration, or peerage. *You* only want information!'[2]

But Salisbury also had a strong supporter in Mudford, and on 31 July 1885 a leader appeared in *The Standard* which warned the Prime Minister to beware of Churchill who was 'at heart a greater Radical than Mr Chamberlain himself' and who had 'done the Conservative Party almost irreparable harm' since taking office. He was accused of having risen to the top by cultivating the editors of newspapers, backed by a shaky combination of public bluster and private opportunism; 'his ignorance and crudity must be measured at their worth, and the fact that he had been ruinously overrated'. The leader continued: 'We will follow Lord Salisbury, but we will not be governed by a sort of overgrown schoolboy, who thinks he is witty when he is only impudent, and who really does not seem to possess sufficient knowledge even to fathom the depths of his own ignorance of everything worthy of the name of statesmanship.'[3]

Churchill's immediate reaction was that Salisbury had been 'reworking a leader'. That same day, in some haste, Alfred Austin wrote to the Prime Minister: 'Have you read the first article in the *Standard* today? I need scarcely say I neither wrote nor inspired it, and fail to see its opportunities.' With Escott ill at home suffering from a nervous depression, there could be only one person responsible – the hand of Mudford was at work once more.[4]

One of the key appointments in the Salisbury administration had been that of Lord Carnarvon, who became Lord Lieutenant of Ireland, and during the summer he held secret meetings with the Irish Nationalist leaders, culminating on 1 August, when he met Charles Stewart Parnell, with the Prime Minister's knowledge, in a vacant house in Hill Street, Mayfair. An assertive Parnell believed that he stood his best chance with the Conservatives, but that same month Gladstone himself became a convert to Home Rule for Ireland. In Dublin, at the end of the month, Parnell declared that his aim was nothing less than national independence for Ireland. In view of this situation, *The Standard*, in a tense message, begged the leaders of both parties to oppose any such motion.

The election was held in November 1885, and the returns showed that the Liberals had eighty-six seats more than the Conservatives, which was exactly balanced by Parnell and his supporters. The Queen's foresight was once again acute, and she observed: 'But of course neither the Govt. or opposition can count upon these.' Thanks to Thomas Wemyss Reid, an old colleague of Mudford who had been 'privy' to Gladstone's proposals, *The Standard* was able to publish the Liberals' plans to concede Irish Home Rule. Five days later, following an investigation by the Liberal party elders, Charles Cooper wrote to Lord Rosebery saying there was not the slightest doubt that Reid had been provided with the sketch of what Gladstone intended to do, passed it to Mudford, as 'the paragraph in *The Standard* was almost a verbal reproduction of it'. He added, tartly, that the *Scotsman* might have beaten *The Standard* but for the fact that its editor prided himself on being 'most unfortunately scrupulous'.[5]

On 21 January 1886, the Queen opened Parliament for the last time. The Government, however, lasted barely a week into the new session, for on 27 January it was defeated by the Liberals, supported by the Parnellites, on an amendment to the Royal Address. It was not even Ireland that brought down Salisbury ... but a vote on agriculture! At first, the Queen wished Salisbury to continue, and it was only through his persistent refusal that she sent for Gladstone. Although the

"Grand Old Man" was to be her new Prime Minister, it was Salisbury whom she was to rely on, even offering him a dukedom.

Determined to introduce Home Rule, Gladstone was prepared to suffer the possibility of a split in his party. He immediately had refusals from Derby, Goschen, Hartington and Selborne, and internal opposition was to increase. Mudford, commenting on Gladstone's appointment, said 'The political outlook is gloomy in the extreme. Either England and Ireland will be torn apart, or we shall introduce a succession of short-lived Administrations, a consequent weakening of the action of the Executive, both at home and abroad, and a shock to the Representative Institutions that will leave its traces for many a day.'[6]

PEAK OF POPULARITY

During all the excitement of the demands for Home Rule, the circulation of *The Standard* continued to rise. The paper was now at its peak of popularity: less than a decade earlier, on 21 May 1877 – fifty years exactly since the paper had been launched – Cooper Brothers & Co., Accountants, had announced that the sales for the week ending 12 May had been 1,088,023, or a daily average of 181,337; by 1887 a regular figure of more than 250,000 copies per day was being attained. (An official return for 23 September 1882 had shown sales of 255,292.)

From its 'port-wine flavour in the solid rhetoric of its editorial pages', the paper had moved to become a radical title with Tory predilections, and ever anxious to preserve British imperial power. On the whole, it was succeeding admirably as a steadying influence on its own party with its healthy and stimulating criticisms. It prided itself on being in close touch with all aspects of contemporary life. It was most certainly aware of the secrets of the Cabinet, and this successful insight had been extended into other spheres.

Sir Clinton Dawkins, at the India Office, was able to furnish the paper with extensive details concerning the creation of a reserve corps for the native army, and the maintenance of Imperial Service troops. Colonel Sturley, of the Scots Guards, was a regular contributor on military matters. Drama and music, too, were well covered by A. E. T. Watson and Desmond Ryan. In total, *The Standard* had in its employ more than 500 people, and paid £1,500 a week in salaries.

The day-to-day management was left to Walter Wood, who had been with the paper for eighteen years. Born in 1830, Wood had begun his career as a reporter in London and from there went to Newcastle. Returning to the capital, he joined *The Standard* under Hamber, and immediately covered the trial of the Manchester Fenians in 1867. During the First Ashanti War he was stationed for some months at Madeira to intercept the mail steamers and to cable the despatches from the Gold Coast to Shoe Lane. His dedication there earned the confidence of James Johnstone, the proprietor, and on Johnstone's death Wood was promoted by Mudford (who assumed full control) to the post of manager. He continued in this post until 1890, and upon his retirement, with a liberal pension, was succeeded by William Mudford, a nephew of the chief executive.

It was during this period that *The Standard* employed its first woman foreign correspondent, Maria Ternan, the sister of Charles Dickens's mistress. Following ten years of marriage, she enrolled in the newly established Slade School of Fine Art. Her marriage, though, broke down, and, divorced, she moved to Rome, where she met Tom Trollope, brother of novelist Anthony. Upon his travelling, which was often, she acted as *The Standard*'s Italian correspondent.

Following Tom Trollope's retirement in 1886, she was appointed by Mudford as the paper's permanent correspondent, and 'for the next twelve years, until she was sixty-one, she wrote a series of articles about life in Rome, including the usual staples of cholera scares, the Pope's health, the eruption of Mount Etna or a strike of cabmen and carters.' Mostly they were signed "from our own correspondent", but occasionally, especially if the subjects were fashion, they were "by a lady".[7]

Five years earlier, in 1881, under her married name, Maria Taylor, her journeys through Tunisia were published as *Some Old Letters from North Africa.* In a choice phrase she described her visit to a harem, 'This was one of the few occasions in one's life in which it was a distinct advantage to belong to the weaker sex.'

HOME RULE FOR IRELAND

Gladstone's third ministry was to be of short duration: barely six months; but as he was intent on introducing Home Rule its brevity was hardly surprising. He brought his first Home Rule Bill to the Commons on 8 April 1886; but even as the debate continued, a monster petition against Home Rule bearing the signatures of 20,000 Ulster women was presented to the Queen. Lord Randolph Churchill was in no doubt as to the proper course if Home Rule were enacted: 'Ulster will fight and Ulster will be right.'

On 7 June, Gladstone made his final plea for the Bill: 'Ireland stands at the bar, expectant, hopeful, almost suppliant, think, I beseech you, think well, think wisely, think not for the moment but for the years to come.' It was not enough ... for in the early hours of the following day the vote was taken, and, with Joseph Chamberlain and his ninety-two Liberals followers committed to opposing the motion, the Government was defeated by thirty votes – 343 to 313.

As a result of their victory in the consequent election, on 20 July 1886, the Tories, under Salisbury, were now able to command a composite majority of 188. Parnell, through his campaign of hate, had ruined the party best suited to provide Ireland with Home Rule. He, however, thought otherwise, blaming it on Chamberlain: 'There goes the man who killed Home Rule.'

But one of the real architects of Gladstone's defeat had been Randolph Churchill. During this period, Lord Randolph Churchill was once more riding high: he was not only Leader of the House, but had also become Chancellor of the Exchequer. A young man in a hurry, he was determined to make a name, and in the autumn, in preparing his budget, he planned to cut the Navy and Army estimates. W. H. Smith, at the War Office, would have none of it, and he was supported by Salisbury.

To an irrational Churchill, there was only one step to take: he tendered his resignation; to his astonishment, it was accepted. The following night, Churchill paid an unexpected call to *The Times* offices and authorised them to publish the full correspondence with Salisbury – and his resignation. Churchill's wife was surprised to read it in *The Times*; but not the wily Salisbury, who told his wife at breakfast: 'Randolph resigned in the middle of the night and if I know my man it will be in *The Times* this morning.'[8]

Alfred Austin in *The Standard* was quick to seize upon Churchill's departure in a slashing attack:

> Lord Randolph Churchill has missed his mark. Englishmen are always ready to respect independence ... but the circumstances and manner of [his] secession effectively deprives him of the sympathy generally extended to Ministers when conscientious conviction separates them from their colleagues. If Mr Goschen were only free to succeed Lord Randolph Churchill we might congratulate the seceding Statesman on the great service he has done to the Unionist cause.[9]

It would appear that this leader by Austin bore the mark of Salisbury himself, for within days the Prime Minister was offering the Chancellorship to Goschen. When Churchill finally knew that he had lost, he confessed to his major error: 'I forgot Goschen'. There could be no return, and as Salisbury was alleged to have said: 'Did you ever know a man who having got rid of a boil on his neck wanted another?'

Throughout Salisbury's years in high office he was in constant touch with Austin: T. E. Kebbel, another *Standard* leader writer, was to note:

> Foreign affairs now fell into the hands of the present Poet Laureate [Austin] who continued for many years to represent *The Standard* on all questions of interest connected with Continental affairs. He was in frequent communication with Lord Salisbury, and it was

generally allowed that on all subjects of this nature *The Standard* occupied a foremost place among the leading London journals.

Kebbel also had some interesting observations to make upon the payment system then in force for the paper's correspondents:

> One advantage of *The Standard* system was that you were paid for your articles as soon as they were sent in. Leaders would naturally be used at once; but reviews and biographies were often, especially the last, kept over for a long time, and on most other papers – I almost think on all – you had to wait till they were published before you saw your money. The Tory *Standard* was a bright exception to this rule.

Mudford believed in looking after his correspondents, and as such had little difficulty in attracting people of the right calibre, but, politically, he attached himself to no man. Despite the close links between Austin and the Prime Minister, Mudford remained as enigmatic as ever. His views on foreign policy – contrary to the official Tory line – in the early spring of 1887 caused the Queen to seek the advice of Salisbury. On 23 March, he replied: 'We have no influence with the paper by which we could keep it from any line of writing or tone of policy that we disapproved. Occasionally it will put in what it is asked to put in: but that is rare. The paper is quite independent: but we have to bear the blame of its proceedings.'[10]

THE NEW JOURNALISM

Politicians were becoming aware that not all editors could be manipulated, and there was a growing consciousness of the phrase 'New Journalism', introduced by Matthew Arnold when writing in the May 1887 issue of *Nineteenth Century*. Arnold observed:

> It has much to recommend it; it is full of ability, novelty, variety, sensation, sympathy, generous instincts; its one great fault is that it is feather brained. It throws out assertions at a venture because it wishes them true; does not correct either them or itself, if they are false; and to get at the state of things as they truly are seems to feel no concern whatever.

Here he was talking of the *Pall Mall Gazette* and its contemporaries. Ever since W. T. Stead had taken over the editorship of that paper in 1883 there had developed a new style of journalism: less reportage of the political speeches; the introduction of heavier headlines and cross-heads; and the use of graphics. It was a style that was to be copied and developed by other papers. It was this gradual change in appearance in the evenings – some, admittedly, from their first issue. *The Star,* under the radical T. P. O'Connor, was one such that now showed up the dull greyness of the mornings. By the end of the decade, O'Connor was able to proclaim: 'Beyond doubt we are on the eve of a new departure ... reflected in the more personal tone of the more modern methods.'

In 1887, a young Ralph Blumenfeld, future editor and chairman of the *Daily Express,* arrived from New York, and was immediately aware of the solemn appearance of the morning papers, all 'great heavy-sided blanket sheets full of dull advertisements and duller news announcements'.[11] But with the New Journalism, a gradual change was already taking place: the trend was towards snappier news stories, and the use of cross-heads and American-style headings. For the politicians, long accustomed to being reported verbatim, this was to be a bitter blow. In November 1885, the Central Press Agency had announced new instructions on the coverage of politicians' speeches; Chamberlain, Churchill, Gladstone and Salisbury were entitled to verbatim reportage; Lords Hartington and Spencer, to one column; and all others merited half a column or less. Even Churchill complained that his speeches were being cut in *The Standard* and *The Times.* As Stephen Koss noted: 'This was the single most striking development in late Victorian journalism.'[12] It was against this changing press background that the political life of the country was to be carried out until the end of the nineteenth century.

Just as the New Journalism was affecting the character of the newspapers, so was the Education Act of 1870 creating a vast new reading public, with simple tastes and eager for enlightenment. To meet this new demand, on 30 October 1881, George Newnes launched *Tit-Bits,* a weekly penny paper full of scraps of information. Within six months its sales had grown to 900,000, three times the circulation of *The Daily Telegraph.* This success was noted by young Alfred Harmsworth,[13] the future Lord Northcliffe, and seven years later, on 3 June 1888, he brought out *Answers.* With the aid of a competition to calculate the amount of gold and silver in the Bank of England, for which the winner received a pension of £1 a week for life, circulation soared to 700,000, and then settled down to more than 350,000 copies per week. It was from this base that Harmsworth was able to found his publishing group, earning profits of £100,000 a year, and to purchase the ailing *Evening News* for £25,000 in 1894. Two years later, on 4 May 1896, he brought out the *Daily Mail,* a newspaper which, within a few years, was to have a considerable effect upon the sales of *The Standard.*

Meanwhile, C. Arthur Pearson,[14] another young publisher (and a future owner of *The Standard*), following brief employment with *Tit-Bits,* had launched out on his own with *Pearson's Weekly.* A great deal of its success was due to the 'Missing Words' competition: this was eventually to be declared illegal, but by that time it was attracting almost half a million entries, with a complementary sales figure.

As the new decade began, so there continued the involvement by Salisbury, through Austin, in *The Standard*'s editorials, although Mudford remained the arbiter. For example, on 11 October 1891, Austin was directed by Salisbury to write 'an article urging that Arthur Balfour should be made Leader of the House of Commons'. However, in Mudford's absence, Byron Curtis had no intention of deciding the matter and telegraphed Austin that the editor was away and he dared not print the article without consultation.[15] The man at the centre of the piece, Balfour, was to remark: 'Such papers as the *St. James's Gazette* or *The Standard* are ... of no earthly value to the party in the way of making opinions, as their criticisms are a foregone conclusion.'

Salisbury had his own ideas on *The Standard* articles and their effect on the public. Writing to Viscount Woolmer, he said:

> I never came across so sensitive a public man [Chamberlain] before. I have known one disgruntled statesman who went half-mad whenever he was caricatured in *Punch*; and another who wished to resign his office, because he was never caricatured in *Punch* – which he looked upon as a slight on his public importance. But I never met anyone before who was disturbed by articles in *The Standard*.[16]

AUSTIN DEPARTS

As for the paper's chief leader writer, after almost thirty years Austin was now beginning to tire, and cynicism was creeping into his work. He wrote to Salisbury in December 1892: 'Newspapers are like Corporations. They have no soul to save.' He then complained of a *Standard* leader which had been ruined by 'the interpolation of a cantankerous editor'.[17] Now in his fifties, Austin was facing a mid-life crisis: on the one hand there was his well-paid work for *The Standard*, on the other his urge for recognition as a poet.

In the summer of 1894, he published a prose work, *The Garden That I Love*, which achieved wide popular success. Because of this, and because of his journalistic services to Lord Salisbury and the Tory party, Austin achieved his life's ambition: on 1 January 1896 he was made Poet Laureate. Although the appointment was greeted with much mirth – especially by *Punch* – Austin's reverence for authority and for official ceremony gave him partial qualifications, but in commemorating certain national events he only revealed his own lack of a sense of the ludicrous.

Austin remained in journalism until 1898, when he decided that he must devote himself full-time to poetry. On 19 February 1898, the Prime Minister wrote to him from Hatfield House, Herts.:[18]

> My Dear Austin – I am very sorry to hear that you are meditating a retirement from public life. The readers of *The Standard* will be great sufferers from your resolution, and so will the interests of the Conservative Party. But health stands before everything and no one can doubt that you do rightly and wisely

His replacement was Sidney Low, who joined the paper from the *St. James's Gazette*, where he had been editor for a decade under the proprietorship of Edward Steinkopff, a millionaire from Glasgow, but described, unflatteringly, as a 'vulgar, loud speaking German'.[19] During his period on *The Standard*, Low was offered, but rejected, the editorship of the *Morning Post* and the *Johannesburg Star*.

Two events dominated the news pages of this time: on 19 May 1898, *The Standard* announced the death of W. E. Gladstone, causing Mudford to write: 'By the death of Mr Gladstone, a great man and, with all his faults, a great Minister has disappeared from the political arena, and with him the last surviving specimen of the old school of British statesman'. And in the late summer, the country was delighted to learn that the Sudan had been conquered by Kitchener. *The Standard* was in buoyant mood in its leader: 'The death of Gordon has been avenged. Omdurman has fallen, and the Egyptian flag, coupled with the British Standard, once more flies at Khartoum. The Sirdar and the whole force under his command are to be congratulated on a splendid victory, won by hard fighting and admirable tactics. It will serve to show that when English interests are in danger, England knows how to defend them, no matter at what distance from the sea or on what apparently inaccessible portion of the earth's surface. In the present crisis of world affairs the lesson will not be thrown away.'[20]

Reporting from the battle of Omdurman for *The Standard* was William Maxwell, later to head a section of the Secret Service. He wrote about an event in which a young Winston Churchill was involved:

> Chief among the isolated incidents of the battle was a great charge of the 21st Lancers. Galloping down on a detached body of the enemy, they found swordsmen massed behind, and were forced to charge against appalling odds. They hacked through the mass, rallied, and kept the Dervish horde at bay by carbine and magazine fire, losing one officer killed and four wounded, with about forty men killed and wounded.

However, it was not only conflict in the Sudan that attracted the attention of *The Standard*'s readers. As the century drew to a close, Britain was to be involved in war in South Africa. Since the failure of the Bloemfontein Conference, held between 31 May and 5 June 1899, the struggle was inevitable. On 21 August 1899, S. H. Jeyes, the assistant editor of *The Standard*, paid a visit to Chamberlain at the Colonial Office, very anxious to know what line to take with regard to the Transvaal crisis.[21] Chamberlain was unable to meet him, and a subordinate who attended him later minuted that 'Mr Jeyes seemed in a great doubt as to whether he should preach peace or war, but I hope that after what I said he will not commit *The Standard* to any definite verdict yet.' Bearing in mind that Mudford remained in supreme control of the paper, and knowing of his practice of not seeing ministers, it would seem that Jeyes, his trusty lieutenant, was just seeking Chamberlain's views. Mudford, however, still remained the final arbiter.

On *The Standard*'s domestic scene, Mudford had recently increased the salaries of the parliamentary reporters: each man who had been on the staff for six years would in future receive seven guineas per week instead of six: those who had been members of the staff for twelve years would receive an advance of two guineas a week. It was also announced that the granting of summer holidays, which had been tried for some time in the composing room, would be further extended. Compositors who had been in the employ of *The Standard* for less than ten years would, henceforth, be allowed one week's holiday; for ten years and under fifteen, ten days; for fifteen years and under twenty-five, two weeks; and for twenty-five years, three weeks each – all, of course, with full pay.[22] As an employer, Mudford was indeed benevolent, following the practices of his predecessors, Baldwin and Johnstone. No doubt this was a major reason why industrial disputes at Shoe Lane were virtually unknown.

MUDFORD RETIRES

On 10 October 1899 the Transvaal, which had been joined by the Orange Free State on 27 September, formally declared war on Britain: 'The date was significant, for experienced South Africans had long declared that if war came it would be in the spring, when the grass of the veldt was at its best for a campaign by a nation of horsemen.'[23] *The Standard*'s coverage of the Boer War in its sober and responsible manner was to be as powerful as ever.

The paper continued in this unspectacular way of presentation, for Mudford was certainly not about to change the habits of a lifetime. Not for him, the brashness of a young Harmsworth or the verve of a purposeful Pearson; rather it was take a more measured view of the news. R. D. Blumenfeld was later to recall those days:

> There was Mudford, the editor of *The Standard*, the morning *Standard* of those days, the most authoritative, the most widely quoted, the best-informed and the least enterprising journal of its

time. It made a great deal of money for the people of importance in the various capitals, and the old *Standard* went on undisturbed, unperturbed and unnoticing the changes of the world. Meanwhile, Mr Mudford, its editor, who in person was amiable and capable, and by reason of his studied anonymity a more or less mythical personage, looked benevolently on while his next-door neighbour *The Daily Telegraph* banged the drum, blew the whistle, rattled the bones and trumpeted the glad news from the second-storey window to the surging masses of top-hats passing up and down Fleet Street.[24]

This New Journalism, however, was not a journalism with which Mudford wished to be associated. Now in his early sixties, he decided that the time had come to retire and hand over to a younger man; he selected as his successor Byron Curtis, who had been the night editor.

Of Mudford's immediate predecessors as editors, Hamber was in semi-retirement; James Johnstone Jnr was in retirement at Hove; and John Gorst was a prominent Tory politician. Now Sir John, Gorst had served as Solicitor General in the short-lived Salisbury Government of 1885, a post which carried a knighthood; and he remained in Parliament until 1906, when he was rejected, as a Free Trader, by the Conservative Unionists. He died in London on 4 April 1916, and is buried in Castle Combe, Wiltshire.

With Alfred Austin retired, there was now no longer the strong link between Salisbury and *The Standard*, and an incident which occurred on 9 November 1899 was perhaps, in a sense, indicative of the change. Writing to J. A. Spender, editor of the *Westminster Gazette*, Sir Robert Edgcumbe, a Liberal supporter, noted:

> I was travelling to London and was alone in my compartment. At Hatfield, Lord Salisbury got into the same carriage and as the train moved off he was handed three evening papers. Shortly after we started he took them up, opened first the *Globe* and immediately threw it on the floor of the carriage, then he opened the *Evening Standard* and treated it in a similar manner, lastly he opened the *Westminster Gazette* and proceeded to read it diligently until we arrived at King's Cross Station. He was on his way to London to speak that night at the Lord Mayor's banquet.[25]

Mudford decided to retire at the end of 1899, and leave the new editor to face the new century. But, despite his many years' service to *The Standard*, there is no mention whatsoever of his departure in the final issue of 1899. In his last leader he commented: 'The year which closes tomorrow is one that is destined to be long memorable in the annals of the British Empire. It has been a period so far, at least as its portion is concerned, of striking events, of dramatic episodes, of humiliations and unexpected reverses, and of a sudden, and almost startling, outburst of Imperialist enthusiasm.' His retirement, though, did not pass without notice in other newspapers, and was greeted with a certain sadness, especially in the provinces. The *Belfast Newsletter* commented: 'He mixed very little in society and seldom accepted an invitation to dine, even with a Cabinet Minister. All his time was devoted to the discharge of the exacting duties of his dual position.' The *Western Daily Press*, Bristol, believed that he had represented the very best traditions of British journalism. The *Aberdeen Free Press* said: 'His high trust is discharged without fear or favour. Statesmen have sought his acquaintance in vain.'

Note was made by the *Leicester Daily Post* of the magnificent terms that he had enjoyed:

> Mr Mudford retires with a pension of £5,000 a year. The late proprietor of *The Standard* made Mr Mudford editor for life at a salary of £5,000, with the proviso that, should he wish to retire at any time, the salary should continue intact. The editorship of *The Standard* has thus been the best paid and the safest post in journalism. Mr Mudford practically created the fortunes of the paper.

Mudford was to live for another sixteen years, dying on 18 October 1916. In a fulsome tribute two days later, *The Times* said:

> We regret to announce that Mr William Heseltine Mudford, formerly editor and manager of *The Standard*, died on Wednesday night at his residence, Westcombe Lodge, Wimbledon Common, from the effect of burns. It appears that on Saturday evening he slipped into the fireplace and his clothing caught fire. Born in 1839, Mr Mudford was brought up in a newspaper atmosphere, his father being the proprietor of the *Kentish Observer* and *Canterbury Journal*.

The long obituary concluded:

> His ear was not attuned to the modern voice; he did not move with the times; and in his arrogant confidence in the unmistakeable ability of his newspaper he failed to recognize the inroads which brasher rivals were making upon its prosperity. But he was one of the masters of older journalism; and as long as his hand was at the helm, *The Standard* was a real force. How largely this was due to his own curious but capable individuality is shown by the rapid decline which set in after his retirement of the editorship.[26]

The Times obituary was correct: Mudford *had* been *The Standard*, and his departure did indeed mark the beginning of a decline in the paper's power and influence.

11

The Greatest Hustler

On 1 January 1900, Byron Curtis,[1] a tall, spare man, with a striking moustache, became editor of *The Standard.* Curtis was born near Worcester on 10 August 1843 and, after being educated privately, he eventually joined the staff of *The Echo* as assistant editor and Parliamentary summary writer in 1869. Six years later he was appointed acting editor, and as such on 4 October 1875 brought out *The Echo* as the first London halfpenny morning paper. It was not profitable, though, and the last issue was published on 31 May 1876. Curtis's work on *The Echo,* however, had won Mudford's approval, and the editor invited Curtis to join *The Standard* as a leader writer in 1877. By 1900, with 23 years' experience as chief assistant editor, Curtis was in an enviable position.

Arthur Jameson, a contemporary considered that

> In the hot race for honour in London journalism the prize is not always to the swift. There have been cases where pushing young men have risen rapidly to the editorial chair, have flashed like comets through the sky of Fleet Street, and have disappeared as quickly as they came, leaving few traces of usefulness behind. The biggest prize in London journalism is held by journalists to be the editorship of *The Standard,* and this recently fell to Mr C. Byron Curtis. The prize was won after 20 years' faithful service as sub-editor on that paper. Mr Curtis is a thin, wiry man, about 55, who possesses a knowledge of Parliamentary secrets and of political doings on the Continent that is coveted by every journalist in London.[2]

Unlike Mudford, who disliked clubs, Curtis was a member of both the Carlton and Junior Carlton, ideal places in which to secure the attention of Conservative politicians. Curtis, quite rightly, regarded the editorship of *The Standard* as the most important in Fleet Street; he certainly did not believe his paper to be in any way inferior to *The Times.* In a sense he was following on the principles of Mudford, who had been said to reign like some Eastern potentate over the paper: 'Thus, Byron Curtis could say, "I know I'm only a humble sort of fellow, but I've a jolly lot of power."'

R. D. Blumenfeld, editor-to-be of the *Daily Express,* and a close friend of Curtis, wrote some years later:

> All London bona-fide departmental Editors are naturally under the Editor-in-Chief and have access to him. It has not always been so. I recall the case of Mr Byron Curtis, the august and personally kind Editor of *The Standard*, Mr Mudford's successor, who was as inaccessible to the staff as the Dalai Lama.
>
> He used to come down to the Shoe Lane office after lunch and sit in his heavily guarded sanctum, write a few letters in his own hand to Cabinet Ministers and Bishops (*The Standard* was largely read by the clergy) and then go off to his Club in Pall Mall for tea. If you had an idea to offer you went to his room at your peril. The idea of offering ideas!
>
> In the evening after dinner he came down, talked to his leader writers, waited to see the proofs of the leaders and took the 12.20 train from Blackfriars. Did the French republic blow up or there were likely to be some grave news later in the night, he took the 12.20 just the same, and the efficient Night Editor did the rest.[3]

One of the key figures on *The Standard* at this time was Sidney Low, the chief leader writer, who had joined the paper in December 1897 after having been editor of *The St. James's Gazette.* Once settled in, Low had to be at *The Standard* offices on Sunday, Monday, Wednesday and Thursday nights; Friday was free but, on the other hand, Tuesday was an 'open' day, when he might be called upon at very short notice. Low led a very busy life at this time, and noted that in one day during the late summer of 1900 he contributed a 600-word article to the *New York Tribune*, which had to be cabled before 10 p.m., plus his normal *Standard* leaders, which might, for example, be 1,600 words on Nietzsche plus a leader of equal length on the railway strike. Educated at Balliol, Low was also an outstanding historian, and in 1900 was appointed Lecturer on Imperial and Colonial History at King's College, University of London.

AILING FORTUNES

The early years of the new century saw a continuing move towards the New Journalism: the *Daily Mail* and the *Daily Express* were now both successful – and were joined by the *Daily Mirror* at its launch in November 1903. As yet another paper entered the daily market, catering for the ever-growing middle classes, so the swing away from the more traditional titles was becoming more and more apparent – and none was more affected by these changes than *The Standard*; by the spring of 1904, the fortunes of the paper were on the wane. The editorship of Byron Curtis had not been the hoped-for success: a new reading public was not interested in the high politics of the Tory press.

For the Johnstone family, now in charge of the paper's ailing fortunes, the heady days of Mudford, in his dual role as editor and manager, belonged to the past. With sales of the paper continuing to fall, the family decided that the time had come to sell. Secret negotiations were opened with the Hon. John Edward Douglas-Scott-Montagu, MP, the future second Baron Montagu of Beaulieu. A keen motorist, Montagu had been successful in persuading Parliament to abolish the 12 mph speed limit, which had led to the 1903 Motor Car Act, the basis of all future motoring laws.

For eight months, Montagu was to be in discussion with the Johnstone family. Negotiations began in April 1904, and afterwards Montagu noted: 'Nothing definite arranged. Figures not discussed but evidence given that they're not averse to JM's proposal to take over'. Within a month, he had been approached by Alfred Harmsworth, who informed him on 4 May that he had heard the news at the opera the previous evening from a mutual acquaintance, Alfred Watson, editor of the Badminton Library.[4]

Harmsworth then said that he had been trying to buy *The Standard* for the previous two years, and suggested that, through Montagu, he should purchase the title. If successful, he proposed that Montagu would become editor-in-chief, with full editorial powers. However, in the event of a government crisis, he, Harmsworth, reserved the right to veto the paper's policy.

To have the backing of the huge and wealthy Harmsworth empire seemed an ideal solution for Montagu, and he felt that the bid could not fail. He was to conduct all negotiations with the Johnstone family; and if there were not enough financial backers Harmsworth had promised to 'see to it' to raise the balance of the finance himself. There was one condition, however: Harmsworth's involvement was to be kept a close secret. Two days later they met in a solicitor's office in Ely Place, Holborn, and there signed a formal agreement setting out the powers and responsibilities if and when they acquired *The Standard*. For Montagu, it would mean a salary of £5,000 a year.

By mid-summer, Castle & Co., solicitors for the Johnstone family, were demanding to know the names of Montagu's backers – and were met with silence. But, following a weekend at Sutton Place, the country mansion of Harmsworth, a relieved Montagu noted in his diary: 'Scheme now takes a big leap forward. Am beginning, now that the thing is so near and probable, to doubt JM's capacity to do the job. It's a very big thing to undertake.' With Castle & Co. still pressing Montagu to sign, and Harmsworth, although professing to be secretly eager to purchase the paper, playing for time, doubts now began to creep into the negotiations. Harold Harmsworth, the future Lord Rothermere, was brought into the secret for the first time and told by his brother, Alfred, that they should hold off until the autumn, as he believed that there would be a slump in advertisement revenue and that the asking price for *The Standard* would fall. Harold had other ideas, and felt that the deal should be struck immediately. It was to be Alfred, though, who won the day.

Despite this, on 21 July, an offer was made for *The Standard* and rejected as being totally inadequate. A fortnight later, on 2 August, Castle & Co. responded: now Montagu felt that their asking price was too high. For the next three months, negotiations went silent, but on 28 October Montagu entertained Arthur Balfour, the Prime Minister, at Beaulieu. There he had an opportunity to inform him of his plans for the paper: 'He was greatly interested and promised his support if we were successful in obtaining *The Standard*. Very pleased to get this from him.'[5]

But, even while Montagu was being assured of the Prime Minister's support, the prize was slipping away ... That same day, Castle & Co. had been trying to contact him with the news of another prospective purchaser. It was not until late on the afternoon of 2 November that Montagu, returning from a day's shooting, was handed a telegram sent by his aide, Eleanor Thornton, urging him to return to London. Arriving at his office at the late hour of 10.20 pm, he found it deserted, and immediately left for the Beefsteak Club. There he was found by Miss Thornton, who told him that Harmsworth now believed that there was another bidder for *The Standard* – probably C. Arthur Pearson – and he wished to counter this.

With Harmsworth out of London on business, Montagu could do nothing the following day, and it was not until 4 November that they were able to meet. Immediately after their discussions, Montagu left for Castle & Co., but it was already too late: Pearson had paid the Johnstone family the full asking price. A chastened Montagu, knowing that Pearson had not actually signed the contract, hastened to Downing Street to tell 'Balfour the news and to warn him that *The Standard*, under Pearson, could not be relied upon to support Government policy as it had in the past'. However, the languid Balfour did nothing.

Returning to Beaulieu for the weekend, Montagu wrote in his diary: 'Coming so suddenly, this is more of a blow than it would have been if worked up. I find, now that the thing slips, how hopes and ambitions were built upon it. Seem to have missed the chance of a lifetime.' When the news of Pearson's success was printed on the front page of *The Standard*, it was greeted with amazement by many of Montagu's hard-line Tory associates, who told him that they would rather have had a person such as himself in charge of the paper. A final entry in his diary summed up Montagu's disappointment: 'Little do they know how he had striven for it and what hopes he had built upon it, not for himself but for the party'.[6]

NEW OWNER

The new owner of *The Standard*, C. Arthur Pearson, was aged only 38, but he already controlled a large newspaper empire, including the *Daily Express* and the recently-acquired *St. James's Gazette*, plus provincial titles in Birmingham, Leicester and Newcastle. Born at Wookey, near Wells in Somerset, on 24 February 1866, the son of a country curate, he was educated at Winchester. After leaving school, he was awaiting a promised position in a bank when he noticed a competition in the recently-launched *Tit-Bits*. The prize was a post in the offices of the magazine at a salary of £100 per year. Pearson was declared the winner of the contest and within days, in September 1884, he had joined George Newnes, the magazine's proprietor, in Fleet Street and, by the following April, at the age of only nineteen, had been appointed office manager.

Nine months later, Pearson was promoted to manager of the magazine and remained on the staff of *Tit-Bits* for another five years. By that time, married and the father of two daughters, he found it increasingly difficult to live on his salary of £350 per year, and to increase his income he began to work in his spare time as a freelance journalist. One of his earliest successes was an article entitled 'Light', which was accepted by *The Standard* on 15 February 1889. When early in 1890 George Newnes[7] and W. T. Stead[8] launched the *Review of Reviews*, Pearson was appointed business manager of the journal. Because of this additional responsibility, he sought a further increase in salary, but Newnes rejected the request, and on 30 June 1890, Pearson left. Three weeks later the first number of *Pearson's Weekly* appeared.

From the initial issue, with sales of more than 250,000, *Pearson's Weekly* was a huge success. Most of the first number was written by Pearson himself, who, of course, also acted as business manager. Launching his paper involved his making a tour of the United Kingdom, visiting every newsagent of importance, often sleeping in third-class carriages, and writing, in the train, articles and stories which were posted to the office. From *Tit-Bits*, Pearson had brought with him Peter Keary and Ernest Kessell, and they helped him to establish Pearson's Limited. His major financial support was a Mr Stephen Mills, who provided Pearson with £3,000 to launch the venture.

Always a person with ideas for circulation-boosters, in the first issue of the *Weekly*, Pearson offered free railway insurance policies of £1,000 with each copy of his paper. There were also prizes for the person with the longest name and for the fathers of twins, and women readers were given the opportunity to win £100 a year for life and a good husband. The name of the first lady selected for the prize appeared in the Christmas issue, but she withdrew after having second thoughts, explaining that 'she had not seen any gentlemen from the photographs who had taken her heart by storm, and did not feel disposed to come to any decision without due consideration'. One of Pearson's best stunts, however, occurred during an influenza epidemic. Travelling in the train to his office, he was told by a doctor that the best preventive for influenza was 'some stuff made from the eucalyptus tree'. Pearson immediately bought all the eucalyptus oil he could find and engaged a staff of fifty commissionaires to squirt the oil through scent sprays on to the copies of *Pearson's Weekly* as they came off the printing presses.

By the turn of the century, Pearson was a wealthy man, having launched *Home Notes, Pearson's Magazine, M.A.P.* and *The Royal Magazine.* It was also at this time that he established the Fresh Air Fund, designed to provide a day's outing in the countryside for as many East End children as possible. During the first year, 20,000 children were accommodated, and within three years similar organisations were operating in forty-two centres. Ultimately, the number of children taken on these outings totalled almost half a million every summer.

Alfred Harmsworth and Pearson had been rivals since 1890, and the success of Harmsworth with the *Evening News* and, later, the *Daily Mail* in 1896, made Pearson even more determined to launch a national newspaper. Even before the *Daily Mail* had been established, Pearson had been planning a daily paper, but one designed for American readers in particular, with extracts from the main newspapers in the United States. He had even gone so far as to open offices near Fleet Street and to send A. W. Rider, one of his close associates, to New York to make the necessary arrangements. But costs were deemed to be too high and the project was abandoned. Then, on 7 February 1900, Pearson wrote from his premises at 17 Tudor Street to the editor of *The Newspaper Owner and Modern Printer*: 'If you think the matter of sufficient general interest, will you be so good as to announce that I am going to produce a London morning newspaper in a few weeks' time? It will be called the *Daily Express.* Its price will be a half-penny. It will be owned by myself and not by Messrs. C. Arthur Pearson.'

As good as his word, ten weeks later, on 24 April, Pearson launched the *Daily Express.* His opening leader as editor proclaimed:

> It will be the organ of no political party nor the instrument of any social clique. ... Its editorial policy will be that of an honest Cabinet Minister. ... Our policy is patriotic, our policy is the British Empire.

From the beginning, the paper was a success, and by the end of the month had an average daily circulation of 232,374.

Within four years, in addition to his successful *Daily Express*, Pearson also owned the *St. James's Gazette*, as well as the *Newcastle Evening Mail*, the *Birmingham Gazette*, the *Birmingham Evening Dispatch* and the *Leicester Evening News* – all profitable titles. However, with these ever-increasing pressures, Pearson realised that the strain of personally editing the *Daily Express* was too much for him, and he handed over the editorship to R. D. Blumenfeld – although for several more years he was to attend conferences and supervise policy.

LAYING HIS PLANS

Despite all this activity, Pearson was not content to rest on his laurels. On 4 November 1904, he bought *The Standard* and the *Evening Standard* from the Johnstone family. While Montagu had been nursing his hopes for the paper, Pearson had been laying his plans, and on 12 October had written to Tariff Reform leader Joseph Chamberlain:

> *The Standard* is on the market and I have secured an option on it. The paper has, of course, gone down very much of late, but not too far to be saved from the total wreck which will befall it if it is left much longer under the present management. From the business standpoint it is conducted on old and extravagant lines by people with no knowledge of practical newspaper work. With the introduction of modern methods it is, I am certain, capable of being brought back to a state of prosperity and of regaining the influence which it has lost.
>
> *The Standard* among newspapers is like a free-fooder in the Cabinet. It is a powerful enemy in our ranks and very much more harmful than an open foe. In my judgment, *The Standard* has from the point of newspaper influence done far more to impede the course of Tariff Reform than any other paper. It has still a great hold among the sober thinking class and particularly among business men, for its commercial intelligence has always been looked upon as the very best.[9]

Writing in his diary at the time, R. D. Blumenfeld noted:

> Thursday, November 3
> Arthur Pearson came into my room this afternoon and said that he had purchased *The Standard* and *Evening Standard* from the Johnstone family for £700,000. Pearson is heavily backed by men of wealth. *The Standard*, which up to three years ago was one of the most prosperous papers in the world, has lost readers and support owing to its policy of Free Trade. I went with Pearson over the

establishment in Shoe Lane tonight and found it archaic and ill-equipped. There are men there who have drawn salaries for years without doing an adequate day's work.[10]

When Chamberlain heard that Pearson had been successful, he wrote to him from Siena, offering his congratulations. He noted the rumour that the purchase price was £700,000: 'If this had been so it would have been the greatest deal that has ever been negotiated.'

On the day after the sale, 5 November, the *Daily Mail* commented: 'that no alterations are contemplated in the price, appearance or general tone of the paper'.[11] The hand of Harmsworth was behind the article, which added that Pearson had bought *The Standard* as a business venture and not as a support for Tariff Reform. It said that although aged 38, he talks with the enthusiasm of a 25-year-old. The sum of £700,000 was given as the purchase price.

A pleased Pearson wrote to Harmsworth that very day, thanking him 'for the nice things you say about me in this morning's *Daily Mail* and for the importance which you gave to my purchase of *The Standard.* It had been intended to complete the business next Tuesday, or Wednesday, but the announcement in your paper made it necessary to complete it at once.'

E. T. Cook, a former editor of the *Pall Mall Gazette* and the *Daily News*, wrote in his diary that the purchase price of *The Standard* was 'not far short of £700,000 as opposed to Harmsworth's offer of £450,000. The present circulation is 80,000 and last year's profits were said to have been £10,000 – at one time £100,000.'[12]

According to *The History of The Times*, however:

> Pearson needed to bargain with the Johnstones. The price of *The Standard* property (£700,000 was originally asked) came down to £300,000. It then became necessary for Pearson to go out and find new money. *The Standard* Newspapers Limited, which was formed for the purpose of acquiring *The Standard* (morning and evening editions) and the *St. James's*, had a capital of £350,000. Most of this cash was contributed by a well-known stockbroker, Sir Alexander Henderson, later Lord Faringdon, a fervent Tariff Reformer.[13]

The official announcement of the change of ownership was contained in a mere four paragraphs in the paper on the morning of 5 November:

> **THE STANDARD**
>
> *The Standard* passes today into the possession of Mr C. Arthur Pearson.

> The recent owners feel assured that, in disposing of their property to Mr Pearson, they are taking a step which will ensure the continuance of the traditions which have given *The Standard* the proud position which it has for so long occupied in the annals of British journalism.
>
> No alterations are contemplated in the price, appearance or general tone of the paper.
>
> The statement cabled from America yesterday that Mr C. Arthur Pearson is acting for the Tariff Reform League is untrue. The transaction is a purely business one, in which Mr Pearson is acting for himself alone, and neither the Tariff Reform League nor any other body or Association has anything whatever to do with it.

Although Pearson was adamant in the statement that there was no connection with the purchase of *The Standard* and the Tariff Reform League, his letter to Chamberlain on 12 October, intimating plans for the paper, proves otherwise – and his chief backer, Sir Alexander Henderson, was a keen supporter of the League. Pearson's rivals and contemporaries were not impressed with the statement. Writing in the *Manchester Guardian* two days later, the author of 'The London Letter' commented: 'I cannot remember any one of the frequent transfers in the ownership of newspapers which caused nearly so much discussion as has been caused by the sale of *The Standard* to Mr Pearson. Its long and solitary defence of the block-house of Tory Free Trade has been watched as something heroic.'

The venerable Frederick Greenwood wrote that the press 'was running down into disgrace as deep as ever it stood in, or deeper. The new managers of Shoe Lane were behaving after the manner of the mudlarks ... under the hotel windows of Greenwich'.[14] Sidney Low noted in his private diary at the time: 'Went down to *The Standard* as usual and was informed by Curtis that the paper had been sold to C. Arthur Pearson who was already in possession. Saw Pearson for a few minutes; he said he would like me to go on.'[15] A few days later, Pearson offered Low a three-year contract as leader writer and literary editor, with the curious proviso that he was to write on general and foreign politics, but not on home party politics, of which he was acknowledged to be an expert.

Pearson's purchase of *The Standard* continued to bring forth criticism from politicians and the press – and J. A. Spender, editor of the *Westminster Gazette*, was quick in his condemnation. Then the Liberal MP for Oldham, Winston Churchill, in a speech at Glasgow, said:

> Only last week had witnessed the capture of *The Standard* newspaper, that great organisation of the middle classes which for so long

possessed a character of its own. When the Great Free Trade controversy arose, *The Standard*, like the *Glasgow Herald*, by remaining perfectly true to the Unionist cause, also remained perfectly true to Free Trade. Few more articles upon the controversy have been more able, none more damaging to the Protectionists than those written by *The Standard.*

They could not answer them. An easier method presented itself. £700,000 was found – I wonder where – *The Standard* passed into the hands of the champion hustler [Chamberlain] of the Tariff Reform League. The group of able writers who exerted so much influence is scattered. Their places are filled by the obedient scribes of a mammoth trust and the protest of the last remaining Free Trade newspaper is silenced.[16]

On 9 November, *The Spectator* published a long letter from Pearson in which he rebuked Winston Churchill:

It is my firm intention to preserve in every way the tone which has distinguished *The Standard* up to the present. My association with other publications does not prevent me from thoroughly appreciating the dignified role played by *The Standard* in the past, and I am determined to uphold the traditions of the paper in the future.

Three days later, *The Standard* reported, in brief, Churchill's statement at the opening of a Liberal club in Coatbridge:

He thought there was not enough of the personal element in journalism. The establishment of a mammoth newspaper trust which operates thus, five, ten or a dozen newspapers at a time, and very often managed from one management, and yet animated by different opinions in politics, but which could turn on its writers on this side or that at the caprice of some individual who was principally out of touch with politics, and the interests of the population was to be deplored. It was the men and not machinery which shaped the fate of nations.

To put an end to the speculation that was now rife in Fleet Street, on 17 November, immediately following the leaders on page 4, Pearson made the following announcement:

THE STANDARD

Mr H. A. Gwynne[17] has been appointed Editor of *The Standard.* Mr Gwynne began his journalistic life as an unattached regular contributor to *The Times* in Roumania. He then joined the staff of

Reuters Agency as correspondent in Bucharest. Coming home in 1895 he represented the Agency with the British Expedition to Coomassi.

Two days after his return to England in March 1896, he proceeded to the Soudan when he took part in the Dongola Expedition. Early in 1897 he followed the operations of the Turkish Army under Edhem Pasha in the war against Greece. On the conclusion of that campaign he again visited the Soudan, and returned home towards the end of the year, only to receive orders to proceed to China. At Pekin he remained until May 1899 when he received instructions to proceed to South Africa and organize an elaborate service of war news for Reuters Agency. As soon as this was done he himself joined Lord Methuen's forces. On Lord Roberts' arrival he followed the operations which resulted in the capture of Johannesburg and Pretoria. Mr Gwynne remained in South Africa until peace was restored.

He then returned home after five years absence but very shortly returned to South Africa, and accompanied Mr Chamberlain on his tour. Soon after returning to England he went to Belgrade on the occasion of the assassination of King Alexander and Queen Draga, and again, after a brief interval in England, went to Macedonia at the time of the insurrection. Since the beginning of this year, Mr Gwynne had been acting as Foreign director of Reuters Agency and has been entrusted with much responsible work in other directions.

Mr S. H. Jeyes, who has been one of the leading members of the editorial staff of *The Standard* for 19 years – for the last five of which he has acted as Assistant Editor – retains this important position, with increased responsibility. Mr Sidney Low and Mr Richardson Evans, who have been the principal leader writers on the paper for a long period, have entered in agreements to continue this work. Mr Sidney Low, in addition to writing leaders on general topics and foreign politics, has accepted the appointment of Literary Editor. Mr H. J. Wigham, the brilliant Special Correspondent, who has done much admirable work for the *Morning Post* in South Africa, the Far East and elsewhere, has joined the staff of *The Standard*.

On Saturday, 19 November, *The Times* reprinted a letter from Pearson – previously in *The Spectator* – in full, and it gave Byron Curtis the chance he had been waiting for. His rebuttal appeared in the following Monday's issue:

'No writer on *The Standard* staff has left. Mr Curtis, the only member of the editorial staff who has gone, has not written in its columns for some 15 years.' I should not have noticed Mr Pearson's letter but for the last sentence. It implies that I was a mere member of the staff who had not written for the paper for 15 years. I, consequently, was

> not a person to be taken into account. Mr Pearson will have to settle that matter with my solicitor.
>
> For 20 years, I was the chief assistant editor under Mr W. H. Mudford, and possessed his full confidence. When he retired at the end of 1899, I was appointed editor, and from that date I have been responsible for everything that has appeared in its columns ... Mr Pearson, when he took possession of *The Standard*, asked me to remain as editor, but I did not see how the proprietor of the *Daily Express* (professedly Liberal) and of the *St. James's Gazette* (avowedly Conservative) but both Chamberlainite agents, could possibly wish to publish *The Standard* as a Conservative free-trader journal, especially as he was the chairman of the executive committee of the Tariff Reform League.

Further letters printed in *The Times* on the controversy were to come from Winston Churchill: 'Why did Mr Pearson buy *The Standard*? ... to make it the mouthpiece of the chairman of the Tariff Reform League'; Pearson in reply; Curtis once more; Sidney Low; and, finally, in humorous vein, on 26 November, from G. K. Chesterton. For Curtis, a man of such high principles, there could be no return to the paper he had served so faithfully for almost thirty years. His days in Fleet Street were over; and less than two years later, in May 1907, he was dead – in a sense the victim of Tariff Reform. As for the new editor, H. A. Gwynne, he believed that *The Standard* should now pursue a strongly imperialistic course, while still supporting protectionism. Pearson had already spoken to the Prime Minister, at the time of the purchase of the paper, and Balfour had been 'merely the listener to a man of business talking with the enthusiasm of an expert upon his own business'.

NEW APPOINTMENTS

Apart from the changes on *The Standard*, Pearson had also been making new appointments on the *Evening Standard*, the chief one being the placement of his cousin, William Woodward, as editor. Other newcomers on the staff included Guy Pollock and Lints Smith. It was said that when Pearson first went over to *The Standard* office he enquired in vain for the editor of the *Evening Standard*. No one had ever heard of such a person. Pearson finally found himself in the composing room, where the head printer was sitting with a pile of manuscripts in front of him. 'By his side were two baskets, one was labelled "copy" and the other "muck". The printer used his own discretion. The "copy" was set. The "muck" was not.'[18]

Having appointed an editor for the paper, Pearson turned his attention early in the New Year to its rivals, and on 14 January 1905 it was announced that the *Evening Standard* and the *St. James's Gazette* were to merge. One commentator in the *Newspaper Owner* noted: 'The *St. James's Gazette* type of paper is the paper that sells for a penny in the evening, and the *Evening Standard* has a certain reputation and distinction. Combine the two papers, thereafter; call the publication the *Evening Standard*, but retain for it the more popular features of style and size that experience has proved to be popular; and you have the elements of probable success.' The *Evening Standard* management were quick to point out that its sales were a great deal larger than that of any other penny London evening paper. In fact, they were as large as any two others: 'It has not a large book-stall sale but a very large sale in other directions'.

Acknowledging this, the *Newspaper Owner* replied:

> We are glad to hear that this well-known paper has so much a larger circulation than has generally been imagined, and if it be really the fact that it beats both *The Globe* and the *Westminster Gazette* put together, even without being strongly in evidence in the evening trains, the explanation must be, we suppose, be sought in the fact that it gets farther afield than most of its competitors, and has come to be regarded as an institution in provincial reading rooms, in country hotels and other newspaper centres.

Gwynne, meanwhile, had been addressing the Authors' Club and told its members – including Sir Arthur Conan Doyle and C. B. Fry – that as editor of *The Standard* 'he was resolved in all matters connected with foreign affairs and with the Army and Navy to view things from a national point of view, and not in a merely party spirit'. He added that this is what he had always been accustomed to do, and he would, consequently, 'find it congenial to him to carry out on *The Standard* those principles of independence in imperial and strictly national matters which have been a distinguishing feature of the *Daily Express*, under the same proprietorship'.

With the purchase of *The Standard*, and the subsequent merger of the *Evening Standard* with the *St. James's Gazette*, Pearson was now able to claim 8 per cent of the daily reading public. His titles were:

Daily Express, London
The Standard, London
Evening Standard and St. James's Gazette, London
Daily Gazette and Express, Birmingham
North Mail, Newcastle upon Tyne
Leicester Evening News.

Pearson's weekly publications, 'which convey the impression that they are edited with a view to appealing to a more educated class', included *Pearson's Weekly, Home Notes, M.A.P., Smith's Weekly, The Big Budget, The Boy's Leader* and *Isobel's Dressmaking and Home Cookery.* His monthly publications were: the *Royal Magazine, Pearson's Magazine, Home Magazine of Fiction, Rapid Review* and *Pearson's Music.*

A breakdown of Pearson's finances showed that the *Daily Express* was a private company with a capital of £1,500 in one shilling shares, of which Pearson held 16,402. Debenture charges amounting to £250,000 had also been registered. Similar arrangements existed in the cases of the *North Mail*, the *Birmingham Daily Gazette and Express* and the *Leicester Evening News.* The Pearson periodicals, which produced thirteen titles, were owned by C. Arthur Pearson Ltd., with Pearson and Peter Keary as joint managing directors. The capital was £400,000, of which £250,000 was in 5½ per cent deferred shares of £5 each and £150,000 ordinary shares of £1 each; Pearson held 79,950 of the latter. The company had paid a regular dividend of 15 per cent, and, in addition, an annual bonus of 5 per cent during the preceding seven years.[19]

IMPERIAL PREFERENCE

On 6 February 1905, Gwynne ran a series of articles over four days in *The Standard* on Imperial Preference, calling for a 5 per cent tax on all imports, with enumerated exemptions from colonial suppliers. Printed with the full approval of Pearson, the articles differed from the Chamberlain doctrine of 10 per cent duty on all foreign manufacturers. Chamberlain, most displeased with the paper's stance, immediately wrote to the secretary of the Tariff Reform League, Professor W. S. Hewins:

> Pearson has been thinking of something of this sort since he took over the paper. I am much disappointed at Pearson's action and do not understand it. It will not do … that the political cause which we have at heart should be in any way prejudiced in order to suit the exigencies of a newspaper, and while we have no right to press Mr Pearson to do anything against his own interest we must I think ask him to separate his fortunes from ours.

Yet, despite Chamberlain's misgivings, he was to write to Pearson on 17 February 'in a very cordial letter' suggesting that Pearson should stand for Parliament. He declined the invitation, believing that he was temperamentally unsuited to the never-ending debates. Less than a month later, on 3 March, Pearson sent in his resignation to the Duke of Sutherland, the League's President:

> With great regret I find myself compelled to place in your hands my resignation from the office of chairman of the Tariff Reform League. During the last few months my business responsibilities have increased to such an extent that I do not find it possible to devote to the work of the league the time and attention by which, in my opinion, should be devoted to it by occupying the responsible position of chairman.[20]

At the next meeting of the League, Chamberlain moved the following resolution:

> That the executive committee expresses its sincere regret that Mr C. Arthur Pearson has felt compelled through the pressure of his business engagements to resign the position of chairman of the league ... and desires to record its high appreciation of the invaluable services rendered by Mr Pearson to the Tariff Reform League.

Throughout the summer of 1905, Chamberlain was securing more and more Conservative support for the League. His plans for a strong, united Empire, and to improve the standard of living in Great Britain by imposing taxes on food and raw material from non-imperial sources, were gaining ground. For Balfour, there was the pressure to declare himself – and on 2 June, at the Albert Hall, he talked of that 'other great branch of fiscal reform which stirs a responsive fibre in the heart of every citizen of the Empire as the most urgent of all the constructive problems with which we had to deal'. However, on 4 December 1905, as a result of the intra-party divisiveness caused by Chamberlain's Tariff Reform campaign and the growing unpopularity of his government, Balfour resigned. At the general election held the following month his party was shattered and, the final ignominy, he himself lost his seat. The new Parliament consisted of 377 Liberals, led by Sir Henry Campbell-Bannerman as Prime Minister; 157 Conservatives; 83 Irish Nationalists; and the emerging Labour Party with 53 members. Chamberlain and his seven cohorts won their seats in Birmingham and, until Balfour's hasty return to the House as member for the City of London, he led the Opposition. For a moment it looked as if Chamberlain would become the new leader of the Conservatives, but it was to be a fleeting illusion.

However, on 7 July 1906, the citizens of Birmingham held a tremendous fête in honour of Chamberlain's seventieth birthday, and his thirtieth year as a Member of Parliament. Two days later, in a great speech in Bingley Hall, he ranged over his political life from the struggle against Home Rule to the need to abandon Free Trade policy:

> The union of the Empire must be preceded and accompanied, as I have said, by a better understanding, by a closer sympathy. To secure that is the highest object of statesmanship now at the beginning of the twentieth century; and, if these were the last words that I were permitted to utter to you, I would rejoice to utter them in your presence and with your approval.

With savage irony, his words proved to be prophetic, because just two days later Chamberlain suffered a paralytic stroke which deprived him of public speech for the rest of his life. It has been said that he was the 'greatest might have been' in modern political history. Possessed of strong ideals, capability and vision beyond any of his contemporaries, he had been destroyed by Ireland and Home Rule. He died on 2 July 1914, four days after the assassinations at Sarajevo – the event that brought about the misery of the Great War of 1914–18.

Less than a week after Pearson had resigned from the Tariff Reform League there appeared on 8 March 1905 the first issue of his combined paper, *The Evening Standard and the St. James's Gazette.* The merger was welcomed in the trade journals, the *Newspaper Owner* commenting:

> We understand that in this combined publication a strenuous effort will be made to create a new style of daily evening journal, which shall, in its main features, typify the penny evening of the future. The great point that is, we gather, to be steadily kept in view, is that, given the necessary telegraphic and mechanical facilities, an evening newspaper may, in the present advanced state of the art of daily newspaper production, be made a practically complete chronicle of the events of the day on which it is published. What would have seemed to be impossible has been successfully accomplished ... the two are rolled into one, and a strong resemblance to both parents is traceable in an exceedingly promising offspring. There is even the same typographical expression combined with a general brightening up of features and rounding of contour, which are so much to the good.

Alfred Harmsworth, however, was not prepared to let Pearson, his arch-rival, steal a march, and he immediately announced that the *Evening News* would be bringing out a new edition – on the same day as the revamped *Evening Standard.* Selling at a halfpenny, its eight pages contained some of its rival's traditional features. Having first regretted the passing of the old *Evening Standard* – and belittling its circulation and revenue – it seemed as though the *Evening News* was itself publishing a carbon copy as a late edition. Harmsworth, though, rejected the idea: 'Of course it will be nothing of the kind. The old *Evening*

Standard was practically a reprint of the morning *Standard*, with some extra telegraphic and other news, and there is about as much resemblance between the *Evening Standard* as it was and the *Evening News* as it is and always will be, as there would be between Noah's Ark and an Atlantic liner.'[21]

A fortnight before the launch of the revamped *Evening Standard*, the statutory meeting of the new company was held at Winchester House, Broad Street, with Pearson, as chairman and managing director, presiding. He said he thought it should be known that the recent share issue of *The Standard* Newspapers Ltd. had been a great success. The preference shares, which were offered to the public, had been over-subscribed nearly twice over, and the issue of the debenture stock had also been largely over-subscribed. He believed he could say without fear of contradiction that *The Standard* was now a much better paper, and its circulation was already more than that of *The Evening Standard and St. James's Gazette.* This would inevitably mean that it would prove to be a valuable advertising medium, and consequently a great asset to the company.

Since the merger of the two papers, only fifty-five letters had been received from readers who had not cared for *The Standard* in its new format – not a very large number, he thought, out of the scores of thousands of people who *were* interested. Turning to Alfred Harmsworth, he said the methods used by the *Evening News* in bringing out an additional issue were not those which would have commended themselves to everybody from the point of view of good taste, but he had no wish to constitute himself a judge of other's people's methods in doing business.

MAINTAINED PRIVATE OFFICE

Within weeks of launching the merged *Standard*, Pearson had moved the offices of the *Daily Express* from Tudor Street into a building opposite *The Standard* offices in Shoe Lane. There he had a bridge built across the lane and maintained a private office in each building. Always a glutton for work, he was at this time spending almost all his waking hours on his papers – a point noted by Harmsworth, who remarked: 'He is an easy man to argue with, most industrious, and his vanity would keep him there 14 hours a day'.

Pearson himself recorded for posterity how he managed his daily business affairs:

> I lead a methodical life, getting up at seven o'clock and going to bed at midnight, although, on average, I was up till four for a number of days after I took over *The Standard.* The first thing I do is read some

> of my papers. Fortunately, I can get over a column of type in half the time that will be taken by anyone else I have ever come across.
>
> I get through with that lot by seven forty-five, then I exercise to eight-thirty, swinging my arms and legs about – all that sort of thing – good hard work, getting a good sweat. A man comes to me every morning and puts me through my paces. I need a lot of exercise and take it in this way in tabloid form. At eight-thirty I read more newspapers for a quarter of an hour. Then I have a bath. After a very light breakfast my secretaries come along with my letters, collected from all the different places, and I usually manage to go through these by ten o'clock, that means I have broken the back of the day's routine and am free to sort out the rest of the morning according to circumstances.
>
> My one great rule is that the busier I am the longer I take for lunch. It is a light lunch, but I take my time over a cigar after it. I am perfectly sure that going back to work directly after lunch is the thing to kill you. Perhaps the hardest fight in my life now is to get rid of detail. I keep seeing things all the time that I fancy I can do better than the man who happens to be doing them; but once you succumb to temptation of that sort there are a thousand temptations of the same kind all equally strong, and your effectiveness is lost. With every new venture, however, I go into details with a microscopic eye; nothing is too small to master and rearrange until it is producing its utmost effectiveness. Then leave it alone as much as you can. One of the great rules of business is to forget things and to get someone else to remember them for you. Here is my pocket notebook, for instance. The minute I think of anything to be done, down it goes in the book and my mind is free of it.
>
> The first thing my personal secretary does when he comes to me is to say 'Notebook', then we work off all the entries accumulated. My secretary is my memory to the greatest possible extent. I save myself in every possible way. I figure that I save several hours of each year by signing only my initials to all of the great number of business letters I dictate – excepting only those, of course, that are of importance.[22]

Although Pearson had been confident at the launch of *The Standard* Newspapers Ltd., twelve months later, at the first annual meeting, he was far less sanguine. He said that the period which had passed since the formation of the company had been one of great difficulty. The directors had been literally and figuratively engaged in simultaneously pulling down and rebuilding on old foundations; the whole business had had to be reorganised, most of its routine changed and the editorial methods revised; and while all this was being accomplished the papers had to be produced day and night without a pause.

Pearson went on to say that the most important event that had happened since the business had come under his control had been the alteration in appearance and character of the evening paper. Owing to improved mechanical facilities and the reorganisation of the editorial department, it was now possible to go to press sufficiently early to catch trains from London to the provinces which had not hitherto been used by penny papers. This would, he had no doubt, exercise a further beneficial effect upon the circulation of the morning paper, which, for some time past, had been steadily increasing.

An interesting account of *The Standard* during Pearson's time was given in later years by William Colley, who in his career between 1894 and 1931 had worked for a variety of papers. Colley was at the *Daily Mail*, when he received a letter from a former colleague, Charles Watney, now news editor for Pearson: '*The Standard* wants a really first-class man. It might be worth your while if you came forward. What are your views on the salary question, etc., etc.?'

To quote Colley:

> I was now entering its halls, deeply impressed by its historic past. It was sick. Hard times had come to it. There was a scent of adventure in co-operating to bring it back to favour and circulation. Particularly attractive was the idea that *The Standard* could resume its old place in world politics and influence foreign governments and peoples. During the whole of my tenure until the Great War that was my fixed and hidden hope. But when I crossed Fleet Street to begin my editorial duties with *The Standard* it seemed like stepping from the market place to the cloisters of a venerable cathedral. Movement was slower, deliberation was halting, decision paused and the past impregnated the whole atmosphere.
>
> It reminded me, in its ineffectiveness, of an elderly man wearing three overcoats, three suits of clothes, three sets of underwear, three pairs of woollen gloves and trying to balance three hats to help him to catch a train. We were appreciably overstaffed.
>
> The office had all sorts of many requisites, but only one size of salary – the big size. At the particular work he was supposed to do I cannot recall a mildly inefficient member of the whole staff. It was a widely read and deeply learned staff, taken throughout. At first I was 'adjutant' to Mr (now Sir) William Maxwell. He resigned after a little while, and I became Chief of the Sub-editorial Staff. A review of the army revealed 'overcrowding' of staff and 'ample, nay, plethoric supplies' of copy.
>
> That a full dose of the desk had fallen to me again was apparent. It was presumed that in my position I knew everything that was going on, and most of the news. I did – most of it. First came Mr

Samuel Jeyes in evening dress, usually from the Garrick Club, with a fat cigar. He was an Oxford 'star', who wrote beautifully, was a fine classical scholar and a devotee of Mr Joseph Chamberlain. In followed Mr (later Sir) Sidney Low, former editor of *St. James's Gazette*, classical scholar and pungent writer, and with them was Mr Wheeler, former Indian judge. They all wanted to know. They were all about to write leading articles, more topical, if necessary, than the leaders they had prepared. They all had to be told as befitted their dignity and high calling. Their work was really high-class if somewhat Victorian.

Mr E. R. Thompson was night editor and read and selected letters 'to the Editor'. He also made-up the paper. Mr (now Sir) Malcolm Fraser was acting editor, as the editor-in-chief, Mr Herbert Gwynne, was only then taking duty during the day. The dramatic critics chose their own work. The musical critics kept their own schedule of duties. Mr Watney managed the rest of the news-getting, a sporting editor removed all responsibility from his shoulders in the department of rod, line, hunting, football, fencing, cricket and the like. These were water-tight compartments: independent departments: and *The Standard* expected every man to do his duty, and he undoubtedly did so, without much let and with little hindrance. But the whole thing was unscientific and not controlled from any given point.

In the editorial department one saw only the results of the daily in-gathering. At command, a brilliant reportorial staff now being built up. After an interval came Edgar Wallace, and Bernard Falk was added on the 'outside staff'. A grave, somewhat juridical, introduction was A. J. Russell, produced in the Isle of Wight, later in life to become several things besides the tallest man in Shoe Lane. A very modest lady, young, sedate, quiet and industrious, was our first woman reporter. She wrote carefully, and gathered her facts methodically. There was something fresh, attractive and compelling respect about her. I watched her copy closely. It usually got into the paper. ... She faded away for a while and became the literary amanuensis of Thomas Hardy, the famous novelist. She is now Mrs (Thomas) Hardy, the devoted wife of that great man.[23]

Others on the reporting staff included Arthur Burrows, an Oxford man, with a most distinctive voice, who later became the first announcer of the BBC; and Andrew Soutar, who was to gain acceptance as a novelist. Apart from three drama critics, and three music critics, the paper also had a number of book reviewers, the chief of whom was Hugh Walpole. He was then to win fame as a novelist and was later knighted.

BIDDING FOR *THE TIMES*

As for Pearson, he was now about to bid for *The Times*. With the assistance of Sir Alexander Henderson, the financier and chief supporter of *The Standard* and *Daily Express*, a meeting was arranged with the Walter family, advised by Lord Rothschild. As a consequence, on 1 January 1908, a printed memorandum setting out details of the sale of *The Times* was prepared. It was, however, provisional and would need the consent of the proprietors and the Court. In the statement it was noted that Pearson held the ordinary shares in The *Daily Express* Limited and the deferred and ordinary shares in *The Standard* Newspapers Limited. Pearson stipulated that his company had ordinary liquid assets equal to their current liabilities and, between them, additional working capital of £20,000; that all these assets with the goodwill of *The Times*, the printing business, and other assets in connection therewith owned by the Walters should be transferred to a new company. The capital was to be £850,000, and the price to be paid by the new company for the Pearson holdings was to be £150,000 in ordinary shares.

It was also agreed that the character of *The Times* would not be changed and its prestige and position as an independent organ would be preserved and maintained:

> The political direction and the appointment of the more important members of the staff of the Company shall, subject to the absolute control of the Board, be vested in the said Arthur Fraser Walter and the said Cyril Arthur Pearson including the following viz; Editor, Assistant Editor, Foreign Editor, City Editor, Principal Leader Writers, Correspondents in Paris, Berlin, Vienna, St. Petersburg, New York, Ottawa, Sydney and Melbourne.

Pearson, as managing director, was to receive a salary of £2,500 a year and commission upon profits after certain deductions had been made.[24]

Four days later, Fleet Street was surprised to read in The *Observer* of Sunday, 5 January 1908:

> **THE FUTURE OF THE TIMES**
> It is understood that important negotiations are taking place which will place the direction of *The Times* in the hands of a very capable proprietor of several magazines and newspapers.

Having lost out to Pearson with *The Standard* in 1904, Alfred Harmsworth [now Lord Northcliffe] saw the opportunity to pay off Pearson and to secure *The Times*. Northcliffe was later to say: 'I put the paragraph in the *Observer* [which he owned] to expose the Pearson conspiracy.'

In its issue of 7 January 1908, *The Times* announced that negotiations were in progress with Pearson who, as the proposed managing director, would reorganise the business side. However, the editorial character of the paper would remain unchanged and would be conducted on lines independent of party politics. That same day, Northcliffe printed the story in the *Daily Mail*; and in one significant paragraph quoted Joseph Chamberlain: 'Mr Pearson is the greatest hustler I have ever known. He is a great believer in the strenuous life. It is one of the sayings that his success is due to the habit he contracted as a young man of never wasting time and always working with extraordinary speed.'[25]

Northcliffe followed up the article with a telegram from the Ritz Hotel in Paris, where he was staying, addressed pointedly to: C. Arthur Pearson, *The Times*, London:

> PLEASE ACCEPT MY WARMEST CONGRATULATIONS AND ADMIRATION FOR YOUR MOST SPLENDID JOURNALISTIC ACHIEVEMENT ON RECORD HAVE WRITTEN PERSONAL SKETCH OF YOU PROOF WILL BE SUBMITTED TONIGHT

By late morning, Pearson had received a wired proof of the article, which noted his achievements and his future plans. He was delighted, and that afternoon wired Northcliffe:

> MY SINCEREST THANKS FOR YOUR MORE THAN KIND TELEGRAM AND FOR THE STATEMENTS ABOUT ME THAT HAVE APPEARED AND ARE TO APPEAR IN THE DAILY MAIL YOUR GENEROSITY IS OVERWHELMING AND I AM DEEPLY APPRECIATIVE

Following the despatch of the telegram, Pearson wrote a letter of thanks to Northcliffe:

> I trust that I may have an opportunity of showing one day how much I appreciate your action. Words are poor things in such cases and written words particularly so. Perhaps you will let me tell you how kind I think it of you, one day when you return. Were all 'opponents' as generous as yourself, business life would be a good deal happier than it is apt to be.[26]

On 7 January Northcliffe sent Pearson a cable, requesting that he be interviewed for the *Daily Mail* on his forthcoming purchase of *The Times.* Pearson replied that all the publicity for him was 'rubbing things in too much' so far as the Walters were concerned, and from their point of view he did not want to be seen as pushing himself: 'Believe me, I very much appreciate all that you have done, and will be very glad, if you still think it worth while, to have a talk with the *Daily Mail* after I have been in *The Times* office a few days.'[27]

Later that day, a confident and relaxed Pearson took the chair at a dinner held in the Savoy for his key staff on *The Standard.* He assured them that he had not the slightest intention of stopping separate publication of *The Standard.* His staff were, quite naturally, elated and drank a toast to their proprietor, wishing him every success at Printing House Square. So sure was Pearson of victory that the Savoy chef had reproduced *The Times* clock in ice as a table centrepiece.

However, even while *The Standard* staff were celebrating, Kennedy Jones, Northcliffe's key executive, and the man who had obtained the *Evening News* for the Chief, was already at work. After considering leading a consortium to bid for *The Times,* Jones turned to Northcliffe and sent the following telegram:

> ARE YOU PREPARED TO COME INTO A DEAL WHICH WILL UPSET NEGOTIATIONS EVENTUALLY ACCQUIRING BUSINESS OURSELVES? PROFITS ON PAPER HAVE FOR EIGHT YEARS NEVER BEEN BELOW THIRTY THOUSAND SCHEME WOULD REQUIRE THREE FIFTY THOUSAND WHICH WE COULD BORROW AND PROMISES GOOD MONEY IN RETURN WOULD HAVE TO BE CARRIED THROUGH BY SOME BIG MAN OR SYNDICATE WHO COULD SAVE ORGANIZATION FOR EMPIRE SUTTON CAN START TONIGHT KAY JAY

The following evening, Jones was in Paris with Northcliffe – and the plans were laid to take over *The Times.*[28]

At the period of Pearson's bid for *The Times,* there had been doubts expressed in the City, even though Sir Alexander Henderson was regarded as the main backer. The latest published figures for *The Standard* and the *Daily Express* for the year ended 30 June 1907 had shown a profit of £33,000, but a recent increase in advertisement rates on the *Daily Express* was expected to yield further profits of £15,000 before commissions. According to the auditors, the circulation of *The Standard* was decreasing and was 'not showing any indication of an increase in income'. There was even talk in Fleet Street that *The Standard* was on the point of closing; but with both papers being printed on the presses of *The Times* plant it was estimated that profits would be in excess of £50,000, and there would be significant sharings in costs, especially with regard to *The Times.*

Northcliffe, meanwhile, had by then also involved Sutton, another of his key executives, in the secret bid for *The Times,* and suggested to him on 9 January 1908 that they stop the Pearson negotiations by a slightly superior offer, but let Pearson remain as managing director, 'under our guidance, in which case I think he would be an excellent one'. Northcliffe insisted that complete secrecy be maintained, as he did not wish Pearson to increase his offer for *The Times.*

For the next three months, Northcliffe played a very clever hand: he attacked Pearson anonymously in *The Observer*: 'he is a little over forty', 'an adventurer', who has done 'well and sensational things'. On 3 February, Northcliffe wrote to his solicitors: 'I am desirous of purchasing *The Times* on behalf of myself and others, and I authorize you up to June 30th 1908, to negotiate for the purchase of the copyright thereof for any sum up to £350,000. I agree to be satisfied with the purchase at that price.'[29]

The next move for Northcliffe was to meet with Moberly Bell, the general manager of *The Times.* As usual, he came straight to the point: 'Well, Mr Bell, I am going to buy *The Times* with your assistance if you will give it; without it, if you will not.' In less than a week a deal had been struck.

Walter, having given a tacit approval to the Bell proposal, now had the task of informing Pearson that his scheme must fail. He had been surprised at the almost unanimous opposition from the other proprietors of *The Times* and from the Establishment. A chastened Pearson realised that he could not now win, and reluctantly agreed to withdraw his name from the scheme.

With Pearson thwarted, Bell determined to have Northcliffe, still hiding under the anonymity of 'Mr X', accepted as the future proprietor of *The Times.*

However, despite withdrawing from the negotiations, Pearson was not finished, and on February 18 told the Press Association that he was still interested in purchasing *The Times.* There were to be three rivals for the paper: Pearson; Miss Brodie-Hall, one of the minor proprietors; and Northcliffe, still shielding under Mr 'X'. Late in the afternoon of March 16, Bell telegraphed Northcliffe at Versailles:

GONE THROUGH AS WE WANTED

For Northcliffe it was exactly as he had predicted – and at £320,000 *The Times* was £30,000 less than had been allowed.

12
Dalziel in Charge

Within days of losing his battle for *The Times*, Pearson, on 18 March 1908, was operated on for glaucoma. Since childhood, he had suffered with his eyesight, and had invariably worn glasses. There was little doubt that the long hours of travelling while he had been building up his publishing empire – reading constantly in poorly-lit railway carriages – had now taken their toll. Unfortunately, following the operation, he was never again able to see well enough to read or write. His doctors advised him to rest completely for six months, and he went to Frensham Place, his country home. There, neither his large aviary nor golf could excite him, and walking was to become his chief pleasure, often up to twenty miles a day.[1] Towards the end of the year, he had recovered enough to enable him to travel up to Shoe Lane each morning to supervise his newspapers and to attend board meetings. However, within three months, the strain was to prove too much, and Pearson realised that there was no hope of his sight improving.

In the spring of 1909 he set off on a walking tour through the Austrian Tyrol, and on his return to England he became involved in establishing the first Imperial Press Conference. Two years earlier, his private secretary, Mr (later Sir) Harry Brittain, while on a visit to Canada, had devised a plan to set up a conference of Empire newspaper executives. In June 1909, under the leadership of Pearson, and assisted by Brittain and Gwynne, a conference was held in London, culminating in a great banquet in the Earls Court Exhibition Halls, with more than fifty Empire delegates attending, plus scores from Great Britain. As originator and organiser, Brittain was presented with a magnificent gold and silver trophy of Britannia and Mercury, representing the press, by the overseas delegates. A barrister, Brittain had been educated at Repton and Oxford, and had joined Pearson in 1902 to assist in the work of the Tariff Reform League, later moving to the management staff of *The Standard*. From this first conference grew the Empire Press Union, with Lord Burnham as president, Lord Northcliffe as treasurer, Pearson as chairman, and Brittain as honorary secretary.[2]

As for *The Standard*, under Gwynne's editorship it was a much less sombre newspaper: on most days it comprised twelve pages with seven $15\frac{1}{2}$-em $24\frac{1}{2}$-inch columns on each. Of these eighty-four columns, approximately thirty were devoted to advertising. The paper, though, still maintained its dignified front page of advertisements. When

Pearson found that ordinary linage did not run to a page he immediately originated a special feature of a Continental Hotel Directory (as in the *Evening Standard* he had made a speciality of flats and houses to let), which now ran to three columns. Page 2 remained a full page of City news and stock market prices, while page 3 covered agriculture, markets, company intelligence and shipping. General news was to be found on Page 4, which embraced such topics as Unionist Party Organisation, new books, country notes, suburban pantomimes, and Progress of Japan. On page 6 were to be found the summary column and leaders, while the facing page 7 covered foreign news. Sport, especially cricket, also featured strongly in the paper, as did stories concerning the motor car.

Throughout this period, Gwynne had been bringing to the attention of A. J. Balfour, the former Prime Minister, the shortcomings of the navy, and the need to increase its strength in view of the growing German navy. The relationship with Balfour and the Unionists was one that Gwynne was determined to maintain; he believed that he and his paper could be of use to the party, especially as it was supporting *The Standard* both financially and through the supplying of exclusive news items. This is clear in a letter that he wrote to Balfour on 8 April 1908, in response to a complaint of an offending paragraph in *The Standard*:

> It will not be necessary for me to put in a defence of the paragraph to which you complain. It happened to be published without being seen by me. On the morning of its appearance I wrote to my Lobby Correspondent and among other things I referred to his note of the night before on the following lines: 'We (i.e. *The Standard*) have endorsed and supported Mr Balfour's attitude (on the Fiscal Question) without questions or doubtings and it is very unfortunate that your note should have slipped in, since it may lead the unwary to imagine that we are still at the carping and doubting stage, whereas we are strong and unswerving in our belief that the Birmingham speech thoroughly closed the ranks of the party in the matter.' I think this will give a better idea of my opinion of the note than anything I could write now. I can only regret, with all sincerity, the misfortune of its appearance in *The Standard.* Would you like anything done to counteract its possible effects? If so, I need not tell you that I shall be most delighted to carry out any suggestion you may have.[3]

Pearson, meanwhile, increasingly troubled with his eyesight, now decided that there should be senior editorial changes on the paper, and at the end of 1908 he wrote to Sidney Low, terminating his engagement. Of all Pearson's autocratic decisions, this was undoubtedly one of his strangest, for Low was not only an assistant editor of the paper – at one time, even, a likely editor of *The Standard* – but one of the most-respected journalists in Fleet Street and Whitehall.

Ever anxious to retain the services of his friend, Gwynne proposed to Pearson that Low should now be employed mostly on foreign missions. After a hiatus of six weeks Pearson relented and an arrangement was made by which Low was to return to *The Standard* and write four leaders and one signed article weekly. For the remainder of his time on the paper, the leaders of Low, written in their classical style, were a strong feature, and, although penned under the cloak of anonymity, were easily identified by discerning readers.

Many years later, Gwynne wrote: 'Sidney Low was an old friend of mine, for whom I had a very great regard and he was a leader writer of *The Standard* under me for a considerable time. We met in the hurly burly of newspaper life; we were very good friends and I found him not merely a supremely skilful craftsman but of a very generous, kindly and sympathetic nature.'[4]

THE PEOPLE'S BUDGET

In the spring of 1909, David Lloyd George, the Liberal Chancellor of the Exchequer, introduced his People's Budget, which, after allowing for the building of eight dreadnought battleships, provided for the introduction of an old age pension scheme – at a total cost of £15 million. To pay for these measures, tax on incomes over £3,000 was increased from 1s to 1s 2d in the pound; death duties were raised; taxes were put on spirits and tobacco; and a land tax was established.[5]

The Budget provoked a furore, and none were more vociferous than the Tory land-owning classes in the House of Lords. All newspapers were now embroiled in the affair, with the party agents ensuring that their doctrines were being followed; throughout the summer the Budget was debated in the Commons and in the press. Concerned that Balfour was preparing to 'surrender to the Government under threat of royal pressure', on October 14 the editors of *The Standard, Daily Telegraph, Daily Mail* and *Daily Express* saw J. S. Sandars, his private secretary, and after having been 'hopelessly on the wrong tack were put on reasonable lines' by an assurance Balfour would stand firm against the Budget.

During this period, *The Standard* – losing circulation and prestige – was considered to be prey to a take-over; and Frederick Huth Jackson, a director of the Bank of England, was to be involved in leading a group of capitalists wishing to purchase the paper to run it as 'a daily organ of central opinion'. Their plans came to naught, and *The*

Standard was to continue with its pro-Tory political stance. The paper was also involved in the setting-up of a Working Men Candidates' Fund, having an early success in an October by-election, when John Dunphrys captured Bermondsey from the Liberals. On 14 December Gwynne was able to announce in his columns that *The Standard* had collected more than £6,000 in support of working-class Tories.

Meanwhile, on 4 November, the Budget had been passed in the Commons by 379 votes to 149, but three weeks later on 30 November, it was rejected by the Lords by 350 to 75. Two days later, Herbert Asquith, determined not to have the Commons overruled, proposed the following resolution, which was prominently displayed in *The Standard*: 'That the action of the House of Lords in refusing to pass into law the financial provisions made by this House for the sessions of the year, is a breach of the Constitution and a usurpation of the rights of the Commons.'

Gwynne commented in his leader:

> In the terms of the Resolution put down by Mr Asquith for discussion today in the House of Commons there is a degree of inexactitude, unusual even in the language of official Liberalism. It is untrue, as a matter of fact, that the Lords have refused to pass into law the financial proposals made by the Commons for the sessions of the year. They did not refuse to pass the Finance Bill; they suspended it until the views of the country had been ascertained. ... On the one hand they [the Unionists] will stand up stoutly for the Peers, who in a memorable crisis have acquitted themselves like men; on the other they will lose no opportunity of explaining the objects and describing the methods of Tariff Reform.[6]

Parliament was prorogued the following day, and in the election which followed there was a confused result: Liberals 275; Conservatives, 273; Labourites, 40; and Irish Nationalists, 82. Naturally enough, Asquith's decision to go to the country on a matter of principle had attracted a large press coverage: A survey of the election, during the eight weeks after 3 December 1909, showed that the *Manchester Guardian* had devoted 39,600 column inches, or 40 per cent of its editorial space, and next came *The Standard* with 26,000 column inches or 29 per cent.

On 14 April 1910, with the support of the eighty-two Irish Nationalist MPs, who sought and expected Home Rule, the Liberals were successful in their three resolutions, which contained the substance of the proposed Parliament Bill. A fortnight later, on 27 April, the Budget was finally passed and allowed through the Lords, so a constitutional crisis which had loomed large for more than a year – with the King guaranteeing to create enough peers to overcome the Lords' opposition – was over, at least for a time.

Hardly had the Commons recovered from this constitutional crisis when the nation was suddenly plunged into deep mourning. On 6 May, King Edward VII died. His sorrowing son, King George V, wrote: 'At 11.45 beloved Papa passed peacefully away & I have lost my best friend & the best of fathers'. For *The Standard,* it was to be a night of high drama; and William Colley, who was chief sub-editor at the time, has left a graphic account of how the news was treated at Shoe Lane:

> We had just finished a difficult period at Westminster, caused by Mr Asquith and the House of Lords' invasion of the realm of finance, when King Edward suddenly passed away. On that night *The Standard* was made-up and formes were about to be locked. Our headlines had reached the 'critically ill' stage. The leading article embodying the news and the grief of the Empire was included. Then, like a bolt from the blue, came the tragic news just seventeen minutes before going to press. Everyone was stunned. The whole office was brought to a standstill. Then for the first and only time in my long career I took my jacket off. Rules (for mourning) were turned, headlines changed, and a new leaderette announcing the death was written and set up at full speed.[7]

Writing many years later, Bernard Falk, a one-time colleague, had this to say of Colley's skill:

> In the twinkling of an eye he would have the main story of the front page changed for something later and better. I have known him to have out at the printers, in twelve minutes, a leader column with headings complete. A reporter had only to come in with a big story for him to seize that story, skilfully extract the gist, and, slip by slip, written up by himself with incredible rapidity, put a new lead on the lino. machines. Such quickness I have never seen since.[8]

Gwynne was determined that *The Standard*'s coverage of the funeral of Edward VII would be second to none, and, taking up the suggestion of Thompson, his news editor, he engaged Frank Brangwyn,[9] the well-known artist, to provide an impressionistic sketch of the King's body at Paddington station. The drawing, which covered an area of 5 columns by 12 inches, showed a shaft of light illuminating the coffin as it was carried onto the train for its final journey to Windsor. The chief role of covering the funeral was given to Edgar Wallace, who had recently joined the paper, and was, no doubt, glad to be working once more with Gwynne, a colleague during the reporting of the Boer War. Wallace was by then one of the most famous reporters in Fleet Street. His first novel, *The Four Just Men,* published in 1905, had been a great success; and in the years following he was to become a prolific and highly-paid author of thrillers. He was also a successful writer of film scripts: his death occurred in Hollywood in 1932 at the age of 57 while working on the script of *King Kong*.

However, in 1910, Wallace was delighted to be back on the national press once more, where 'he flung himself into the reckless routine of the reporters' room with something like enthusiasm'.[10] He even considered it a pleasure to have been reporting the funeral of King Edward; but he considered it even more delightful to report Ascot for the paper, with a new grey morning coat and all expenses paid; he accepted his substantial winnings on Gold Cup Day as a happy omen.

Wallace's description of the scene in Westminster Hall, where Edward lay in state, was especially fine. The queue of the King's subjects wishing to pay their last respects stretched back five miles, and more than a quarter of a million mourners filed past:

> It was the day the earth was due to pass through the tail of Halley's Comet whose appearance called forth reminders that it was traditionally the prophet of disaster. ... Silence profound reigned in the ancient building; beams of sunlight melted the shadows in its grey recesses, and fell softly, caressingly on the coffin of the King, flashing on the jewels in the crown and glowing into flame on the motionless scarlet-clad figures of the King's guards.

One of the first acts of the new King George was to ask the Conservative and Liberal party leaders to attempt an amicable solution of the political crisis. To stave off another general election – which neither party wanted – the decision was taken to hold a Constitutional Conference. This met on 16 June at Downing Street, and was to last five months. Lloyd George was one of the chief participants – and was a notable source of leaks to the press. It was said of him that he never ventured to deliver a speech without first supplying polished copy to one reporter on condition that a proof was sent for final correction.

On 10 September, Gwynne wrote to J. S. Sandars in confidence: 'I was very interested in your summary of the situation. On one point I am in cordial agreement with you and that is the failure or success of the Conference depends upon Lloyd George and upon him alone. Asquith doesn't seem to count at all.' The Conference, which had dragged on into the autumn, now ran into difficulties over Home Rule. On 28 October, Gwynne wrote to Balfour, saying that 'such an ending due to such a contentious subject would not have greatly surprised or displeased the great mass of Unionists'. Gwynne considered that the breakdown of the Conference would be a national disaster, and informed Balfour 'in the most respectful way I can that you must not count upon me to conceal my opinions if the Conference breaks down'.

DRAMATIC CHANGES

While the People's Budget had been going through its final stages in the Commons, dramatic changes had also been occurring at Shoe Lane. Throughout the previous decade, *The Standard* had continued to support the Conservatives, and as such was the recipient of party funds – sometimes alleged to be as much as £10,000 a year. Arthur Steel Maitland, in charge of the Conservative Party's Central Office, considered 'that the recognized channel had to be a man of substance so as to make the transaction plausible; and the individual usually added some genuine investment of his own.'[11] One such person was Sir Alexander Henderson, a Liberal Unionist MP from 1898 to 1908 and again from 1913 to 1916, when he received a peerage and took the title Lord Faringdon. Henderson had backed Pearson when he launched the *Daily Express*, purchased *The Standard* and bid for *The Times*. Now he was supporting Davison Dalziel to buy *The Standard* from a sick and disappointed Pearson. For the previous six years, Pearson had striven to make a success of *The Standard* but, despite his fanatical enthusiasm and hard work in improving the contents and style of the paper, circulation and advertising had never been satisfactory.

In January 1909, *The Advertising World* had published the following tables, which showed the amount of advertising (in numbers of columns) of the London daily and evening papers:

> MORNING: *The Times*, 1,126; *Daily Telegraph*, 1,571; *Daily Mail*, 1,223; *Daily Chronicle*, 719; *Morning Leader*, 426; *Daily Express*, 697; *Daily News*, 752; *Daily Mirror*, 600; *Daily Graphic*, 555; *The Standard*, 794; *Morning Post*, 770.
>
> EVENING: *Westminster Gazette*, 388; *Evening Standard*, 608; *Globe*, 378; *Pall Mall Gazette*, 398; *Evening News*, 609; *Star*, 231.[12]

From those statistics, it was apparent that although *The Evening Standard* and the *Evening News* were almost equal in leading the way with the evenings, it was a very different story with regard to the morning papers – and the number of *The Standard*'s advertising columns, at 794, was only half that of *The Daily Telegraph, The Times* and the *Daily Mail*. Here was reason for the great concern.

Sidney Dark, in his biography of Pearson, wrote:

> The army of new newspaper readers were amply catered for by the half-penny newspapers, the *Daily Mail*, the *Daily Express*, the *Daily News* and the *Daily Chronicle* and *The Standard* had fallen so far behind in its bad years that it could never be re-established as a serious rival to *The Times*, the *Morning Post* and *The Daily Telegraph*. The public interest in the Tariff Reform agitation was for all intents and purposes destroyed by the Radical victory at the General Election of 1906, and by the stroke which took Mr Chamberlain permanently out of the ranks of the fighting politicians.
>
> Arthur Pearson was a man of splendid courage, but he detested being beaten. His early career had been one long romance of success, and it bored him to be responsible for a publication which showed no signs of becoming a genuine financial proposition. He grew weary of the losing battle. He once said that every time there was a fog or an east wind *The Standard* lost at least one of its elderly readers, and that there were never any young readers to replace the veterans.[13]

With his eyesight now failing badly, Pearson had had enough, and on 22 April 1910, he sold both *The Standard* and *The Evening Standard*, and, with his family, immediately left for Switzerland, remaining there for four months. By this time, Pearson knew that within a few short months he would be quite blind.

ENTER THE ENTREPENEUR

The new proprietor of *The Standard* was Davison Alexander Dalziel,[14] who was described as 'an entrepeneur in finance and service industries'. Born in Camden Town, London, on 17 October 1852, he was the son of Davison Octavian Dalziel, the youngest of eight brothers. Of these, seven were artists, four becoming well-known as the Brothers Dalziel, and experts in engraving.

From an early age, when he travelled to New South Wales as a youth and worked as a reporter on the *Sydney Echo*, Dalziel had led a varied and colourful life, and, after marrying Harriet Sarah Dunning, of the Exchange Hotel, Sydney, he became a journalist in the United States. In February 1886 he was sued by the Hanover National Bank of New York, who alleged that his purchase during the previous year of the National Printing Co. from C. H. McConnell was fraudulent, as was his subsequent sale of the firm to the Dalziel Printing Co., of Chicago. Dalziel immediately issued a counter-suit for $100,000 for libel, defamation and false oaths.

Four years later, another bank, S. A. Kean, of Chicago, obtained judgement against Daziel, and in the autumn of 1890 he sailed for

England, where, with American backing, he launched Dalziel's News Agency to challenge Reuters' supremacy in London. He immediately secured a coup, when on 7 October 1890, he signed a contract with Moberly Bell, the new manager of *The Times.* Bell saw the agreement as a clever move to play off one agency against another, and in the first two months *The Times* paid the new agency £700 for telegrams, almost double its normal subscription for the same period to Reuters.

With *The Times* as a key first customer, Dalziel now tackled the provincial newspapers, who were annoyed at Reuters' subscription rates. In a clever ploy, he took half the subscription to this news service in cash and the residue in free advertising space, which his agency then offered for re-sale. His speciality was lurid American sensationalism, and nothing was too small or too sensational: 'A murder in Canada was followed by a series of crimes, cyclones, and ravages of escaped animals, all suffered by obscure townships in the United States. In every case full details were given; and the names and mishaps of unknown citizens of Utah or Ohio suddenly provoked intense interest among the British public'.[15]

Reuters, with a fight on its hands, now launched a special interpretative service, quite separate from the normal telegrams, and at the same time greatly increased the supply of news from the United States. By April 1891, *The Times* had decided to take this special service, and twelve months later Dalziel was dismissed by Moberly Bell, who said that his task 'to infuse a spirit of competition into the agencies was now accomplished'. The following year almost every message from Dalziel was, according to Bell, 'absolutely devoid of foundation – and every line is pure invention'.[16] For Dalziel and his agency, the writing was on the wall, and the end came when Reuters was able to show that what had purported to be a Dalziel original New South Wales Budget message was in fact the Reuter message of the Budget rehashed. In September 1895, *The Times* paid Dalziel £1 for his telegrams for the month – Reuters had emerged victorious.

Dalziel, for the next six years, abandoned journalism and became involved in company promoting. Among the companies he worked with were Southern Development Ltd.; Copper King Ltd. – a mine near San Francisco; and Broomhill Collieries Ltd. But it was in transport that he was to achieve his greatest success, becoming involved in the 1890s with the Cie Internationale des Wagons-Lits (CIWL), and in 1902 joining the Conseil d'Administration of CIWL 'to re-organize railway operations and to fund investment in rolling-stock'. As the next step, in 1906–7, Daziel purchased the British Pullman Car Co., and was ruthless in making the business profitable, scrapping loss-making services. That same year he launched the General Motor Cab Co. Ltd., of which he was initially vice-chairman, becoming chairman from 1906 to 1912. This, together with the United Cab Co., of which he was the first chairman, in 1907–8, introduced motor taxicabs to London, following their success in Paris. In *The Times* of 2 July 1907, Dalziel proudly announced 'that a new English industry, with immense prospects, has been established'.

His finances, however, seemed to bring about a mixed reaction from banking sources. That same year, the National Bank stated that he had kept 'an excellent account with them for many years'. On the other hand, it was noted from another source that 'in the past he had undertaken transactions which left him apparently without anything. Although he had made a lot of money lately ... great care should be taken in any transactions with him, as again and again he has shown himself perfectly able to take care of himself without consideration for any liability he may have incurred in by way of guarantees'.[17]

In the general election of 1906, Dalziel had stood as Unionist candidate for Brixton, but lost the seat after a close contest. However, by siting his General Motor Cab's great garage in the constituency the following year, he was victorious in the general election of 1910, and was to represent Brixton for almost seventeen years. Always the entrepeneur, Dalziel was not above venturing into new markets, and in 1906 he founded the De Mellor Rubber Co. Ltd to develop 700,000 acres on the River Acre in Brazil. He was also involved with the Liberian Rubber Corporation. It was therefore with this much varied business background of mines, transport and rubber that Dalziel, abetted by Henderson, decided to buy *The Standard*. The Conservative Central Office was also involved in the deal, and Arthur Steel-Maitland, the party chairman and part proprietor of *The Sunday Times*, was to monitor the fortunes of *The Standard* and *Evening Standard*. During the first year of Dalziel taking over, the company made profits of £29,000, but the next year the figure was down to £16,000.

Within twelve months of Dalziel assuming control of *The Standard*, Max Aitken, the Canadian-born millionaire businessman and newly-elected Unionist MP for Ashton-under-Lyne, was making approaches to buy the newspaper. On 9 March 1911, Rudyard Kipling wrote to Aitken and hoped 'very greatly' that he would be able to get *The Standard*, adding: 'I just pray your £10,000 cheque will soften his heart if he has one. Evidently he has no brains.'[18] However, Dalziel was in no mood to sell. Northcliffe, however, was pleased that Aitken had not been successful in his bid. Years later, Aitken was to recount how before he had entered journalism he had been instructed by Northcliffe: 'Spreading the old *Morning Standard* on the floor, he turned over page after page, paying no attention to the text: he examined and commented on the advertisement columns – he condemned the character of the advertisements. Then he declared: "This newspaper will die" and it did die.'

DEPARTURE OF GWYNNE

Almost from the onset, Davison Dalziel's handling of the *Standard* had been a source of worry to Arthur Steel-Maitland and the other officials of Conservative Central Office. As Stephen Koss has said: 'Dalziel was an obliging backbencher with more money than experience.'

And from the first weeks of Dalziel's proprietorship, there had developed an antipathy between him and his editor. Gwynne, very much his own man, told Dalziel that his place was in the boardroom and not in the editorial department of which Gwynne was the head. From these differences there could really be only one outcome. Barely a year after Dalziel had taken over, Gwynne realised that he was in an intolerable position, and on 6 May 1911, he wrote to the Leader of the Tory Opposition:

> My dear Balfour,
>
> I feel that I owe it to your uniform kindness and courtesy for me to tell you that I am about to sever my connections with *The Standard.*
>
> I have struggled hard to sink my personal likes and dislikes in order to retain control of a paper in which I might do useful work for the party and the Empire but there are differences of journalistic principles so wide between my present proprietor and myself that I am afraid they are quite insuperable ...
>
> Will you allow me to thank you most heartily for all your kindness to me during the time I have edited the paper and to assure you of my determination to fight as a private since it is no longer permitted to me to fight as a captain.[19]

Less than a month later, Gwynne's resignation from the paper was imminent, and on 7 June he wrote to Bonar Law, a prominent Tory and future Prime Minister:

> My dear Law,
>
> I would not like you to see first of all in the press the announcement of my resignation. I am most anxious that you should not think that I have been petulant or unreasonable in the matter. There are irreconcilable differences of principle involved which no sort of compromise could bridge over for any time. I have been willing to meet Dalziel reasonably but when I found that we were fundamentally opposed in our views as to the proper conduct of the paper I found it only right and just both for him and myself to retire.[20]

Two days later the formal announcement of Gwynne's resignation appeared in *The Standard.* He had already written to J. L. Garvin, editor of the *Observer*: 'I look upon a paper as a very sacred trust. Dalziel regards it as a money making machine and must therefore ruin it.'

To the end of his long life, Gwynne was to remain a master craftsman, never losing his integrity and honesty of opinion. In later years he wrote:

> The Victorian era in journalism may have been dull, but it was very honest. Each newspaper hoisted its own flag, and it fought cleanly and honestly under it. They were hard hitters in their days, but they were polite, impersonal and content to limit their criticisms to ideas rather than to persons. And, above all, they were outside the political arena and political temptations. Today this is all changed. Honours, preferments, promotion and participation in administration seem to be the ambition of proprietors and editors. ... It is impossible to serve two masters. Either a newspaper, to the best of its ability, puts before its readers the truth, as it sees it, or it must deceive them. It is impossible to combine honesty of thought and personal ambitions. But above all, we should bear in mind the very great responsibilities we carry. I remember, when first I entered a newspaper office, being given a piece of advice by a very experienced old journalist. 'Do not forget,' he said to me, 'that a whisper in an editor's room becomes a roar when it has passed through the case room.'[21]

Almost coincidentally with Gwynne leaving *The Standard*, Fabian Ware was dismissed from the editorship of the *Morning Post*. To Rudyard Kipling, an old friend of Gwynne, there could really be only one man to take over, and on 15 June he wrote to Lady Bathurst, the paper's proprietor: 'Have you ever thought of Gwynne as a successor for Ware?' Five days later, Kipling reassured her: 'I quite see your point in not wanting to take a man from one of the other papers but Gwynne is by no means the type of man one finds in London journalism. ... As I see it, his seven years on *The Standard* has simply given him further knowledge ... but it has in no way blunted him nor weakened his convictions; and, as you know, he is a good fighter.'

Kipling's second letter was to be successful, and on 7 July Lady Bathurst offered Gwynne the editor's chair at a starting salary of £2,000 per annum. She gave just one order: 'I want the Lords to be urged to resist at all costs.' To Gwynne, a die-hard Unionist, this would not prove a problem, and as for the Tories, they 'now have one daily London paper of repute under the editor of a man of character'.[22] For the remainder of his life, Gwynne was to owe a great debt of gratitude to Kipling; his most treasured keepsake in later years was a pencil given to him by the writer's widow.

According to Bernard Falk, Gwynne 'alone among newspapermen, living or dead, has edited two separate London dailies [on] the same day '. At 3 a.m. on July 17, 1911, he saw *The Standard* safely to press, and at 11 a.m. he was supervising the staff of the *Morning Post.* The interval he had spent in snatching a few hours' sleep. Gwynne was to edit the *Morning Post* for twenty-six years until it was merged on 30 September 1937 with the *Daily Telegraph.* For his long and distinguished services to journalism he was rightly rewarded the following year when he was appointed a Companion of Honour.

During the hot summer of 1911, while Gwynne had been in the throes of changing editorships, two non-political stories had dominated the pages of *The Standard.* The first was the Coronation of King George V on 22 June. For this great occasion the paper produced a Special Illustrated Coronation Supplement of eight tabloid-size pages tucked into the main paper, the centre-spread of which was dominated by an impressionistic drawing by Frank Brangwyn of the Coronation ceremony in Westminster Abbey, showing the King and Queen in a shaft of light.[23]

The other main story to grip the public was the Great Air Race[24] – the Circuit of Europe – organised by *The Standard* in conjunction with *Le Journal,* of Paris. Backed by *The Standard*'s new owner, Daziel, it created tremendous interest for more than a fortnight, and on 19 June the paper published a full page of photographs of ten of the intrepid aviators. The circuit – most adventurous for those times – started at Paris, went on to Rheims, Liege, Utrecht, Brussels, Calais, Dover, Brighton and Hendon, and back to Paris for the finish.

Through the use of a private wire, *The Standard* readers were informed that thirty-eight had started out, but, at the end of the first stage, three had been killed (two burnt to death), eight had reached their initial target and the remaining twenty-seven had met with minor accidents and delays owing to high winds. Before the start of the race, the local parish priest, in an emotional address, had wished them good fortune, and bestowed upon them the blessing of the Archbishop of Paris – a solemn and touching ceremony in the light of subsequent events.

Following the race, a reception was held at the Savoy Hotel on 4 July and among the guests was Lord Northcliffe, who was himself a patron of aviation, having provided the prize for the first crossing of the English Channel by aeroplane. Northcliffe said that he was proud that an English journal should be the means of helping to secure this historic feat of a European Circuit. A delighted Dalziel responded and declared 'that all connected with *The Standard* were grateful to Lord Northcliffe for the manner in which he had referred to the paper ... The interest that *The Standard* had taken in the circuit was wholly that of furthering the great work by Lord Northcliffe and others.'[25]

DEATH OF JEYES

During the preparations for the Coronation, Samuel Henry Jeyes, a key figure on *The Standard* editorial staff, was seriously ill, and on 27 June, at the age of 54, he died. Born in 1857, he was educated at Uppingham School and Trinity College, Oxford; and from 1879 to 1883 was lecturer in classics at his old college. During his final two years on *The Standard,* his health had been failing fast and a serious operation for cancer became necessary, but the disease spread. From the early spring of 1911 he was too ill to go to the office, but insisted that proofs, correspondence and reviews should be sent to his home. There he could read the letters and articles and, with the aid of his wife, dictate replies. On the afternoon before he died he was still working on papers brought by a messenger from Shoe Lane.

His great friend and colleague, Sidney Low, has movingly described his final hours: 'I saw him for the last time a few days before his death. It was in that thronged and feverish week of King George V's coronation, when all London was tossing restlessly under its trappings. But the decorations and the tumult left the quarter of groves and gardens untouched. Peace and sunshine were on the green lawn where Jeyes was lying in a little tent, such sunshine and such peace as made the coming of death more poignant in its pathos.'[26]

Jeyes had been one of the pillars of *The Standard* for more than twenty years, having joined the paper as assistant editor from the *St. James's Gazette* in May 1891. It was said of him that he was interested in all aspects of journalism and newspaper management, 'whether he were interviewing a Cabinet Minister on some delicate international question, or mollifying an exasperated printer struggling with belated copy, or making sense of cryptic telegrams from St. Petersburg and Vienna, or toning down the exuberances of descriptive reporters and dramatic critics.' Above all, he was a person of great compassion, and one such example is indicative of his style of management. One evening, an indoor messenger was discovered attempting to cut his throat with a blunt table-knife. Despite proposals to send for the police and fire the boy, Jeyes vetoed all such action. He said that to send away the lad to face the magistrates would bring on certain ruin, but for him to remain with his friends on *The Standard* would make him ashamed of his foolishness.

For a senior executive on a morning paper, life was very exacting, but there still remained plenty of time for the social life, as a typical Jeyes day showed. Although he invariably kept late hours at *The Standard,* he would be up for breakfast at nine o'clock, take a stroll along Piccadilly and into the park before returning to his rooms to read through a dozen London, provincial and foreign newspapers, and perhaps the latest parliamentary report, before going off to the

Garrick Club for lunch. Here he was at his best and was a member of its committee for many years. After lunch, and perhaps a game of billiards, he would take a cab to *The Standard* offices, then back to his rooms to dress for a dinner party, before returning to the office to write up a leader and supervise the edition. The hours in Fleet Street were much more indulgent in those days, and seldom were the papers off stone [ready for the press] before midnight. Despite his high social profile, Jeyes never let it interfere with his work, and even the occasional attack of gout did not prevent him from appearing: he would write his leaders, instruct reporters and deal with the printer while resting his inflamed foot on a chair.

During the summer of 1911, striking railwaymen brought havoc to the distribution of newspapers, and Dalziel, always the great motoring enthusiast, decided to employ a fleet of thirty motor cars to get supplies of *The Standard* into the provinces. These were used on runs to Nottingham and Derby, Birmingham, Kettering, Peterbrorough, Bath and Bristol, and Gloucester and Cheltenham, thus enabling the paper to steal a march over the other London nationals. Encouraged by these successes, Dalziel instituted a daily motor service to Norwich, thereby gaining three hours over the old time. *The Evening Standard*, too, had increased its small number of cars by employing fifteen vehicles for runs to Reading, Gravesend, Watford, Redhill and Dorking.

In the December of that year, a dinner was given at the Carlton Hotel for W. A. Woodward, the retiring editor of the *Evening Standard*, by Davison Dalziel. Supporting the chairman were four other directors: the Earl of Fingall, F. S. E. Drury, E. H. Johnstone and R. D. Norton. The guests included R. D. Blumenfeld, editor of the *Daily Express*, and H. A. Gwynne, now successfully editing the *Morning Post*, plus forty members of the staffs of *The Standard* and the *Evening Standard*.[27]

An incident which caused a great deal of mirth in the Shoe Lane offices at the time was the 'case of the boiled leg'. One evening a director of the company was crossing Ludgate Circus at 8.20 p.m. when he met a *Standard* sub-editor, who told him that all the sub-editors went to supper at the same time. As this did not happen at the *Daily Express* it was considered that in future all *Standard* sub-editors should remain on the premises, taking their supper in the large Reporters' Room. On the second evening of the edict, Colley, the managing editor, was approached by an elderly sub-editor who protested: 'I cannot eat in that room and I will not.' 'Why?' demanded the managing editor. 'Because there's a woman's leg being boiled over the fire and the place smells horribly.' Colley descended to find that a reporter (also a medical student) was poised over a large saucepan. He explained that he wanted the flesh stripped off the deceased lady's leg, which he had bought for the purposes of study.[28]

CIRCULATION PLOYS

In a bid to increase sales of *The Standard,* Dalziel now sent Colley on a tour of Great Britain, visiting the political constituencies, interviewing Conservative candidates, sitting members, agents and local leaders – and each day he was expected to write at least a column for the paper. Large numbers of copies of *The Standard* were ordered in the localities visited and paid for by the Members of Parliament or others on the day of publication. Although the tour – which lasted nine months – was a success at the time, the sales did not hold. Upon his recall, Colley took charge of the news desk, and he later wrote: 'There was something attractive in returning to the quiet glades of Shoe Lane, for I was once again installed in the chair of news editor, with 18 reporters on the staff and five good men "on space".'[29]

At this time the circulation managership of *The Standard* and *Evening Standard* fell vacant, and the successful applicant was B. M. Hansard of the *Daily Mail,* who succeeded Ivor Fraser. Many years later, Hansard wrote:

> There was no hurry and no excitement, *The Standard* was very old, and as its readers died, so the circulation fell. It was dying fast. *The Evening Standard,* carrying the morning paper on its back, left the staff weary and worn. There was no life in the place and precious little money.
>
> We had two batteries of presses, one for *The Standard* and the other for the *Evening Standard,* and it was a nerve-wracking noise when the presses of *The Standard* started to revolve. It sounded like so much old iron whirling round in tin cans, and I thought that at any time, the presses might fall to pieces. Those of the *Evening Standard* were more modern and produced a very good sheet. A printing schedule did not exist – the papers went to press when the editorial departments thought fit.
>
> I was in charge of what had been two of the greatest papers in London. My first attention was *The Standard.* I took it over with a very doubtful circulation of 40,000, with the *Evening Standard* about 45,000. At the end of the month, by concentrating on *The Standard,* I had increased its circulation by something like 5,000 copies a day, but the *Evening Standard* had gone back.[30]

To increase the circulation of *The Standard,* Hansard suggested to Herbert A. White, who had succeeded Gwynne as editor, that he should devote a page to enable women to express their political views on suffrage. The effect was electric; within a month sales had increased by more than 20,000 copies. However, after a woman suffragist had tied herself to the grille in the House of Commons,

White cancelled the feature, saying that he was not going to support a lot of howling female dervishes.[31]

Tired of *The Standard*, with its lack of direction, Hansard now turned his attentions to the *Evening Standard*, and in discussions with the new editor, James A. Kilpatrick, it was agreed that the editorial staff should issue contents bills. The main edition of the paper was the 'Special', which was published after 6 p.m. and was bought for its late City news and the complete racing results, upon which the bookmakers paid out. Ensuring that the paper went to press promptly at 6 p.m. – and including the very latest results in the 'stop press' column, despite objections from the sports editor – meant that the sales increased. However, even with these circulation stunts, *The Standard* and the *Evening Standard* still continued to lose ground; from a figure of £29,000 in 1910, the year Dalziel took over, profits fell to £12,000 in 1912. *The Standard*'s advertising receipts in the first six months of 1912 were £54,430, with £52,238 and £51,298 respectively for the same six months in 1913 and 1914; but within a fortnight of the outbreak of the First World War on 4 August 1914, advertising revenue had dropped from £2,075 to £757 per week.[32]

Hansard later wrote of those days: 'The position of *The Standard* had become serious. Dalziel to help the financial landslide started the *Daily Call* as a competitor to the *Daily Mirror.* It had no hope or chance of success. It simply accelerated bankruptcy. Dalziel had divorced the *Evening Standard* from the parent company, and had purloined it as his personal share of the wreck.[33] Hansard also said that Dalziel was: 'a financier, and not a newspaper man'.[34]

So concerned were the Tory party's Central Office at the parlous state of *The Standard* that in December 1914, Arthur Steel-Maitland wrote to Bonar Law, the party's new leader, saying that it looked as if *The Standard* with the *Evening Standard* was coming to grief. He rated 'the *Evening Standard* a good property and the morning *Standard* a bad one'. As Stephen Koss has written: 'Davison Dalziel had taken control of this dual concern in 1910, with a heavy investment from Sir Alexander Henderson. Since then, Henderson had been kept at arm's length and had grown "very sore". In December 1914, Dalziel found himself "in the strait", and his silent partner was disinclined to bail him out. Instead, Henderson has discussed the whole position with Steel-Maitland.'[35]

Less than a week later, on 23 December, Steel-Maitland wrote once more to Bonar Law reaffirming the political need that the 'object is to keep the *Evening Standard* in your hands. The morning *Standard* can be dropped without loss'. He added that as 'a good evening is a strength to a morning paper' Lady Bathurst might be induced to publish the *Evening Standard* in tandem with the *Morning Post.* He believed that Gwynne should now put pressure on his proprietor, but not too strongly, otherwise she would 'tend to turn down anything connected with *The Standard* without much consideration'. Ever faithful to the party, Gwynne met Henderson, who expected to 'come into control of *The Standard* on New Year's Day, owing to Dalziel's default in the payment of debentures'. Following this, Gwynne spoke to Lady Bathurst and suggested that the morning *Standard* should be allowed to die but that 'the *Evening Standard* which is a first class paying property should be taken over by you and run by you as an evening paper'.[36]

Bonar Law, too, believed that there was merit in the proposal and he told Gwynne that 'he thought the idea worth considering and that he would be glad to talk it over with you or Lady Bathurst'. Henderson, also, had his reasons, the chief one being that he was afraid the papers might fall into the hands of Lord Northcliffe. However, despite the efforts of Gwynne, Steel-Maitland and other prominent Tories, Dalziel was to retain control of *The Standard* and the *Evening Standard* until, in the late spring of 1915, Fleet Street was stunned to learn that Edward Hulton Junior had become involved.

13
The Man from Manchester

Edward Hulton Junior was born in Hulme, Lancashire, on 3 March 1869, the son of a former bill setter on the *Manchester Guardian,* and Mary, a woman of severe and puritanical ideals. The story of Edward Senior, or Ned as he was known, is one of the great romances of newspaper lore. He was born in 1838 in Clock Alley, Manchester, the son of James Hulton, a self-employed tinplate worker, who owned a small foundry in the Ancoats area. When Ned was aged only 12, James Hulton's foundry burned down and the father left, penniless, for America, never to return. Now responsible for his mother and five sisters, young Ned sold newspapers on the streets for 2s 6d per week, telling her that one day he would fill her apron with gold sovereigns. It was even said that if customers did not pay their bills, then Ned would dance in clogs outside their homes until the debts were honoured.[1]

From selling newspapers it was a natural step to be involved in producing them, and as a teenager he spent some years printing the contents bills of the *Manchester Guardian.* Always interested in horses and betting – he had even issued a racing sheet in his spare time – he joined forces in 1871, at the age of 23, with E. O. Bleackley, a wealthy cotton broker, who had been impressed with Ned's study of form. With Bleackley's advance of £100, he bought a printing press, and from a cellar in Spear Street, Manchester, launched a four-page sheet called *The Prophetic Bell.* Produced on a shoestring from cramped premises, Hulton not only edited the paper but also published his tips under the name of 'Kettledrum'. The paper quickly became a success among the working classes in Lancashire, and within four years *The Prophetic Bell* had become *The Sporting Chronicle,* a paper which was to last for more than a century.

In 1875, Hulton also started *The Athletic News,* the first title devoted entirely to that sport; and a decade later, when he was an increasingly-successful proprietor, he launched his biggest gamble, *The Sunday Chronicle.* It was a paper which quickly caught the imagination of the public, with its diet of police reports, politics, sport, sensational news and columns of advertisements. Always a restless figure, Hulton, after Mass on Sundays, used to walk through Manchester's parks counting the number of readers of his paper.

In 1885, Hulton withdrew Edward Junior from St. Bede's Roman Catholic College, Manchester, and set him to learn the newspaper business.[2] Within ten years his son, having gained a wide experience in most departments, was running the company, and in 1897 was mainly responsible for launching a halfpenny paper, *The Manchester Evening Chronicle*, which was to have the largest evening circulation in the provinces. From splendid new offices at Withy Grove – for many years the largest newspaper plant in the world – the paper was delivered to newsagents by teams in carriages drawn by smart Welsh cobs.

Bernard Falk, the first apprentice journalist to be engaged by Edward Hulton Senior, and himself later a Fleet Street legend, has left a vivid account of those early days on *The Manchester Evening Chronicle*. Concerning Edward Hulton Junior, he said:

> I did not think the young man as picturesque as his father. On the other hand, if less pliable and more self-opinionated, he disposed of a wider range of ability and subtlety. What the father did by instinct, the son did by calculation. In his last days papa Hulton dressed extremely well, but he never reached the stylish heights of his offspring, who excelled in marvellous silk ties and waistcoats cut very low. I would often catch the father's admiring eye bent on his son's smart set-up.[3]

For Edward Hulton Junior, the success of *The Manchester Evening Chronicle* meant that he could launch a daily counterpart – and in 1900 *The Daily Dispatch* was born, a paper developed for the ever-increasing Northern middle classes. By catering for this new area, all sections of the market were being reached, and in 1905 *The Umpire*, for long a main rival of *The Sunday Chronicle*, was taken over.

Although destined to be a very rich man, Edward Hulton was never to forget his early days on *The Sunday Chronicle*, under the editorship of Robert Blatchford, and the following incident was long to remain with him:

> In the early '80s, Blatchford published a sensational series of articles about the Manchester slums, as horrifying as Engels' classic *Condition of the English Working Class*, which had not yet been published in Britain.
>
> Even Edward the second, then working under his father, thought the paper had gone too far. 'I took him into a slum hovel,' Blatchford wrote, 'where the husband had just died of consumption and was laid out dead on a deal table. There was no fire and no bed. Three young children cowered together on the floor with a couple of sacks over them and the widow sat on an empty box crying to herself. Young Hulton looked round, emptied all the money out of his pockets and walked out without a word … he would not go into another house. He had seen all he needed to bring home the naked truth.[4]

The death of Edward Senior in 1904, leaving an estate of £557,000, meant that the Hultons were now the largest newspaper proprietors outside Fleet Street. There was, however, an immediate family difference, and two of Hulton's sisters, Aggie and Theresa, disagreeing with Edward's lifestyle and its possible effect on the business, withdrew their support and money. He was fortunate, though, to retain the assistance of his two other sisters, Maggie and Mary.

Despite his new responsibilities as head of the family firm, Hulton continued to follow his main outside interests – horse racing and greyhound coursing – and in 1908 he won the Waterloo Cup with his dog Hallow Eve, at odds of 1,000 to 15.[5] Two years before he had registered his racing colours under the name of H. Lytham (using an assumed name so that his mother would not hear of it) and he set out to invest large sums in developing a fine racing stable, which was to meet with some success. It was even said that if there were the inkling of an industrial dispute on the *Evening Standard* then he would walk around the composing room floor, dispensing tips of likely winners from his stable. Hulton's only Classic victory, though, was in 1924 when his filly, Straitlace, won the Oaks.

In his newspaper office, Hulton's presence was everywhere and he possessed a shrewd business manner:

> He was particularly down on people who came to him with schemes for which they had made out all sorts of specious claims. He would listen until they had finished, his patience unruffled, his demeanour apparently friendly, induce them once more to repeat their confident assertion that success was a certainty; then, if it was a particularly bad case of bluffing, would turn on his smooth-tongued visitors with the withering taunt, 'You must think I'm a damned fool.'[6]

A DAILY IS LAUNCHED

In 1909, Hulton decided that the time was right to launch a daily illustrated newspaper. He had been very much influenced by the success of Northcliffe's revamped *Daily Mirror*, and from his Withy Grove base Hulton introduced the *Daily Sketch*. Despite the initial success of the *Daily Sketch*, it was found that it could not compete with the Fleet Street dailies on an equal footing, so the decision was taken by Hulton to secure a London base. His first choice was the recently-vacated *Daily Express* offices in Tudor Street, but within a matter of months the growth of the paper meant that its offices were too small and it was forced to move to purpose-built premises in Shoe Lane.[7]

The first editor of the *Daily Sketch* was James Heddle, later to become managing director of Hulton's titles in London. From its early days, the paper's picture coverage was excellent, and it secured outstanding reportage of the sinking of the *Titanic*, in 1912; the suffragist tragedy at the Derby, in 1913; and, later, the first pictures of the Irish Rebellion, in 1916. In the early days of the First World War, by spending thousands of pounds on pictures, the paper succeeded in presenting to the public some of the horror of the Western Front, and it led the way by publishing photographs of British troops 'going over the top'.

With the *Daily Sketch* having proved a success, Hulton now turned his attention to a Sunday title. The move from the narrow confines of the Tudor Street premises to the spacious new building on the corner of Shoe Lane and Plum Tree Court meant that there was room for expansion, and the opportunity to keep this modern plant running seven days a week. For some years, Hulton had contemplated a London edition of his successful *Sunday Chronicle.* The plan was to send down some pages of the Manchester publication in matrix form, but difficulties with the London Society of Compositors proved insuperable. Although a matrix could be sent to Manchester from London, thus saving the cost of a second setting, it could not be sent from Manchester to London without involving the cost of double composition. While provincial newspapers were on 'basic' rate, piece scales reigned supreme in Fleet Street.[8]

Early in 1915, Hulton announced that a national Sunday newspaper was to be launched from London, on March 28. The new title, the *Illustrated Sunday Herald,* was to constitute a separate company from the *Daily Sketch,* and there was to be a strong picture bias. However, once the news was announced, Lord Rothermere immediately launched the *Sunday Pictorial,* and that same year T. P. O'Connor started *T. P.'s Weekly.* The circulation of both the *Sunday Times* and the *Observer* rose dramatically because of readers' desire for war news, and even the *Daily Mail, The Daily Telegraph* and *The Times* experimented with Sunday issues, when important items of news warranted. Lord Camrose was later to observe: 'The anxiety for news overcame religious scruples and Sunday newspapers acquired for the first time an odour of respectability.'[9] In fact, newspapers had never been more eagerly sought than at this period, and it was estimated that more than £10,500,000 was spent on them each year. There were 2,400 titles in the United Kingdom, and within the London postal radius there were 460, of which twenty-seven were morning dailies and six evening dailies.

While the newspaper world as a whole was enjoying its increased prosperity, there was the occasional casualty – and first among these was to be *The Standard.* Early in April 1915, rumours were rife in Fleet Street that *The Standard* was about to be taken over 'by a newspaper magnate whose extensive interests already assure him a powerful influence in the world of journalism and publicity'. The rumours were soon to be partially fact, as less than a month later Hulton had taken over the *Evening Standard* as 'a metropolitan launching pad ... purveying a diluted form of [Tory] Unionism'.[10] It was noted that the change of ownership did not involve any disturbance in the staff. It was intended that the paper would still sell at a penny and, for the time being, would continue to be printed in its old home until plans had been finalised for a move higher up Shoe Lane.

William Colley has left an interesting account of the first moves by Hulton in taking over the paper:

> One early morning while sitting alone in a large room engaged on the [*Notes and News*] column, there entered a smart, alert man wearing glasses. He had a Scottish accent and a pleasing voice. ... Seeing I was unoccupied, after delivering my column, he said; 'You are Colley? I'm Heddle.' We shook hands. 'We are taking the *Evening Standard* over, you know, lock, stock and barrel. ... The end of April or May at the latest.'[11]

By the end of that summer, the *Evening Standard* was still being produced in the offices of its morning namesake, although there was now no connection between the two titles. It was noted that 'Messrs. Hulton and Co., who bought it from Mr Dalziel for £50,000, are waiting for new machinery in order to print it in their *Daily Sketch* offices: This delay means a bit of good fortune for *The Standard* and brings the proprietor a substantial sum per week.'[12] The final move to the new premises came at five o'clock on a Saturday afternoon, and by the following Monday the staff were in their new premises. There they joined their colleagues on the other Hulton newspapers: *Daily Dispatch, Sunday Herald, Sunday Chronicle, Empire News* and *Daily Sketch.* Hulton believed that when he had purchased the *Evening Standard* from Dalziel it had been for some time handicapped by the serious financial position of the morning *Standard.* He considered that with extra expenditure on the editorial and production sides the paper could respond and he hoped that 'an evening of the highest class may be established and maintained'.

Within a matter of months of the take-over, the paper had a new editor, A. Wyatt Tilby being replaced by Arthur H. Mann.[13] Born in Warwick in 1876, Mann had started in journalism with the *Western Mail,* Cardiff, proceeding to the *Birmingham Mail* and later to the *Birmingham Dispatch,* of which he was the editor. He then went to Fleet Street as the London editor of the *Daily Dispatch.* Of the various editors of the *Evening Standard,* Mann made the 'Londoner's Diary' a distinct feature. It became an authoritative three columns of outstanding, distinctive news. Mann personally went to Whitehall and did things himself and he was on first-name terms with all the leading politicians

To quote Colley once more:

> The Lancashire accent reigned supreme – a labiodental language which the Southerner generally dislikes. But this was redressed by the editor's staccato, clean-cut Shakespearean country English and the chief sub-editor's Dundee blend of expression – the former Mr Arthur Mann (now editor, *Yorkshire Post*), and the latter, Mr David Phillips. Taken as a whole, the reportorial staff of the *Evening Standard* got the news. Members of the Lancashire invasion edited, sub-edited, headed and knew 'darn well better stuff could be done in Manchester'. But all worked together loyally and time spent away the 'O'Dam' language from the rumble it was to the occasional tinkle it is today.[14]

CHANGE IN FORMAT

Meanwhile, conditions at *The Standard,* still owned by Dalziel, continued to deteriorate. A change in format was ordered, and its pages were cut to a 'more convenient' size: 'It was as if *The Times* came out, suddenly, the size of *Answers.* The paper lost in a night the look of authority and the atmosphere of high responsibility.'[15] It continued to exist during 1915, but gradually staff left and were not replaced:

> The year 1916 had turned. On many nights the staff of *The Standard* assembled not knowing whether the paper would be published tomorrow or not. They waited about until Thompson, the editorial chief, had been to the City to endeavour to obtain the money to carry on yet another day. For the staff, the position was dreadful: for *The Standard,* tragic. Thompson was a hero, but, alas, he failed. On my visits from the *Evening Standard* I saw the empty rooms and many vacant chairs. Life slowly ebbed. A sort of newspaper continued until the early months had passed, when suddenly, although it had been expected, the long history of *The Standard* ended.[16]

On 16 February, 1916, *The Times* announced that *The Standard* was to be sold by auction: 'Notice is given in our advertisement columns that, by order of the Court, the goodwill and copyright of *The Standard* newspaper will be offered for sale by public auction by Messrs. Walter Phelps and Son, at Anderton's Hotel, Fleet Street, at 3 o'clock on February 23.' History was about to repeat itself; for the second time in less than seventy-five years the paper was in the hands of the receivers, but this time there was to be no James Johnstone to act as a last-minute saviour.

When the auction began there was a large crowd at Anderton's Hotel, but most were there as onlookers. Very few had any intention of bidding for what had once been the leading rival to *The Times.* At the beginning of the sale, the auctioneer, Frank Phelps, announced that the machinery and plant would not be sold unless the copyright and goodwill were also sold and any sale of the plant would be subject to its use during the daytime for three months for the production of the *Evening Standard*, with the proprietors of which, Messrs. Hultons' contract covering the next two months was still in force. Another condition was that 25 per cent of the purchase price of either lot must be paid at once by way of deposit.

Asked whether the printing of the *Evening Standard* would not interfere with the production of *The Standard*, the auctioneer replied that 'the one had been practically the child of the other' and both had been printed most of the time in the same premises. Indeed, the mechanical facilities were more than sufficient for both. Other points explained were that the assets included £4,376 worth of definite unexpired advertisement orders in addition to 'till countermanded' orders of £300 weekly and £50 monthly. As to the machinery, it was pointed out that all equipment, including the up-to-date Linotype machines, and the elaborate office furnishings were also included. He added that the purchaser would also have the option of securing two octuple straight-line Goss printing machines that were on order, but had not yet been delivered, and for which the pits had already been constructed and the electrical equipment installed. These machines were capable of producing 30,000 copies per hour. As to the book debts, it was explained that these amounted to between £8,000 and £9,000, could be bought for a fair price and could be collected at a reasonable consideration for a purchaser.

Before putting up this first lot – that of the entire property – the auctioneer explained that the most favourable terms would be made with a purchaser as to the tenancy of the buildings in Shoe Lane and in Fleet Street. There then ensued a long silence: no one was prepared to make the first move, until, as the auctioneer was raising his hand for the 'third and last' time before withdrawing, an offer of £5,000 was made. It was to be nowhere nearly enough, the auctioneer stating that double that amount would not reach the reserve that had been fixed by the Court.

Dealing with what he considered the most important part of the paper – the spiritual as compared with the physical – the copyright and goodwill, it was pointed out that *The Standard* had originated at a time that went back beyond the recollection of those present and had had a prosperous and distinguished history. But it was difficult to translate into words the energies that had been in operation over so many years to produce what was to be understood by the words 'copyright and goodwill'. At the time of the auction the paper was not a profit-earner, but as recently as 1910 it had made a profit of £29,000 and in 1911 a profit of £16,000. Even in 1912 the profit was £12,000.

The gross advertisement revenue in the first half of 1912 was £54,430; and in the first half of 1914 it was £51,298, showing practically no drop whatever. Then came the war, and in the first week there was a drop from £2,705 to £757, and things continued in pretty much the same state. In the year of the auction there had been in every week except two a considerable increase on the figures of the corresponding week of the previous year; and there were doubtless gentlemen in the room who had ideas which they could put into operation for bringing back the advertisement revenue of this well-known paper and restoring it to something of its old-time property.

The auctioneer, having withdrawn the property as a whole, now put up the copyright, goodwill and advertisement orders, and explained that a purchaser would, if he desired, be able to lease or rent the present offices for a long or short period, or could have the paper printed elsewhere (there had already been offers of this kind), or it could be printed for him by the vendors. Despite these inducements, the only bid was one of £100, later increased to £200 by the same person. Neither figure was acceptable and the lot was withdrawn, the auctioneer stating that the vendors would now be prepared to deal privately with any intending purchasers.

It was, indeed, a sad afternoon for a great newspaper – it was a newspaper that no one seemed to want. However, despite the lack of interest at the auction, *The Standard* managed to struggle on for a further three weeks, thanks to the efforts of a group of Cardiff businessmen. After Lord Faringdon had finally withdrawn his support, H. J. Thomas, a well-known South Wales stockbroker associated with Mr Oswald Stoll's enterprises, made strenuous efforts to raise new money. The head of one of Cardiff's largest fleet of steamers, W. J. Tatem, undertook to find funds for a short period, but, with costs running in excess of £1,000 per week, they were unable to find other backers to support them.

On 17 March, *The Times* announced as its lead on page 5:

THE STANDARD

—

PUBLICATION SUSPENDED

—

AN HONOURABLE CAREER

—

The Standard newspaper has suspended publication: but we are asked to state that the necessary steps have been taken to preserve its copyright.

The disappearance of this old-established newspaper will be regretted, not only by the world of journalism, but by a wide circle of readers of newspapers. For several years *The Standard* had been struggling against troubled waters.

High hopes were raised two years ago when the paper was altered in size and form and seemed for a while to thrive, but these hopes were finally destroyed when the newspaper's goodwill, copyright and plant were put up for auction three weeks ago and failed to draw anything like a satisfactory offer.[17]

A week later, *The Times* reported that the premises and machines of *The Standard* were now being used by Messrs Wynne, the government printers. Writing in *The Newspaper World*, during the week after the auction, 'A Special Correspondent' noted:

Several statements are current in Fleet Street concerning the reasons why *The Standard* went downhill after Mr C. A. Pearson paid £300,000 for the property. In some quarters political reasons are instanced for the decline, and in others they are discounted.

I hear that two or three distinct attempts were made to save *The Standard* and that the Official Receiver was in touch with those who endeavoured to secure the capital. When, however, the fact evolved that not less than £100,000 would prove sufficient to finance the journal over the present troubles times no further steps could be taken. Some people had hopes of Lord Faringdon, but though it was understood he felt keen at one time he did not pursue the matter. Probably, many people have overlooked the fact that the man who gave *The Standard* its pre-eminence in the later part of the 19th century is still living on Wimbledon Common. He is now 77 years, having enjoyed nearly 16 years of freedom from newspaper control. If it were possible to have his reflections upon the happenings in Shoe Lane during those 16 years we might print some piquant copy.

In a footnote the editor of *Newspaper World* said that he had ascertained some weeks previously that Mr Mudford was not prepared to give an interview on the subject.

A graphic account of *The Standard*'s last hours was given by J. Maynard Saunders, night editor, in the 1 April 1916 issue of *The Newspaper World*:

It was ten p.m. The paper had been dead fifteen minutes. The editor had bidden his farewells, and the staff – editorial, sub-editorial and printing – had been dismissed. But all through the evening work had gone on in every department for the possible production of the paper next day; the copy prepared and head-lined had been dispatched to the composing room in readiness for the word that should set the machinery in motion. But instead of the 'carry on' there came the 'dismiss'. Yet so hard was the realization thereof, that a quarter of an hour after the departure of the last compositor the head printer came to the night editor, who was clearing up, to ask: 'I suppose all that copy on my desk is no good now?' To him there came the sad reply, 'No, it's all cancelled matter now.'

The paper had existed for nigh on one hundred years – a power at home and abroad. The night editor himself had survived two changes in the proprietory and three editors, and this was the end. But none had cause to be ashamed on the manner of their death. They formed but one of the many business casualties in journalism owing to the war. For four nights the staff had come in on the sporting chance that there would be a paper on the morrow. On three the morrow had seen the old journal appear. But the strain had been great. On one of the nights the 'line' was not on until 8.45 instead of at 5.30 owing to the uncertainty of the outlook; on another night not until nine o'clock. But on the fourth – the fatal night – the agony was prolonged to a quarter to ten. Then it was that the strain became well nigh intolerable, for the question arose: Could the paper then be produced in time to catch the trains?

Up to that hour was shown, in all its wonderful efficiency, the rigid discipline of a newspaper office. Everything revolved except the wheels of the composing machines – the Parliamentary sketch writer sent up his sketch – it was to be received, sub-edited and sent to the composing room; so with the notes of the Lobby correspondent; the Parliamentary report came in and as it arrived it was dealt with and cut to the space which had been alloted to Parliament at the editorial conference in the afternoon.

The editor was available for consultation; the leader writers had their subjects and only waited the word to begin. In one of the theatres the paper's representative was making notes of an important new play of which he was to write a notice – for the morrow's paper. He, poor innocent, ventured between the acts to telephone to the office for the latest news of the internal situation. The night editor, anxious to relieve the strain he dare not show before the staff, bade him sharply to have his copy prepared, paper or no paper, or stand the consequences the next day.

Even the messenger boys, under the compelling eye of the head messenger – a man of forty years' service – did not dare question the futility of their half-hourly pilgrimage with copy to a composing room which was in idleness and semi-darkness. Then came a summons to the night editor to attend his editor, who, in words husky by emotion, declared that the fight was over and there would be no paper on the morrow. He was bidden to tell the staff and to say that the editor would take his farewell of the printers and then of the sub-editors.

Later, standing at the printer's desk, with the printers forming a dense semi-circle before him, in the semi-glow of lowered lights, the editor told of the efforts which he and others had made to carry on the paper and how their efforts had come to nought, and of the great sorrow for the older members of the staff. It was a very manly and very moving speech. Then spoke the Father of the Chapel, who, on behalf of the printers, bore testimony to the excellent relations which had always existed between that department and the heads of office. He was followed by the chief stone hand – a man of 41 years' service on the paper.

Thus ended a sad and historic evening in the newspaper world. It is doubtful if more than one other journal in London can show such records of service among its staff, for there passed out of Fleet Street that night men who had found their daily occupation on the paper for sixty, fifty, forty and thirty years.

A STRANGE MIX

Meanwhile, to the employees of the *Evening Standard,* their new chief, Edward Hulton,[18] was a strange mix. At first he was regarded as being somewhat reticent, but the paper's staff soon threw impressions to the wind when they got to know him better; by then he was regarded as a prince among millionaires and proprietors.

Hulton's involvement in his newspapers – and this was especially so with the *Evening Standard* – was almost entirely commercial. Unlike his contemporaries, he was not politically motivated, and seldom used his papers to publicise his own personal opinions. Apart from the *Evening Standard* his papers were mainly popular and non-pretentious, providing simple news stories rather than party politics, with particular emphasis on sporting news.

As increasing numbers of servicemen returned from the First World War, so there was demand from the reading public for more and more news. This was especially so with the London evening newspaper market, where the circulations of the *Evening News* and the *Star* were ahead of the others. In an effort to improve the sales of the *Evening Standard,* in the summer of 1919 Hulton introduced the first delivery of newspapers by air – to Dover,[19] and plans were in hand to extend the service to Brighton and Eastbourne. Papers were taken by van from Fleet Street to Hendon for loading on to an Avro aeroplane, and 45 minutes later the pilot would be landing in Dover. It was certainly a novel means of transport for the newspaper industry – and a notable first for the paper.

DEATH OF PEARSON

On 9 December 1921, the *Evening Standard* announced with deep regret the tragic death of Sir Arthur Pearson, one of the 'greats' in the history of the British Press, and a former owner of *The Standard* Company. Since approaching blindness had forced Pearson to sell *The Standard* and the *Evening Standard* in April 1910, his life had taken on a new dimension. The following year, having disposed of his interest in the *Daily Express*, he went with his wife to Vienna to consult Professor Fuchs, a famous Austrian occulist. Pearson was told that he would certainly be blind within two years, and was advised to give up active business and put his affairs in order. His wife, not entirely satisfied, telephoned the specialist from their hotel and was told that the two years would probably be less than one year. Returning to their room, she found her husband lying on a sofa. 'I shall soon be blind,' he said, 'but I will never be a blind man. I am going to be *the* blind man.'[20]

From that moment, Pearson determined to do all in his power to help the blind, and in October 1913 he joined the council of the National Institute of the Blind, being appointed its treasurer the following January. His first act was to raise £30,000 to equip the Institute's headquarters in Great Portland Street and to form an endowment fund for the production of embossed books. With the active support of Sir Vansittart Bowater, the Lord Mayor of London, donations flooded in, and among the first were £1,000 from Lord Northcliffe, £1,000 from Lord Rothermere and £1,000 from Pearson himself. So successful were Pearson's fund-raising activities that in only eight years he increased the annual income of the Institute from £8,010 to £358,174.

In his appeal through the press he said:

> I am venturing to make myself the mouthpiece of the many blind and particularly blind folk who will benefit by your kindly and able advocacy. ... The lives of the blind – particularly of the poor blind – are very dull and monotonous, and, short of restoring to them their sight, nothing can be given them of greater value than books. ... I do not want these poor blind people to go on being content to sit with folded hands. I want those folded hands to be busy passing to and fro along the lines of Braille type, and these unimaginated minds to be filled with pictures of the great and wonderful world which their owners cannot see.
>
> Braille is not difficult to learn. I mastered its principles in a fortnight; and once that is done it only remains to acquire speed by practice ... I want to help to spread Braille reading, for, as you know, the loss of sight takes the spirit out of a man; and I only began to get mine back when I mastered Braille.[21]

After King George V had opened the new premises of the National Institute for the Blind on 19 March 1914, Pearson immediately launched a world-wide appeal for funds. Ever conscious of the use of the media, he was the first person to use wireless in this fashion. With the assistance of the Marconi Company the message was sent free to 'all on board British ships, and even sympathetic friends on ships flying other flags who are grateful they are not blind'.

This dramatic, first-ever appeal, rightly earned Pearson columns of newspaper publicity and praise. One writer, Filson Young, commented:

> A flash of wireless over half the world on Saturday night, enlisting the greatest of invisible forces in the service of those who cannot see – how beautiful an incident in the history of mankind. Wireless telegraphy is the most modern of man's powers; charity, I suppose, the most ancient of his virtues. I am glad that it was Arthur Pearson who thought of this dramatic way of helping his fund for providing books for the blind; it is worthy of the hustler as he was called in the days before he, too, entered the dark kingdom. It is the old touch, the grand manner asserting itself once again.

Headed by the King and Queen, this first campaign for books for the blind was a great success and won the support of all the parties, with Arthur Balfour, Bonar Law, Lloyd George and Ramsay MacDonald figuring prominently. Less than six months later, following the outbreak of the First World War, Pearson, at the request of the Prince of Wales, transferred his activity and enthusiasm to the Prince of Wales's Fund, and in less than a year succeeded in raising more than £1 million for families of serving troops.

But Pearson was about to embark on his greatest venture – a venture that was to be recognised as his living memorial. From the opening of his first hostel for blinded soldiers early in 1915 he had found his true vocation – and St. Dunstan's was born. On 26 March of that year the hostel was moved from Bayswater Road to St. Dunstan's, a mansion situated in Regent's Park. The house belonged to Otto Khan, a New York banker, who gladly placed it at Pearson's disposal free of charge. From the small beginnings of sixteen men being cared for, by the end of the war more than 1,700 members were on his books, and he could proudly say that 'with practically no exception all the blinded soldiers and sailors of the British Imperial forces came under my care'.

In recognition of his great work at St. Dunstan's, Arthur Pearson was, deservedly, created a baronet in 1916, and the following year received the GBE. With the war over and St. Dunstan's firmly established, Pearson was considering entering Parliament as a spokesman for the blind.

On the morning of 9 December 1921, he was awakened at 7.15 and, unaided, went to his bathroom. He always insisted on preparing his bath himself, but the previous day he had mentioned that the enamelled bath had been rather slippery. This particular morning, apparently, he slipped forward, striking his head on the tap. Stunned, he fell face downwards into the water and drowned.[22] Pearson normally breakfasted at 8.30, but with no sign of him at that time his secretary contacted his son, who went to the bathroom, where he found his father dead.

His death caused a great sense of shock throughout the country. In his old paper, the *Evening Standard*, it was noted:

> The career of Sir Arthur Pearson is at once a romance and a glory. This fight against the foe of physical darkness – a magnificant struggle – undoubtedly owes the major part of its success to the virile personality, the optimism, and the genius of a man who would never acknowledge defeat. He treated blindness from a new angle: he cut out entirely the word 'pity' and the word 'affliction', and insisted that blind people, above all others, must be cheerful, with a wide humorous outlook.

R. D. Blumenfeld, so long one of his friends, wrote in the *Daily Express*, the paper that Pearson had founded: 'A man of achievement, strong, vivid, a radiant figure of energy, enthusiasm and human affection has come to a sudden and tragic end of his picturesque career. Arthur Pearson, the blind leader of the blind, whose death is regretted today, was one of those rare men who are born for a purpose and who, having achieved that purpose, are taken away as flaming examples to posterity.'[23]

Arthur Pearson was buried at Hampstead Cemetery, and the King and Queen, Queen Alexandra, the Queen of Norway and the Prince of Wales sent representatives. Members of the government, Commissioners from the Dominions and the high and the mighty of Fleet Street were also there to pay their final respects. But, above all else, there were hundreds of blind mourners, brought especially from all over the country, who gathered by the graveside:

> Never before had such scene been witnessed at a public funeral. It enhanced, if that were possible, the pathos of Sir Arthur's tragic end.
>
> Guided gently by big guardsmen in grey overcoats and by nurses, they moved slowly past the grave in groups of two and three, arm in arm. Humbly dressed and smartly dressed, some wearing dark spectacles, some with the blank expression of the blind man whose eyes look normal, the sightless procession moved uncertainly in the December sunlight.

The feeling of the nation was to be summed up in the wreath from Queen Alexandra:

Life's race well run,
Life's work well done,
Life's crown well won,
Now comes rest.

14

Empire Crusader

In 1923, Sir Edward Hulton – he had been created a baronet two years earlier for services during the war – was considering selling his newspapers. He had been dogged by ill-health for more than twenty years, and all his life had been 'tormented by the Victorian, Puritan urge to get up early and work hard, and always be doing something "useful". He was a conscientious worker to an almost pathetic degree, being ... too suspicious to delegate'.[1] It now seemed that this desire for always working and constant action had finally proved to be too much. Many years later, Hannen Swaffer wrote of meeting him at Ascot and offering congratulations on his improved appearance: 'You are wrong,' replied Hulton, 'I am dying and I am the most miserable man on earth.'[2]

By the early 1920s, E. Hulton & Co. Ltd, a private company, owned eight newspapers – including, of course, the *Evening Standard* – plus a number of periodicals. The average circulation of the morning papers in the first six months of 1920 was 1,267,343; of the evening papers 868,639; and of the Sunday and weekly papers 4,518,349. Despite a loss in 1920 of £216,433, average profits before tax for the previous five and a half years had been £377,702; and profits for 1922, which included fifteen months of the *Empire News*, were £818,438.

Initially, Hulton decided to sell his chain to the Berry brothers from Merthyr – later Lords Camrose and Kemsley. In April 1923, negotiations were at an early stage when their lawyer fell ill. Lord Rothermere, fresh from purchasing his late brother's newspapers, now entered the fray, but Hulton would not sell to him. Never one to miss an opportunity, Lord Beaverbrook saw his chance and suggested to Rothermere that he should buy the newspapers on Rothermere's behalf, taking the *Evening Standard* as commission. Rothermere agreed. Beaverbrook started with one great advantage: as a near neighbour of Hulton he was a close friend, and his Cherkley estate was within walking distance of Sir Edward's home at Downside, near Leatherhead.

On 28 September 1923, Beaverbrook learned that the Berry-Hulton deal was to be signed three days later, on 1 October: 'The price was to be £6 million with an immediate down payment of £300,000'.[3] It was an easy matter, therefore, for Beaverbrook to stroll through the french windows of Hulton's home on 28 September to greet his friend lying ill in a ground-floor bedroom. Hulton needed little persuasion to sell his newspapers for £5 million. Beaverbrook wrote the details on a sheet of Midland Bank writing paper, and Hulton scrawled 'I accept', and signed it:

> The family had been ready to stop Beaverbrook entering the bedroom on the grounds that Hulton was too ill. They were horrified to find the note, and at once rang the Midland Bank to check on Beaverbrook's resources. The bank replied that Beaverbrook had no account with them, but within 20 minutes the manager rang back to say that the sum would be met. Beaverbrook had hurried home, and telephoned his friend, Reginald McKenna, former Chancellor of the Exchequer and now chairman of the Midland Bank.[4]

He had asked McKenna if the bank would honour his cheque for one million pounds. With McKenna's assurances, Beaverbrook remitted this amount, with the balance to follow within a week. But, even before the final payment had been made to the Midland, the ever-astute Beaverbrook had sold the package to Rothermere, deducting the *Evening Standard* as his commission.

Ever prescient, on 3 October 1923, H. A. Gwynne, editor of the *Morning Post*, wrote to Stanley Baldwin that he had heard 'on good authority that Beaverbrook is in with Rothermere in the purchase of the Hulton concerns'. On less good authority, Gwynne informed Baldwin that Lloyd George was behind the deal and that he had 'declared that he was coming back to sweep the country on an Empire policy'.[5]

Ten days after the purchase, Beaverbrook was interviewed by the bureau chief of the *New York Times*: 'He [Beaverbrook] dropped around to see Hulton late at night. There he was shown all the documents necessary for the sale of Hulton Press.' Beaverbrook then told the bureau chief:

> Of course there was Berry and it was just worth trying him, so information was conveyed to him that he could if he liked have the rest of the publications, but Berry did not seem to grasp the idea and said nothing.
>
> Lord Beaverbrook then thought of Rothermere. It was common gossip that he was not satisfied with the position of his newspapers in Manchester, and it had even been rumoured that he was about to start a northern daily. Lord Beaverbrook called him up on the telephone and told him in his own offhand manner the proposition he had to offer and Rothermere equally nonchalantly accepted without ringing off. That is the inside story of the biggest newspaper deal that Fleet Street has ever known.[6]

Less than a fortnight later, on 14 October, Beaverbrook was able to announce that he was in control of the *Evening Standard*. He kept 51 per cent of the company and the Daily Mail Trust took 49 per cent, paying for it with 40,000 of their shares. As A. J. P. Taylor has written:

> It is true that he now had a well-balanced empire – a morning paper, an evening paper and a Sunday paper. But the *Evening Standard* did not fit in with the pattern he had previously created ... More probably, he welcomed the *Evening Standard* as something different. Those who thought that Beaverbrook could only inspire one kind of newspaper did not grasp the many-sidedness of his nature. He wanted political influence. He wanted mass circulations for some of his papers on the Northcliffe pattern. But he also wanted fun, and the *Evening Standard* provided an outlet for his excessive radicalism.[7]

With the sale of his papers, Hulton retired from full-time business and gave £75,000 to be distributed among his staff. For a time he lived in Cannes, but returned to London and then to his Surrey home, where he died, aged 56, on 23 May, 1925.[8]

THE YOUNG BEAVERBROOK

As for Beaverbrook, the new proprietor of the *Evening Standard*, he was already owner of the *Daily Express* and had launched the *Sunday Express* in 1918. He was born William Maxwell Aitken,[9] the son of a Church of Scotland minister, on 25 May 1879 in Maple, Ontario, and throughout his long life was never to lose his rasping Canadian accent. As a youth he had a series of jobs: selling newspapers; a clerk in a lawyer's office; a drug-store assistant; running a bowling alley; peddling insurance – and even starting a small newspaper, *The Leader*, from home, until his father put an abrupt stop to it when he discovered the young Aitken working on a Sunday.

As a young, forceful entrepreneur, he entered the expanding field of selling bonds, and promoting companies and company mergers, for during the boom years at the turn of the century, takeovers and consolidations flourished in Canada, and with each transaction completed Aitken would move on to the next lucrative venture. In 1906, at the age of 26, he married Gladys Drury, daughter of a Canadian general. The honeymoon was spent in New York and the West Indies, giving Aitken the opportunity to purchase the Puerto Principe Electric Light Company in Cuba, for $300,000; 417 acres of land; the old Mule Train franchise; and the electric railway franchise. Twelve months later he had bought himself a seat on the Montreal Stock Exchange, becoming an investment banker, and buying the Montreal Trust company for $350,000. Within less than two years he had sold it, making more than $200,000 profit; and by the end of the decade, through his expertise in mergers, had become a millionaire. Working with different syndicates over a 12-month period he had set up combines worth more than $100 million – and all created in tariff-protected industries. He was not, however, without critics, and his final deals – the formation of the Canada Cement company and the birth of the Steel Company of Canada – were to find him under severe attack. Following the cement deal, questions were asked by leading businessmen and politicians, and Aitken was formally warned by a minister of the Liberal government that there would be strictures if he embarked upon further mergers.

Undeterred, within weeks Aitken had involved himself in purchasing the Montreal Rolling Mills for $4,200,000. This immediately incurred the wrath of the other Canadian steelmasters, who wanted to prevent him from linking up with the United States Steel Corporation. Determined to protect their cartel, the Canadian steelmasters paid Aitken more than $6 million for his property. As for Aitken, he positively revelled in the intrigue, having taken a trip to London to sell bonds and borrow $5 million from Parr's Bank, just in case he needed the money for the mills. In the event, the $4,200,000 was not required, as the cartel paid the bill – and a jubilant Aitken pocketed more than $2 million in profit.

On 17 July 1910, the Steel Company of Canada came into being, and that same evening Aitken and his wife left Montreal for New York and then England, for new conquests and fortunes. Aitken, a small man, was ever a restless, crusading person, and his attitude can be summed up in the following; 'On the rockbound coast of New Brunswick, the waves beat incessantly. Every now and then comes a particularly dangerous wave that breaks viciously on the rocks. It is called "Rage". That's me.'[10]

Throughout his life he was to believe that fire and brimstone awaited the souls of the damned. Randolph Churchill was later to write: 'They've been getting the place ready for him specially all these years.' Another of his friends, H. G. Wells, wrote: 'If Max gets to Heaven he won't last long. He will be chucked out for trying to pull off a merger between Heaven and Hell ... after having secured a controlling interest in key subsidiary companies in both places, of course.' Aitken, himself, though, took a more basic view of his faith: 'My Christianity is quite simple ... God is Moderator of the Church of Scotland.'[11]

As a first business venture in England, Aitken bought heavily into Rolls-Royce and immediately demanded that the company should turn over to mass production. A horrified management pleaded with Northcliffe, himself a motoring pioneer, who took a non-financial interest in the firm. He wrote to Aitken asking him not to interfere with 'the delicate orchid' of Rolls-Royce. Aitken sold his shares, and received from Northcliffe the accolade of being 'one of the straightest men in the country'.

In 1910, Aitken, thanks to fellow-countryman Andrew Bonar Law, stood as Conservative candidate for Ashton-under-Lyne, a Free Trade stronghold, and home of the many spinners and weavers at the cotton mills. Using his best business methods, Aitken reorganised the local party machine, undertook a most detailed canvassing and had all the voters card-indexed. Despite lack of support from Lord Derby, vice-president of Lancashire Conservatives, Aitken continued in his dynamic manner, culminating in a huge procession through the streets on the eve of polling day. His tactics were successful, and he defeated his Liberal opponent by 4,044 votes to 3,848, a majority of 196.

MEETING WITH BLUMENFELD

The strain of electioneering had, however, proved too much for Aitken, and he was told by his doctor that he needed to recuperate in the South of France. Christmas for the Aitkens, therefore, was spent in Nice, and it was there, on the Riviera, on 2 January 1911, that he began an association that was to have a significant effect upon his future.

As he was descending the steps of the Casino at Monte Carlo he was approached by R. D. Blumenfeld, with a note of recommendation from Bonar Law. With C. Arthur Pearson having withdrawn his interest from the *Daily Express* because of his blindness, Blumenfeld was now urgently seeking help. Although the circulation was beginning to climb, the paper remained heavily in debt to newsprint suppliers. The Unionist party had offered to take over the paper, but Blumenfeld, being a keen Tariff Reformer, was reluctant. Late in December he had consulted Law at the Carlton Club who had told him: 'I know the man for you. Max Aitken is enormously rich. He knows nothing about newspapers and is not interested in them. But he wants to have a big political career, and he'll be glad of a paper which will back him.' Blumenfeld left at once for the South of France. Aitken listened to his story, walked over to the Hotel de Paris and wrote out a cheque for £25,000 as a personal loan.

Many years afterwards, Blumenfeld was to recall:

> A month or so later [after lunching with Aitken and F. E. Smith] I was standing on the steps of the Casino at Monte Carlo, chatting with Sir Gilbert Parker, when what we used to described as a 'powerful automobile' (it must have been 15 h.p.) drew up, and out jumped our new M.P., Max Aitken. He was vociferous in his greetings, and then informed me that 'You and I are going to do big things together.' I did not agree; but I have found in the past twenty years since he and I have been associated, that, even if I did not always agree, he generally succeeded in doing what he wanted to do.

So we became close friends. We breakfasted and dined incessantly. I learned a lot about mergers and share-splitting and cement and Canada, and he learned more about people and journalism.[12]

As an MP, Aitken was not a success, rarely bothering to vote and conducting most of his intrigues in the committee rooms of the House of Commons. However, on 20 April 1911, he met Sir Alexander Ackland-Hood, the Tory chief whip, who informed him that he had 'Two peerages, two P.C.s, two baronetcies and six knighthoods in his giving for the Coronation'. He offered a knighthood to Max Aitken 'for the purpose of rewarding me for services to come and to the [Tory] Unionist party'.

For the next few years, Sir Max, among his many other activities, continued to support the *Daily Express*, although Blumenfeld remained the titular head. But on 15 January 1915, the paper was once more in trouble, owing £9,000 in newsprint bills, and a receiver was about to be appointed. Steel-Maitland, once more the mediator, suggested that three safe Tory MPs should be appointed as receivers. Sir Max, as mortgage-holder, would have none of this, and successfully proposed the appointment of Blumenfeld, the editor, as the receiver. On 5 May 1916, he wrote to Walter Runciman, the President of the Board of Trade: 'The *Daily Express*, in which I am interested, is short of paper. I should like to have the opportunity of discussing with you the means by which I could secure the release of a ship to bring over a cargo of paper from the mills of Price Brothers and Company Ltd. of Quebec.'

Blumenfeld has left an interesting account of those difficult days on the *Express*:

I was wallowing about in the trough of the sea somewhere NNE by SSW off Ludgate Circus, two points to leeward of Fleet Street – in Shoe Lane to be exact. My good ship *Daily Express* was strong enough in hull and frame and steering gear and all that, but short of steam. Like the Mississippi steamer of note, she was underpowered and overwhistled, i.e., every time the whistle blew the engines stopped. My friend Aitken came along and showed me how to balance things and keep the steam pressure always on top. He also pointed at the chart, and indicated that I had been travelling along the old course, which was full of danger and storms and fogs, whereas he knew a short cut which would land my craft quicker and with greater ease.

Then he became more and more interested, until one day he joined me on the Board, and from that time on there was no holding him. Away went his cherished desire to return to Canada and grow up with the country. He got the sniff of printers' ink in his nostrils, and those

> who know what that means will understand why everything went overboard. I have often observed that revitalising effect on men who were once connected with my trade. The moment their olfactory senses come into contact with that strange overpowering heaven-induced tank of ink and type and rollers and paste, their eyes twinkle, their nerves tingle, and the years slough off almost visibly.[13]

Sir Max was hooked, and later, as Lord Beaverbrook, he recalled with clarity his very early days as a newspaperman and his decision to become involved with the *Daily Express*:

> The first farthing I ever made in my life was selling one cent or half-penny newspapers in the little town of Newcastle, New Brunswick. Afterwards I consolidated the whole newspaper distribution in the village, but I was not satisfied, I felt I could do better.
>
> I became a newspaper publisher. I was the publisher and the sole proprietor of a paper, *The Leader*. I also set up the type. I stood at the case, and could do so now but for those new-fangled machines. Not only that but I ran the printing press, and I did it not by touching a button, but had to do it by turning a handle in the same way as you turn a mangle. I did everything but distribute type after it had been used. That I would never do. It was too boring.[14]

Talking of how he entered Fleet Street, he said:

> Then the same friend came to me and asked me take an interest in another newspaper [he had previously been involved with *The Globe*, a London evening]. That paper was the *Daily Express*. That was in 1915 and we turned a £40,000 loss into a a profit. It was a very good thing we did. But there were branches of the newspaper industry that came along, demanding more pay and remuneration. Well, we managed to wriggle along until year 1920.

Four years later, in his book, *Politicians and the Press*, he once more returned to his acquisition of the *Daily Express*:

> I had for a number of years a considerable connection with the *Daily Express* of an indefinite character, but was never interested much. Towards the end of the war that newspaper wanted money very urgently to keep its supply of newsprint. Finally, the editor came to me and suggested that I could purchase the controlling shares in the newspaper for £17,500.[15]

Before buying the shares, he spoke to Lord Rothermere, who told him that to take the shares at this price implied a great deal of courage as he would need to devote a considerable amount of money and energy to the business. Aitken then consulted Lord Northcliffe, who asked him: 'How much are you worth?' 'Over five million dollars,' replied Aitken. 'You will lose it all in Fleet Street,' retorted Northcliffe.[16]

WAR CORRESPONDENT

During this period of becoming proprietor of the *Daily Express*, Aitken was also serving as a distinguished war correspondent, including a much-talked-about account of Canadian heroism at the Battle of Ypres in April 1915.[17] He also started the first newspaper devoted exclusively to the troops, the *Canadian Daily Record*, with a free distribution of 250,000 copies, which lasted until 31 July 1919.

In 1916, for his 'wartime services to Canada', Aitken received a baronetcy. Later that year, on 6 December, Asquith resigned as Prime Minister and was never to hold office again. His replacement, Lloyd George, immediately did away with the old-style cabinet, replacing it with a committee of five people. Having been used by Lloyd George to secure the premiership, Aitken was confident that he would secure a post in the new administration, probably as President of the Board of Trade.

However, on 9 December, Lloyd George wrote to Aitken offering a peerage: 'There are two or three important business departments which have no representatives in the House of Lords and therefore no spokesmen. Would you allow me to recommend your name to the King for a Peerage. You could answer for these departments in the H. L.' By return, Aitken replied; 'My dear Prime Minister, I am grateful to you for your offer and I shall be glad if I can be of any help to you in the way you indicate.' That same day, Bonar Law added his thoughts: 'My dear Max, I hope you will accept L. G.'s offer, Yrs A. B. L.'

Not everyone, however, was pleased at the news that Aitken was to be elevated to the peerage, as Lord Beaverbrook, and one of his severest critics was King George V, who did not 'see his way' to approve since he did not consider that the 'public services of Sir Max Aitken called for such special recognition'. Practising journalists were strong in their opposition to the new peer, and Leo Maxse, in writing to Bonar Law, noted:

> 'We are all terrified of having men like Max Aitken ... thrust upon us.' Gwynne also had grave misgivings, as he said to Edward Goulding: 'I didn't make any comment about Aitken's peerage in the *Morning Post* because I did not want to foul the nest of the new Govt. Just when they were starting. I'm not sure I've done right.'[18]

Nevertheless, despite these criticisms, Aitken was made a peer, mainly due to Lloyd George's insistence. He had informed Lord Stamfordham, the King's private secretary, that any refusal would 'place him in a position of great embarrassment' and asked him to discuss the matter with Bonar Law, as the announcement had already been made unofficially. A reluctant King George gave way, but insisted that any future honours should not be offered until he had been informally consulted.

On 18 December 1916, in the visitors' book at his Cherkley country estate there appeared the following entry: 'Beaverbrook formerly W. M. Aitken'. The small boy from Maple, Ontario, had finally arrived ... For Fleet Street's latest Press Baron, the time had come to take stock of his new property, and for Beaverbrook, seemingly no longer required to act as a political go-between, the first task was to purchase a thousand tons of newsprint from Northcliffe at favourable terms.

Beaverbrook was later to write: 'I claim to have become a full-blooded journalist just before the general election of 1918.'[19] Earlier that year, on 10 February 1918, Lloyd George invited Beaverbrook to become Minister of Information. As such, Beaverbrook made a great feature of inviting the editors of newspapers in the Dominions and in neutral countries to visit Britain: 'But no editor in the world was satisfied to leave England unless he could say that he had seen Mr Lloyd George'.

Despite criticism in a House of Commons debate on 5 August when propaganda was discussed, Beaverbrook remained in office until 21 October when he resigned his post through ill-health – and was immediately operated on for a glandular swelling on the neck.

Free of office, Beaverbrook could once more turn his energies to the *Daily Express*. Bonar Law, though, suggested that he should remain in politics or, if he must, run an official Tory newspaper. 'No. In politics I am bound – for no man can really be a politician without submitting to the necessary trammels of the party,' Beaverbrook replied: 'In the Press, on the contrary, I am free and can work from the outside ... I never mean to hold a public office again except during a period of war.'

LAUNCH OF *SUNDAY EXPRESS*

On 29 December, 1918, Lady Diana Manners (later Lady Diana Cooper) started the presses for the first issue of the *Sunday Express*. Assured by Blumenfeld that the new paper would cost only a few thousand pounds to launch, this figure was to prove woefully inaccurate; in the first two years it cost Beaverbrook almost £500,000, and he was to spend another £2 million before it moved into profit.

Although Blumenfeld edited the first issue, he did not see working seven nights a week as his role. A succession of top editorial people were then engaged to direct the paper, but none lasted for long. Beaverbrook later wrote; 'The corpses of *Sunday Express* editors were spread up and down Fleet Street in every direction.' For a short time he even edited the paper himself, but found the constant conferences and planning too restrictive; it was not until John Gordon, a dour Scotsman from Dundee, took charge that the *Sunday Express* began to establish its own identity. Unlike most press barons, who preferred to remain anonymous, Beaverbrook used his new paper as a platform to expound his views. In 1921, he wrote 25 articles for the *Sunday Express*; in 1922, 35 articles; in 1923, 24 articles; and in 1925, 10 articles. Talking of those early years, he was later to recall: 'I sometimes used to go out into my garden and shake myself like a dog ... I always wrote off the very considerable sums I had invested in, or advanced to the *Sunday Express* as a potential total loss.'[20]

Meanwhile, because of an unparalled run of luck with its racing tips, the circulation of the *Daily Express* had begun to rise dramatically; and in the month of June 1920 the sales soared from 530,000 to 701,000. Because of the heavy involvement of the racing fraternity, many regular readers were unable to obtain their copies, and it was almost with a sigh of relief that its luck ran out with the horses, and the circulation was able to settle down at 550,000 copies per day.

The previous four years had seen a hard battle to raise the paper's figures from 350,000 to 550,000, but the growth of sales had caused a consequent pressure on advertising space. Despite the pleas to put advertising on page 1, Beaverbrook would have none of it. He was correct in his decision, for the more dramatic presentation of news on the front page was now helping to push the circulation over the 600,000 mark. Demand continued to soar, and by August 1922, with sales of 942,591, certain restrictions had to be put into force.

Beaverbrook's comments were:

> It may seem astonishing that a newspaper should be compelled to check its production. But let any man consider the practical position. The publication of every additional copy involved us in a loss. It compelled expensive arrangements for extra printing facilities outside our own office, and for handling and despatching the newspaper. It was necessary to start printing in our own office and to close the formes of type against extra late copy hours before the proper time. In spite of precautions the *Daily Express* was frequently late for delivery to the newsagents. Then came a further difficulty. By November 1922, it had become absolutely necessary to produce a

> sixteen-page newspaper. The growth in the sales had increased the demand for advertisement space, and this in turn created a further need for news space.
>
> But the consequence was to magnify the difficulties of producing the number of copies the public wanted. For the production of a sixteen instead of a twelve-page paper slowed down the rate at which several of the printing presses could turn out their sheets by nearly 50 per cent. It became necessary to ration the output of the *Daily Express.* I remember that in one single evening we took a decision which cut down the numbers of an issue by 30,000 copies – and this out of sheer necessity.[21]

Earlier that year, on 14 August 1922, the newspaper world had been stunned to learn of the death of Lord Northcliffe at his London home. The man who had changed the course of the British press, he was described by Beaverbrook as 'the greatest figure who ever strode down Fleet Street'. Within weeks of Northcliffe's death, his empire had been broken up, his brother Harold – Lord Rothermere – buying control of Associated Newspapers: the *Daily Mail, Evening News, Weekly* (later *Sunday*) *Dispatch* and *Overseas Daily Mail.* He was unsuccessful, though, in his bid for his brother's shares in *The Times,* which were purchased by the Hon. J. J. Astor.

J. L. Garvin's prediction of the break-up of the Northcliffe newspapers had been absolutely accurate. In his tribute to Northcliffe he wrote: 'I feel as one might if Niagara itself were to cease and vanish. There will not be another Lord Northcliffe. To that Alexander's Empire of journalism, however it may be divided, no one man can succeed.'

Within little more than fourteen months, the face of the newspaper world had changed: Beaverbrook was now in control of the *Evening Standard* with 51 per cent, plus owning 40,000 Daily Mail Trust shares. Rothermere, for his part, as well as proprietorship of his late brother's papers, also owned 49 per cent of the *Evening Standard.* And the Berry brothers, with the aid of Edward Iliffe, were extending their Allied Newspaper group, thanks to the purchase of the former Hulton titles.

FIRST MEETING

On 30 November, 1923, the first meeting of the Evening Standard Company Limited[22] was held; and on December 21 the new Board met to consider the undertaking entered into between E. Hulton and Co. Ltd, the Company, the Daily Mail Trust and Lord Beaverbrook, 'being an agreement for the acquisition by the Company of the goodwill and copyright of the *Evening Standard* and certain freehold and leasehold premises and machinery connected therewith'.

A little over a month later, on 25 January, 1924, Hultons were 'pressing for immediate payment of the purchase of the goodwill and payment of the purchase consideration of £250,000'. In view of the urgency, it was agreed to complete that day. A breakdown of the price showed that Lord Beaverbrook had purchased 12,750 shares at £12,750 and 114,750 debentures at £114,750. The Daily Mail Trust were to buy 12,500 shares at £12,500 and 110,250 debentures at £110,250. Beaverbrook was immediately involved in paying off debts of £12,000 to press manufacturers.[23]

By mid-March, the *Evening Standard* was able to join the Newspaper Proprietors' Association and to appoint a general manager, Alfred Wilson, who also acted as company secretary. Although the paper was not now owned by Hultons it was still 'printed and published by E. Hulton & Co. Ltd., of 46–47, Shoe Lane', and it was resolved that the wording 'for the proprietors Evening Standard Co. Ltd.' be added. Less than a month later, on 4 April, the Board were discussing the issue of a series of debentures for £225,000 in denominations of £1,000, £500 and £100 each, carrying interest at seven per cent and redeemable by annual drawings over twenty-five years.

By early May, with the tacit approval of Beaverbrook, the newly-constituted board of the *Evening Standard* was in being. Messrs Goss, Francis and King, the legal people, had departed and had been replaced by A. Wilson, chairman, who was also general manager and company secretary, and R. B. Jackson and W. Harman.

One of the board's first acts was to cease publication from Saturday, 3 May, of the *Midday Standard*, 'because the financial position was very unsatisfactory and there was no prospect of any immediate or future improvement'. The gentlemen's agreement between the *Evening Standard*, the *Evening News* and the *Star*, whereby no copies of these papers were to be sold before 9.30 am, also came under discussion, and it was agreed that one month's notice of termination should be given.

The effect of late news and sporting results in the *Evening News* and the *Star* was very much in the minds of the *Evening Standard* directors, and on 3 June it was decided that the company should run one late press to provide for close of play cricket scores, 'when, in the opinion of the publisher, this course is advisable'. The decision was also taken to look closely into purchasing 40 Multistamp machines to print news and results in the 'stop press'. It was, however, agreed that seven racing tipsters each day was too many – and the decision was taken to axe 'Captain Cuttle' and 'Morning Star'.[24]

15

The General Strike

While Beaverbrook had been busy expanding his newspaper empire, he was still deeply involved in the political scene. But after having been one of Lloyd George's main supporters in 1916–18, helping him to win the general election, a certain coolness had developed between the two men. Under Beaverbrook's direction, the *Express* had conducted several campaigns against the government: taxation of war fortunes by means of a special once-only levy; Winston Churchill's intervention against the Bolshevik government in Russia; embargo on Canadian cattle; and criticism of Lloyd George's policy in encouraging the Greeks in their war against the Turkish nationalists under Mustapha Kemal. However, defeat of the Greeks at Smyrna meant that Kemal was intent on carrying the war across the Dardanelles and into the European territories assigned to Greece at the recent Treaty of Sèvres (1920). In London, the government feared that the Allied occupation forces guarding Constantinople would be attacked; so, despite hesitancy from the French and the Italians, Lloyd George and Churchill ordered reinforcements of the British detachment in Chanak, the area on the Asiatic shore of the Dardanelles.

The Chanak Incident,[1] as it came to be known, was a major contributory cause of the fall of Lloyd George's government in the autumn of 1922. In August of that year, at Deauville, Beaverbrook had discussed the heightening crisis with the Aga Khan, who made arrangements for him to meet Kemal in Ankara. Before leaving for Turkey, Beaverbrook invited Lloyd George, Churchill and Lord Birkenhead (F. E. Smith) to his Cherkley estate. It was not a successful meeting: Beaverbrook, who sought 'some kind of power to negotiate' was to be disappointed. Lloyd George, anxious not to offend Lord Curzon, the Foreign Secretary, was 'indefinite and evasive'. Word of the meeting was leaked to Gwynne on the *Morning Post* and he was able to publish 'detailed and alarming accounts' of Beaverbrook's movements.

On arriving in Turkey, Beaverbrook found that the situation had changed dramatically, and, with the Greeks already routed, he hurried back to England, telling Bonar Law: 'These men [Lloyd George and his supporters] mean war'. The planned articles in the *Daily Express* were now abandoned and a short notice announced that 'he disagreed with the Government's policy but did not want to embarrass the Government during delicate negotiations'.

On 18 October 1922 it was announced that Bonar Law would be going to a meeting of the Carlton Club the following day. Beaverbrook later wrote:

> The moment it was decided that Bonar law should go to the Carlton Club I informed the Press Association and authorised them to publish the fact to all the newspapers – and the issue was decided in favour of Conservative Independence in spite of the most frantic efforts of pro-Coalition Ministers to secure the support of Tory members ... The historian of the future may find it difficult to connect the Chanak Incident with the Tory revolt. The clue is a simple one. It was Bonar Law's letter opposing the war with Turkey. After that Toryism simply slid like an avalanche in the direction of its natural leader.[2]

Sensing the desire of the Conservatives for a new leader, Viscount Rothermere was quick to support Bonar Law and other press chiefs were swift to offer aid: Riddell endorsed him in the *News of the World*; there was support from the *Evening Standard*; and Wickham Steed, in the twilight of his editorship, saw Bonar Law on three consecutive evenings and promised him 'whatever influence *The Times* possesses'. Steed believed that the Conservatives would win an election with a majority of seventy-five seats. His forecast was to be amazingly accurate.

Polling day was on 15 November 1922 and, in a campaign of increasing bitterness, Beaverbrook was once more to the fore, backing Independent Conservatives in constituencies where local pacts had been made between Coalition–Liberals and Conservatives. The result was victory for Bonar Law and the Conservatives with a majority of seventy-one, and for Beaverbrook it was a happy day – once more he had shown that he was a power behind the throne.

Randolph Churchill, in his biography of Lord Derby, was to be in no doubt as to who was the architect of the Conservative victory:

> The prime mover and principal agent in the plan to bring down the Coalition Government [of Lloyd George] was Beaverbrook ... He had played a leading part behind the scenes in the election of Bonar Law in 1911 as Leader of the Conservative Party upon the resignation of Arthur Balfour. He had been active in the formation of the first Coalition Government under Asquith and he had probably done more than anyone else except Lloyd George to pull Asquith down and to set up Lloyd George in his place ...[3]

Unfortunately for Bonar Law it was to be a short-lived return to public life ... Within months of taking office, it became clear that he was a sick man, and under increasing pressure from members of his party. Beaverbrook, who was visiting Palestine to investigate the Zionist question, was disturbed by a telegram from the Prime Minister urging him to come home at once:

> I found the Premier undoubtedly worried by the persistency of the attacks delivered against him by dissident Conservatives ... The latest attempt was to secure Lord Rothermere and his newspapers as the spearhead of a general movement against the Conservative administration. As a matter of fact this particular intrigue turned out in the exact reverse of the way its authors intended.[4]

On 23 April, 1923, Rothermere wrote to Beaverbrook pledging support: 'If Bonar places himself in my hands I will hand him down to posterity at the end of three years as one of the most successful Prime Ministers in history, and if there is a general election I will get him returned again. This may sound boastful but I know exactly how it can be done.'[5]

Although cheered immensely by this support, Bonar Law was still desperately ill, and on 1 May he left England on a Mediterranean cruise, hoping to recuperate. His condition, however, worsened, and a week later he left the ship at Genoa, going straight to Aix-les-Bains, where he was joined by Beaverbrook. Alarmed at his friend's condition, Beaverbrook at once proposed a move to Paris, where Sir Thomas Horder, a leading specialist from London, could meet them. After examining Bonar Law, Horder took Beaverbrook for a walk down the Champs-Elysées. The news was grave: Bonar Law had an incurable cancer of the throat and would be dead within six months. Beaverbrook, adopting an air of forced cheerfulness, went back to the Prime Minister, saying: 'My friend I encourage you to resign. You have become so determined to go on that you will not recover until you get nervous relief.'[6]

STRUGGLE FOR LEADERSHIP

There now ensued a struggle for the leadership of the Conservative party – and the Premiership. Two candidates stood out: Lord Curzon, a former Viceroy of India, 'a man who would scorn to be called a bird of paradise because he felt equipped to govern all the earth and possibly paradise as well', and Stanley Baldwin, a wealthy country squire from Worcestershire. In a quandary, Bonar Law was undecided whom to put forward as his successor. Although he could not recommend Baldwin he felt that Curzon would not be strong enough to hold the Cabinet together. But it was Arthur Balfour, the elder statesman and a former Prime Minister, to whom King George V turned for advice. So sure was Curzon of being appointed that when he heard that the King had sent for Baldwin he declared: 'Not even a public figure ... And of the utmost insignificance.'[7]

Patently annoyed at not being the 'king-maker', Beaverbrook wrote in the *Daily Express* on 21 May 1923 'Bonar Law was the greatest Conservative Prime Minister since Disraeli'.[8] For Beaverbrook, the appointment of Baldwin was to be deplored: he had never liked the man – and the feeling was mutual. Many years later, Baldwin recalled: 'I disliked him from the first moment I saw him. Years ago I told some people that I would not put my feet under the same table with Beaverbrook. One of them went off and reported it to him. He has never forgiven me – and I still wouldn't put my feet under the table with him.'

Throughout the long summer of 1923, Beaverbrook had been the perfect friend, refusing social and political engagements so as to be near Bonar Law. They played bridge in the afternoons and dined together in the evenings. At 3 a.m. on 3 October, Bonar Law died after having, some hours earlier, murmured his final words to his friend: 'You are a curious fellow'. A deeply-distressed Beaverbrook later recalled: 'Something was severed forever in my political associations. I had never cared much for the purely political life, but Bonar Law's charm, his urbanity, his wisdom, his firm and reasonable attitude towards problems, held me in a silken chain.'[9] Baldwin's view, though, was somewhat different: 'We fought for the soul of Bonar Law. Beaverbrook wanted to make him a great man after his own fashion. I showed him there were better things to be'.

Within days of taking over the premiership, Baldwin announced that only protection would cure unemployment and that he must, therefore, call a general election in order to absolve himself of Bonar Law's pledge not to abandon Free Trade. To the majority of the Conservative Party this was a wrong move, none being more vociferous than Beaverbrook, who condemned Baldwin's decision as 'a serious blunder'. Several years later Beaverbrook was to tell Stanley Morison, the distinguished typographer and historian of *The Times*: 'Protection attracted Baldwin for the wrong reason; it was a catch-penny reason. The grandeur of an all-embracing association between the Empire parties, of fiscal union giving benefit to all and harming none, was something Baldwin did not understand.'[10]

On 1 November 1923, Rothermere telegraphed Beaverbrook from the South of France that he had 'given my newspapers strict instructions not to commit themselves ... until I can judge whether Baldwin understands the subject and has the imagination to go through with it'. In reply, Beaverbrook was 'very glad to know that you are delaying decisions about protection until Baldwin develops his plans'.[11] A flurry of telegrams then flowed between 'Harold' and 'Max' until, on 14 November, Beaverbrook wired: 'Have seen Derby who declares he is against election and opposed to general tariff. Will you let me on your behalf run policy of Hulton

Manchester newspapers on Conservative Free Trade lines?' Rothermere replied by letter the following day, swearing that the nation, empire and the press were collectively heading for disaster: 'Tariffs or no tariffs there is a bad time coming. Make as much as you can now ... If I were you I should cut down your expenditure to the bone, then float the *Express* and the *Standard*. You could get millions & still control the business thro' deferred shares.'

Three weeks later, on 8 December, Baldwin 'went to the country', and just as Beaverbrook had predicted 'Law's majority, which he had helped to create, was wantonly thrown away'. The Conservatives secured 258 seats, eighty-seven fewer than they had won under Bonar Law's leadership; and, although the largest party, they had lost their overall majority. The Liberals, with 158 MPs, and occupying a quarter of the seats, were a powerful minority, but it was to Labour, with 191 members, that people now looked to provide the next government.

Immediately following the result of the general election, the *Evening Standard* announced that Baldwin was to resign and that Ramsay MacDonald would form the new government. On 11 December, however, E. R. Thompson, the editor, was forced to retract: 'Mr Baldwin has decided not to resign. He will meet Parliament as Prime Minister'. His tenure, though, was to be brief; on 22 January 1924, the *Standard*'s Late Night Final edition proclaimed: 'Mr Baldwin resigned office at 11.30 a.m. today and Mr Ramsay MacDonald had an audience of the King at which he was invited – and consented – to form a Government.'[12] Three weeks later, on 12 February 1924, Ramsay MacDonald led his colleagues to the Front Bench – and the first Labour government was in power. Apart from the *Daily Herald*, with its relatively low circulation of 400,000, support came only – and then condescendingly – from the Liberal Party. As Beaverbrook later wrote: 'Heretofore, no British Government for a hundred years had been without considerable newspaper backing. The Socialists could only claim one organ with a small circulation, and this newspaper could not be depended on by the new Prime Minister, for it really represented the extreme Left of his own supporters.' MacDonald himself had declared in *The New Leader*, a week after the General Election: 'Liberal papers like the *Daily News* have never been more dishonest nor more gleeful in their gloating over the prospects of a Labour defeat. I think that the way that the *Daily News* and the *Westminster Gazette* behaved was contemptible. We expect nothing better from the *Daily Mail* and such miserable products.'

DISINTERESTED PATRIOTISM

Gwynne, meanwhile, as editor of the *Morning Post*, was having his own problems, and wrote to Baldwin that 'up to the present Lady Bathurst [his proprietor] has been and is today a shining example of disinterested patriotism'. He was very much concerned that Beaverbrook or Rothermere would become involved. Gwynne believed that the paper would suffer. Plainly disenchanted at Labour being in office, Lady Bathurst could complain that politics afforded her no incentive, and that costs on the paper had increased by more than £130,000 a year: 'If journalists wish to kill newspapers they are going about it the right way.'[13] Concerned at the possible loss of the *Morning Post*, a consortium of prominent Conservatives handed over £470,000, of which £100,000 was paid in cash and the remainder in debentures. Lady Bathurst was delighted that the paper would be 'owned by men of right principles and whose ideas are the same as ours'. She told Gwynne that she had only been interested in selling the paper to die-hards, and that it grieved her to think that he 'believed that I would sell the *Morning Post* to Rothermere or anyone – just as you were afraid before the war that the German Ambassador might influence me by flattery'.

On 14 May 1924, an account of the recent negotiations appeared in 'Londoner's Diary' in the *Evening Standard*, incurring the wrath of Gwynne, himself a former editor of *The Standard*. He complained that the article contained a 'mass of mis-statements' that he wished to contradict. Writing that same day to Beaverbrook, he commented;

> You say the *Morning Post* has for some time past been considered practically the official organ of the Conservative Party, and certainly has close relations with the Conservative Central Office. I rescued the *Morning Post* from the Central Office. And as for the close relations, party officials would not hesitate to say that they regard the *Morning Post* as a thorn in their side ... I have never had any pressure of any kind put upon me by any single Director in this Company ... so if I have sinned, I have sinned on my own.[14]

A few months later, on 8 August, a contented Ramsay MacDonald wrote to the King: 'So the first stage of the Session comes to an end. From more than one point of view the Session has been historical. The Prime Minister may perhaps justly claim that he has shown the Country that the Labour Party is fit to govern ... Looking back on the Session, the Prime Minister has every reason to be satisfied.' The satisfaction, however, was to be short-lived. Less than a month earlier, on 25 July, *The Workers' Weekly* – later to be *The Daily Worker* – had urged British soldiers to 'let it be known that, neither in the class war nor the military war will you turn your guns on your fellow-workers'.[15] With full Cabinet approval, the Attorney-General took steps to prosecute J. R. Campbell, the acting editor of *The Workers' Weekly*. After an outcry from the ranks of the Labour movement – influenced, perhaps, by the fact that Campbell was a disabled war veteran – the case was dropped.

A Conservative censure motion, with Liberal backing – despite Asquith's protests – was enough to defeat the government. MacDonald now demanded a general election, which the King granted. On 25 October, four days before the election, the fate of the Labour Party was sealed; the Zinoviev letter, alleged to have been written by Gregori Zinoviev, the Russian Bolshevik leader, was published in the *Daily Mail*, calling on all British Communists to promote revolution. On 30 October, the *Evening Standard* proclaimed: 'A Conservative government with a handsome majority over all parties in the next House of Commons is announced. While Labour has again lost heavily, the Liberals have been almost wiped out, and, as a party, will be a negligible force in the near future.' The Conservative Party won 413 seats, obtaining a clear majority over Labour, who had lost forty-two seats, and the Liberals down to a mere forty Members. Beaverbrook had no doubt as to where the praise should be accorded, and on 30 October telegraphed Rothermere: 'I congratulate you on your magnificent victory. You have made the new Baldwin ministry. Now control it if you can.'[16]

GENERAL STRIKE

Ever since the First World War, there had been industrial unrest in the coalfields, and attempts had been made by the miners' leader, A. J. Cook, to secure sympathetic support from fellow trade unionists in the heavy industries. Threatened by further wage cuts, the miners – calling upon a resolution from the 1925 Congress – urged the Trades Union Congress (TUC) to call a General Strike. Accordingly the TUC called out transport workers, printers, builders, workers in heavy industries and, later, engineers. In response, the Baldwin-led government recruited special constables and volunteers to run essential services, and used troops to maintain food supplies. The strike lasted nine days, from 4–12, May, 1926, and during that period the government was determined to keep up a flow of information from both the press and radio.

On 1 May the *Evening Standard* commented upon the forthcoming strike in its leader column:

> A coal stoppage is a frightful disaster and an act of stark unreason. But if the miners decline to work under certain conditions, they have, after all, the right to do so. It is an entirely different matter if other trades seek to compel the government to subsidise miners' wages by the threat of a general paralysis of trade and com-

munications. Such action goes far beyond the limits of an industrial dispute ... Such action would be an attempt to dictate to the nation and those who took it would have no reason to complain if the nation through its organ, the Government, reacted against it with the utmost vigour. It may be hoped that a sane spirit will prevail ... but if trouble of the kind does come the Government will have the nation behind it in resisting any attempts to force it to surrender.[17]

That same day, Beaverbrook was summoned to the offices of the *Sunday Express*, where the Fathers of the Chapels were objecting to a government advertisement appealing for strike-breakers.[18] He rang up Birkenhead, who urged compromise. Churchill, though, was all for making a stand, saying: 'Close it down. You can afford it.' Beaverbrook, however, compromised by removing a few words from the advertisement. The *Sunday Express* was saved, but a statement in the leader left readers in no doubt that a General Strike must fail. And in the *Daily Express*, taking an almost conciliatory approach, Blumenfeld wrote a leader which the workers were prepared to print. At the *Daily Mail*, however, its editor, Thomas Marlowe, ran into difficulties because of his outspoken comments. Many of the production staff objected and sought to intervene. The editor refused – and the paper was not published; it was this act that finally gave Baldwin the excuse to break off negotiations with the TUC.

Nevertheless, Beaverbrook was determined to print his papers, even if it meant giving way, and in his own words: 'I should have been perfectly prepared to go on publishing at almost any cost ... even though the actual editing of the *Evening Standard* was interfered with by the Fathers of the Chapels.' The paper did appear on 3 May, but in a much-reduced size of eight pages – and cuts were made to the leader to placate the chapels.

However, a statement did appear on page 1, giving details of the stoppage.

THE DAILY MAIL

The editor of the *Daily Mail* has issued the following:

The Natsopas (National Society of Operative Printers and Assistants) at Carmelite House took exception to the leading article which had been prepared for publication in the *Daily Mail* of Monday, May 3, under the heading 'For King and country' and demanded that alterations should be made by the editor, who refused to comply.

They were supported by the machine minders, the stereotypers and the packers. Several unions, including the compositors, the process workers and the telegraphists, declared that it was not within their province to discuss the policy of the newspaper, and resolved to carry on their work in the usual way.

The Natsopas and the members of the unions supporting them ceased work and consequently there will be no issue of the *Daily Mail* from Carmelite House this (Monday) morning.[19]

On the *Daily Express*, Blumenfeld, the venerable editor-in-chief, took off his black coat, wrapped a white apron around his middle and became Head Printer, while Sidney Long, the Works Manager, fresh from his labours under the editorshop of Winston Churchill on the official *British Gazette*, for which he was awarded an OBE, was the chief Linotype operator:[20]

It was lucky for 'Blum' that Sidney Long was a brilliant Linotype operator – he could set a column of type without a single literal and at such a fantastic speed that in his pre-managerial career he took home more money on piece rates than the star reporters or even the leader-writers. In every respect Long was in splendid form .... Having assembled the type, he made up the pages, he supervised the casting of the stereo plates, and he got the presses rolling. [21]

There he was assisted by Beaverbrook himself, and Viscount Castlerosse, the society columnist, in blue dungarees, on the folder.

Meanwhile, negotiations with the *Evening Standard* chapels had broken down, as J. Wilson, the chairman of the company, would not agree to 'publishing at almost any price'. Beaverbrook offered to return and meet the men, 'but the directors demurred'. As the principal shareholder but not a director, 'I had no right to give a direction or an order though I had made my opinion clear.'

With the production staff now out on strike, plans were put in hand to issue emergency editions, and these were produced between Tuesday, 4 May and Saturday, 15 May. They ranged from a two-sided mimeograph on A4 paper to a small, four-page tabloid printed letterpress and complete with pictures; but, because of using a variety of small printers, different mastheads were printed on the same editions.[22]

On Thursday, 6 May, in a typed issue, the paper announced:

THE GENERAL STRIKE WILL FAIL

The Trade Unionists know it is failing. Every good citizen should help to make it fail quickly by standing firm and giving support to the authorities.

TAKE NO NOTICE OF RUMOURS AND DO NOT SPREAD THEM

Monday 10 May:

SEVENTH DAY OF STRIKE

The Chief feature of the 'Great Trek' to work today in London was the maintained cheerfulness of the people.

Wednesday, 12 May:

BREAKING UP

Important developments in the crisis are possible today. It seems clear that the leaders of the strike realise that it is failing and talks were initiated by them last night with the object of finding a speedy way out.

Later that same day:

STRIKE SETTLED: OFFICIAL

The TUC has unconditionally withdrawn the General Strike.

Thursday, 13 May:

GETTING BACK TO WORK

Despite the good news it was not well received in the more militant areas – especially among the London dockers – and the back page of this issue reported civil disturbances and police charges:

> Riotous scenes occurred at Poplar following the announcement that the strike had been called off. Dock workers gathered at the headquarters of the Transport and General Workers' Union and expressed dissatisfaction at the termination of the strike. Numbers increased with threatening attitudes. Following a baton charge the crowd fled in all directions, leaving many of their number injured on the ground. The Mayor of Poplar, Councillor J. Hammond, and the Rev. Cyril Maguire, of All Saints Parish Church, were among those who received injuries.

On 17 May with the strike finally over, the *Evening Standard* came back with a bumper 16-page issue. In his leader, the editor looked back on the dispute:

> Today the nation begins work once more, after an interruption of its activities which in many respects has had no parallel since the Great War. If we must survey with some ruefulness the result of the fortnight's folly we can yet start on the task of making good with some sense of relief if the situation is no worse. A fortnight ago, in

> the course of an article which was prevented from reaching the public, we wrote: 'The general strike must fail, as it has always failed.' The nation has won, the costly lesson, it is hoped, has been duly digested. Let recrimination cease, and all classes settle down, on terms of amity and mutual respect, to make good the damage of the great folly.

Afterwards, Beaverbrook told his old friend Tim Healy;

> I think everybody enjoyed the strike – on both sides – volunteers and strikers alike. It was treated in a holiday spirit; and the pickets outside the *Daily Express* office were quite as amused as the amateurs working the mechanical side of the newspaper within. I am almost inclined to favour the idea of having a General Strike once every year by law.[23]

One direct result of the strike was to be a split in political cooperation between Beaverbrook and Churchill. In his role as director of the government newspaper, *The British Gazette,* Churchill sought a monopoly of the news, even commandeering newsprint from *The Times.* A similar threat against the *Evening Standard* and the *Daily Express* ended in a terrible row between the two men, with Beaverbrook enlisting the support of his friend, William Joynson-Hicks, the Home Secretary, who refused to sign the requisition order. Churchill, said Beaverbrook, 'was in one of his fits of vainglory and excessive excitement'.

The failure of the General Strike left the miners deserted once more, and it was to be another seven months before, in November 1926, they were forced back by hunger on the worst possible terms. The eight-hour day was imposed by law, and wages were back to the low point they had been in 1921, and in some places back to the level of 1914. Lack of support from the TUC had left a legacy of disaster for the miners. Baldwin, though, was very much the man of the hour and praise was heaped on him for his skilful leadership and successful conclusion to the strike. Beaverbrook took a much more sardonic view, writing on 24 May: 'The laudations which are being poured upon Baldwin are pure hysteria. I have worked with him intermittently at one time for ten years at a stretch, and he is a man absolutely without a mind or a capacity to make one up.'[24]

IMPROVING CONTENT

Meanwhile, Beaverbrook was gradually improving the editorial content of the *Evening Standard,* and he was determined that the paper should employ only the finest writers. In one key area, the book review, he was very fortunate; the man selected, Arnold Bennett,[25] was already one of the country's leading authors and a playwright, and in his new role he was to be rightly celebrated.

Born in Hanley, Staffordshire, in 1867, the son of a self-educated solicitor, he went to London at the age of 21, to work as a clerk. His first stories were published in *Tit-Bits* (1890) and *The Yellow Book* (1895) and it was during this period that he became the editor of *Woman*. However, it was with his novels: *Arnold of the Five Towns*, in 1902; *The Old Wives' Tale*, in 1908; and the Clayhanger series (*Clayhanger*, 1910; *Hilda Lessways*, 1911; *These Twain*, 1916; and *The Roll Call*, 1918) that he was to make his name. He also wrote many lighter works, including *The Grand Babylon Hotel* in 1902; and *The Card* in 1911.

Beaverbrook first met Bennett in 1917, when he had invited him to sit on the Imperial War Committee and to act as Director of Propaganda in France; they were to remain close friends. A few weeks after Beaverbrook had taken control of the *Evening Standard* in 1923 Bennett, while spending the weekend at Cherkley, had urged him to make it a sophisticated paper, advice which was gladly acted upon. Bennett then wrote a three-page letter to Beaverbrook, expounding his views on the *Evening Standard*:

> This is the only evening paper that appeals even a little to educated people, and it ought to be made to appeal a great deal more to them than it does. Hence I wouldn't let it be yellow ... Your policy about retiring from Europe may be sound, but I don't think you'll get any Government to adopt it. There is a moral side to this matter that counts heavily. You might, and would, argue me to a standstill, but I should continue to think that to clear out of Europe was not right ... if you think only of circulation you won't get prestige, and if you think only of prestige you won't get circulation.[26]

Bennett wrote a weekly column for the paper from 18 November 1926 until his death in 1931.

Bennett didn't confine himself simply to reviewing new books, but he would chat about the state of literature in general, about old books that he wished to be remembered, about favourite authors and grievances. It was read eagerly and had the reputation of being the best selling book column in print.

Although Bennett had a strong involvement with the theatre – he had had some success as a playwright – it was not an interest that Beaverbrook shared, possibly because he was the largest shareholder in the country's leading cinema chain. He had identified correctly that the masses were seeking to be entertained – especially with the coming of 'the talkies' – and were not greatly interested in seeing live plays, and especially not the opera.

After writing to Arnold Bennett's wife, 'I went last night to a play called *Seventh Heaven.* I sat through two acts and registered a solemn vow that I would not enter a theatre again for a long time', Beaverbrook instructed his editors to give more space to films than to plays, saying, '100,000 people go to the cinema for every 1,000 who go to theatre'. To E. R. Thompson, the editor of the *Evening Standard,* he complained: 'If you will read the names of the persons who went to the Opera on Monday night you will see that they were a lot of "duffers". Most of them are too old to be out in the cold night air.'[27]

Other writers prominent in the *Evening Standard* at this time included Dean Inge, the Dean of St. Paul's, who in his weekly articles provided a cultivated total disbelief in established laws and institutions, earning himself the title of the 'Gloomy Dean'. His career on the paper was not without its drama, as on at least two occasions he had resigned and then rejoined. Hilaire Belloc and G. K. Chesterton also featured regularly in the *Standard*'s columns. However, Hilaire Belloc was to present something of a problem, and on 4 March 1927 Beaverbrook sent Rothermere cuttings from *The New Statesman* and *G. K.'s Weekly,* and wrote:

> All this stuff emanates from one source. I have given an order to the Express Newspapers that neither G. K. Chesterton nor Hilaire Belloc are to appear in the columns of these papers. They spend so much time in writing articles in abuse of me elsewhere, that I feel they have not got time to do good work for the newspapers with which I am connected. In the *Evening Standard* Diary there was a perfect passion for mentioning the names of Chesterton and Belloc. I have cut down the space allotted to advertising them. Now their names seldom appear. Besides their journalism is so dull, and their statements are utterly unreliable.

During the mid-1920s, London was served by three evening papers: the *Evening News,* which for many years proclaimed itself to have 'The World's Largest Evening Sale'; *The Star,* irreverent, down-to-earth, appealing directly to the working classes – and the *Evening Standard,* having the smallest circulation of the three, with 314,633 copies per night, catering mainly for the well-to-do of the City, the West End and the suburbs. The *Evening Standard* at that time was the combination of what had, not long before, been four independent journals. In 1921 *The Globe* had been amalgamated with the *Pall Mall Gazette,* which in 1923 had been absorbed by the *Evening Standard,* which itself, in 1905, had incorporated *The St. James's Gazette.*[28] Although Beaverbrook regarded the *Evening Standard* as his 'plaything', a vehicle with which he could have fun, and, on occasion, cause mischief, he was determined that it should continue to be an up-market product. Nevertheless, it should not be run at a loss. He was to be fortunate on both counts, because by the end of the decade the circulation had risen by more than 50,000 copies to 366,991 per night, while the advertisement revenue had also shown an increase, from £512,793 to £707,103 a year.[29] Much later, Beaverbrook wrote to Tom Blackburn, a former general manager of the paper and now chairman of the group, that for twenty-five years he had stood around in odd places observing the sales of the *Evening Standard* – 'watching outside Harrods sometimes for an hour at an end ... It is an exacting occupation, the ownership of newspapers. It is only for the very young, the very healthy, the very vigorous.'[30]

It was also during the 1920s that Beaverbrook secured his biggest catch for the paper, David Low, the cartoonist: 'Low was an artist of genius with strong political views ... and his scathing pencil did not spare Beaverbrook himself'. As the 'Empire Crusader' he appeared in many of the cartoons, as a small figure breathing mischief. A New Zealander, Low had arrived in London after the First World War to work on *The Star*, which he described as 'a miserable little sheet, badly printed'.[31] Low developed a comic strip for *The Star* featuring Beaverbrook and Rothermere as the wicked uncles in 'Babes in the Wood', calling the series 'The Plot Press'. The two figures, the little Beaver and the Fat Rother, in mock-sinister cloaks and hats, were naturals to draw – and for the cartoonist and *The Star* it became an immediate success. Beaverbrook, attracted by the cartoons' wit and draughtsmanship, determined that Low should work for his newly-purchased *Evening Standard*, making him an offer of twice his salary on *The Star*. It was to be three years, though, before Low ultimately agreed to join the *Standard*, obtaining for himself 'complete freedom in the selection and treatment of subject-matter for your cartoons and in the expression therein of the policies which you believe'.

16

Celebrating 100 Years

For Beaverbrook, the 1920s were not only a period when he was to meet continuing success with his newspapers, it was also to be a time of great personal loss. Throughout those years he behaved like a playboy with a purpose: 'The powerful, the promising, the storytellers, the witty and the beautiful were welcome at his table: he did not suffer the foolish or the plain. He became a figure in the social scene, flitting between Deauville and Monte Carlo with his guests. He became a racehorse owner, acquired a yacht, and multiplied his millions by entry into the film industry.'

In 1926, his wife, Gladys, with their daughter, Janet, went on a round-the-world trip, but while in Canada, Gladys became seriously ill, and on returning to England, after a short holiday with Beaverbrook at Le Touquet, went to Brighton for rest.[1] He wrote her a letter there which summed up his feelings for her: 'How I wish you well again ... And I declare that you are the only permanent love in my bad and wicked life. So come back soon and strong too.'[2] She returned to Stornaway House, their London mansion, and died on 1 December 1927. Beaverbrook, unfortunately, did not see her immediately before her death – which subsequently caused him great distress. Lord Birkenhead, his close friend, wrote in condolence: 'She had a breeding, a beauty, a poise and a judgement which would have recommended her to any society in Europe.'

Earlier that same year, on 21 May 1927, the *Evening Standard* celebrated a distinguished century of publishing with a 24-page paper, including special articles and messages of congratulations. The page 1 headline of this issue, number 32,069, read:

ONE HUNDRED YEARS OLD TODAY

We publish below the messages of congratulations from His Majesty the King, His Royal Highness the Prince of Wales, His Grace the Archbishop of Canterbury, and His Grace the Archbishop of York.

The message from the King is as follows:

BUCKINGHAM PALACE

The King has learnt with interest that on the 21st the *Evening Standard* celebrates its Centenary: and I am commanded to express to you His Majesty's congratulations on this memorable event in the history of journalism.

From the Prince of Wales

St. James's Palace, 20th May, 1927

I am desired by the Prince of Wales to send His Royal Highness's congratulations to the *Evening Standard* on the occasion of its hundredth anniversary.

From the Archbishop of Canterbury

The completion of the *Evening Standard*'s hundred years of publication is a matter of much interest. I am thankful for all the newspapers that maintain a high standard, and wish you all success.

From the Archbishop of York

The Archbishop of York desires to congratulate the *Evening Standard* on the completion of a hundred years' existence and the quality of its present articles.

Two former Prime Ministers also sent their best wishes: Lloyd George wrote:

> To the newspaper is entrusted the responsibility of seeing that the great British ideals of justice and fair play are kept ever before the people, not alone in these islands, but throughout the larger Empire which the courage and determination of our forefathers so firmly established. The *Evening Standard* by upholding the traditions of the great journalists who have been enlisted in its service has played a worthy part in the progress of our nation.

And Earl Balfour said: 'I am very happy to offer my congratulations to the *Evening Standard* on the completion of its 100th year of journalistic service.'

In his leader on page 6, the editor devoted the column to the state of English literature:

> But if, as is proper on a centenary occasion, we make ourselves think in centuries, we shall be rendered less melancholy by the relative emptiness of a decade. A hundred years ago we were just recovering from the turmoil and the disillusionment of the Revolutionary Wars. Today we are just recovering from a struggle which affected the whole population with infinitely greater intimacy. We shall have no good reason for despair if our emptiness lasts for even a longer period. We shall be recompensed if we have a flowering like that now ending.

The main story on this auspicious day was the first solo flight across the Atlantic, by Charles Lindbergh, but it was played down, with only a single-column heading; and on 23 May there was even less prominence, with no picture of his arrival in Paris. It was, however, noted that the Royal Aero Club had invited Captain Lindbergh to London as a guest at a reception.

ASK FOR DISSOLUTION

By the spring of 1929, the Tory-dominated Parliament elected in October 1924 had almost run its course, so Baldwin decided to ask for a dissolution. Under his leadership, the Conservatives hit upon the slogan 'Safety First'. Labour, though, believed that they alone could cure the increasing problem of unemployment. On 24 March 1929, Beaverbrook wrote to J. M. Patterson, of New York: 'The Conservative Party stands no chance of coming back with a majority. Baldwin has frittered away his heritage again. He cannot help it. He sits in the garden with his arms folded and talks about the beauty of it, while the weeds grow all about him.'[3]

To the voters, it was an election without fire, and the *Evening Standard* did little to disturb the calm:[4] 'The public apathy is astonishing ... I have never known anything remotely resembling the indifference of the public on this occasion. Nor can I think of a satisfactory explanation.' On 6 May, F. G. Doidge, who was covering the election for the *Evening Standard*, reported privately to Beaverbrook: 'The Labour candidates have been invariably the best platform speakers. The Conservatives have been the worst. If these meetings are to be accepted as any criterion of the public mind then it would seem that there exists a strong enmity towards Lloyd George whose name elicited real hostility whenever it was mentioned.'

Polling took place on 31 May, and, in the largest-ever general election, each of the three parties put up some 500 candidates. The result was a Labour victory with 287 seats, with the Conservatives 261 and the Liberals 59. The Conservative figure was just as predicted by Beaverbrook in a telegram to Rothermere almost three weeks earlier. On 5 June Baldwin motored down to Windsor, where King George V was convalescing, to hand in his resignation and that of the government. That same evening, at a Derby Eve dinner, Lord Birkenhead put the blame for the Conservative defeat fully on the heads of Beaverbrook and Rothermere.

The following morning, Beaverbrook fired off a telegram to Birkenhead: 'That Jemmy Twitcher should peach me I own surprised me.'[5] The quotation, possibly supplied by Arnold Bennett, was regarded as offensive. And, as already noted, in 1765 Lord Sandwich, a notorious rake, denounced John Wilkes in the House Lords for his obscene *Essay on Woman.* That same evening Sandwich had attended

The Beggar's Opera, and at the reference to Jemmy Twitcher the whole house rose in delighted applause. [In *The Beggar's Opera,* Jemmy, an associate of Captain Macheath, betrays him.] Sandwich was forever afterwards known as Jemmy Twitcher.

Birkenhead replied immediately. Not only was he incensed at the way that Baldwin had been treated but also commented: 'While during my political career you have often shown me great friendship and very valuable support, you have very often caused me deep mortification and done me great injury. Your Cartoonist over a long period of time published filthy and disgusting cartoons of me which were intended and calculated to do me deep injury.'[6] Beaverbrook at once sprang to the defence of Low and the *Evening Standard*:

> I rejoiced in Baldwin's downfall. I wanted the defeat of the Government because I believe it was bad. If I am right in assuming that you did not regret it, then my Jemmy Twitcher telegram is to the point. You are out of touch with the times, and I am too old at fifty. The new generation like the Low caricatures. For my part, Low outrages my feelings when he makes me crawl out from under the table or peep through the door. But I hold the view that a caricature cannot give ground for complaint. Perhaps I am wrong, but I stick to it. The Conservatives are trying to blame everybody but the right persons for their failure at the polls. They had better concentrate on their jockey.[7]

Within a matter of months, Birkenhead and Beaverbrook were once more friends, but it was a friendship that was to be of a short duration, as on 30 September 1930, the *Evening Standard,* as its front page lead, announced with regret 'that the Earl of Birkenhead died today at his house in Grosvenor Gardens, S. W. He was 58 years of age'. In 'Londoner's Diary', the main item noted:

> In the death of Lord Birkenhead the nation will mourn the loss of one of its most versatile and brilliant men. With no start in life to help him except his own brains he achieved, in an incredibly short time, the highest distinction both at the Bar and in the House of Commons ... As a talker and wit, "F.E." was in the very highest class, and many of his epigrams and retorts will go down in history.

Since its inception by Arthur Mann in 1916, 'Londoner's Diary' had always been one of the most widely-read features in the *Evening Standard,* and never was this more popular than when edited by Bruce Lockhart[8] in the decade from 1928. Lockhart had begun his career as a diplomat in Moscow in 1911 and rose to fame as a British agent at the time of the Russian Revolution, knowing personally V. I. Lenin,

Leon Trotsky and Alexander Kerensky. He first met Beaverbrook on his return from Russia in 1919, but shortly afterwards was posted to Czechoslovakia as the Commercial Secretary at the British Legation in Prague.

In the spring of 1926, Lockhart, back in England, was invited by Beaverbrook to stay at Cherkley, the first of a series of invitations that were to span thirty years. Beaverbrook suggested to Lockhart that he should write his memoirs and that he (Beaverbrook) would immediately take up the serial rights. At the same time he fixed Lockhart up with an appointment with the editor of the *Evening Standard.*

The paper's editor at this time was E. Raymond Thompson, who had held the chair since 1923 and was to serve until 1928. Known to the general public as E. T. Raymond,[9] the writer of political portraits, he was born in 1872 and had received his training as a journalist in Brighton and Leeds. In 1897 he joined the staff of *The Star* in London, but within twelve months had decided to go to Japan, where he spent the next four years, firstly on the *Japan Mail* and then as night editor of the *Japan Gazette* in Yokahama. On his return to Fleet Street he joined the staff of the *Daily Mirror,* and afterwards filled various posts on *The Standard* until in 1916 he became leader writer on the *Evening Standard,* and was appointed editor seven years later at a salary of £4,000 a year. As E. T. Raymond, he was the popular author of sketches of political figures: 'All and Sundry' followed by studies of Lloyd George, Arthur Balfour and Lord Rosebery, 'Portraits of the Nineties', and 'Portraits of the New Century' – all written with a clever pungency. He died in London on 11 April 1928.

However, on 28 April 1926, he met Lockhart for the first time and agreed to receive articles, and paragraphs for 'Londoner's Diary'. From the first, Lockhart was a success and within less than two years was offered a job as a leader writer for the *Evening Standard* and the *Daily Express* at a salary of £2,000 per year. Lockhart, however, demurred until 23 April 1928, when he accepted the position of editor of 'Londoner's Diary', but on the understanding that he should have some months free to travel around Europe before joining.

On 9 May 1928, he wrote to Beaverbrook, who was then staying at Newmarket preparing for the racing: 'I am seeing Wilson and Gilliat tomorrow, today being inconvenient for all of us, but I should like to thank you ... for your kindness. I hope that now I am going to work for you, you will never have any cause to regret the offer you made me.'[10] Lockhart's two interviewers at this time were George Gilliat, newly-appointed editor of the *Evening Standard,* and J. B. Wilson, news editor of the *Daily Express* from 1912 until 1940.

Lockhart started on the 'Diary' on 17 September 1928; among his colleagues were Edward Shanks, poet and literary adviser to

Beaverbrook; Stella Gibbons, soon to win fame with her novel, *Cold Comfort Farm*; and Arnold Bennett. The following day, Lockhart noted: 'I am enjoying my new life. The hours are from 9.30 to 1.15 during which time I am working at full pressure. The afternoons and evenings I use for ferreting out information.'[11] At the end of the year he visited Doorn, Holland, where he met Kaiser Wilhelm II, who gave an exclusive interview – the first time since the War that he had been willing to speak to a British journalist.

Lockhart's personal diaries – more than fifty in total – provide a most valuable insight into the political and social life of Britain and the Continent during the twenties and thirties. Mislaid for almost 10 years, the diaries are now in the House of Lords library. Beaverbrook himself revelled in the use of the 'Diary' to insert paragraphs – sometimes malicious – of prominent people; and it was a practice he never stopped.

Returning from holiday on 25 June 1929, Lockhart was informed by Beaverbrook that he would be starting a new job and should find a replacement on 'Londoner's Diary'. His new job, which he later thought had been 'impossible from the start', was to be constantly with Beaverbrook, to be his liaison with the *Daily Express*, to write leaders on Saturdays for the *Sunday Express* – and still write for the *Evening Standard* 'Londoner's Diary'. He estimated that he wrote some 400,000 words a year for Beaverbrook's newspapers, and was 'nailed to his desk'.

It was during this time, on 29 November 1929, that the *Evening Standard* was featured in *World's Press News*. There 'Our Newspaper Critic' reported:

> The *Evening Standard* is an able paper; but I have no affection for it. I find it faintly depressing, like talking in a strange club to an elderly, well-informed gentleman in a black suit who never laughs but may from time to time indulge in a very discreet smile. The paper depresses me before I begin to read it. I like the size of the page – the only reasonable size for an evening paper at least – but I dislike the size of the type used in the headings. I think it is too large. I dislike the way the lower heading sits tight on the top of the story. There is a lack of daylight. The effect is one of overcrowding and gloom. *The Star* and *Evening News* headings are, in my opinion, much better and brighter.

Discussing the *Standard*'s main writers, he admired the intellectual courage of Dean Inge, but found him long-winded and dull: 'I think he writes too much. They all do.' On the dramatic front, he considered that critic Hubert Griffith suited the paper very well, but should do more interviews with actors. Sport, he believed, was well served by W. J. A. Davies with his rugby reports, which he read with interest: 'His is human, intelligent stuff.' The news side, too, came in for praise, especially its reporting from abroad: 'When every paper is printing the same story it is a relief to turn to something different.' Two people stood out in his summary of the paper: David Low, 'who leaves all the other cartoonists standing'; and Arnold Bennett, whose weekly feature on books he considered the finest reading in the *Standard.*

Meanwhile, Lockhart, in the quest for his successor as editor of 'Londoner's Diary', had turned to his old friend Harold Nicolson,[12] then aged 42 and Counsellor – the second-ranking officer – at the British Embassy in Berlin. Nicolson, the son of a diplomat, was born in Tehran in 1886 and in 1913 married the aristocrat, Vita Sackville-West. He had already published biographies on Verlaine in 1921; and Swinburne, in 1926. Much later (in 1952) he was to write an acclaimed biography of King George V, and in 1953 was appointed KCVO. He is best remembered, however, for his *Diaries* (in 3 volumes, 1966–68), which were edited by his son Nigel.

In July 1929, Lockhart informed Nicolson that Beaverbrook was looking for a man of ability, and would pay a very considerable salary. His job would be to write and edit a page like 'Londoner's Diary' in the *Evening Standard*: 'I have suggested your name, and he would be glad to "capture" you.'[13] Nicolson replied on 22 July: 'The offer which you make me is flattering in the extreme. It is also tempting. I long to get back to London and into the whirl of real life again.' He did, however, have certain reservations about his salary, hours of work and contract. As for his political stance, he was a left-liberal or right-labour: 'On the one hand I am a pacifist and believe strongly in good relations with America ... On the other hand I am an Imperialist in the modern sense of the term, and I am by no means a passionate free-trader. I could not agree to express opinions which conflicted with these principles.'[14]

After further negotiations, it was agreed that Nicolson would join the *Evening Standard* at £3,000 a year and 'edit a page upon Politics, Life and Literature'. After coming to England on leave and finalising negotiations, Nicolson returned to Berlin, where he had copies of the *Evening Standard* and *Daily Express* posted to him. He was not impressed, as this letter to his wife written on 14 November 1929, shows:

> I have been reading three-days-worth of the *Express* and *Standard.* They really fill me with alarm. I shall simply be unable to write the sort of sob-stuff they want. They seem to have an unerring eye for just the sort of thing I loathe. What shall I do in such a *galère*? I shall be thought highbrow and cloacal. For this I shall be glad when my

> *Express* and *Standard* reach me by the post in small doses. I really feel ill when I consume a whole fill of them.[15]

Despite his misgivings, he started on 'Londoner's Diary' on 2 January 1930, writing to his wife that afternoon:

> Came up with Desmond McCarthy who was charming and full of talk. Rather too full of talk, as I wanted to do my lessons, which now consist in reading all the papers in the hope of finding a good paragraph. I suppose I shall get into the way of finding these paragraphs leaping ready-armed to the mind. At present they are rather a bother to think or, rather a bother to write, and terribly feeble when written. But I shall settle down in time.

While this major editorial change was taking place, the *Evening Standard* continued in its profitable way. At a board meeting of 14 March 1930, it was revealed that the previous year's accounts showed a profit, after tax, of almost £40,000, to which could be added £19,000 brought forward. Later that year, on 12 December, it was agreed 'to provide for the continued erection of the advertising clock facing down Shoe Lane for a period of five years from the 29th day of September 1930 at an annual rent of £50'. (The clock still exists and now adorns the *Evening Standard* offices in Kensington.)

Since the paper had come under the control of Beaverbrook, board meetings had been regularly chaired by A. Wilson, the general manager, with Viscount Castlerosse as one of the main attendees. Items discussed during those years ranged from withdrawing the horse service in 1925 (housed at Bowling Green Lane and run as a joint arrangement with the *Daily Sketch* and *Sunday Herald* – and costing the paper £122 a week), to engaging David Low as cartoonist at a salary of £4,500 a year. Four years later, in 1929, the Board agreed that Wilson's new remuneration as general manager should be £4,000 a year, replacing the previous arrangement of £2,000 plus 10 per cent of the profits in excess of £60,000 a year, with a guaranteed minium of £1,000.

EMPIRE FREE TRADE

On the political front, Beaverbrook continued to be heavily involved with his pet project, Empire Free Trade,[16] and had recently published a penny pamphlet setting out the manifesto: 'The foodstuffs that we need in this country could all be raised either on our own soil or in the British Dominions, Colonies or Protectorates. The coal, machinery and textiles that the increasing populations of our new territories overseas demand could be supplied by the mines and factories of Great Britain and its Dominions.'

Discussions with Neville Chamberlain and, later, Stanley Baldwin in November 1929 had, on the surface, been friendly enough, and Beaverbrook had been urged to work through Parliament in his efforts to secure Empire Free Trade. Despite these meetings, he was not convinced that either man was a fit person to lead the Conservative Party at this time, and had, in fact, written to William Randolph Hearst, the American newspaper magnate: 'Churchill should be their leader. But the Conservatives will have none of him. He has served too many parties. If Baldwin is dismissed Neville Chamberlain will take his place. He is as bad as Baldwin.'

Although often taking an autonomous line in his newspapers, 'The Empire Crusade' was Beaverbrook's only venture into independent political leadership. It was not merely a newspaper campaign led by Beaverbrook and backed by Rothermere, it was also an organisation that enlisted supporters, set up local committees, held mass meetings at which Beaverbrook was the star speaker, raised money and put up candidates at by-elections. To further the campaign, Beaverbrook demanded total support from his editors, and informed George Gilliat, editor of the *Evening Standard*, that where politicians spoke in favour of Empire Free Trade then 'the reporter must stay until the end of the meeting'. Meanwhile, Lockhart, having stepped down from running the 'Londoner's Diary', was now Beaverbrook's chief lieutenant in the campaign; it was he who wrote the pamphlets and provided the statistics and other material for the platform speakers. On 17 February 1930, Beaverbrook officially launched the United Empire Party, with a fighting fund of £100,000, of which he was to provide £70,000, with support from Rothermere.

Two months later, on 3 April, Beaverbrook announced that he was 'no longer a journalist – and for good'. The following month, on 20 May, he declared: 'My association with the *Daily Express* is now at an end. I hear nothing of them and I give them no assistance.' This was patently untrue, for he still continued to send a stream of notes to his editors and managers, offering criticism and advice: 'Why was the *Evening Standard* not on sale at Maidenhead? at Boulogne? at Dover?' In each case he was told that such sales were not an economic proposition. This answer did not satisfy Beaverbrook when he saw the *Evening News* or *The Star* on the bookstalls. He wrote to Gilliat on 12 June: 'Many readers hate cricket. Most of them know nothing about it. The cricket public is dwindling every day.' [17] A month later, on 18 July he was defending the paper and Low from objections by Neville Chamberlain: 'Beaverbrook must call off his attacks on Baldwin and the Party, cease to include offensive cartoons and paragraphs in the *Evening Standard*'. He, of course, did nothing of the sort – and the campaign was renewed.

It had not been a good summer on the paper, though, with talk of redundancies; and on 2 August, twenty of the staff were dismissed, which prompted Gilliat seriously to consider resigning. Three days later, Lockhart observed: 'The economic campaign in *The Standard* continues. Everyone is in a state of nervous tension, and both Wilson and Gilliat are cracking under the strain. Gilliat is too immersed in detail to be a great editor. He wilts, too, in a crisis.' Throughout the year, Beaverbrook continued to fire off notes to the editor. On 23 September: 'The public likes to know the fortunes men leave behind them. They like to know what diseases men die of – and women too.' On December 19: 'Lord Beaverbrook reminds you that the *Evening Standard* is a Capital Punishment paper.'

Meanwhile, on 30 October 1930, the first of the Empire Crusade candidates fought a by-election. He was Vice-Admiral Taylor, and thanks to the support of Beaverbrook – and eleven members of the household staff at Cherkley as canvassers – was successful by 941 votes over the official Conservative candidate. A shock defeat for the Tory Party leadership meant that there were divisions among the Conservatives. Indeed, dissent in the party's ranks meant that by early 1931 Baldwin's position was now in question, and on 25 February Sir Robert Topping, the chief Conservative agent, wrote to Neville Chamberlain urging the need for a new leader. Less than a week later, on 1 March, Chamberlain faced Baldwin with the latter, afterwards noting in his diary: '4.30. S. B. has decided to go at once'.

ST. GEORGE'S BY-ELECTION

In Baldwin's terms, 'at once' did not mean immediately, but it was to be Beaverbrook, ironically, who was to save the day through his intervention in a by-election at St. George's, Westminster. This was an impregnable Conservative seat, and it was to become a straight issue over Baldwin's leadership. Following the refusal of two prominent Conservatives to support Baldwin, the party looked to Duff Cooper, a former Member for Oldham, who, with his wife, Lady Diana, were two of London's leading socialites. Opposing him was to be Sir Ernest Petter, an industrialist from the West Country, backed by Beaverbrook and Rothermere.

Beaverbrook rightly considered that the primary issue of the by-election was over the leadership of the Conservative Party: 'If we win this fight the Conservatives will select a new leader and take up our policy and we'll all live happily ever after.' Even before the fortnight's canvassing began, Beaverbrook, 'in the friendliest manner', tried to dissuade Duff Cooper from standing: 'He felt that I should lose, that my support of Baldwin, who would have to retire, would do me no good in the party.'

In his autobiography, *Old Men Forget*, Duff Cooper has left a memorable account off the contest:

> Servants have little time to read a newspaper in the morning, but if they do cast an eye on one in the West End of London it will almost certainly be either the *Daily Express* or the *Daily Mail*. In the afternoon when they have more time at their disposal they will turn to the *Evening News* or the *Evening Standard*. These four papers were my chief opponents, and every issue of each of them was devoted to damaging my cause. The only other evening paper, the *Star*, was neutral, as was the rest of the press with the exception of the *Daily Telegraph*, which gave me support.

Beaverbrook fought hard for his candidate, speaking at sixteen meetings and paying all Petter's expenses. There was also support from Lord Castlerosse, in an article in the *Evening Standard* entitled 'Enjoying himself in St. George's':

> The inhabitants of the West End are having a golden age. 'City Lights' turned the limelight on them, and there is ending an election which has even put 'The Circus' into the shade. Sir Philip Sassoon made a mistake in going to Berlin with Charlie Chaplin: he should have stayed here in London, where the fun is far more furious. To have a vote in St. George's today invites fame. I have been asked out to dinner by people, who, ordinarily speaking, would offer me but an occasional cup of prussic acid.[18]

As a rule, party leaders did not involve themselves personally in by-elections, but Stanley Baldwin now decided that the time was right – and he had an opportunity to put Beaverbrook and Rothermere in their places. He chose 18 March, the eve of the poll, as the date to make his attack, and all the passionate resentment and indignation that had been contained over the years was now about to be unleashed at Queen's Hall, before a stunned audience.

The theme of Baldwin's speech was persecution by the press, and it was to be developed relentlessly:

> I have said little. It is not worth it. I am going to say something today. The newspapers attacking me are not newspapers in the ordinary sense. They are engines of propaganda for the constantly changing policies, desires, personal wishes, personal likes and dislikes of two men.
>
> What are their methods? Their methods are direct falsehood, misrepresentations, half-truths, the alteration of the speaker's meaning by publishing a sentence apart from the context, such as

> you see in these leaflets handed out outside the doors of this hall; the suppression and editorial criticism of speeches which are not reported in the paper. These are methods hated alike by the public and by the whole of the rest of the press ... What the proprietorship of these papers is aiming at is power, and power without responsibility – the prerogative of the harlot throughout the ages.[19]

The crucial final sentence that was to haunt Beaverbrook for the rest of his life was the work of Baldwin's cousin, Rudyard Kipling, and, long before, Max Aitken's first friend when he arrived in England.

For Duff Cooper, the last-minute intervention of Baldwin meant that the result was no longer in doubt, and he was elected with a majority of 5,700. Less than a week later, when he took his seat in the House of Commons 'Mr Baldwin walked on my right – a rare honour to be accorded by the leader of the party. He knew how important the result of the election had been to him.'[20] Baldwin, having survived this test, was to remain leader of the Conservatives for a further six years, but perhaps of more significance was the decline in influence exercised by newspaper proprietors from this time.

While Beaverbrook had been involved in the St. George's by-election, Harold Nicolson was becoming associated with Sir Oswald Mosley's New Party. Having resigned from the Labour government in May 1930, Mosley had put forward his ideas during the Party's Conference in October of that year for the relief of the country's high unemployment. His speech had made a great impact and he had been only narrowly defeated. He renewed his challenge at a special meeting of the Parliamentary Labour Party on 27 January 1931, and, receiving no support, decided to found his New Party, a decision which led to his being expelled on 10 March for 'gross disloyalty in seeking to create a new party ... with Parliamentary candidates in opposition to Labour members'.

As an old friend of Mosley, Nicolson was one of the first to be approached to join the New Party – especially as it was hoped that his association with Beaverbrook would lead to support from the *Evening Standard* and the *Daily Express.* On 4 March, Nicolson wrote to Mosley from the *Evening Standard* office:

> I spoke to Max [Beaverbrook] about joining your party. He was most appreciative ... He said I had his blessing (his sorrowing blessing) in joining you. I might serve on any of your committees if I wished. I must not boost you unduly in the *Evening Standard.* Nor must I devote to the New Party the time that I ought to devote to the *Standard.*[21]

Six weeks later, on 22 April 1931, with a by-election in the offing, Nicolson wrote to Beaverbrook seeking permission to stand. Within two days Beaverbrook, staying at the Hotel Adlon in Berlin, replied: 'I think you would be mad to contest the by-election, which, I presume, is Brentford and Chiswick ... But the decision rests with you, and I have no objection so far as concerns the newspaper work.'

The fact that Nicolson was becoming more and more disenchanted with his work on 'Londoner's Diary' was not evident in his writings. Four months earlier he had summed up his first year on the paper:

> I have found my feet in the *Standard* office – and Beaverbrook likes me. But that is all very well. I was not made to be a journalist and I do not want to go on being one. It is a mere expense of spirit in a waste of shame. A constant triviality which is bad for the mind. Goodness knows what I shall do next year. I am on the verge of politics. I am on the verge of leaving the *Evening Standard* and either writing books of my own or sitting in the House of Commons. 1931 assuredly will be the most important year, for good or ill, in my whole life.[22]

Lockhart was by then having misgivings for having introduced Nicolson to the paper, and he was to be even more upset when on 2 April he lunched with Mike Wardell, the *Evening Standard*'s managing director, at the Savoy. Wardell informed him that he wanted the 'Diary' modelled on Harold Nicolson: 'He intends to make Harold virtually responsible for the Diary. I think this would be a grave mistake. Harold's tastes are not the public's tastes. He is altogether too precious.' By the following Monday, 6 April, though, at Beaverbrook's directive, Nicolson was firmly in charge – much to Lockhart's chagrin, as his diary jottings for that week show:

> Tuesday, April 7, 1931
> The Diary arrangement made by Wardell has gone through, and Nicolson is not only to sub-edit and 'give a Nicolson twist' to all paragraphs, but is actually to select the paragraphs for the Diary. The arrangement is bad. Harold Nicolson has no experience of day-to-day journalism. In any case his tasks are not those of the average Diary public. Gilliat is now superseded except for his right of veto for libel, etc. He does not like it. Neither do I. The position is humiliating for me. Two years ago, when I recommended Harold, I wrote that I was hanging myself with a silken cord. The noose is now drawn. The curious thing is that all this upset is due to Harold's complaints about his paragraphs not being taken and to his desire to be relieved of the Diary.
>
> Thursday, April 9, 1931
> Had an unsatisfactory morning in Shoe Lane. Wrote about eight paragraphs, none of which went into the Diary. Gilliat and Toulson

> are now hopeless. They yield and defer to Harold Nicolson in everything – not because they believe in his judgment – on the contrary – but because they are terrified of offending Beaverbrook and think that Harold Nicolson is Beaverbrook's star.

Lockhart now had every reason to be worried, for, unbeknown to him, on 18 June Beaverbrook offered Nicolson the editorship of the *Evening Standard* on condition that he abandoned the New Party and his proposed standing as a candidate in the Chiswick by-election.

After discussing the matter with his wife that evening, Nicolson wrote in his diary:

> After dinner I discuss with V. [Vita Sackville-West] the situation by my luncheon with Beaverbrook. Clearly I am likely to fall between two stools. Were I to enquire further into Beaverbrook's offer, I might well be put in a position of authority on the *Evening Standard* which would mean not merely a very high salary but also an opportunity to make a decent and influential paper out of it.
>
> There is no limit to the possibilities opened by such a prospect. B. [Beaverbrook] is quite likely to become an invalid and to hand over the administration of all his papers to a Directing Board. It would be quite possible to evolve out of this a position of great influence and power. Alternatively, there is a chance that the New Party within five years would be in such a position as to force a coalition upon one of the other two parties. In such a coalition, I should certainly be able to ask for the Foreign Office, and here again there is no limit to the avenue of extensive power.
>
> I said that possibly it might be open to me to tell B. that I would take on the editorship of the *Standard* on condition that he allowed me twice a month to devote a column to New Party news. This would reconcile my two allegiances. I could run the paper in the Party interest for say four years, and at the end of that period I might rejoin the Party and enter politics with greater authority and even greater prospects.[23]

The following day, he told Mosley of the meeting, and was immediately offered £3,000 per annum to edit *Action*, the soon-to-be-launched weekly of the New Party. Less than a week later, Beaverbrook contacted Nicolson once more:

> I am very sorry that you are getting more deeply involved in the New Party. I think that the movement has petered out. It might be saved by immense sums of money, and brilliant support, but of course there is a conspiracy of silence in the newspapers, except for the particular newspapers I am connected with. I hope you will give

up the New Party. If you must burn your fingers in public life, go to a bright and big blaze.

Despite Beaverbrook's warning, Nicolson decided to plunge ahead, and left the paper on 22 August, 1931, writing in his diary:[24]

My last day at the *Evening Standard.* I have learnt much in this place. I have learnt that shallowness is the supreme evil. I have learnt that rapidity, hustle and rush are the allies of superficiality. My fastidiousness has been increased and with it a loathing of the uneducated. I have come to believe that the gulf between the educated and the uneducated is wider than between the classes and more galling to the opposite side. I have not been popular in the office. I make perfunctory farewells. As I leave the building I shake my shoes symbolically.

17

The Abdication Crisis

The departure of Nicolson meant that the 'Londoner's Diary' was once more under the direction of Bruce Lockhart, and two years later he noted on 2 September 1933:

> My birthday – forty-six today and still feebler in character and self-control. Fleet Street is no place for me. With very few exceptions I loathe and despise everyone connected with it, and the exceptions are failures. Most of the successful ones have trampled over their mothers or their best pal's body to lift themselves up. They are dead to decency.[1]

The 'Diary', however, was not proving a success, and on 14 September Nicolson was invited to lunch by Mike Wardell, who asked him if he would return to the *Evening Standard* to edit 'Londoner's Diary', with complete control of the staff. Nicolson listed a number of conditions[2] before rejoining, to all of which Wardell agreed.

Nicolson, though, was having great doubts about returning to the paper: 'On the one hand it would solve our financial worries and the conditions at Shoe Lane might be a little better than last time. On the other hand it means becoming a journalist which I loathe and abhor.' It was to be another month before he made up his mind, and he explained his actions in a letter to Lockhart on 31 October 1933: 'I have written to Mike telling him that I cannot accept his offer. The more I came to think about it the more I realised that after having tasted the joys of freedom I could not possibly contemplate going back to an office.'[3]

Early in 1934, Nicolson once more turned down the offer of editing 'Londoner's Diary', which was now sadly lacking in leadership. On 9 May 1934, Lockhart wrote: 'More trouble over the Diary which goes from bad to worse. *Telegraph* diary [Peterborough] is now better. It is based on our old Diary. Chief trouble is total lack of co-ordination. No one makes any attempt to organize a Diary. [Percy] Cudlipp himself has not the Diary mind. Ramsden is ineffectual, and the Fleming experiment has been a complete failure.'[4]

Less than two months later, Lockhart was busy revising Adolf Hitler's obituary for the *Evening Standard*: a hurried phone call from the proprietor had made him rewrite the galley proofs, as Beaverbrook was concerned that Hitler would be assassinated. Lockhart said: 'He has now turned solidly, fanatically anti-Hitler, refers to him as Al Capone and to the Nazis as gangsters.' The past few weeks had seen a hardening in Beaverbrook's attitude: violently anti-Führer, an opinion which was expressed in his papers – and especially with Low's cruel cartoons in the *Evening Standard.*

On 25 July 1934, the Chancellor of Austria, Engelbert Dolfuss, was assassinated by Austrian Nazis. Armed and financed by Hitler's supporters, these attacks by the Austrian Nazis brought a swift response from the British press – and no one was more vociferous than Winston Churchill. Lockhart noted:

> Violent attacks on Germany continue in the Press. This morning I wanted to do a paragraph comparing Winston (who has had about six articles in the papers during the weekend) to [Alexandre] Dumas who once had six serials running in the Paris papers at the same time. Cudlipp, our editor, said: 'The idea is first class but I think you had better keep off it. The Chief (Max) will say that you are giving publicity to Winston. He hates paragraphs about Winston. He pulled me up the other day. I know this is true; (1) because Cudlipp does not lie; (2) because I have heard the same thing from the little man when I was with him.[5]

Low's cartoons in the *Standard* were now attracting great attention and were becoming increasing hostile to the new Nazi regime. Low had first used Hitler in a cartoon in 1930, and that same year Lockhart, returning from Germany after interviewing the Führer, told him that: 'Hitler was an artist, that he was interested in my cartoons and would appreciate the gift of a few originals to hang around the Brown House. I passed on a couple as from one artist to another.'[6] For the following six months, Low devoted himself to a detailed study of Communism, Fascism and Nazism: 'I had for my pains a wall of my studio divided into four compartments (I had added Liberal Democracy) within which I entered for future reference, neatly typed by my secretary Jean, the philosophical fundamentals and working principles of each system.'

With his plans laid, Low now attacked Hitler and the Nazis in earnest, culminating in his cartoon of the Führer attempting to set fire to the League of Nations building over the title 'It worked at the Reichstag – Why not here?' The allusion was to the destruction of the Reichstag by fire in Berlin in 1933 by Hitler's cohorts, and their accusing the German Communists of the deed. The effect of the cartoon was immediate: the *Evening Standard* and all other newspapers printing Low's cartoons were officially banned in Germany.

Within months, Low and the *Standard* were also to be banned in Italy, a cartoon entitled 'The girls he left behind him' incurring the wrath of the Italian censor. The press even entered the fray, when the

Rome newspaper, *Il Travere*, printed a banner caption: 'Our Answer to the Degraded Low of the *Evening Standard*' over a cartoon of John Bull floundering in the Suez Canal. And the introduction of Low's dog, Musso, into his cartoons even brought an excited attaché from the Italian Embassy to the *Standard* offices in Shoe Lane complaining bitterly about this slight to Mussolini.

NEW EDITOR

The new editor of the *Evening Standard* at this time was Percy Cudlipp,[7] who had succeeded George Gilliat in October 1933. Gilliat had come to London from Manchester, where he had served for many years with the Hulton group, and was 'regarded as one of the shrewdest students of politics in the country'. Following the resignation of Beverley Baxter from the editorship, he was appointed joint editor with Arthur Christiansen of the *Daily Express*.

Many years later, in his autobiography, *Headlines All My Life*, published in 1961, Christiansen wrote:

> They placed [with me] George Gilliat, an elderly journalist who had been editing the *Evening Standard* for some years. It was made clear to me that Gilliat was the senior, and that while I was to run the paper, his decisions on all matters must be recognised. This arrangement seemed fair enough. Gilliat interfered as little as possible and was such a kindly, diffident man that I had no difficulty in getting my own way ... [He] was withdrawn from the scene six weeks later and went into happy retirement. I was therefore Editor. But nobody can give me the exact date in December 1933.

Percy Cudlipp, Gilliat's successor on the *Evening Standard*, was born in Cardiff in 1905, the eldest of three brothers, all of whom were to edit national newspapers – the others were Hugh, of the *Sunday Pictorial*; and Reg of the *News of the World*. Percy Cudlipp had left school at the age of only thirteen to work for the *South Wales Echo*, which had already published his verse and had advertised him as 'the boy poet of Cardiff'. After six years, in 1924, he joined the *Evening Chronicle* in Manchester, as a reporter while at the same time contributing to London papers, and within twelve months was in Fleet Street as drama critic and columnist on the *Sunday News*. Always keenly interested in the theatre, Cudlipp also began to provide topical lyrics to the Co-optimists Revue then running in the West End. He was becoming well known, and in 1929 was engaged by the *Evening Standard* as a special writer. His most famous article during this period was a half-page interview with Noel Coward, written in verse as a parody of 'the Master's' style – and all within a few hours.

In 1931, Cudlipp was appointed assistant editor, and two years later, when aged 27, replaced Gilliat as editor – the youngest editor of any British national newspaper at that time. His new role moved him from being a witty writer to being an executive, but he was not altogether happy in his relationship with Mike Wardell, the paper's dashing managing director, who had succeeded A. Wilson two years previously. Although Cudlipp, like other *Evening Standard* editors, was not politically attuned to Beaverbrook, he did nevertheless consider that his role was to follow the proprietor's lead, saying: 'I am an advocate, like a lawyer in court, rewarded for my skill in putting my client's case.'

A key editorial figure on the *Evening Standard* at this time was George Malcolm Thomson, who was to serve the Beaverbrook organisation for more than 40 years, and in 1994, at the age of 94, was still writing erudite book reviews for newspapers. In 1930, though, he had succeeded his friend Percy Cudlipp as leader writer on the *Evening Standard* – and one such leader had brought him to the attention of Beaverbrook himself. As a result Thomson became closely involved with the 'Beaver' for almost 30 years as a political adviser and writer, and during the Second World War he moved in government circles as his principal personal secretary. Thomson remained with the organisation until 1970 when he retired as senior editorial adviser.

TRADING PROFITABLY

In June 1934, Wardell, as well as being managing director and chairman of the *Evening Standard*, became involved, as chairman, in the launch of *Farmer's Weekly*.[8] As a consequence, L. A. Plummer was appointed general manager of the *Evening Standard*, moving from a similar role on the *Sunday Express*. During this period, the *Evening Standard* continued to trade profitably: in 1930 profits were £32,414; in 1931, £13,775; and in 1932, £70,645. One interesting new appointment to the board had taken place on 22 April 1931, when the Hon. John William Maxwell Aitken [later Sir Max Aitken] was appointed a director. On 21 February 1933, Wardell, as chairman, announced that the chief shareholders – Lord Beaverbrook and the London Express Newspapers Ltd had agreed that the Evening Standard Co. Ltd. could be converted into a private company. Two months later, on 3 April at an Extraordinary General Meeting, the special resolution 'that the Company henceforth be a Private Company' was duly passed.

Throughout the early years of the 1930s, the average daily sales had not risen dramatically. In 1930, the circulation was 366,991, and in 1933 it was 373,753. However, the existing plant was now becoming obsolete, especially in the machine room. Here 'the method of changing the reels is quite out of date and wastes time'. The board was told that 'we have to face very soon the question of the introduction of colour printing. It is impossible under present conditions to add colour decks to our existing machines.'[9]

Thoughts to take over part of the old premises recently vacated by the *Daily Express* and to print the *Evening Standard* at either *Daily Express* or *Star* size were discounted, owing to the risk of *The Times* or *Daily Telegraph* producing a new evening paper in a form closely resembling the *Evening Standard* in its present size. The board 'were satisfied that this risk should not be taken, particularly in view of the present progress of the paper'. It was decided, therefore, to look at either (a) taking over adjoining premises to the present Shoe Lane property in order to provide more room for the line presses to be installed; or (b) finding a new site within a mile or two of Fleet Street. It was estimated that costs would be between £300,000 and £500,000.

At a board meeting on 25 January 1934, A. Wilson resigned as chairman and was succeeded by Capt. J. M. S. Wardell. An interesting aside to emerge from this board meeting concerned the Red Lion public house, Shoe Lane, purchased as part of the *Standard* expansion plans. As it had lain unoccupied since the previous September it was agreed that 'Until our plans for the development of that property were complete it was thought desirable that the licence should be renewed in case it might be necessary to continue the business of Licensed Victuallers.' Accordingly, it was agreed that Albert John Talbot, company secretary, should apply and hold on behalf of the company the licence of the Red Lion.[10]

Meanwhile, under Cudlipp's leadership, changes had been taking place on the editorial front: George Slocombe, foreign editor, had returned to live in France; Herbert Gunn, news editor, had left after five years for the *Daily Express* and had been succeeded by William K. Bliss, his deputy for the preceding three years; and Edward Grice, special writer, had become deputy news editor. In the summer of 1935, a young John Betjeman resigned as film critic for the paper, leaving to handle Shell Mex publicity, but within a few weeks the *Standard* was to gain another young man who was later also to achieve fame: Malcolm Muggeridge. In August 1935, after returning from Russia as the *Manchester Guardian*'s correspondent, he was in India, working in Calcutta on *The Statesman*, and it was there 'out of the blue that he received a telegram from Percy Cudlipp, editor of the *Evening Standard*, offering him a job on the 'Londoner's Diary' at twenty pounds a week. He wired off his acceptance ... he was coming home.'[11]

LONDONER'S DIARY

In his diary on 28 September, after his first day on the paper, Muggeridge wrote:

> The *Evening Standard* where I work is a nightmare. There are tables scattered about a room. I write paragraphs for the 'Londoner's Diary'. Most of them get taken out by the Editor ... He's ferociously energetic and yet somehow unsure of himself. I dress immaculately, or as immaculately as I can, but inside there's the old loathing, disgust. I hurry along Fleet Street to and from the office library with papers in my hand, but there is no reason why I should hurry.[12]

Lockhart also noted Muggeridge's first day on the paper:

> Malcolm Muggeridge, the author of an anti-Bolshevik book on Russia and of a suppressed novel on the *Manchester Guardian*, joined us today. Clever, nervous and rather 'freakish' in appearance. Holds strong views. His arrival gives the Diary Room the appearance of an old *Manchester Guardian* office. We have Howard Spring, Thomson, Stephen Williams and Muggeridge. They are of a type in the same way that Wykehamists are.[13]

Howard Spring, soon to become the paper's chief book reviewer, had begun his career in journalism as a 13-year-old messenger boy on the *South Wales Daily News.* After seven years he was a fully-fledged reporter, later serving on the *Manchester Guardian* before joining the *Evening Standard.* He was to leave Fleet Street at the age of 50 in 1939 to devote himself to writing more than a dozen novels with great success, including *Fame is The Spur* and *My Son, My Son.*

Spring had first attracted Beaverbrook's attention when covering a political meeting for the *Manchester Guardian* at Darwen, at which Beaverbrook was the chief speaker. The description of Beaverbrook as a 'Pedlar of Dreams'[14] was to win instant approval from the press lord – and an invitation to Fleet Street:

> It was a Saturday night, and the weekly market was being held in the big square of the town. I lingered there, looking at the flaring naptha lamps, the hucksters shouting their wares, the gay ephemeral traffic of the cheapjacks' lies and promises. Adjoining the fair-ground was the hall where Lord Beaverbrook was to speak; and I began to see his meeting and this chattering tumult as all part of the one thing: the pedlars of promise without, the pedlar of dreams within.

On 3 October, Abyssinia was invaded by the Italian armies, an act which prompted the League of Nations to propose sanctions. Beaverbrook, however, remained sceptical: 'We will not be involved beyond mild economic sanctions. Government is now ratting on pacifists who wish to make war.' A fortnight later he wrote in the *Daily Express* that he had sent 80,000 letters to professional men seeking their views on the Isolationist Cause; 'Of course we should pity the Abyssinians. But we must not on that account inflict sorrow and grief and death on those who live outside the zone of war.'

Convinced, however, that the upsurge of Fascism in Italy and Germany posed a serious threat to the peace of Europe, Beaverbrook determined to meet foreign leaders to seek their points of view. He had been converted to flying on a trip to Paris in 1934, and he used a special charter plane to visit the heads of state in 1935: Mussolini in the spring, and in November a trip to Germany, to see Hitler. Earlier, Beaverbrook had written to Joachim von Ribbentrop, congratulating him on his appointment as German Ambassador to the United Kingdom: 'You have praise from the press and from the people. You may save the peace of Europe, I truly believe, by your conduct here.'[15]

This letter to Ribbentrop was not one 'which Beaverbrook was subsequently proud of'. Lockhart – on the Hitler meeting – noted in his diary on 27 November 1935:

> Max and Mike [Wardell] came back last night. They received a wonderful reception in Berlin – Mike said that no crowned head could have been better received. Max dined with Ribbentrop. Foreign Office experts were told to stand by in case Max wanted information .... Max and Hitler talked through former Geneva interpreter Schmidt. Mike immensely impressed by his efficiency. General [Erhard] Milch, Reichswehr general, transferred to Air, is the big noise. Turning out a thousand planes a week.[16]

Lockhart also found time to make further notes on Muggeridge: '[He] hates the big press proprietors ... [He] coined the phrase for Max Beaverbrook – Robin Badfellow.' As for Muggeridge, he found the work on the paper both boring and tiring. He wrote on 1 January 1936: 'I've been back in London three months. The *Evening Standard* is pretty grim, revoltingly futile, and yet exhausting. Whenever I say anything to Bruce Lockhart, who edits 'Londoner's Diary', he says he's heard if fifty times.'[17] Three weeks later, on 24 January, over lunch, Muggeridge told Lockhart that he intended to retire to a farmhouse near Battle in Sussex, bought by his mother-in-law, and write his novel: 'He will have only £400 to do it with. But he is only thirty-two and I advised him strongly to take the risk.' On 22 May, Muggeridge left London for Battle to commence his new life. His final week at the *Evening Standard* had been:

> The last lap of that fantastic episode, sitting in the twilit room with twelve others, typewriters tapping. Bruce Lockhart modulating his voice accordingly, to whom he was telephoning, and Cudlipp coming and going, etc. I used to feel dazed there all the time.

> The memory of it is like nightmare – grubby and unhappy and hysterical, looking up things in encyclopaedias, poring over newspapers, scribbling. 'Let's have a look at the stiffs,' Leslie Marsh used to say, meaning the obituaries. Bruce Lockhart ... used to tell me often how he longed to get out of it all. Not happy with money and wireless talks and best-selling books. Either I find goodness and truth, or die, because I've cut away everything. I shall find it, but only when I've hunted myself and conquered myself and shed fear.[18]

SILVER JUBILEE

Meanwhile, with King George V having reigned for almost twenty-five years, the nation prepared to celebrate the great occasion with due pomp and ceremony. In the previous seven years, however, the King had suffered two serious illnesses which had left their mark on his health. The then Prince of Wales was later to write: 'These were my thoughts that momentous spring of 1935, as the country prepared to celebrate my father's Silver Jubilee, although the unstinted outpourings of affection from all parts of the Empire gratified him, the continuous ceremonies and functions wore him out.'

Jubilee Day was 6 May, and the *Evening Standard*, naturally, covered the occasion in great detail. In his leader, the editor commented:

> The King has been the visible sign of the unity of our race, as our loyalty to him has been the sign of our determination to remain united. The historians looking back will have much to say of King George V. They will say that with his calm courage he inspired the British to fortitude in adventures sterner than had ever befallen them. They will say also that he won the confidence of all his peoples all over the world. It was in his reign they will say that the British Empire took its final and most glorious shape, a free alliance of nations held together in friendship by the King's hand, resolved never to break that bond but to work out together the British destinies. Perhaps another man could have done this. What we know is that King George V has done it. It is of that that his subjects have been thinking during his progress at St. Paul's today. They thank him and they trust him. That is his achievement. That is his reward.

But, even in the midst of the Silver Jubilee celebrations, there was the underlying fear of the British Establishment at the rise of Nazi Germany. An article by Rothermere in November 1933 had painted a horrifying picture:

> ... the Commander in Chief of the enemy nation will press a button and 20,000 – perhaps – 50,000 aeroplanes, laden with bombs and

gas, will rise into the air and set off at more than 200 miles an hour to rain destruction on this country.[19]

In the summer of 1935, he was calling for Britain to build 10,000 planes and had even subsidised a National League of Airmen. Rothermere realised that just as naval power had been all important in the years prior to the First World War now, in the thirties, it had been superseded by the threat from aeroplanes. He pointed out that, with Germany having an air force of 20,000 by the end of 1936, the time had come for Britain to re-arm, and he believed that Britain needed an aircraft supremo to ensure that the country was prepared.

By July, with Rothermere's stance having firmed, an editorial in the *Daily Mail* commented: 'It is madness for Great Britain to remain unarmed when Germany and Italy are armed to the teeth and able at any moment to attack our vital interests.' Rothermere was to press, with limited success, for British rearmament – especially in the air – but in the year 1936–7 the national expenditure on arms was less than half of Germany's. Even Beaverbrook at that time had grave doubts about any intervention by Britain in a Continental conflict, and on 20 September 1934, he wrote to F. C. Davies: 'The airplane had destroyed the only argument there ever was for taking part in the quarrels of Europe. A modern airplane can fly across Belgium in twenty minutes. Belgium is no longer of any interest to us. By intervention we embrace the possibility of war. By isolation, we flee from it.'[20]

While a growing tension was emerging with Germany and Italy, the health of King George V continued to deteriorate. On December 9 he received Anthony Eden at Buckingham Palace and had discussions concerning Italy and Abyssinia, and possible war. Less than a fortnight later the King travelled to Sandringham to spend a traditional Christmas with other members of the Royal Family. He was now unwell, and on 17 January made his final, almost illegible, entry in his diary: 'A little snow and wind'. That same day the Prince of Wales flew to Sandringham in his own aeroplane: 'The air was clear; and as the semi-circle of the Wash came slowly into view, leaden grey under the winter sun, a sudden impulse made me signal the pilot to make a wide circle around the estate. Here was my father's home, a place he preferred to palaces ... It was impossible for one to believe that his life might be coming to an end.'[21]

On 18 January, the King's condition worsened, and the following morning the Prince of Wales drove to 10 Downing Street to inform Baldwin, the Prime Minister, that the King's death was imminent. He was met by Mrs Baldwin, who invited him to join them at her birthday tea. When the Prince had finished telling the Prime Minister the grave news, Baldwin murmured his sympathy, adding almost wistfully: 'I wonder if you know, Sir, that another great Englishman, a contemporary of your father's died yesterday.

But, of course, Sir, you have a great deal on your mind. I should not have expected you to know that it was Rudyard Kipling, my first cousin.'

At 9.25 pm on 20 January Lord Dawson, the King's physician, drafted a notice for the waiting press at Sandringham: 'The King's life is drawing peacefully to its close.' For more than 50 years the King had kept a diary in his careful script, but the final entry is in the handwriting of Queen Mary: 'My dearest husband, King George V, was much distressed at the bad writing above and begged me to write his diary for him next day. He passed away on January 20th at 5 minutes to midnight.'[22]

The following day, the *Evening Standard* produced a Special Edition of twelve pages, all heavily ruled in mourning borders:

> Britain and the Empire have learned with the deepest sorrow of the news of the passing of King George. Within a few minutes of his death almost every corner of the earth had received the message today. The world pays tribute to King George as a great Monarch and stresses his part in promoting peace. From every capital, from famous men and humble subjects messages of sympathy came to the Queen Mother, the new King and other members of the Royal Family.

Later that day, in the main edition of thirty-two pages, there were many photo-features illustrating the life of King George V.

Among the messages of sympathy from world leaders was one from Hitler, the German Chancellor: 'The news of the death of his Majesty has deeply grieved me. I beg your Majesty to accept my and my Cabinet's sincere sympathy and the assurance that the whole German nation mourns with the great loss of the Royal Family and the British nation.' In Doorn, the Netherlands, it was reported: 'the ex-Kaiser had been aroused from his sleep shortly after midnight to be told of the death of King George V in accordance with special instructions given to his household before he went to bed. He expressed the deepest regret at the sad tidings.'

On the day of the funeral, the *Evening Standard* noted in its leader column:

> The peoples and the princes who for the past week have stood bowed in mourning for King George V today salute him for the last time. Multitudes press forward everywhere along the funeral route to see with their own eyes the passing of the solemn cavalcade. To their silent homage is joined the tribute of a vaster throng, which, far removed in body, is no less keenly grieved at the passing of a Father and a King. It is, indeed, not a City not a Kingdom – no, not an Empire only – which makes its pilgrimage in body or in mind and heart to the tomb at Windsor.

ABDICATION CRISIS

In the autumn of 1936 a crisis which had long lay dormant at last broke out into the open. For a number of years the new King Edward VIII had embraced a close relationship with Mrs Wallis Simpson, an American lady, married to an Englishman and living in London. Beaverbrook, like so many of the Establishment, was aware of the stories circulating in the American press about this affair.

On 27 October 1936, Mrs Simpson's divorce petition was put down for hearing at Ipswich Assizes. With the foreign newspapers having heard of the impending proceedings, the King, through Mike Wardell, a close friend, and chairman of the *Evening Standard*, approached Beaverbrook for assistance:

> At my request, Max Beaverbrook came to the Palace on October 16. I told him frankly of my problem. I had no thought of asking him to use his influence on other newspaper publishers for the purpose of hushing up the news of the imminent divorce petition. My one desire was to protect Wallis from sensational publicity at least in my own country. Max heard me out. 'All these reasons,' he said, 'appear satisfactory to me – I shall try to do what you ask.' Without delay he began a prodigious task, unique in the annals of Fleet Street, where the mere suggestion of censorship offends.[23]

Following the meeting, Beaverbrook immediately contacted Esmond Harmsworth (Lord Rothermere's heir), a director of the *Daily Mail*, and Sir Walter Layton, in charge of the *News Chronicle*, writing also to newspaper friends in Dublin and Paris. To Percy Cudlipp, editor of the *Evening Standard*, who had asked if details of the divorce should appear in the paper, Beaverbrook had replied: 'Publish.' But, following the King's intervention, 'Mrs Simpson's divorce received only brief formal reports and went through unnoticed by the public.'[24]

With the King giving no indication that he intended to marry Mrs Simpson – and her solicitor, Theodore Goddard, an old friend of Beaverbrook, confirming this – Beaverbrook left for America. 'And I believed it,' he was later to write, 'The sole purpose of the application to you is to escape as far as possible the publication of unjustifiable gossip concerning the King.' While a sanguine Beaverbrook was en route to the United States, the crisis deepened. The King was now even more determined to marry Mrs Simpson – and retain the throne.

On 16 November 1936 he met Baldwin at Buckingham Palace, and at once came to the point: 'I understand that you and several members of the Cabinet have some fear of a constitutional crisis developing over my friendship with Mrs Simpson.' Pulling deeply on his pipe, the Prime Minister confirmed that he and his senior Cabinet colleagues were disturbed over the prospect of the King marrying someone whose former marriage had been dissolved by divorce: 'I believe I know,' he said, 'what the people would tolerate and what they would not. Even my enemies would grant me that.'

One of the key social personalities of this time, 'Chips' Channon, MP for Southend, but, more importantly, a leading light in London society – and a confidant of the King – has left in his diaries an absorbing account of the crisis. On 19 November, he had achieved the pinnacle of his social ambition, having the King, with Prince Paul of Yugoslavia, to dinner: 'At once I saw he was in a gay mood – no doubt a reaction from his depressing Welsh tour, two dreadfully sad days ... The King called to me, "Sit on my left, Chips. Come next to me Paul." We thus had a three-handed conversation – two reigning sovereigns and Chips.'[25]

Two days later, Channon noted in his diary:

> London is suddenly seething with rumours: sinister, unlikely rumours ... Mr Baldwin had spoken separately to all the Cabinet, telling them that he had seen the King, and had with all respect protested at his association with Wallis, and declared that unless the King promised never to marry her, his Government would resign. He gave the King three weeks in which to make up his mind ... Beaverbrook is rushing across the Atlantic in order to help him ... [he] apparently sailed ten days ago for America en route for Arizona in the hope of curing his asthma, and was bombarded all the way over with cables and appeals from the King to return urgently. The crossing in the *Bremen* was bad and Beaverbrook, tired and ill, cabled back that he would return in a few days' time, after a short rest in New York. The King cabled through his solicitors that it was urgent, and that there was not a moment to be lost and Beaverbrook sailed seven or eight hours after his arrival in the same ship.[26]

Newly-arrived from New York, and having heard of the Cabinet meeting, an agitated Beaverbrook hurried to Buckingham Palace: 'Sir,' he exclaimed, 'you have put your head on the execution block. All that Baldwin has to do now is to swing the axe.' Beaverbrook asked the King if he had seen the cables which Baldwin had sent to the governments of Canada, Australia, New Zealand, South Africa and the Irish Free State: 'Do you recommend the King's marrying morganatically? Or if the King insists upon marrying, do you recommend abdication?' To the King's reply of 'No', Beaverbrook urged that he should stop their being sent. 'I am a Canadian. I know the Dominions.

Their answer will be a swift and emphatic No.' The King, eager for the right answer from the Dominions, did nothing.

Less than a fortnight later the storm broke – and from a most unexpected quarter. On 1 December 1936, the Bishop of Bradford, the Right Reverend A. W. F. Blunt, made a startling speech in which he referred to the coming Coronation and the King's unawareness of his 'need of Divine grace'. It only needed this criticism to bring the affair of his into the open. The story was picked up by the provincial press, led by the *Yorkshire Post*, still under the control of A. H. Mann, a former *Evening Standard* editor. Not only was the Bishop's speech reported in full but there were also strong condemnatory leaders: 'Dr Blunt must have had good reason for so pointed a remark. Most people are by this time aware that a great deal of rumour has been published of late in the more sensational American papers.'[27]

Having received the first press agency report of the Bishop's speech, Beaverbrook at once telephoned the King who was taken by surprise: 'What are the London papers going to do?' I asked him. 'They will report Dr Blunt's speech.' 'With editorial comment?' 'No,' he answered, 'that will be reserved until the results of tomorrow's Cabinet meeting are available.'[28] The gentlemen's agreement in Fleet Street lasted less than 24 hours. Led by *The Times*, under the editorship of Geoffrey Dawson, the facts were printed in detail for the first time. Dawson later wrote in a memorandum:

> In the late evening [December 2] as I was struggling with the paper he [Baldwin] rang me up twice himself – the only time, I think, that I have ever heard his own voice on the telephone – to say that His Majesty was worrying him to find out, and if necessary stop what was going to appear in *The Times*. He understood that there was to be an attack on Mrs Simpson and 'instructed' the Prime Minister to forbid it. In vain S. B. had explained that the press in England was free, and that he had no control over *The Times* or over any other newspaper. When he spoke to me, full of apologies, the second time, it was to say that the King would now be satisfied, and leave the Prime Minister alone, if the latter would read the leading article for him, Could I possibly let him see it for the sake of peace? By this time, as I told him, the paper was just going to press; but towards midnight I sent a proof of the leader by messenger to Downing Street and heard no more about it.[29]

The leading article in *The Times* entitled 'King and Monarchy', referred to the recent revelations of the affair in the American press and 'a marriage incompatible to the Throne'.

With the news being broken in Britain, the *Evening Standard* was able to announce in large headlines on page 1 on 3 December:

THE KING: PREMIER ASKS M.P.s NOT TO QUESTION HIM YET

Mr Baldwin was questioned in the House of Commons this afternoon about the issues which have arisen between the King and his Ministers concerning the King's desire to marry Mrs Ernest Simpson. Mr Attlee, the Opposition leader, asked: 'May I ask the Prime Minister a question of which I have given him a private notice – whether any constitutional difficulties have arisen and whether he has any statement to make?' Mr Baldwin replied: 'I have no statement to make today. While there does not at present exist any constitutional difficulty, the situation is of such a nature as to make it inexpedient that I should be questioned about it at this stage.'

Mr Attlee: 'May I ask the Prime Minister whether, in view of the anxiety reports on this matter are causing in the minds of many people, he can assure the House that he would make a statement at the earliest possible time that a statement can be made?' Mr Baldwin: 'I have all that the right honourable gentleman says very much in mind.'

Mr Churchill: 'Would my right honourable friend give us an assurance that no irrevocable step will be taken before a formal statement has been made to Parliament?' The House broke into cheers as Mr Churchill asked the question. Mr Baldwin replied: 'I have nothing to add to the statement that I have made at this present moment. I will consider and examine the question that my right honourable friend has asked.'

While the Abdication Crisis was, of course, the main news, cricket lovers were being regaled with reports of the First Test between Australia and England in Brisbane. For the *Standard*, its reporting team was C. B. Fry, Douglas Jardine, Neville Cardus and Bruce Harris. Another *Standard* writer on cricket was E. W. Swanton.

However, on the leader page, the editor was in a far more sombre mood:

Today the whole world knows of a situation which has been discussed by the well-informed and the partly-informed for months past. A constitutional crisis of the gravest character has arisen. It has arisen because the King wishes to make a marriage of which the Cabinet disapproves. The British Cabinet is justified in its disapproval by the opinion of the Dominion Governments. In particular, the Australian Government views unfavourably the marriage which the King desires to make. The *Evening Standard*, though in possession of the facts, has hitherto refrained from mentioning or commenting upon them. Silence was the proper course while there was any possibility that an acceptable solution might be found. The crisis has reached a state where it is no longer advisable, or indeed possible, for newspaper to remain silent.

With the press having broken its silence at long last, for the majority of the country there was now almost a total disbelief that their King should be determined to put his throne at risk. There swiftly grew a faction in support of the King, and in London crowds paraded through the streets singing 'God Save the King', and assembled outside Buckingham Palace all night. 'After the first shock the country is now reacting, and demands that their King be left in peace.' In the House of Commons, on 4 December, Baldwin could add nothing to his statement of the previous day. But later on that evening he drove down to Fort Belvedere, near Windsor, to see the King once more.

Beaverbrook, ever eager to help his King, was revelling in the drama and could tell Chips Channon: 'Our cock would be all right if only he would fight, but at the moment he will not even crow.' Channon ventured: 'Cocks crow better in the morning.' 'Not this one,' Beaverbrook laughed.[30] On the following day, 5 December, the *Evening Standard* published on page 7 a story by George Bernard Shaw, which parodied the whole affair:

THE KING, THE CONSTITUTION AND THE LADY
Another Fictitious Dialogue

In the Kingdom of the Half Mad, that same prince whose difficulties over his father's illness I formerly chronicled succeeded to the throne on the death of the same father, and almost at once found himself in difficulties with his Cabinet and with the Church. For the new King, though just turned 40, was unmarried; and now that he was a King he wanted to settle down and set a good example to his people by becoming a family man. He needed a gentle, soothing sort of wife, because his nerves were very sensitive, and the conversation of his ministers was often very intimidating. As it happened he knew a lady who had just those qualities. Her name, as well as I can remember it, was Mrs Daisey Bell; and as she was an American she had been married twice before and was, therefore, likely to make an excellent wife for a king who had never been married at all.

During the next few anxious days, the King's friends – led by Beaverbrook and Churchill – fought desperately to save the situation, but the replies from the Dominions were decisive: marriage or throne. On 7 December, Mrs Simpson flew to Cannes after issuing a statement, which appeared in the *Evening Standard* on 8 December: 'Mrs Simpson throughout the last few weeks has invariably wished to avoid any action or proposal which would hurt or damage the King or the Throne. Today her attitude is unchanged, and she is willing, if such action would solve the problem, to withdraw from a situation that has been rendered unhappy and untenable.' Only the *Evening Standard*, *Daily Express* and *Daily Mail* now supported the King, the *Daily Express* even announcing 'End of Crisis'. *The Times* and *The Daily Telegraph*, though, were determined that the King should abdicate.

On the morning of 10 December, the day of the fateful announcement, the *Evening Standard* proclaimed in its leader column:

> The *Evening Standard* has never written in favour of the morgantic marriage which the King desired to make. That is not because the *Evening Standard* was opposed to such a marriage. It would gladly have supported the plan rather than accept the alternative – abdication. The *Evening Standard* has also recognised from the outset that there could be no divergence between the King and the Cabinet on the Constitutional problem. His Majesty emerges from the crisis strong in the respect and affection of his people. We are to lose our King for no other reason save that he wished to marry a lady who has been a successful petitioner in the Divorce Court.

Within hours of the paper appearing on the streets, at two o'clock on a grey winter's afternoon, to a crowded House of Commons, the Speaker, through tears, announced that the King had renounced his Throne, the first abdication since Richard II in 1399. That same evening, the King, now Prince Edward, made his moving abdication speech, a speech in which the hand of Churchill was clearly visible. When Churchill had left the King, there had been tears in his [Churchill's] eyes: 'I can still see him standing at the door: hat in one hand, stick in the other.' Listeners throughout the world were very much moved by the broadcast in which he said. 'But you must believe me when I tell you that I have found it impossible to carry out the heavy burden of responsibility and to discharge my duties as King as I would wish to do without the help and support of the woman I love.' On hearing these words, Churchill, at Chartwell, wept once more.

Writing in his diary that night, Malcolm Muggeridge noted:

> In the evening we sat listening to the wireless broadcasting the news of the King's abdication. I had the feeling that the affair somehow symbolized the whole horror of life, the struggle between Man's noblest, richest impulses and the shoddy fabric of Time ... We drove Hughie back. Blackshirts were selling their papers in the streets surrounded by a circle of admiring girls, Kit saying to me: 'Everything's going to be all right, isn't it?' and I nod without conviction.

18

Munich and Appeasement

Throughout the 1930s Beaverbrook was to rely heavily upon two management figures: Mike Wardell, chairman of the *Evening Standard*, and E. J. Robertson, the managing director of the *Daily Express*. The Captain, as Mike Wardell was always known, was a man of high social connections, including, as noted, a close friendship with King Edward VIII. After a distinguished war record, Wardell had entered Beaverbrook's social circle and employment in 1926, and for the ensuing decade was to share many of his business trips and pleasures abroad. Another member of this circle was Viscount Castlerosse, a one-time director of the *Evening Standard*, and a famous *Sunday Express* columnist.

As A. J. P. Taylor wrote: 'Castlerosse and Wardell were now his most constant companions, but both were employees as well as friends, and this made some difference. In the last resort neither would stand up to him.'[1] Malcolm Muggeridge, in reviewing his days at Shoe Lane, has described Wardell as Beaverbrook's man on the premises:

> The Captain, as we called Wardell, had an office upstairs, though what his precise functions were I never knew. He had a patch over one eye ... and as one of Beaverbrook's familiars was treated with considerable awe and respect. His eye, it seemed, had been injured in a hunting accident, and in his day paragraphs about hunting and related matters were frequent in the Diary. In his upstairs office he gave regular luncheon parties, to which I was occasionally invited. At them, one would meet such figures as Brendan Bracken, Beverley Baxter, Bob Boothby and other kulaks of journalism, politics and finance.[2]

It was at this time that the phrase 'Beaverbrook's young eagles' gained a certain vogue. It was coined by George Malcolm Thomson, chief leader writer on Beaverbrook's papers and for many years his political adviser. One of the brightest of these young eagles was Peter Howard, a former Oxford University and England rugby captain, who had joined Beaverbrook Newspapers in June 1934 at a wage of £9 12s 3d per week and within five years was to be one of the highest paid political writers in Fleet Street, earning nearly £60 a week. Another was Randolph Churchill, who had been engaged by the *Evening Standard* in June 1937. With the distinct advantage of having Winston Churchill as his father and being a family friend of Beaverbrook, for the young

Randolph the horizon seemed limitless. Once described by Lord Rothermere as 'England's young man of destiny', Randolph, with the departure of Bruce Lockhart through ill-health, took over the editorship of 'Londoner's Diary'.

By the late spring of 1937 Lockhart had made up his mind to leave, and on 7 June, after working on the 'Diary', he saw Wardell, who was not surprised or unsympathetic. He believed that Lockhart was a tired and sick man and that should he take two months' leave to recuperate. Four days later, after having seen Beaverbrook, Lockhart left 'Londoner's Diary'. It was a very hot day and he lunched at the office with Wardell, Cudlipp and a recently-returned Muggeridge, who had been forced back because of the unexpected expenses of his wife's illness. Cudlipp was certain that Lockhart would soon return and bet him £100, while Wardell told him that he too was suffering from nervous indigestion and would soon be like him.[3]

Lockhart's next task was to 'see Randolph who has also been engaged for the Diary and hopes to succeed me as Chief Diary writer'. Lockhart's final thoughts on leaving prompted the following remarks:

> Two of the greatest evils in British social life are venereal disease and the Press. One reason is that they cannot command the services of first-class men. No young medical student who has any hopes of success dreams of taking-up venereal disease because there is a social stigma on 'pox doctors'. For the same reason no decent man goes into journalism.

For Randolph Churchill, work on 'Londoner's Diary' was to be a happy haven. Here he was in the centre of things and paid a good salary; and, unlike the other writers, the only person to whom he was accountable was Beaverbrook. The ever-observant Muggeridge later wrote:

> Politics rested largely in the hands of Randolph Churchill, who, to the considerable awe of the rest of us, could telephone almost without fear or rebuff. That you, Bobbity? Duff? Fruity? Bob? Rab? There was also, of course, his father to whom he could always turn, and who contributed a highly paid weekly article to the *Evening Standard*; in those days very much out of things, and, I thought from a fleeting glimpse I had of him, showing it.[4]

Randolph's contacts were of the highest order, and in October 1937 he was able to inform *Evening Standard* readers that he had visited the Duke and Duchess of Windsor (ex- King Edward VIII and his new wife, the former Mrs Wallis Simpson) in Paris. They had told him that they had no intention of returning to England. He added that, following visits to Germany and the United States, the Duke would return to

Europe but had 'abandoned all ideas of ever returning to England'. This exclusive was, naturally, the page 1 lead, and was to be picked up by newspapers throughout the world.

Others on the 'Diary' at this time included Patrick Balfour, the son of a Scottish peer, who was responsible for cultural affairs; Philip Page, a one-time theatre critic; and Howard Spring. The hours were short. The staff were expected to be at Shoe Lane by 10 am; the 'Diary' went to press at half-past twelve and there were very few changes before the afternoon editions. As Muggeridge wrote: 'With so many of us working on it, two, or at most three, paragraphs was our daily stint. Quite often one made no contribution at all. Every Friday at the accountant's office on the ground floor we collected our pay in cash, mine being four white crinkly five-pound notes.'

During those years, the 'Diary' was Beaverbrook's plaything. It was he who indicated the 'must' stories; it was he who determined who was to be praised and who maligned; and it was he who had insisted that after the death of King George V and until the royal funeral had taken place, every story in the 'Diary' must deal with the bereavement. This meant, in all, some 120 paragraphs! For Muggeridge, by 1937 the depressing effect of the *Evening Standard* was again proving too much and the time had come to move on: 'My own part in the Beaverbrook circus was, happily, for me only a minor and insignificant one. Even so, it became increasingly distasteful, and I decided to take a chance, and spend the remaining time before the next war being engaged in my own pursuits rather than Beaverbrook's.'

ONLY ONE ENDING

To most intelligent people, it was now not just a question of if there were to be a war, but when it would begin: since the mid-1930s, the demands of Hitler had become more and more insistent. From the Nuremberg Rally in September 1934, when the slogan of the Nazi Party was first heard, '*Ein Reich, Ein Volk, Ein Führer*' (One Realm, One People, One Leader), there could be only one ending: the reunification of the German-speaking peoples. The first move was to be the reoccupation of the Rhineland, and, transgressing the Treaty of Locarno, four German brigades crossed the Rhine in March 1936 with secret orders to withdraw if the French took military action to stop them. There was to be no resistance, and Baldwin announced: 'If there is one chance in a hundred that war might result, I cannot commit Great Britain.'

Writing in the *Sunday Express* nine days after the invasion, Beaverbrook pointed out that his criticism of the Locarno Treaty had been justified by events: 'The bond to fight for France which we gave at Locarno was bad, but the new bond would be worse. It would simply postpone the day of payment.' The following week he was far more critical: 'If we make this alliance, we must fight to maintain the integrity of Czechoslovakia, an ally of France, an ally of Russia, a country with a German population of over three million. If we make this alliance, we commit ourselves to a war – a war near or remote, but nevertheless inevitable.' Here was Beaverbrook, the complete isolationist, an isolationist who was sanguine enough to think that there would be no conflict: 'I do not believe that war is at hand. I do not think that Germany means to fight at the present time at all. I believe that Germany is intent upon assembling all Germans under the Reich banner. My view is that this purpose will be accomplished without resorting to war.'

Winston Churchill, who had recently been engaged by the *Evening Standard* to write a fortnightly column, took a more cautious view when making his debut on 13 March 1936:

> There has rarely been a crisis in which Hope and Peril have presented themselves so vividly and at the same time upon the world scene. When Herr Hitler on Saturday last repudiated the Treaty of Locarno and marched his troops into the Rhineland, he confronted the League of Nations with its supreme trial and also with its most splendid opportunity. If the League of Nations survives this ordeal there is no reason why the horrible, dull, remorseless drift to war in 1937 or 1938, and the preparatory piling up of enormous armaments in every country, should not be decisively arrested.

So popular were these articles in the *Evening Standard* that they were also syndicated throughout the world, and in 1936 appeared in the United States, Canada, France, The Netherlands, Denmark, Sweden, Norway, Greece, Czechoslovakia, Switzerland and Luxemburg. During May 1936 Churchill wrote three articles for the paper: 'How Germany is Arming', 'Our Navy Must be Stronger', and 'Organizing our Supplies'. The Spanish Civil War – 'a sinister and, perhaps, a fatal milestone on the doomed path of Europe' – was next to attract his attention, and in early August 1936 he asked Anthony Eden, the Foreign Secretary, if he would read the article. On 12 August, Eden replied: 'I was most interested to read your article in the *Evening Standard* ... [it was] timely and helpful ... I do agree emphatically with its concluding paragraphs.'

For Churchill this was a most successful period from a literary – and financial – point of view, and on 28 December 1936, he noted that he had contracted for a total income for 1937 of £13,630, including £2,880 from the *Evening Standard.* Throughout the following year, Churchill's articles were to continue to attract attention, and on 5 February 1937 he showed that Czechoslovakia , with its fifteen million inhabitants, was now 'living under the fear of violent invasion, with iron conquest in its wake. At any moment a quarrel may be picked with them by a mighty neighbour. Already they see the directions given to the enregimented German Press to write them down, to accuse them of being Communists, and, in particular, of preparing their airports for a Russian assault upon Germany'.

Surrounded by this air of impending gloom, the people of Great Britain and the Empire were about to celebrate a great event: the Coronation of King George VI. For this occasion, the *Evening Standard* published on 12 May 1937, a 32-page souvenir issue, including twelve pages of photographs from Westminster Abbey and the processional route. Howard Spring, who was the paper's special correspondent, wrote: 'Westminster Abbey is a great cross. The point of interest is today the focal point of the Empire's thoughts, and of the thoughts of much of the world outside the Empire.' In his leader, Cudlipp, as editor, declared:

> The King spoke to the Empire yesterday. He said: 'I stand on the threshold of a new life ... I shall do my utmost to carry on my father's work for the welfare of our great Empire. To fulfil this promise – the promise to put first the well-being of others – is to tread the way of sacrifice. It is in this expectation – indeed this belief – that his subjects today in this land and throughout the Empire will join their voices to those which are within the Abbey. God Save The King!'

Within days of the Coronation, Baldwin felt that the time had come to resign. Chips Channon noted in his diary on May 28: 'The great Baldwin reign has drawn to a magnificent and splendid end; this morning at 9.30 he was received by the King who accepted his resignation as Prime Minister, created him Earl and conferred the Garter on him.'[5] Three days later, in a crowded Caxton Hall, the Conservatives met to elect their new leader. There was never any doubt that Neville Chamberlain would be the one selected. Moved by Lord Derby and seconded by Churchill, the resolution was overwhelmingly received. Beaverbrook, however, was to remain bitter to the end, and on 29 May wrote in the *Daily Express*:

> Mr Baldwin makes his bow. He takes farewell of the political stage. Let the audience not stint its applause. This has been a remarkable performance. The turn has lasted for just fourteen years ... And in those fourteen years the chief actor has given us our money's worth – not in statesmanship, not in solid gain to the public welfare, but in variety, in interest and bewilderment. What will the historian make of a record as baffling as Mr Baldwin's? He will look for a man embarrassed by the inconsistencies of his policy and the contradiction of his statements. But he will not find that man.

For Neville Chamberlain, the new Prime Minister, immediately dubbed 'the coroner' because of his dress and manner, there was much to be done: continuing high unemployment – especially in South Wales and the North East – and the looming crisis in Europe were to remain foremost in his thoughts. On 25 June he addressed the House of Commons in calm, sensible tones, proclaiming Britain's desire to be at peace with everyone, especially Germany. This was a theme quickly taken up by the people of Britain, for, with the German reoccupation of the Rhineland having been accepted by France, albeit grudgingly, 'there was now a calm stretch when it was supposed that a new balance of power was coming into existence.'

Even Churchill, for a while, seemed to be lulled into accepting peace at any price, and on 15 September 1937, he wrote in the *Evening Standard*: 'I declare my belief that a major war is not imminent, and I still believe there is a good chance of no major war taking place in our time.' Two days later he was to repeat the theme:

> I find myself pilloried by Dr Goebbels' Press as an enemy of Germany. That description is quite untrue ... no one has the right to describe me as the enemy of Germany except in war time. We cannot say that we admire your treatment of the Jews or of the Protestants and Catholics of Germany ... To feel deep concern about the armed power of Germany is in no way derogatory to Germany. On the contrary ... when a people who have shown such magnificent military qualities are arming night and day, its neighbours, who bear the scars of previous conflicts, must be anxious ... One may dislike Hitler's system and yet admire his patriotic achievement. If our country were defeated, I hope we should find a champion as indomitable to restore our courage and lead us back to our place among the nations.

To Churchill, it was the power that Mussolini was now wielding that was causing concern, and the following month he wrote in the paper: 'It would be a dangerous folly for the British people to underrate the enduring position in world history which Mussolini will hold; or the amazing qualities of courage, comprehension, self-control and perseverance which he exemplifies.'

EDEN RESIGNS

As for Chamberlain, ever since taking over as Prime Minister, he had felt that the Foreign Office, under Anthony Eden, was too anti-German – hence the visit by Lord Halifax to Hitler at Berchtesgaden in November 1937. Early the following year, Chamberlain proposed an open discussion with Mussolini to obtain a general settlement in the Mediterranean, including the recognition of the Italian conquest of Abyssinia. Eden was opposed to these measures, and was later to write in his memoirs: 'A leading democracy in negotiating with a militant dictatorship must not go cap in hand in search of fresh negotiations to cover long-standing differences, until there is evidence that the dictator is going to carry out the engagements he has already undertaken.'

There could be only one result to these differences between Prime Minister and Foreign Secretary, and on 20 February Eden resigned. The following day the *Evening Standard* covered the resignation speech in depth:

> This is for me, both on personal and political grounds, a most painful occasion. No man would willingly sever the links which bind him with the colleagues and friends. But there are occasions when strong political convictions must override all other considerations. Of such occasions only the individual himself can be the judge. No man can be the keeper of another man's conscience ... Propaganda against this country by the Italian Government is rife throughout the world. I am myself pledged to this House not to open up conversations with Italy until that horrible propaganda ceases.[6]

In the leader column, the editor noted:

> What is the cause of the break leading to the resignation of Mr Anthony Eden? It is of the highest importance that this question should be clearly understood by the public ... yet the break between Mr Chamberlain and Mr Eden does not take place upon what should or should not be given to Italy or expected from Italy. It took place on whether we should talk to the Italians or not.

On the facing page, George Malcolm Thomson, Beaverbrook's chief political writer, had a long article entitled 'Shepherd Without a Fold':

> Mr Eden was the best dressed of Foreign Secretaries. He was – he is – a credit to the athletic figure which public school education sometimes bestows on a man, and also the tailors of London. But the garb he wore in the eyes of a great public was the prophetic mantle. It is, as history recalls, a dangerous garment.

The new Foreign Secretary was to be Viscount Halifax, who, as Lord President of the Council, had not been burdened by a government department, and he could say of Eden's departure: 'Confidence faded as misunderstandings grew, so that at the end the parting was unavoidable.' Beaverbrook also had his say:

> Eden decided to get out of the Foreign Office. He got out because he could not get on. All the harvest he could reap from that field he had gathered in ... The great new factor in British politics is the rise of Chamberlain ... If he succeeds in separating Italy from Germany – which is not easy – he will be a big man. If he is triumphant in his plan for an understanding with Germany then he can be Prime Minister for life.[7]

While Eden had been resigning on a matter of principle, Hitler had been meeting with the Austrian Chancellor, demanding concessions for the Austrian Nazis, including co-operation with the government. Writing in the *Evening Standard* on 4 March 1938, Churchill noted: 'They [the Austrians] could now probably face a plebiscite ... under fair conditions without fear.' However, no one could tell 'what the reaction in Nazi Germany will be, or what new shattering blows impend upon a small unhappy State'. A little over a month later, on 10 April, a Nazi-controlled plebiscite recorded a vote of 99.75 per cent in favour of the *Anschluss* – the unification of Austria and Germany had been achieved: As George Steiner later wrote: 'when Nazism came home to Vienna in the spring of 1938 the welcome accorded it exceeded in fervour that which it had received in Germany'.

The previous month, on 17 March, in an article headed 'And So Heil Hitler', George Bernard Shaw had written in the *Evening Standard*: 'Happily, Czechoslovakia is not part of the Führer's dream; he was not born there; and to invade Czechoslovakia would mean taking on a devil of a fight ... We cannot interfere.' To Lord Beaverbrook, this article by George Bernard Shaw set just the tone which he now sought for his paper. But for Winston Churchill there could be no compromise, and there swiftly developed a coolness between Beaverbrook and himself, a coolness which Peter Howard noticed:

> Churchill sat all by himself in the moonlight, or almost, it seemed in the sunset of a career which had somehow missed greatness. His war song against the Nazis was almost a solo. Just the same he sang it fortissimo in the columns of the *Evening Standard*. Meanwhile my boss, Lord Beaverbrook, was advocating the cause of Splendid Isolation. He was coining phrases such as 'There will be no war this year or next year either.' He was paying me a large salary to write leaders on the subject. And he was entirely opposed to Mr Churchill's big idea.[8]

However, Winston Churchill's days as a writer on the paper were, by then, numbered. On 18 March, he once more drew his readers' attention to the growing crisis in Czechoslovakia. Although advocating that the German-speaking minority should be granted equal citizenship, he welcomed the declaration that France should satisfy its Treaty obligations if Czechoslovakia were to be attacked: 'A further declaration of the intentions of the British Government in such an event must come soon.' Less than a month later, on 4 April, Churchill's last article appeared in the *Evening Standard*, and the following week he wrote to Reginald J. Thompson, the new editor:

> With regard to the divergence from Lord Beaverbrook's policy, that of course has been obvious from the beginning, but it clearly appears to me to be less marked than in the case of Low's cartoons. I rather thought that Lord Beaverbrook prided himself upon forming a platform in the *Evening Standard* for various opinions, including of course his own. With regard to the method of terminating the contract by a month's notice, this was clearly within the formal agreement but the understanding which I had with Mr Cudlipp certainly never led me to expect such abrupt treatment, and I admit I was surprised by your communication.

Reginald John Tanner Thompson, the new editor of the *Evening Standard*, had succeeded Percy Cudlipp in December 1937. (Cudlipp was later to tell his brother, Hugh, another famous Fleet Street editor: 'No cause is really lost until we support it.') After serving with the Royal Fusiliers on the Western Front in the First World War, Thompson had joined the *Daily Express* as a reporter, later being attached to the *Evening Standard*, *Evening News* and *Scottish Daily Express*. In 1931, he rejoined the *Daily Express* as night editor from the *Standard*, where he had been managing editor.

Although Beaverbrook wrote in March 1938 that 'The *Daily Express* is the largest, most active and most nervous paper in the world [and] the *Evening Standard* is the most sluggish, leisurely and conservative newspaper in the world', he had no intention whatsoever of allowing his *Standard* editors full freedom. His dismissal of Cudlipp was proof of this, and interference with leader writers was another, even if a young Frank Owen was one of his favourites, as this note written in June 1938 shows:

> Frank, be careful of your attacks on Ribbentrop. If you keep making attacks on Ribbentrop you are going to disturb the immense efforts that are now being made for an accommodation with Germany. And we want it for the sake of our people, and we can't put any impediment in the way of it, no matter how much we may feel like doing it ... We have got to give over our criticism of those foreign powers for the time being. It is a great misfortune, a terrible deprivation that we face, but at the same time we must be big enough to do it for ourselves, by ourselves, and for the benefit of the people.

During the long, hot summer of 1938, while holiday crowds were flocking to the seaside and Len Hutton was breaking batting records at the Oval, trenches were being dug in Hyde Park and gas masks were being issued by the thousand. But for Beaverbrook, who still believed in staying out of any European conflict, life remained good, as he reminded Sir Edward Grigg on 20 June: 'As we have isolation in fact, although not in name, I have not much to complain about'. So confident was Beaverbrook of a continuing peace that on 1 September he announced in the *Daily Express*: 'There will be no European War.' This phrase and subsequent similar headlines were to be used time and time against him by opponents – even appearing in Noel Coward's film, *In Which We Serve.* However, despite his apparent confidence, Beaverbrook did write to Lord Halifax, the Foreign Secretary, on 16 September, saying: 'Newspapers are all anxious to help the Prime Minister and to help you. But they are greatly in need of guidance. A Minister should be authorized to have direct contact with the newspaper.'

Randolph Churchill, meanwhile, had left 'Londoner's Diary' and was now a reserve officer in the Fourth Hussars at Aldershot, a position, obtained by his father after writing to the colonel of his old regiment: 'Not only did Churchill provide encouragement, but, during Randolph's training period, he agreed to safeguard his son's job on the *Evening Standard* by contributing paragraphs to 'Londoner's Diary'. He insisted, however, that the salary for these paragraphs should continue to be paid to Randolph.'[9]

BRINK OF WAR

With Hitler pressing strongly his claims on Czechoslovakia, Europe was now on the brink of war, and on 7 September *The Times* published a leader[10] which put forward the case for the dismemberment of Czechoslovakia:

> Drafted by Leo Kennedy, the text was hurriedly revised by Dawson [the editor] who regarded it 'as a very mild suggestion and one that had been constantly made before, that no avenue should be left unexplored which might lead to settlement of the Sudeten question.' Acknowledging that it was exceedingly 'difficult to predict anything in these days with events changing from hour to hour', Dawson believed that this leading article, 'which caused so much hubbub', did good rather than harm.

It was not a point of view, however, shared by the government, which issued a statement 'that a suggestion appearing in *The Times* this morning to the effect that the Czechoslovakian Government might consider as an alternative to their present proposals the secession of the fringe of alien populations in their territory in no way represents the view of His Majesty's Government.'

Britain – and Europe – were by this time awaiting Hitler's speech, to be made at Nuremberg on 12 September. On that day, as its page 1 lead, the *Evening Standard* announced:

> Sir Neville Henderson, British Ambassador in Berlin, saw Herr von Ribbentrop, German Foreign Minister, at Nuremberg today ... Sir Neville sought to convince Herr von Ribbentrop that Britain, as the Prime Minister had stated in the House of Commons, could not finally remain disinterested in the event of a general European conflict. Herr von Ribbentrop, it is believed, was previously reluctant to accept the prospect of joint action by Britain and France if peaceful methods fail.

In the leader column, now written by Peter Howard, the reader was made aware of the importance of Hitler's forthcoming speech: 'The week has begun with Europe still at peace. War is not here, and every day of unbroken peace is a day gained. War, until it arrives, is never inevitable.' Facing the leader page, the main article was by the paper's special correspondent from New York, C. V. R. Thompson, who posed the question: 'If War Came to Britain Would America Keep Out?' So important was Hitler's speech regarded that the paper announced that it would be printing special late editions with full details.[11]

The news was bad: 'Hitler has staked his claim, the Czechs will not budge, and the French say they will march if one inch of Czech territory is violated'. With the increasing prospect of the peace being shattered, Chamberlain took the dramatic – even despairing – step of telegraphing Hitler for an urgent meeting. His request was granted, and on 15 September, at the age of 69, he took his first flight – to Berchtesgaden. Low's cartoon of the event showed an airborne Chamberlain, with the captions: 'STILL IN THE AIR. PEACE: It all depends on where we come down, doesn't it?'

Duff Cooper was later to write in his diary:

> At the Cabinet meeting on September 17 ... the Prime Minister told us the story of his visit to Berchtesgaden. Hitler struck him as 'the commonest little dog' he had ever seen ... After ranting and raving at him, Hitler had talked about self determination and asked the Prime Minister whether he accepted the principle ... From the beginning to the end Hitler had not shown the slightest sign of yielding on a single point.

In this highly-charged atmosphere of impending war, while huge processions were marching down Whitehall crying, 'Stand by the Czechs' and 'Chamberlain must go' Beaverbrook was writing in the *Daily Express*: 'Britain never gave any pledge to protect the frontiers of Czechoslovakia ... no moral obligations rest on us'. On 26 September, Frank Owen, deputising as editor, announced in the *Evening Standard*: 'If war comes, there is one statesman at least whom history will acquit of all the responsibility for the catastrophe. At the cost of exposing himself to bitter criticism, Mr Chamberlain has done everything humanly possible to preserve peace.' Two days later, with the navy already mobilised, the Prime Minister rose in the House of Commons to give his verdict of recent events: 'Hitler had decreed that his mobilization will begin today at two o'clock'. An official from the Foreign Office then frantically handed Chamberlain a note. He cleared his throat and paused, before telling the Members that he had telegraphed both Hitler and Mussolini that morning. He then read the message and said: 'That is not all. I have something further to say to the House'; Hitler had invited him, along with Benito Mussolini and Edouard Daladier, the French Prime Minister, to go to Munich the following morning. Among the first to congratulate the Prime Minister was Beaverbrook, who, that same evening, wrote to Chamberlain: 'My dear Neville, My faith is very great, but not so immense as my joy and delight over your reward. Don't answer. Yours ever, Max.'

The following morning 29 September, at dawn, the whole Cabinet was at Heston Airport to see off the Prime Minister to Munich. However, the result of the meeting was, not unexpectedly, total victory for Hitler and his policies. Sudetenland was to be ceded to Germany, and Polish and Hungarian claims for frontier adjustments were to be made at the expense of Czechoslovakia. And all frontier fortifications, along with more than a third of its population, were to be transferred to Germany. When these changes had been made, all four of the Powers represented at Munich agreed to guarantee the rump of Czechoslovakia against unprovoked aggression. For Chamberlain it was to be his hour of triumph. From the moment, on 30 September 1938, when the Prime Minister stepped off his plane at Heston waving his scrap of paper and averring 'Peace for our time' it was to be a glorious return to Downing Street and the admiring crowds. As Lord Halifax later wrote: 'That drive from Heston is perhaps worth recording. It was not easy to talk at all, for flowers were being thrown into the car, people were jumping on the running board, seizing his hand and patting him on the back.'

Meanwhile, on the following day, Lockhart went down to Shoe Lane, met Wardell and agreed that he would return to the *Standard* on his old terms with involvement in the 'Diary' and page 7: 'Mike very bitter about Beaverbrook whose interference, he says, makes it quite impossible to produce a good *Evening Standard*, as our *Evening Standard* readers dislike most of the things which Lord Beaverbrook likes and tries to do.' That weekend, Reginald Thompson's tenure as editor came to an end: a policy difference with Beaverbrook meant his instant dismissal and the appointment of Frank Owen as acting editor. From the *Standard*, Thompson moved to the *Essex Chronicle* series, where he was editor and managing director.

While the unfortunate Thompson was being dismissed, Duff Cooper was leaving the Cabinet. In his resignation speech he was to refer to that 'miserable scrap of paper', suggesting

> that for the Prime Minister of England to sign, without consulting his colleagues, without any reference to his allies and without any communication with the Dominions and without the assistance of any expert diplomatic advice, such a declaration with the dictator of a great state is not the way in which the foreign affairs of the British Empire ought to be conducted.

Harold Nicolson's comment 'That is fine of him. He has no money and gives up £5,000 a year plus a job he loves'[12] was not, however, to have too depressing an effect, for within hours Duff Cooper had accepted a lucrative contract with the *Evening Standard*: 'Immediately after the resignation, I accepted an offer from the *Evening Standard* to write a weekly article in their columns. The political views of the proprietor were very different from mine, but the editor undertook to alter nothing that I wrote, reserving only the right not to publish it, in which case he would pay for the article none the less.'

Lockhart, a close friend, was delighted, and on 3 October, once more at Shoe Lane, wrote a long article on Duff Cooper. He later wrote: 'My first day back in Fleet Street; a hectic one, too, for I arrived at the office at 9.45 and I did not leave it until 7.15 p.m. Great disorganisation in office; Frank Owen is acting editor in place of Thompson who has been sacked. Staff do not know yet. Owen is erratic and has no sense of time or organisation.'[13] Apart from Duff Cooper's articles, Owen was now running a series based upon Hitler's *Mein Kampf*. It was to be an immediate success, adding many thousands of copies to the circulation. As the 'blurb' announced: '*Mein Kampf* (My Struggle) is the book that Hitler wrote when he was in prison for attempted rebellion in 1923. It was his testament of faith. It has become the Nazi Bible and today every German has read it. In *Mein Kampf* Hitler sets forth his programme of 25 unalterable points. Are they compatible with peace for the rest of the world? Or must Hitler's doctrines mean inevitable war?' To the readers of the *Standard*, Hitler's edicts were only too clear: Munich was but a breathing space.

19

On the Brink

To be an editor of a Fleet Street newspaper in the days immediately after Munich was, indeed, a heady experience: J. L. Garvin, after thirty years, still laboured at the *Observer*, Arthur Christiansen, of the *Daily Express*, exhibited nightly his typographic pyrotechnics, while remembering 'the little man in the backstreets of Derby';[1] and Francis Williams, on the *Daily Herald*, was steadfastly proclaiming the policies of the Labour Party. But the newest and brightest of the editors was Frank Owen, who had first attracted Beaverbrook's attention as the youngest Liberal MP in the 1929–31 Parliament.[2] And after losing his Herefordshire seat, Owen became Beaverbrook's ghost writer for most articles on economic policy.

One of Owen's colleagues on the *Evening Standard* was the young Michael Foot, afterwards to be leader of the Labour Party, and who was later to recall:

> In the autumn of 1938 he was just the man who might be expected to take the *Evening Standard* by the scruff of the neck, and transform it from what it was, the house-journal of exclusivist London West End, into a real rival to the *Star* and the *Evening News* with their larger circulations ... That autumn, it was Frank more than any of his major rivals who discovered just how Hitler's awful name sold newspapers. He started, just for a week at first, to write a serial on Hitler's *Mein Kampf*, a work little studied in the England of Chamberlain's appeasement epoch. Then when sales soared he continued the enterprise for weeks on end.
>
> Two or three times a week, each night after the paper had been put to bed, he would attend a session at Stornoway House [Beaverbrook's London home] where the successes and failures of the day and the prospects for the next day were compared with those of our rivals by our most relentless reader. One answer was supplied by Frank, much to the horror of Captain Wardell, the manager, and was suggested by the columns of advertising puffs, 'musts' which the management required to be printed. One night Frank supplied a stack of this scandalous material to prove his charges. Captain Wardell received his instructions; and the victory was celebrated long before we returned to Shoe Lane.[3]

During this period there was 'a smell of peace in the air', for even Lloyd George, now in semi-retirement at Churt, in Surrey, was bombarding the American press with syndicated articles, while George Bernard Shaw, in the *New Statesman*, was preaching a compromise peace, and certain Establishment figures were advocating appeasement. And even in *The Standard*, Beaverbrook had been talking of 'Splendid Isolation'. The previous autumn, on September 9, 1937, a half-page advertisement had declared: 'Why I want another 600,000 readers for the *Daily Express*'.

> The *Daily Express* has yet to accomplish other objects that it desires in national policy, chief of all the ideal of Splendid Isolation.
>
> We persist in our plea for the detachment of Britain from Continental quarrels; we put forward unremitting argument that Britain is not the outpost of Europe, but the heart of the British Empire.

Now in these early days of 1939, the *Evening Standard* was to discuss the position of Jewish immigrants fleeing from Germany and Czechoslovakia. Lord [Stanley] Baldwin's appeal for the Jewish refugees had met 'with generous and unstinting response from the British people' and had raised more than £350,000 in less than four weeks. The paper commented:

> The horror which swept this country at the news of the Nazi pogrom has not been dissipated in a mere display of verbal sympathy. Such a response to the call of humanity was right and urgent. British tradition would have been sadly betrayed had it not been forthcoming.

The rest of the leading article of January 16, though, showed a certain reservation:

> Yet those who have organized the public subscription would be the first to admit that financial assistance is not a remedy ... It is not possible, for instance, to contemplate permanent increased Jewish settlement in this country. British traders and those employed in the professions cannot be expected to view a large influx of competitors with equanimity ... Another and equally important side of the problem is raised by the belief which seems to have grown in dictator countries that the democracies are willing to aid their policies of expulsion by unlimited financial support for the refugees ... It is not possible for the British Government to allow immigrants to pour into this country.

Meanwhile the paper was proposing to stage an exhibition of underground roads and air raid shelters, an exhibition to which E. J. Robertson and Leslie Plummer, his deputy, were both opposed. They wrote to Beaverbrook on 24 February 1939:

> We do not believe that such an exhibition could be run, except at a substantial loss...We assume that it would take six months to organise the exhibition, by which time we think that either we will be in the middle of another international crisis, or the chances of war will be receding. If the crisis is on, no one will be interested to see an exhibition of plans for providing air raid shelters five or ten years hence.

It has been said that the Ides of March (15 March) 1939 marked the beginning of the end of 'a low dishonest decade'.[4] Chamberlain, however, still refused to face the fact that Hitler was once more casting his eye on Czechoslovakia: on 9 March 1939, he called representatives of all the Fleet Street newspapers to a private conference at 10 Downing Street, and told them that the international situation had much improved. He added that as a result of the Munich Agreement there were high hopes of reaching political, economic and military understanding throughout Europe, and as a first step he intended to call a disarmament conference later that year. The next day, prompted by the Prime Minister's 'off the record' talk, the *Standard* ran an optimistic leader headed 'Bright Morning'.

Realistically, however, Owen and his fellow editors had greeted Chamberlain's statement with astonishment, for their correspondents in Prague and Berlin had daily been informing them of an impending German invasion. They were to be proved right, for less than a week later the Munich Agreement was in tatters and Germany had annexed Czechoslovakia. On that day, March 15, Chips Channon wrote in his diary: 'Hitler has entered Prague, apparently, and Czechoslovakia has ceased to exist. No balder, bolder departure from the written word has been committed in history ...'[5] Beaverbrook's comments on the invasion were: 'Our Government could never have defended Czechoslovakia, and that combination of races could never have worked together in their common defence against Germany. The structure was bound to fall as soon as the weight of reality was imposed upon it.'

For Francis Williams, editor of the *Daily Herald*:

> The time between Munich and the declaration of war was, I suppose, the worst ever lived through by those who had not been old enough to feel the full weight of the First World War. We knew that war was certain. We were ill-prepared for it and expected it to be indescribable in horror. By an unfortunate coincidence a film based on H. G. Wells' *War in the Air* [*Things to Come*] had been showing at the cinemas at the time of Munich and had added a macabre horror to the sight of slit trenches being dug in the parks by the light of acetylene flares as darkness fell.[6]

TIME TO RETIRE

During most of the 1930s, the financial position of the *Evening Standard* had been causing Beaverbrook some concern. For instance, in 1931, the paper had made a small profit of £8,000, which led him to write to Lord Rothermere: 'The *Evening Standard* is a luxury-advertising medium. It is used by all the first-class drapers and rejected by the popular drapers.' Having decided to transfer the title to the *Evening Standard* and having secured tacit approval, he was surprised to learn from Rothermere: 'The Daily Mail Trust have an option, which I did not know they had, to buy the *Evening Standard* and will not surrender it without some considerable consideration.' On 4 July 1931, Beaverbrook had proposed that control of the paper should be transferred to his son Peter, writing: 'I am divesting myself of all my newspaper interests. I am doing so because I am returning home to Canada.' Once more, the Daily Mail Trust sought to enforce its option and the idea was abandoned.

Towards the end of that year, Beaverbrook planned to move the *Standard* to the new black-glassed *Express* building in Fleet Street, and reduce the size of the paper from $25^1/_8$ in. cut-off to the more traditional $23^9/_{16}$ in cut-off, thereby bringing it into line with Rothermere's *Evening News*. Rothermere, however, was appalled, and suggested that the change would be a great shock to advertisers and would cost £400,000. Nevertheless, the constant nagging from Beaverbrook was to have its effect, and on 9 December Rothermere lost his patience, writing: 'Go ahead with the *Evening Standard* in whatever way you think its interests are best served ... You are fully able to decide.' Ever obdurate, Beaverbrook did nothing.

Determined to shake off Rothermere's involvement, in the winter of 1932–3 Beaverbrook paid more than £500,000 for the 80,000 shares which the Daily Mail Trust held in the *Daily Express*. And sold his Daily Mail Trust shares for a much higher figure. His next task was to secure the future of the *Evening Standard*. In February 1933 he asked for an option on the shares held by the Daily Mail Trust, and gave an assurance that he would gradually dispose of them. In response, the Trust wished for a firm purchase and asked for £324,405. Beaverbrook's retort was to offer £282,030, which was immediately rejected. Beaverbrook, however believed that he would not have long to wait before the shares fell into his lap, and on 17 May 1933, he was successful with a bid of £275,483. As a result, there were no longer any mortgages or debentures on Express Newspapers and 'he could transfer the *Evening Standard* to the ownership of the *Express*'.

Six years later, in the spring of 1939, Beaverbrook, now aged 60, had decided to retire and sell the *Evening Standard* to its staff, and on 27 April Robertson wrote to Beaverbrook:

> Referring to the agreement dated 29th day of March 1939, for the purchase of the *Evening Standard* by the London Express Newspaper Limited, you very kindly agreed to allow us to pay the purchase price of £500,000 in ten annual instalments of £50,000. It is understood that the first payment will be made by us on the 1st January, 1940. Last night when discussing the *Evening Standard* new building, and the programme for developing the net sale and advertising revenue of the newspaper, you stated that you were prepared to allow us to postpone the first payment of £50,000 until our plan of development has been carried out. I shall be glad if you will please confirm that offer.[7]

A week later, on 4 May at the *Evening Standard* board meeting, the chairman, Captain Mike Wardell, reported that 'negotiations had been concluded with the London Express Newspaper Ltd. in which it had been agreed that the London Express Newspaper Ltd. would be appointed Managers of the *Evening Standard* Co. Ltd. Newspaper and the general trading of this company. An agreement embodying the terms of the appointment was now being prepared and would be submitted to the board for approval when completed.'[8] Robertson, who sat on the *Evening Standard* board, wrote to Beaverbrook on 19 May: 'Critchley, in consultation with Francis who has been advising the *Evening Standard,* has decided that a formal agreement is necessary in connection with our taking over the management of the *Evening Standard* company. I attach the final draft which I think is all right, but before having it signed and sealed by the two companies, I shall be glad to know if it meets with your approval.'

Almost two months later, on 18 July, Beaverbrook informed his accountant, T. M. Till: 'I am now returning to Canada. I sail on the *Empress of Britain* on the fifth of August, and I shall not be back again, except as a visitor. I have agreed to sell my various holdings in London Express Newspapers Limited to members of the staff of that company for three million pounds.'[9] In the event, the deals did not go through because the war intervened. By September 1939, Beaverbrook was once more at the helm.

Throughout the summer of 1939, Beaverbrook, ever conscious of the sales of his newspapers, had been urging Robertson to higher and higher circulation because, even though the *Daily Express* could now claim the world's largest daily figure and the *Sunday Express* was selling almost 1,500,000 copies each week, there still remained problems with the *Evening Standard.* On 5 June, Robertson wrote to Beaverbrook:

> Plummer, Blackburn [the new general manager] and I had a conference this morning with reference to your demand for *Evening Standard* net sale. We all feel that while that increase of 16,000 on last May does not sound much, yet it is a beginning, and our June

figure, which we hope will be over 400,00, will be on a firmer basis than the 402,000 of June of last year. We feel that we have arrested the chronic decline which had set in and while it is impossible to promise the spectacular monthly increase which you would like to see, we are hopeful that there will be a steady and continuous move towards the 500,000 mark.

The chief rivals of the paper during this period were the *Evening News* and the *Star.* Tom Blackburn, a former circulation manager, and not long before appointed to the *Standard* board, was later to write:

> In 1937, 1938 and 1939 I believe the progress of the *News* was due to its consistent policy of giving a multiplicity of small news items, good sport and features appealing to the suburban or typists' mind. They always had this sale while the *Standard* appealed to the highest class in the West End and the City and the *Star* in the artisan area. The *News* was assisted at this time by two factors. The *Standard* during this period was a very heavy newspaper, overloaded with advertising; its news lacked variety and it was long winded. I recall such things as only five items of news on Page 1, middle spread entirely devoted to cricket and such features as the life of Lady Houston which did not appeal to the popular mind. At the same time it held its supremacy among grade 'A' readers. It only penetrated the suburban and artisan field on its racing and big news days which, I might add, were many during this period, with Franco, Mussolini and Hitler holding the stage. On days of big news I believe the *Standard* sold better than the other two but it never held and always reverted back to the old figures the following day. In politics we were rather too right wing for the man in the street at that time.
>
> The other factor was the *Star.* It was living on its racing edition, the *4 Star* [late edition]. On its main editions it made no progress either, depending upon the working class sale. It had not recovered from its experiment in 1934 of changing from a tabloid sheet to a full size paper which cost them 20,000 a day in sales and they had quickly to revert back to the smaller size. From 1939 we developed a more stable policy editorially. I believe our news was better handled; our features much more informative and topical and our outlook, although vigorously independent, slightly more liberal. With the war, people became more serious minded and I think that they turned to the *Standard* because it was a more responsible paper.[10]

WEEKEND AT CHERKLEY

Although the new editor was making his mark on the *Standard,* he was not without his critics, especially with regard to his off-stone performances. Robertson was to inform Beaverbrook: 'I have talked with Blackburn this morning and you may rest assured that both of us will do everything possible to see that Owen forms good time keeping habits.'[11] Owen's closest colleague on the paper, and now its chief leader writer, was Michael Foot. Having spent some time under Kingsley Martin on the *New Statesman*, and 'a few odd months learning typography from the Master, Alan Hutt, of the *Daily Worker*',[12] Foot joined the *Tribune*, remaining there for two years. Then, through the efforts of Aneurin Bevan, he quite unexpectedly received a call from Beaverbrook inviting him to spend a weekend at Cherkley. Foot has written a choice account of their first meeting:

> Beaverbrook came downstairs in his riding-attire and asked whether I had read the newspapers. When I replied, 'Yes, a few', he insisted: 'Read them *all*. Albert, see that Mr Foot is supplied with all the newspapers in the library. I will return in an hour or two, Mr Foot, and perhaps you will be good enough to tell me what is in the newspapers.' When he did return, he made a bolt for the swimming pool, calling me to follow, and prepared to plunge, naked-ape-like into the water. 'You've brought your notes with you, Mr Foot; now let me hear what is in *all* those newspapers.' But I had no notes, instead what might have passed muster as a photographic memory. I had memorised the Sunday newspapers as no one, I trust, has felt required to do before or since. 'Come with me with no delay,' he said, as the recital concluded, and he led me where the assembled score of house guests, one of his usual congregations of the incongruous, were drinking their pre-lunch drinks on the spacious porch overlooking the Surrey woodlands. 'Mr Foot will now tell you what most of you no doubt have been too damned lazy to read for yourselves.'[13]

As a result, Foot was offered a job on the *Evening Standard* at the union minimum of £9 per week, exactly double his salary on the *Tribune*. Within weeks of joining the paper, he was taken by Beaverbrook on the Blue Train to Cannes, Monte Carlo and back to the Ritz in Paris. The object was twofold: to inform his Lordship what was in the newspapers; and to receive instruction on writing a column. To this end he was told to study the modern masters of American journalism, Arthur Brisbane and Westbrook Pegler. Back at Shoe Lane, an enthusiastic Foot was eager to put his ideas into practice, and with Owen's blessing it was decided to make the leader column more lively and with a distinct London flavour.

The first test came on 2 March, when, under the headline 'PULL DOWN THE RAILINGS' Foot began: 'Henry VIII built a fence round Hyde Park. The fence was changed to a wall and the wall to railings. And there those railings stand today, ugly iron monuments to the tyranny of a rapacious monarch. Someone ought to pull them down.' Before publication, however, the column had been seen and vetoed by Captain Wardell, who was deeply shocked:

> He knew, and also took the precaution to check, the long-standing objection of the police to the removal of Hyde Park railings; it was hard enough to guard against the spread of vice in any case, but, with the railings down, the task would become useless. However, Beaverbrook would have none of it, and his message was conveyed to the pious and passionate Captain in his presence and in a manner not calculated to advance my popularity in the office. 'No more of it, Captain Wardell; you have beautiful beds in Claridges and all over London where you can do your f[...]; what about the rest of us?'[14]

Throughout the spring and summer of 1939, Foot was in a key position to view Beaverbrook and his friends:

> When I arrived on Beaverbrook's scene, had he not become an arch-appeaser, the prophet of peace when there was no peace, the defender of Neville Chamberlain and Samuel Hoare, even enduring their presence at his dinner table? He had indeed, and may his Presbyterian God forgive him this sin more scarlet than all the others ... leading journalists, headed by Frank Owen, were moving into the anti-Munich camp. Beaverbrook remained unconvinced; he still clung wretchedly to his dream of splendid isolation.[15]

On 5 August 1939, Beaverbrook sailed for Canada and into retirement, firmly convinced that his newspaper days were over. Less than a week later, on 11 August, the *Daily Express*, for the eighth and last time that year, averred: 'Britain will not be involved in a European war.' That same day, on arrival at Quebec, Beaverbrook said: 'I would not be here if I did believe that war was imminent.'[16] Robertson, though, was far less sanguine, and with the signing of the Nazi-Soviet pact on 23 August, told him that war *was* imminent and that he should return to England. Six days later he informed his Lordship that sales of all newspapers were

> going up like smoke. The *Standard* is printing approximately 850,000 and according to Blackburn selling pretty well ... If the crisis condition continues into next week, the suggestion is that all newspapers would reduce to 12 pages, and of course, in the event of war, we would come back to eight pages at once. If the worst should happen, and war comes, I think we have done everything possible to make our three offices as safe and secure as possible. The staff have been well drilled and we have done our best to create in them a

feeling of confidence, which would enable us to continue production as long as possible.[16]

Back in England once more, Beaverbrook was greeted with the news that Germany had invaded Poland: Hitler's plan to annexe Danzig and the Polish Corridor was now being put into effect, and by the end of that first day, 1 September 1939, more than a million troops had been thrusting into Poland, with many cities having been bombed. At 6 p.m. the following day, a hushed House of Commons heard Neville Chamberlain say that His Majesty's Government would be bound to take action unless the German forces were withdrawn from Polish territory. From the Labour Opposition there was complete agreement. Less than twenty-four hours later, Great Britain was at war. Chamberlain had informed Parliament that a further communication had been given to the German Government at nine o'clock that morning asking for an assurance that their forces would, as previously requested, suspend their advance into Poland; if a satisfactory assurance to this effect had not been received by eleven o'clock a state of war would exist between the two countries.

At 11.15 a.m. Chamberlain broadcast to a waiting nation. No satisfactory assurance had been received: 'Consequently this country is now at war with Germany.' He told the House of Commons: 'This is a sad day for all of us, but to none is it sadder than to me. Everything that I have worked for, everything that I have hoped for, everything that I have believed in during my public life, has crashed into ruins.' For almost everyone on that September day there was a feeling of high tension: 'It was a warm and bright Sunday morning, on which the early services in all the churches were packed with worshippers, many of whom had not been seen in church for a long time.'[17]

Viscount Castlerosse, a one-time director of the *Evening Standard*, and Captain Michael Wardell, its chairman, were playing golf that morning, Castlerosse was later to write a splendid, atmospheric piece about the occasion:[18]

It must have been round about half past eleven o'clock in the morning and Walton Heath was looking at its best. The sun was shining. The turf was green and springy ... The little larks were flying joyfully in the sky. A man in a green shirt had hit a good drive off the fourteenth tee when suddenly we heard a distant sound. It sounded as if all the banshees of the world had joined together to give voice to a united wail. 'That must be war.' I said to Captain Wardell. After a while ... [he] turned to me and said: 'Yes, without doubt war has been declared and we had better make up our minds here and now that this will alter everything.'

20

The Standard at War

With war having been declared, one of Chamberlain's initial moves was to invite Winston Churchill into the Cabinet to serve as First Lord of the Admiralty. But for Beaverbrook there was to be no place; instead, he was sent to the United States to find out what President Roosevelt thought about the war. One of Beaverbrook's last acts before leaving was to inform Robertson of the need for American support. On 19 September, Robertson replied: 'A written instruction has been given to Christiansen, Gordon [editor *Sunday Express*] and Frank Owen, making it clear that Mr Kennedy [the American Ambassador] is not to be criticised in the columns of our papers, but that he is to receive favourable comment. Also that this applied to all Americans.'[1]

On 2 October, Robertson wrote to Beaverbrook in Washington:

> Everyone I meet is saying why don't they send for you and put you in charge of the Ministry [of Information]. Our friends in Fleet Street are all saying you should be in charge ... The trading results for last week should again be quite satisfactory as far as the *Daily* and *Sunday Express* are concerned. In the case of the *Standard* we are still a long way from break-even, and if the price of newsprint goes up I think we shall have no alternative but to face some heavy cuts in salary.[2]

Twice a week – and sometimes more frequently – Robertson would write to Beaverbrook giving details of the papers' performance and general news from Whitehall and Fleet Street. On 4 October he commented:

> The *Evening Standard* [newsprint] stocks in London amount to 9,400 tons which at the present rate of consumption of 160 tons a week is equivalent to approximately 60 weeks' supply. As Blackburn will no doubt have told you, the *Standard* loss for last week was again very high at £2,300. Long [production director], Plummer and I spent several hours with Blackburn on Monday, examining the costs of every department, and we have taken decisions to make very drastic cuts in the number of employees all the way round. There appears to us to be no alternative if we are to get anywhere near a break-even figure, even with low priced newsprint.

A week later, he wrote: 'I think the high standard of our papers is being maintained. The *Standard* is inclined to be too much of a propaganda sheet, and I am urging Frank to avoid that tendency, and give more and more space to news, particularly to strive after news of a human character as a relief from war news.'[3] This continuing correspondence between Robertson and Beaverbrook only confirms that the editors were totally reliant upon the proprietor for their instructions. There was to be no question of editorial independence.

Throughout this period of the 'phoney war', while the French stood firm behind the Maginot Line and the Germans behind the Siegfried Line, the sales of the *Evening Standard* continued to cause concern, and on 11 December Robertson once more returned to the subject when writing to Beaverbrook:

> I agree the fall in the *Standard* net sale is most unpleasant, and I am afraid that the fall has been more precipitated than that of either the *Star* or the *News* ... I don't think there is any doubt that the *Standard* has suffered more than either the *News* or *Star* through the vacation of large business organisations. Over 1,200 organisations have transferred their headquarters from London into the country, mostly to the western parts of England. It is safe to estimate that that fact alone must have affected the *Evening Standard* sales to the extent of 40/50,000 copies per day.

Beaverbrook, in an effort to improve the *Standard*'s profitability, suggested that the paper should revert to its 1922 make-up: five columns per page instead of four. This appeared to make sound business sense, increasing the column yield by 25 per cent. Robertson, however, thought differently, and on 14 December he wrote:

> By adopting the five column make up as against four columns, the advertising rate, which remained at £300 a page, was automatically reduced from £75 to £60 a column. As the average number of columns carried in a 16 page paper [then the *Standard* size] is 25, the loss in advertising revenue was £375 a day, or £2,250 a week. The experience of that time was that advertisers did not take additional space because of the reduced rate per column, and still booked 1 or 2 columns as usual. Talbot [advertisement director] states that after two months the result on advertising revenue and profits of the *Evening Standard, Daily Sketch* and *Sunday Herald,* all of which adopted the 5 column measurement, was so disastrous that all three papers reverted to the 4 column basis.[4]

Nevertheless, Beaverbrook was to have his way, and on 18 April 1940, the *World's Press News* reported:

> Without preliminary announcement, the *Evening Standard* first edition on Monday of this week appeared on the street with new make-up, five columns to the page. The *Evening Standard*'s new format has been introduced to combat the newsprint shortage and the increase in production costs. No new advertisement rate is to be brought into operation, but advertisers are being charged the same rate for the narrower columns. The new layout and smaller type, it is claimed, give the paper an additional eight columns of text in a 20-page issue.[5]

Earlier in the year, on 17 February 1940, Londoners were amazed to see copies of the *Evening Standard* being dropped by German aircraft as a propaganda exercise. This 'Issue No. 35,941'[6] was a fictitious newspaper, showing Churchill in party mood!

ABOUT TO BREAK

In the spring of 1940, the war at sea continued, but in Western Europe there was virtual stalemate. Beaverbrook believed firmly that Hitler would not go into The Netherlands or Belgium.[7] The storm was about to break, however, and on 9 April the Germans invaded Norway, where the intervention of British forces ended in a humiliating withdrawal. Almost a month later, on 7 May, a two-day debate began in the House of Commons to discuss the fiasco. The first day was notable for the intervention of two speakers from the Conservative benches: Roger Keyes came to the House wearing his uniform of Admiral of the Fleet, a gesture which dramatically enhanced his speech; but the main attack came from Leo Amery, who, in quoting Oliver Cromwell, seemed to sum up the feelings of the House. He told the Prime Minister: 'You have sat too long for any good you have been doing. Depart, I say, and let us have done with you. In the name of God, go!'[8] For Chamberlain the signs were ominous: in a division forced by the Labour Opposition forty-one supporters of the government voted against him and some sixty abstained.

In the early hours of 10 May, German armies invaded The Netherlands and Belgium. Beaverbrook telephoned Peter Howard, the *Standard* leader-writer: 'You can record in your diary, if you have one, that today Hitler lost the war.'[9] The *Evening Standard* that day, in huge headlines, announced on page 1:

> **NAZIS INVADE HOLLAND,**
> **BELGIUM, LUXEMBURG:**
> **MANY AIRPORTS BOMBED**
>
> HITLER HAS INVADED HOLLAND, BELGIUM AND LUXEMBURG. HIS PARACHUTE TROOPS ARE LANDING AT SCORES OF POINTS AND MANY AIRPORTS ARE BEING BOMBED.

THE DUTCH HAVE OPENED THEIR FLOODGATES AND CLAIM TO HAVE BROUGHT DOWN A DOZEN BOMBERS.

It was confirmed in official quarters in London shortly after 8 a.m. today that appeals for assistance have been received from both the Belgian and Dutch Governments, and that these Governments have been told that H.M. Government will, of course, render all the help they can.

That same day, Kingsley Wood led a revolt against Chamberlain within the Cabinet and, with the Labour leaders also refusing to serve under Chamberlain, that afternoon Churchill became Prime Minister. Past differences forgotten, Beaverbrook was once more established as Churchill's intimate adviser, lunching and dining with him on that momentous day. One of the first acts of the new Prime Minister was to appoint Beaverbrook as Minister of Aircraft Production.

Michael Foot's recollections of that time make interesting reading:

In those first weeks we had another interest, too. Right up till the moment when Hitler's tanks smashed through the Ardennes, Beaverbrook had continued to exercise his perpetual, erratic, inescapable surveillance over the newspaper; he was the editor-in-chief and everyone inside the office knew it. Then, one fine memorable morning, peace descended. The blitz was just about to burst upon us in all its fury. All Beaverbrook's improvising energies were devoted to the task, night after night, for weeks on end. So, led by Frank Owen, we on the *Evening Standard* went about our task all the more zestfully, producing the best paper sold on the streets of our beleaguered city. Day after day, I dare say, our tone became exhilarated and revolutionary – that was the mood of the time. And one fine morning I embroidered a leading article with a quotation from Cromwell on the eve of the battle of Dunbar 'We are upon an Engagement very difficult … But the only wise God knows what is best. All shall work for Good ….'

Within hours, it seemed more like minutes, of that paper reaching our street-sellers, the blitz-laden peace of the previous weeks was broken by a thunder-clap. It was Beaverbrook on the telephone: 'How dare you, Mr Foot, how dare you use the columns of the *Evening Standard* to attack the Presbyterians. The tale is spread in Westminster and Whitehall that Beaverbrook no longer takes an interest in his newspapers. I would have you understand, Mr Foot, that his newly-developed good nature does not extend to some damned dispensation permitting attacks on Presbyterians. And Cromwell at Dunbar, I would have you know, had no title to pray to the god of battles to destroy his Presbyterians.'[10]

Meanwhile, the battles in Europe were at a critical stage, and after five days of fighting, and the destruction of Rotterdam, The Netherlands capitulated. This was followed on 28 May by King Leopold of the Belgians surrendering his country. With the remnants of the British and French armies encircled at Dunkirk after constant attack from massed Panzer divisions and devastating air power, there seemed to be little hope. But on the fateful weekend of 31 May–2 June an armada of little ships crossed the Channel to evacuate the British army from the beaches; and in an epic operation more than 250,000 British and 150,000 French troops were saved.

Owen, Foot and Howard, on the afternoon of 31 May 1940, sat in the offices of the *Evening Standard* discussing the news as it came in. They blamed the debacle directly on Chamberlain and his colleagues, and they decided to write a book in which they would take to task the neglect by these men. The title of the book, *Guilty Men*, was selected by Foot from the life of the French revolutionary St. Just: 'The leader of the angry crowd replied. "The people haven't come here to be given a lot of phrases. They demand a dozen guilty men."' They decided that the author should be 'Cato', the man who had cleaned out the sewers of Rome. On 3 June they returned to Shoe Lane, each with eight chapters written during the weekend. The book was finished on 4 June, and accepted for publication by Victor Gollancz the following day. From its launch in July 1940, *Guilty Men* caught the mood of the public and swiftly became a legend. A delighted Victor Gollancz could not keep up with the demand. As an advertising ploy he even sold it in barrows along Fleet Street, but from the conservative W. H. Smith there was a brief ban. Sales had been expected to reach 5,000, but more than 200,000 copies were sold in three months. Foot himself wrote the review in the *Evening Standard*:

A Mystery Here
by MICHAEL FOOT

Pamphleteering is a forgotten weapon, yet once it was perhaps the most potent in English politics. A pamphlet by Swift broke the Duke of Marlborough. How many others of the great name in English literature were associated with this particular art: Milton, Burke, Junius and hundreds more.

The weapon has now been drawn from its scabbard with a vengeance. *Guilty Men* written by a mysterious and bashful 'Cato' (Gollancz, 2s 6d) promises to become the most sensational political publication of the war.

It is a searing, savage but documented attack on the men responsible for the failure to provide Britain with the armaments to fight this war. It is an amazing vindication of the foresight of the present Prime Minister, and it pays full tribute to the men who have intensified the war effort in recent weeks. The story is told by one who appears to have watched the drama from the floor of the House of Commons itself. Some of the judgements are unfair. It has some flagrant omissions. But, whatever verdict is passed on the whole, none can dispute that its total effect is terrific. Who is this 'Cato'? M.P.? And why does he hide his fireworks under a bushel?[11]

Beaverbrook, who had his doubts over the authorship of *Guilty Men,* never pressed Owen or Foot for the name of the writer, but somehow believed that he was in on the secret: 'Later still the story circulated that Lord Halifax (one of the guilty men, for sure) had condescendingly remarked to his fellow-cabinet Minister, Beaverbrook: "You must find it hard to live on your Cabinet salary of £5,000 a year", to which Beaverbrook allegedly replied: "Ah, but I've always got my royalties from *Guilty Men.*"'

The following month, Samuel Hoare, now Special Ambassador in Spain, wrote from Madrid to Robertson on 27 July 1940, complaining of attacks from the Beaverbrook press:

> The great thing is to keep Spain out of the war as long as we can … This being so I am asking you to keep an eye upon the *Express* and the *Standard* with a view to avoiding any unnecessary embitterment of the present delicate situation. Rightly or wrongly the Minister for Foreign Affairs complains to me about the attitude of the *Express* and the *Evening Standard.*[12]

HIS FINEST HOUR

Beaverbrook was now about to enter his finest hour, and his appointment as Minister of Aircraft Production was just the shot in the arm that the Royal Air Force needed. In the savage withdrawal from France, the RAF fighter strength had been badly mauled, and aircraft were at a premium. In his official report, Lord Dowding, head of Fighter Command throughout the Battle of Britain, wrote:

> I saw my resources slipping away like sand in an hour glass … The effect of Lord Beaverbrook's appointment can only be described as magical and thereafter the supply situation improved to such a degree that the heavy aircraft wastage which was later incurred during the Battle of Britain ceased to be the primary danger.

Years later, Dowding informed Lord Templewood (formerly Sir Samuel Hoare): 'The country owes as much to Beaverbrook for the

Battle of Britain as it does to me. Without his drive behind me I could not have carried on during the battle.' To Beaverbrook, the man who only nine months before had sailed into retirement, it was the challenge of a lifetime, and he ran his enterprise as he ran his newspapers: all was high drama. Throughout that summer of cloudless days, while he led the crusade for more aircraft, his son, Max, was flying as a fighter pilot. Each evening, Beaverbrook would be on tenterhooks until he had received that very important telephone call from his son to say that he had survived another day. Family pride, quite rightly, had not prevented Beaverbrook from writing to Harold Balfour, Under Secretary of Air, on 30 May: 'Max Aitken is nerveless. He should be given some squadron at once. His promotion is long overdue. And he can carry any burden.'

The proof of Beaverbrook's success is contained in a memo written to Churchill on 2 September 1940, in the midst of the Battle of Britain:

> On May 15th last there were 884 aircraft available for operations in the Squadrons – excluding Lysanders. Now there are 1,325, excluding Lysanders. There is an increase of about 450 to 500 in operational aircraft in operational units. So it will be seen that the RAF has drawn from the Aircraft Ministry nearly a thousand operational machines since your Government was formed, for the purpose of strengthening units. In addition all casualties had to be replaced. And 720 aircraft were shipped abroad. 'Nobody knows the trouble I've seen.'

Churchill minuted: 'I do.' By 15 September, the Battle of Britain was reaching its climax, and that evening Peter Howard, still writing for the *Evening Standard*, received a telephone call from Beaverbrook: 'Peter, do you keep a diary? Well, if you had a diary, I would tell you to record in it that this day our country has won a victory that will be recorded in the annals of history in the same terms as Trafalgar or Waterloo are recorded.'[13] The number of German aircraft shot down on that fateful day over south-east England totalled 185.

But for Beaverbrook the incessant pressures of working seven days a week and suffering many sleepless nights had brought on fresh attacks of asthma, and on 1 October the *Evening Standard* announced in 'Londoner's Diary': 'Today asthma has laid its hand as firmly on [Beaverbrook] as a gaoler receiving an old prisoner back after a brief release. On 30 September 1940 the Prime Minister had received Beaverbrook's letter of resignation:

My Dear Winston,

I gathered from our conversation tonight that you expect me to undertake more responsibilities. But my asthma drives me to the unhappy conclusion that the cold weather and sharp winds bring my labours to nothing. I have tried many devices but nights pass in procession without any sleep for me.

If I live through the war I shall give you thanks for winning it, even though you may die now. For the example you gave the nation in the last four months, and the leadership of the dark days of the flight from France decided the battle in our favour.

Your devoted Max[14]

In his diary the following day, John Colville, the Prime Minister's Private Secretary, wrote: 'In another letter he says he is going to resign. Of course, he is a crafty man and what he says is not necessarily the truth, but Brendan [Bracken] tells me that he really is suffering a great deal.' Despite Beaverbrook's pleas, Churchill would not hear of his resigning, and in January 1941 paid eloquent testimony in the House of Commons to his friend's efforts. Beaverbrook was quick to respond: 'You have given me a certificate of character which will carry me through my days. And that is good for me. Because there is a difference between us. You will be talked of even more widely after you are dead than during your lifetime. But I am talked of while I live, and, save for my association with you, I will be forgotten thereafter.' Commenting on Beaverbrook's letter, Colville noted in his diary on 26 January 1941: 'Lord B. knows how to lay it on – and also how to forward his own cause in his unceasing struggles with the Air Ministry, of which the P.M. said to me on Friday that he was heartily sick.'

On 1 May 1941, Beaverbrook's pleas were finally heeded and he ceased to be Minister of Aircraft Production. Churchill, though, was determined not to lose Beaverbrook's experience and immediately appointed him Minister of State. That evening at Cherkley, Beaverbrook and Michael Foot composed the leader for the next day's *Evening Standard*: 'The King has been pleased to appoint Lord Beaverbrook Minister of State. What that means is anybody's guess. We have our own private explanation. It is to distinguish him from his father, who was a Minister of Gospel.' The leader continued: 'Is he promoted or is he demoted? Is he climbing the ladder or has he started down the drain? ... What have they done with our proprietor? Is he coming back to flay us or is he going to flay somebody else?'[15] However, second thoughts prevailed and the leader was not used.

Beaverbrook's new role was certainly not going to be a sinecure, because in September 1941 he visited Moscow, when he and Averell Harriman led the Anglo-American Supply Mission and in the

December accompanied Churchill to Washington. There he told the Vice-President and his aides that they had yet had no experience in the losses of material incidental to a war of the kind we [the British] are now fighting. He also felt that they had very little conception of the productive facilities of the Axis powers.

ROBERTSON AS CHAIRMAN

With Beaverbrook having been strenuously engaged in the War Cabinet since May 1940, even more of the work of running his newspapers fell on the shoulders of Robertson, and since March of that year Robertson had also assumed the role of chairman of the *Evening Standard*. The Minutes of the *Evening Standard* board meeting for 29 March 1940 reveal:

> Letter received from Mr Wardell resigning his office as Chairman and Managing Director of the Company was read. It was Resolved that under the provisions of Article No. 83 Mr E. J. Robertson be and is hereby appointed as director of the Company to fill the vacancy. It was Resolved that Mr Robertson be and is hereby appointed Chairman of the Board of Directors. Mr Robertson notified his acceptance and occupied the chair.

Wardell, the previous Chairman, had resigned to rejoin the Army, and was to end the war as a brigadier.

The first full year of war had seen a dramatic increase in the *Standard*'s circulation, with sales of 401,009 daily, an improvement of almost 20,000 copies over the previous period. However, the reduction in pagination in the autumn of 1939, through voluntary newsprint rationing, meant a maximum of twenty-four tabloid pages a day – and a dramatic drop in advertising revenue of more than £200,000 to a low of £347,654. Pagination was to be depressed further when, through the German occupation of Norway in April 1940, the flow of Scandinavian newsprint came to an abrupt halt. Frank Waters, manager of Express Newspapers in Scotland, wrote in his diary of 28 April: '[Newsprint] has become rarer than gold. Sizes of paper have been further limited to 8 pages [broadsheet]. Now actually embarrassed by extra sales. Like many other things newspaper life has become so standardised and stereotyped that originality will count for nought. That for a newspaper is pure hell.'[16]

The *Evening Standard* was, of course, similarly affected and its maximum size was now sixteen tabloid pages. Newsprint was to be even more restricted when on the night of 12 September Beaverbrook Newspapers lost 1,000 tons of newsprint by fire through enemy action.

The Luftwaffe struck again on the night of 26 September, 'when the sky glowed crimson over London's dockland from uncontrollable fires that consumed more than 16,000 tons of newsprint, representing to the *Express* a loss of £370,000 or roughly a fortnight's consumption.'[17]

Despite the restrictions in newsprint usage, the aggregate sales of the national press were higher than in pre-war days: four men out of five and two women out of three were reading at least one paper a day. The public, desperate for news, was now willing to pay more for less. For instance, *The Times*, which in April 1941 was to raise its cover price to 3d, could announce that its circulation was bigger than in pre-war days, and that profits were higher. Symptomatic of this craving for news, a young Colin Perry – 'proud to be one of the Londoners under bombardment' – could write in his diary, peppered with quotations from the *Evening Standard*: 'Well I must buy all the papers for the next few days.'

Even though the City – and Fleet Street – was now under great pressure from the almost nightly attacks of the Luftwaffe, the cry continued to be 'business as usual'. In September 1940, the *Evening Standard* offices in Shoe Lane suffered a direct hit from a large calibre bomb. This struck a 15,000-gallon water tank on the roof, wrecking it and the tower, and penetrating the composing room, where considerable damage was done. The huge volume of water cascaded down ten flights of stairs into the basement; there the engineers and machine minders worked valiantly to 'bail out' the pressroom which was under two feet of oily water.[18]

The *Standard* was fortunate in that Tom Blackburn, the general manager, and A. L. Cranfield, the managing editor, together with a number of executives, were sleeping on the premises, and were thus able to take immediate steps to retrieve the damage and maintain production. The *World's Press News* later reported that the editorial and composing activities were transferred to the *Daily Express* building at 121 Fleet Street, and printing was started on the south side of the river, with the result that no delay whatever was caused in publication.

The prompt steps taken, and the fact that the ensuing edition carried a cartoon by Low showing that a bomb had suffered damage by contact with the *Standard* building drew from Churchill a congratulatory telegram: 'Bravo, *Evening Standard*'. Throughout these almost nightly raids, Beaverbrook, when not required at the Ministry, would return to his specially-fortified flat high in the *Standard* building, from where he could see at first-hand the efforts of his paper's firewatchers in their defence against the incendiaries. On the odd occasion, he would even be joined by Churchill, and the two old friends would watch London under attack.

While an ageing staff was now producing the paper, more than 1,000 of their colleagues were in the Forces. Each month these servicemen and women would be sent special 'house' newspapers, giving details of their friends. Foremost of the *Evening Standard* staff serving in the Forces was, undoubtedly, Max Aitken, a former general manager. He had joined the County of London Squadron of the Auxiliary Air Force in 1935 and went straight into the RAF when war was declared. In all, he was to fly 161 operational missions, amounting to 2,000 flying hours.

Despite the exodus of key personnel, the *Standard* – under Owen and later, Foot — continued to attract the best writers, from among those waiting to be called up or declared unfit for service. Of these, one name stood out: George Orwell, later to win fame as the author of *1984* and *Animal Farm.* In January 1941, Orwell wrote:

> The *Standard* is the sounding-board for young journalists of left-wing views who are allowed to say what they like so long as they don't attack the boss directly. ... The tone of the popular press has improved out of recognition during the last year ... All of them print articles which would have been considered hopelessly above their readers's heads a couple of years ago. Nearly the whole of the press is now 'left' compared with what it was before Dunkirk – even *The Times.*[19]

To the likes of Michael Foot, this was an ideal situation, which was to be exploited even more that summer. On 22 June 1941, Foot was a weekend guest at Cherkley, where, waking early, he heard on the radio the news of the German invasion of Russia:

> I heard it again, and then ran down the stairs and ransacked from the gramophone cupboard the record I knew was there of *The Internationale,* and turned it on full blast. The whole place was awakened, and as they poured downstairs I was happy to inform Beaverbrook's household, guests and butlers alike, that they were now allies of the Soviet Union. No one seized the moment more exuberantly than Beaverbrook. That morning he went to Chequers; all day he assisted in the preparation of Churchill's famous broadcast, and a reception committee awaited at Cherkley for his return.[20]

Although Foot and Owen believed that they had been given virtually a free-hand, their proprietor thought otherwise, as he was to recall before the Royal Commission on the Press on 18 March 1948:

> I did issue very many of what were called directives. It was really advice, particularly to Michael Foot. He is a very clever fellow, a most excellent boy. And then suddenly he was projected into the

editorship of the paper before he was ready for it ... Michael Foot himself believed that I made him a journalist. He took the view that I allowed him immense freedom of expression, and he certainly thought that he had more freedom of expression with me than he could have with anyone else.

Nevertheless, in 1941, clearly identifying the needs of its growing army of readers, the *Evening Standard* had a circulation of 461,107, an increase of more than 60,000 over the previous year. Beaverbrook, however, believed that his papers – especially the *Daily Express* – had a duty to perform and a message to convey. Circulation was no longer his god as this letter to Robertson on September 24 shows:[21]

I have been reading the paper. You should improve it. It is not nearly as valuable a paper as you could give at the present time.

You should have much better foreign correspondents, and a good deal more attention should be paid to the foreign service of the paper. Your centre page article ought now to be more informative and it should have some valuable contribution from abroad – really valuable, written by men who are trained to see and have a reputation for doing so.

Add more – a good deal more – to your editorial charges.

Give up now the popular presentation of small events. The front page should be a document of the war. You do not want any more net sales, and you should make no popular appeal whatsoever.

Here is an opportunity for you young fellows to build up the greatest newspaper in the world – the greatest ever imagined. On your net sale you can build so soundly and so well.

All this must be done with serious thought. And when the decision has been taken and the line settled, it will be still more difficult to sustain.

FOOT AS EDITOR

In the spring of 1942, Frank Owen resigned his editorship to join the Royal Armoured Corps. His departure was covered in the following day's 'Londoner's Diary':

We of the *Evening Standard* – and a few of our closest friends – met last night to say farewell to the editor of this newspaper, Frank Owen, now a member of the Royal Armoured Corps. Of course the Pope of Fleet Street – Hannen Swaffer – was there, and one or two of the cardinals. There were speeches by Mr Percy Cudlipp, editor of the *Daily Herald*; Mr Arthur Christiansen, editor of the *Daily Express*; and Mr Arthur

> Cummings, of the *News Chronicle.* There has never been a greater fighter for liberty and justice than Frank Owen. Now he is in the ring for the biggest fight. When this is over we hope to welcome Frank back to Shoe Lane. In the meantime, Michael Foot, often Frank Owen's second at the ringside, will sit in the editor's chair. The resolve of the whole staff is that the *Evening Standard* will remain the same newspaper which Frank Owen made it.

Michael Foot's new appointment was noted in that week's *News of the World*:

> Fleet Street's youngest editor will now be Mr Michael Foot, who succeeds Mr Frank Owen as editor of the *Evening Standard.* Mr Owen has become a Trooper in the Royal Armoured Corps. Mr Foot has been the leader writer on the *Evening Standard* for the past five years and is now only 28. He is a son of Mr Isaac Foot, a famous Liberal politician and Methodist orator, and a brother of Mr Dingle Foot, MP, Parliamentary Secretary to the Ministry of Economic Warfare. Another brother, Mr Hugh Foot, is adviser to the Emir of Transjordania.

Michael Foot, a sufferer from asthma and therefore not fit for military service, has left a most interesting account of his war-time editorship:

> For two years, since the departure of Frank Owen for the forces, I had the enthralling job of editing the paper which he above all others had created, the war-time *Evening Standard,* the *Standard* in its very greatest days I naturally contend, although it has had some other great ones since. The war, as one of its minor by-products, raised the quality of British journalism as a whole and especially London journalism in a manner which has never been properly and collectively acclaimed. For one thing, the profit test, advertising pressures, were overnight tossed out of Fleet-street's bomb-threatened windows, and there prevailed instead a genuine competition of merit to use the precious supplies of newsprint to serve the common interest of the hour. We believed on the *Standard* that we changed to meet the new conditions and caught the new atmosphere better than any rival. For a start, we reported the new kind of war itself more freshly, analysed strategy more contentiously. For this, Frank Owen, an inspired military reporter himself, was chiefly responsible.[22]

Owen had been far-seeing in engaging the two best military correspondents for the paper: Liddell Hart and, later, although anonymously, Major-General J. F. C. Fuller, the 'father of the tank'. Owen and Foot were also assisted by fellow-sympathisers who religiously monitored broadcasts from Europe:

> Down towards Ludgate Circus was a little I.L.P. bookshop where Frank and I made purchases of such essential topical documents as the writing of Leon Trotsky or Tom Wintringham and which was run by a Swiss Socialist called Jon Kimche. He listened to the babel of Europe's battling radio stations in God-knows how many languages, and out of it distilled another original approach to the new kind of war, and a new profession for himself.[23]

Within days of Foot taking over as editor, Beaverbrook was off once more to the United States: this time to deliver a speech – previously agreed by President Roosevelt – at a newspaper dinner in New York. The speech was broadcast throughout America on a coast-to-coast hook-up and caused a sensation. Beaverbrook ended with this message: 'Strike out to help Russia. Strike out violently. Strike out even recklessly. How admirably Britain is equipped in weapons of war for directing an attack on Germany I well know. Britain should imitate Russia's spirit of attack by establishing somewhere along the two thousand miles of occupied coastline a Second Front.' The following day, 24 April 1942, Foot wrote to his proprietor to say that the speech had been stupendous: 'We are resolved to maintain the stalwart conservative line of the *Standard*, and outbursts of Communist fervour from whichever side of the Atlantic they may appear are viewed by us with grave concern.'

From the beginning, Beaverbrook had realised the potential of the young Foot and was determined to aid his career: 'You and I are the last two Radicals'. He was not, though, prepared to share his protégé's services with any other paper. Being short-staffed, Kingsley Martin had asked if Foot might be allowed to write the occasional article for the *New Statesman*. On 18 November 1942, Beaverbrook replied: 'If the newspaper opened the door, it would swing very wide. The newspaper pays Foot nearly £4,000 a year. If he were to do similar work for another paper, the directors would ask "Is Beaverbrook losing his punch? Is he going down the valley where all the newspaper men before him have gone?" And they might be right.'

One of Foot's earlier memories of the *Standard* had been when he was called to the office of the then managing director Captain Wardell, who was wearing his eye-patch and chairing a management meeting. In answer to a query from Wardell, Michael Foot, in all innocence, had replied: 'Well, in the land of the blind the one-eyed man is king!' This still raised a smile more than fifty years later.[24] In looking back on those memorable years, Foot was later to say that all types of independent people were attracted to Shoe Lane or to the 'surrounding consulting rooms' at this period. One such visitor was Orde Wingate, yet to be famous as leader of the Chindits, who 'Throughout one whole night at Frank's flat in Lincoln's Inn drank even Frank under the table. At five o'clock in the morning, with Frank's last bottle of sparkling Burgundy deflated and dead, all seemed possible.'

As Foot so aptly noted, the wartime *Evening Standard* was not just concerned with military matters. It did, indeed, capture some of the special flavour of London under fire: 'The people of London did truly play an heroic role, and the *Standard* reported their daily and nightly ardours, gave voice to their protests against blind or tardy bureaucracy, and endlessly argued about the way in which the supreme objective could be achieved.' Special issues were produced with verses of the *Marseillaise* printed on the front page to celebrate the blowing up of Vichy French battleships in Toulon; and the news that Mussolini had been overthrown by a handful of brave Italians resulted in a souvenir edition, telling his whole story from the march on Rome to Abyssinia and to Spain, embellished with Low cartoons.[25]

Encouraged by the huge success of his *Guilty Men* some two years earlier, Foot now wrote a sequel, *The Trial of Mussolini* by 'Cassius'. This time, however, he could not rely upon the support of Owen and Howard, and his authorship was not to remain secret for long. Beaverbrook was not amused and told Foot that he could be either an editor or a pamphleteer but not both at the same time:

> And, incidentally, what had happened to the form, circulated in the *Guilty Men* aftermath, requiring all Beaverbrook employees to inform the management about prospective books they had in mind? No I had not signed it: I had put it in the wastepaper basket where indeed, after a suitable interval, we would assign all the awkward messages from the Beaverbrook dictaphone which we hoped would not stir future animosities.

Foot had also been in trouble with his proprietor in securing a scoop with the publication of the Beveridge Report, much to the dismay of Churchill and his Cabinet.

A clash was inevitable: here were two independent-minded men who, although sharing a deepening friendship, could not agree. Foot resigned as editor, but for a number of months he continued to write editorials, until in June 1944 he decided that even this was too much, informing Beaverbrook:

> Your views and mine are bound to become more and more irreconcilable. As far as this Socialist business is concerned my views are

unshakeable. For me it is the Klondyke or bust, and at the moment I am doubtful whether I am going the right way to Klondyke. There does not seem to be much sense in my continuing to write leaders for a newspaper group whose opinions I do not share and some of whose opinions I strongly dissent from.

I know you never ask me to write views with which I disagree. But as this works out it is good business neither for you nor for me. The leaders which I now write are hardly worth writing since they are non-commital and from my point of view I am associated with a newspaper group against whose policies (but not against the proprietor) I am resolved to wage perpetual war. Somehow things were different before. The compromise worked and certainly greatly to my advantage. But I do not see how it could work very much longer. The business of maintaining allegiance to my own political ideas and to a newspaper which fundamentally must be opposed to them is too difficult. It seems foolish to raise a personal matter like this at a time when much bigger things are happening. But it would also be foolish to disguise the fact that my feeling is I am wasting my time and there is so much I want to do and accomplish. Your kindness to me has given me great advantages in this world. I do not forget them. But I am sure it is right for me to make a change and I dearly hope you will understand my reasons.[26]

PROBLEMS WITH CENSORS

While Michael Foot had been preparing his resignation letter, the *Evening Standard* had been incurring the wrath of the military censor – and Churchill himself. For weeks, talk of the Second Front and the invasion of Europe had been on everyone's lips: D-Day was imminent. On 30 May 1944, the paper printed an apparently innocuous paragraph in its 'Londoner's Diary' concerning an 80-year-old general who was to watch London Home Guards beating retreat. Within twenty-four hours the offending paragraph had been brought to the attention of the Prime Minister and a stinging rebuff was immediately sent to the editor of the *Standard*. Since 1942, the man responsible for 'Londoner's Diary' had been Tudor Jenkins, who had started on the *South Wales Evening Post*, Swansea, and had then moved to London, becoming chief sub-editor on the *Standard* until promoted to being in charge of the 'Diary'.

This difference between the *Standard* and the authorities was only the latest in a long series. In November 1940, for instance, Marshal of the Royal Air Force, Lord Trenchard had complained bitterly about two leading articles in the *Standard* which had advocated the transfer of Coastal Command to the Royal Navy. So incensed was he that he intended asking a question in the House of Lords. Beaverbrook, however, forestalled him, raising the matter in Cabinet. Churchill, sending him a copy of Sir Archibald Sinclair's letter of complaint, added pointedly: 'Of course if articles appear in the *Evening Standard* which are observed to reflect the views you are pressing in Cabinet, the Air Force will start up their agitation the other way. It would be a great pity if this became a matter of public controversy.' In reply, Beaverbrook pointed out that he was not directing the *Evening Standard.* The paper was a supporter of the government and of all its members. Still, fellow-Ministers considered it more than a coincidence that quite often points discussed in Cabinet would appear as subjects for leaders in the *Standard* the next day.[27]

Less than a month later, Churchill was to complain once more. This time it concerned a Low cartoon which made fun of Arthur Greenwood, the Labour Minister without Portfolio: 'All these Ministers conceiving themselves threatened to bank up against you and your projects, and owing to my friendship with you they will think that I am condoning the attacks made upon them.' Continuing, Churchill pointed out that '[Low] is a great master of black and white, but he does you and your work disservice by these cartoons, and he is only too well aware of what he does.' Once more, Beaverbrook denied that he had any control of the *Standard* or of Low, 'but it was a matter of real agony that he should be the occasion of such attacks upon my Prime Minister'.

In the summer of 1941, Brendan Bracken was appointed Minister of Information. One of his close companions for more than a decade, Beaverbrook was determined that the new Minister should be given every assistance, and instructed Owen that he was to provide the loyal co-operation that had been withheld from Duff Cooper. Bracken, however, preferred, as a rule, to work through proprietors rather than editors. On the day after he had taken up office, 26 September 1941, the *Standard* carried a report of a mutiny among the sailors on the sinking *Bismarck* two months before. A horrified Bracken discovered that the story, which had been obtained from the Admiralty, had never at any stage been cleared by his Ministry. He immediately wrote to A. V. Alexander, the First Sea Lord, on the lack of background news being provided on the Battle of the Atlantic, the most important theatre of war at that time: 'I deplore entering into a controversy with such a good colleague. But I do want to point out to you that the irritability and unreasonableness of a section of the press is due to the feeling that the service departments seem to show little sympathy with the real needs of the press. This fact has been recognized by the Secretaries of State for War and Air.'

Less than two months later, the paper was once again involved in controversy. This time it concerned Evelyn Waugh, a one-time correspondent in October 1928, and now a serving officer in the Royal Marines. Waugh was already one of England's leading novelists with *Decline and Fall* (1928) and *Scoop* (1938) and was shortly to write *Brideshead Revisited*. He noted in his diary at the time:

> November 1941
> Writing an article. On my first leave home I was asked by *American Life* to write an article on the Commandos. I said I must get leave first and the editor arranged it with Brendan Bracken. I wrote about the Bardia raids and got £200 for it. Then, without my knowledge, Peters sold it to the *Evening Standard*. It was announced; the other papers complained; the War Office then issued my article as a news bulletin. The Marine Office became agitated, Brendan backed out of his responsibility, and I got reprimanded.[28]

Despite these pressures, the paper was never threatened with closure, unlike the *Daily Mirror* for its famous Zec cartoon; but the next major incident was to involve the Prime Minister himself and his son, Randolph, now serving in the Middle East. In February 1943, Randolph Churchill was stationed in Algiers, where, having received a batch of British and American newspapers, he was so incensed at what was being said of the Vichy French in North Africa that he promptly wrote a letter to the *Evening Standard* – a letter which was not published until 2 March:

> There seems to be a widespread tendency to assume that any Frenchman who has occupied an official position under the Government of Vichy, whether at home or abroad, must necessarily be a traitor or possessed of a Fascist mentality. Such an intransigent outlook can only serve to perpetuate disunity among the comparatively few Frenchmen who are lucky enough to be outside the power of the enemy ... This Pharisaical attitude which is, I fear, fostered by certain French elements in London, is devoid of any real moral justification. Surely it is time a truce was called in this campaign of recrimination. In the last analysis it is Frenchmen who must settle such differences among themselves.

When the letter appeared there was an outcry and none was more vociferous than Aneurin Bevan, who tabled a question to the Prime Minister in the House of Commons. Bevan wanted to know if Churchill had been aware 'that a letter appeared in the *Evening Standard* written by a serving officer attached to an intelligence unit in North Africa and whether he could inform the House if that letter was passed by a senior officer, and whether he had any comment?' Amidst laughter, Churchill replied: 'This question should normally have been addressed to the Secretary of State for War but since Mr Bevan, no doubt from those motives of delicacy in personal matters which are characteristic of him, has preferred to put it to me, I will answer it myself.' Continuing, he said that he had indeed read the letter and had been advised that it did not fall under 'the restrictions of paragraph 547(a) of the King's Regulations as it dealt with political and not military matters. It had not been passed by a senior officer because the base censorship dealt only with security matters, not matters of opinion. In his view the letter expresses a perfectly arguable point of view and one which is shared by many responsible people.' For the benefit of those Members who had not seen the letter Churchill arranged for it to be published in the House of Commons Official Report.

A further instance of censorship and the *Evening Standard* was to occur in 1943 and concerned Douglas Wilkie who was representing the paper in the India-Burma theatre. During a 2,000-mile tour, he wrote a dozen articles describing his experiences and the conflict with the Japanese. However, Wilkie was to discover that the censor in New Delhi had rejected three articles and had severely cut the remainder before sending them on to London.

Wilkie was so incensed at this treatment that he wrote to the head of Army Public Relations in protest: 'If war correspondents are to be allowed to write only what the Army wants, then it would be easier if you confined your publicity to official handouts ... It is my concern in every sense that my professional reputation should be endangered because of my editor's compulsory ignorance of your policy ... My articles as dispatched are not a fair index of my industry, views or conception of the functions of a war correspondent.' Following the despatch of the letter, Wilkie returned to England.[29]

Throughout those difficult days, Bracken was in regular contact with Beaverbrook and Robertson, chairman of the *Evening Standard*, and where possible was always anxious to help. Not all correspondence, though, which passed between Beaverbrook, Bracken, and even Churchill, was of a serious nature. On one occasion the Prime Minister complained against the use of the word 'tensed' in the *Evening Standard* columns. Beaverbrook answered: 'The just indignation of the Prime Minister should be addressed to the Minister of Labour, who has deprived newspapers of staffs of compositors and proof-readers, adequate to prevent such outrages. In manning the defences of England, Mr Bevin has weakened the defences of the English language.'

Bracken, too, could also have his lighter moments, as this letter to Beaverbrook on 22 June 1944, which commented on Beaverbrook's church livings, shows: 'Mr Bracken thinks there is now a good case for dis-establishing the Church of England. He considers it the ripest of scandals that a bigoted Presbyterian should become a patron of church livings. Were it not for the flying bombs, the weather and the reading of Mr Lyttelton's speeches he would have reported this matter to the Archbishop of Canterbury.'

It is possible that on this occasion Beaverbrook was not amused, for in the following month 'Londoner's Diary' revealed that forty years earlier Bracken's father, as an Irish Nationalist, had been refused a gun licence. Once again, Beaverbrook pleaded innocence and described its publication as 'a desperate thing to do'. He was not, however, pleased when Bracken used his power as Minister of Information and tried to have the story suppressed.

D-DAY AT LAST

On Tuesday 6 June 1944, the Allied invasion of Europe had at last begun, and in large, front-page headlines the *Standard* proclaimed:

> **Churchill Announces Successful**
> **Massed Air Landings Behind**
> **Enemy Lines in France**
> **4,000 SHIPS, THOUSANDS OF**
> **SMALL VESSELS**
>
> An immense armada of more than 4,000 ships, with several thousand smaller craft has crossed the Channel, said Mr Churchill today, announcing the invasion.

With the Allied armies having secured their beach-head, the drive was now on through Normandy – despite the bitter battle for Caen. Hitler, meanwhile, was about to launch his secret weapon, the V1 flying bombs; and, less than a week after D-Day, at 4.13 am on 13 June the first V1 bomb landed on British soil at Swanscombe, near Gravesend. Herbert Morrison, the Home Secretary, arranged with the Ministry of Information that the press should publish no information about this attack. The War Cabinet agreed that no statement should be made until the enemy had made it public, or until the weight or extent of attack made a statement necessary.

But, unknown to the War Cabinet, the damage had already been done. That afternoon, the Air Ministry, believing that the defences had been successful, had issued a communiqué, which duly appeared in the late editions of the *Evening Standard*:

> RAIDER SHOT DOWN IN EAST LONDON
>
> Two short alerts, the first since April 27, were sounded in London early today. Some districts had three warnings. A raider was brought

down in the East End of London. Several people were killed during the second alert, when bombs fell in a working-class area. Other German aircraft operated over districts in East Anglia, South-Eastern and Southern England, as well as over the Thames Estuary. They did not appear to be carrying out any well-defined attack.

Beaverbrook, who had long been aware of the threat of attack from flying-bombs and rockets was to write: 'Duncan Sandys strongly supported the view that Peenemünde was building V1s and V2s [rockets]. Cherwell opposed the notion that rockets would fall in Britain. He said they would ricochet back to France; that they would fall in the Channel; that the Germans would not waste an engine in such a venture; that they would rather send an airplane that could bring the engine back.' Before the launching-sites were finally over-run, during the main ten-week campaign in the summer of 1944 several thousand rockets – each containing a ton of high explosive – had landed in Southern England, killing 6,000 civilians.

On 25 August 1944, Paris was liberated and a few days later Evelyn Irons, of the *Evening Standard*, having received licence No. 976 from the War Office and Air Ministry, became one of the first official woman war reporters. Within hours she was in France, but soon discovered that she was not allowed into the front line, the army preferring her to cover stories of military hospitals.

Later, she was to tell Anne Sebba: 'Finally, I ran into Janet Flanner of the *New Yorker* in Paris and she suggested the French Army. The French? With their attitude to women? But a woman ceases to be a sex object – if ever there was one – when she gets into uniform, Flanner explained, here in France.' The ruse worked. Early in 1945, Evelyn Irons joined the Première Armée Française and crossed the Rhine into Germany with General de Gaulle. Several French correspondents were also accredited, but she was the only British.'[30]

Among her early despatches was one of the French crossing the Rhine and occupying part of Germany. 'The French troops were terribly ill-equipped – the Allies wouldn't let them have anything – and in the middle of February, a bitter winter that year, half of them wore old tennis shoes because there were not enough boots. But de Gaulle had them all lined up and with a band playing and a tricolour fluttering he marched them in their tennis shoes across a pontoon and onto German soil.'[31]

Another vivid episode was the capture of a village in Bavaria: 'We somehow had got ahead of the advance, and four of us in a jeep came to this village and found no Allied troops had arrived. So we took it ourselves. We were armed – the French would have none of this nonsense about war correspondents not carrying weapons – so we held everyone up at gun-point and accepted their surrender.'

The most notable event, though, for Evelyn Irons was at Pforzhiem on 13 April, 1945, for which she was to become the first woman to receive the Croix de Guerre with Silver Star. The citation stated: '...under violent enemy fire she went in with advance troops volunteering to serve as liaison officer taking part in the transport of wounded.'[32]

Another correspondent very much in the front line had been Gordon Holman, the paper's naval correspondent, and he had been one of the few journalists on the St Nazaire commando raid in 1942. The youngest war correspondent, though, was 19-year-old Tom Pocock, then filing for the Hulton Press – *Picture Post* and *Leader.* He was later to be on the *Daily Mail, Times* and *Daily Express* before joining the *Evening Standard* in 1959. There, until 1973, he acted as 'fireman' and war correspondent, covering hostilities in Algeria, Aden, Borneo, Cyprus, India and Vietnam. He was to remain on the paper until 1988 and in those years was travel editor and, later, special features writer.

However, back in 1945, on 17 March, the Americans had crossed the Rhine at Remagen, to be followed a week later by the British under Field Marshal Montgomery. The advance units of the British Army were now about to see at firsthand the horrors of the concentration camps at Buchenwald and Belsen. Writing in the *Evening Standard,* Patrick Kirwan reported: 'The idea of torture is so abhorrent that it is not easy to believe that practices associated with the Spanish Inquisition could be carried out by twentieth century Europeans.' For the BBC, Richard Dimbleby was to broadcast a most heart-rending account from Belsen: 'I picked my way over corpse after corpse in the gloom, until I heard one voice raised above the gentle undulating moaning. I found a girl. She was a living skeleton.'

Barely a fortnight later, Hitler committed suicide in his bunker in Berlin. At 9.30 in the evening of 1 May 1945, Hamburg Radio, one of the few German radio stations still broadcasting, announced:

> Our Führer, Adolf Hitler, has fallen this afternoon at his command post in the Reich Chancellery, fighting to the last breath against Bolshevism and for Germany. On April 30 the Führer appointed Grand-Admiral Dönitz as his successor. Our new Führer will now speak to the German people.

The war in Europe was now almost over, and on 7 May Dönitz agreed to the unconditional surrender of all German forces to the Allies – Britain, Russia and the United States.

22 (*left*) H. A. Gwynne, editor of *The Standard.*

23 (*below*) *The Standard* auction announcement in the *Newspaper World.*

BY ORDER OF THE COURT.

"THE STANDARD" NEWSPAPER.

MESSRS. WALTER PHELPS & SON

are instructed to Offer for SALE by PUBLIC AUCTION,

At ANDERTON'S HOTEL (Pillar Room), FLEET STREET, LONDON, E.C.

at 3 o'clock on the afternoon of

WEDNESDAY, FEBRUARY 23, 1916,

THE GOODWILL AND COPYRIGHT OF "THE STANDARD" NEWSPAPER.

The GOODWILL AND COPYRIGHT will be sold free of all liabilities, but with the benefit of all subscriptions, together with the advertising and other contracts. The book debt can be taken over by arrangement, or at valuation.

The whole of the Receiver's Interest in the

MACHINERY and PLANT

and general contents of the building situate at 102-3-4-5, Shoe Lane, London, E.C., will also be offered for sale in one lot, subject to such contracts as may have been entered into, of which particulars will be given. The

FREEHOLD and LEASEHOLD PREMISES,

including the Advertisement Offices at 132-134, Fleet Street, can be purchased, or they will be leased at a moderate rental.

Alternately, the Receiver is prepared, with the sanction of the Court, to enter into a favourable agreement with the Purchaser of the Copyright and Goodwill for the rental of the buildings occupied by The Standard Newspaper, together with the plant and facilities for its production.

Full particulars can be obtained on application to Messrs. W. B. Peat & Co., Chartered Accountants, 11, Ironmonger Lane, London, E.C.; or to Messrs. Walter Phelps & Son, New Street Chambers, Birmingham.

24 *Evening Standard* and the first aeroplane newspaper service.

25 Sir Edward Hulton and Lord Beaverbrook (both proprietors of the *Evening Standard*).

26 *Evening Standard* editorial staff during the General Strike 1926.

27 *Evening Standard* composing room, showing a battery of Linotypes, during the 1930s.

28 Abdication Crisis 1936.

29 (*above*) Frank Owen and (*right*) Michael Foot, both editors of the *Evening Standard*.

Late Blighters Final

Evening Standard

Black-out To-night

Black-out To-morrow

No. 35,941 LONDON, SATURDAY, 17. FEBRUARY 1940 ONE PENNY

The Massacre of the R.A.F.

Secret session of Parliament demanded

Premier perturbed – one out of ten planes only return. Another Cabinet reshuffle in sight

Despite the Hush-Hush tactics on the part of our defence chiefs the true facts of the air war situation are gradually leaking out. At the Air Ministry a secret report has been prepared which contains the true balance of the war in the air.

Our airforce has not only lost a perturbing number of its most up-to-date bombers and fighters, but a far higher percentage of its crack flyers than has been admitted. The policy of publishing a weekly casualty list containing between two or three score names of the dead and missing will be overhauled completely. It has misled even people of high rank into a far too optimistic attitude *as regards Britains true position.*

Everybody of course is aware of the fact that the German claim of having shot down 36 out of a total of 44 British bombers in that famous air battle over the Bight of Heligoland is perfectly correct.

But it now transpires that the German airforce does not publish all the losses of its British adversaries. If a flight of British machines is destroyed without trace, no report is given. The underlying idea of this policy is to overawe the British people with concealed terror. The only source of information for people on this side are rumours.

People ask what has happened to pilot officer so and so, and nobody knows anything at all. He is missing, that is all. *The whole matter is to be the principal* question for the next secret session of the *House of Commons.*

M. P.s who were at first inclined to disbelieve these hair-raising stories have meanwhile come round to regard the present state of affairs as highly disquieting.

In Whitehall there reigns an atmosphere of gloom. Mr. Kingsley Wood, who *is conducting a sort of personal investigation,* feels that he has been misled by certain subordinate quarters. The Prime Minister is said to be rather uneasy.

Apart from the losses of the R. A. F. in action, the numbers of machines and *men "destroyed" in accidents has been very* high. Whereas the normal losses in training were expected not to exceed a certain figure per week, it is now reported that this estimate has been at least trebled.

Some of the not very distant relations of Mrs. Oliver Stanley, Lady Wood and Lady Primrose, are seen here discussing the more intimate aspects of the war. You see them both worried. They realise that the dismissal of Mr. Hore-Belisha brings the more delicate issues connected with Jewish influence in Britain to the fore. They represent, so to say, the hidden hand in Downing Street, and, as we say, "Some" hand too.

Is Britain at war with Denmark?

The by now famous exploit of the R.A.F. against the German Northsea coast has been a colossal geographical error. The planes purported to have attacked the island of Sylt and to have damaged the Hindenburg Damm have in reality attacked the Danish island of Roem. Although the Danish Government has treated the incident with commendable reserve, because the damage done to Danish property was comparatively slight, it may be pertinently asked „Are we at war with Denmark? And if so, why?"

His last Trip to the Front

Mr. Hore-Belisha enjoying Paris

Britain no longer secure

Government prepares flight to Canada

As the „Evening Standard" is able to reveal, the British Government are preparing to go to Canada when the grim phase of the war, as predicted by the Prime Minister in his Mansion House speech, is about to begin. The Majority in the Cabinet consider Britain as no longer secure. They have come to the conclusion that a real aerial attack on the British Isles, even if it were strictly limited to military objectives, would create such general disorganisation and chaos, that it would be better to establish a political nerve centre outside of Britain.

The Royal Family would, of course, have to leave the country too. The Royal Tour undertaken last year is regarded as a full dress rehearsal for what will happen in the not too distant future. The Royal Party and the Government would on this occasion be found on men of war. The only ship available is the Battle Cruiser Renown. The Hood and Repulse are undergoing what is politely described as their annual overhaul. They are in Dry Dock, extensive repairs have been necessary after the devastating hits by German bombs and torpedoes.

Meanwhile Mr. Chamberlain is busy forming a shadow Government for the Home country. Obviously the Chiefs of the Fighting Departments would not be sent away. They have to stay behind. Mr. Hore-Belisha has offered his services to act as Liaison Minister in Montreal. He would keep in contact with the fighting services. But all the members of the Inner War Cabinet are certain to leave.

I hear that March 14th has been chosen as a provisional date for the Governmental exodus: it is the day when Hitler seized Czecho-Slovakia. Nothing of the sort is, of course, expected in Downing Street, but the Prime Minister refuses to take any risks.

For the Rich **Rationing in Britain** **For the Poor**

30 German propaganda newspaper dropped over London.

31 *Evening Standard* is bombed 1940.

32 Group Captain Max Aitken with his father, Lord Beaverbrook, 1945.

Evening Standard
45,121 MONDAY, JULY 21, 1969 5d.

MOON LANDING SOUVENIR

THE FIRST FOOTSTEP

Man's first footstep on the moon — a reconstruction of the historic moment.

Human footsteps crunch noiselessly on lunar soil—never to be erased for perhaps a million years.

One of two brave men gazes at this alien world through gold visors with almost unbelieving eyes. No wind, no rain, no sounds shatter the eerie silence. They are there!

Since time flowed, man has gazed at the moon and wondered. Neil Armstrong and Edwin Aldrin today are the first to touch it.

And, as TV screens glow 240,000 miles away, the watching earth pauses in its moment of destiny . . .

More moon colour on centre and back pages

33 Moon Landing 1969.

34 Charles Wintour, editor *Evening Standard*, 1959–76 and 1978–80.

35 Back bench, Shoe Lane. Charles Wintour (third right).

36 Jocelyn Stevens, managing director of Express Newspapers, in 1978.

37 Victor Matthews, chairman of Express Newspapers, at the launch of the *Daily Star*, February 1978. He had led Trafalgar House in the successful takeover.

38 (*left*) Simon Jenkins, editor of the *Evening Standard;* during the merger crisis, 1977.

39 (*below*) Louis Kirby, editor (right), at the *Evening Standard* Drama Awards 1985 with Princess Alexandra and Lord Matthews.

40 John Leese, editor, cuts the cake in December 1988 as the *Evening Standard* leaves Fleet Street for Kensington.

41 Viscount Rothermere in the *Evening Standard* editorial room, Northcliffe House, Kensington.

42 Stewart Steven (editor of the *Evening Standard*), Viscount Rothermere (Chairman, *Daily Mail* and General Trust), Sir David English (Chairman, Associated Newspapers) and Paul Dacre (editor of the *Daily Mail*).

21

Peace in Shoe Lane

Despite a proposal by Winston Churchill to continue the National Government until Japan had been defeated, the Labour Party would agree only until the autumn. On 23 May 1945, therefore, Churchill ended the Coalition. With so many voters overseas, this third 'khaki' election of the century was to be a long-drawn-out affair. On 31 May, Beaverbrook was pleased to hear from Lord Woolton that 'the mixture we want is Churchill the war-winner, Churchill the British bulldog bred in international conference, and Churchill, the leader of a government with a programme of social reform.'[1] In the run-up to the election, from 16 June to 5 July, Beaverbrook was to ensure that his papers were 100 per cent in support of the Conservatives; it has been calculated that one-fifth of the space alloted to election coverage – or 241 column inches in the *Daily Express* – was lavished upon Churchill's campaign tours.

Polling took place on 5 July, but on the previous day Beaverbrook had forwarded to Churchill his letter of resignation: 'You were kind enough to say that, when the election was over, I might be permitted to retire from the Government ... In parting, I want to give you my grateful thanks for so much personal kindness and understanding during the crowded and trying years in which I served under your leadership.' With three weeks having been allowed for the Services' votes to be received from overseas, the result was not declared until 25 July. For Churchill and his party, it turned out to be a rout: Labour 393, Conservatives 189, Liberals 12. To most of the press – the *Daily Mirror* and *Daily Herald* were notable exceptions – the Conservative defeat had been unforeseen, but not for a young John F. Kennedy, covering the campaign for the Hearst papers in America.

On the night of the results, Beaverbrook had arranged a party at Claridge's, confident of a celebration but, with defeat certain, he was to stand up and say to his guests: 'This occasion was intended as a victory feast. In the circumstances it now becomes a last supper.' The next day, in bold headlines, the *Evening Standard* proclaimed:

BRITAIN SWINGS TO THE LEFT – and the Churchill Government goes in a landslide

SOCIALISTS IN
26 LIBERALS OUT: LONDON AND BIRMINGHAM CAPTURED
MASSACRE OF THE LIBERALS

In its leader column, the paper noted: 'The people after an uneasy hiatus have returned a Socialist Government to office with a sweeping majority. There has been some relaxation during that time in the main branches of our national effort. Now the pause is over. The new Prime Minister, Mr Attlee, must form his Cabinet without delay, and begin promptly the business of government ... This is a time to get busy not to theorise.'

While the nation was immersed in the general election, Herbert Gunn, who had succeeded Sidney Elliott as editor, was under pressure from his chairman to improve the quality of the paper. On 14 May 1945, E. J. Robertson wrote that a daily count was being taken of the literals (typesetting errors) in each edition of the paper:

> The *Evening Standard* used to be the cleanest of the three evening papers, now it is by far the worst. I urge you most strongly to take all steps necessary to get back our reputation. It appears that the cause is due to excessive over-setting which inevitably leads to bad edition times. My experience is that an increase in sub-editors very often results in the sending down of too much copy and over-setting which inevitably leads to bad edition times.

Robertson concluded his list of complaints with some comments regarding 'Londoner's Diary':

> I still believe there is room for improvement ... both as regards livelier subjects and also in better writing. On many days recently it has inclined to unnecessary dullness. I should have thought that in these days of small papers every paragraph should not only be hot news but also full of personality about interesting people.[2]

Gunn replied the next day that he had taken all possible steps to avoid literals in the paper:

> It was unfortunate that in the edition of last Friday you sent over, one short front page story got in uncorrected and that this story contained 9–10 literals. The cause does not appear to be excessive over-setting but rather an excess of zeal in trying to get into the paper very late stories. I have also arranged for the Head Reader to tip us off if there is a danger of a 'dirty' story being used and we can take action.[3]

Prior to Gunn taking over the editorship in March 1945, Sidney Elliott had been in the chair, having succeeded Michael Foot one year earlier. Born in London in 1902, Elliott was educated at Glasgow's

Govan High School, and when aged only 20 wrote the *Life of Sir William Maxwell.* He was editor of the *Glasgow Eastern Standard* in 1923 and of the *South Side Standard* the following year. Following spells as assistant editor, *Scot Co-operator* in 1927, and the *Co-op News & Millgate Monthly* in 1928, he joined *Reynolds News* as managing editor in 1929. He moved to the *Evening Standard* in 1942 as a leader writer under Michael Foot and by 1944 was himself editor, but left in the spring of 1945 when the wartime coalition was breaking up, and the *Standard* was preparing to support the Conservative Party. At the time of his leaving, *World's Press News* could report that he had joined the *Daily Mirror* in the advisory executive capacity, for 'political reasons'.[4]

By 1949, however, he was in Melbourne, Australia, as managing editor of the *Argus and Australian Post.* He returned to Britain in 1952 to be general manager of the *Daily Herald,* and the following year became its editor. Five years later he left to become a director of South Wales newspapers. A journalist of strong Socialist convictions, he was also the author of *Co-operative Storekeeping: Eighty Years of Constructive Revolution* (1925) and *England, Cradle of Co-operation* (1937). He died on 9 October 1987.

Herbert Gunn, however, was a very different person. Born at Gravesend, Kent, in 1904 he became a junior reporter on the *Kent Messenger* in 1920 and stayed with that paper until 1925, when he left for the Far East to work as a sub-editor on the *Straits Times* in Singapore. Within twelve months, however, he was back in England, employed by the *Manchester Evening News,* where he remained until 1929, before going to Fleet Street to join the *Evening News.* Two years later he moved to that paper's arch-rival, the *Evening Standard,* as a sub-editor, and in 1933 was promoted to news editor. His next appointment within the Beaverbrook Group took him back to Manchester as northern editor of the *Daily Express* under Arthur Christiansen. Gunn served in Manchester from 1936 until 1938, when he returned to Fleet Street as assistant editor of the *Daily Express,* where in 1943 he was appointed managing editor. It was during those years that Gunn wrote a manhunt headline that has gone down in Fleet Street folklore: 'Man with staring eyes has egg-shaped head'. He also coined the phrase 'It's that man again (ITMA) the famous war-time radio show, starring Tommy Handley'.[5]

As editor of the post-war *Evening Standard,* Gunn achieved a European scoop on 24 September 1945, with the publication of extracts from Hitler's engagement book covering 'the first detailed and authentic account of the Fürher's life in the dying days of the Nazi Reich'. Discovered in a bomb-ruined cellar beneath the Chancellery in Berlin, the charred book had been kept by Hitler's personal adjutant, Sturmbannfürher Heinze Linge, and in it he had related Hitler's every movement, appointment and conference during vital weeks in 1944.[6]

DISGRUNTLED TORIES

Six months after Labour had gained office, Gunn's coverage of the election – prompted by Beaverbrook – was to come under attack from disgruntled Tories. On 25 January 1946, his proprietor received a letter from Ralph Assheton, on behalf of defeated Conservative candidates, complaining of the role taken by the *Standard* and its sister papers:

> Many of the speakers at the meeting took the view that, however inadvertently, you had done the Party no small disservice in the previous years of public opinion by the employment on your papers of some of the ablest and most consistent Left Wing propagandists of the day. Their view was that if you have employed a brilliant propagandist such as Low, an amusing (but none the less deadly) propagandist in Nat Gubbins, a vitriolic propagandist such as Michael Foot, or a subtle propagandist such as J. B. Priestley (to mention but a few) over a period of years, no whirlwind campaign of a few weeks can undo the long-term anti-Conservative work of these men ... I admit, of course, that many of these Left-Wing propagandists are, journalistically, extremely talented – but taking a long term view I suggest that you can sometimes buy this talent for too high a political price.[7]

On 1 February Beaverbrook replied in his usual vein:

> As to the criticism of my newspapers, I can do nothing to meet it. The papers were built up on a conception of freedom which gives a hearing to every Party. In this respect they have always differed from the *Daily Herald*. The cartoons are valued on their merits and not on the opinions they illustrate. The columnists and humorists are treated in the same way. But of course the leader column is different. That is the property of the newspaper and not open to anyone who opposes the paper's policy. But on one matter you all go wrong. Owen and Foot never gave a left turn to the politics of the *Evening Standard*. This will surprise you. But an examination of the files of that newspaper will confirm what I say. There was considerable action in the *Evening Standard* for a Second Front. This may have been misunderstood as a movement of the left. But it was no such thing. And indeed I was responsible for it after I retired from the Government.[8]

With the *Evening Standard* and the *Evening News* locked in a circulation battle – though still restricted in pagination because of newsprint rationing – the activities of the fledgling Labour administration were given extensive news coverage. Both newspapers, apart from their normal parliamentary correspondents, employed extensive use of 'contacts'. Although known by all parties that these practices existed, there was not any great disapproval until April 1947, when Garry Allighan, the Labour MP for Gravesend and a former wireless correspondent of the *Evening Standard,* wrote an article in *World's Press News*:

> THIS MAY BE DYNAMITE!
> Labour MP reveals his concept of how Party News Gets Out.
>
> Every newspaper in the Street has anything up to half a dozen MPs on its 'contacts' list. They always have had – what's the contacts file for, otherwise? Some of the 'contacts' are on a retainer, some get paid for what they produce, some are content to accept 'payment in kind' – personal publicity.
>
> Some of the *Evening Standard* stories have been verbatim reports and having been present at such meetings I would go further and say that they were accurate verbatim reports. Who could have taken the speeches down? I reply: Any one of the score or more MPs who can be seen at every party meeting making voluminous notes.

After the Speaker of the House of Commons had ruled that there was a prima facie case, the article was referred to the Committee of Privileges. Summoned before the committee, Allighan made an unreserved withdrawal and apology. Next to appear was Herbert Gunn, who was asked to name the source of his information about a private meeting of the Parliamentary Labour Party. Gunn replied that he would prefer not to answer the question, as it had always been considered sacred that the names of informants were not disclosed. The Attorney-General ruled that the interest of the public was supreme, in the committee's view. It was important that he should answer, but they could not insist. If he refused, the matter would be reported to the House which would take such action as it thought proper. Gunn agreed that he had no alternative and named his source, a newsagency named Transatlantic Press. Then pressed as to where the agency got the information, Gunn replied: 'An MP'.

'I am afraid I must ask you his name,' said the Attorney-General. 'His name is Garry Allighan,' replied Gunn, adding that Mr Allighan was not paid directly, but that the agency received £30 a week. Allighan was then recalled and admitted that he had supplied the *Evening Standard* with stories. He was paid £120 a month and took 65 per cent of the profits of Atlantic Press. Allighan was found guilty of gross breach of privilege, and was later expelled from the House. Much later, Charles Wintour wrote: 'Apparently on his own and to the immense surprise of his colleagues, he [Gunn] abandoned the principle of protecting his informant.'[9]

ROYAL COMMISSION

Earlier that year, on 26 March, 1947, the Prime Minister had appointed the first Royal Commission on the Press. Clement Attlee and his colleagues had been influenced through the presence at Westminster of 'a large number of Members who had worked inside newspaper offices'. The idea had first been raised almost twelve months earlier at a conference of the National Union of Journalists held in Liverpool on 19 April 1946. A resolution had been passed calling for a public inquiry into the 'ownership, control and financing of national and provincial newspapers, newsagencies and periodicals'. On 29 October, following a six-and-a-half-hour debate the motion for a Royal Commission was passed by 270 votes to 157. Five months were to elapse, however, before Attlee named the commissioners, under the chairmanship of Sir William David Ross, Provost of Oriel College, Oxford. Sixty-one meetings were to be held, thirty-eight of them devoted to the collection of oral evidence from a total of 182 witnesses.

There was little doubt that the Labour government had been concerned at the manner in which the press had supported the Conservatives in the recent election. This was a point emphasised by former *Standard* editor Percy Cudlipp by this time occupying a similar role for the *Daily Herald* when he chaired a meeting on 27 November 1946. The main speaker was the veteran Socialist, Kingsley Martin, who stressed: 'that our serious newspapers with a comparatively small circulation have a political influence quite out of proportion. The vastly circulated press had nothing like a political influence to its circulation.'

As usual, Beaverbrook was quick to comment on any threat to his newspapers; and to Robertson, on his Soundscriber – an early form of tape-recorder – said:

> I will be glad to hear about the Royal Commission on the Press which is one of the Government Agencies in the persecution of newspapers. Sorrow, sorrow ever more. There is nothing I can say about it except to bow my head in misery. It wouldn't be a bad thing if the Socialists cut off all newsprint entirely. I don't care Mr Robertson what the Government tries to do to us. The intention is without doubt to persecute the press, but let the effect of that persecution fall more heavily upon the government press than upon the independent newspapers. Now the way to carry that situation to a conclusion is to refuse to increase your selling price, tighten your belt and let the suffering and misery descend upon the wretches who supported the Socialists in the last election.[10]

As one of the early witnesses to be called before the Commission, E. J. Robertson was an immediate 'Star' before its members. Particular attention, though, was paid to the White List – a list of people whose names were not to be mentioned in any of Beaverbrook's newspapers.

But, as was to be expected, the star witness was Beaverbrook himself, who spoke on 18 March 1948, and had a field day. It was particularly agreeable for him to score off his old antagonist Lady Violet Bonham Carter, and he made the most of his opportunity. What he said was no novelty. He had mentioned it many times in his newspapers, but it apparently surprised the Commission:

> I ran the paper purely for propaganda, and with no other purpose ... In order to make propaganda effective the paper had to be successful. No paper is any good at all for propaganda unless it has a thoroughly good financial position. The policy is that there shall be no propaganda in the news. There is a strong, stern rule, and the most tremendous attempt ... to carry the rule into effect. But we do stumble. It is terrible how we stumble; it is heartbreaking sometimes.[11]

Discussing the lists, he said: 'Some people call it a black list. In the *Evening Standard* it is called the cautionary list, and in the *Daily Express* office it is called the warned list.' On the question of giving directions to his editors he remarked that it was really advice.[12]

The report of the Royal Commission was not published until 26 July 1949. In the words of Stephen Koss: 'The commissioners were defeated by their own prodigious industry, which produced a mound of indigestible and sometimes contradictory material.'

LONG-SERVING JOURNALISTS

As editor, Gunn had inherited a staff containing a number of long-serving journalists, and in November 1948 – at a ceremony organised by the paper's National Union of Journalists (NUJ) chapel – he was able to speak highly of these, including in particular, Alfred E. Whelham, who had joined the *Evening Standard* in 1892, and had only recently retired, and Miss M. T. Hogg, who had started with the paper in 1910. Toasting the long service brigade, the editor mentioned that when Alfred Whelham had joined the paper it had just one telephone, copy came in by runner and there was only one direct telegraph wire to the House of Commons. Time brought promotion to young Alfred and he graduated from 'printer's devil' in the composing room to a copy holder in the readers' department before joining the subs staff with 'Puzzle Corner' and the *St. James's Budget*, the weekly publication, as special – and spare-time – jobs. From there he graduated to the City Desk. Speaking of Miss M. T. Hogg, the editor said: 'She is one of the nicest women I have had the pleasure of meeting. She became woman editress in 1916. "Corisande" was born and lasted from one war to the next. Miss Hogg was an outstanding name in Fleet Street and her personality had impressed itself upon fourteen editors of the *Evening Standard*.'[13]

While these long-serving journalists were being rightly honoured, newcomers – soon to make their names – had been joining the paper. George Gilliat, a former editor, after acting as assistant to Gunn had left for Canada, and he was succeeded by Charles Curran, previously assistant editor of the *Evening News*. Among the writers attracted to the *Standard* at this time were Sam White, to be the paper's Paris correspondent for forty years; Milton Shulman, distinguished film and theatre critic; and Rebecca West, destined to be the Grande Dame of the English literary world. Her memories of that period make interesting reading:

> My closest relationship with the *Evening Standard* was in the few years after the war and during that period I formed a great affection for the paper. All papers have a tendency to be barmy because they are run by loose organisations consisting largely of the barmier sex; and there was something engaging but extreme in the barminess of the *Evening Standard*. It was full of gifted people, no trace of whose gifts ever got into the paper. The features editor in my time, Charles Curran [later Tory MP for Uxbridge] was not very good at his job, but he was one of the great wits of his time and a real authority on political history and political science. No hint of this was to be found in the columns of the *Standard*, which showed no trace either of the superb journalistic flair and the knowledge of how the world works which were the specific gifts of the then editor, Herbert Gunn. The office was a wild, wild garden and its routine appeared efficient and was not. It was a peculiar, amiable, self-satisfied bedlam that never sought to correct its faults. And it was a great paper. Somehow or other, though, the journalists who worked there did not contribute their specific talents, the fact that they were perceptive and intelligent people got through to the paper in some mysterious way hard to define.
>
> They were pleasant and civilised to work with, they were pleasant and civilised to read; and in time their pleasant and civilised interests declared themselves so that the *Evening Standard* can be reckoned to as one of our civilising forces. It has done what Fleet Street and nothing else can do, and has done it superbly.[14]

Sam White, one of Fleet Street's legends, had first wished to join the *Standard* in the mid-1930s but it was not until ten years later that he was to be successful:

If ever I got to London, I thought at the time, this was obviously a newspaper for which I would dearly love to work. Came the great day when, after a £27 steerage passage to England, I arrived on the boat train at Paddington in the midst of the Abdication crisis and there was the *Evening Standard* on sale with a Low cartoon of an impish Beaverbrook. I felt instantly at home, almost as though I had reached a predestined destination. However, a job on the *Standard* or any other Beaverbrook newspaper – or for that matter on any Fleet Street newspaper – eluded me until 1942. In that year, discharged from the British Army with a badly broken leg which I fortified with long sessions in Fleet Street's El Vino bar, I was made a war correspondent for the *Sydney Daily Telegraph*, and the *Standard* bought my services along with other *Telegraph* correspondents. That is how the association started. When I returned to Sydney after the War I was offered the coverage of the North Sydney police court. When I returned to London, after throwing up this job in the winter of 1946, the *Standard* offered me Paris, with no tedious questions regarding my qualifications. And there I still am, an old man surveying a cemetery of alleged scoops.[15]

Milton Shulman, a former intelligence officer in the Canadian Army, was to be another who was to serve the paper for more than forty years. From his war-time experiences he had written *Defeat in the West*, the first study of the conflict as seen by the Germans. It was highly praised, especially by George Malcolm Thomson, at that time book critic of the *Evening Standard.* Thomson mentioned the book to Beaverbrook who asked to see Shulman – then working on Reuters' foreign desk – and as a result he was engaged for 'Londoner's Diary'. From there, Shulman was selected by Beaverbrook as the paper's film critic.[16]

As such he pioneered a new style of reviewing, 'with an enthusiasm, a wit and a talent that was soon being quoted all over London. But the big film companies were not pleased', and in December 1952 the London representatives of the Motion Picture Association of America decided to withdraw all advertising from the *Evening Standard* and from the *Sunday Express*, 'whose critic, Logan Gourlay, had also offended them to a lesser extent'. After the ban had been in effect for a month – with a possible annual loss to the group of £250,000 – the news was leaked. In retaliation, Beaverbrook barred the film companies concerned from advertising in the *Daily Express*; and as newsprint rationing was, in effect, restricting the size of the paper, there was no lack of advertisers willing to fill the gaps. The American film companies sought assistance from the British groups but were rebuffed, Sir Alexander Korda describing their actions as 'disgustingly silly'.

As Charles Wintour was later to write in his classic *Pressures on the Press*: 'Eventually hostilities ceased. The advertising returned to the *Evening*

Standard, and, in due course, Shulman moved on to drama criticism. Later, he entered the television industry, and, later still, to my great pleasure, returned to the *Evening Standard* as drama critic and columnist where he demonstrates every week that his pen has not lost its cutting edge.' Shulman later stood down as drama critic and went on to write a witty and much-read weekly column on the arts. In this, on 9 October 1992, he discussed that attempt in 1953 to censor critics:

> Although there had been occasional attempts by film companies to pressurise newspapers into ridding themselves of critics with astringent views, this was by far the most concerted attempt ever organised by a production cabal to dictate the terms upon which they would advertise. But in threatening Lord Beaverbrook the companies had taken on the wrong man ... It is perhaps the only time in his controversial career that he was acclaimed by rival papers and congratulated by commentators who normally reviled him ... In the 16 years I worked for him as a film and theatre critic, I cannot recall a single time when he asked me to modulate my views or write to his or his editor's instructions.

Of the young men who had joined the *Evening Standard* after the Second World War, the best-known was to be Charles Wintour, who was eventually to be on the paper for almost thirty years. Educated at Oundle School and Peterhouse, Cambridge, he served in the Army, being awarded the MBE (Mil.), the Croix de Guerrre and Bronze Star, and was mentioned in Despatches. As a young officer attached to Supreme Headquarters, Allied Expeditionary Force in Paris, he was friendly with Arthur Granard, aide to Air Chief Marshal Tedder, the Deputy Supremo. As Lord Forbes, Granard had written the gossip column in the *Sunday Express,* and 'he said out of the blue, "If ever you want an introduction to Lord Beaverbrook, let me know".'[17]

After the war, Wintour wrote to Granard, and a fortnight later 'I was amazed to receive an invitation to visit Lord Beaverbrook at his flat in Park Lane ... Beaverbrook suggested that I should write an article on the difference between British and American methods of work'; and shortly after Wintour had sent off the article he was engaged by the *Evening Standard* on a three-month trial as a leader writer at a salary of £14 a week. After five months he approached the editor, Herbert Gunn, and asked if the trial had been satisfactory. 'Oh, don't bother about that,' Gunn replied. Among the many leaders written by Wintour during this period was one concerning the assassination of Mahatma Gandhi on 30 January 1948: 'Written with Morris Finer in 15 minutes against the clock it was a seamless leader.'[18] Wintour was later to say 'He [Gunn] was a very kind man and a real professional' and 'I owe him a real debt of gratitude for what he taught me'.

LOW DEPARTS

While these new names had been joining the paper, the *Standard* was now about to lose probably its greatest asset. With the government-dictated small-size newspapers, the *Standard* could no longer afford room for the full-sized cartoons by Low 'and my past had spoilt me for settling down tamely to a life of making small drawings that gave me no pleasure ... No more would I work for one paper alone. I would arrange a home base, expand my foreign connections and take on "special" jobs abroad.' On 2 December 1949, therefore, he wrote to Beaverbrook: 'The Oldest Inhabitant will inevitably decline into dullness and boredom'.

Looking back on their long friendship, Beaverbrook was greatly distressed and replied from his Jamaica home:

Dec. 9 1949
Black Friday

My Dear Low,

Your letter is an unwelcome message.

I always look over my letters here before opening them myself, for I have no Secy. or Typist. Then I select the pleasant-looking lot and read them. The rest I put off until after lunch.

Your letter was in the first batch because I expected to hear that you wished me well for Christmas or that you and Mrs Low would visit Jamaica or that you had changed your mind about Churchill. Instead I got the worst letter first. That's the way life has treated me far too often.

Your decision is a disaster. It is unnecessary and inadvisable. That's what I think of it ...

Don't forget your old friend,
Yours ever,
BEAVERBROOK

Earlier that year, Beaverbrook had been involved in a great row with Churchill. On 11 February 1949, the *Standard* had printed a leader declaring that the Liberals should run more candidates in the next general election: 'The Liberal cause must be kept constantly before the people. If the Liberals refuse to fight for their faith, they will lose their battles by default.'

Upon reading this, a furious Churchill immediately despatched a telegram to Beaverbrook in Jamaica:

Leading article *Evening Standard* February 11 is so obviously intended to injure Tory chance in impending by-elections that alas I cannot while remaining leader accept your most kind and attractive invitation to be so publicly your guest in Jamaica stop I am making arrangements at hotel I do not exaggerate importance of your newspaper action in our affairs nor of course is our friendship affected stop Trust you will be able to give me good news of your health and that we shall meet when I arrive 8th or 9th [March] it is a sad world Winston.[19]

Churchill also expressed his anger when telephoning Robertson, the paper's chairman, in a 'bitter conversation'. Beaverbrook immediately telegraphed back, hoping that Churchill would propose 'no such change', following it up with another telegram that same day:

> Personally I deplore *Standard* leader and I have asked Robertson for enquiry into circumstances stop I can tell you more when I hear results stop Surely Conservatives should grasp simple truths that Express Group help their cause more than any other newspapers on account of widespread circulation and independent policy.

Although sending this telegram, Beaverbrook had not even read the leader – a fact he was to reveal to Brendan Bracken later, but he did not wish to hurt Churchill's feelings. Two days later, Churchill telegraphed: 'My reaction was too impulsive but I feel that all we have worked for all our lives is at stake in the near future.' He agreed to go to Jamaica and then abandoned the idea because of the political situation in Britain. With a possible general election in the offing, Churchill thought he should not be away from England.

In August 1949 Churchill stayed at Beaverbrook's villa, La Cappocina, in the South of France, and while there became seriously ill with the first of his strokes. The press were informed that he had contracted a chill while bathing. Churchill's health soon improved, however, and he told fellow house-guest Mike Wardell, once the *Standard*'s managing director but now a publisher in Canada: 'The dagger struck, but this time it was not plunged to the hilt. At least, I think not.'[20]

Six months later, on 24 February 1950, in a fiercely-fought election, Labour retained power with an overall majority of six – 315 to 309. The *Evening Standard* reported:

> **LASSOED AND FINISHED**
>
> The Government has been lassoed by Churchill. Scarcely a hair's breadth separates Socialists from Tories and that margin is useless to the Socialists for the working of a programme which the country, by a majority of votes, has condemned. The Socialist steamroller has been smashed to scrap ... An early election is inevitable, but it by no means follows that it must be left to the Socialists to choose the

time. Given the inevitability of a new election the Socialists may well concentrate their efforts on some desperate measure to snatch popularity from the Tories. Any such stunt is doomed to failure.

One of the MPs returned in the Labour administration was John Strachey, as Member for West Dundee. He was appointed Secretary of State for War, leading to a front-page attack in the *Evening Standard* 'suggesting that his Communist past made him unreliable, which represented a kind of nadir in scurrility'.[21] Strachey was to remain in the government. The *Standard* was wrong and its attack led to fierce condemnation from political leaders and other sections of the press.

For some two years, Gunn had been subjected to an almost daily stream of memos from Beaverbrook:

June 27, 1949

MR GUNN: I have received your letter of the 21st June. I hope you will believe me that nothing justifies you presenting stale news. Such a proceeding is not justified by a lunch to one of your staff.

July 3, 1950

MR GUNN: I see the British Magazine in Moscow, called *British Ally*, is threatened and that the circulation is down to 15,000. You should attack that publication, Mr Gunn, It doesn't serve any useful purpose at all, save only the waste of taxpayers' money.

July 13, 1950

MR GUNN: I think your leader column was very good on the subject of newsprint. I wish that the newspapers might expose that situation in its entirety. It wouldn't be enough for one newspaper to take it up.[22]

During the final months of his editorship, Gunn had been endeavouring to make the paper more sensational and down-to-earth as a direct rival to the *Evening News*. Beaverbrook, however, was determined that it should remain sophisticated, catering especially for the City and the West End. The result was inevitable: Gunn resigned without recrimination or bitterness, leaving for the *Daily Sketch* where in the following eight years, through brilliant and aggressive leadership, he was to build up the circulation to 1,340,000. As Francis Williams later wrote: 'For years the *Daily Sketch* fumbled from disaster to disaster under a succession of editors ... only when a large degree of authority and independence was given to its editor Mr Herbert Gunn did it – whether one liked his methods or not – begin to increase its circulation at a phenomenal rate.'[23] Unfortunately, Gunn was to pay a high price for his success, dying before he was sixty.

22

Death of Beaverbrook

The new editor after Herbert Gunn left was Percy Elland. Aged 41, he came from the North-East, where his family owned a chain of stores. His first job in journalism was as a reporter in Doncaster before joining the *Manchester Evening News*, and from there he progressed to the *Daily Express*, Manchester, where he rose from sub-editor to northern editor.[1] Called by Beaverbrook to Shoe Lane to take editorial charge, one of Elland's first priorities was to consider the *Standard*'s coverage of the forthcoming general election. Elland was fortunate in having the newly-promoted Charles Wintour as political editor and William Alison as the paper's political correspondent, a position he had held with distinction for almost thirty years.

As for the Labour government, with its majority of only six, its days were bound to be numbered, and in October 1951 another general election was held. Beaverbrook believed that 'the Conservatives will get a majority of 100'. However, he was now openly lacking in faith in their policy and on 15 October the Crusader logo on the front page of the *Daily Express* appeared in chains and remained so for the rest of his life. As for the result, the Conservatives were returned with a majority of only 16. The *Evening Standard* reported:

IT'S CHURCHILL
But it's a close finish
MAJORITY MAY BE AS LOW AS 15

In its leader column on 27 October the paper commented:

Winston's task

> Mr Churchill's immediate task is not to assemble a coalition but to form a Tory Government as strong as possible and to produce an immediate programme. The future of the British Empire, and with it the future of the Tory Party waits upon the conduct of that office in the next few months.

As editor of the *Standard*, Percy Elland was very much a man in the Beaverbrook mould: he knew what his proprietor wanted and was determined that it would be provided. Beaverbrook appeared to be delighted with his choice, as this message from Nassau in 1955 was to indicate: 'Mr Elland, there is nothing I miss so much as the *Evening Standard* when night comes and I am waiting for dinner. I am sure many of your readers feel the same way.'[2] There were, though, the occasional criticisms: 'In Friday's *ES* there are three turnaways. You should cut down your turnaways into the inside of the paper. You should never have three stories that have to be turned, except in great crises, immense events. In the ordinary course of news, there is nothing that will justify three turnaways.' And on another occasion: 'Mr Elland I do not admire your front-page cartoons but evidently you do so I bow to you and bend the knee and submit and do it gracefully at that.'[3]

At Beaverbrook's promptings the paper ran a campaign against the British Council and was also vociferous in its protests at the practice of the National Trust taking over historic houses, while allowing the previous owners to continue to live in them. But 'essentially it remained a fun paper'.

DEATH OF A KING

On 6 February 1952, the nation was stunned to learn of the sudden death of King George VI, who had seemingly recovered from an operation for lung cancer.

The *Evening Standard* announced:

THE KING DIES
IN HIS SLEEP
A peaceful end
this morning

> The *Evening Standard* announces with deep regret that the King died early this morning. The announcement came from Sandringham at 10.45 a.m. It said: 'The King, who retired to rest last night in his usual health, passed peacefully away in his sleep early this morning.' With him at Sandringham were the Queen, Princess Margaret and the King's grandchildren, Prince Charles and Princess Anne. The King was 56. It is 136 days since the operation on his lung. Yesterday he was out rabbit shooting for several hours. To everybody he appeared to be in the very best of health.'

On the same page, the paper announced that Princess Elizabeth would be returning from East Africa, where she and Prince Philip had been about to commence their world tour: 'The new Queen is flying back to London immediately. She did not hear the news until 45 minutes after the announcement from Sandringham. Her aircraft will arrive in London at 4.30 p.m. tomorrow.'

In the House of Commons that afternoon, the Prime Minister, Winston Churchill, said: 'Mr Speaker, the House will have learned with deep sorrow of the death of His Majesty King George VI. We cannot at this moment do more than record a spontaneous expression of our grief.'

In its leader column, the *Evening Standard* commented:

THE KING

All had seemed well with the King's health. The operation on his lung had apparently been successful. His convalescence seemed satisfactory. Only a few days ago he appeared to be in good health when he waved good-bye to Princess Elizabeth and Prince Philip as they left on the tour they had undertaken on his behalf ... He came to the throne unwillingly. As Duke of York he had always assumed that his brother Edward would either have children or outlive him – and in that latter expectation he was proved correct ... In all that he did the Queen sustained him, devoting her brilliant gifts to strengthening the institution of monarchy and to lightening the heavy burden ... Today as the innumerable cares of State fall on the young and gracious shoulders of Elizabeth the Second, the nation is comforted with the knowledge that on her return, with her able husband, Prince Philip, her mother will be there to offer comfort and guidance.

In a 12-page Royal Funeral Edition on 15 February the *Standard* paid full respects:

THE LAST SALUTE
The Queen scatters a handful of red earth from a silver bowl on her father's coffin
FROM THE SHADOWS

All this week, under the dark oaken vaults of Westminster Hall, the candles cast radiance over the coffin they encircled, waking fire on the Crown, the Orb and the Sceptre that lay upon it, and on the splendid uniforms of the soldiers keeping vigil. Out of the half-light, into the radiance, filed a nation on pilgrimage, paying the silent tribute of the heart to their departed King ... A young generation now steps forward led by a young Queen. Together, on the enduring foundation of her father's reign, they resolve this day to build a new Elizabethan Age of heroism, daring and success.

EDITORIAL CHANGES

Meanwhile, on the *Evening Standard* itself there were to be a number of key editorial changes, and in 1953 John Junor was appointed by Beaverbrook as deputy editor. Educated at Glasgow University, after war-time service as a pilot in the Fleet Air Arm, Junor had stood as a Liberal candidate in the 1945 general election, losing by only 642 votes. He next turned to journalism, joining the London office of the *Sydney Sun*, but was sacked two weeks before Christmas 1947: 'In retrospect it turned out to be the luckiest thing that ever happened to me.'[4] He was then taken on by Arthur Christiansen as a reporter on the *Daily Express*, but within months was in charge of the Cross-Bencher political column on the *Sunday Express*. In 1951 he was promoted to the post of assistant editor and chief leader writer of the *Daily Express*, remaining there for two years before transferring to the *Evening Standard* as deputy editor.

In 1954, John Junor was appointed editor of the *Sunday Express*, and was to remain in control until 1986 – a Fleet Street record. For much of that time he wrote the hugely successful 'JJ' column. He was knighted in 1980, and retired as editor of the *Sunday Express* six years later. In 1989, he joined the *Mail on Sunday*, where he was to write a hugely popular column.[5]

Writing in his memoirs, *Listening for a Midnight Tram*, he could say of his days on the *Evening Standard*:

> I served on that newspaper for over a year and found it a happy experience apart from the fact that I was in enormous pain from a stomach ulcer ... Percy Elland, the editor of the *Evening Standard*, was a great-hearted, plump, rosy-cheeked man with twinkly eyes and a splendid sense of humour. He also had an enormous sense of duty ... At times Percy found the going a little tough. He was not a political editor, and so found himself at a disadvantage with Beaverbrook.[6]

One such example concerned putting racing on the front page of the first edition, a decision taken by Beaverbrook's son, Max Aitken, but which drew the wrath of the proprietor:

> Beaverbrook turned on Elland but Percy gamely held his ground. He argued that the first edition was essentially bought by people wanting to know which horse to back, that sales had been falling off recently, especially in the suburbs, and that this was a calculated and deliberate attempt to regain some early edition sales. His argument was that people who bought the first edition for racing would subsequently buy later editions to see the race results.[7]

On 26 May 1954, the day after Beaverbrook celebrated his 75th birthday, a luncheon attended by 600 of his staff was held at the Dorchester Hotel. In 'The Big Lunch Edition' of the *Standard*, under the headlines:

Today the Beaverbrook Boys meet to toast
the dynamo they are proud to call their boss
75 IN THE SUN

the article went on:

> So far as we are concerned he is simply the head of our newspaper family. He is famous, important and – it is widely believed – very rich. But it is our privilege today to take these matters for granted and approach him on a more intimate footing … Once more he is among those who have added the pleasure of liking him. Here – look at him – is the hardest-working labourer in our vineyard, worn out by toil! Here is the true story of the Beaverbrook legend.[8]

With the departure of John Junor to edit the *Sunday Express*, Charles Wintour, having been assistant editor of that paper during 1952–4, returned to the *Evening Standard* as deputy editor, and one of his first successes was to bring back Randolph Churchill. Having noticed Churchill's brilliant invective in *The Spectator*, Wintour telephoned him and asked if he would comment on the Crichel Down affair, which was bringing the Ministry of Agriculture into dispute. Randolph Churchill agreed immediately and so, after a gap of some sixteen years, he was back once more at Shoe Lane: 'The fact that his father was still Prime Minister added power to his pen.' Wintour offered a contract of £65 per week, for which, apart from his regular contributions, he agreed to write two articles on the forthcoming general election.[9]

By the time the general election came around, on 27 May 1955, Winston Churchill had resigned and had been replaced by his deputy, Anthony Eden, who was to lead the Conservatives to a splendid win:

NINE SEATS TO GO – AND EDEN HAS A FINE VICTORY
MAJORITY IS SIXTY
Tories canter home

> The Tories are back in power with a handsome majority. Later this afternoon they had a clear majority of 59 seats, with only nine remaining to be declared. If these seats stay the same as last time, 60 will be the final Tory majority.

In its leader column, the *Standard* commented: 'The Tories have swept to a splendid victory. For the first time in nearly 100 years a Government is returned to power with an increased margin of seats.'

Throughout Eden's premiership, Randolph Churchill proved to be a thorn in his side. Travelling to the United States on the same ship as the new Prime Minister in January 1956 Churchill was refused an interview. 'Very curious,' was Randolph's reaction. However, on 2 February he was able to return to the attack when the paper carried his report on the Washington conference being held to discuss on Anglo-American agreement on the Middle East. He wrote:

> When statesmen and politicians can't think of anything else to say they always drag in God. Last night's declaration did it twice over, both in preamble and peroration. It was obvious from the start of the conference ... that as no planning had been done by either side, no joint plan could be produced. The declaration and the communiqué were full of pious platitudes and impeccable opinions.

The Times was to say of Randolph: 'As a political journalist he was usually astute and, sometimes, brilliant.' However, Eden was to remain the target, and under the headline 'Britain in Danger' Randolph wrote: 'I was told that the Prime Minister was doing his best. I do not doubt it, and that is why I am sure there has got to be, quickly, a change in the occupancy of 10 Downing Street.'[10] In the debate that followed, Eden was taunted in the House of being afraid of the Churchill pen.

NEW LEADER WRITER

Meanwhile, the *Evening Standard* had recently engaged a new leader writer: Robert Edwards, later to be editor of four national newspapers. Born in Farnham, Surrey, he had entered journalism on the *Reading Mercury* and, following service in the RAF, joined the *Tribune* under Michael Foot. From there, he moved in 1950 to *The People* as a reporter, then returned to edit the *Tribune* for three years. During the 1955 newspaper strike, on a radio programme with other editors, he argued with John Junor over the merits of the new Prime Minister and as a result, Junor recommended him to Lord Beaverbrook.[11] He joined the *Evening Standard*, ostensibly as a leader writer, 'at a salary of £50 a week ('and you can have what proportion of that you like in expenses')', but wrote few leaders and many articles on social subjects.[12]

Edwards was later to say in his book *Goodbye to Fleet Street*: 'most of the leaders were written in time for the main editions by the chief leader-writer, the young, studious Rudolph Klein. Jack Waterman, who became a stylish sports writer, and I struggled with first edition leaders on a wide variety of London topics. They were usually melted down by 1.00 p.m., especially when Beaverbrook was in town.'

On 13 March 1956, Randolph Churchill once more assailed Eden in the paper: 'WHY I ATTACK SIR ANTHONY, IT IS NOT A VENDETTA.' Embarrassed by these criticisms of the Prime Minister, Beaverbrook invited Edwards to his home and said: 'Bob. It is good journalism to say the opposite to everyone else. Why don't you write a defence of Eden in the *Evening Standard*?'

From this meeting, Edwards, using the pseudonym Richard Strong, sprang to the defence of Eden:

> I was hidden with a typewriter in a room in the *Evening Standard* basement and only Percy Elland and Charles Wintour were supposed to know that I was the author. At great speed I wrote two ludicrous articles, parodying Beaverbrook's style, in defence of Eden ... Beaverbrook read through the drafts. 'It's a wonderful thing, he said, 'defending the indefensible,' and did not alter a word.[13]

Randolph Churchill, instantly dubbing the new columnist 'Lord Richard Strong', was in no doubt as to who was behind the affair: 'Within a few days of Beaverbrook's return he has given new proof to Fleet Street and Westminster that he is still firmly in the saddle by discovering and establishing an outstanding new political journalist, a Mr Richard Strong.'

A few months later, Edwards was asked by the editor to write all the leaders on the Suez War: 'I began to tell Percy that unfortunately I was so opposed to Eden's invasion that I could not possible write leaders in support of him ... It seemed to me my career was in some jeopardy.' He then wrote to Beaverbrook, who replied promptly:

> I have written to Mr Elland. I am sure he will make more and more use of your extraordinary abilities. Before long you will be a pillar in the temple. It was Dean Inge when attacked as a pillar of the *Evening Standard* who replied that he was no pillar; he was two columns.[14]

A few weeks later, Edwards was appointed deputy editor of the *Sunday Express*. He then became deputy editor of the *Daily Express* in 1959, and editor of the *Express* in 1961, from which post he was fired nine months later. A Siberian period followed, as editor of the Beaverbrook-owned *Glasgow Evening Citizen*, which he adored, but a year later he was restored as editor of the *Daily Express*.[15] He survived this time for three years until he was fired by Max Aitken. He then became editor of *The People* from 1966 until 1972, and of the *Sunday Mirror* for a record thirteen years. He was later awarded the CBE.

SUEZ CRISIS

Throughout the summer of 1956, Eden and his Cabinet were enmeshed in the problems of Egypt. Colonel Nasser, the Egyptian President, had recently nationalised the Suez Canal, the main commercial artery between Britain and the Far East; and, following Nasser's refusal to negotiate, the decision was taken by Britain and France to invade Egypt and regain control.

On 2 November 1956, the *Evening Standard* reported:

PARATROOPS TAKE PORT SAID AIRFIELD, THEN FAN OUT
FIRMLY IN AFTER
TOUGH FIGHTING
Red Devils fight
Nasser's tanks
BIG NEW FRENCH FORCE MAKES AIRDROP THIS AFTERNOON

> Wave after wave of British and French paratroops today landed in Egypt. The main force, dropping from 600 feet, seized the airport of Gamal, five miles from Port Said. They have had some tough fighting, said the Allied C-in-C, General Sir Charles Keighley, this afternoon. But, he added, the paratroops are now firmly established, and are setting out from the airfield.

In its leader column on 5 November the paper noted: 'The troops are in. It is a critical time for Britain. The time for partisan argument is past. The thoughts of the nation must now be to giving the fullest possible support to the men who are in action on Egyptian soil.'

Among the correspondents sent out to cover the Suez conflict, Randolph Churchill was flown to Tel Aviv to obtain the Israeli viewpoint. There he met Anne Sharpley, who was in charge of gathering hard news while Randolph telephoned his opinionated articles to the office. Being a Churchill he was given every facility by the Israelis and he positively revelled in the political intrigue. Anne Sharpley had joined the *Evening Standard* two years earlier, following a period on the *Manchester Evening News*, and was quickly to become one of the leading journalists of her generation. Apart from war despatches, her work ranged from crime reporting and the coverage of state occasions – including Grace Kelly's wedding to Prince Rainier – to light accounts of London life. As a foreign correspondent, she had nerves of steel: 'She was shot at in Cyprus, expelled from Egypt, and coped simultaneously with war and Randolph Churchill in Algeria.' Her colleague, Angus McGill, was later to write: 'Possibly her biggest scoop occurred on her own doorstep, when terrorists took over a flat in Balcombe Street, London, where she lived. The street was sealed off by police, no one was allowed in except residents. Anne, all opposition thus annihilated, covered the famous siege from her sitting-room window.' Charles Wintour, for many years her editor, said: 'Anne Sharpley was so talented; she was able to dictate from her notes quite fluently.' In later years she contracted a recurrent tropical fever, forcing her to give up full-time journalism. This had affected her during her coverage of the Churchill funeral 'when she dried up'.[16] She died in 1989.

HUNGARIAN INVASION

While the British and French were involved in Suez, Russian troops had been invading Hungary. Reporting the story for the *Standard* was Evelyn Irons, their distinguished war correspondent. She was later to recall:

> In November 1956, when I was once more based in Shoe Lane, there was another revolution, this time in Hungary. In Budapest they were singing and dancing in the streets, burning piles of books and records from sacked shops. Next morning the Soviet tanks rolled in. With Basil Davidson of the *Herald* I tried to stay out in the streets to see what they were up to, but we found it a bit too much, and took refuge, like the other correspondents from London, in the British Legation. Eighty people were jammed in there for a week, with minuscule rations but plenty of bull's blood of Eger to drink, which inflamed our fury at being unable to communicate our reports. After five days, some of us made up an international convoy and tried to get out of the city. After 12 miles, a Russian officer stopped us, and admired our cars. Next time the British tried it on their own, and made it to Vienna, and telephones. That was my last big story for the paper. A few months later I told Percy Elland, the editor, that I wanted to go back to New York. He said no. So I quit, and went.[17]

Meanwhile, stunned by the Suez fiasco, and the lack of support from the people, Eden, a sick man, resigned. Everyone believed that R. A. (Rab) Butler would be his successor. Randolph Churchill, however, thought differently, and was about to gain his greatest political scoop. All the leader writers were plumping for Butler, but Randolph declared that Harold Macmillan would become Prime Minister. While the rest of Fleet Street were desperately trying to find out who the next Prime Minister would be, Randolph , on the phone for half the night, advised Anne Sharpley to telephone Lady Dorothy Macmillan. Summoned from her bath, Lady Dorothy came to the telephone: 'Is it out already?' she asked, and realised that she had inadvertently confirmed her husband's appointment.

During this period of change in the decade after the Second World War, the managing director and chairman of the *Evening Standard* had been Owen Rowley, who was to serve Beaverbrook for thirty-three years. As publicity manager for the Express group in the 1920s he had helped to introduce the crossword into British newspapers. However, his greatest contribution to the financial success of British newspapers was his determination to expand massively the small-ads.[18] In April 1959, Percy Elland stood down as editor to become chairman and managing director. However, it was not to be a long tenure, for he died less than twelve months later, on 3 March 1960. His predecessor, Owen Rowley, said of him: 'He was a natural journalist with a brilliant sense of news, always at his best on the big occasion ... The editorship of a London evening newspaper and the *Evening Standard* in particular is an assignment calling for a journalist of the toughest fibre and the fact that Elland retained that post with distinction for eight years is a tribute to his endurance as well as his worth.'[19]

WINTOUR TAKES OVER

Now in his early thirties, Charles Wintour was to edit the *Standard* from 1959–76 and from 1978–80 – a longer period than any other editor with the exception of Dr Stanley Lees Giffard. During this time he was rightly described as 'the finest editor in Fleet Street, if judged solely by his ability to spot and encourage nascent talent'.[20] This talent was to include six future Fleet Street editors: Trevor Grove (*The Sunday Telegraph*); Max Hastings (*The Daily Telegraph*); Simon Jenkins (*The Times*); Magnus Linklater (*London Daily News* and *The Scotsman*); Derek Marks (*Daily Express*); and Roy Wright (*Daily Express*).

As the new editor, Wintour inherited 'Vicky', one of the great cartoonists. Thanks to Wintour's efforts, he had joined the paper the previous autumn, on 3 November 1958, after leaving the *Daily Mirror.* The contract, drawn up by Wintour, without Percy Elland being aware of it, was at a salary of £6,000 a year and he was to enjoy 'complete freedom in the selection and treatment of subject matter for your cartoons and in the expression therein of a policy in which you believe.'[21]

Within a week of starting, Vicky was more than to prove his worth with the introduction of 'Supermac' on 6 November 1958. Vicky's most famous creation, it showed Prime Minister Harold Macmillan as Superman, the American comic-strip character. However, 'Supermac' backfired on Vicky and 'became one of Macmillan's assets in the General Election of 1959'. Vicky was to say: 'This figure, Supermac, has really boomeranged on me now'. Other well-known characters in the Vicky gallery included 'White Rabbit' (Eden) and 'Totempole' (Charles de Gaulle).

However, despite his world-wide acclaim, Vicky suffered greatly from depression, and on 13 February 1966, he took an overdose of sleeping pills and died in London. Charles Wintour was later to say: 'Vicky was my greatest triumph. He had been trained by Gerald Barry, of the *News Chronicle*, and had been told to read Shakespeare and Dickens, to go to Lord's and to absorb everything English. Prior to his death, Vicky didn't know what to do about Rhodesia. He was deeply, deeply depressed, but said: "Whatever happens I've never been happier than at the *Standard*".'[22]

During the early months of Wintour's editorship, however, his relationship with Randolph Churchill was to come under strain, Randolph wanted to go to America and the paper refused to send him. As a consequence, after lunch at the Savoy with Sir William Carr, owner of the *News of the World*, he resigned from the *Standard*. On 5 September 1959, Wintour wrote to Beaverbrook: 'I am disappointed that Randolph Churchill has left us at the moment when he might have repaid some of the time and money we have spent on him. His election reports might have been quite entertaining.' Beaverbrook, in a pensive mood, replied: 'I am sorry that Randolph Churchill's gone away, but there are advantages and you got most of the disadvantages.'

Randolph, though, was to have regrets later, and contacted his former editor. The following day, 28 November 1959, Wintour wrote to Beaverbrook: 'Randolph Churchill rang yesterday to ask if the *Evening Standard* was interested in taking him back ... Personally, I would like to see Randolph Churchill back in the *Standard* although he is of course the most troublesome contributor I have ever met. He does bring news into the paper, and he is someone who creates interest in the paper.' After contacting Randolph direct, Beaverbrook informed Wintour three days later: 'Randolph Churchill would prefer to stay with the *News of the World*'.[23] This was to be a 'nagging sore' with Beaverbrook, who had refused to pay Randolph's expenses.

Although Beaverbrook was now in his eightieth year, time had certainly not mellowed him and he was as alert as ever, daily dictating to his editors: 'Mr Wintour your Diary paragraphs are too long.' On another occasion he wrote to Charles Wintour, who had sent him a message on *Evening Standard* headed paper, though trying to minimise his offence by typing his message on the reverse side of a previously used sheet, 'Don't waste valuable letter paper.'[24]

THE ELDERS

Churchill and Beaverbrook, now very much the elders, continued to see each other regularly, whether in Jamaica, the South of France or in London, and in May 1960 Beaverbrook was thrilled to receive, on his 81st birthday, an engraved silver box from Churchill, destined for the archives at Fredericton, New Brunswick. A delighted Beaverbrook remarked: 'Many will see it and they will say, 'Our Boy' must have been a "somebody".' Friendship, however, had not prevented Churchill complaining of two cartoons by Vicky which had appeared in the *Standard* in February and March. Both had referred to Britain's difficult relations with Rhodesia and South Africa, and he had thought that they were contrary to Beaverbrook's way of thinking as well as his own, and that they would help no one 'but our enemies'.

On 2 December 1961, shortly after Beaverbrook had attended Churchill's 87th Birthday dinner at Hyde Park Gate, Churchill wrote to him: 'I think you know how much your friendship has meant to me over the years.' Beaverbrook could look back on the previous decade with particular pleasure, as during that period he had published six books. He told Charles Wintour in May 1963: 'In ten years' time, if I am remembered at all, it will not be for my newspapers. It will be for my books.'[25]

The book reviewer on the *Evening Standard* at this time was Malcolm Muggeridge, who had been brought back to the paper by Wintour. Muggeridge's tenure, though, was to come to an end following an article for *McLean's*, a Canadian magazine, about Fredericton, where Muggeridge said that his former employer had memorialised himself in his own lifetime 'to a degree which might have been considered excessive if accorded to Napoleon in Corsica or Shakespeare in Stratford-upon-Avon'. After seeing the article, Beaverbrook wrote to Wintour:

> I make no objection to Muggeridge's attacks. On the contrary, I find them amusing. But it is all old stuff. I could have helped him with some fresh material. No one is asked to look after my reputation. That stands on the foundation of fifty years of hard work. Errors there have been. Mistakes many. Much service.

Muggeridge's contract was not renewed, the news of which he received with some relief. On 4 May 1964, he wrote to his former editor:

> My dear Charles, I have thoroughly enjoyed our association and the fact that it is ending is good news has nothing to do with you. Would you please convey to Lord Beaverbrook the contents of this letter. I am particularly anxious that he should know that, far from wanting to hang on to his employment, I only entered it reluctantly at your persuasion, and that I most urgently wanted to leave it the moment I sniffed a breath of displeasure from his direction.

Much to Beaverbrook's delight, Michael Foot, fresh from the *Daily Herald*, and following his appraisal of a biography of Lord Lyttleton, returned to his old paper as principal book-reviewer.[26]

FINAL YEARS

Beaverbrook was now entering his final years, and early in 1964 he wrote to a friend: 'I am now in my eighty-fourth year and that is approaching the moment when I must bring out my Late Night Final!' In January that year he telephoned Charles Wintour: 'It looks as though I've got better! That's bad news, isn't it?' The following month, taking the winter sunshine at his Riviera residence, he wrote to Wintour in criticism of a leader which had been published supporting the unification of the Anglican and Methodist churches:

> Next we'll have a leader saying that there should be an amalgamation between the *Evening Standard* and the *Evening News*. What will be the result of that? The circulation of one or the other will disappear. And that is what will happen to the church congregations if they unite. I think you must be a Baptist or a Second Day Adventist. They will gain when Methodists become Episcopalians.[27]

A reply from Wintour that he thought that the agreed policy of the *Evening Standard* was to support the established church, brought forth the retort: 'The *Evening Standard* should certainly support the Church of England. I am unable to do so. But I bow to the superior judgement of the Editor.'

On 25 May 1964, Beaverbrook was to be eighty-five, and as a tribute Lord Thomson of Fleet, a fellow-Canadian and newspaper proprietor, had planned a great dinner with 600 guests. Beaverbrook, confined to a wheelchair, had been unwell for weeks and knew that he was dying of cancer. He feared the great dinner would be too much of an ordeal: there would be the walk to his place of honour, and then the speech. For days before the great occasion he had scribbled fragments of his speech on scraps of paper. He had tried recording the speech but it was no good: his voice was too feeble. He was advised not to go – but Beaverbrook must have realised that this was to be his final public appearance. He was driven to the Dorchester in the late afternoon and taken upstairs in a wheelchair: 'When the moment came he rose from his chair, balanced himself on Max Aitken's arm and walked sturdily to his place practically unaided.'

As Hugh Cudlipp, a guest, later wrote:

> There were six hundred of us, of all ages and most professions, happy or proud for one reason or another to be at the last gathering of the tribe, regarding the guest of honour either with awe or, with qualifications, affection. Nobody present, I reckon, has forgotten the nerve-tingling atmosphere of the occasion, as spellbinding as the last act of a Verdi opera without the need for scenery or music

or lighting effects. The compelling personality of the man, now physically frail and dying, was undiminished. Everybody knew, including Beaverbrook, that it was the last performance.[28]

Speaking in strong, firm tones, Beaverbrook declared that his theme was that of the 'Apprentice'. First an apprentice to finance in Canada: that was a life of daring adventure. Then London:

> And then I decided to become an apprentice in politics. After the war I became an apprentice in Fleet Street. And that was a real exciting experience. At last, I thought, I will be a Master. Fancy free. Instead, I became the slave of the Black Art. I did not know freedom again for many a year.

He then spelled out his definition of a good journalist:

> First he must be true to himself. The man who is not true to himself is no journalist. He must show courage, independence and initiative. He must also, I believe, be a man of optimism. He has no business to be a pedlar of gloom and despondency. He must be a respecter of persons, but able to deal with the highest and the lowest on the same basis, which is regard for the public interest and a determination to get at the facts.

The peroration was perfect:

> This is my final word. It is time for me to become an apprentice once more. I have not settled in which direction. But somewhere, sometime soon.

To uproarious applause and the strains of 'For he's a jolly good fellow', he was escorted by Max Aitken into an anteroom. There he met his host, Lord Thomson, once more and Eric Cheadle, Thomson's right-hand man, who had organised the affair. Cheadle played back a recording of Beaverbrook's speech. With a twinkle in his eye, Beaverbrook then looked up at his son and said: 'There, Max, that's the way to do it!'[29]

Beaverbrook returned to Cherkley that night and died two weeks later, on 9 June 1964.

23

Decline and Fall

For the new proprietor, John William Maxwell Aitken, known for most of his life as 'Young Max', it had been a long wait. Aged 54, when he took over, he had served an extensive apprenticeship within the company, starting as a Linotype operator during vacations from Cambridge University in the 1930s. For this work, the London Society of Compositors had even presented him with a membership card.[1] His management roles had included spells of running the Glasgow operation, the *Evening Standard* and the *Daily Express* before becoming chairman of Beaverbrook Newspapers Ltd in 1955. His father, though, remained head of the Beaverbrook Foundation, which controlled the majority of the voting stock, while a long-serving executive, Tom Blackburn (later knighted), became executive chairman of the company.

Relationship between father and son had – despite the odd differences – been extremely close. Beaverbrook, had even told an interviewer: 'Well, I'm proud of my son. He's a fine fellow. He's a nicer man than I was. A much nicer man.' However, a few months before Beaverbrook's death, his almost-daily criticisms of the management of the papers had led a disillusioned Max Aitken to remonstrate for the first time:

> I respect your judgement and along with all Fleet Street acknowledge your absolute leadership in journalism. For some thirty years I have gratefully accepted your criticism, usually I hope with good grace. But lately all we do or don't do is muddle and muddle. I agree some of our mistakes are silly but some of our successes are magnificent. . . When you used to work at the office with your coat off, you drove everyone hard but you also made them laugh and feel that they were on the 'sunny side of the street'. This is still necessary and some of it must come from the master however far away he may be. Therefore I hope you will continue to hold us by the hand each and every day and beam an occasional smile our way.[2]

As a pilot during the war, Max Aitken had been among the bravest of the brave, being in the midst of the fighting at the fall of France and in the Battle of Britain. During the remaining war years he commanded a Czech night fighter squadron, before in 1943 leading a fighter group in the Middle East. From 1944 he commanded an anti-shipping strike wing based in Scotland. Refusing all promotion above group captain, so that he could continue flying, he ended the war in charge of the largest wing of Mosquitos in Britain. A much decorated man with the DSO, DFC and Czech War Cross, he was always proud to recall that he was in the air on the day war began and still in the air on the day it ended.[3]

Max Aitken was about to inherit an organisation which, during the previous decade, had seen dramatic changes in its leading personnel: E. J. Robertson, for more than thirty years the business head of the group, had suffered a stroke in 1955 and had lingered on for another five years; and in July 1956, Christiansen, the great editor of the *Daily Express*, had a heart attack while staying with Beaverbrook in the South of France. With his stamina gone, he was no longer fit for full-time work, and a benevolent Beaverbrook suggested that he direct the syndication of the *Evening Standard* feature articles: 'I have always had an advantage over some other journalists because I knew both the commercial and the editorial side of newspapers. When you emerge from your contact with the *Evening Standard* you will roll me over in commerce as you have always done in journalism.' Two years later, Christiansen left, embarking on a new career in television, but he was to collapse and die in the studio of Anglia Television in Norwich, on September 27, 1963.

New management names were joining the *Evening Standard* during these years. Early in 1966, John Coote, a former submarine captain and close friend of Max Aitken, was appointed managing director, and other senior appointments were to include John Dawson, David Aitken, Jimmy O'Brien and Leo Simmonds. Coote has described his appointment in *Altering Course: A Submariner in Fleet Street*:

> The *Evening Standard* [was] in a run-down building on Shoe Lane near the Holborn Viaduct ... Beaverbrook was rightly proud of having started the Sunday newspaper from scratch in 1919 and built it up to become the hottest property in Fleet Street, but he was prouder still of the *Standard*'s place as required reading in the City, Westminster and Belgravia ... it was an alternative voice for promoting views and interests outside those governing the editorial policies of the two national newspapers in the Group.[4]

Coote was managing director for two years, and was to say later: 'The nett sale steadied not far below 700,000 and, to general astonishment, each week we started to contribute real profits to the group's exchequers.' During his tenure, he was responsible for engaging Brian Nicholson from the *Sunday Times* to take charge of the paper's advertising, and a further recruit was to be Colin Owen-Browne as classified advertisement director.

Meanwhile, on the editorial side, Charles Wintour was extending the paper's news and arts coverage. His deputy at this time was Derek Marks, a former political correspondent and leader writer on the *Daily Express*: 'He emerged during the 1950s as the leading parliamentary correspondent of his day. For him there were no short cuts.' Marks remained on the *Standard* until 1965 when he returned to the *Daily Express* as editor, a post which he held with distinction until ill-health overwhelmed him.

After becoming ill, he resigned his editorship and began writing regular political columns for the *Daily Express* and *Sunday Express*. He was also a director of Beaverbrook Newspapers, and special adviser to Sir Max Aitken. Although wracked with pain and illness, Derek Marks continued to write his columns with punch and vigour, without a word of self-pity, until his death in February 1975. Sir Max said of him: 'He was a fine editor, a great journalist and a magnificent colleague.'[5]

MAJOR STORIES

Of all the important stories during the early years of Wintour's editorship, among the biggest were the assassinations of John F. Kennedy and, five years later, of his brother, Robert.[6]

The assassination of John F. Kennedy in Dallas was 'flashed' in Britain at 7.40 pm on 22 November 1963, two hours after the *Evening Standard* presses had finished their run and too late for any special edition. However, the following day the paper provided full coverage and was to say in its leader:

> It was his youth, zest and optimism he brought to American government. He led the advance to the new frontiers of science … Few, if any, politicians, have exerted so great an influence outside their own countries by virtue of their personalities rather than their policies … For it was in the field of race relations that the Kennedy Administration made its biggest impact in American politics. And it is one of the bitterest twists of history that his death should come within a few days of the centenary of Abraham Lincoln's speech at Gettysburg which set out the ideal of the American way of life.

This point was noted, too, by Vicky, who, in a moving cartoon, showed Lincoln at the grave of Kennedy. It was captioned: 'My fellow American: Ask not what your country will do for you – ask what you can do for your country.' President Kennedy – his inaugural address, January 20, 1961.

On November 25, Jean Campbell, Beaverbrook's granddaughter and a fine journalist, reported the President's funeral from Washington, and said of Jacqueline Kennedy: 'She had suffered horrors enough to send most women to the limbo land of Ophelia.'

Meanwhile, Jeremy Campbell, the *Standard's* distinguished American correspondent, wrote: 'Washington, Monday. In the sedate suburb of Georgetown yesterday I watched what must be the first nationally televised murder in history, the shooting of Lee Harvey Oswald. "Pray Oswald dies," said the man next to me fervently. "And pray the guy who killed him is a member of the John Birch Society." The first prayer was answered; the second was not.'

Five years later, on 6 June 1968, the shooting of Bobby Kennedy in a Los Angeles hotel provided the *Standard* with a 'skinner'. He died just after 9 a.m. London time, enabling the paper to lead the field. Under the page 1 streamer HE'S DEAD, the main story announced; 'Bobby Kennedy is dead. The 42-year-old Senator victim of an assassin gunman like his brother, President John, died as his family gathered in prayer at his bedside. The time was 1.44 this morning (9.44 in London) just 25 hours after he had been gunned down at the moment of his greatest triumph.' On that same front page, the *Standard* also announced: 'Randolph Churchill dies at the age of 57.'

The death of Randolph's father, Winston Churchill, on 24 January 1965, had naturally, been accorded much greater coverage, and in his main leader on that day the editor had said: 'Tears and black drapery are for lesser men. But with the true princes of this world, esteemed as much for their genius and the quality of their contributions, death seems irrelevant ... The man of this troubled century is and will be Winston Churchill. No better ever existed to share such a century with.' On the facing page, in an article entitled 'The Uncommon Man', part of an obituary notice written by the late Sir James Grigg, Churchill's War Minister, he concluded: 'Happy the state or sovereign who finds such a servant in years of danger.'

On 27 January 1965, the whole of page 1 of the *Standard* was taken over by a photograph of Churchill lying in state in Westminster Hall, and reference made to the one-mile-long queue of mourners. Three days later, Anne Sharpley described the funeral service at St Paul's, while others reporting the occasion included Robert Carvel, Jeremy Campbell, Judy Hillman, Milton Shulman and Sam White. Possibly the most poignant scene recorded was a full-page photograph under the heading: IN FLEET STREET – THE OLD JOURNALIST. The caption read: 'The funeral cortege passes along Fleet Street. Sir Winston, master of the English language, once said: "I love journalism, for I'm an old journalist ... I pushed a pencil in Egypt, and India, and South Africa".'

NEWCOMERS TO PAPER

In that same year (1965), the *Evening Standard* was named the Evening Paper of the Year by Granada Television's 'What the Papers Say'; and there was a further honour, from the *World's Press News*, when 'Londoner's Diary' was voted the best diary of the year.

Among the writers making their names on the paper at that time – writers who had been engaged and/or encouraged by Wintour – were Angus McGill, Alexander Walker and Nicholas Tomalin. McGill had joined the paper in 1957 from the *Newcastle Evening Chronicle* , and spent the next four years working on 'Londoner's Diary'. In 1961 he began writing a humorous column, which was to grace the paper for more than thirty years. He was Descriptive Writer of the Year in the British Press Awards 1968 and that same year began the 'Augusta' comic strip, drawn by Dominic Polensa. He was awarded the MBE in 1990. Also on the 'Londoner's Diary'– as editor – in the early years of Wintour's editorship was Nicholas Tomalin, who was later killed when covering the Yom Kippur War for the *Sunday Times* in October 1973. Alexander Walker joined the *Standard* in 1960 as film critic and has held that position for more than thirty years. He was named Critic of the Year in 1970 and 1974. Frank Dickens, of Bristow cartoon fame, was another to join during this period.

Other 'names' in the editorial firmament included James Cameron and Nigel Lawson. Cameron was later to recall:

> I was working for the *Evening Standard* in Israel [1967] when I had the now legendary encounter with authority that has haunted me for years. We were all down there waiting for the war. We did not know that it was to be the Six Day War: we were standing by for something much more like Armageddon. In fact, we fully expected the Egyptians to blow Tel-Aviv and us to kingdom come at any moment, and that was the story I wrote. Israel has always had a military Press censorship for the very good reason that all the 30 years of its life it has been technically at war. At times of stress, like waiting for wars, the army reinforces the staff of censors with a bunch of soldiers, like university lecturers and PhDs and experts in every known language, and scholars and students, all now captains and majors and so on for the duration of the emergency. They have a low opinion of newspaper men on the whole. To such a lordly one did I submit my *Evening Standard* copy to be cleared for filing. He gave me a courteous *Shalom*, adjusted his glasses and read the stuff. From time to time, he sighed slightly. He read it again. Finally, he returned it to me with an indefinably weary air. He said: 'I find the emotions trite, the theme sentimental and the style pitifully banal. But I have nothing against it militarily, so by all means send it, if you must.' Now the trouble about this was that in my mortification I read the story again, and everything the man had said was true. I screwed it up and threw it away.[7]

Nigel Lawson, much later to be Chancellor of the Exchequer, recalled another time:

> During much of 1970 and 1971, when I was beginning the painful process of changing from journalist into politician – that is, to say, moving from one universally execrated profession to another – I was engaged to write a weekly economic commentary for the *Evening Standard.* In fact, fearful that the dreaded word 'economic' would frighten away readers, Charles Wintour insisted on labelling it a 'financial commentary', but since he gave me complete freedom and a generous ration of space I could scarcely complain. Let me give one example of that freedom: In 1970 the *Standard* ran a series of five special leading articles on the economy on successive days in which it argued that the Government should not worry too much about inflation or the balance of payments, and instead ought to go all out for expansion – buttressed, if need be, by an incomes policy. The following week I asked Charles Wintour for extra space so that I could shoot down all the arguments advanced in the *Standard* leaders. He gave it to me without demur, and my piece appeared under the heading, 'A reply to the *Evening Standard*'. How many other papers, I wonder, would have shown a similar tolerance? In the event, the then Government took the *Standard's* advice on the economy, and not mine. Whether it was wise to do so is another story.[8]

HARSH INSIGHTS

In 1966, The Economist Intelligence Unit produced a study of the national newspaper industry which contained some harsh insights into Fleet Street in general and Beaverbrook newspapers in particular. The report noted that of the potential savings of £4,875,000 obtainable through proper production levels more that £1 million could be achieved by Beaverbrook Newspapers: the *Daily Express*, £671,550; *Sunday Express*, £210,250; and *Evening Standard*, £264,470.

Discussing Beaverbrook Newspapers, it was noted that:

> There is a much greater concentration of editorial and non-executive representation on the board than would normally be considered ideal ... There may, therefore, have been a tendency to neglect the foundation of efficient and continuing management ... the general standard of middle and senior management with a few notable exceptions was not high ... communication within the company seemed to be poor, and at times senior management even up to general manager level did not always appear to be clear on the policy adopted by the Company.

Because there were no formal systems of budgets or profit planning, it was 'difficult to see how costs could be controlled at all levels.'

Arising from this report, John Coote, at that time joint managing director of the Group, with Sir Max Aitken announced the formation of a Forward Planning Group to investigate the efficiency of the production side and to make recommendations. The committee was to comprise senior management and production executives from the *Daily Express* offices in London, Manchester and Glasgow, plus the *Evening Standard* and the *Evening Citizen* in Glasgow. I, acting as representative of the *Standard,* was the youngest member of that committee, and can still recall its recommendations:

> Integrate the *Evening Standard* into the *Express* building, possibly leading to the loss of 200 jobs; develop the *Standard* premises as lettable office space; develop a site beside the *Daily Express* building in Fleet Street (known as Racquet Court, and already owned by the company, this would house the combined *Express/Standard* operation and also provide space to let); replace old printing machinery with 71 new units, thereby reducing the number of presses from 185 to 157; develop property in Glasgow and Manchester where the northern and Scottish editions of the *Daily* and *Sunday Express* were printed. [9]

It was estimated that the cost of these recommendations would be £17 million. The new pressroom equipment would cost £5.5 million and the cost of property development some £11.2 million. It was predicted that production costs would drop, and that the redeveloped property would be worth almost £20 million, with an annual rental income of £1.6 million. With this movement into property away from newspapers, profits from which, more and more, were becoming cyclical, it appeared that the Group was now on course to meet the challenge of the 1970s.

While the Forward Planning Group had been embarking on its task of projecting the company's future, Sir Max himself had been summoned by Harold Wilson, the Labour Prime Minister, to travel to Rhodesia to open up the way for fresh talks with Ian Smith. (Wilson had assumed power in October 1964, replacing Sir Alec Douglas Home – Harold Macmillan's successor – and the Conservatives.) At the time, Robert Carvel wrote in the *Standard*: 'Labour will rule tonight because it picked the right leader and the Tories picked the wrong one. . . For most of the nation it is a time to fasten the safety belts. The journey towards the New Jerusalem will be exciting but a little bumpy in places.'

Four years later, Wilson, in trying to settle Rhodesia's Unilateral Declaration of Independence – following months of fruitless discussions – had discovered that Sir Max Aitken was one of the few

Britons who was trusted by Ian Smith, Rhodesia's Prime Minister – both had been fighter pilots during the war. In August 1968, therefore, accompanied by Lord Goodman, a prominent London solicitor, Sir Max travelled to Salisbury, Rhodesia. Smith greeted him as an old friend and agreed to meet Harold Wilson on HMS *Fearless* off Gibraltar in October 1968. Unfortunately, these talks were to prove abortive, but Sir Max and Lord Goodman were to maintain communications with the Rhodesian Premier and help to develop other contacts between the two governments.

ENTER JOCELYN STEVENS

Sir Max was now about to engage a personal assistant, soon to be made managing director of the *Evening Standard* – and a man who was to play a key role in the fortunes of the Group during the next decade. He was Jocelyn Stevens, grandson of former *Evening Standard* owner, Sir Edward Hulton. Born on 14 February 1932 (he shared the same birthday as Sir Max) Stevens had inherited £750,000 at thirteen days of age. After being educated at Eton and Cambridge, he enrolled at the London College of Printing under its Principal, Leslie Owen, and with his family background – his uncle had founded *Picture Post* – publishing and printing came naturally, and he finished the two-year course in twelve months.[10]

As a 25th birthday present to himself, he bought an obscure magazine called *Queen*, and, with himself as editor-in- chief and various friends from Cambridge days, including Mark Boxer and Tony Armstrong-Jones, plus sundry debs, he turned it into one of the most talked-about magazines of the decade. He laughingly declared that it was 'directed at the fresh upper crust – crumbs held together by a lot of dough'. It was the magazine for the up-and-coming set, and in the advertising world it was considered to have the cream of the AB young readership.

Watching his progress with interest, Beaverbrook, in the early 1960s, had offered Jocelyn a job, but Stevens, at this period, was more interested in backing Radio Caroline, the first off-shore radio station. Stevens was then wooed by Cecil King, head of the Daily Mirror Group, who offered him the position of editorial director of IPC's 200 magazines. But, having sold his *Queen* magazine, it was to Sir Max Aitken that Stevens turned, and in the autumn of 1968 joined Beaverbrook Newspapers, with an office in Shoe Lane. He was immediately involved in organising the Great Car Race to Australia and on his return was appointed managing director of the *Evening Standard* on 1 January 1969, at the age of 36. His brief from Sir Max, was: 'Save it.'[11]

With the *Star* long since gone, the London evening newspaper market had developed into a bitter battle between the *Evening Standard* and the *Evening News*, owned by Associated Newspapers. Since taking over the *Star*, circulation of the *Evening News* now topped the one million mark, almost double that of the *Standard.* However, under its new and dynamic managing director, the *Standard* now epitomised the 'Swinging Sixties': it was the newspaper of 'the bright young things', the first to introduce high-class pre-printed colour, the first to build up its classified advertisement revenue.

One example was to typify Stevens' style: on 21 July 1969, Neil Armstrong became the first man to step on the moon. Six weeks before this momentous event, Stevens called his executives into his office, saying that the Americans had spent millions of dollars to put a man on the moon. To commemorate the occasion, he announced, the *Standard* was going to produce Monday's edition on Saturday, including colour, 24 hours before the planned landing – saying that the Americans had succeeded. I can still remember the hush in Stevens' crowded office.

In the utmost secrecy, colour pictures of the blast-off were received from NASA, and a facsimile of Armstrong on the moon was produced for the front-page. With the pages locked up on the Saturday night, printing commenced early on Sunday morning. By lunch time, all the colour reels had been inserted, and happy management and press crews adjourned to a nearby public house in tentative celebration. With the papers under strict guard, there then came the wait of further eight hours until the successful landing.

At that time, there was a 9.30 a.m. embargo between the *Standard* and the *News*, but, with such a great publishing day in prospect, the *Standard* went on sale at 7 a.m., Monday, July 22, and was an immediate hit with incoming commuters. For happy management and guests there was a special 'Moonday Breakfast' at the Savoy. Production of the paper was frentic, and, with colour reels fast running out, further supplies were despatched from the colour printers. By eight o'clock that evening, when Armstrong's crew had successfully blasted off the moon on their journey back to earth, the *Standard* had printed more than 1,200,000 copies in eleven editions – 100 per cent above normal. And a champagne party in Charles Wintour's office was a fitting end to one of the greatest days in newspaper publishing.[12]

The success of this colour was to lead to 'Specials' covering football and pop star editions. The Treasures of Tutankhamun was also a great seller, advertisers flocked to the *Standard* – and the paper was back in profit. The flair of Stevens and Wintour was also to be apparent following a strike in Fleet Street of all national papers.

On 9 June 1970, with the threat of a national newspaper strike imminent, Sir Max Aitken, Chairman of Beaverbrook Newspapers, wrote an article in the *Standard* headed: 'In danger – the job we all love'. In it he said: 'Conventional financiers and industrialists would suggest we need our heads examining for conducting a business involving such outgoings and risks for so diminutive a profit, but we publish newspapers because we are in the business to do so and because it has been our job for years.' Four days later, under a front-page heading: 'Hello again! We're back', the *Standard* noted: 'The strike which shut down national and London evening newspapers is over. It ended shortly before midnight last night when representatives of the NPA [Newspaper Publishers' Association] and union leaders agreed on a £5 million pay and holiday deal covering all the print unions.' In his leader column, the editor remarked: 'The vigorously negotiated settlement of the newspaper dispute will be greeted with widespread relief. Not only for those who work in the industry but all those who believe that for the country to hold a General Election without newspapers is a travesty of the democratic process will feel happier today. The industry owes a special debt of gratitude to the new chairman of the NPA, Lord Goodman.'

On another page, Harold Wilson, the Prime Minister, in an interview, said: 'You realize I couldn't say much about it while it was on, but perhaps I may make this clear: the reason I intervened on Monday night and Tuesday morning was because the situation was in a state of total deadlock on procedural grounds.'

After the announcement of the agreement, shortly after midnight, by means of a well-organised communications network, the *Standard* staff were called in and printing started at 5.43 a.m. (05.43), producing the only paper on sale in London that day. Sales were in excess of one million, but the rival publishers were incensed at this alleged breach, and summoned a hasty meeting of the NPA council. Invited to explain how it had been done and how much money had been paid, Sir Max told his fellow-publishers that Stevens' reward to each man who had worked in those early hours had been a necktie decorated with the image of an *Evening Standard* van and the numerals '05.43.'[13]

The close understanding between Stevens and Wintour was now bringing about better and better papers, and once more the cream of young talent was attracted to Shoe Lane. Assisted by Roy Wright, as deputy editor, Wintour was able to engage such up-and-coming youngsters as Maureen Cleave, Ray Connolly, Simon Jenkins, Max Hastings, Mary Kenny, Suzy Menkes, Emma Soames and Janet Street-Porter. Sydney Edwards was arts editor and was one of those involved with the paper's Drama Awards. And Marius Pope and, then, Dick Garrett were features editors.

ADDED TENSION

However, despite the continuing editorial successes of the paper, there were still pressures from the production unions. In 1968, the *Standard* had introduced computer typesetting, but claims from the composing chapel, which insisted that its members should only spend one day on the system before returning to the traditional hot metal machines, meant that it was totally uneconomical, and was soon abandoned.[14] Charles Wintour was later to discuss these pressures:

> An added cause of tension between managements and unions is the fact that the stakes on both sides are getting so high. I recall with nostalgia the atmosphere when I took over the editorship of the *Evening Standard* in 1959. There was no great strain about finance in those days. If the *Evening Standard* made money that was excellent. But if it lost money, that was no disaster because the loss was unlikely to be substantial. I was given no information about how much money the editorial department was spending as a whole, no financial targets of any kind, and my knowledge of the financial side of the business was largely limited to figures anyone could read in the company's annual report.

The most serious dispute between unions and management was to concern 'Jak', the paper's cartoonist, who had replaced Vicky, 'whose tragedy was that he took politics really seriously and found the problems he wished to illustrate too complex for cartooning'. Indeed, Vicky had written into his contract that he was to be given complete freedom of comment, subject to the law of libel. Jak was, therefore, the inheritor of a fine tradition. Educated at the Willesden School of Art, he later moved to an advertising agency, and, spotted by Roy Wright, he joined the *Standard* in 1952 and since that time has been one of the most successful-ever cartoonists, with his work syndicated worldwide.[15]

In December 1970, however, Britain was suffering from a power workers' strike which seriously affected everyday life, including production of newspapers. Jak produced one of his toughest cartoons, depicting a power worker without brains or compassion. The cartoon appeared in the first edition of the *Standard*, but while the next edition was being prepared a stoppage occurred.[16] Wintour and Stevens immediately met representatives of the Federated House Chapel. To quote Wintour:

> This did not seem a moment for raising temperatures but for cooling them. So I spoke in a fairly low key. I expounded on the traditional independence of the cartoonist in the *Evening Standard*. I explained that strike action would simply ensure the widest possible

publicity for the cartoon. I spoke about the virtues of toleration. I refused to withdraw the cartoon but offered to run a letter setting out their objections or even, at a later stage, a cartoon giving their viewpoint. In offering them this right of reply, I went no further than I would have gone with any reputable body that wished to object to an article or cartoon in the *Evening Standard*.[17]

Following a forceful argument from Ted Simpson, Father of the NUJ Chapel, it was agreed that a reply should be drafted for publication. Meanwhile, the NUJ Chapel had passed a resolution 'that it would not countenance any attempt at censorship of the *Evening Standard* by any union. It is, and must be, the decision of the editor what the editorial columns contain ... [we protest in] the strongest fashion at the action of the maintenance and production chapels in stopping production'.

Drafted by the NUJ Father of the Chapel, the following appeared in the last edition:

> WHY WE OBJECT TO JAK
> The cartoon by Jak which appears on Page 14 expresses his own opinion. We wish to make it clear that the opinion is not shared by members of the *Evening Standard* Federated House Chapel, which represents trade unions within this newspaper. The Federated House Chapel most strongly deprecates the cartoon and feels that it goes above and beyond the bounds of humour and fair comment. However, to show that we are not boneheaded as portrayed and because we firmly believe in the freedom of the Press we have not refused to print once given this opportunity to express our opinion.
>
> ES
> Federated House Chapel

Aside from stoppages for the Day of Action and the Jak cartoon, production of the newspaper had been relatively trouble-free, which was reflected in profits of £1.2 million in 1971–72. In July 1971, with the *Evening Standard* on a firm footing, Stevens saw Sir Max and told him that he was contemplating going back into magazines. Sir Max's immediate response was to promote him to the board's five-man executive committee. 'Ambassador from Shoe Lane to the Court of Sir Max,'[18] was Jocelyn's jocular reaction to the appointment.

Four months later he left the *Evening Standard* to take over as managing director of the *Daily Express*. His parting from the *Standard* was the occasion for a memorable dinner at the Café Royal, given in his honour by the unions. There he was presented with an antique blunderbuss, engraved with a list of the paper's achievements during his time in charge.[19] Amid much *bonhomie* and emotion, Stevens thought it was one of the nicest things that had ever happened to him: 'Everyone blubbed; it was agonizingly marvellous'[20]

Meanwhile, John Coote, who had been appointed vice-chairman of the Group in June 1971, had twelve months later been able to declare a record pre-tax profit of £3,348,000. Unfortunately, these days of record profits were not to last, and in the summer of 1973 Lloyds Bank called in Sir Max and John Coote, warning them that Beaverbrook Newspapers had reached the limit of its credit. With losses on the *Daily Express* of £1 million for 1972–3 and a forecasted deficit of £4.8 million for 1973–4, it was estimated that the loss per issue of the *Daily Express* was sometimes as high as £18,000.

On 23 January 1974, it was announced that: 'Mr John Coote, vice-chairman, becomes deputy chairman and managing director of properties, newsprint and subsidiary companies. Mr Jocelyn Stevens is appointed deputy chairman of Beaverbrook Newspapers and managing director for the group's newspapers.' Some fourteen months later, John Coote 'offered to leave early in 1975'.[21]

With basic materials and wages having risen dramatically in the previous four years – and circulation falling – severe steps needed to be taken: On 19 March 1974, therefore, Stevens flew to Glasgow to inform a stunned workforce that the *Evening Citizen* was to close – the title had already been sold to Sir Hugh Fraser, owner of the rival *Evening Times*, for £2.75 million – and that printing of the *Scottish Daily Express* and the *Scottish Sunday Express* would be transferred to the Beaverbrook plant in Ancoats Street, Manchester. Of almost 2,000 employees in Glasgow, some 1,800 were to lose their jobs, with the £2.75 million from Fraser paying for the redundancies.

The closure was a bitter affair, Stevens being showered with soot by irate printers. Interviewed afterwards, he said:

> I hated shutting the Glasgow office and getting rid of 1,800 people, but I was completely cold about it because I knew that otherwise we would not survive. You have to be strong to survive in Fleet Street. It's the open boat syndrome ... the fewer people in the boat the longer the water will last out ... In fact, the Glasgow closure has provided the most immense savings. It has given us breathing space which will get us into the future.[22]

The breathing space was not to last long, however, for although Sir Max was able to announce a pre-tax profit of £3.2 million for the year ending June 1975, it did not come anywhere near covering the cost of replanting. Old presses at 121 Fleet Street – 'black Lubianka' – were being replaced by the most modern Ampress units, capable of speeds of up to 75,000 copies per hour, double that of the current plant. First to use these Ampress units was the *Evening Standard* which, after fifty years in the Beaverbrook Group, had finally moved from its Shoe Lane premises, enabling it to share the same cut-off size as the *Daily Express* and *Sunday Express*.[23] The group's borrowings were soon to be in excess of £14 million ... and the day of reckoning was about to come.

POLITICAL CHANGES

While the *Standard* and its sister papers in the group were about to undergo dramatic changes, there had also been a good deal of activity on the political scene during this period. On 19 June 1970, immediately following the end of the national newspaper strike, the Conservatives had been successful in the general election, with Edward Heath replacing Harold Wilson as Prime Minister. In the *Standard* page 1 lead story, Robert Carvel wrote: 'The Tories are back. Back in power tonight to fulfil their Election promise to give Britain: "A better tomorrow".' In its leader, the paper commented: 'The result of yesterday's election is little short of sensational. Shoals of pundits and pollsters are utterly confounded and a dozen political maxims on their heads.'

Four years later, following the 'winter of discontent' and the dispute with the miners, Heath called a general election, but for the Tories, failing to reach an agreement with the Liberals, the result meant defeat. Following a weekend of uncertainty, Heath resigned, and on 5 March 1974, the *Standard* said in its leader: 'It is one of the more paradoxical results of this election that Mr Wilson returns to Number Ten with what is now, in all likelihood, a greater degree of goodwill from the electorate than if his party had won an outsize majority.' On the same page, under the headline, 'Can Labour mop up London's mess?', Simon Jenkins wrote: 'There is little doubt that the Conservative Government have left London in a mess. Labour love saying they can get us out of Tory messes. Now they have a golden opportunity.'

Within seven months, Wilson 'went to the country', and in the general election on 11 October 1974, Labour won an overall majority of just three. 'This is viable and my government can endure,' said Wilson. 'After the General Election which nearly backfired in his face,' commented Robert Carvel in the *Standard*, 'Mr Harold Wilson returned to 10 Downing Street this afternoon with the cheeky promise not to stay in office as long as Gladstone.' On page 7 of that issue, there was a prescient photograph of Margaret Thatcher, with her son Mark, after her victory at Finchley, with the caption: 'In a Ladbroke's book on who will lead the Tories in the next General Election she is quoted at 50–1.'

Four months later, on 11 February 1975, Margaret Thatcher was, indeed, the new leader of the Conservatives, having defeated William

Whitelaw by 146–79, with Sir Geoffrey Howe, John Peyton and James Prior all recording fewer than twenty votes each. As she said: 'I beat four chaps. Now let's get down to work.' A little over a year later, there was also a change in the Labour Party leadership when, on 16 March 1976, Wilson resigned as Prime Minister, informing his press secretary: 'Tell the lobby correspondents you've got a little story that might interest them.' In the contest for the new leader held on 5 April, James Callaghan defeated Michael Foot by 176–137 and assumed the premiership.

TALKS WITH ASSOCIATED

Later that year, in the autumn of 1976, the position at Beaverbrook Newspapers had become so serious that it was decided, in the strictest confidence, to hold talks with arch-rivals Associated Newspapers over the possibility of a merger. Discussing the age-old rivalry between the groups, Michael Davie, in *The Observer,* could note: 'For longer than anyone still in the newspaper business can remember, two dinosaurs, the *Mail* and the *Express* groups, have been slogging it out in the mud. Forests have been levelled, aeroplanes needlessly hired, expense accounts fudged and marriages smashed in pursuit of victory.'[24]

Talks between the groups had been held once before, in 1970, when it had been proposed to merge the *News* with the *Standard* and introduce a joint *Mail/Express* with a possible circulation of more than five million. The *Sunday Express,* however, was to remain outside the deal. The results looked promising: monopoly of the London evening scene and a huge middle-market daily, plus contracts to print the papers on the *Express* plant – and the opportunity to develop the Associated buildings as offices. But, despite its apparent attractions, the deal did not go through.

But, six years later, with Sir Max recovering from a stroke in King's College Hospital, and his son, Maxwell, still only 25, the weight of the negotiations was to fall on Stevens. And it was he who was chosen to lead the three-man team, the others being Maxwell Aitken and Peter Hetherington, the finance director. In the previous few years, the *Daily Express* had seen three editors: Ian McColl, 1971–74, later chairman of Scottish Express Newspapers Ltd; Alastair Burnett, 1974–76, under whose guidance the paper was taken upmarket – before leaving for ITN's 'News At Ten'; and Roy Wright, from deputy editor of the *Evening Standard.* An excellent technician, he was to be involved in changing the *Daily Express* from broadsheet to tabloid. On the *Sunday Express,* John Junor still continued his successful editorship and column, but on the *Evening Standard* there was to be a change.

After seventeen years in the chair – longer than any other serving editor of a Fleet Street daily – Charles Wintour, now aged 60, offered his resignation. He was then appointed managing director of the *Daily Express*, with special responsibility for the tabloid launch scheduled for 24 January 1977. Although the rest of Fleet Street had predicted disaster, the changeover of the *Daily Express* was a complete success, production finishing 44 minutes ahead of schedule.[25]

Wintour's successor at the *Standard*, whom he had long groomed for the role, was Simon Jenkins, who became, at the age of 33, Fleet Street's youngest editor. Educated at Mill Hill and St. John's College, Oxford, he joined *Country Life* magazine in 1965, and the following year was a research assistant at the University of London Institute of Education. From 1966 to 1968, he was news editor of *The Times Educational Supplement*, and then moved to the *Evening Standard* to work on the leader page. During the next four years, he gained a wide reputation by writing about the threat to London's architectural environment. He was 'Insight' editor of the *Sunday Times*, 1974–5 and then returned to the *Standard* as deputy editor, before succeeding Wintour.[26] His deputy was to be Brian MacArthur.

Meanwhile, Sir James Goldsmith, having been unsuccessful in his bid for the *Observer*, had been picking up Beaverbrook shares, but, because of the complex share structure, only 'voting' shares – mainly owned by the Beaverbrook Trust – had voting rights. Goldsmith argued, correctly, that if the company plunged further into trouble it would have to raise fresh capital by issuing new shares. Under current stock exchange practice these would be voting shares.

On 3 February 1977, the Beaverbrook team had a meeting with Viscount Rothermere III – Vere Harmsworth, chairman of Associated Newspapers; and his managing director, Mick Shields, at the Master's Lodge, University College, Oxford. The son of Viscount Rothermere II, Vere Harmsworth was born in 1925 and educated at Eton and Kent School in the United States. From 1948 to 1950 he was with the Anglo-Canadian Paper Mills, Quebec, and since 1952 had been with Associated Newspapers. He became chairman in 1970 and the following year relaunched the *Daily Mail* as a tabloid.

Now, in the residence of Lord Goodman, former chairman of the NPA, discussions began. The key point to come out of the talks was a proposed merger between the *Evening News* and the *Standard*. In the seven months up to January 1977 the *Standard* had lost £1.3 million. The *News*, though, was estimated to lose more than £4 million in 1977. Although the *News* still outsold the *Standard* by 536,000 to 418,000, its market profile was lower and not so attractive to advertisers. After much discussion, it was suggested that through the establishment of a joint printing company Associated would take a 50 per cent stake in Beaverbrook's plant. Beaverbrook would also get an infusion of much-needed capital in return for giving Associated control of the new evening paper.[27]

Wintour's reaction the following day was that as far as he was concerned the new paper would have to be a continuation of the *Standard*, even if owned by Associated. Throughout February and March, secret talks continued and as a result it was possible to put forward conclusions: Associated would buy the *Evening Standard*, valued at £7.5 million, and Associated and Beaverbrook would share the payment of an estimated £4.3 million redundancy which would result from a merger of the two papers. A joint company would be established to buy Beaverbrook's properties and printing plant in Fleet Street. The new company would be called 'Fleet Street Printers' and would produce the *Daily Express, Daily Mail, Sunday Express* and the merged evening paper. Associated would buy a 50 per cent share in the company, in the process assuming responsibility for half the £8 million loan made to Beaverbrook by the Finance Corporation for Industry.

The deal now looked to be a clear winner. However, Charles Wintour, as chairman, was determined to fight for his *Standard*, and on 18 March 1977, he wrote to Lord Goodman:

> Jocelyn Stevens has kindly kept me informed about the general progress of negotiations with Associated Newspapers. Obviously the proposals under discussion would represent an enormous coup for Beaverbrook Newspapers. But as you can imagine the point that concerns me is the identity of the surviving evening newspaper. If it is to be the *Evening Standard*, then there are no problems. The present editor and editorial staff can perfectly well maintain the character and quality and integrity of the paper under different ownership and management. If however the survivor under the scheme were to be the *Evening News* then a great injustice is contemplated and an act which is contrary to the public interest. For the *Evening Standard* is close to breaking even now while the *Evening News* by all accounts is making desperate losses. Above all the *Evening Standard* does attempt to play some serious role in the life and community and the *Evening News* does not. If therefore the deal involved the closure of the *Evening Standard*, I would clearly have to oppose it and I would do so on the grounds that another buyer might be found, and that the *Evening Standard* need not stop publication. Whether this would lead to delays in securing Department of Trade approval for the arrangement under the Monopolies legislation, I don't know, but it is a possibility. I am sending a copy of this letter to Jocelyn Stevens who is already aware of my view and understands my reason.[28]

On 22 March, Wintour told Simon Jenkins that his paper was now under attack from Associated. To Jenkins this was total anathema: both men realised that they must try and find an alternative purchaser for the *Standard* – 'every political and social weapon we could bear'[29] However, Wintour's calls to Lord Barnetson, of United Newspapers; Gordon Brunton, of Times Newspapers; and S. Pearson, publishers of the *Financial Times*, all drew blanks – but all offered sympathy. Jenkins, in his meeting with Sir Denis Hamilton, Chairman of Times Newspapers, was also unsuccessful. By the end of the month, Wintour and Jenkins realised that there were not going to be any saviours in Fleet Street. They now decided to get Goldsmith to make a statement regarding the *Standard* and to sound out Nigel Broackes, chairman of Trafalgar House, who some months earlier had expressed a mild interest in Beaverbrook Newspapers, should they ever need help.

Throughout April, while talks continued between Associated and Beaverbrook Newspapers, Wintour kept up the pressure. He was now aided by the *Evening Standard* chapels, and none was more vociferous in the defence of the paper than Reg Brady, Imperial Father of the Federated House Chapel. Brady was in the forefront of the fight, leading marches down Fleet Street and lobbying at 'secret' meetings.[30]

WINTOUR MEETS HARMSWORTH

On 21 April 1977, Wintour and Jenkins were invited to Vere Harmsworth's Eaton Square home to discuss the editorial future of the combined paper. There they were joined by David English, editor of the *Daily Mail*, and Louis Kirby, editor of the *Evening News*. During lunch, Harmsworth suggested that an advisory committee should be set up to select staff for the new paper and according to Wintour, 'they might well find that eighty per cent ... should be drawn from the *Standard* ... He [Vere Harmsworth] did not however go so far as to suggest that Jenkins should be the editor. By this time I was so wound up at any idea that the *Standard*, a paper I loved and whose staff I cherished, might die that I rejected all thoughts of compromise.'[31]

The following day, Simon Jenkins dined with Vere Harmsworth, and was later to be offered deputy editorship of the merged paper, with Louis Kirby as editor. Simon Jenkins refused: had he been offered the editorship of the *Standard* the deal would almost certainly have been concluded. This decision was to be a key factor in the subsequent negotiations.[32]

Seeking further support, three days later Charles Wintour wrote to Michael Foot, Lord President of the Council and Leader of the House of Commons, and, of course, a former editor of the *Standard*, explaining in great detail the difficulties facing the paper. He ended: 'If Vere made Simon the editor I would support the deal and believe it is the best we can hope for. If Kirby is the editor, I will resign and oppose the deal publicly. We should know by Thursday at the latest.' Writing to Foot a week later, Wintour was a little more optimistic:

> Just to keep you informed, there is a very slight chance that we may have a solution which will keep the *Evening Standard* alive as a separate entity. This depends on Sir James Goldsmith ... [his] condition would in no way affect the editorship of the *Evening Standard* for which I am glad to say he has the highest regard.

Support for the paper was now coming from all quarters – especially from the 'quality' press – and none was more vociferous than the *Daily Telegraph* in its leader column of 29 April 1977:

> **FLEET STREET'S STANDARDS**
>
> THAT 'DOG DON'T EAT DOG' is one of Fleet Street's most hallowed clichés. National newspapers, so quick to make judgment upon other people's troubles, prefer judicious silence about their own. It is arguable that this discretion has contributed to the Press mortality of recent years. Now that at least one more title may soon disappear, perhaps it is time to speak out. The current negotiations between Associated Newspapers and Beaverbrook Newspapers, in which Sir James Goldsmith has dramatically intervened, call for at least two comments.
>
> The first is that while there can be no painless solutions to Fleet Street's dearth of profits, one that involved the disappearance of the *Evening Standard* would be hard to define. Here is a group that has one newspaper (*Daily Express*) which enjoys neither profitability nor particular prestige, one (*Sunday Express*) which enjoys profitability, and one (*Evening Standard*) which enjoys prestige and the prospect of a return to profitability. The second comment was that it is hard to accept that London can really only afford one evening newspaper – and, apparently, no 'quality' evening paper at all ... A main virtue of the Press is the diversity. That virtue would be sadly diminished by the loss of one of London's two evening newspapers – and that, in the eyes of all persons seriously interested in public affairs and the arts, unquestionably the better of the two.

A GREAT CELEBRATION

While the war of words raged in the quality press of the impending takeover of the *Standard*, and Associated Newspapers were refining their proposals more and more, Sir James Goldsmith now suggested that: 'The *Evening Standard* should be saved; there should be union agreement to an effective reorganization of the company; and enfranchisement of all Beaverbrook shares on the principle of one share, one vote.' Meanwhile, the paper at the centre of all the discussions, the *Evening Standard,* was about to celebrate its 150th birthday, and on 20 May 1977, it produced its largest-ever issue, a bumper 64-page edition printed on pink paper. Despite the trauma it was going though, the paper, quite rightly, was on the offensive, and Simon Jenkins in his special page 1 leader could say:

The first 150 years

We are 150 years old today. In the course of a century and a half, we have braved many storms and come through with the *Standard* still flying from the masthead. We have been bought and sold many times. We have survived two world wars, publishing even after being hit by a bomb in the second. We have continued to modernise our appearance to meet the changing nature of our market. As a result, we have today the youngest and liveliest readers of any paper in Fleet Street. They are our greatest strength and security. Just now we are passing through another crisis similar to, if more immediate than, that afflicting most London papers. It is not a terminal crisis. Too many people assume newspapers are a dying industry. Yet within our own history, we have heard that said of painting (with the invention of photography), and the theatre (with the coming of the cinema). Neither has died. We shall not.

Demand for a simple and flexible medium of communication will continue. 'Quality' paper sales in particular have long been buoyant with increasing mass education. And readers will always show loyalty to newspapers such as the *Standard* which seek not just to inform but to entertain and involve them in the life of their community. Reading the *Standard* is part of being a Londoner. The industry which produces us is undeniably archaic. However, it is no more archaic than a host of other British industries, and its much-abused industrial relations perform relatively well compared to those of other industries and public services we shall forbear to mention. Restructuring this industry will be an agonizing process, but it will require sympathy rather than criticism from outsiders. In such reorganisation, newspapers may well say to themselves what they have often said to others: think small. The *Standard* is a small operation and derives much of its character from the close relations which exist between its workers. Smallness has been shown to yield efficiency. It would also make it easier for a plurality of titles to be maintained.

All the talk there has been of there only being 'room' for one London evening paper should deceive no one. New publishing techniques – and new editorial ideas – could in years to come give the people of London the exciting prospect of not two but four or five evening titles. London is entering a new era of renaissance. It is the most attractive and popular of great world cities. It survived the recent recession well, and the growing prosperity of this paper is just one index of its incipient recovery. Economic revival in a framework of environmental conservation has long been at the centre of the *Evening Standard* policy for London. Already the renewal of the inner areas of the City is proving the fruits of that approach. For newspapers do not only observe and record events. They seek to play at least some part in them. In this year of the Royal Jubilee and our 150th anniversary, we have tried to play a part in London life. We are determined to play a full and growing role in the future.

Messages of congratulation poured into the paper, including one from the Queen:

Whatever the future may hold, Her Majesty is happy to have had this opportunity of sending her congratulations on this notable anniversary.

James Callaghan, Prime Minister, said:

I am very glad to send congratulations to the *Evening Standard* as it celebrates its 150th anniversary. It is a record of which all those who produce it, and the Londoners who read it, can be justly proud. I hope you will be able to maintain your standards for many more successful years.

Leader of the Opposition, Margaret Thatcher, said:

The *Evening Standard* is required reading. I would like not only to congratulate the paper on the magnificent contribution which it has made to London life, but also to thank it for giving so many people so much pleasure and food for thought for so many years.

Amid all the celebrations – and doubts – Charles Wintour was about to fire off a salvo which would seriously wound Associated's chances. On 25 May 1977, he addressed the Automobile Association's annual luncheon. He began his prepared speech in a light-hearted manner, discussing events at the *Standard* in the language of the second-hand car trade. Then the mood changed dramatically as he attacked Vere Harmsworth and his company's efforts to take over the *Evening Standard*.[33] The speech was to cause a sensation and brought a letter of congratulation from Michael Foot: 'What a speech! I'm sure it is the first time for months that the old man [Lord Beaverbrook] in his grave can have had a night's sleep.' For the *Standard* employees, Ted Simpson, NUJ FOC, reported: 'Morale has now gone up a few more significant notches.' And the Imperial Father of the *Express* Federated House Chapel sent congratulations for a speech that 'echoed the views of all Beaverbrook employees'.

ENTER TRAFALGAR HOUSE

With Associated Newspapers still anxious to gain control, and Sir James Goldsmith submitting fresh proposals, there came forward two more candidates: Rupert Murdoch and, at last, Trafalgar House; the ultimate victor was about to enter the fray. Already owner of the wildly-successful *Sun* and *News of the World,* Rupert Murdoch came from Australian newspaper stock and, after Oxford University, had begun his career as a trainee sub-editor on the *Daily Express.* Early in June 1977, Murdoch met Sir Max Aitken for dinner and proposed that he should supply £10 million for working capital and a new management team. By the end of the month, Murdoch proposed, in addition to the £10 million loan, to buy out Sir Max's personal 20 per cent of voting shares.

While the other three would-be purchasers were still discussing terms, on 30 June Trafalgar House made their play. After a day of intense pressure, with Jocelyn Stevens dividing his time between the Associated Newspapers headquarters and the Berkeley Street offices of Trafalgar House, the board of Beaverbrook Newspapers gave unanimous approval that Sir Max be empowered to accept any improved offer which satisfied him. They 'found themselves pushing against a door that was already ajar'. Within minutes, the improved offer of £13.69 million had been provisionally accepted. It meant that the Beaverbrook Foundation would receive £3 million and Sir Max more than £1 million. At 2.30 p.m., Sir Max formally announced the trustees' decision to the directors, and 20 minutes later Stevens telephoned Victor Matthews at Trafalgar House with the news.

Accompanied by a BBC television team, Victor Matthews immediately left for Fleet Street, telling the interviewer: 'I am just like any other chap that we see walking across the street now who has got to the top and if that can happen in a country in a straightforward way, by hard work, then I am very anxious to maintain that.' For Victor Matthews, the one-time able seaman, it was the fulfilment of a dream: the former clerk of works for Trollope and Colls, builders at the *Daily Express,* was now the new proprietor.

But for Sir Max, walking to his car, it was a different story: 'I've given up because I got ill. No, I'm not disappointed. I think he [Beaverbrook] would have sold up long before.'

The days of the Aitkens had ended ....

24

Harmsworth Victorious

Described as 'the most unlikely newspaper publisher of the century',[1] Victor Matthews was aged 58 when he became the new chairman of Beaverbrook Newspapers. Born in London, he had begun work as an office boy and during the Second World War had served in the Royal Naval Volunteer Reserve. On demobilisation, he became a trainee with Trollope and Colls, the City of London builders, and rose to become contracts manager. During the next thirty years, he was to play a prominent part in the building and contract world, and with Nigel Broackes (later Sir Nigel) developed Trafalgar House into an international force, with interests in civil engineering, the Ritz Hotel and the Cunard shipping line, including the *Queen Elizabeth II*.[2]

But Matthews was to have a key role in the affairs of Express Newspapers – which had reverted to its old title within weeks of the Trafalgar success – and Fleet Street. Upon taking over, he asked for three months' industrial peace, but this was soon shattered when the engineers sought parity with the highest-paid printers, which would have increased their wages from £140 to £250 per week. Matthews refused to pay, and the engineers held a meeting during working hours and declined to return when instructed to do so. As a result they were dismissed. Key elements from foundry equipment were found to be missing, and, as a consequence, production was not possible. The 'black-glass' building, 121 Fleet Street, was then – on management's orders – surrounded in scaffolding and wire mesh and each evening plans were put into effect for possible production.[3] It was not, however, until seven days later on a following Saturday evening – when the number of working Linotypes had been reduced through non-maintenance to just six (instead of eighty) – that agreement was reached. Nevertheless, a London edition of the *Sunday Express* was produced.

When the *Daily Express* resumed publication on the following Monday, in a front-page leading article, written by new editor Derek Jameson on behalf of Matthews and under the headline 'WE SHALL NOT BE MOVED', the paper stated: 'Far too many within the industry have cashed in on the vulnerability of newspapers in a shrinking and highly competitive market. Fleet Street has become a jungle where anyone who dares to oppose excessive and often outrageous demands does so at the eternal risk of instant stoppage and imminent bankruptcy ... We shall not be moved.'

That same year, 1978, Matthews told *The Sunday Times* that 'Fleet Street is not overmanned; it is underworked'. Subsequently, in November 1978, the *Daily Star* was launched from the group's Manchester offices – the first new national newspaper for seventy-five years. Editor of the paper was Peter Grimsditch, an Oxford classics scholar (later to edit the *Daily Sport* and in 1994 *Tonight*, a free London evening), with Derek Jameson as editor-in-chief. Jameson had succeeded Roy Wright as editor of the *Daily Express* the previous year, who then became senior assistant editor on the *Daily Mail.*[4]

Meanwhile, there were also editorial changes on the *Standard.* In 1978, Simon Jenkins left the paper. As a young and forceful editor, he had been in the forefront of the fight to save the paper from takeover. The following year he became political editor of the *Economist*. He was then columnist on *The Sunday Times*, 1986–90 and during this period was Granada Journalist of the Year, 1988. Afterwards he was to edit *The Times* between 1990 and 1992.[5] Following his spell as managing director of the *Daily Express*, Charles Wintour returned to edit the *Standard* in 1978 and the next year was joined, once more, by Roy Wright as deputy editor.

CLOSURE OF THE NEWS

In the New Year Honours List in 1980, Matthews was made a life peer. It was also an important time for the *Standard*. On 6 October 1980, the *UK Press Gazette* announced on its front page: 'The Secretary of State for Trade has today given consent for the merger of the *Evening News* and the *Evening Standard*', and on Friday 31 October the *Evening News* ceased publication after 99 years. The *Standard* emerged victorious as the sole survivor of the London evenings war. The previous day, on 30 October the *Evening News* had published a Special Commemorative Edition: 99 OF THE BEST. Tomorrow we say goodbye after 99 years as London's leading newspaper. But today we tell the story of the evening paper that has written its own chapter in London's history:

> A red light goes on. Below Northcliffe House an overalled printer standing by one of the great rotary machines pushes a button. The presses begin to slow down and then cease to turn. A klaxon horn blares out with the finality of the Last Post. The time: just after about five o'clock tomorrow night. That is how a newspaper ends its life ... On Monday, we shall not be there. Or rather, our name will be found writ small under the title of *The Evening Standard* with whom we are compelled to amalgamate ... It was on the evening of July 26, 1881, that the newsboys first shouted our name through Victorian London. This means that had we survived the bitter wind now

> blowing down Fleet Street, the *Evening News* would have celebrated its 100th birthday next year. That is not a bad survival record on the fiercely competitive battlefield of journalism ... Through our pages we have forged friendships for 99 years. It has been a privilege to speak to, and on behalf, of the people of London.

The paper's final edition had, naturally, led with its demise:

After 99 years the News reports its last big story

GOODBYE LONDON

Describing the closure of its sister paper, Brian James reported on 1 November in the *Daily Mail*: 'First duty for John Leese, the editor who has had to put the final 14 grim editions to print, was morning conference. It was about as cheerfully meaningful as an Entertainment Officer's meeting on the *Titanic*.'[6] At the mammoth wake, which followed the 'banging out' of the paper's final edition, four former editors – Guy Schofield, Reg Willis, John Gold and Don Bodie, plus John Leese – were present; and later Lou Kirby, the paper's previous editor, arrived and spoke of his sadness: 'I am looking forward to the job of editing the *Standard* but I will still have the feeling of desolation at the demise of the *News*.'

Among those present was Lord Rothermere, having flown specially from Paris, and for an hour he mingled among the *News* men and women. Later he told Brian James: 'I know we have done everything we could to keep this paper alive. And we have failed. We simply could not get our share of what was left once television started taking the bulk of advertising. All other problems stem from that: and when it came down to it we were losing £4 million for every £1 million lost by the *Standard*. So we had to be the one to go.'

Secret negotiations between Associated Newspapers, led by managing director Mick Shields, and Eric Parker, for Trafalgar House, to merge the papers had been in progress for a number of months prior to the closure. The *Evening News*, which had already lost some £38 million, was expected to lose a further £20 million in the next five years, while the *Evening Standard*, after a profitable period, was anticipated to show a loss of £1 million that year.

THE NEW STANDARD

From the negotiations, it was agreed that the *Evening News* redundancies, anticipated to cost £6 million, would be paid by Associated, and that a new company would be formed, Evening Standard Co. Ltd (ESCO), with the shares held equally between Associated Newspapers Group Ltd and Express Newspapers Ltd. Production of the *New Standard,* as the paper was to be called, would continue, under contract, on the Ampress units at the Daily Express building. It was further agreed that the chairman would be Victor Matthews – and if he left the chairmanship would alternate between the groups. In the event of Trafalgar House selling their 50 per cent, Associated would have first option on the shares, thereby becoming sole owners. This was, as Vere Harmsworth (Lord Rothermere III) was later to say, a key factor in the negotiations.[7] Another point to emerge from the discussions was that Charles Wintour should resign the editorship: 'Vere Harmsworth had not forgotten an attack I made on him at the height of his previous attempts to obtain the *Standard.* As I had already resigned the editorship voluntarily some years earlier, believing that it was a job for someone under sixty, I had no problem about resigning again, particularly as everyone else on the editorial staff kept his job.'[8]

The new editor was to be Louis Kirby, former editor of the *Evening News.* Upon hearing of the appointment, Jocelyn Stevens told Lord Matthews: 'It was like the RAF winning the Battle of Britain and finding Goering in charge at the end of the war.'[9] When he was appointed, Simon Jenkins wrote: 'I don't envy you having to ride that particular tiger.'[10] Born in Liverpool, Kirby had entered journalism as a junior reporter on the *Express & Star,* Wolverhampton, and during 1949–50 was a reporter with the *Royal Gazette,* Bermuda, and a freelance for two years before joining the *Daily Mail* as a general reporter in Manchester in 1953. The following year he ran the Liverpool bureau and then moved to Dublin in 1955 and on to London in 1956. There he was, in turn, courts reporter, parliamentary gallery writer and lobby correspondent.

He joined the *Daily Sketch* in 1962 as a reporter, and was successively leader writer, political writer, assistant editor, executive editor, and then acting editor during preparations for the merger of the *Sketch* with its sister paper, the *Daily Mail,* relaunched as a tabloid in 1971. He was appointed deputy editor of the *Daily Mail* during 1971–4, then became editor of the *Evening News* when relaunched as a tabloid in August 1974, and moved it upmarket. He was vice-chairman of the *Evening News,* and a director of Associated Newspapers between 1975 and 1980. As a prelude to taking over the editorship of the *New Standard* he informed the staff:

> From next Monday I intend to offer you a newspaper that is significantly different from any other publication in Britain. Firstly, it will, of course, be London's only evening paper. Secondly, it will comprise a unique combination of two great newspapers, the *Evening Standard* and the *Evening News.* You will find that it blends

the best of both. But not only that: I strongly believe that the time has also arrived to make an important leap forward. To present a newspaper which is more relevant, more attractive, more in tune with the needs and aspirations of every intelligent man and woman living and working in London today. It will be a quality product, but totally lively and entirely unpretentious: reflecting a wide interest in every aspect of life in the Capital, but keenly aware of the world outside. That may sound a tall order. I am happy to be able to say that we have the resources, the writers and the total commitment to be able to carry it out. Together we shall launch ourselves into the future determined to turn two good papers into one that is truly superb. In our drive to create every day a better and better product, we shall inform, we shall entertain, we shall involve you all. We want to bring you the highest Standards possible.[11]

Joining Kirby on the *New Standard* from the *News* were Bill Nutting for the back bench and Keith Turner as assistant editor features. Jeremy Deedes moved from the back bench of the *Standard* to take charge of the two 'Diaries'. The new editor said: 'I want it ['Londoner's Diary'] to go back to what it was in Beaverbrook's days.' His concept was to have 'really interesting disclosures about big business, publishing politics and the arts.' Also from the *News* came Richard Compton Miller, to write a society diary; Patrick Collins, sports columnist; Patric Walker, astrologer; Delia Smith, cookery writer; and John Blake, pop music commentator.

The first day's issue of the new paper, on Monday 3 November 1980, though, was not without its problems, as the printers restricted the number of copies produced. Previously, the combined circulation of both titles had been some 800,000. But the new paper, basing its commercial future on hopes of achieving 600,000 sales, was forced through chapel pressure to hold its figure to under 400,000 – the *Evening Standard*'s former print run – pending settlement of a pay claim.[12] And only two days earlier, Margaret Thatcher, the Prime Minister, had told the Conservative Trade Union Conference at Reading that the closure of the *Evening News* and the decision of Lord Thomson II to sell Times Newspapers could be blamed on the unions: 'You have only to look at the closures in Fleet Street to realise that restrictive practices can lose jobs.'

Three months after his appointment, Kirby was interviewed in *Campaign*, the advertising trade weekly, and said: 'I had to keep a strong contingent of AB readers and obviously I'm happy to take on C1 readers, but not lose the AB section. So I've built on the *Standard* rather than the *News*. People have accused it of looking like the *News* because of the bigger headlines but I've kept on the columnists and I was taking the *News* upmarket gradually.'

Another senior executive to join the *New Standard* at this time – as chief executive – was Bert Hardy, who had been invited to join the paper by Lord Matthews on 9 October. Hardy's previous experience in advertising and general management had included the *Daily Mirror, Sunday Pictorial* and IPC-owned *Sun.* When Rupert Murdoch, freshly arrived from Australia, bought the *News of the World* in 1969 he appointed Hardy as advertisement director, and a few months later Hardy was also to be responsible for the relaunched tabloid the *Sun,* again purchased by Murdoch. Following a period with the new London Weekend Television, in which Murdoch had a stake, Hardy was subsequently promoted to the post of managing director of News International. In October 1977 Murdoch announced he was giving up his role as News International chief executive, while continuing as chairman, and that Hardy would take over the title while also continuing as News Group Newspapers' managing director. Hardy remained with News Group until September 1979. During his time there, he had been deeply involved in the building of the Wapping plant.

Within eight months of becoming chief executive of the *New Standard,* Hardy was to face a possible newcomer to the London evening newspaper scene, when it was announced that Lonrho, owners of *The Observer,* were looking at launching a London evening. Joint managing director of *The Observer,* Brian Nicholson – and a former *Standard* senior executive – said in June 1981: 'We're going into this very carefully; it's not going to be an instant newspaper, if it happens.' Pointing out that 150,000 readers of London evenings had been lost since the merger of the *News* and *Standard,* he remarked: 'Naturally it would be worth finding out whether the new paper is not attracting those readers because they are dissatisfied. Why there's such a low level of advertising, why there's such a comparatively low level of sales and why the *Standard* hasn't had the effect on the market that a monopoly paper should.'[13]

Responding, Bert Hardy could say: 'Too much money, too much time and too much heartache have been spent to give way to a newcomer. There is going to be a very aggressive, very cut-throat war between ourselves and the new paper. We are not simply going to walk away. There will be a battle for every inch of copy, every centimetre of advertising.'[14]

In the event, a new evening paper was not launched: that was to wait for another day.

THATCHER AS PRIME MINISTER

Meanwhile, on the political scene, Margaret Thatcher had been Prime Minister since 4 May 1979, when the Conservatives had succeeded Labour as the new government. The result had been a resounding win:

Conservatives 339, Labour 269, Liberals 11, Ulster parties 12, Nationalists 4 – a majority of 43. The *Standard* noted in its leader:

> The great Tory victory is above all a personal triumph for Margaret Thatcher. As the first woman Prime Minister of Britain she has achieved an amazing breakthrough. Over the coming months and years it will be fascinating to watch how the nation as a whole, accustomed to paying respect of quite a different kind to the Queen, will adopt to a woman at Number 10.[15]

Max Hastings, writing on 'A woman driven by a vision' said: 'She has yearned for power with passion far beyond even the usual politician's lust for office, because she thinks she can lead their great movement of liberalism. ... If she fails, at least it can never be said that it was because she set her sights too low.' Thatcher herself, remarked, when reaching the steps of No. 10: 'Where there is discord may we bring harmony ... where there is despair may we bring hope.'[16]

The return of a Conservative government, loudly supported by Express Newspapers, was now about to bring about a change in the Group's fortunes, for under the Finance Act of 1981 it became possible for subsidiaries to demerge from their parent companies. Consequently, the decision was taken by Trafalgar House to demerge Express Newspapers – including the Morgan-Grampian magazine arm, bought for £20.5 million in 1977 – as Fleet Holdings. However, an idea was put forward by Jocelyn Stevens, managing director of Express Newspapers, and Graham Sherren, head of Morgan-Grampian; the suggestion was made to Lord Matthews that they should lead a management buy-out. This was not to be, however, and within a few days both had left the organisation.[17] After returning to magazine publishing, with Graham Sherren – and making a huge success of it – Jocelyn Stevens then became Rector of the Royal College of Art, and later chairman of English Heritage. Long-serving executive Mike Murphy succeeded Stevens as managing director, and on 5 March 1982, Fleet Holdings was 'floated' at 20p per share, but soon slumped to 15p, 'nonetheless the profits to September 1982 were less than £3 million but more than the final prospectus forecast'.[18]

While Fleet Holdings was facing this challenge there had been an even sterner challenge for Margaret Thatcher when, on 2 April 1982, Argentina invaded the Falklands. The following day *The Times* said:

> In a pooled and censored dispatch from Port Stanley, Simon Winchester, our correspondent, reported yesterday that the Argentine flag was flying over Government House on Port Stanley. 'I understand that the British Governor will be flying to Buenos Aires tonight. The action began at 0600 and ended at 0900 (local time)

and quite a few Argentine troops were involved. None of the British or any of the Royal Marines has been injured although three Argentines were hurt during the invasion'.[19]

Amid great national fervour, a Task Force was assembled by Britain and despatched 8,000 miles to the Falklands. With the correspondents covering the campaign was Max Hastings, of the *Standard*. A former editor of 'Londoner's Diary', he had joined the paper from Oxford University, and for much of his time had served as a roving correspondent, reporting from more than sixty countries, and covering wars and conflicts in the Middle East, Angola, Vietnam, India-Pakistan, Cyprus and Rhodesia. His despatches from the Falklands made him the outstanding correspondent of the campaign, and he was rightly honoured as Journalist of the Year, 1982, and Granada TV Reporter of the Year, 1982. The finest of all his despatches was on 14 June, 1982, the last day of the Falklands War, when he entered Port Stanley before the British troops:

> I wandered down to the road. It stretched empty ahead, the cathedral clearly visible perhaps half a mile away. It was simply too good a chance to miss. Pulling off my web equipment and camouflaged jacket, I handed them up to Roger Field in his Scimitar, now parked in the middle of the road and adorned with a large Union Jack. Then with a civilian anorak and a walking stick that I had been clutching since we landed at San Carlos Bay, I set off towards the town, looking as harmless as I could contrive. 'And where do you think you are going?' demanded a Parachute NCO in the traditional voice of NCOs confronted with prospective criminals. 'I am a civilian,' I said firmly and walked on unhindered.
>
> Just round the bend in the road stood a large building fronted with a conservatory that I suddenly realized from memories of photographs was Government House. Its approaches were studded with bunkers, whether occupied or otherwise I could not see. Feeling fairly foolish, I stopped, grinned towards them, raising my hands in the air, and waited to see what happened. Nothing moved. Still grinning and nodding at any possible spectres within, I turned back on to the road and strode towards the Cathedral, hands in the air. A group of Argentinian soldiers appeared by the roadside. I walked past them with what I hoped was a careless 'Good morning'. They stared curiously, but did nothing.
>
> Then, ahead, of me, I saw a group of obviously civilian figures emerging from a large, official-looking building. I shouted to them: 'Are you British?' and they shouted back 'Yes'. Fear ebbed away, and I walked to meet them. After a few moments' conversation, they pointed me towards the Argentinian colonel on the steps of the

administration block. I introduced myself to him quite untruthfully as the correspondent of *The Times* newspaper, on the basis that it was the only British organ of which he might have heard. We talked civilly enough for a few minutes. He kept saying that most of my questions could be answered only after four o'clock, when the British General was due to meet General Menendez. Could I meanwhile go and talk to the British civilians, I asked? Of course, he said. I walked away towards that well-known Stanley hostelry 'The Upland Goose' down a road filled with file upon file of Argentinian soldiers, obviously assembling ready to surrender. They looked utterly cowed, totally drained of hostility. Yet I did not dare to photograph their wounded, straggling between comrades. It was only when I saw officers peering curiously at me from their vehicles that I realized that my efforts to look civilian were defeated by my face, still blackened with camouflage cream.

Walking into the hotel was the fulfilment of a dream, a fantasy that had filled all our thoughts for almost three months. 'We never doubted for a moment that the British would come,' said the proprietor, Desmond King. 'We have just been waiting for the moment.' It was like liberating an English suburban golf club.[20]

While the nation had been gripped by events in the Falklands, executives at Associated Newspapers, led by Lord Rothermere, had also been heavily involved in the launch of the tabloid *Mail on Sunday* on 2 May 1982. An initial sale of 1,250,000 copies had been hoped for, but within six weeks circulation had dropped to 700,000. Bernard Shrimsley, the launch editor, was succeeded by David English, who was also, of course, editing the *Daily Mail*, and he brought with him some twenty staff.[21] A colour magazine, edited by John Leese, was also added to the revamped paper, and given the title *YOU* by the editor. Within five months, the *Mail on Sunday* was making real progress, and as a result David English was appointed group editor-in-chief, while Stewart Steven, from the *Daily Mail*, became the new editor – and the battle to overtake the *Sunday Express* had begun in earnest.

On the political scene, twelve months after Britain had regained the Falkland Islands, the Prime Minister called a general election – and there was to be little doubt as to the outcome: she swept to power once more with an overall majority of 144: Conservatives 397, Labour 209, Liberals-Social Democrats 23, others 21. Thatcher said: 'It is wonderful.' Michael Foot, now Leader of the Labour Party, called the result a national disaster.

The *Standard* of 10 June 1983 led with the front-page headlines: 'Now the reshuffle – I'm no butcher but I've learnt to carve.' In the leader it noted: 'Whatever the challenges and struggles that lie ahead, this is Mrs Thatcher's day. It was uniquely her election campaign. She led her forces from the front from start to finish. She did not just win: she smashed the opposition.' Brian Walden, a former Labour MP and by the early 1980s a prominent television interviewer, commented in the paper: 'Out of date, out of touch. For the last fortnight Labour has lain like a beached whale ... The age of fudging is over for Labour's Right. They must radically overhaul their Party or surrender all hope of future victory.'

A month prior to the Election, the *Standard*, too, had made a 'small slice of history' when it became available in New York on the afternoon of publication. On 5 May to celebrate 'Britain's Salute to New York', 50,000 extra copies of the paper had been flown across the Atlantic on British Airways' Concorde and Air India flights. New York city's mayor and Nancy Reagan, who was visiting the city, had copies delivered to them. *Standard* chief executive, Bert Hardy, commenting on the exercise, said it was a complete success: 'British Airways really pulled out all the stops. It was expensive but we made some money on the operation by selling special advertising.'[22]

For the next two years, the *Standard*'s editorial department – since 1979, mainly through the efforts of managing editor Jeremy Deedes, operating successfully in the 'black glass' building – continued to expand its news and arts coverage. And on 29 April 1985, an important change was made in the title of the paper to *The London Standard*. Announcing the fact on page 2, Louis Kirby said:

> The *Standard* today gains a new title – *The London Standard* – for three good reasons. To proclaim a message, to acknowledge a responsibility and to reaffirm a purpose.THE MESSAGE is that we do indeed speak for London, and about London, as no other news medium can. THE RESPONSIBILITY is to report and record as fully and as faithfully as we are able. THE PURPOSE is to hold to that path without compromise, for and on behalf of all the people in the capital ... We have always been more than a metropolitan newspaper. London is a cosmopolitan city, and its newspaper needs to focus a wide-angle lens on the world. That we shall continue to do. The name of a newspaper is its first word to its readers. As such, it is a prized asset, not to be lightly tampered with or changed. That is all the more true when our masthead has, from necessity, already seen changes not so long ago. We believe that *The London Standard* is a title that speaks loud and clear. It is a name we will wear with pride.

UNITED NEWSPAPERS TAKE OVER

During the previous three years, since Express Newspapers, as part of Fleet Holdings, had been demerged from Trafalgar House, various changes had taken place in the editorial direction of the *Daily Express*.

Prior to the demerger, Derek Jameson had been the editor between 1977 and 1980, leaving to become the editor of the *News of the World*, and later to achieve much success as a radio and television personality, and Arthur Firth had held a brief tenure during 1980–1. He was succeeded by Christopher Ward. In 1983, Sir Larry Lamb, former editor of *the Sun*, was in charge. By August of that year, shares of Fleet had risen sixfold, to £1.22, and soon group profits of £9.5 million were declared. By June 1984 the figure had risen to more than £22 million.

With Fleet Holdings now providing an entry into Fleet Street, the group became 'in play', and among the interested parties were to be Robert Holmes à Court, Dr Ashraf Marwan and, finally, Robert Maxwell. Apart from the increasing profitability of the group – due largely to the Morgan-Grampian division – there was now the *Express*'s 9 per cent share in Reuters, whose recent flotation had owed much to Lord Matthews' persistence. (Ultimately, these shares were to be worth more than £130 million.)

In January 1985, David Stevens, as chairman of United Newspapers, purchased the 15.76 per cent stake held by Robert Maxwell in Fleet Holdings for £30 million,[23] and the battle was on. By March the United Newspapers' shareholdings in Fleet stood at 20.1 per cent. Once clearance had been gained from the Monopolies Commission, the result was no longer in doubt, and by October 1985 United were victorious, but having had to raise their offer to £3.75p a share, nearly twenty times their original value. Victor Matthews, after a hard battle to save Fleet Holdings, retired to Jersey; and as Charles Wintour later wrote: 'His two really big achievements for the newspaper industry were the break-up of Reuters Trust into a public company, and his employment of the law in securing a greater measure of industrial discipline.'

Within weeks of United Newspapers assuming control of Fleet Holdings, on 18 December 1985 the following announcement appeared on page 1 of the *Standard*:

Sole owners for The London Standard

Associated Newspapers, whose interests include the *Daily Mail* and *Mail on Sunday*, have become sole owners of *The London Standard*. Negotiations between the company and Trafalgar House – joint shareholders in *The London Standard* for the past five years – were concluded yesterday when Trafalgar House sold its 50 per cent holding. Lord Rothermere, chairman of Associated Newspapers Group, has become chairman of the Evening Standard Company Limited. The previous chairman, Lord Matthews, has resigned from the board, together with the three remaining Trafalgar House representatives. A statement issued by the two groups today said:

> The shareholding in ESCO was Trafalgar House's only remaining newspaper interest, following the demerger of Fleet Holdings in 1982. Both Trafalgar House and Associated Newspapers believe that it is in the best interests of *The London Standard* and its employees that ESCO should be wholly owned by a major newspaper group. The two groups became joint owners in October 1980, when their newspapers, the *Evening News* and the *Evening Standard*, were merged. Negotiations for the purchase by Associated Newspapers of the Trafalgar House shareholding intensified last month after Fleet Holdings – whose chairman was Lord Matthews – was taken over by United Newspapers.

After exactly eighty years – when Alfred Harmsworth had lost out to Arthur Pearson for possession of the *Standard* – the paper was finally in the ownership of his family.

Louis Kirby remained as editor of the *Standard* until October 1986 when he was promoted to the position of editorial director of Mail Newspapers. His successor was to be John Leese. Born in 1930, he had entered journalism on local newspapers in the Midlands, and in 1963 had been appointed editor of the *Coventry Evening Telegraph*. Six years later he went to Fleet Street as deputy editor of the *Evening News*, and was to work for Associated Newspapers for more than twenty years. In 1976, he had moved into a management role with the group as editorial director in Harmsworth Publishing, and, after his short spell of editing the final issues of the *Evening News*, was sent to New York as editor and publisher of *Soho News*, a lifestyle magazine for the emerging 'yuppie' market. He returned to London in 1983 to edit *YOU Magazine*, the colour supplement of *The Mail on Sunday*, and did much to assist the paper at a critical moment.

SEEING OFF MAXWELL

As the new editor of the *Standard*, his first challenge was to see off Robert Maxwell's *London Daily News*, launched on 24 February, 1987. With Charles Wintour as editorial consultant and Magnus Linklater as editor, the *London Daily News* had engaged a first-class editorial staff – dedicated to fight in the same ABC1 market place as the *Standard*. But, as Charles Wintour was later to write:

> The most serious mistake was to launch with the twenty-four hour concept. When Maxwell told a small executive group that this is what he wanted I said it would increase costs by at least sixty per cent. Maxwell simply shrugged his shoulders. I believe he thought he could get two newspapers for the price of one and a

> half ... Senior editorial executives never knew whether they were fighting the *Mail* or the *Standard.* There were other major weaknesses, particularly in production and distribution ... too much instant decision-making too much over-optimism, too much waste.[24]

To counteract Maxwell's plans, Lord Rothermere, in a brilliant move, while visiting Tokyo, decided to relaunch the *Evening News.*[25] Meanwhile, Bert Hardy on the *Standard* put forward a masterly promotion, offering five free houses as prizes to readers, while at the same time tightening up the paper's distribution network, using the company's vans to carry both the *Standard* and the *Evening News.*

Under the guidance of John Leese, Lori Miles, fresh from editorial charge of *Chat,* was appointed editor of the *Evening News* – one of the first of the new band of woman editors, and she controlled a small team of 'some thirty-five *Standard* journalists and freelances detailed to get on with it'.[26] The scene was now set for a three-way battle for the London evening market: 'The *Daily News,* like the *Standard,* was offered to the public at 20p a copy and the *Evening News* cut its price to 10p. When Maxwell was rash enough to match this, Leese halved its price again to a derisory 5p. It was the last set-piece battle of the Old Fleet Street, won by Leese with a poker-player's panache.' And caught between the *Standard* on the one hand and the more down-market *News* on the other, Maxwell's *London Daily News* folded on 24 July 1987, with heavy losses. The job done, the *Evening News,* selling 30,000 copies per issue, was closed down. Lori Miles left to make a great success with *Take a Break,* later editing *TV Quick.*

Discussing his victory, Lord Rothermere told Raymond Snoddy of the *Financial Times*:

> What gave me the greatest pleasure recently was the squashing of Bob Maxwell's *Daily News.* His product was aimed at the wrong market. It was badly thought out, poorly constructed and mechanically he didn't have the means of getting it to places he should have got it to. The whole thing was an ill-thought-out performance from beginning to end. It would have died anyway, The whole question was whether we could speed up its demise.

Politically, while the *Standard* had been seeing off the Maxwell opposition, Thatcher had also been seeing off the Labour opposition, and on 12 June 1987, she made history by becoming the first Prime Minister this century to win three successive general elections, with Conservatives 375, Labour 229, Alliance 22, Nationalists 6, and others 18.

In December 1988, the *Evening Standard* became the first of the Associated newspapers to move into the magnificent new Northcliffe House in Kensington.[27] *The Mail on Sunday* followed in July 1989; the last to cross were the *Daily Mail* and the chairman (Lord Rothermere) himself.

One senior executive, Ivor Cole, the paper's long-time legal adviser, commented on the changes in the *Standard*. As the person with the longest line of actual continuity on the paper, he reflected that at Shoe Lane there had been a 'cottage industry feeling, It had been a very intimate atmosphere'. Continuing, he said that the transfer to Kensington had seen a move from paper to new technology: 'It had been a long journey from the white tiles and shabby mahogany of Shoe Lane to the hi-tech of Northcliffe House.' Having served under seven different editors, he noted that each editor had been intent on leaving his mark on the paper, and said: 'I'm your legal adviser. Long live the editor.'[28]

Meanwhile, John Leese was to continue as editor of the *Evening Standard* until ill-health led to his resignation in March 1991, and during his tenure he was to see circulation increase by 12 per cent and the improvement of its profile, so that 72 per cent of its readers were from the affluent ABC1 categories. He died six months after he resigned, on 23 September 1991, and was described by Sir David English, then editor of the *Daily Mail*, as 'a newspaperman's newspaperman, a brilliant technician gifted with excellent judgment'.[29]

ROLE OF MANAGEMENT

During his editorship, John Leese had worked closely with the new managing director, Anthony Hilton, a former City editor on the paper – and only the second journalist to be appointed managing director of the *Standard* in more than a hundred years. It was, as he recalled, a complete surprise: 'I was telephoned at home on a Thursday in November 1989 by Bert Hardy and told he wanted me to start my new job on the following Monday.'[30] Discussing the role of management, Anthony Hilton said that this had changed greatly in recent years and with 'the vacating of power by the print unions had switched from industrial relations to marketing. The key aspect now was understanding the market place.

'Although, through the recession of the past three years, the number of commuters had dropped by 20 per cent, the circulation of the *Standard* was still constant.'

Continuing, he said that with the increased use and efficiency of new desk-top technology it was now possible to change colour pages six times a day. He quoted, as instance, the announcement of John Major winning the leadership of the Conservative Party in November 1990. Dissension within the Conservative backbenchers had finally led to Michael Heseltine challenging Margaret Thatcher for the leadership. The result showed Thatcher polling 204 votes and Heseltine 152. For Thatcher, however, the majority was not enough, and she was forced to stand down. In the subsequent ballot for the leadership – and the premiership – John Major polled 185 votes, Michael Heseltine 131 and Douglas Hurd 56. The result was announced at 6.40 p.m., and 35 minutes later a special edition of the *Standard* was on sale at Westminster, even after allowing 20 minutes for the copies to be despatched from the printing plant at Surrey Docks to the Houses of Parliament.[31]

'The paper would always respond to readers needs and innovate,' Anthony Hilton concluded, and cited a special Saturday edition in January 1991, during the Gulf War, and, more recently, the gradual roll-out of the *Standard* from London to areas where it had previously circulated – Brighton, Oxford and Kent.

For the new editor of the *Standard*, Paul Dacre, it had meant a move from being deputy editor of the *Daily Mail* to its sister paper on an adjacent floor. Born in 1948, he was educated at Leeds University before joining the *Daily Express* as a reporter in 1971. There he rose to become a features writer and then associate features editor. From 1976 to 1979, he was the Washington (and later New York) correspondent of the *Daily Express*. In 1980, he became bureau chief of the New York office of the *Daily Mail* and in 1983, returned to Fleet Street as news editor, *Daily Mail*. Three years afterwards he was appointed assistant editor (news and features). He then became, in succession, assistant editor (features) in 1987; executive editor in 1988; and associate editor in 1989, before transferring to the *Standard* as editor.

Discussing the *Standard*, he said:

> It is unique in world journalism – a power way beyond its circulation. There is a two-fold immediacy with its West End and City coverage and because of its unique time window, 8–9 hours, it is possible to change the course of politics in a day: the government, as an example, has taken a 360 degree turn during a day. It is a paper with tremendous force and integrity and has always been very powerful at No.10. For instance, it was critical of ERM and the only paper to consistently offer such criticism.
>
> Throughout the years, the paper has always had wonderful columnists, Alexander Walker and Milton Shulman, for instance; and for this Charles Wintour must be given much credit. During my editorship the female readership went up by 50 per cent, with 66 per cent of all readers aged under 44 and still more than 70 per cent in the ABC1 social group – and we introduced pink pages for the business section and improved the features and news coverage. The *Standard* can offer such a fast and direct conduit to its readers. There's really no other paper quite like it. Anybody who lives or works in London has to buy it. All in all it is a tactile paper. I was very proud to have been editor.[32]

Paul Dacre continued as editor until July 1992, when he turned down an offer to edit *The Times.* There he would have succeeded Simon Jenkins, another former *Standard* editor, who had announced that he would be standing down to return to writing for *The Times.* As a result of this offer – and his refusal – Dacre was appointed by Lord Rothermere as editor of the *Daily Mail,* succeeding Sir David English, who, after twenty-one successful years, was elevated to chairman and editor-in-chief of Associated Newspapers Ltd.

As a consequence of these changes, the new editor of the *Standard* was to be Stewart Steven, editor of *The Mail on Sunday.* Born in 1937, he was educated at Mayfield College, Sussex, and became a political reporter with Central Press Features in 1961, two years later moving to the *Western Daily Press,* Bristol, as political correspondent. In 1964, he came to Fleet Street, joining the *Daily Express* as a political reporter, and rose to become diplomatic correspondent during 1965–7 and foreign editor, 1967–72. He left to join the *Daily Mail* as assistant editor, and in 1974 was promoted to the post of associate editor. He was then editor of *The Mail on Sunday* during 1982–92.

Steven says, as editor of the *Standard,* he has found running a great metropolitan newspaper the most exciting thing he has ever done in journalism:

> The sheer adrenaline which courses through this floor on a big news day is something I have never experienced before. On Black Wednesday, Nigel Griffiths, our production editor, actually used the phrase, and not in any ironic sense, 'Hold the front page'. I actually heard the phrase used ... and they did hold the front page ... and I thought it would have been a pretty good moment to retire![33]

Discussing the *Standard* and its continuing success, he described it as an exciting paper with a unique constituency:

> Because we are in London, our base is the City, the political establishment – here, the coverage of John Major leading the Conservatives to a fourth successive general election victory in April 1992 is an excellent example – the civil service, the artistic establishment ... all these people are our readers. And between the hours of 10 and 6, we're really their only source of information and comment on the day's events. It is imperative that we have an energy, a drive, which other evening newspapers don't ... My job, in so far as we do have a monopoly, is to protect it. And the best way of doing that is to make it a paper which is so good that no one would dream of coming in against us.[34]

Steven's methods were to be well illustrated in the *Standard* of 11 January 1993, when in a full-page leader, headed 'It's the truth that really frightens them', he commented on possible new legislation to curb the power of the press:

> The press does not have the power to make people behave badly or in a way which is opposite to their public image. All the press can do is to report. When it gets it wrong and when, indeed, it lies it can be sued ... Let us be clear about this: if legislation is framed which means that the Royal Family can only be reported upon in terms of drivelling and lying sycophancy, the Royal Family is doomed. Republicanism will at last become respectable ... It needs to be remembered that the freedom of the press is not simply the freedom to practise 'responsible journalism'. It is the freedom, subject only to the constraints of defamation, sedition, blasphemy, obscenity and incitement, to express views, however wrong or unacceptable, to do so in language which may be trenchant, florid or tabloid.
>
> In 1819, Lord Ellenborough attempted to defend the suppression of Chartist agitation, declaring: 'It was not against the respectable press that this Bill was directed but against the pauper press.' It is ever thus. For pauper press read tabloid press. The issue really is: do we really want a free press, even though a free press can sometimes be cruel, or do we not? If we do not then remember that a licensed press is a press of the Establishment. It will print news that the governing classes wish the people to know. A free press is a press of the people. It tells the people what the governing classes wish to conceal from them ... And yes there may be a gutter press and yes it does sometimes offend not only those of a finer sensibility but us all. But it may be that journalists belong in the gutter because it is in the gutter that the secrets of the ruling class are to be found.

Powerful stuff, and a leader of which the first editor, Dr Stanley Lees Giffard, more than 150 years earlier, would have been proud ... the paper was still 'maintaining its *Standards*'.

Two years later, on September 30, 1995, Stewart Steven, on reaching the age of 60, announced that he intended retiring at the end of the year. Lord Rothermere, paying tribute to Mr Steven, said: 'He has been one of the finest editors of his generation, immensly innovative and with a special skill of bringing on great writers to the titles he ran.'

The new editor was to be Max Hastings, who for almost the past ten years had been editor of *The Daily Telegraph*, and was now to return to the *Evening Standard*, where he had achieved great success as a special correspondent. Sir David English said: 'We have achieved the ultimate situation where a great editor is taking over from a great editor.'

References

Chapter 1 An Outspoken Publisher

1. Apprentices' Register Book 1666 to 1727 (MS, Stationers' Hall, London).
2. Reference Department, High Wycombe Library, Buckinghamshire.
3. Harold Herd, *The March of Journalism*, p. 24.
4. Ibid., p. 31.
5. Ibid., p. 31.
6. A. E. Musson, *The Typographical Association*, p. 5.
7. R. Rosenberg, *English 'Rights and Liberties'.* Richard and Anne Baldwin, Whig Patriot Publishers, p. 373.
8. Times Publishing Co., *Tercentenary Handlist of English and Welsh Newspapers, Magazines and Reviews.*
9. R. Rosenberg, op. cit., p. 374.
10. H. Herd, op. cit., p. 36.
11. S. Morison, *The English Newspaper,* p. 67.
12. Court Book, 103 (MS, Stationers' Hall).
13. J. Dunton, *Sketches of The Printers, Stationers and Binders of the City of London 1689–1705*, p. 118.
14. D. Nichol Smith, *The Newspaper. Johnson's England.* Ed.: A. S. Turberville.
15. *Purnell's New Encyclopedia.* vol. 4, p. 1840.
16. William B. Ewald, Jr., *The Newsmen of Queen Anne,* p. 109.
17. Press Club Collection, London.
18. D. M. Griffiths, *Encyclopedia of the British Press,* p. 399.
19. R. Rosenberg, op. cit., p. 411.
20. H. Herd, op. cit., p. 53.
21. John Gay, *The Present State of Wit,* p. 11.
22. John Morley, *The Spectator.*
23. *The Spectator,* issue no. 452.
24. Jonathan Swift, *Journal to Stella.*
25. *The Spectator,* issue dated 31 July 1712.

Chapter 2 *The Chronicle* is Launched

1. H. Herd, *The March of Journalism,* p. 65.
2. M. Harris, *Newspaper History,* ch. 4: 'The Structure, Ownership and Control of the Press, 1620–1780', p. 84.
3. Ibid., p. 85.
4. Apprentices' Register Book, 1666 to 1727 (MS, Stationers' Hall).
5. Court Book (MS, Stationers' Hall).
6. S. Morison, *The English Newspaper,* p. 144.
7. Charles H. Timperley, *Literary Anecdotes of the Eighteenth Century, VIII,* pp. 478–9.
8. S. Morison, op. cit., p. 144.
9. Richard P. and Marjorie N. Bond 'The Minute Books of *The St. James's Chronicle*', *Studies in Bibliography,* p. 28.
10. Bath Postal Museum.
11. M. Harris, *Newspaper Distribution during Queen Anne's Reign,* p. 141.
12. *The St. James's Chronicle,* Issue no. 1, Guildhall Library, London.
13. Richard P. and Marjorie N. Bond, op. cit., p. 22.
14. D. M. Griffiths, *Encyclopedia of the British Press,* p. 561.

15. Ibid., p. 164.
16. Richard P. and Marjorie N. Bond, op. cit., p. 27.
17. James Boswell, *The Life of Samuel Johnson*, p. 111.
18. H. Herd, op. cit., p. 99.
19. Francis Williams, *Dangerous Estate*, p. 44.
20. File copies, Guildhall Library, London.
21. G. Binney Dibblee, *The Newspaper*, p. 165.
22. Richard P. and Marjorie N. Bond, op. cit., 27 February 1770; 3 August 1770; 21 December 1770; 4 September 1771.
23. D. Johnson, House of Lords Records Office.

Chapter 3 A Phalanx of First-class Wits

1. Court Book (MS, Stationers' Hall).
2. *Annual Register*, 17 (1774). 'The Minute Books of the St. James's Chronicle'.
3. Bond, Richard and Marjorie N. 27 October 1774; 29 June 1775.
4. *Poetical Works of William Cowper*, 'Introduction'.
5. *Purnell's New Encyclopedia*, vol. 11, p. 5363.
6. Francis Williams, *Dangerous Estate*, p. 49.
7. Dewi Morgan, *Phoenix of Fleet Street*, p. 143.
8. *Evening Standard* Library files.
9. Sir Philip Gibbs, *The Journalist's London*, p. 150.
10. *Gentleman's Magazine*, August 1781.
11. E. Howe & Harold Wait, *The London Society of Compositors*, pp. 43–64.
12. A. Aspinall, *Politics and The Press c. 1780–1850*, p. 68.
13. *History of The Times*, vol. I, pps. 3–8.
14. *Evening Standard* Library files.
15. John Child, *Industrial Relations in the Printing Industry*, p. 51.
16. Richard and Marjorie N. Bond, op. cit., 4 May 1808; 8 June 1808; 6 July 1808.
17. H. Herd, *The March of Journalism*, p. 102.
18. *History of The Times*, vol. I, pps. 109–19.
19. *The St. James's Chronicle* file, Guildhall Library, London.
20. Ibid.
21. Conversations with Earl of Halsbury, great-grandson of Dr Stanley Lees Giffard.
22. Ibid.
23. Aspinall, A., *The Formation of Canning's Ministry*, p. 166.

Chapter 4 Plant here *The Standard*

1. *Evening Standard* Library files.
2. A. Aspinall, *Politics and the Press*, p. 79.
3. *Standard* files, British Library Newspaper Library, Colindale, London.
4. Ibid.
5. Earl of Halsbury conversations with author.
6. Croker Papers, 397, 399.
7. Ibid.
8. *Standard* files, British Library Newspaper Library.
9. Ibid.
10. Elizabeth Longford, *Wellington – Pillar of State*, vol. II, p. 189.
11. A. Aspinall, *Politics and the Press*, p. 228.
12. Wellington MSS. Eugenius Roche to Planta, 24 August 1829, The Library, Southampton University.

13. Wellington MSS. Scarlett to Wellington, 18 September 1829.
14. *Evening Standard* Library files.
15. T. H. Macaulay, *History of England.*
16. Lonsdale MSS. Lord Lowther to Lord Lonsdale, 7 May 1831.
17. Ibid. 12 February 1832.
18. Correspondence of Grey and William IV, ii, p. 374.
19. Le Marchant's MSS. Journal.
20. Wellington MSS., The Library, Southampton University.
21. Ibid.
22. Peel MSS., British Library.
23. Ibid.
24. *Standard* files, British Library Newspaper Library.
25. E. Howe, *The London Compositor,* p. 140.

Chapter 5 Bright, Broken Maginn

1. D. M. Griffiths, *Encyclopedia of the British Press,* p. 396.
2. Robert Blake, *Disraeli.*
3. *Evening Standard* Library files.
4. *History of The Times,* vol. I, pps. 392–5.
5. Margaret Forster, *William Makepeace Thackeray,* p. 59.
6. Grantley Berkeley, *My Life and Reflections.*
7. Giffard Correspondence, British Library.
8. Ibid.
9. Alexander Andrews, *The History of British Journalism,* p. 169.
10. *Dictionary of National Biography,* p. 976.
11. Halsbury Collection and conversations with author.
12. Ibid.
13. Ibid.
14. *Standard* files, British Library Newspaper Library.
15. *Greville Memoirs* (second part) Vol. I, p. 158.
16. *The Times* Newspapers Archives.
17. Peel papers, British Library.
18. *Standard* files, British Library Newspaper Library.
19. Ibid.
20. Ibid.
21. R. J. Evans, *The Victorian Age 1815–1914,* p. 37.
22. *Evening Standard* Library files.
23. Halsbury Collection and conversations with author.
24. Ibid.
25. Ibid.
26. Ibid.
27. Conversations with Dr Nigel Cross, Royal Literary Fund.
28. *Evening Standard* Library files.
29. H. Herd, *The March of Journalism,* p. 149.

Chapter 6 Enter Edward Baldwin

1. James Grant, *The Newspaper Press. Its Origins, Progress and Present Position,* p. 317.
2. Ibid., p. 319.
3. Ibid.
4. *Standard* files, British Library Newspaper Library.

5. *The Times* files, British Library Newspaper Library.
6. Conversation with Curator, Dickens Museum, Doughty Street, London.
7. *Standard* files, British Library Newspaper Library.
8. A. W. Palmer, *A Dictionary of Modern History 1789–1945*, p. 211.
9. *Standard* files, British Library Newspaper Library.
10. Ibid.
11. Halsbury Collection and conversations with present Earl.
12. A. P. Wadsworth, *Newspaper Circulations 1800–1954*.
13. *Standard* files, British Library Newspaper Library.
14. James Grant, op. cit.
15. *Punch* Archives.
16. Stephen Koss, *The Rise and Fall of the Political Press in Britain*, Vol. 1, p. 103.
17. Ibid.
18. *The Times* files, British Library Newspaper Library.
19. R. Wilkinson-Latham, *From Our Special Correspondent*, p. 37.

Chapter 7 A Change of Ownership

1. *The Times* files, British Library Newspaper Library.
2. D. M. Griffiths, *Encyclopedia of the British Press*, p. 86.
3. James Grant, *The Newspaper Press*, vol. II, pps. 111–113.
4. J. C. Francis, *Notes and Queries* (1916).
5. *Standard* files, British Library Newspaper Library.
6. Report from the Select Committee of the House of Commons on Newspaper Stamps, Parliamentary papers, xvii (1851), British Library Newspaper Library.
7. *Daily Telegraph* files, British Library Newspaper Library.
8. *Punch* Archives.
9. *History of The Times*, vol. II, pps. 297–9.
10. D. M. Griffiths, op. cit., p. 597.
11. *Sell's Dictionary of the World Press*, 1904, obituaries.
12. Conversation with Librarian, Oriel College, Oxford.
13. Halsbury Collection.
14. *Standard* files, British Library Newspaper Library.
15. T. H. S. Escott, *Platform, Press, Politics and Play*, p. 236.
16. Ibid.
17. Hughenden (Benjamin Disraeli, Earl of Beaconsfield) Papers, Bodleian Library, Oxford.
18. Ibid.
19. *Punch* Archives.
20. *Standard* Archives.
21. Hughenden Papers.
22. Lucy Brown, *Victorian News and Newspapers*, p. 63. See also Basil L. Crapster, 'Thomas Hamber, 1828–1902, Tory Journalist', *Victorian Periodicals Newsletter, 1978–80*, 117, quoting Hotze MSS, in the Library of Congress.
23. Ibid.
24. Conversation with Justine Taylor, Archivist, Reuters; and Reuter's contract with James Johnstone.
25. D. M. Griffiths, op. cit., p. 304.
26. R. Wilkinson-Latham, *From Our Special Correspondent*, p. 90.
27. St. Bride Institute Library.

Chapter 8 Captain Hamber Departs

1. James Grant, *The Newspaper Press,* 1871.
2. Disraeli Papers, Bodleian Library.
3. Ibid.
4. Ibid.
5. Alfred Austin, *Autobiography,* ch. VII.
6. A. W. Palmer, *A Dictionary of Modern History,* pp. 48–9.
7. Alfred Austin, op. cit. ch.1, pp. 24ff.
8. Ibid.
9. Ibid.
10. Ibid.
11. *Standard* Archives.
12. *Sell's Dictionary of the World Press,* 1899, obituaries.
13. A Journalist, *Bohemian Days in Fleet Street,* p. 168.
14. *Sell's Dictionary of the World Press,* 1905, obituaries.
15. Disraeli Papers, Bodleian Library.
16. *Morning Herald* files, British Library Newspaper Library.
17. Disraeli Papers, Bodleian Library.
18. T. H. S. Escott, *Master of English Journalism,* pp. 197–202.
19. Stephen Koss, *The Rise and Fall of the Polical Press in Britain.* vol. I, p. 182.
20. Disraeli Papers, Bodleian Library.
21. Stephen Koss, op. cit., p. 183.
22. Obituary, Stationers' Company.
23. *Dictionary of National Biography.*
24. Sir John Gorst, *The Maori King,* p. 220.
25. Alfred Austin, op. cit., p. 108.
26. Blackwood Papers, National Library of Scotland, Edinburgh.
27. T. H. S. Escott, *Masters of English Journalism,* op. cit., pp. 197–202.
28. Basil L. Crapster, 'Thomas Hamber'.
29. Stephen Koss, op. cit., p. 184.

Chapter 9 Mudford Takes Over

1. *Standard* files.
2. Ibid.
3. Obituary, *The Times,* 20 October 1916.
4. Ibid.
5. Alfred Austin, *Autobiography,* p. 94.
6. *Standard* archives.
7. *The Times* archives: MacDonald correspondence.
8. William Colley, *News Hunter,* pp. 162–3
9. Stephen Koss, *The Rise and Fall of the Political Press in Britain,* vol. I, p. 237.
10. Ibid, p. 237.
11. Escott Papers, British Library.
12. H. Massingham, *The London Daily Press,* p. 80.
13. St. Bride Printing Library archives.
14. H. Massingham, op. cit., p. 115.
15. Robert Wilkinson-Latham, *From Our Special Correspondent,* p. 139.
16. Ibid, p. 143.
17. Ibid.
18. *Standard* files, British Library Newspaper Library.
19. Wilkinson-Latham, op. cit., p. 152.

20. *Standard* files, British Library Newspaper Library.
21. Wilkinson-Latham, op. cit., p. 175.
22. *Standard* files, British Library Newspaper Library.
23. Ibid.

Chapter 10 The New Journalism

1. Enoch Powell, *Joseph Chamberlain*, p. 18.
2. Lady Gwendolen Cecil, *Salisbury*, vol. III. p. 142.
3. *Standard* files, British Library Newspaper Library.
4. Cecil, Lady Gwendolen: op. cit.
5. Stephen Koss, *The Rise and Fall of the Political Press in Britain*, vol. I, p. 278.
6. *Standard* files, British Library Newspaper Library.
7. Anne Sebba, *Battling for News. The Rise of the Woman Reporter*, p. 30.
8. *The Times* archives.
9. *Standard* files, British Library Newspaper Library.
10. Salisbury Papers.
11. R. D. Blumenfeld, *The Press in My Time*, p. 32.
12. Stephen Koss, op. cit., p. 346, (see also J. O. Baylen, 'The New Journalism in Late Victorian Britain,' *Australian Journal of Politics and History*, XV III (1972), 367ff.
13. Reginald Pound and Geoffrey Harmsworth, *Northcliffe*, ch. 4.
14. D. M. Griffiths, *Encyclopedia of the British Press*, p. 459.
15. Stephen Koss, op. cit., p. 331.
16. Ibid., p. 316.
17. Austin to Salisbury: Salisbury Papers.
18. Salisbury papers (copy).
19. Stephen Koss, op. cit., p. 317.
20. *Standard* files, British Library Newspaper Library.
21. Memorandum to Chamberlain, 21 August 1899. Chamberlain Papers.
22. *Standard* archive.
23. R. J. Evans, *The Victorian Age 1815–1914*, p. 317.
24. R. D. Blumenfeld, *All In a Lifetime*, p. 226.
25. Stephen Koss, op. cit., p. 386.
26. *The Times* files, British Library Newspaper Library.

Chapter 11 The Greatest Hustler

1. *Standard* archives.
2. *Newspaper World*, February 1900, St. Bride Printing Library.
3. R. D. Blumenfeld, *In My Time* (The Press) pp. 73–4.
4. Paul Tritton, *John Montagu of Beaulieu. Motoring Pioneer and Prophet*, p. 107.
5. Ibid, p. 110.
6. Ibid, p. 112.
7. D. M. Griffiths, *Encyclopedia of the British Press*, p. 435.
8. Ibid, p. 532.
9. Sidney Dark, *The Life of Sir Arthur Pearson*, p. 114.
10. R. D. Blumenfeld, *R.D.B.'s Diary*, p. 197.
11. *Daily Mail* files, British Library Newspaper Library.
12. Stephen Koss, *The Rise and Fall of the Political Press in Britain, vol. II: The Twentieth Century*, p. 26.
13. *History of The Times*, vol. III, *The Twentieth Century Test, 1884–1912*, p. 122.
14. Stephen Koss, op. cit., p. 28.
15. Desmond Chapman-Huston; *The Lost Historian*, p. 99.

16. *The Times* files, British Library Newspaper Library.
17. *The Standard* files, British Library Newspaper Library.
18. Sidney Dark, op. cit., p. 121.
19. *Standard* archives.
20. Sidney Dark, op. cit., p. 102.
21. *The Newspaper Owner*, March 1905.
22. Sidney Dark, op. cit., p. 121.
23. William Colley, *News Hunter*, p. 156.
24. *History of The Times*, vol. III, p. 532.
25. *Daily Mail* files, British Library Newspaper Library.
26. *History of The Times*, vol. III, p. 532.
27. Ibid., p. 311.
28. *History of The Times*, Vol. III, p. 536.
29. *The Observer* files, British Library Newspaper Library.

Chapter 12 Dalziel in Charge

1. Sidney Dark, *The Life of Sir Arthur Pearson*, p. 127.
2. *The Newspaper Owner*, June 1909, St. Bride Printing Library.
3. Balfour Papers, British Library.
4. Desmond Chapman-Huston, *The Lost Historian*, p. 344.
5. R. J. Evans, *The Victorian Age*, pp. 401–2.
6. *Standard* files, British Library Newspaper Library.
7. William Colley, *News Hunter*, p. 167.
8. Ibid., p. 166.
9. *Standard* files, British Library Newspaper Library.
10. Margaret Lane, *Edgar Wallace. A biography*, p. 229.
11. Stephen Koss, *The Rise and Fall of the Political Press in Britain*, vol. II, p. 122.
12. *Advertising World* files, January 1909, St. Bride Printing Library.
13. Sidney Dark, op. cit., p. 125.
14. R. P. T. Davenport-Hines, *Dictionary of Business Biography*, vol. 2, p. 5.
15. Graham Storey, *Reuters Century*, p. 108.
16. Ibid., p. 110.
17. R. P. T. Davenport-Hines, op. cit., p. 7.
18. Anne Chisholm and Michael Davie, *Beaverbrook. A Life*, p. 105.
19. Balfour Papers, British Library. See also Stephen Koss op. cit. p. 177.
20. Bonar Law Papers, House of Lords. Ibid.
21. *Newspaper Editor* files, 1915, St. Bride Printing Library.
22. Stephen Koss, op. cit., vol. II, p. 179.
23. *Standard* files, British Library Newspaper Library.
24. Ibid.
25. Ibid.
26. Sidney Low, *Samuel Henry Jeyes. A sketch of his personality and work*, p. 142.
27. *Newspaper Owner*, December 1911, St. Bride Printing Library.
28. William Colley, op. cit., p. 158.
29. Ibid.
30. B. M. Hansard, *In and Out of Fleet Street*, p. 169.
31. Ibid., p. 174.
32. R. P. T. Davenport-Hines, op. cit., p. 9.
33. B. M. Hansard, op. cit., p. 176.
34. Ibid., pp. 176–7.
35. Koss, Stephen, op. cit. vol. II, p. 263.
36. Ibid.

Chapter 13 The Man from Manchester

1. Michael Burn, *The Guardian*, 26 August 1985, p. 6.
2. D. M. Griffiths, *Encyclopedia of the British Press*, p. 324.
3. Bernard Falk, *He Laughed in Fleet Street*, p. 25.
4. Michael Burn, op. cit.
5. *Newspaper Editor* files, 1909, St. Bride Printing Library.
6. Bernard Falk, op. cit., p. 29.
7. *Newspaper Editor* files, 1909, St. Bride Printing Library.
8. Personal knowledge.
9. Viscount Camrose, *British Newspapers and their Controllers*, p. 83.
10. *Newspaper Editor* files, April 1915, St. Bride Printing Library.
11. William Colley, *News Hunter*, p. 196.
12. *Newspaper Editor* files, August 1915, St. Bride Printing Library.
13. D. M. Griffiths, op. cit., p. 400.
14. William Colley, op. cit., p. 197.
15. Ibid., p. 192.
16. Ibid.
17. *The Times* files, British Library Newspaper Library.
18. William Colley, op. cit., p. 201.
19. *Evening Standard* files, British Library Newspaper Library.
20. Sidney Dark, op. cit., p. 139.
21. Ibid., p. 199.
22. Ibid., p. 204.
23. *Daily Express* files, British Library Newspaper Library.

Chapter 14 Empire Crusader

1. Bernard Falk, *He Laughed in Fleet Street*, ch. II.
2. Ibid., p. 29.
3. Lord Hartwell, *William Camrose. Giant of Fleet Street*, ch.9, pp. 111–19.
4. Conversations with Jocelyn Stevens, grandson of Sir Edward Hulton, and later managing director of the *Evening Standard*. See also Charles Wintour, *The Rise and Fall of Fleet Street*, pp. 88–9.
5. Gwynne to Baldwin, October 3, 1923 (copy), Bodleian Library, Oxford.
6. Lord Hartwell, op. cit., ch.9.
7. A. J. P. Taylor, *Beaverbrook*, p. 215.
8. Conversations with Jocelyn Stevens.
9. Harold Oxbury, *Great Britons. Twentieth Century Lives*, p. 3.
10. R. P. T. Davenport-Hines, vol. 2, *Dictionary of Business Biography* Beaverbrook.
11. A. J. P. Taylor, op. cit., p. 215.
12. R. D. B. Blumenfeld, *All In a Lifetime*, p. 204.
13. Ibid., p. 206.
14. *Daily Express* archives, 24 February 1922.
15. Lord Beaverbrook, *Politicians and the Press*, p. 10.
16. Tom Driberg, *Beaverbrook*, p. 139.
17. Ibid., p. 84.
18. Stephen Koss, *The Rise and Fall of the Political Press*, vol. II, p. 307.
19. *Daily Express* archives.
20. Lord Beaverbrook, op. cit., p. 17.
21. Ibid., p. 34.
22. *Evening Standard* Minutes Book, 30 November 1923.

23. Ibid., 25 January 1924.
24. Ibid., 3 June 1924.

Chapter 15 The General Strike

1. Lord Beaverbrook, *Politicians and the Press*, ch. VI.
2. Ibid., p. 50.
3. Randolph Churchill, *Lord Derby. A Biography.*
4. A. J. P. Taylor, *Beaverbrook*, p. 207.
5. Ibid.
6. A. J. P. Taylor, op. cit., p. 208.
7. Harold Nicolson, *Curzon: The Last Phase.*
8. A. J. P. Taylor, op. cit., p. 211.
9. Anne Chisholm and Michael Davie, *Beaverbrook: A Life*, pp. 11–32.
10. Beaverbrook to Stanley Morison, 4 May 1951.
11. Stephen Koss, *The Rise and Fall of the Political Press*, vol. II, p. 428.
12. *Evening Standard* files, British Library Newspaper Library.
13. Stephen Koss, op. cit., p. 436.
14. Gwynne to Beaverbrook, 14 May 1924. Beaverbrook Papers. C/148, House of Lords, quoted by Koss, op. cit., p. 437.
15. *The Workers Weekly* file, British Library Newspaper Library.
16. A. J. P. Taylor, op. cit., p. 224.
17. *Evening Standard* files, British Library Newspaper Library.
18. *Daily Express* archives.
19. *Daily Mail* file, British Newspaper Library, Colindale.
20. *Daily Express* archives.
21. Arthur Christiansen, *Headlines All My Life*, p. 46.
22. Author's collection.
23. A. J. P. Taylor, op. cit., p. 232.
24. Ibid.
25. Margaret Drabble, *Arnold Bennett. A Biography*, p. 313.
26. Anne Chisholm and Michael Davie, op. cit., pp. 240–1.
27. *Evening Standard* archives.
28. Ibid.
29. *Evening Standard* Minutes Book, March 1931.
30. Sir Thomas Blackburn Papers, *Evening Standard* archives.
31. David Low, *Low's Autobiography*, p. 85.

Chapter 16 Celebrating 100 Years

1. A. J. P. Taylor, *Beaverbrook*, p. 241.
2. Anne Chisholm and Michael Davie, *Beaverbrook. A Life*, p. 257.
3. A. J. P. Taylor, op. cit., p. 259.
4. *Evening Standard* files, British Library Newspaper Library.
5. A. J. P. Taylor, op. cit., p. 261
6. Ibid.
7. Ibid.
8. D. M. Griffiths, *Encyclopedia of the British Press*, p. 132.
9. *The Times* newspaper files, obituary, 12 April 1928, Guildhall Library, London.
10. Bruce Lockhart Diaries, *Daily Express* archives (now House of Lords)
11. Kenneth Young (ed.), *The Diaries of Sir Robert Bruce Lockhart*, p. 72.
12. Harold Oxbury, *Great Britons* pp. 262–3.

13. Nigel Nicolson (ed.)., *Harold Nicolson. Diaries and Letters 1930–39*, p. 34.
14. Kenneth Young (ed.), op. cit., p. 99.
15. Nigel Nicolson, op. cit., p. 35.
16. A. J. P. Taylor, op. cit., ch.12.
17. *Evening Standard* archives.
18. *Evening Standard* files, 17 March 1931, British Library Newspaper Library.
19. Hugh Cudlipp, *The Prerogative of The Harlot*, p. 274.
20. Duff Cooper, *Old Men Forget*, p. 177.
21. Nigel Nicolson, op. cit., p. 69.
22. Ibid., p. 62.
23. Ibid., pp. 78–9.
24. Ibid., p. 88.

Chapter 17 The Abdication Crisis

1. Bruce Lockhart Diaries, *Daily Express* archives.
2. Nigel Nicolson (ed.), *Harold Nicolson. Diaries and Letters 1930–39*, p. 154.
3. Kenneth Young (ed.), *The Diaries of Sir Robert Bruce Lockhart*, p. 276.
4. Ibid., p. 293.
5. Ibid., p. 301.
6. David Low, *Low's Autobiography*, p. 250.
7. D. M. Griffiths, *Encyclopedia of the British Press*, p. 179.
8. *Evening Standard* Minutes Book, June 1934.
9. Ibid., July 1934.
10. Ibid., July 1934.
11. Malcolm Muggeridge, *Chronicles of Wasted Time, The Infernal Grove*, p. 49.
12. John Bright-Holmes (ed.) *Like It Was. The Diaries of Malcolm Muggeridge*, p. 50.
13. Kenneth Young (ed.), op. cit., p. 329.
14. Howard Spring, *Autobiography*, p. 186.
15. A. J. P. Taylor, *Beaverbrook*, p. 352 (see also Anne Chisholm and Michael Davie, *Beaverbrook. A Life*, pp. 330–3).
16. Kenneth Young (ed.), op. cit., p. 333.
17. John Bright-Holmes, op. cit., p. 141.
18. Ibid., p. 145.
19. Richard Bourne, *Lords of Fleet Street. The Harmsworth Dynasty*, p. 114.
20. A. J. P. Taylor, op. cit., p. 349.
21. H. R. H. The Duke of Windsor, *A King's Story*, p. 243.
22. Harold Nicolson, *King George V*, p. 531.
23. H. R. H. The Duke of Windsor, op. cit., p. 291.
24. A. J. P. Taylor, op. cit., p. 369.
25. Chips Channon, *Diaries of Chips Channon*, p. 105.
26. Ibid., p. 107.
27. *Yorkshire Post* files, 2 December 1935, British Library Newspaper Library.
28. H. R. H. The Duke of Windsor, op. cit., p. 321.
29. *History of The Times, 1921–1948*, Part II, p. 1036.
30. Chips Channon, op. cit., p. 118.

Chapter 18 Munich and Appeasement

1. A. J. P. Taylor, *Beaverbrook*, p. 334.
2. Malcolm Muggeridge, *Chronicles of Wasted Time, The Infernal Grove*, p. 50.
3. Bruce Lockhart Diaries, *Daily Express* archives.

4. Malcolm Muggeridge, op. cit., p. 55.
5. Chips Channon, *Diaries of Chips Channon*, p. 162.
6. *Evening Standard* files, British Library Newspaper Library.
7. Ibid.
8. Anne Wolrige Gordon, *Peter Howard. Life and Letters*, p. 85.
9. Anita Leslie, *Cousin Randolph. The Life of Randolph Churchill*, p. 41.
10. *History of The Times*, vol. IV, pps. 929–34.
11. *Evening Standard* files, British Library Newspaper Library.
12. Nigel Nicolson (ed.), *Harold Nicolson, Diaries and letters* 1930–39, p. 374.
13. Kenneth Young, (ed.) *The Diaries of Sir Bruce Lockhart*, p. 399.

Chapter 19 On the Brink

1. Arthur Christiansen, *Headlines All My Life*, p. 163.
2. Gron Williams, *Firebrand: The Frank Owen Story*, pp. 21ff.
3. Michael Foot, *Debts of Honour*, p. 86.
4. W. H. Auden, quoted in ibid., p. 165.
5. Chips Channon, *Diaries of Chips Channon*, p. 230.
6. Francis Williams, *Nothing So Strange*, p. 147.
7. E. J. Robertson papers, *Daily Express* archives.
8. *Evening Standard* Board Minutes, 4 May 1939.
9. A. J. P. Taylor, *Beaverbrook*, p. 394.
10. Sir Thomas Blackburn papers, *Daily Express* archives.
11. E. J. Robertson papers, *Daily Express* archives.
12. Michael Foot, op. cit., p. 76 and conversations with author.
13. Ibid., p. 78.
14. Michael Foot, conversations with author.
15. Michael Foot, op. cit., p. 77.
16. E. J. Robertson Papers, *Daily Express* archives.
17. John Colville, *The Fringes of Power*, p. 19.
18. George Malcolm Thomson, *Viscount Castlerosse*, p. 154; and conversation with author.

Chapter 20 *The Standard* at War

1. E. J. Robertson Papers, *Daily Express archives.*
2. Ibid.
3. Information from the late John Robertson, son of E. J. Robertson.
4. Ibid.
5. *World Press News* files, 18, April 1940, St. Bride Printing Library.
6. Information from Geoffrey Hamilton, then Head of the British Newspaper Library, Colindale.
7. Letter to Lowell Thomas, 5 March 1940, quoted by A. J. P. Taylor, *Beaverbrook*, p. 402.
8. Duff Cooper, *Old Men Forget*, p. 278.
9. Anne Wolridge Gordon, *Peter Howard*, p. 103.
10. Conversations with Michael Foot.
11. Ibid.
12. E. J. Robertson papers, *Daily Express* Archives.
13. Peter Howard, *Beaverbrook. Max the Unknown*, p. 134.
14. John Colville, *The Fringes of Power*, Vol. I, p. 299.
15. Conversations with Michael Foot.
16. Stephen Koss, *The Rise and Fall of the Political Press in Britain* vol. II, p. 602.
17. *Evening Standard* archives.

18. Conversation with Roy Oliver, chief engineer, *Evening Standard*.
19. Stephen Koss, op. cit., vol. II, p. 608.
20. Conversations with Michael Foot.
21. E. J. Robertson papers, *Daily Express* Archives.
22. Conversations with Michael Foot.
23. Ibid.
24. Ibid.
25. Ibid.
26. Ibid.
27. A. J. P. Taylor, *Beaverbrook*, p. 432.
28. Michael Davie (ed.), *The Diaries of Evelyn Waugh*, p. 517.
29. Philip Knightley, *The First Casualty*, p. 291.
30. Anne Sebba, *Battling for News. The Rise of the Woman Reporter*, p. 170.
31. Philip Knightley, op. cit., p. 326.
32. Phyllis A. Deakin, *Press on*, p. 62.

Chapter 21 Peace in Shoe Lane

1. A. J. P. Taylor, *Beaverbrook*, p. 565.
2. E. J. Robertson papers, *Evening Standard* Archives.
3. Herbert Gunn papers, *Evening Standard* Archives.
4. *World's Press News* files, March 1945, St. Bride Printing Library.
5. Conversations with Charles Wintour.
6. *Evening Standard* files, British Library Newspaper Library.
7. A. J. P. Taylor, op. cit., p. 566.
8. Ibid.
9. Conversations with Charles Wintour.
10. E. J. Robertson papers, *Daily Express* Archives.
11. A. J. P. Taylor, op. cit., p. 585.
12. A. J. P. Taylor, op. cit., p. 586.
13. *World's Press News* files, November 1948, St. Bride Printing Library.
14. *Evening Standard* 150th anniversary number, 21 May 1977.
15. Ibid.
16. Conversations with Charles Wintour.
17. Ibid.
18. Ibid.
19. A. J. P. Taylor, op. cit., p. 592.
20. Ibid., p. 593
21. Conversations with Charles Wintour.
22. *Evening Standard* Archives.
23. Francis Williams, *Dangerous Estate. The Anatomy of Newspapers*, p. 260.

Chapter 22 Death of Beaverbrook

1. Conversations with Judith Dunn, News International Newspapers Ltd.
2. A. J. P. Taylor, *Beaverbrook*, pp. 621–2.
3. Ibid.
4. Discussions and correspondence with Sir John Junor.
5. Ibid.
6. Sir John Junor, *Listening For A Midnight Tram*, pp. 79–80.
7. Ibid.
8. *Evening Standard* Archives, special edition.

9. Conversations with Charles Wintour.
10. *Evening Standard* files.
11. Conversation with Robert Edwards.
12. Robert Edwards, *Goodbye to Fleet Street*, p. 55.
13. Ibid., p. 58.
14. Ibid., p. 62.
15. Conversation with Robert Edwards.
16. Conversations with Charles Wintour.
17. *Evening Standard* 150th anniversary number, 21 May 1977.
18. *UK Press Gazette*, 2 November 1987.
19. *World's Press News*, 11 March 1960.
20. John Coote, *Altering Course. A Submariner in Fleet Street*, p. 51.
21. Conversations with Charles Wintour.
22. Ibid.
23. Ibid.
24. A. J. P. Taylor, op. cit., p. 594.
25. Conversations with Charles Wintour.
26. Ibid.
27. A. J. P. Taylor, op. cit., p. 654.
28. Hugh Cudlipp, *The Prerogative of the Harlot*, pp. 296–7.
29. Conversations with Sir Eric Cheadle.

Chapter 23 Decline and Fall

1. Information from *Daily Express* Father of Chapel.
2. A. J. P. Taylor, *Beaverbrook*, p. 654.
3. Obituary, *Daily Express*,
4. John Coote, *Altering Course, A Submariner in Fleet Street*, p. 51.
5. Obituary, *Daily Express.*
6. Conversations with Charles Wintour.
7. *Evening Standard* 150th anniversary number, 21 May 1977.
8. Ibid.
9. Personal knowledge.
10. Conversations with Jocelyn Stevens.
11. Ibid.
12. Personal knowledge.
13. Ibid.
14. Ibid.
15. Conversations with Charles Wintour.
16. Personal knowledge.
17. Charles Wintour, *Pressures on the Press*, p. 86.
18. Conversations with Jocelyn Stevens.
19. Ibid.
20. Ibid.
21. John Coote, op. cit., p. 110.
22. Lewis Chester and Jonathan Fenby, *The Fall of the House of Beaverbrook*, pp. 55–7.
23. Personal knowledge.
24. Lewis Chester and Jonathan Fenby, op. cit., p. 62.
25. Personal knowledge.
26. Conversation with Simon Jenkins.
27. Lewis Chester and Jonathan Fenby, op. cit., p. 99.
28. Ibid., p. 109, and conversations with Charles Wintour.
29. Conversation with Simon Jenkins.

30. Personal knowledge.
31. Conversations with Charles Wintour.
32. Conversation with Simon Jenkins.
33. Conversations with Charles Wintour.

Chapter 24 Harmsworth Victorious

1. Charles Wintour, *The Rise and Fall of Fleet Street*, p. 151.
2. Ibid., pp. 152–3.
3. Personal knowledge.
4. Personal knowledge.
5. Conversation with Simon Jenkins.
6. *Daily Mail* files, 1 November 1980.
7. Conversation with Vere Harmsworth (Lord Rothermere III).
8. Conversations with Charles Wintour.
9. Conversations with Jocelyn Stevens and, later, Louis Kirby.
10. Conversation with Louis Kirby.
11. Ibid.
12. Personal knowledge.
13. *Campaign*, June 1981.
14. Ibid.
15. *Evening Standard* files, 4 May 1979.
16. Ibid.
17. Conversation with Jocelyn Stevens.
18. Charles Wintour, op. cit., p. 165.
19. *The Times* files, 3 April 1982.
20. *Evening Standard* files, 14 June 1982. See also: Max Hastings and Simon Jenkins, *The Battle for the Falklands* (1983), pp. 348–50.
21. Charles Wintour, op. cit., p. 184.
22. *Evening Standard* Archives.
23. Charles Wintour, op. cit., p. 168.
24. Ibid., p. 212.
25. Conversation with Vere Harmsworth (Lord Rothermere III)
26. Personal knowledge.
27. Conversations with Angus McGill.
28. Conversations with Ivor Cole.
29. Obituary, *Daily Telegraph*, 24 September 1991.
30. Conversation with Anthony Hilton.
31. Ibid.
32. Conversation with Paul Dacre.
33. Conversation with Stewart Steven.
34. Ibid.

Appendix 1
Chronology

1653 Richard Baldwin born
1681 Launches *Mercurius Anglicus*
1682 Launches *The London Mercury* and *The Protestant Courant*
1694 With wife, Anne, launches *The Post-Man*
1698 Richard Baldwin dies and Anne takes over the business

1709 Anne Baldwin becomes publisher of *Female Tatler*
1710 Launches *The Medley*
1711 Launches *New Tatler*
1713 Anne Baldwin dies
1734 Henry Baldwin born
1761 Launches *St. James's Chronicle*
1774 His son, Charles, born
1789 Charles apprenticed in business

1803 Edward, son of Charles, born
1808 Charles Baldwin becomes majority shareholder
1809 Purchases *London Evening Post*
1813 Henry Baldwin dies
1819 Charles Baldwin purchases *London Chronicle*
1827 Launches *The Standard*
1844 Charles Baldwin retires, succeeded by his son, Edward, who buys *Morning Herald*
1857 Edward Baldwin declared bankrupt and *The Standard* and *Morning Herald* bought by James Johnstone (born 1815), who converts *The Standard* to a morning paper
1859 Launches the *Evening Standard*
1860 Charles Baldwin dies; James Johnstone closes down *Morning Herald*
1878 James Johnstone dies; William Mudford, editor, appointed manager for life to represent Johnstone family interests
1890 Edward Baldwin dies
1899 William Mudford retires

1904 *Standard* purchased by C. Arthur Pearson, founder of *Daily Express*
1905 Pearson merges *St. James's Gazette* (bought 1903) with *The Standard*
1910 Due to increasing blindness, Pearson sells *Standard* and *Evening Standard* to Davison Dalziel
1915 *Evening Standard* sold by Dalziel to Edward Hulton Jr
1916 *The Standard* ceases publication
1916 William Mudford dies from burns
1921 Pearson drowns in his bath
1923 *Pall Mall Gazette* incorporated into *Evening Standard* having itself absorbed *The Globe* two years earlier
1923 *Evening Standard* purchased from Hulton by Lord Beaverbrook (Max Aitken, born 1879)
1940 *Evening Standard* premises bombed by German aircraft. Germans produce a fictitious *Evening Standard* as propaganda exercise

1960 *The Star* merged with *Evening News*
1963 Death of Lord Beaverbrook; proprietorship of Beaverbrook Newspapers, including *Evening Standard*, passes to Sir Max Aitken
1977 Beaverbrook Newspapers – *Evening Standard, Daily Express* and *Sunday Express* – purchased by Trafalgar House, and renamed Express Newspapers; Victor Matthews becomes chief executive
1980 *Evening News* (owned by Associated Newspapers) closes and is absorbed by *Evening Standard*; joint company set up with Trafalgar House having 50 per cent and Associated Newspapers 50 per cent of the *New Standard*; Lord Matthews appointed chairman
1982 Trafalgar House demerges Express Newspapers into Fleet Holdings
1985 Fleet Holdings purchased by United Newspapers; Sir Max Aitken dies; Associated Newspapers, under proprietorship of Lord Rothermere III (Vere Harmsworth) assume full control of *Evening Standard*
1987 ES Magazine launched as a monthly
1988 *Evening Standard* leaves Fleet Street for Northcliffe House, Derry Street, Kensington
1990 Business Day section, pink pages, launched
1993 ES Magazine converts to a weekly in newspaper colour format
1994 Business Day interactive electronic pages launched

The Great Survivor

The oldest evening newspaper in Great Britain, the *Evening Standard* is the great survivor; and as the sole London evening has absorbed nine other titles in its 168-year history: *Traveller, Lane's Star, The British Traveller, The Albion, St. James's Gazette, Pall Mall Gazette, Globe, Evening News* and *Star.*

Appendix 2
Editors

The Standard: 1827–1916

1827–57	Dr Stanley Lees Giffard
1857–72	Thomas Hamber
1872–74	James Johnstone Jr
	John Eldon Gorst
1874–99	W. H. Mudford
1900–04	G. Byron Curtis
1904–11	H. A. Gwynne
1911–16	Herbert A. White

Evening Standard: 1915–

1915–20	A. H. Mann
1920–23	D. Phillips
1923–28	E. R. Thompson
1928–33	G. Gilliat
1933–37	Percy Cudlipp
1937–38	R. J. T. Thompson
1938–42	Frank Owen
1942–44	Michael Foot
1944–45	Sidney Elliot
1945–50	Herbert Gunn
1950–59	Percy Elland
1959–76	Charles Wintour
1976–78	Simon Jenkins
1978–80	Charles Wintour
1980–86	Louis Kirby
1986–91	John Leese
1991–92	Paul Dacre
1992 –	Stewart Steven

Note: In June 1857, *The Standard* converted to a morning paper and two years later launched the *Evening Standard*, an edition for London and the City. Editors of this edition reported to the editor of *The Standard* and sales were included in the overall figures of *The Standard*. Editors were:

1859–60	Charles Williams
1860–64	John Moor Philp
1864–88	Unknown
1888–97	Sidney Low
1897–98	S. J. Pryor
1898–1905	Unknown
1906–12	William Woodward
1912–14	J. A. Kilpatrick
1914–15	A. Wyatt Tilby

Note: For many years, the *Evening Standard* was produced without an appointed editor, the paper, as noted, coming under the aegis of the editor of *The Standard*. In 1915, Davison Dalziel sold the *Evening Standard* to Edward Hulton, who appointed Arthur H. Mann as editor. Dalziel, however, retained the ownership of *The Standard*, which ceased publication in 1916.

Appendix 3
Circulation

	Jan–Dec
1926	314 633
1927	335 941
1928	379 848
1929	363 401
1930	366 991
1931	366 161
1932	367 212
1933	373 753
1934	380 024
1935	389 594
1936	405 504
1937	388 040
1938	388 381
1939	382 238
1940	401 009
1941	461 107
1942	483 273
1943	521 120
1944	599 340
1945	656 422
1946	717 634
1947	763 440
1948	781 141
1949	839 998

	Jan–Jun	Jul–Dec
1950	861 671	871 380
1951	839 458	788 321
1952	786 695	764 995
1953	777 669	766 687
1954	761 292	755 311
1955	710 776	678 244
1956	662 608	680 239
1957	665 428	628 078
1958	589 706	592 485
1959	576 618	586 097
1960	584 061	659 469
1961	761 325	745 996
1962	742 126	741 337
1963	729 241	770 509
1964	758 799	704 264
1965	680 446	661 993

1966	666 446	659 337
1967	676 607	652 939
1968	657 050	594 734
1969	583 366	560 596
1970	549 667	530 040
1971	527 255	506 246
1972	519 154	496 655
1973	519 604	511 681
1974	522 000	518 499
1975	485 481	435 969
1976	431 094	414 349
1977	411 538	396 457
1978	398 316	361 474
1979	376 870	363 553
1980	371 903	–
1981	641 449	569 305
1982	568 762	522 664
1983	506 998	479 609
1984	500 207	487 704
1985	508 893	486 525
1986	523 000	504 388
1987	522 407	487 961
1988	493 317	460 106
1989	478 800	467 582
1990	517 372	501 624
1991	518 789	485 964
1992	528 718	476 367
1993	488 131	466 855
1994	470 722	452 140

Notes:
Circulation figures from 1926–49 are those supplied by Beaverbrook Newspapers; from 1950–92 they have been supplied by Audit Bureau of Circulation.
The *Star* ceased publication in 1960 and the *Evening News* in 1980.
Evening Standard changed name to *New Standard* during the July–December 1980 audit period.
New Standard changed name to *Evening Standard* during the July–December 1981 audit period.
Evening Standard changed name to *London Standard* during the January–June 1985 audit period.
London Standard changed name to *London Evening Standard* during the July–December 1986 audit period.
London Evening Standard changed name to *Evening Standard* during the July–December 1987 audit period.

Appendix 4
Evening Standard Senior Staff, January 1995

Editor	Stewart Steven
Deputy Editor	Peter Boyer
Associate Editor	Sarah Sands
Executive Editor	Philip Evans
Managing Editor	Craig Orr
Associate Editor (Politics)	Stephen Glover
Political Editor	Charles Reiss
Features Editor	Alex Renton
Arts Editor	Michael Owen
Film Critic	Alexander Walker
Theatre Critic	Nicholas de Jongh
Art Critic	Brian Sewell
Literary Editor	A. N. Wilson
Restaurant Critic	Fay Maschler
News Editor	Stephen Clackson
Deputy News Editor	Pat Malone
Chief Reporter	Keith Dovkants
Education Correspondent	Howard Smith
Transport Correspondent	Dick Murray
Motoring Correspondent	Ian Morton
Medical Correspondent	Jo Revill
Travel Editor	Roger Bray
Londoner's Diary Editor	Marcus Scriven
Picture Editor	David Ofield
Deputy Picture Editor	David Theobald
Fashion Editor	Alison Veness
Washington Correspondent	Jeremy Campbell
Assistant Editor (Production)	Nigel Griffiths
Production Editor	Victoria Summerley
Chief Sub Editor	Keith Martin
Editorial Production Co-ord	Doug Wills
Systems Editor	David Maude
City Editor	Ian Griffiths
Deputy City Editor	Michael Harrison
Assistant Editor (Sport)	Michael Herd
Sports Editor	Brian Alexander
Deputy Sports Editor	Mick Dennis
Golf Correspondent	Renton Laidlaw
Racing Editor	Chris Bond
Racing Correspondent	Christopher Poole
Cricket Correspondent	John Thicknesse
Cartoonist	JAK
Chief Football Writer	Michael Hart

Astrologer	Patric Walker
Columnists	Peter Mckay
	Craig Brown
	Alison Pearson
	A. N. Wilson
Leader Writers	Peter Bradshaw
	Melanie McDonagh
ES Magazine Editor	Adam Edwards
ES Magazine Deputy Editor	Miles Chapman

Management

Managing Director	Anthony Hilton
Finance Director	Simon Dyson
Advertisement Director	Peter Clifton-Gould
Classified Ad Director	John Trickett
Circulation Director	Ed Ram
Systems Manager	Stephen Moorby

Bibliography

Aspinall, A., *Politics and the Press, c.1789–1850* (Home and Van Thal Ltd., 1949).
Austin, Alfred, *Autobiography* (1909).
Baxter, Beverley, *Strange Street* (Hutchinson, 1935).
Beaverbrook, Lord, *Politicians and the Press* (Hutchinson, 1925).
Beaverbrook, Lord, *Don't Trust to Luck* (Daily Express Publications, 1955).
Beaverbrook, Lord, *Men and Power 1917–1918* (Hutchinson, 1956).
Blumenfeld, R. D., *R.D.B.'s Diary* (William Heinemann, 1930).
Blumenfeld, R. D., *All in A Lifetime* (Benn, 1931).
Blumenfeld *et al.*, *Anywhere for a News Story* (The Bodley Head, 1934).
Bourne, Richard, *Lords of Fleet Street. The Harmsworth Dynasty* (Unwin Hyman, 1990).
Bower, Tom, *Maxwell The Outsider* (Heinemann, 1991).
Boyce, George *et al.*, *Newspaper History from the 17th Century to the Present Day* (Constable, 1978).
Brake, Laurel *et al.*, *Investigating Victorian Journalism* (Macmillan, 1990).
Brendan, Piers, *The Life and Death of the Press Barons* (Secker & Warburg, 1982).
Bright-Holmes, John (ed), *Like It Was. The Diaries of Malcolm Muggeridge* (Collins, 1981).
Broackes, Nigel, *A Growing Concern* (Weidenfeld & Nicolson, 1979).
Brown, Lucy, *Victorian News and Newspapers* (Clarendon Press, 1985).
Bryant, Mark (ed.), *The Complete Colonel Blimp* (Bellew Publishing, 1991).
Cameron, James, *Point of Departure. An Autobiography* (Arthur Barker, 1968).
Camrose, Viscount, *British Newspapers and their Controllers* (Cassell, 1947).
Channon, Sir Henry (ed. Robert Rhodes James), *Chips. The Diaries of Sir Henry Channon* (Penguin, 1967).
Chapman-Huston, Desmond, *The Lost Historian. A Memoir of Sir Sidney Low* (John Murray, 1936).
Chester, Lewis and Fenby, Jonathan, *The Fall of the House of Beaverbrook* (André Deutsch, 1979).
Chisholm, Anne and Davie, Michael, *Beaverbrook. A Life* (Hutchinson, 1992).
Churchill, Randolph, *What I Said about the Press* (Weidenfeld & Nicolson, 1957).
Christiansen, Arthur, *Headlines All My Life* (Heinemann, 1961).
Clarke, Tom, *My Northcliffe Diary* (Gollancz, 1931).
Clarke, Tom, *Northcliffe in History* (Hutchinson, 1950).
Cockett, Richard, *Twilight of Truth* (Weidenfeld & Nicolson, 1989).
Cockett, Richard (ed.), *Dear Max: the Correspondence of Brendan Bracken and Lord Beaverbrook, 1928–1958* (The Historians' Press, 1990).
Cockett, Richard, *David Astor and The Observer* (André Deutsch, 1991).
Coleridge, Nicholas, *Paper Tigers* (Heinemann, 1993).
Colley, William, *News Hunter* (Hutchinson, 1936).
Colville, John, *Footprints in Time* (Century, 1985).
Colville, John, *The Fringes of Power* (Hodder & Stoughton, 1985).
Cooper, Duff, *Old Men Forget* (Century Publishing, 1954).
Coote, Colin R., *Editorial* (Eyre & Spottiswoode, 1965).
Coote, John, *Altering Course. A Submariner in Fleet Street* (Leo Cooper, 1992).
Crewe, Quentin, *Well, I Forget the Rest* (Hutchinson, 1991).
Cudlipp, Hugh, *Publish and be Damned* (Andrew Dakers, 1953).
Cudlipp, Hugh, *The Prerogative of the Harlot* (The Bodley Head, 1980).
Dark, Sidney, *The Life of Sir Arthur Pearson* (Hodder & Stoughton, 1922).
Dark, Sidney, *Mainly About People* (Hodder & Stoughton, 1925).
Davie, Michael (ed.), *The Diaries of Evelyn Waugh* (Little, Brown, 1976).
Davies, Russell and Ottaway, Liz, *Vicky* (Secker & Warburg, 1987).

Deakin, Phyllis A., *Press on* (Worthing, 1984).
Douglas, James, *Down Shoe Lane* (Herbert Joseph, 1930).
Drabble, Margaret, *Arnold Bennett. A Biography* (Weidenfeld & Nicolson, 1976).
Driberg, Tom, *Beaverbrook. A Study in Power and Frustration* (Weidenfeld & Nicolson, 1956).
Driberg, Tom, *'Swaff'. The Life and Times of Hannen Swaffer* (Macdonald, 1974).
Driberg, Tom, *Ruling Passions* (Jonathan Cape, 1977).
Dunton, J., *Sketches of The Printers, Stationers and Binders of the City of London 1689–1705.*
Edwards, Robert, *Goodbye Fleet Street* (Jonathan Cape, 1988).
Escott, T. H. S., *Platform, Press, Politics and Play* (J. W. Arrowsmith, 1895).
Escott, T. H. S., *Masters of English Journalism* (T. Fisher Unwin, 1911).
Evans, R. J., *The Victorian Age, 1815–1914* (Edward Arnold, 1948).
Falk, Bernard, *He Laughed in Fleet Street* (Hutchinson, 1937).
Falk, Bernard, *Five Years Dead* (The Book Club, 1938).
Ferris, Paul, *The House of Northcliffe* (Weidenfeld & Nicolson, 1971).
Foot, Michael, *Debts of Honour* (Davis, Poynter, 1980).
Gilbert, Martin, *Winston Churchill, Vols. I–IV* (Collins, 1968–).
Glendenning, Victoria, *Vita. The Life of V. Sackville-West* (Weidenfeld & Nicolson, 1983).
Goodhardt, David and Wintour, Patrick, *Eddie Shah and the Newspaper Revolution* (Coronet, 1986).
Gourlay, Logan (ed.), *The Beaverbrook I Knew* (Quartet Books, 1984).
Grant, James: *The Newspaper Press: Its Origin – Progress – and Present Position*, 3 vols. (Tinsley Brothers, 1871; Routledge, 1872).
Gray, Tony, *Fleet Street Remembered* (Heinemann, 1990).
Griffiths, Dennis (ed.), *Encyclopedia of the British Press* (Macmillan, 1992).
Grundy, Bill, *The Press Inside Out* (W. H. Allen, 1976).
Haines, Joe, *Maxwell* (Macdonald, 1988).
Hansard, B. M., *In and Out of Fleet Street* (Hansard, 1935).
Hart-Davis, Duff, *The House the Berrys Built* (Hodder & Stoughton, 1990).
Hartwell, Lord, *William Camrose. Giant of Fleet Street* (Weidenfeld & Nicolson, 1992).
Hastings, Max and Jenkins, Simon, *The Battle for the Falklands* (Pan Books, 1983).
Herd, Harold, *The March of Journalism* (Allen & Unwin, 1952).
Heren, Louis, *The Power of the Press* (Orbis, 1985).
Hoggart, Simon and Leigh, David, *Michael Foot. A Portrait* (Hodder & Stoughton, 1981).
Howard, Peter, *Beaverbrook. A Study of Max the Unknown* (Hutchinson, 1964).
Howe, E. and Waite, Harold, *The London Society of Compositors* (Cassell, 1948).
Jenkins, Simon, *Newspapers. The Power and the Money* (Faber & Faber, 1979).
Jenkins, Simon, *The Market for Glory. Fleet Street Ownership in the 20th Century* (Faber & Faber, 1986).
Jones, Kennedy, *Fleet Street and Downing Street* (Hutchinson, 1920).
Jones, Mervyn, *Michael Foot* (Victor Gollancz, 1994).
Junor, John, *Memoirs. Listening for a Midnight Tram* (Chapmans, 1988).
Kee, Robert, *The World We Left Behind: 1939* (Hamish Hamilton, 1984).
Kee, Robert, *The World We Fought For: 1945* (Hamish Hamilton, 1985).
Koss, Stephen, *Fleet Street Radical* (Allen Lane, 1973).
Koss, Stephen, *The Rise and Fall of the Political Press in Britain, Vol. I, The Nineteenth Century; Vol. II, The Twentieth Century* (Hamish Hamilton, 1981 and 1984).
Knightley, Phillip, *The First Casualty* (Quartet, 1975).
Lane, Margaret, *Edgar Wallace. A Biography* (The Book Club, 1939).
Leapman, Michael, *Dangerous Estate. The Press after Fleet Street* (Hodder & Stoughton, 1992).
Lee, Alan J., *The Origins of the Popular Press in England 1855–1914* (Croom Helm, 1976).
Leslie, Anita, *Cousin Randolph. The Life of Randolph Churchill* (Hutchinson, 1982).
Linton, David and Boston, Ray, *The Newspaper Press in Britain. An Annotated Bibliography* (Mansell, 1987).

Linton, David (introduction Ray Boston), *The Twentieth Century Newspaper Press in Britain. An Annotated Bibliography* (Mansell, 1994).
Lockhart, Sir Bruce, *Guns and Butter* (Putnam, 1945).
Low, Sir David, *Low's Autobiography* (Michael Joseph, 1956).
Mackenzie, A., *Lord Beaverbrook* (Jarrolds, 1931).
Massingham, Henry William, *The London Daily Press* (Religious Tract Society, 1892).
Martin, Roderick, *New Technology and Industrial Relations in Fleet Street* (OUP, 1981).
Melvern, Linda, *The End of the Street* (Methuen, 1986).
Morgan, Dewi, *Phoenix of Fleet Street* (Charles Knight, 1977).
Morison, Stanley, *The English Newspaper: some account of the physical development of journals printed in London between 1622 and the present day* (Cambridge University Press, 1932).
Moseley, Sydney A., *The Truth About a Journalist* (Sir Isaac Pitman & Sons, 1935).
Muggeridge, Malcolm, *Chronicles of Wasted Time*, 2 vols. (Collins, 1972, 1973).
Musson, A. E., *The Typographical Association* (OUP, 1954).
Needham, L. W. 'Bill', *Fifty Years of Fleet Street* (Michael Joseph, 1974).
Nicolson, Harold, *George V* (Constable, 1952).
Nicolson, Nigel (ed.), *Harold Nicolson Diaries and Letters 1930–1939* (Collins, 1966).
Palmer, A. W., *A Dictionary of Modern History* (Penguin, 1962).
Pound, Reginald and Harmsworth, Geoffrey, *Northcliffe* (Cassell, 1959).
Powell, Enoch, *Joseph Chamberlain* (Thames & Hudson, 1977).
Read, Donald, *The Power of News. The History of Reuters* (OUP, 1992).
Renshaw, Patrick, *Nine Days in May. The General Strike* (Eyre Methuen, 1975).
Rosenberg, R., *English Rights and Liberties. Richard and Anne Baldwin, Whig Patriot Publishers* (Yale University Press, 1965).
Sebba, Anne, *Battling for News. The Rise of the Woman Reporter* (John Curtis, Hodder & Stoughton, 1994).
Simonis, H. *The Street of Ink* (Cassell, 1917).
Snoddy, Raymond, *The Good, the Bad and the Unacceptable* (Faber & Faber, 1992).
Spring, Howard, *The Autobiography of* (Collins, 1972).
Stannard, Russell, *With The Dictators in Fleet Street* (Hutchinson, 1934).
Symon, J. D., *The Press and Its Story* (Seeley, Service & Co., 1914).
Taylor, A. J. P., *Beaverbrook* (Hamish Hamilton, 1972).
The Times, History of, vols. I–VI (The Times Publishing Co., 1935, 1939, 1947, 1952, 1982, 1993).
Thomson, George Malcolm, *Lord Castelrosse* (Weidenfeld & Nicolson, 1973).
Vines, C. M., *A Little Nut-Brown Man. My Three Years with Lord Beaverbrook* (Readers' Union, 1969).
Williams, Francis, *Dangerous Estate* (Longmans, 1957).
Williams, Francis, *Nothing So Strange* (Cassell, 1970).
Williams, Gron, *Firebrand. The Frank Owen Story* (Worcester, 1993)
Windsor, H. R. H. The Duke of, *A King's Story* (Cassell, 1953).
Wintour, Charles, *Pressures on The Press. An Editor Looks at Fleet Street* (André Deutsch, 1972).
Wintour, Charles, *The Rise and Fall of Fleet Street* (Hutchinson, 1989).
Wrench, John Evelyn, *Geoffrey Dawson and Our Times* (Hutchinson, 1955).
Young, Kenneth (ed.), *The Diaries of Sir Bruce Lockhart* (Macmillan, 1973)
Ziegler, Philip, *Lady Diana Cooper* (Collins, 1981).

Manuscript collections

Austin, Alfred	The Library, University of Bristol
Baldwin, Henry	Courtesy I. Maxted, Librarian, West Country Study Centre, Exeter

Baldwin, Richard	High Wycombe Reference Library
Beaverbrook, Lord	House of Lords Records Office
Blackburn, Sir Thomas	Daily Express Archives
Blumenfeld, R. D.	House of Lords Records Office
Bracken, Viscount	Churchill College, Cambridge
Bruce Lockhart, Sir Robert	House of Lords Records Office
Chamberlain, Joseph	The Library, University of Birmingham
Disraeli, Benjamin	Bodleian Library, Oxford
Escott, T. H. S.	British Library
Giffard, Stanley Lees	British Library Earl of Halsbury
Gladstone, W. E.	British Library
Gwynne, H. A.	Bodleian Library, Oxford
Hamber, Thomas	Oriel College, Oxford
Low, Sir David (cartoons, etc.)	Centre for Cartoons and Caricature, University of Kent
Nicolson, Sir Harold	Balliol College, Oxford
Orwell, George	University College, London
Owen, Frank	House of Lords Records Office
Peel, Sir Robert	British Library
Robertson, E. J.	John Robertson
'Vicky' (Weisz, Victor)	Centre for Cartoons and Caricature, University of Kent
Wellington, Duke of	The Library, Southampton University

Other sources

Daily Express, *Evening Standard* and *The Times* archives.

Report from the Select Committee of the House of Comons on Newspaper Stamps, Parliamentary Papers, xviii (1851), British Newspaper Library, Colindale.

Royal Commission on the Press Reports, 1947–9; 1961–2; 1974–7, British Newspaper Library, Colindale.

Newspaper files: *Daily Express, Daily Mail, Evening News, Evening Standard, The Standard* – all at British Newspaper Library, Colindale. *St. James's Chronicle, The Times* – Guildhall Library, London.

Evening Standard picture library; (pre-1980) – Hulton-Deutsch Picture Library; *Daily Express* picture library; *Daily Mail* picture library.

Index